ΑΓΑΠΕΜΟΝΗ
THE ABODE OF LOVE

Bernard Shaw
VOLUME III
1918–1950

Books by the same author

Hugh Kingsmill
Lytton Strachey
Unreceived Opinions
Augustus John
Bernard Shaw 'The Search for Love'
Bernard Shaw 'The Pursuit of Power'

Edited by the same author

The Best of Hugh Kingsmill
Lytton Strachey by Himself
The Art of Augustus John
(with Malcolm Easton)
The Genius of Shaw
The Shorter Strachey (with Paul Levy)
William Gerhardie's *God's Fifth Column*
(with Robert Skidelsky)

Endpapers

Front: Scene from *Too True to be Good*,
New York production 1932 (photo Vandamm).

Back: Scene 3, *The Simpleton of the Unexpected Isles*,
New York production 1935 (photo Vandamm).

Bernard Shaw

MICHAEL HOLROYD

Volume III · 1918–1950
The Lure of Fantasy

Chatto & Windus

LONDON

Published in 1991 by
Chatto & Windus Ltd
20 Vauxhall Bridge Road
London SW1V 2SA

A CIP catalogue record for this book
is available from
the British Library.

ISBN 0 7011 3351 1

Typeset by Redwood Press Ltd
from author's discs
prepared by Richard Bates, London
Printed in Great Britain by
Redwood Press Ltd, Melksham, Wiltshire

Designed by Ron Costley
Index by Vicki Robinson

The lines from 'Encounter' in *The Ancient Britons*
by Brendan O'Byrne published 1979 by
Outposts Publications and reprinted by kind permission of the author.

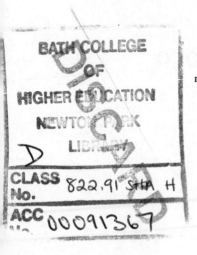

CONTENTS

v

ILLUSTRATIONS

BERNARD SHAW

1918–1950

To men who are themselves cynical
I am a pessimist; but to genuinely religious men
I am an optimist, and even a fantastic
and extravagant one.
Shaw to Norman Clark (circa 1929)

CHAPTER I

[1]

*It is to be impressed on all officers and men that a state of war exists
during the armistice.*
The Times, 21 November 1918

The Cabinet had already decided on a quick post-war general election. A
few days after the Armistice, Lloyd George dissolved Parliament and
announced 14 December 1918 as polling day. It was a degrading election,
exploiting people's hatred of the Germans and their delirious gratitude for
peace, to grab a renewed mandate for the old coalition of Tories and
Liberals. To cries of 'Vote for the Man who won the War', and 'Make
Britain a fit country for Heroes to live in', the electioneering was hurried
through before the heroes themselves had a chance of getting their opinions
known, or the opposition (silenced so long by the Defence of the Realm Act)
could form up and make itself effectively heard. 'I feel physically sick when I
read the frenzied appeals of the Coalition leaders ... to hang the Kaiser,
ruin and humiliate the German people, even to deprive Germany of her art
treasures and libraries,' Beatrice Webb wrote in her diary. 'The one
outstanding virtue of the Labour Party ... is its high sense of international
morality.'

Shaw was now in his sixty-third year. He dropped almost all his
engagements to go campaigning. While his wife Charlotte stayed at home he
toured the country for a fortnight, speaking every day to enormous crowds
of working people at Liverpool and Manchester, Birmingham and
Wakefield, Leicester and Wolverhampton, where the streets were full of
men and women unable to get into the halls and squares. He spoke in
support of Ramsay MacDonald, who had preferred to resign his leadership
of the Labour Party rather than endorse Grey's Liberal foreign policy in
wartime, and on behalf of other Labour candidates who rejected the
'coupon' of Lloyd George's coalition. He warned the electorate against
making it a Jingo versus Pacifist contest: voters must look for the solid
brickwork under all that political whitewash. Ramsay MacDonald had been
'fighting the Kaiser all his life' – but that fight was now over and it was time
to stop poisoning the human soul with crude rancours and darkening the
human mind by lies. He gave them facts; he gave them figures: more than

3

50,000 German children had died in 1917 alone, the civilian mortality rate had increased by thirty-seven per cent – and 'these are only the deaths'. He was to call for the raising of the Allied blockade of Germany which Lord Balfour had declared 'cannot cause the death of a single civilian' but which later caused 763,000 persons to die of malnutrition, 'a polite name for starvation'. Did any primitive want *more* revenge? 'When we break a German's leg with a bullet and then take him prisoner,' he explained, 'we immediately set to work to mend his leg, to the astonishment of our idiots, who cannot understand why we do not proceed to break his other leg.' He continued to inveigh against reparations for as long as the clamouring lasted: 'When Dempsey defeated Carpentier did he demand reparations?' He argued that if we wanted to prosper by restoring trade with our best customer, or even if we demanded a colossal war tribute to be handed over to us, then we must not bankrupt Germany. While others denounced the Kaiser as a Satan who must be interned on some distant island if not condemned to the gallows or the guillotine, Shaw maintained that 'he has a right to live where he pleases . . . If his rights are not as sacred as those of the poorest peasant in Europe then the war has been fought in vain.'

Britain was vibrating with exultation over the most magnificent military triumph in her long record of victories. It was enormously important, Shaw insisted, that she should check the evil that could easily fester after the guns had stopped, and 'set the world an example of consideration for vanquished enemies'. The question was no longer 'Daddy, what did you do in the Great War?' but 'What did you do when the war was over, Daddy?' The socialists and internationalists of the Labour Party 'well know that the traditions of the British Lion have no future', Shaw asserted, 'and that the interests of all proletarians are identical, and, as between one country and another, pacific'.

By his own self-competitive estimate, Shaw's series of campaign speeches that winter was 'my greatest platform success'. But on 14 December, Lloyd George's coalition careered back to Parliament with 516 seats – a huge majority of 340 over the other parties. Most of the Labour candidates Shaw had championed – including Ramsay MacDonald – lost their seats because of their opposition to the war. However, with sixty-two seats over the twenty-seven of Asquith's Liberals, Labour now sat in the House of Commons as the official opposition.

Shaw ended the war as he had begun it: with a brochure. 'I have a war book coming out in a few days,' he notified his pacifist friend, Henry Salt. 'Peace Conference Hints. Hints! Ha ha!' Ten thousand copies of *Peace Conference Hints* were published on 12 March 1919. It has been described as 'a seventeenth-century puritan sermon on twentieth-century politics'.

Partly an admonition to Britain against exploiting her self-righteousness at the Versailles Peace Conference, and in part a collection of 'hints' to nerve President Woodrow Wilson against the wiles of Clemenceau and Lloyd George, the pamphlet represents a continuation of Shaw's election campaign and the summation of his political writings about the war. It is a story retold and completed.

When asking for a mandate for his peace offensive against Germany, Lloyd George had demanded: 'Is no one responsible? Is no one to be called to account? Is there to be no punishment? Surely that is neither God's justice nor man's?' Shaw's answer, which was a categorical rejection of each question, invoked another justice and brought the matter before a different court of morality, one which treats us all as being inevitably connected to one another as parts of the same human narrative. He believed that by fixing the guilt of history collectively or individually on others, Lloyd George was making a classic evasion of the human spirit. Through this duplicity of mind we risked restarting the mechanism that would bring the same tragedies back into our lives.

Peace Conference Hints is a Bunyanesque tract on the moral consequences of the war and those ethics of Christian chivalry Shaw had examined in his Preface to *Androcles and the Lion*. He surveys botched-up British diplomacy between 1906 and 1914 to strengthen his case for the international acceptance of new rules of conduct in war and peace. He grinds out a history lesson to sharpen a moral point. 'The moral cleaning-up after the war,' he states, 'is far more important than the material restorations.' But moral steam, like physical steam, is not independent of engines and organization – and this, he believes, is why the Versailles Peace Conference must be made a nucleus for the League of Nations. Like an illuminated picture, the League of Nations that appears in Shaw's missal is a 'very vigorous organization of resistance to evil', protected by an international police force but making conquests through the power of conscience. This power, enshrined in supra-national law, is defined as a 'mystic force of evolution applied through the sort of living engine we call the man of principle' – the very force that had animated Dick Dudgeon in *The Devil's Disciple*. 'Principle is the motive power in the engine,' Shaw explains: 'its working qualities are integrity and energy, conviction and courage, with reason and lucidity to shew them the way.' This technology for human progress is shown being forced upon us not only by the inevitable march of civilization but by our fear of Armageddon. For the next war, if permitted to occur, 'will be no "sport of kings", no game of chance played with live soldiers and won by changing them into dead ones, but a scientific attempt to destroy cities and kill civilians', Shaw warns. 'Not the soldiers alone, but all of us, will have to live miserably in holes in the ground, afraid to look at the sky lest our white faces should betray us to a hostile aeroplane; for our houses will be heaps of charred bricks ... The notion that war is a beneficent gymnastic, moral and spiritual, is reduced to absurdity ... '

Having raised up his Architecture of Nations above these charred bricks, Shaw constructs various defences against the swarming unrealities of idealism. The League could not prevent its constituents from relapsing into barbarism if they were bent on it, he concedes, but gradually 'when the widespread feeling that war is a crime against humanity finds at last an organized executive power behind it, it will become much easier to deal with war agitations as incitements to crime'. To prevent the League from subsiding into paralysis, he wants to set limits on its composition and aims. The practicability of the scheme resided neither in 'a single Spartan Superstate nor a single obviously unworkable and unstable League of All Mankind from China to Peru', he adds, 'but several combinations, psychologically homogeneous within themselves, all equally interested in keeping the peace in their own way'. He looked forward to its beginning as an assembly of those states with settled democratically-elected governments, including Germany whose presence he emphasized as being essential to the peace of Europe.

Shaw's collection of tactical difficulties – the double-edged spear of the economic boycott, the refusal of the Great Powers to consent to unilateral disarmament and the problems of achieving multilateral disarmament, the growing demand for security, the unrealism of neutrality (Belgium was neutral and invaded by the Central Powers, Greece was neutral and occupied by the Allied Powers), and the pressure for interdependence over spurious independence (he foresaw the NATO and Warsaw Pact blocs) – have a prescience that give his dreaming Palace of Nations the shadow of a substance.

On the throne of this enchanted Palace is the man Shaw tries to set up as its mystical prophet from the New World, President Woodrow Wilson. But, with the rusty accoutrements of his fourteen points, he resembles a benighted Quixote of the Peace. The week after Wilson was to lay his patched-up rag of a treaty before the United States Senate, Shaw was declaring that he had known all along the Versailles Conference would come to nothing and that 'in spite of anything that could be urged by the wisest and most powerful statesmen, the victorious side would skin the other alive ... '

'Wilson has failed as completely as Bismarck to prevent the skinning alive ... War is a game at which the victor is as inexorably bound to take his winnings to the uttermost farthing as the vanquished is to pay his losses. I had no illusions on that subject when I backed Wilson for all I was worth; and therefore I am not disillusioned nor disgusted now.'

He may have had no illusions; he did have hopes. Woodrow Wilson's godlike procession through Europe before the conference had stirred people's goodwill. 'Nothing like this had ever been seen before,' records one witness. 'The full-throated acclamation of Londoners, Parisians and Romans was not the normal cordiality which crowds accord to a visiting monarch. The ovation surged from the depth of the wounded contrite universal heart to a deliverer, the shaper of a new world...'

Some echoes of these aspirations, like distant trumpets, sound through Shaw's pamphlet. For if the war had not gained new moral territory for human beings, then it had been a defeat for everyone. The possibility of defeat is written into his text, which is some 20,000 words long and to which may be added copious letters to the press. 'I have done my best to avoid conciseness,' he wrote. But his prolixity seems to be less of a device for avoiding the reduction of complicated truths to simple falsehoods than the compensation for a probable lack of any volume of action. Pessimism and optimism are cross-stitched into the narrative, and in his subsequent reaction to the incompetent document Woodrow Wilson took away from Versailles may be glimpsed the extent of Shaw's hopes. 'The treaty of Versailles, which was perhaps the greatest disaster of the war for all the belligerents, and indeed for civilization in general,' he wrote, 'left nothing to be done in foreign affairs but face the question of the next war pending the consolidation of the League of Nations.'

Like Bunyan, Shaw had urged the peacemakers to climb the hill Difficulty. But they had shied from Danger and fallen into the pit Destruction. The silence that trailed after *Peace Conference Hints* was to be invaded at the end of that year by another work of moral tension and stylistic force, Maynard Keynes's *The Economic Consequences of the Peace*. After a succession of dreadful weeks at Versailles, Keynes had quitted 'the scene of nightmare' and written up his account of 'the devastation of Europe'. 'A great sensation has been made here by Professor Keynes of Cambridge, who was at Versailles as economic expert, and resigned that position and came home as a protest against the peace terms,' Shaw reported to Siegfried Trebitsch, his German translator. 'He has now published a book in which he demonstrates that the indemnity demanded from Germany is an economic impossibility; and nobody ventures to dispute this.' *The Economic Consequences of the Peace* seemed to have endorsed the central thesis of *Peace Conference Hints*: Keynes's demonstration was Shaw's vindication.

But while Keynes, the informed insider, became in the urgency of his despair 'an outlaw from British official circles', Shaw was to move still further outside, occupying the position of enemy rather than outlaw. The peace conference had been a battle lost for Keynes; for Shaw it looked like unconditional surrender. 'He felt that capitalism had caused the war,' commented William Irvine, 'and that democracy had lost the peace.' Keynes dedicated his book to 'the new generation [that] has not yet spoken and silent opinion [that] is not yet formed'. But Shaw, being a generation older than Keynes, felt his precarious faith in this generation diminishing. At the peace table, over the heads of his colleagues, Woodrow Wilson had again and again appealed to the conscience of the public. But the public's conscience had been subtly changed by the European free press; and the man whom no one dared criticize during the war was now openly jeered at and called a 'dangerous radical' by businessmen who controlled the newspapers. 'He stood in great need of sympathy, of moral support, of the enthusiasm of the masses,' wrote Keynes. '...And in this drought the flower of the President's faith withered and dried up.' Such personal reliance on applause, and journalistic manipulation of popularity, came as additional evidence to Shaw that government by the people was unworkable. Only 'government of the people and for the people' was practicable, and it seemed to him that this democratic goal could most effectively be reached by applied communism. 'What Wilson expected I do not know,' he wrote to Kathleen Scott. '...Lenin is the only interesting statesman left in Europe.'

[2]

Is this England, or is it a madhouse?
Heartbreak House

Shaw's response to the Great War is most deeply revealed in *Heartbreak House*. His depression had seeped into the play: his anger over what he saw at Versailles inflamed the Preface. The whole work grew into a national fable ending with an Old Testament sermon that damned England as a ship of fools and prophesied nuclear holocaust – an apocalyptic dream that T. E. Lawrence thought was 'going into nightmare'.

It 'began with an atmosphere', the unjudgemental atmosphere of Chekhov's plays. Shaw had made enquiries about Chekhov's work as early as 1905, but the Stage Society had not put on *The Cherry Orchard* for another six years – and then the intellectual English audience, finding its

8

Russian manner aimless and impenetrable, became bored, began tittering, and eventually walked out. 'An exquisite play by Tchekoff was actually hissed,' Shaw reported to George Moore. 'You cannot conceive how inferior we are (a small circle excepted) to the common playgoer.' He was to subtitle his own play 'A Fantasia in the Russian Manner on English Themes', and to add that he hoped it would be taken by his Russian friends as 'an unmistakably sincere tribute to one of the greatest of their great dramatic poets'. This was also an apology for the failure of the English highbrow congregation to recognize its own place in Chekhov's declining world. *Heartbreak House* is full of 'the same nice people, the same utter futility' as *The Cherry Orchard*, and though the style may be in imitation of the 'Russian Manner', the contents are specifically labelled 'English Themes'. For here, as the Preface makes clear, is Shaw's view of 'cultured, leisured Europe before the war'. These 'heartbroken imbeciles', as the paralysed man-of-action Hector Hushabye describes them, are recognized by Mazzini Dunn, the man drunk on fashionable ideals, as 'rather a favorable specimen of what is best in our English culture ... charming people, most advanced, unprejudiced, frank, humane, unconventional, democratic, free-thinking, and everything that is delightful to thoughtful people'.

At the centre of this atmosphere Shaw placed the supernatural storybook character of Captain Shotover. His model had been the actress Lena Ashwell's seafaring father, Commander Pocock, 'who was also a preacher and a captain of souls' and whose first adventure, as an eleven-year-old midshipman, was the capture of a slave ship. In retirement he went to live on a sailing vessel on the River Tyne, fitting out the stern as his own quarters, placing bars on Lena's nursery portholes, and equipping the upper deck with a drawing-room and greenhouse. As he lay dying, he had consented to take Communion, but 'when it was administered he absolutely refused to eat the consecrated bread without cheese'. Shaw laughed when Lena told him this story in 1913, 'but in that moment Captain Shotover of *Heartbreak House* was born', he later wrote to Lord Alfred Douglas. 'All truly sacred truths are rich in comedy.'

Heartbreak House was intended as tragedy. 'Laughter is a fatiguing thing and I had imagined that I had nearly eliminated it from this particular play,' he was to say after an apparently successful performance to mark the opening of the Oxford Playhouse in 1923. The director of that production, Richard Denham, recorded Shaw's speech to the audience. 'This has been one of the most depressing evenings I have spent in the theatre,' he told them. 'I imagined I had written a quiet, thoughtful, semi-tragic play after the manner of Tchekov. From your empty-headed laughter, I appear to have written a bedroom farce...' He then sat down amid vociferous applause.

'Behold my Lear,' he later gestured from his puppet play, *Shakes versus Shav*. He regarded *King Lear* as pure tragedy: 'even the fool in Lear is tragic'. Like Lear, Captain Shotover's heartbreak has apparently been caused by his two daughters, Ariadne and Hesione. 'I don't find them much more popular that Goneril and Regan,' Shaw wrote to Lillah McCarthy, '(they are, by the way, the daughters of the old gentleman of 88)'.

Ariadne Utterword, who is 'as strong as a horse', speaks for Horseback Hall which is mentioned in the Preface as 'the alternative to Heartbreak House', a very Irish alternative 'consisting of a prison for horses with an annex for the ladies and gentlemen who rode them'. At the age of nineteen, Ariadne escaped from the overheated atmosphere of Heartbreak House, where everybody lived and loved without a care in the world, and became part of the wooden-headed, outdoor tradition of English life, stocked by people who could see, hear and speak no good except on matters of sport, into which they converted all their religion and politics. The Preface prepares us for a Peacockian dialogue in the style of *Headlong Hall*, satirizing these two poles of contemporary English life, but it is only during the last act of the play (in which Ariadne announces that 'the stables are the real centre of the household') that the condition of England is debated. Having run away from the eccentricity of her upbringing and the world of her emotions, Ariadne has pursued respectability which is represented by her decorous 'numskull' of a husband, a colonial Governor of the British Empire. Sir Hastings Utterword could 'save the country with the greatest ease,' she boasts, once he was given the necessary powers and 'a good supply of bamboo to bring the British native to his senses'. Ariadne is an utter philistine. For much of the first act Captain Shotover has pretended not to recognize her. 'You left because you did not want us,' he eventually tells her. 'Was there no heartbreak in that for your father? You tore yourself up by the roots; and the ground healed up and brought forth fresh plants and forgot you. What right had you to come back and probe old wounds?'

Shaw contrasts Ariadne's pseudo-blonde hair with her sister's magnificent but phoney black hair. Hesione is the opposite of Ariadne, but also false. As the chatelaine of Heartbreak House she is a siren of romance and sexual infatuation who lures people into her web and leaves them suspended. She has disabled the two 'inventors' in the house, her husband and her father, who are the sort of people the country needs for its salvation. Hector Hushabye is a man of action reduced from being a creator of exploits to an inventor of stories, a hero whom the habit of loving has made into a fancy-dress poseur; Shotover is the thinker whose intelligence has been trivialized into money-making and diverted by the exploitation of his fatherly love from creative to destructive ends. 'Money is running short,' Hesione informs him after his patent lifeboat has failed to earn them more than £500. '... Living at the rate we do, you cannot afford life-saving inventions. Cant you think of something that will murder half Europe at one bang?'

Shaw's Cordelia is Ellie Dunn, a spiritual offspring of Shotover's rather than his blood relation. She has been invited to the house by Hesione, and her unsentimental education is the play's single continuous thread of narrative. She arrives as an innocent Desdemona, 'an ingenue of 18' taught nothing by her idealist father except how to mistake Shakespearean romances for reality. When the curtain rises she appears as a solitary figure on stage dreaming over *Othello*. 'There are men who have done wonderful things: men like Othello, only, of course, white, and very handsome,' she rhapsodizes to Hesione – only to find a few minutes later that her own handsome white Othello, a man of wonderfully adventurous stories whom she has known by the name of 'Marcus Darnley', is actually Hesione's husband Hector. 'I have a horrible fear that my heart is broken,' she declares. But refusing to be a sweet little sexual attraction for this 'exceedingly clever lady-killer', she pronounces herself 'cured', passing rapidly in the stage directions from '*great distress*', through anger to hard thought, and '*"disengaging" herself with an expression of distaste*' from Hesione. She now becomes '*scornfully self-possessed*', looks '*curiously older and harder*' and adopts the worldly ways of Ariadne. Before the lady in her was killed she had been going to marry a fifty-five-year-old 'perfect hog of a millionaire' nicknamed Boss Mangan, acting against her instincts but from sentimental gratitude for the financial help he had given her father. In Act II, as part of her disillusioning education, she learns that Mangan has in fact made a profit out of her father by assisting him into bankruptcy. But she is still determined to marry him, her motive now being to gain use of the money he has tricked out of her father, even though Mangan, who has followed her to the house, has fallen in love with Hesione. 'If we women were particular about men's characters,' she explains, 'we should never get married at all,' an attitude endorsed by Ariadne who declares that 'it all turns on your income'.

In the last act Ellie reveals to Mangan that she 'never really intended to make you marry me ... Never in the depths of my soul. I only wanted to feel my strength: to know that you could not escape if I chose to take you.' In the depths of her soul she has reached a mystical union with Shotover, who lies in her arms as fast asleep as a baby while she tells the others that she has given 'my broken heart and my strong sound soul to its natural captain, my spiritual husband and second father'. During a strange interlude in Act II where Shotover and Ellie are left together he has made her face the fact that to steal all the money back from Mangan would simply make her another business-burglar. 'Are you one of those who are so sufficient to themselves that they are only happy when they are stripped of everything, even of hope?' Shotover asks her. Gripping his hand she replies: 'It seems so; for I feel now as if there was nothing I could not do, because I want nothing.' From romantic hell she has travelled through financial purgatory to 'life with a blessing', and wants nothing from 'a vile world' in which the 'bloated capitalist' exploits human weaknesses for unenriching profit. What she has come to share with the Captain is a religious sense of values. Her emotional transformation-in-a-day is an accelerated dash through the long pilgrim's progress of his life. All the optimism of the play centres on Ellie, since Shotover is by now an ancient mariner with 'nothing but echoes ... [whose] last shot was fired years ago'. Shaw's hope focused beyond the generation to which Keynes's *Economic Consequences* was dedicated to one that would attain 'the seventh degree of concentration' which Shotover has failed to reach. This is shorthand for a religious concentration of thought (Shotover), and will (Ellie) and action (Hector) to combine the divided forces of power (Ariadne) and culture (Hesione) that have been exploited by capitalism (Mangan). In an early draft Shaw had written 'the seventh degree of contemplation'. The change signifies that Shotover (as his name suggests) has more of the powerful Undershaft than the dreamer Keegan in his nature. His vocabulary of dynamite and psychic rays 'mightier than any X-ray' that will 'explode all the explosives at the will of a Mahatma' before his adversary 'can point his gun at me' is the terminology of intellectual star-wars. Ellie too welcomes the bombs that fall at the end of the last act, recognizing that although the advent of a religious life depends on moral power, it must also possess the physical ability to destroy an enemy. It is the end of 'cultured, leisured Europe before the war' and the beginning of Shaw's flickering dream set in the headquarters of the League of Nations.

*

'Mr Shaw does not know what heartbreak is,' objected Desmond MacCarthy on first seeing the play. 'He conceives it as a sudden disillusionment ... as a sharp pain, but not as a maiming misery.' Shaw's point was that 'heartbreak is not what I thought it must be', as Ellie Dunn says, and that it is different for everyone. To Ellie herself, who 'has remarkable strength of character', it is 'only life educating you', as Hesione tells her – which is to say it is the process of growing up and 'the sort of pain that goes mercifully beyond our powers of feeling'. To the 'pettish and jealous and childish' Randall Utterword, worthless brother of Hastings, who will never grow up and whose love for his sister-in-law Ariadne is as immature as Octavius's love for Ann Whitefield in *Man and Superman*, heartbreak means little more than 'a change from having his head shampooed'. Between these extremes are ranged the others, most of them in some measure victims of the strange powers of the two Shotover sisters.

But Shaw also makes his Goneril and Regan victims of heartbreak. Hesione suffers from the dangerous after-effects of a love that came once in her lifetime, then passed. What she shared with Hector, whom she has now reduced to the 'household pet' of their marriage, cannot be regained. All her flirtations and seductions will bring no more than fading reflections of that dream. She is already forty-four and has no other interests; what can she do but cry to dream again? For her sister Ariadne heartbreak is paradoxically lack of heart. She is as fearful of emotion as Mangan is of poverty, and has fashioned herself into a rigidly conventional woman of the world whose tragedy is that 'her heart will not break', Shotover tells Ellie. 'She has been longing all her life for someone to break it. At last she has become afraid she has none to break.'

Both sisters, we are given to understand, have been damaged by their wayward upbringing. 'Old Shotover sold himself to the devil in Zanzibar,' Hector romances. 'The devil gave him a black witch for a wife; and these two daughters are their mystical progeny.' In *Heartbreak House* the devil is not the intellectual debater from *Don Juan in Hell*, or even the positive force derived from Blakean imagery that dominates *The Devil's Disciple*. He is a symbol of self-surrender. In a letter to Trebitsch, Shaw explained that by heartbreak he meant a 'chronic complaint, not a sudden shock' – that is, the chronic effects of heredity and childhood, rather than the sudden setback of an unhappy love affair. Ellie's disillusion with her father, her intended husband and herself make up a chain of shocks that pulls this control of childhood apart. For her heartbreak emerges as 'the end of happiness and the beginning of peace'. But even Shotover is prevented from advancing freely to his seventh degree of concentration by forces that swamped Shaw's own childhood. He describes Heartbreak House itself as 'my kennel' – the word Shaw used for his birthplace in Synge Street – and, having retreated into 'my second childhood', he is diverted by habitual rum-drinking from pursuing his thought 'so long and so continuously' that it issues into action. 'To be drunk means to have dreams' – or Shavian fantasies – instead of entering the real world. 'You must never be in the real world when we talk together', Ellie soothes him. But this incapacity of the most gifted characters, Shotover, Hector and even Ellie, to use their abilities in the real world has by the last act developed into the collective heartbreak of the play.

'We sit here talking,' cries Hector, 'and leave everything to Mangan and to chance and to the devil.'

*

At the beginning there is no heartbreak. The house is 'a palace of enchantments', as Shaw described it to the critic J. C. Squire, 'as in the second act of Parsifal'. To this miraculous enchantment all the arts conspire. It was, he told Elgar, 'by far the most musical work' he had written. 'Most of my plays are almost independent of scenery,' he explained to Nugent Monck, 'but the scenery as described in the book is an integral part of Heartbreak House. The captain's house and garden are not only a place but an atmosphere.' The house is all-inclusive. It contains light and dark, land and sea, sleeping and waking, fantasy and fact. The first act, with its complicated jigsaw of almost sixty entrances and exits, its ensemble playing of what appears to be a chaos of informality, is 'as dependent on atmosphere and on subtleties of personality in the performers as any of Tchekov's' plays. Shaw felt he had seen in *The Cherry Orchard* a method of advancing the general disquisitory technique of *Getting Married* and *Misalliance* which preserved the unities and removed the action outside the theatre – with the odd dramatic break-in by pilot, burglar or would-be assassin. In later acts he made a number of references to Chekhov: the 'splendid drumming in the sky' accords with the snapping of the string in *The Cherry Orchard*; and the topsy-turvy burglar is the equivalent of Chekhov's ominous tramp. But these points of structural similarity draw attention to a difference in sensibility. Chekhov's world, with its fusion of impressionistic touches, is naturalistic; in Shaw's house, which is full of surreal and disorientating episodes, 'the very burglars cant behave naturally'.

From the moment the curtain goes up on *Heartbreak House* and the audience sees Ellie Dunn's copy of *Othello* sink to her lap, as her eyes close and she dozes in slumber on the draughtsman's chair, the theatre has moved into a world of dreams. Asleep in her bedroom upstairs lies Hesione, the mistress of *Heartbreak House*, who has changed her name from Shotover to the somnambulistic Hushabye as the result of her 'enchanting dream' of love with Hector. In the second act Mangan is sent into a hypnotic trance, and in the third act, as the thunderous bombers approach, it is the Captain who sleeps. This sleeping and dreaming allows Shaw additional licence for exploring his characters' unconscious minds and provides him with a number of symbolic devices for tapping hidden layers of meaning. In the pathetic scene in which Hector, left alone on stage, 'falls into a daydream' and performs a desperate duel with an imaginary opponent and then in 'another reverie' mimes a thrilling love scene with an invisible woman, we witness all the qualities of courage and imagination he has never been able to employ in waking life – qualities that, when Shotover enters, are immediately contracted into 'a series of gymnastic exercises'.

Growing-up becomes allied to a process of waking-up. Ellie Dunn has the strength to wake herself and the power to mesmerize Mangan so that he cannot resist hearing the truth about himself. 'You dreamt it all, Mr Mangan,' Hesione apologizes. But Mangan answers: 'I believe in dreams.' For however much he protests, he has been powerless against Ellie's and Hesione's removal of his pretensions. 'Let's all strip stark naked,' he later cries. 'We may as well do the thing thoroughly when we're about it. We've stripped ourselves morally naked.' Though Ellie and Shotover are 'only happy when they are stripped of everything', Mangan is terrified to death by a game that casts off his clothing of self-approval and exposes him as a whimpering nonentity. Even more infantile than Randall Utterword, he exhibits the essential babyhood of capitalism. This is a revelation to Hesione, who has accepted him as he has presented himself to the world: a businessman 'Boss' with plenty of money and no heart at all. 'It comes to me suddenly that you are a real person: that you had a mother, like anyone else.' But it is too late for Mangan to grow up. 'I suppose his soul was starved when he was young,' remarks Ellie.

'What is true within these walls is true outside them,' announces Shotover. Heartbreak House has splendid views of reality which no one inside can reach. For the Palace of Dreams is a revelation as well as a refuge, and recalls an earlier dream sequence in Shaw's plays: the hell scene in *Man and Superman*. Hector is the reluctant Don Juan of this hell and Hesione a Doña Ana who has long ago given birth to her children and now gives herself over to pleasure. Her house is a moral vacuum. 'What do men want?' she demands, reversing Freud's question on women. 'They have their food, their firesides, their clothes mended, and our love at the end of the day. Why are they not satisfied? Why do they envy us the pain with which we bring them into the world, and make strange dangers and torments for themselves to be even with us?'

Before the strip poker begins, Shaw shuffles the cards of identity with comic virtuosity. 'In this house we know all the poses,' says Hector: 'our game is to find out the man under the pose.' It is a matter of Shavian orthodoxy that every person should contradict the pose he adopts. 'The great question is, not who we are, but what we are,' sententiously remarks Mazzini Dunn, little realizing that he is to be shown up as a gullible sentimentalist wrong about everything except his daughter ('you become quite clever when you talk about her', Hesione admits). Even comfortable Nurse Guinness, who asks disbelievingly: 'now is it likely I'd kill any man on purpose', is shortly afterwards demanding why the burglar (who turns out to be her husband as well as one of the Captain's old crew) had not been shot. 'If I'd known who he was, I'd have shot him myself,' she swears, and to show us that this is no empty hypothesis, Shaw has her running at the end of the play 'in hideous triumph ... laughing harshly' to the gravel pit where her husband has been blown up.

This disrobing is complicated by the coverings of personal association and layers of derivation that went into the creation of these characters. For Mazzini Dunn, Shaw has borrowed some of the trappings of Ebenezer Howard, idealistic pioneer of the Garden City Movement, in which G.B.S. had taken both a humorous and a financial interest (he was generously to cancel a loan when Howard died almost penniless in 1928). This was an aesthetic variation on the Fabian route to reform. It had been Ebenezer Howard's book *To-morrow, A Peaceful Path to Rural Reform* that Tom Broadbent had carried round with him as a blueprint of heaven and model for his business expansion scheme in *John Bull's Other Island*. And it had been Ebenezer Howard's dream-town that Shaw put on the stage as Perivale St Andrews, 'beautifully situated and beautiful in itself', in *Major Barbara*. At the beginning of the war, Howard had petitioned Shaw with a plan for bombing the Germans with millions of friendly messages dropped by aeroplane. This 'gorgeous notion' served to remind Shaw of those high-flying sentimentalists who, on matters of life and death, miscalculated everything (Mazzini Dunn decides that the only two people in *Heartbreak House* who are in fact killed, Mangan and the Burglar, 'are acting very sensibly; and it is they who will survive'). But because 'people dont have their virtues and vices in sets: they have them anyhow: all mixed', Mazzini is both a 'boresome elderly prig' and (as Hesione concedes) rather likeable. So it was with Ebenezer Howard who, for all his amazing impracticality, did eventually get his schemes for Garden Cities and pamphlet propaganda by air (and even his shorthand typewriting machines) implemented – though for the advantage of others. Despite looking like an 'elderly nobody' and a 'negligible crank' he was also, Shaw wrote, 'one of those heroic simpletons who do big things while our prominent worldlings are explaining why they are Utopian and impossible. And of course it is they who will make money out of his work.'

The person making money out of Mazzini's work is Boss Mangan, whom Shaw modelled on Hudson Kearley, head of a wholesale grocery firm. Kearley, who was created Viscount Devonport, had been a Liberal Member of Parliament before the war and was brought into the coalition government as Food Controller during the period when Lloyd George was rejecting Shaw himself, both for a place on his Reconstruction Committee and on the

Irish Convention. The Palace of Enchantment is darkened by the intrusion of Mangan, who is possibly the least sympathetic character in all Shaw's work. He is the alternative captain to Shotover: a captain of industry, morally unfitted for administering a country, who sees his job as getting the better of 'other fellows in other departments'. His announcement that the Prime Minister had asked him to 'join the Government without even going through the nonsense of an election, as the dictator of a great public department', provokes a dismay which is part of the general humiliation of Mangan in *Heartbreak House* before his miserable death in a gravel pit. Nurse Guinness's 'Serves un right!' is the signing-off of Shaw's revenge on the egregious Devonport.

This quality of revenge also fires the creation of Hesione, which is Shaw's first portrait of Mrs Patrick Campbell since the end of their affair. Hesione is a creature of poetry. She is also an arch-seductress whose talent for incapacitating those she seduces makes Hector liken her to a vampire. 'You are the Vamp and I the victim,' Shaw was later to write to Stella Campbell when advising her to put *Heartbreak House* out of her mind, 'yet it is I who suck your blood and fatten on it whilst you lose everything!' This was to be part of his revenge set in the future when Hesione will become 'a sluttish female, trying to stave off a double chin and an elderly spread, vainly wooing a born soldier of freedom'. The exploding bombs at the end of the play sound like the 'glorious experience' of an overture to death with a bang instead of a whimper, which, unless she moves into mystical experience, is all Hesione has to look forward to when her sexual magic fails. 'When I am neither coaxing and kissing nor laughing,' she says, 'I am just wondering how much longer I can stand living in this cruel, damnable world.' It is a percipient forecast. Mrs Pat had predicted that her life 'is sure to be a short one. I wish it to be.' Being denied her wish, she was to demand pathetically in old age 'who is there here who still *loves* me?' and receiving no reply, ask: 'Why am I alive – what for?' It is this expanding emptiness that Hesione conveys, foreshadowing the career of a great actress who was to die '*sans profession*'.

'I wish I was a man and old enough for Shotover,' Stella wrote to Shaw after he had read his play to her. Nobody could speak Hesione's lines as she could, he told her, 'or give the quality of the woman as you could if you would'. But, though in her fifties and growing stout, she fancied playing the eighteen-year-old heroine, Ellie – and that was impossible. For, merged with his intuition of Virginia Woolf's floating inner being, Ellie had been conceived from Shaw's visionary memories of that hypnotic young girl, Erica Cotterill, who had lived in 'a fanciful world of her own' and now occupied a special place within the fanciful world of his plays. In the real world, drafting a letter on behalf of Charlotte, he had been obliged to banish her from his house. 'Yet she was an exquisite sort of person', and he followed her in his imagination to Heartbreak House. As 'Incognita Appassionata' in *Getting Married*, she had embodied the sexual passion lacking in his marriage; and as Ellie Dunn she is his spiritual intimate, which may be one reason why the play was (so Shaw told Nancy Astor) 'loathed by Charlotte'.

There was little in *Heartbreak House* with which Charlotte could identify and which would have pleased her. 'It's a dangerous thing to be married right up to the hilt, like my daughter's husband,' Shotover says to Ellie. 'The man is at home all day, like a damned soul in hell.' Elsewhere marriage is described as 'a safety match' in comparison to the wild rites of romantic love. 'It was damned dangerous. You fascinated me; but I loved you; so it was heaven,' Hector says to Hesione: and he speaks Shaw's love for Stella.

Charlotte's loathing of this play is reproduced in Ariadne's disapproval of the house. Ariadne is the last word in social propriety. Her emotional rigidity, as well as her early determination to make marriage unacceptable to her living parent, were Charlotte's attitudes. Shaw had entered the world of Horseback Hall on visits to Charlotte's friends and relations, when he put up in the castles and big houses belonging to the county families of Anglo-Irish society. But Ariadne's affinity with Charlotte is well-disguised by several other factors, such as her appearance, which, it has been suggested, was taken from Virginia Woolf.

The Shaws, the Woolfs and the Webbs had come together during the weekend of 17 to 19 June 1916 at a big house called Wyndham Croft in Sussex. 'We talked quite incessantly,' Virginia remembered. '...I liked it better than I expected. At anyrate one can say what one likes, which is unusual with the middle aged.' Surrounded by all this talk and in Shotover-style, Shaw 'went fast asleep apparently', Virginia observed, '...and then woke up and rambled on into interminable stories about himself ... Poor Mrs Shaw was completely out of it.' In the mornings Shaw would go into the garden where Leonard saw him writing his play 'on a writing pad on his knee'. From this garden, which is described in the last act of *Heartbreak House* (it had a lamp post on the terrace which cast its circle of light like 'a moon on its opal globe'; and a quarry beyond the gardener's cottage), could be heard the guns of the Somme offensive which he turned into the 'splendid drumming' that Mazzini characteristically identifies as the sound of a goods train and Hector interprets as 'Heaven's threatening growl of disgust at us useless futile creatures'.

This weekend, with its coming together of Bloomsbury and the Fabians, helped Shaw over some of his difficulties with the play – which he gratefully acknowledged in a letter to Virginia twenty-four years later when the bombs of the Second World War had begun to fall. 'There is a play of mine called Heartbreak House which I always connect with you because I conceived it in that house somewhere in Sussex where I first met you and, of course, fell in love with you,' he wrote. Though the Bloomsbury Group had published and exhibited little of its work before 1916, the principles of aesthetic sensibility and personal relationships which animated that work, and to which it gave priority over the economic and political values of the Fabians, would have become sufficiently apparent to Shaw during these days of incessant talking – and it is these Bloomsbury values which he now injected into the play. 'Shaw visits upon the age of Bloomsbury with its cult of sentimental personal relations the same scorn Carlyle visited upon the age of Brummel with its Byronism and its pococurantism', commented the critic Louis Crompton. And this was truly Shaw's intention. But the inhabitants of Heartbreak House are more convincingly made up from that coterie of gallants and graces known as 'the Souls', who were far more aristocratic than the Bloomsbury Group and went on polishing their veneer of culture, went on sipping the sweet life, even after the declaration of war. Shaw added Bloomsbury to his mixture so as to make his play contemporary, but the Souls still haunt his house because he had earlier and better knowledge of them than of Bloomsbury.

The habit of writing is Shaw's equivalent of Shotover's addiction to rum. His frustration over the limitations of writing is echoed by Hector who exclaims: 'Think! Whats the good of thinking about it? Why didnt you do something?' Like Sergius Saranoff, the tragic hero of *Arms and the Man*, Hector owes something to the adventurer Cunninghame Graham ('to live up to your biography of me, I shall have to ruin myself in hats & boots', he told Shaw) and he flaunts, too, some borrowed plumes from Hubert Bland and from Wilfrid Scawen Blunt. But even the 'handsome Arab costume' which he prefers to a dinner jacket (and which goes completely unremarked by all the other characters) cannot distract us from hearing in his exclamations of 'worthlessness' at 'playing the fool' the voice of Shaw's own failure to work the clogged machinery of political life by extravagant comic methods.

Shaw's pessimism had grown from his experience of contemporary history; his optimism was increasingly tied to a visionary future where the action of human will has broken the cyclical pattern of behaviour. *Heartbreak House* is less a visionary than a contemporary play, and Shotover, as the most authoritative voice of the Life Force, gets the better of his exchange with Hector, though it is a misanthropic victory which seems to overshadow Shaw's last years. 'I cannot bear men and women. I have to run away,'

Shotover cries out. '. . . Old men are dangerous: it doesnt matter to them what is going to happen to the world.' Yet the play marries Shotover spiritually to Ellie Dunn, and in doing so points to an alternative history which the surreal works of Shaw's last period were to explore.

*

Shaw described his play as being, like himself, an inexplicable phenomenon. But its thicket of personal, historical and literary associations have made it a rich text for critics. They likened Hastings Utterword to Warren Hastings, Mazzini Dunn to the Italian revolutionary Giuseppe Mazzini, Shotover to Carlyle's Undershot, 'Marcus Darnley' to the husband of Mary, Queen of Scots, Ariadne to the daughter of Minos, King of Crete, and the metaphorical title *Heartbreak House* to Dickens's *Bleak House*. In a late draft, Shaw changed Mrs Hushabye's name from Hecuba to Hesione – from the wife of King Priam to King Laomedon's daughter whose beauty provoked a war in which she and Hector were on beaten sides.

> Another Troy must rise and set,
> Another lineage feed the crow,
> Another Argo's painted prow
> Drive to a flashier bauble yet.

Like Yeats, in his contemporary symbolist poem 'Two Songs from a Play', Shaw reinforces his drama of the downfall of the British Empire and the end of pre-war English culture with this mythological precedent, the fall of Troy.

Heartbreak House belongs more than any of Shaw's other plays to the mood of its time. The throbbing pessimism, bolts of anger, shivers of violence that build to its ambiguously explosive climax are also ingredients active in the great apocalyptic works of the war: Eliot's *The Waste Land*, Lawrence's *Women in Love* and Yeats's 'The Second Coming'. Yet Shaw's solitary voice is not happily joined to the modernist movement. He felt unusually possessive about 'my masterpiece', as he protectively called it, suspecting it of being a flawed masterpiece. Though giving it to be understood that the play had been largely written before the war, its actual composition in 1916, and the successive detailed revisions throughout 1917, were interrupted by the stream of war events to which he was continually responding in other writings – a draft of his appeal against Casement's execution, for example, actually appears on the other side of one page of the *Heartbreak House* typescript. These breaks in his normally fast method of composition disrupted the tone. 'I have *no* hesitation in feeling that I listened to a very fine play,' Mrs Pat wrote to him after he had read it to her in June 1917, 'the first act delights me – you beget your own dramatis personae like a God – but as you went along you lost respect for their bones. They didn't always stand steady on their feet ... the people become mere mouthpieces of the general scheme – without bones flesh or blood – I feel *disorder* where you probably feel "there I was inspired".'

What is in question is Shaw's *control* of disorder. He is in surreal territory several years before the arrival of the surrealists who courted loss of control to explore connections between dream and reality. The sudden spiralling of his wit, the curious patches of farce, the sideslips of tone (such as the nursery incantation at the end of Act I which seems to sound from the world of T. S. Eliot), all fill gaps in the play's organic unity. He had written a revenge tragedy without blood. As they drift in and out of this visionary house, these elemental characters seem to grow disembodied, as if made of air and fire. Perhaps influenced by Ibsen's *The Master Builder*, Shaw lowered their ages in the typescript but also eliminated the sexual explicitness – a change that, while moving them towards the Bloomsbury generation, was contrary to the Bloomsbury ethos. It is the play of an older man. 'I have children,' says Hector. 'All that is over and done with for me' – as it is for Hesione and Ariadne. In his early trilogy of plays Shaw had tried to join material reality with spiritual passion and concentrate his optimism on waking life; but the explosives shed in *Major Barbara* had blown up in Captain Shotover's gravel pit and destroyed reality. Larry Doyle in *John Bull's Other Island* had longed for a place where the facts were not brutal and the dreams not unreal; but the brutality of the war had driven Shaw deeper into dreams. The love charades of *Heartbreak House* are the games that go on in 'the house of the unreal and of the seekers for happiness' which is Don Juan's definition of hell in *Man and Superman*. Shotover's inventions and Hector's fantasies are also parts of that eternal romancing and pretension; and Ellie Dunn, having escaped the tyranny of the flesh by virtue of her love affair with the non-existent 'Marcus Darnley' and her white marriage to Shotover, now qualifies for hell as one of those inhabitants whom Don Juan describes as 'not animal at all ... in a word, bodiless'. There is no physical plane on which Hector, Ellie and Shotover, all with their divine sparks, can join as there had been in *Major Barbara* for Cusins, Barbara and Undershaft. In the last act, where 'the house breaks out through the windows, and becomes all England with all England's heart broken', intelligence, will and action have not been fused together by the heat of the explosion; and the past, present and future are still left in suspension.

Shaw came as close as he dared in *Heartbreak House* to 'the blasphemous despair of Lear', as an antidote to which, in his next play, he would create a new race of beings. He overlooked those who accepted the opportunities as well as the bereavements of war (such as women who drove ambulances, worked on the land, ran hospitals and became VADs). He responded to the stupidities paraded in the newspapers and practised by such good people as the Lambeth Guardians, who had discontinued the practice of giving workhouse children an egg on Christmas morning in order to bring home to them the lesson of self-denial. 'And yet no thunder falls from heaven,' he had written to Stella Campbell on reading this. 'Do we two belong to this race of cretins?' His play provides that thunder from heaven and numbers Stella and himself among the endangered.

*

Some 20,000 copies of *Heartbreak House*, *Great Catherine*, and *Playlets of the War* were published in North America and Britain during September 1919. In Britain the critical response was generally unfavourable. A. B. Walkley, having survived the war unchanged, failed to notice any change in G.B.S. 'You take up the familiar squat volume in the familiar greenish-grey binding, and find the inside familiar, too,' he wrote in *The Times Literary Supplement*: 'the old point of view, the old logic, the old people, and the old preface. After so much upheaval in the world at large it is comforting to have at least one antique way to stand upon.' He dismissed the Chekhovian parallel and substituted as a precedent the artifice of an eighteenth-century light romantic playwright. 'All this is sheer Marivaux,' he concluded after a brief résumé of the plot.

Walkley doubted whether the 'fun' of *Heartbreak House* 'would stand the glare of the footlights', and other critics shared this doubt. The *Nation* thought it was perhaps 'unplayable'; the *Spectator* saw the characters as too elusive, reflections of Shaw's lessening contact with people; in the *Athenaeum*, Middleton Murry wrote that it would probably 'be intensely amusing on the stage', but he viewed it all simply as farce: 'half-procession, half-pandemonium ... all the characters seem to be scurrying about with the intense crazy logic of lunatics'. None of this could have helped Shaw to decide for a production in London. He had withheld his play from the stage during the last year of the war and his reluctance to see it performed persisted after the war. 'No: you let "Heartbreak House" alone,' he instructed Esmé Percy, who had successfully staged *Man and Superman* in its entirety, 'you cannot cast it. And you are too young to play the Captain.'

Eventually, in the summer of 1920, he signed a contract with the newly-incorporated Theatre Guild of New York, where his volume of war plays had been less condescendingly received. He would not, however, let them open until the presidential election that autumn was over – 'and very thankful you will be to me for having saved you from a disastrous blunder', he assured its founder, Lawrence Langner. The world première took place at the Garrick Theater in New York on 10 November 1920. It was well reviewed, and the production ran for more than 100 performances over almost five months. 'See what has happened recently in America!' Shaw exhorted his French translator Augustin Hamon. '...I gave Heartbreak House to the Theatre Guild of New York, who ... engaged a famous producer. The famous producer found the play quite impossible at full length: no audience could endure three hours "talk". I withdrew the play and ... the Theatre Guild capitulated; sacked the famous producer; and pledged themselves that not a comma should be omitted, no matter how disastrous the consequences. Result: a great success.' So loyal to this pledge was the American company that the actress playing Hesione, a glorious blonde who disdained a wig, had to be offered slurred congratulations each night on her magnificent head of black hair.

The American production was good, but it provided Shaw with a bad precedent. In Vienna, where Trebitsch's translation was staged later that November 'with great respect for the intentions of the author', Shaw's loquaciousness seemed to weaken the effect. 'Like Richard Strauss in music, he never seems to know when to finish his parlando,' one critic wrote. '... The audience at first listened with great interest ... later, however, the interest lessened visibly, the signs of impatience were not wanting at the end.'

Shaw was to learn something of this difficulty for himself a year later during rehearsals of the English production which he directed with the new leaseholder of the Court Theatre, the Irish playwright and manager J. B. Fagan. He was meticulous over the details of stage business ('which is as much part of the play as the dialogue'), trying to work up the explosion, manipulate the lights, control the pitch, pace, inflection, movement, mood and even make-up of the actors. He resented lunch breaks, but allowed interruptions by the theatre cat and did not mind holding up his rehearsals with his own anecdotes. He made endless notes, gave endless instructions, bullied and cajoled, taking the actors aside to whisper conspiratorial advice ('I want you on the first night to make up like Cunninghame Graham,' he told James Dale, who was playing Hector. 'He will be in the front row.') He was 'a born *ad-vis-er*' remarked Edith Evans who played Ariadne.

'I am rehearsing Heartbreak House at the Court Theatre,' he wrote to Elgar. 'It was like old times rehearsing John Bull there.' But there was a difference. 'The book of the words has been so widely read and so much discussed,' wrote the critic of the *Westminster Gazette*, '... that the real hush of expectation was absent. Indeed, the people in the stalls around me talked almost as much as the people on the stage, and at the same time...' In the old times, publication of Shaw's plays had sharpened the public's demand for their performance; now it seemed to dull the curiosity of an audience that already knew about the eccentricities of Shotover and the climax of the bombing raid. The reviewers were specially abusive. 'If the Press could kill a playwright I should have been a dead man twenty years ago,' Shaw wrote. The play was retitled 'Jawbreak House' and the action which, readers were told, took place in 'a private lunatic asylum with many patients and no keeper' was described as having 'half-emptied the stalls before it was over'. As a play it was judged to be 'about the worst there ever was'. The only reputation to be significantly lifted was Chekhov's. 'Tchekov always has an atmosphere,' commented the *Sunday Times*; 'this play has only a smell.'

Shaw blamed the lack of rehearsal time. 'I have been rather unhappy because I let the play go before it was safely ready,' he wrote to Fagan, 'and before we had polished it.' He immediately set about polishing it himself with a blue pencil – exactly what he had forbidden the American and Austrian directors to do. 'I cut some dead wood out of Act III,' he told St John Ervine who had criticized the slow pace of the production and the casting of the Irish actress Ellen O'Malley as Ellie Dunn. Shaw defended his casting and the cuts. 'I never cut anything merely to save time ... [but] there are always lines which are dud lines with a given cast. Change the cast and you get other lines dud.' This truth, however, obscured another truth: the play lacked the seventh degree of concentration.

On the first night the stage machinery had seized up, which delayed the performance of the third act by nearly half an hour. This technical hiccup left some reviewers wondering whether the play's reception had been fair. 'As an entertainment pure and simple it is dull and incoherent ... [with] all the author's prolixities and perversities,' reported James Agate in the *Saturday Review*, and yet 'I found it quite definitely exhilarating and deeply moving, and it therefore ranks for me among the great testaments.' Responding to this feeling, the *Sunday Express* helped the management to arrange a second press showing at a matinée on 25 November. Most of the second notices were less ungenerous. The *Sunday Express* itself reported that 'judicious cutting and quickening have transformed the piece into an intellectually exhilarating entertainment'.

Shaw was 'much touched' at having been given this opportunity to change critical opinion. At the end of the performance, in front of a full house, he made a brief speech, concluding: 'We will keep it going as long as we can. Come again.' But it was too late. After sixty-three performances the shutters went up, and J. B. Fagan was left with massive debts, £7,676 of which were unpaid royalties. 'He can pay me entirely at his convenience,' Shaw wrote to Fagan's solicitors. 'If the other creditors force a bankruptcy I shall of course put in my claim ... but otherwise he may dismiss it from his mind until his next period of prosperity.'

'The fault is mine if there is any fault,' Shaw had told St John Ervine. But having protected Fagan and the actors, he made it clear where he thought the fault really lay. Granville-Barker and Vedrenne's experiment at the Court Theatre had demonstrated that a classical theatre could only just be kept alive if the theatre itself were free of rent, rates and taxes. Twenty years later, when the expense of running a theatre had been greatly increased by a new entertainment tax, England needed an endowed theatre more urgently than ever. 'We have municipal morgues and national racecourses, but no municipal theatres and no national one,' Shaw complained in the *Sunday Express*. '... the vain appeal of the Shakespeare Memorial National Theatre has shown that you can get money in England for sport, for religion, for party politics, for charity, and even for nothing discoverable (as in the case of the Prince of Wales' Fund), but not for art, least of all the art of the theatre. We are in that respect barbarians, which means, not that we are indifferent to high art, but that we actively dislike it.'

Like the great pushes of the war, *Heartbreak House* seemed almost to have succeeded – before turning into a victory for the culture of Horseback Hall. Coming at the start of the 1920s, this was a bad omen.

[3]

You *are becoming too famous.*
Shaw to Blanche Patch

'Would you care to be my secretary?' Shaw enquired of a forty-year-old clergyman's daughter. Like Judy Gillmore before her, Ann Elder was deserting him for a husband. She had abandoned him previously when deciding to train as a solicitor at the end of the war (her sister Una then stepping into the part of his secretary). She had even abandoned him for a spring honeymoon (when Shaw used a Miss Pyke as understudy). But now, in the summer of 1920, she was transferring to India, where her husband had an engagement as an electrical engineer.

Blanche Patch, the clergyman's daughter, seemed perfect casting for the vacancy. In appearance she reminded Shaw of Harold Laski – and since he was a prominent socialist at the London School of Economics, this counted in her favour. It may even have influenced Charlotte on whom, when inspected, Miss Patch made a 'pleasant impression'. She had emerged from a Sussex rectory to become a Norland nurse, a handloom weaver, a pharmacist's assistant in Wales and was currently typing for a London optician. She was 'not a university woman', had little shorthand, but came recommended by the Webbs and impressed Shaw by knowing pretty well nothing about the literary or political world.

As a non-Shavian, Miss Patch was unaware of her advantages. Shaw's 'quick, witty, friendly way ... [which] was new to me then' increased her diffidence, and she wrote back declining his offer. Recognizing the uncertainty behind this refusal Shaw tried again. 'I hardly like to steal you away from another man. Still, I will not take your first No for an answer; so will you let me have a second one, or a Yes, before I let loose a general announcement that the post is vacant?'

This tactful renewal gave her confidence to take the risk and do what she really wanted – after all 'he had only himself to blame'. She started work as Shaw's secretary at the end of July 1920 and remained with him until his death. Towards the end of this time, when giving her permission to quote some correspondence for her book *Thirty Years with G.B.S.*, Shaw wrote: 'The engagement as my secretary negotiated in the enclosed letters has now lasted 28 years and has never been regretted by me.' The tone of this commendation is a key to their partnership. He treated her like a typewriter, and she went on typing for him, usually without approval, often without understanding. There was nothing odd in this: she had sometimes disagreed with the diagnosis of doctors whose prescriptions she had made up in Wales. 'Nothing that you could possibly write,' Shaw confidently told Stella Campbell, 'could produce the slightest effect on her.' Certainly nothing that he wrote ever affected her. This arrangement suited them both well. Though 'Shaw-proof', she became such a curiously appropriate Shavian *alter ego* that some correspondents suspected 'Blanche Patch' of being his pen name.

Ann Elder had observed that 'my successor, Miss Blanche Patch, was older and more mature than I, but I'm not sure that her sense of humour was ever very strongly developed.' This lack of humour was amusing to Shaw. 'Patch is a born comedian,' he insisted in a letter to Beatrice Webb, 'and shews me photographs of herself as a Pierrot.'

She had been nervous at first. 'Does he throw things at you?' she asked one of the maids. But what responsible employer would deliberately damage his office equipment? During her thirty years' employment only twice could she remember him losing his temper – and then it was not with her. 'Even-tempered he always was, and that made working for him easy; but never a word of praise came from him.' Though she may have had regrets, as Shaw hints, there could be few fantasies. He was less a father to her than a maintenance inspector. 'The trouble you have NOT given me,' he

complimented her, 'and the help you HAVE given me are immeasurable.'
Who could say which was the greater?

He never misused her, never spoilt her. 'No man knows your value better
than I do,' he told her: and it was true she was wonderfully economic. 'Will
you think £3-10s per week too much?' she had asked him and he
immediately agreed to this, not telling her that it was ten shillings a week less
than Ann Elder had been getting. He was not 'fundamentally mean', Miss
Patch decided. Over the years, she was to witness him handing away many
thousands of pounds, but such gifts were conferred 'without human
warmth', she noted, and often to people she felt were undeserving. It struck
her as odd too that he should be so spontaneous with strangers while
remaining so cautious with someone invaluable like herself. He appeared to
believe that money was out of place in a civilized community. This scorn for
capitalistic money-making affected her awkwardly. Shaw had been paying
Ann Elder more than union rates ('it will make you more effectually my slave
if you live at that rate') and acknowledged that he would have paid her still
more if she had asked. But by the time Blanche Patch took over he preferred
to *calculate* his finances. These calculations, sometimes hampered by an
elderly adding machine (a cumbersome contrivance that was later replaced
by a portable implement with which he loved playing) seemed to her 'finicky'
and pedantic. 'The meaning to the ordinary worker of the increased cost of
living never reached his conscious mind,' she complained. '...Pounds,
shillings and pence were in truth as remote from his active comprehension
as the meaning of figures ranged in their thousands.' She was not to know
that he added a codicil to his will in the late 1920s leaving her an annuity of
£260, which he raised to £365 in the late 1930s and to £500 in 1950. What
she did know was his inability, as he grew older and taxation rose, to
recognize the facts of inflation and add significantly to her salary. If only she
had asked for more, earlier. For a long time she puzzled over his financial
aberrations – until it suddenly occurred to her that he simply had no head
for numbers. 'He could never, for instance, remember how many brothers
and sisters I had.'

Shaw had warned her that the Adelphi Terrace apartment was protected
by a strongly fortified obstacle giving it 'the appearance of a private
madhouse'. When she had got through this barbed-wire gate, she ascended
to the study, a long 'horribly pokey room' on the third floor overlooking the
Water Gate arches upon Hungerford Bridge, with Shaw's desk at one end
and hers at the other. His shorthand, which was without contractions or
grammalogies and gave him a regular writing speed of twelve words a
minute, had all the vowel signs written in and difficult words spelt out in
longhand, so it was easy for her to transcribe. He wrote 1,500 words of

prime work a morning, without corrections, on blocks of water-lined paper with a green tint to rest his eyes, and would give her his shorthand draft in batches. 'I used to rest his manuscript on a stand, such as violinists have, placed behind my typewriter and raised to eye height,' she wrote. '... A double-spaced typescript was the working copy for his revision. Carbons of anything that was to be published were made on yellow paper...' Very occasionally she made an error – 'the profiteers of the theatre' instead of 'the proprietors of the theatre', which struck Shaw as an improvement, and 'porter' for 'torture', which for some reason made him laugh.

Apart from his hobbies of swimming at the RAC, walking, motorcycling and motoring (with a little hedge-trimming and log-sawing in the country), Shaw did nothing but work, so far as Miss Patch could see. 'His industry was terrific,' she wrote. 'I have always thought that he wrote too much.' She did not air her opinion of his plays, which was a stroke of tact. Privately she found *Back to Methuselah* 'hard pedalling' and *On the Rocks* 'dull', while *Too True to be Good* 'bored me a bit'. The first two plays she worked on were *Jitta's Atonement*, which was 'slight' and 'rather dismal', and *Saint Joan*, which she acknowledged to be not his best. She was still less enthusiastic about his non-dramatic work. 'He would be an uncommonly devoted Shavian who to-day would cheerfully set out again to read through *The Intelligent Woman's Guide*, followed by *Everybody's Political What's What* not to say explore once more the Sahara of the novels,' she wrote shortly after Shaw's death.

It was a pity that writing had become such an obsession with him. Miss Patch didn't believe he ever had a thoroughly frivolous afternoon. Often she was obliged to put aside her 1,500 words of play-typing for the articles and long letters 'which rained upon me in a torrent'. Early subjects ranged from Beethoven and Churchill, to Walt Whitman and Santa Claus; while the topics moved from proposals for sex training and the question of rejuvenation by monkey glands, to whether dogs have an after-life and why he could not afford a peerage – all implacably typed out. Then there were what she called the 'pests' and 'busybodies', who wanted autographs, prefaces, cheques, speeches and appearances, whom she would 'fob-off' with one of the printed cards from his coloured pack or a paragraph of careful explanation. 'To most of them,' she objected, 'he was much too polite.'

Miss Patch herself was not so polite. Some of those who at first had been enchanted by her name ('it suggests a vivacious person in a play by Sheridan' proposed Charles Ricketts) were soon addressing her: 'Dear Miss Cross Patch.' She referred to 'my pretended irascibility' as a necessary component of 'our firmness'. The only person who really exasperated her was G.B.S. 'Oh, go away and write another play!' she would exclaim when he came between her and her typescripts. She didn't much like him pacing near her typewriter either – 'he created a considerable draught as he swung past me' – and eventually instructed him to indulge these Life Force manoeuvres when she was absent. His formal manners were invariably courteous, she admitted, but he was a shy man who shrank from people: how envious he must be, she often told herself, of the way she herself got on with everyone. 'He always appeared to be astonished that I knew much more about the working classes than he did.'

But what exasperated her most was the way he took her for granted. 'I resented being looked on simply as a shorthand typist.' Occasionally he would be flatteringly observant, remarking one morning, for instance, that she must have been very well brought up as she always wiped her shoes on the doormat whether it was wet or dry. At other times he would behave as if she wasn't there at all, except apparently when she actually wasn't there. 'I might be away for a week or so with influenza and he would receive me when I returned to work as if I had been there all the time.'

Planted beneath the cool surface of their relationship was a perpetually unflowering seed of emotion. Although she never showed it openly, Charlotte was 'jealous of the fact that I had to read and transcribe his shorthand', Miss Patch noticed. It didn't surprise her. Phonetic shorthand was a form of intimacy that 'a lonely type of person' like Charlotte would have loved. Miss Patch could appreciate that. What she could not appreciate was Shaw's behaviour when, from time to time, he passed on 'certain of my duties' to another woman – by which she meant his former secretary and relative, Judy Gillmore. That really put a spark in the gunpowder. Why G.B.S. should still feel so fond of Judy Miss Patch could never comprehend. Judy had made her bed with Harold Musters in 1912; and that should have been that. Of course Shaw was contrite: 'you hate to have anyone stealing your work', he acknowledged. But this gesture hardly atoned for his repeated acts of unfaithfulness. Take, for example, the matter of the big toe of her right foot. She must have injured it in her school days, for it had stiffened over the years and by the time she settled down at Adelphi Terrace it had become an agony to her. News of her toe never failed to stimulate G.B.S., who often corresponded about it when away and entertained several notions as to the effect of high heels on toes. By way of experiment, he even sent her at his own expense to a 'Scandinavian Naturpath' who applied hot fomentations to almost every part of her body except the foot, bringing no relief whatever. Shaw was anxious that she avoid 'the operation panacea' but all the extra walking during the General Strike finally disabled her and she decided to go into St Thomas's Hospital to have her toe joint removed. 'I throw up my hands and ask desperately, is there ANYBODY who is not being operated on?' Shaw remonstrated. 'Who is your proposed *locum tenens*? You will probably find her on the table also.' It was when she went down to Frinton for what she hoped would be a peaceful convalescence that Shaw exploded his surprise. He had engaged Judy Gillmore as *locum tenens*, 'so you need not hurry back if your foot needs a little more rest'. She hurried back. It was typical of him to get fun out of teasing her. If she had been able to afford it, she would have left him on the spot, and for once she gave him a jolt by making her feelings plain.

But to do him justice, he seemed greatly relieved to have her back not wholly disabled. 'I am distracted and lost without you,' he had appealed to her, and he had 'footed' the bill for her operation. So they settled down again until the next upheaval. Miss Patch realized that some people thought her attitude to G.B.S. was unfriendly; one of them (probably St John Ervine) was to send her an anonymous card marked JUDAS when she published her reminiscences of him. But Shaw himself understood the nature of their long fragmentary partnership. He cared for her as he did for his paste and scissors, which also contributed to the manuscripts and proofs of his life. And she looked after him as a matron of a nursing home might look after a long-term patient – with detachment and efficiency, noting his fads and the long periods of abstracted silence, and occasionally telling him off when his foolishness went too far. 'The faithful Patch', he once called her. She prized this tribute from one who had the tribute of the world.

*

'Travelling is still very troublesome,' Shaw had written to Trebitsch in the summer of 1919. For more than six years following the war the Shaws did not travel outside the United Kingdom, though Charlotte regularly hustled G.B.S. over England, Scotland, Wales and Ireland on a series of purposeful holidays and political speaking trips, on theatrical tours and to Fabian Summer Schools. Kilsby, going off to make aeroplane engines at Woolwich, had taken a long farewell of them during the war, and in May 1919 Charlotte engaged Fred Day from Codicote as their new chauffeur at Ayot St Lawrence. At this time, and until he was almost seventy, G.B.S. was still a fiery motorcyclist, and he soon egged on Day to 'ginger up' his two-stroke machine – after which it would hurtle away, bucking him off and sometimes landing on top of him. Before Day's arrival he had taken hypothetical instruction from the local chemist, E. P. Downing, on how to steer this motorcycle round corners, but he could not bring himself to accept the theory that it was necessary to slow down and to lean over at an angle. The chemist, impressed by Shaw's 'outstanding deficiency in mechanical sense', had no more luck with his extra hints on reversing motorcars, Shaw once taking half an hour to turn the car round, and demolishing some flowerbeds while doing so.

By the time Fred Day took over, the village had grown proud of Shaw's notorious road exploits. Local dogs, knowing him well, would play dead under his car while he anxiously crawled after them – when they would bounce out, barking triumphantly. In Day's opinion his employer was 'rather reckless' at the wheel, though 'always very considerate' afterwards. Whenever anything happened, such as a bump or a crash, 'Mr Shaw was always ready to take the blame.' He would leap out, offer to pay all expenses, scoop up the other driver and passengers and drive them trembling home.

According to Miss Patch up in London, Shaw was 'extremely lucky with his staff'. Fred Day, for example, stayed with him for thirty-one adventurous years and owned that he 'would do anything for Mr Shaw', though he was not paid particularly high wages. The Shaws were excellent employers, never interfering but always treating him kindly. Once, during a storm, Shaw noticed Day give a small wave to a woman and child at a bus stop. 'Who's that?' he asked. 'My wife,' Day answered. 'Stop,' Shaw commanded, ' – turn round. We must take them home.' Day had schooled his family never to recognize him if they met him on duty since 'in those days [1925] it was definitely not usual for the gentry to have anything to do with the staff socially. But Mr Shaw was different. He put his arm round her shoulders and helped her into the car. She was terrified . . .' Later on, Shaw even offered to pay for his daughter to train as a schoolteacher though personally admitting 'I'd rather be a crossing-sweeper.'

It was an interesting job being the Shaws' chauffeur. You got to drive all sorts of machines – a Vauxhall or a Bianca with mechanical windscreen wipers, a straight-eight Lanchester with a harmonic balancer (which Mr Shaw spoke of as if he believed it to be a musical contraption), followed by a 'run-about' Lanchester ten, then a chocolate-coloured Rolls-Royce and finally a 25-30 m.p.h. Silver Wraith. Mr Shaw would ask Day's advice on cars – such as the A. C. coupé they bought in 1923 – quiz him about helical pinions or differential gears and take him to the dealers. He would ride next to Day up front, and take the wheel until lunch, while Mrs Shaw, still rather nervous, preferred sitting at the back. Mr Shaw had the back seat specially upholstered for her, with the compartment sealed from draughts and fitted with a heater. Mrs Shaw designed the front seat for him, with a cushion at the head propping him bolt upright. In this manner, at various speeds, they travelled the country, usually very slow when Mrs Shaw was with them, invariably very fast when she wasn't and Mr Shaw was driving. You never quite knew what he would get up to next. His favourite trick, Day noticed, was to mistake the accelerator for the brake. Sometimes, when visiting their friends, his employers would travel by train and arrange for Day to follow with the bags. It seemed to him a funny sort of logic, using a Rolls-Royce for carrying luggage.

[4]

I dont expect anybody but myself to see as far as I do.
Shaw to the Webbs (1916)

I am doing the best I can at my age.
Preface to *Back to Methuselah* (1921)

'Messrs Constable & Co have to announce the publication early in the forthcoming season of an important and even extraordinary work by Mr Bernard Shaw,' wrote Shaw in a press release for his publishers in the spring of 1921. The book would, he promised, 'interest biologists, religious leaders, and lovers of the marvellous in fiction as well as lovers of the theatre. It is the author's scientific, religious, and political testament as well as his supreme exploit in dramatic literature...

'The author, in a massive historical and biological preface entitled The Infidel Half Century, seriously contends that the extension of human life contemplated in his play is a scientific possibility, and must be included as such in the religion of Creative Evolution which ... is now ready for adoption as the New Faith of the world.'

Shaw had begun this colossal affair, its 30,000-word Preface leading to a sequence of five plays under the collective title *Back to Methuselah*, more than seven months before the war was over, and completed it at the end of May two years later, though continuing to revise and prepare it for publication into the early months of 1921. Like *Heartbreak House*, it was struck out of him by the war; but where *Heartbreak House* exploits the forces of death, *Back to Methuselah* explores new powers of life. It is a vastly hopeful composition, produced at a period when he suspected 'my sands are running out', and either a world classic or nothing, he added, on its appearance in the Oxford University Press library of World Classics.

Relieved to see him less restless than usual, and warmed by the religious flavour of his work, Charlotte supported him faithfully. 'We are very happy & even G.B.S. doesn't want to go away,' she reported from Parknasilla in

32

south-west Ireland a few days before he sent his manuscript to the printer. 'He gave up the Fabian Summer School to stay on here! He is finishing his book. I am quite sure it is going to be his *magnum opus*.' Charlotte's aspirations echoed Shaw's own hopes that here was 'one of my most important works (or so I fancy)'. For he had put much other writing aside, working with great urgency and intensity at what seemed must be 'the last work of any vigor I shall produce'.

In his mid-sixties Shaw sensed the encroachments of age not in ill-health and sexual loss, but more obliquely as philosophical pessimism and financial threat, a sense of falling out of step with the contemporary world and losing contact with his audience. It was an age of fancy dress. Men wore co-respondents' shoes, brilliantined their hair and stuck on big bow ties; women plucked their eyebrows, raised the hems of skirts and painted their nails. Everyone wanted to be young and to have a good time in a bad world. There were crazes for cocktails, for cosmetics, jazz and jasper, the night club and the *thé dansant*. The Continent was miraculously transformed from a battlefield into a playground. Don Juan's picture of hell had been visited on earth. Below the syncopated rhythms and vibrant colours, the high kick and the quick step of this whirling triviality, Shaw sensed a disillusionment. He was fighting disillusionment in himself. The world was still bleeding dangerously in these terrible post-war years, which sometimes seemed to him more frightful than the war itself. He felt 'the uncertainty of my own position and my impotence in the face of a collapse of civilization'. The men-of-one-idea – Lloyd George, Poincaré and Clemenceau – who had successfully prosecuted the war and emerged as the victors of western Europe, wanted to build the peace upon the bankrupt bodies of the vanquished. Every day Shaw received appeals to save babies who were starving overseas. Every week some unfortunate German author or professor would 'write me the whole history of his life, more to console himself and persuade his wife that he was doing something that might bring them the price of a sack of coals, than in any real hope of escaping from his miseries', he told the German playwright Julius Bab. '... it became part of the day's routine to hear that So and So and his wife were starving and that there was not a child under 7 years of age left alive in Poland'. Before the war Shaw had been remarkably generous to all manner of people who appealed to him for money. But the financial calamity now seemed beyond all reckoning. His generosity persisted but, seeming almost pointless, grew capricious – after all, one tragedy more or less, here or there, was hardly noticeable when the whole world was breaking up. He complained that as a result of the inflation of the German and Austrian currencies, he was now paying off the war debt himself. 'But everyone stands ruined to-day,' he wrote, 'except the war profiteers. It is a case of "Let us eat and drink: for at the next budget we die".'

In these circumstances his decision to devote more than two years to a play that 'alas! [has] no money in it' dramatically illustrated his view that effective argument with public opinion was no longer an economic but a moral argument. 'In writing *Back to Methuselah* I threw over all economic considerations,' he wrote. The play distanced him from the unbearable inadequacy of mere cheque-signing and obliged him to look beyond his social work. 'I was forced to take refuge in complete callousness,' he explained. '...I soon lost the power of feeling anything.' He tried to make this more acceptable through self-mockery, describing himself as one of the poor rich who did not know where to turn to pay his supertax without selling his stocks. 'I am the sort of man who devotes his life to the salvation of humanity in the abstract,' he declared, 'and can't bear to give a penny to a starving widow.'

Back to Methuselah belongs to an abstract world from which the ignorance and errors of post-war statesmen look infantile. The one idea of victory having been replaced in their minds by the one idea of security, the war was still not over: 'the dread of defeat, instead of being removed by victory, is merely transferred to the next war', Shaw prophesied to an American journalist. The remedy was to stop warfaring and organize peace; 'but nobody seems to have the slightest intention of doing it. So much the worse for civilization!'

Shaw explained such lack of intention as a lack of ability. Again and again, he had turned down invitations to enter Parliament, refusing to stand for Northampton in 1919 and for the constituency of West Edinburgh in 1922. 'It would be easier and pleasanter to drown myself.' He could not help feeling his superiority over the elected Parliament man, but superiority seemed to him an impediment in the capitalist phase of our democratic system. It attracted dread and mistrust, an inevitable result of the unevenness of evolution. 'I have no doubt that if tigers and monkeys were to express their opinion of mankind they would vote us cold, passionless, calculating, and mysteriously dreadful.'

After the war he felt increasingly convinced that the world was being tragically mismanaged by unqualified pretenders who, at best, meant well but had no idea that government was a science for which only a small percentage of the population had any aptitude. 'My conclusion was that we need very urgently a sound anthropometric method to guide and limit the present adult suffrage,' he was to write, 'and that even the discovery of such a method would only make it clearer that we must live longer (say 300 years) if we were to solve the social problems raised by our huge modern populations and developments of powers of communication, transport, destruction and slaughter.' *Back to Methuselah* combines Shaw's most scarifying satire of contemporary politicians with this utopian formula for a biologically advanced society, where he himself would progress to refreshing inferiority, shedding G.B.S. on his way to much-desired oblivion. 'If I am to leave my headaches and my imbecilities and brutalities behind,' he wrote, 'I shall leave Bernard Shaw behind, and a good job too.'

It was an immense relief to work in this futuristic world, phasing out the miseries of life around him. 'The whole world is ill, in ruins, starving,' he wrote to the artist Bertha Newcombe: 'I am tired of its troubles & follies.' Hardship abroad was compounded by cynicism at home. A war-damaged generation, suddenly dropped from peaks of combat terror into a tarn of disillusion, seemed unable to make any further moral effort after doing its bit on such an exorbitant scale. It appeared to Shaw that the strain of war had forced humanity into an unnatural shape. The country was filled with 'shell-shocked rakes and deflowered flappers' – 'boys who for years did not believe they could escape death for many weeks more ... excited girls who could refuse these doomed boys nothing: "Virtue" in them would have been an unthinkable meanness. When it was over the girls had lost the habit of virtue and the boys had acquired the habit of drink...'

The expectation of death (with which *Heartbreak House* concluded) had utterly exhausted people who had learnt to feel, think and act as if there were no future. In *Back to Methuselah*, Shaw struggled to discover what this discouraged generation needed to have said to it. He wanted to give it back a future with new prospects of living, and by rekindling its hopes to restore the certainty of his own position.

His cycle of plays is a metaphysical (or what he called a metabiological) enquiry into the causes of pessimism in the development of thought since Darwin, and a search for a legitimate philosophical basis on which to re-engage optimism. Yet his own political experience suggested that men and women were incapable of solving the social problems raised by their civilization and had therefore been doomed to the poverty and slavery against which socialism vainly protested. He insisted that this was no reason to abandon socialism (as Edmund Wilson, in his criticism of *Back to Methuselah*, was to claim he had done). 'I take the view that the worse a job is the more reason for trying to make the best of it,' he wrote. 'But my creed of creative evolution means in practice that man can change himself to meet every vital need, and that however long the trials and frequent the failures may be, we can put up a soul as an athlete puts up a muscle. Thus to men who are themselves cynical I am a pessimist; but to genuinely religious men I am an optimist, and even a fantastic and extravagant one.'

35

Back to Methuselah is the vision of an extravagant fantasist, a *Paradise Lost* and *Paradise Regained* which seeks to demolish our concepts of normality, reintroduces the imaginative quality of free will as an unconscious process, and treats the present as a passing phase of history in which crisis and even collapse might be interpreted as vital changes for the future – where all progress logically resides. There was a peculiar satisfaction for Shaw in responding to what he believed were the needs of the present by removing himself into the future. 'The present occupies all my time,' he wrote. But his chief contact with the historic present comes through newspapers and his animosity towards journalism – which pretends to be an organ and not the exploiter of public opinion – is partly the awareness of its inadequacy as a primary source. Writing in reaction against an atmosphere of lazy opportunism in which no one seemed 'to have any real concern for the future of England provided his immediate passions are gratified', he dreamed of a renewal of faith that would measure conduct by the longest conceivable perspective, and of an imaginative rather than academic lens through which to regard our history. He wanted to go as far as thought, and much further than facts, could reach. After all, historical truth was a matter of interpretation. Therefore an instinctively trained eye was needed to recognize the tiny shoots and buds sent out by the Life Force – for example, the natural tendency for people in the twentieth century to live longer. Maynard Keynes caught the mood of the moment when in 1923 he wrote that in the long run we were all dead. But what would happen if, in the long run, we were still alive?

*

'The original preface ... I regard as one of my most important writings,' Shaw remarked near the end of his life. He had written a treatise, using the machinery of rationalism to advance his mystical theory of evolution both as a frame of reference for his thinking and as a means of coming to terms with keeping alive at a time of hideous fatalism. 'Our will to live depends on hope,' he was to write; 'for we die of despair, or, as I have called it in the Methuselah cycle, discouragement.' He believed that civilization needed a religion 'as a matter of life or death'. But churches became clotted with superstitions and credulities unless, like a spring clean, there was a Reformation. Christ had reformed the vindictive morality of Moses with his perception of the futility and wickedness of punishment and revenge, so that the Old Testament gods were now perceived as little more than nursery bogies. But after almost 2,000 years another Reformation was needed to adapt Christian morality to the mental habits of the twentieth and twenty-first centuries. Shaw believed it was necessary to redistil the eternal spirit of

36

religion by scientific methods. This meant a change in vocabulary: a matter of replacing the word 'God' with the impersonal concept of an evolutionary appetite operating by trial and error towards the achievement of greater power over the environment. But it was also a matter of seeing the future as part of our history. From our past alone it was easy to prove that mankind was incorrigible, that potential saviours like Swift and Ruskin had died mad from despair, or been executed like Jesus and Socrates, or idolized as classics like Plato and shelved out of reach. But though all civilizations known to us had collapsed, and contemporary civilization was showing all the recorded symptoms of a collapse, nobody could prove that we would not succeed this time, or next time, or sometime. And even if the human species were scrapped, like the megalo-organisms which we knew only through fossils, that was no cause for pessimism. 'Man may easily be beaten: Evolution will not be beaten.'

Shaw called for the same sort of healthy admission from the strong-minded that Copernicus, Galileo and Darwin had demanded. He too removed human beings from their central position as unique instruments through which a divine will operated, but he restored to them their own will. As subjects of literary biographies will collaborate with their unknown biographers in the future writing of their lives, so our general history may be considered as part of an unfinished narrative that did not cater for our self-interest, but would be influenced by our acts and thoughts. This collaborative hypothesis would bring back our self-respect and sense of responsibility, emphasize the importance of collective self-help, and restore the value of instinct and the use of intelligence as controls for human destiny.

'If I must explain what I dont understand,' Shaw wrote, 'I prefer to do it in an inspiring way and not in a stultifying one.' His treatise is the compounding of a prescription against the madness of Ruskin and Swift. It announces not only the taking down from the shelf of Plato's *Republic*, to put it back in readers' hands, but also a modernizing of the first five books of the Old Testament (he subtitled his play 'A Metabiological Pentateuch') in which the Garden of Eden is comprehensively weeded. *Back to Methuselah* is Shaw's version of *Gulliver's Travels*, with longevity replacing size, and the element of the future added as a preventative against morbidity. For it had been a crude blunder, he argued, to treat causation as a process by which the present was determined by the past and would determine the future. 'The true view is that the future determines the present,' he wrote. 'If you take a ticket to Milford Haven you will do so not because you were in Swansea yesterday but because you want to be in Milford Haven tomorrow.'

37

In promoting Creative Evolution as 'the genuinely scientific religion for which all wise men are now anxiously looking', Shaw placed himself after the isolated figure of Samuel Butler, and encouraged everyone to share this isolation by treating themselves, under a strictly impartial rent act, as tenant-caretakers of this planet. He regarded Butler as a pioneer in the metabiological crusade against the environmental consequences of Darwinism. Butler had revealed his genius to Shaw in *Life and Habit*, the essay on evolution where he compressed his objections to the dogma of Natural Selection into six words: 'Darwin banished mind from the universe.' It was Butler who first perceived the moral abyss of determinism – what Shaw called 'the unspeakable horror of the mindless purposeless world presented to us by Natural Selection'. In 1887 Shaw had been sent Butler's *Luck or Cunning?* for review by the *Pall Mall Gazette*. 'I was indignant because the review was not printed at full length,' he remembered, 'presumably because the literary editor did not consider Butler important enough ... From this time on I was acquainted with Butler's view of evolution, though I do not think I grasped its full significance until years afterwards when I had arrived at it in my own way.'

The review treats Butler's opinions as being of equal merit to Darwin's. 'The question at issue is – granted the survival of the fittest, were the survivors made fit by mere luck, or did they fit themselves by cunning?' he wrote. 'Mr Butler is for cunning; and he will have it that Darwin was all for luck.'

'The quarrel is a pretty one; for if you decide in favour of cunning, the Darwinian will reply that it was a great piece of luck in the survivor to have that cunning; whereas, if you back luck, the Lamarck-Butlerian will urge that the survivor must have had the cunning to turn his luck to account. Now, evidently the essence of pure luck is that it brings more than average good fortune without the exercise of more than average ability. Luck is luck only in so far as it is independent of cunning. Otherwise luck and cunning are convertible terms, in which case the dispute is about words, not about ideas ... The controversy is one of those in which the last word is everything.'

In this truncated piece, Shaw leaves undecided the matter of whether the controversy was one of semantics or metaphysical truth. Yet the review had felt almost epoch-making to Butler himself, who was not accustomed to being treated so tenderly. Butler 'admits pure luck as a factor in evolution', Shaw wrote, 'but denies its sufficiency as an explanation of all the phenomena, and insists that organisms that have the luck to be cunning make further luck for themselves by the deliberate exercise of that cunning, and so introduce design into the universe – not design as we used to conceive it, all-foreseeing from the first, but "a piecemeal, *solvitur ambulando* design", which, as it becomes more self-conscious and intelligent, tends to supplant natural selection by functional modification.'

In the decade following this review, Butler and Shaw met on several occasions. They did not like each other. In his *Notebooks*, Butler admits to having 'long been repelled' by Shaw, though 'at the same time attracted by his coruscating power'. At the Fabian Society, after Butler had advocated his ingenious theory that the *Odyssey* was written by a young woman living at Trapani, Shaw got up and 'spoke so strongly that people who had only laughed with me all through my lecture began to think there might be something in it after all. Still,' Butler continues, 'there is something uncomfortable about the man which makes him uncongenial to me.' Shaw did not mind being disliked: he had long been uncongenial to himself. By celebrating Wagner at the expense of Handel or trifling over Shakespeare, and generally blaring his Shavianisms, he was giving Butler a demonstration of how to be outspoken without malice or vituperation. Shaw regarded Butler as the sort of person he himself might have turned into if he had not invented G.B.S. – someone who, having gone around 'undermining every British institution, shocking every British prejudice, and deriding every British Bigwig with irreconcilable pertinacity', was dismissed by the public as an oddity and a vulgarian, and could make no headway with his writings. Failure, like success, being cumulative, the longer he lived the less successful Butler was. 'He died in 1902,' Shaw wrote; 'and, outside a small but highly select circle, nobody cared.'

As an 'ardent Butlerite' and 'one of the select few who read "Erewhon" and swore by it', Shaw may have counted himself within this circle. By suggesting that poverty should be attacked as a crime instead of being coddled like a disease, Butler 'made me reconsider a rather thoughtless contempt for money, and thereby led me towards the theme of Major Barbara', he acknowledged. In the Preface to *Major Barbara* he had described Butler as being 'in his own department the greatest English writer of the latter half of the XIX century' and an exponent of Undershaft's doctrine of the importance of money. Thereafter he makes many references to Butler which reveal the kinship he felt for this uncomfortable man. He pictures Butler as being 'naturally affectionate' as a child, as having 'sought for affection at home' and gone on 'assuming that he loved his dear parents' whose good names he later slew in *The Way of All Flesh* 'so reasonably, so wittily, so humorously, and even in a ghastly way so charitably'. He defends Butler's epigrammatic wit, as he would have wished his own wit to be defended, from confusion with W. S. Gilbert's. Both men were natural adepts in a particular vein of humour, but 'Gilbert never saw anything in the operation but a funny trick ... Whenever Butler performed it he presently realized that the seeming trick was an inspired revelation.'

In a letter to Butler's biographer Festing Jones, Shaw wrote: 'Butler can stand on his own legs and carry most of us on his shoulders as well.' It was as an evolutionist, and particularly in *Back to Methuselah*, that Shaw stood on Butler's shoulders. As a great moralist, a writer whose *Erewhon* Shaw called 'the only rival to Gulliver's Travels in English Literature', who used his instinctive knowledge of human nature instead of a collection of evidence based on guinea-pigs in laboratories, Butler had stood alone against an army of purblind naturalists and, so Shaw insisted, 'won all along the line'.

If this victory were not apparent to all, Shaw argued, it was due to the class upbringing and education at public school and university that had damaged Butler's character. 'England is still governed from Langar Rectory, from Shrewsbury School, from Cambridge, with their annexes of the Stock Exchange and the solicitors' offices,' he concluded his review of Festing Jones's life of Butler, '... and even if the human products of these institutions were all geniuses, they would finally wreck any modern civilized country ... Unless we plough up the moral foundations of these places and sow them with salt, we are lost. That is the moral of the great Butler biography.'

Shaw transplanted this moral into his Preface to *Methuselah*, where contemporary schools are presented as factories producing rows of educated idealists for philistine warfare against Creative Evolution. Such tactics, which flattered converts to Creative Evolution as having minds so abnormally strong as to have thrown off the paralysis of conventional education, were beyond Butler himself. His insulting public manners were, Shaw tells us, symptoms of his schooling, which forced him to commit the gross strategic error of handling Darwin like a moral delinquent. In his Preface Shaw comes to praise Darwin, not to dig him up and throw stones. He was, Shaw insists, 'an amiable and upright man' and an 'honest naturalist' who 'never puzzled anybody'. Realizing that he cannot dull Darwin's popularity, he congratulates him on 'having the luck to please everybody' and makes him out to be everybody's good and simple neighbour. 'Darwin, by the way, was no more a Darwinist than I am a Shavian,' he adds. But in order to separate Darwin from his followers and repair the damage done by Butler's insults, he pushes exaggeration into factual error. Darwin had declared himself 'convinced that Natural Selection has been the main but not exclusive means of modification'. Shaw paraphrases this by declaring that Darwin 'did not pretend' that Natural Selection 'excluded other methods, or that it was the chief method'. Taking this extra step enables him to get beyond range of Darwin and to concentrate on the Neo-Darwinians whose minds Darwin himself had influenced only 'unintentionally'.

Shaw's Preface, as well as many of his other writings during the last third of his life, were operations to degrade the methods and devalue the conclusions of these Neo-Darwinians. Charles Darwin becomes a figure from *The Doctor's Dilemma*: someone whose evolutionary 'discovery' had often been made in the past – by his own grandfather Erasmus Darwin among others. By describing Natural Selection as Circumstantial Selection, Shaw made it all seem rather unremarkable.

He used all his dialectical skills to undermine the authority of determinism, accusing its adherents of having damaged Darwin by reducing the whole conception of Evolution to the level of external accident, 'as if a tree could be properly said to have "evolved" into firewood by the storm which blew it down'. He also attempted to remove the historical legitimacy of its scientific 'discoverers' and 'demonstrators' by giving them, as patron saint, St Thomas, who 'with Christ staring him in the face, refused to believe that he was there until he had put his fingers into his wounds, thereby establishing himself as the prototype . . .'

Shaw felt a strong aversion to 'the barren cruelties of the laboratories'. But he also held intellectual objections to 'manufactured evidence in a secret chamber' because it produced knowledge that, being based on constructed and controlled events, was necessarily mechanistic. Finally, his opposition was personal and cultural. For if the central debate in a scientific age was to be limited to the laboratory findings of people who would 'guess eggs if they saw the shells', then he was once more the complete outsider. He wanted to erase the distinction between scientists and imaginative artists such as Leonardo, Goethe and 'that very remarkable scientist Samuel Butler'. All problems, he believed, were finally scientific problems, and he too was, among other things, a man of science. 'I have made observations and experiments in the spacious laboratory of the world with a marvellous portable apparatus compactly arranged in my head.'

Shaw's Preface to *Back to Methuselah* is an example of that compound of Will and Hope called wishful thinking. He took his readers to a high place and made them look round. What better evidence was there of where a belief in the 'survival of the fittest' had led than the contest of a world war? What more logical outcome could we expect from regarding ourselves simply as Darwinian combatants for survival than the struggle of one half of Europe, having knocked the other half down, to kick it to death?

But was all this necessary? Shaw says not, if we regard such disasters as evidence of the results and not as evidence of the truth of Neo-Darwinism.

For we are co-authors of our world and our 'imagination is the beginning of creation'. Because of its time-scale, organic Natural Selection was unrepeatable in our life-span and so neither provable nor falsifiable. Shaw therefore used the time-scale of his imagination. 'I have sought for knowledge and studied error,' he wrote, 'postulating intellectual integrity as an indispensable quality in scientific work.' He stood as the natural man thinking about the nature of the universe. But he had been thinking less about the scientific origins than the social effects of Darwin, whose theory of competitive survival could so conveniently be used to justify the horrors of individualistic capitalism. So, for political ends, he flew in the face of observable facts. 'I argue out the statements until I reach a verdict – often comic in its simplicity – and then I give the verdict,' he declared. But Shaw's verdicts were to sound as predetermined and his statements, hammered out in the secret chamber of his head, as much 'put up jobs' as any laboratory trial. He had urged readers to plant their trust in their instincts and not to be demoralized by facts. But instinctively they sensed his pragmatism to be fantastic and his optimism strange. How could you mix design and randomness, as he appeared to do? It seemed chaotic.

Shaw claimed to have been 'at once completely misunderstood by people who had not read' *Back to Methuselah*. He made new and cheaper editions available in the hope of gaining understanding. 'Posterity will believe what it wishes to believe; and if its wishes jump with my guesses I shall be among the prophets,' he wrote. 'If not, I shall be only Simon Magus.'

*

After this appeal to the intellect came a demand of the imagination: after the treatise, his testament. Like seeds in the wind, the mysterious force in Creative Evolution needed to be spread through the world by legends, parables and dramas which were the heritage of the human race and 'the natural vehicle of dogma'. Even the history of science carried its tales of witchcraft and wonders, from Archimedes in his bath to Newton under his apple tree. Shaw had begun to make a dramatic parable of his religion in the dream sequence of *Man and Superman*; and in the science fiction of *Back to Methuselah* he attempted to provide it with an iconography. 'I abandon the legend of Don Juan with its erotic associations, and go back to the legend of the Garden of Eden,' he announced. 'I exploit the eternal interest of the philosopher's stone which enables man to live for ever.' There is a curious parallel between the theme plot of *Back to Methuselah* and that of Karel Čapek's *Makropoulos Secret*, written in 1922 and not translated into English until five years later, which links Shaw to the expressionists' epic use of political awareness and the machine of God.

The hell scene in *Man and Superman* took a Mozartian form; the Methuselah cycle, though it quotes from Mozart, advances as a series of Wagnerian leitmotifs. 'Back to Methuselah is my Ring,' Shaw confirmed to Trebitsch. Despite its machinery of ghosts and miracles, with a cast that includes a couple of lethal Pavlovian dolls, one huge badly-behaved egg, a hooded serpent that whispers, a terrifying Oracle, and hairless He-Ancients and She-Ancients, Shaw did not intend it as a work of remote antiquity or impossible futurism, but as a contemporary drama of philosophic and social significance. He combined a fable of Creative Evolution with an allegory of man's moral development, gathering up the styles of political satire and drawing-room comedy, disquisition and extravaganza he had developed in earlier plays, and pointing the way to his future mystical fantasies. But as a compendium of his dramaturgy, the cycle of plays is unwieldy and uneven, containing 'some of Shaw's best writing', as well as displaying him 'at his worst as a playwright'.

The long journey begins in the Garden of Eden, where Adam and Eve come across a fawn that has stumbled and broken its neck. It is their discovery of death, and Shaw's illustration of how accident controls dying rather than living. The discourse that follows this discovery between the two of them and the serpent is a wonderful seminar in which vocabulary and understanding advance together. In the beginning there was Lilith, the Mother of Creation. 'I was her darling as I am yours,' says the Serpent, which represents Shaw's evolutionary belief that all habits are acquired *and* inherited – inherited by infinitesimal instalments and, when discarded, recapitulated in leaps and bounds.

While Lilith remained alone, all humankind was vulnerable to extinction by a single accident. So, like the snake, she renewed herself and overcame death by the miracle of birth. Lilith's miracle ('a miracle is an impossible thing', the Serpent explains, 'that is nevertheless possible') was created by the potent combination of forces from which all life develops. She imagined; she desired; she dared; she willed – and then she conceived. But since the labour of renewing life was too dangerous for one, she divided herself in two and created Adam and Eve to share this burden in the future.

Adam and Eve have been created immortal. They are suspended between two terrifying possibilities – the prospect of living forever, and the accidental extinction of themselves. This legend enables Shaw to introduce the observation he had taken from August Weismann's *The Evolutionary Theory*. In Weismann's view the individual died so that the species had space to go on living. Shaw improved this theory by suggesting that the individual's will to die was part of a collective will to form higher organisms. But Adam and Eve have not been created equal. Adam's limited wish to improve arises from self-dislike: 'I want to be different; to be better; to begin again and again; to shed myself as a snake sheds its skin. I am tired of myself.' This tiredness, extending over eternity, amounts to a fear of life that outweighs his apprehensions of death. 'Fear is stronger in me than hope,' he says. 'I must have certainty.'

But hope is stronger than fear in Eve. She identifies improvement with the species rather than with herself, and accepts uncertainty, even death, as an inevitable risk in the process of creation. From all their calculations Shaw removes any hope of heaven or fear of hell in some other world since he neither believes in personal immortality himself nor credits others with a serious motivating belief in it. Adam and Eve decide to 'take a short turn of a thousand years, and meanwhile hand on their work to a new pair', expounds the ex-clerical convert to Creative Evolution, Franklyn Barnabas, in the twentieth-century second part of the cycle. 'Consequently, they had to invent natural birth and natural death, which are, after all, only modes of perpetuating life without putting on any single creature the terrible burden of immortality.'

The first scene of the play ends with the Serpent whispering the secret of conception to Eve. The stage directions read: *'Eve's face lights up with intense interest, which increases until an expression of overwhelming repugnance takes its place. She buries her face in her hands.'* This passage was criticized by St John Ervine as 'strange and unconvincing', exposing Shaw's morbid puritanism and the restricted understanding of sex imposed on him by his childless marriage. Was it not more likely, Ervine demanded, that Eve 'leapt with joy'? In his response Shaw denied that he was 'a misogynic St Paul' and defended his representation of a woman 'in a state of complete pre-sex innocence as making a wry face when it was explained to her that in consequence of the indelicacy with which Nature, in a fit of economy, has combined a merely excretory function with a creatively ejaculatory one in the same bodily part (she knowing only the excretory use of it), she is to allow herself to be syringed in an unprecedented manner by Adam ... It is true that the indignity has compensations which, *when experienced*, overwhelm all the objections to it; but Eve had not then experienced them.' Shaw had experienced these compensations, but less frequently than many men, and they were sometimes less 'overwhelming' than his repugnance. Coming at the end of this magical first scene which shows life expanding in an atmosphere of strangeness, as idea gives birth to idea in the sunny stillness of that garden, Eve's repugnance is theatrically powerful. At the distant conclusion of his play Shaw will fill his new Eden with 'children' dancing, playing and mating in the sunlight before they mature out of love-making and into adolescence four years later.

In the second scene 'a few centuries later' at an oasis in Mesopotamia, Adam and Eve have given birth to their family. What had taken place, according to Franklyn Barnabas (speaking of the Fall 5,925 years later) was a series of moral descents. The moment Adam invented death and 'became a tenant for life only', it was 'no longer worth his while to do anything thoroughly well'. That was the first step of the Fall; the second came as a result of inventing birth, before which Adam dared not risk killing Eve because he would have been 'lonely and barren to all eternity'. But the invention of birth has meant that anyone who is killed can be replaced. One of Adam's sons 'invented meat-eating. The other was horrified at the innovation,' Franklyn Barnabas continues with his gloss on what Shaw has written. 'With the ferocity which is still characteristic of bulls and other vegetarians, he slew his beefsteak-eating brother, and thus invented murder. That was a very steep step. It was so exciting that all the others began to kill one another for sport, and thus invented war, the steepest step of all. They even took to killing animals as a means of killing time, and then, of course, ate them to save the long and difficult labor of agriculture.'

Which is the stage reached in Mesopotamia in 4004 BC. Adam's fear has stopped his development with the invention of the spade. He has turned into a worried-looking farmer-conservative and the essential philistine. 'Always dig, dig, dig,' complains his son Cain. 'Sticking in the old furrow. No progress! no advanced ideas! no adventures!' Cain is an early example of the Superman who sets the standards for further human advancement. Like his brother Abel, whom he envied, copied and killed, he is 'a discoverer, a man of ideas, a true Progressive'. By using this up-to-date terminology and asking the actor playing Cain to 'open this scene in quite a modern vein', Shaw intends to remind us that such military conquerors are still seen as models of the successful and illustrious in the twentieth century which must therefore be counted as a primitive phase of our history. Cain has set himself up above his parents. 'No woman shall make me live my father's life,' he declares. '... Man shall be the master of Woman, not her baby and her drudge.' From his father he has inherited fear which he overwhelms daily with acts of courage and the ecstasy of fighting. 'I know all there is to be known of the craft of digging,' he tells Adam. 'By quitting it I have set myself free to learn nobler crafts of which you know nothing ... in a word, the craft of killing.' From his mother, Cain has taken hope, but he has no imagination to make creative use of his will and daring. 'I do not know what I want,' he tells Eve, 'except that I want to be something higher and nobler than this stupid old digger.' In Cain, the first murderer, Shaw embodies his belief that what we have learnt to call evil is technically an error in the experimental process of trial and error by which the Life Force must advance.

Despite the disgust she feels for both Adam and Cain ('I hardly know which of you satisfies me least'), Eve does not lose faith in the Life Force. She has seen glimpses of 'newly created things. Of better things.' There are signs of her own dreams coming true in the dreams of her grandchildren who 'can dream without sleeping' and who 'can remember their dreams'. Her imagination revives when she sees other grandchildren who 'make little mammoths out of clay, or make faces appear on flat stones', and when she hears others again who 'cut reeds of different lengths and blow through them, making lovely patterns of sound . . . raising my soul to things for which I have no words.' None of this family of artists, musicians, scientists and saints, who will be commissioned in Shaw's army of realists, are presented to us except through Eve's words. Cain is the only member of her family to appear on stage because in the kingdom of the short-lived he is the dominant man. Cain is also the minister of death whose fearful inventions of murder and war are reducing life to its new brevity. 'Through him and his like,' Eve declares, 'death is gaining on life.' She blames Lilith's mis-calculation in sharing the labour of creating so unequally between man and woman. 'That is why there is enmity between Woman the creator and Man the destroyer.'

But there is another reason, too, why death is gaining on life. When Franklyn Barnabas declares that Adam and Eve's decision to live a thousand years had been mutually agreed, he is misrepresenting what Shaw actually wrote. The decision was made by Adam and imposed on Eve, from which it follows that there was a greater current of fear than hope let loose in the world. From the need to quell this fear arose the early dominance of Cain, the Nietzschean hero. Franklyn and Conrad Barnabas, the religious man and the scientist, are two of the 'clever ones' from Eve's dreams. There are no artists or musicians in this second part of the cycle, perhaps because Shaw, like Eve, could 'have no words' for their creations. But the significance of these absent poets and storytellers on human history is again endorsed: 'the poem is our real clue to biological science', proclaims Franklyn Barnabas.

The two Barnabas brothers are the spokesmen for Creative Evolution, representing its component parts of biology and religion. Its real originator is an absent figure, Mrs Etteen, who exists only in a discarded act of the play, 'A Glimpse of the Domesticity of Franklyn Barnabas'. This thrice-married super-Shavian female conveys Shaw's sense of continuing time: 'My roots are in the past: my hopes are in the future.' With her violet eyes and inscrutable age, Rosie Etteen is *élan vital* itself. It is she who, adoring Franklyn Barnabas, has converted him to Creative Evolution, and has understood the implications of his brother Conrad's biological theory. 'He had the skeleton of the great faith,' she says, 'but it was Franklyn who put the flesh on it. And it was I, the woman, who made that flesh for him out of my own.' Rosie Etteen embodies imagination and desire, which must be added to the Barnabas brothers' thought and faith to bring Creative Evolution alive: she provides what in the twentieth century is called love. 'Without love ladies there would be no love children,' she tells the Christian philosopher Champernoon. ' . . . There are more love children born in wedlock than out of it: at least I hope so. But there are very few born at all, either in or out of wedlock.' Shaw was not a love child and he could find no creative place in his cycle for this intimate figure who inhabits a 'mystic region between the public meeting and the playground . . . [where] men and women meet when they are alone together'.

Rosie Etteen is the contemporary equivalent of Eve. She recognizes the twentieth century as being populated by Adam's successors who have made a world where 'ugly practical people, and people who can deal with money and material things, and be thoroughly mean about them, succeed, and the beautiful people who live in noble dreams and continually strive to realize them are ruined and despised'. In 'The Gospel of the Brothers Barnabas', the second part of his cycle, Shaw stages his revenge on these ugly, mean, material people whom he typifies in Joyce Burge and Henry Hopkins Lubin, his lampoons of Asquith and Lloyd George. These are his contemporary idealists. They have one quality, which is Will, necessary to the Life Force. But it is Will without imagination, loveless, and by itself destructive. 'The Gospel of the Brothers Barnabas' is designed as a humiliation of these two Liberal leaders, from whom all authority is removed. They have no power to summon the Shavian Barnabas brothers, but arrive at Franklyn Barnabas's house as a couple of campaigning political candidates. They have come on fools' errands, having carefully read between the lines of several newspaper reports and made the erroneous conclusion that Barnabas is going to enter politics and contest the approaching general election. Almost everything they hear they misunderstand; almost everything they say is trivial or untrue. Shaw likens their views on politics and their belief in an immutable law of political economy to the determinists' blind faith in the rigid rules of science.

The play demonstrates the incompatibility between Adam's offspring and the children of Eve – that incompatibility which Shaw felt to be his own inheritance. His criticism of the democratic system has, on the near horizon, the satiric target of the next election. Lubin and Burge cannot take a long view even of the possibilities of longevity. They imagine the gospel of Creative Evolution to be a marketable elixir ('The stuff. The powder. The bottle. The tabloid. Whatever it is. You said it wasnt lemons') which must be kept strictly secret. When they discover it to be an idea (or 'moonshine'), they have no further use for it (except, Burge suggests, as a 'stunt' in his election programme). They leave: and Shaw follows them with a savage lash put into the mouth of the local rector. 'To me the awful thing about their political incompetence was that they had to kill their own sons. It was the war casualty lists and the starvation afterwards that finished me up with politics . . . '

Shaw had burdened himself with a narrative at a point where he seemed to have jettisoned the storytelling with which he had felt impatient ever since *Widowers' Houses*. For half an hour in the third part of the cycle, 'The Thing Happens', almost no progress (apart from some bureaucratic rearrangements and technological innovations) is detectable. We have edged forward another 250 years. The Lilliputian President of the British Islands, a man 'like Joyce Burge, yet also like Lubin, as if Nature had made a composite photograph of the two men', is named Burge-Lubin, symbol of soldered fixity. Equally unchangeable is Barnabas, the Accountant-General with a likeness to his ancestor Conrad Barnabas, a commonplace, repressive bureaucrat who has made a god of statistics but, having no other god, presents the Shavian view of one-dimensional science purified of all creative instinct. Two other characters resemble figures in the previous play of the cycle: the Archbishop of York is 'recognizably the same man' as the Reverend William Haslam who was engaged to Franklyn Barnabas's daughter Cynthia; and the Domestic Minister, Mrs Lutestring, seems remarkably similar to Franklyn Barnabas's parlour-maid. A statistical survey leads accidentally to the dramatic revelation that they are indeed the same people, and since, 'like all revolutionary truths, it [longevity] began as a joke', this gives Shaw's absurdist talent excellent scope. He chose for this experiment two of the least promising candidates from 'The Gospel of the Brothers Barnabas' so as to demonstrate that the change would not take place as the result of individual self-interest ('It wont happen to me: thats jolly sure' predicts Haslam when a schoolboyish clergyman). This choice also enables Shaw to make the transformation from short to long life as dramatic as possible, for unlike Natural Selection there is nothing selective about Shaw's Creative Evolution. 'If the geniuses live 300 years,' he explains, 'so will the chumps.' Since there are more chumps like Haslam (who admits to being 'the fool of the family') than geniuses, most of those to whom the thing happens will be ordinary people, like the parlour-maid.

The revelation of this longevity releases differing reactions among the short-lived of Shaw's Laputa. For the two long-lived themselves, their knowledge that the miracle has happened to more than one of them marks a new beginning. It is the story of Adam and Eve once again, with a vital difference. When this new word is made flesh, the mother and father of the long-lived (their own ages presently totalling more than 557 years) are animated solely by hope.

The impact of 'The Thing Happens' is dissipated by Shaw's avenging spirit driving him all over the place to fire off his ridicule at those who had branded his own political writings as ridiculous. 'Take your convictions easily,' he was to write, 'or they will become phobias and manias.' In *Back to Methuselah* his convictions began easily but fanned out into obsessions. His two long-livers have experienced a hostility and strangeness among the short-lived that reflects Shaw's own isolation. 'I have been very lonely sometimes,' reflects Mrs Lutestring; and the Archbishop reveals that it is 'in this matter of sex [more] than in any other, you are intolerable to us'.

All this is reversed in the fourth part of the cycle, 'The Tragedy of an Elderly Gentleman', which propels us forward to a colony of long-lived people at Galway Bay in the year AD 3000. The deputation of short-lived visitors which comes to consult their oracle has to be escorted by nurses in case their own sense of moral abnormality swells into a disease called 'discouragement', that can kill. By now almost no understanding between the long-lived and the short-lived is possible. There exists a law of Nature about the 'fixed relation between conduct and length of life', so that human nature itself has changed among the long-lived, who hear their visitors speaking dead thoughts in a dead language, and witness their lack of moral sense and reasonable social habits.

The three acts of this 'Tragedy of an Elderly Gentleman' provide a synopsis of the last 1,000 years of history. Following 'the War to end War' among the short-lived, came another war that obliterated the capital cities of the world and ended the 'pseudo-Christian civilization'. The last civilized discovery – that cowardice is a patriotic virtue – was commemorated by a public monument to its original discoverer, a fat old sage named Sir John Falstaff. After this, human nature being unchangeable without voluntary longevity, the whole business of warfare apparently started up again. The long-lived have retired from this fighting to a sacred grove of self-sufficiency once called the British Isles (the capital of the British Commonwealth now being in Baghdad). They are divided into two great political parties. The Conservatives believe that, since their power and peace depends upon their remoteness, they should stay in these islands 'wrapped up in the majesty of our wisdom on a soil held as holy ground for us by an adoring world'. The Colonizers believe it is their destiny to increase their numbers and, by exterminating the short-lived if necessary, take over the world.

Among the deputation is Napoleon, 'the finest soldier in the world' and Cain's most perfect descendant. He brings a peculiar dilemma to the

Oracle. 'War has made me popular, powerful, famous, historically immortal,' he explains. 'But I foresee that if I go on to the end it will leave me execrated, dethroned, imprisoned, perhaps executed. Yet if I stop fighting I commit suicide as a great man and become a common one.' The Oracle answers that his only escape is death, and he is immobilized, gibbering impotently at the base of the Falstaff statue. For this scene Shaw developed the electric emanation, Vril, with which the subterranean sages of Bulwer-Lytton's *The Coming Race* (a favourite book of his boyhood) slayed at sight. The invisible mesmeric field, naturally accumulating round the long-lived, is that same fantasy of intellectual power that Captain Shotover had struggled to invent – a 'psychic ray' to 'blow up the human race if it goes too far' that will explode 'at the will of a Mahatma'. By using this force finally to arrest the progress of his own 'Man of Destiny', Shaw seals the destiny of the short-lived.

'The Tragedy of an Elderly Gentleman' is perhaps the weakest play of the cycle. At a length that parodies Shaw's theme, it explains differences between the two species that could be more imaginatively charted through the use of differing languages. Shaw recognized this growing challenge of vocabulary: he would get round it in the final play by having an 800-year-old She-Ancient tell a three-year-old that 'we have to put things very crudely to you to make ourselves intelligible'. Yet the short tragi-comic scene with which the fourth play ends is a peculiarly effective blend of bathos and pathos. Inside the temple, the Prime Minister of the British Isles, terrified and half-drunk, asks unwittingly for the identical reply that had inspired his predecessor to sweep back triumphantly to power after his consultation with the Oracle fifteen years before. The reply comes: 'Go home, you fool.' The sudden realization that the Prime Minister will have to fake up a pompous answer, as his predecessor must have done, to gain an election victory profoundly dismays his father-in-law, the Elderly Gentleman. This character, who has come on a pious pilgrimage to 'one of the numerous lands of my father' – in short, to Ireland – was supposed to be modelled on the Dean of St Paul's, W. R. Inge, but is Shaw's partial self-portrait: 'harmless babbles unintelligibly with moments of sense ... foreign dress very funny has curious fringe of white sea-weed under his chin', is the description of him given by one of the young long-lived. In the short-lived world the Elderly Gentleman has prided himself on daringly advanced thinking which, in the long perspective, becomes mere obscurantism. At home in neither world, he must choose between the despair of living among people to whom nothing is real, and (perhaps as an example to the rest of us) consenting to be phased out among the superior long-lived. 'I take the nobler risk,' he decides, like Gulliver seeking to escape the Yahoos. The

Oracle agrees and offers him her hands. *'He grasps them and raises himself a little by clinging to her. She looks steadily into his face. He stiffens; a little convulsion shakes him; his grasp relaxes; and he falls dead.'*

Unlike the handshake in *Don Giovanni*, the Elderly Gentleman's grasping of hands is a commitment to the spiritual future set out in the fifth and last play of the cycle. 'As Far as Thought Can Reach' combines past, present and future that parade before a viewing platform set in the year AD 31,920. We are given 'a glimpse of the past' through a grotesque puppet play performed by two 'artificial human beings' that have been manufactured in the laboratory, using the best skills of science and art, by the children of the future. This synthetic couple, like toys that are all reflexes, proclaim themselves to be the products of Cause and Effect, and offer a pantomime of the determinists' concept of human life. But they are also ourselves, motivated by fear, enveloped in lies and illusions, playing fantastic tricks that kill their Frankenstein-creator, the fanatical scientist Pygmalion, and finally, though shrinking from death at any cost, dying of terror and discouragement. These automata, posturing in their little brief authority as persons of importance, have none of those particles of imagination, love, hope, will, courage, faith and thought by which the short-lived have evolved into a superior species. Without these properties they are 'abominations' whose noxious, doll-like flesh degenerates into cancer and horribly taints the atmosphere, and who convey Shaw's fastidious disgust at physical decay. These dolls are destroyed with the 'rest of the laboratory refuse' to avoid contaminating the long-lived. 'There is,' warned Shaw, 'a dangerous side to Shavianism.'

Their present – our future – is a stateless society inhabited entirely by perfect specimens of the long-lived. They have been born from artificially hatched eggs in which they were incubated for two years, developing from all sorts of creatures that no longer exist, to emerge as newly-born, long-lived human beings roughly equivalent to our short-lived sixteen-year-olds. Before them stretch four years of what is called childhood, devoted to arts, sports and emotional pleasures, during which they pass through the immaturity that members of the audience begin to shed at the age of fifty. But whereas the short-lived audience will soon die of decay, the long-lived cast are like the original Adam and Eve who went on living until death by accident, and they will evolve over hundreds of years into a breed of intellectual voluptuaries known as the Ancients, who are Shaw's version of Swift's Houyhnhnms.

Such a prospect appals the children, just as it appals the audience, for we cannot sense anything in the existence of these naked, sexless, bald-headed Olympians to enchant us. 'What is the use of being born if we have to decay

51

into unnatural, heartless, loveless, joyless monsters in four short years,' protests the bearded two-year-old Strephon. To this objection, which is also made on behalf of readers and audience, an Ancient gives the answer: 'Infant: one moment of the ecstasy of life as we live it would strike you dead.' It is logical that, being infants like Strephon, we cannot share or even apprehend this ecstasy, but it is hardly satisfactory if, like the youths and maidens who hear the Ancient speak, we merely feel 'much damped'.

Shaw's artistic problem is one experienced by many creators of utopias. 'I could not shew the life of the long livers, because, being a short liver, I could not conceive it,' he wrote to the Strephon-like St John Ervine. 'To make the play possible at all I had to fall back on an exhibition of short-livers and children in contrast with such scraps of the long life as I could deduce by carrying a little further the difference that exists at present between the child and the adult . . . ' The imaginative effect is handed over to the actors, directors and designers.

Shaw's utopian adults are composed of body, will and thought. They exist because they have a future, which is to be made by concentrating their powerful will to free themselves altogether from the flesh and to evolve into pure thought. 'None of us now believe that all this machinery of flesh and blood is necessary,' explains the She-Ancient. It is the body that, by making them subject to death, prevents them from achieving their immortal destiny. 'The day will come,' prophesies the She-Ancient, 'when there will be no people, only thought.'

In the final minutes of *Back to Methuselah* we see this future from the perspective of the beginning, as the ghosts of Lilith, Adam and Eve, Cain and the Serpent appear. Cain acknowledges that there is no future role for his offspring in the world; Adam too can make nothing of a place where matter does not rule the mind. But the Serpent feels justified. She has chosen wisdom and the knowledge of good and evil, and she sees a new world in which, hope having vanquished fear, 'there is no evil; and wisdom and good are one'. Eve too concludes that all is well: 'My clever ones have inherited the earth.' Finally, as an epitome of the whole cycle, Lilith delivers her apocalyptic vision of the eternal evolutionary movement:

'Is this enough; or must I labor again? . . . They did terrible things . . . I stood amazed at the malice and destructiveness of the things I had made . . . The pangs of another birth were already upon me when one man repented and lived three hundred years . . . so much came of it that the horrors of that time seem now but an evil dream . . . Best of all, they are still not satisfied . . . they press on to the goal of redemption from the flesh, to the vortex freed from matter, to the whirlpool in pure intelligence that, when the world began, was a whirlpool in pure force ... when they attain it they shall become one with me and supersede me, and Lilith will be only a legend ... Of Life only is there no end ... for what may be beyond, the eyesight of Lilith is too short. It is enough that there is a beyond.'

Earlier in the play, the She-Ancient defined art as a 'magic mirror you make to reflect your invisible dreams in visible pictures' – a device no longer needed by the Ancients who 'have a direct sense of life'. Lilith's speech is Shaw's magic mirror, its imagery reflecting his sense of life. Here is the final statement of his spiritual autobiography: a logical working-out of where his instincts ultimately led. Following his courting of disorder in *Heartbreak House*, he had made a greater effort than in any play since *Major Barbara* towards a new coherence. Beneath the inspirational rhetoric lies the tragedy of all such resurrection legends. He had attempted to play a miraculous three-card trick, but none of the combinations he tried – Father, Child and Holy Ghost; Emotion, Will and Intellect; Body, Spirit and Mind – had come out, and eventually he was left with one card in his hand: Intelligence. The discarded act of *Back to Methuselah* is the symbolic evidence of his inability to use the Child, the Emotion, and the Body – because these cards had not been dealt to him. 'I rather jib, myself, at the dualism of mind and matter,' he was to write to a correspondent, 'but if I had to dogmatize I should say that I see in mind the promise and potency of all forms of matter.' But the end of *Back to Methuselah* foretells the dissolution of matter and, with it, all that had vexed his mind. Such a conclusion, inherent in his birth and upbringing, was a victory for destiny over the free will he championed. But his dilemma was also part of the culture of the times. Shaw's perpetual romance of thought, 'disentangled from the matter that has always mocked it', dispenses with his humour and abandons the long pilgrimage to find what, remembering Ibsen, he had called 'the third empire' over which shall reign 'the God of earth and the Emperor of the spirit in one'. To escape the magnetic field of determinism he sent his optimistic signal infinitely far beyond personal experience. The distant echo he received underscores Lilith's words with a poignancy that against all odds makes them perhaps the most moving of all Shaw's speeches for the theatre.

*

'The sale of the book here and in America has been greater than that of any other of my works,' Shaw told Karel Musek, his translator into the Bohemian language. It seemed to answer a need of the times. Printings of 10,000 copies in the United States and Britain were followed within the year by five additional printings of 3,000 copies each in the United States and by a second printing of 5,000 copies in Britain early in 1922. His friend William Archer wrote to accuse him of being almost indecently young and irresponsible. 'Your mind was never more infernally agile, your intellectual muscle was never better,' he reassured G.B.S. 'To put it another way, you never were further from years of discretion ... When a man can walk on a tightrope over the Falls of Niagara, turning three sumersaults to a minute, it's no use his appealing to the census paper to prove himself decrepit.' More surprising was Max Beerbohm's opinion – that *Back to Methuselah* was the best book Shaw had written because he had got away 'from representation of actual things ... and thought out a genuine work of art ...'

'Act I of "In the Beginning" is far and away the best thing that you have ever done ... you no longer, as in "The Revolutionist's Handbook", shelter yourself behind the person of John Tanner in order not to discourage old friends and comrades, but come manfully forth, saying "I G.B.S., *know* and in my own person *assure* you that there isn't a ray of hope for the improvement of man's lot on earth".'

Shaw sent complimentary copies of the book to any number of old friends and comrades, including one inscribed 'to Nicolas Lenin the only European ruler who is displaying the ability character and knowledge proper to his responsible position'. Though he was never certain this was received, Lenin in fact read it carefully and seems to have found in the Preface some confirmation of his view that Shaw was 'a good man fallen among Fabians'. In those places where the shortcomings of capitalism were exposed, Lenin wrote his favourite expression – '*Bien dit!*' – in the margin. But where Shaw appeared to be 'in the power of his Utopian illusions there are marks of disapproval'.

Notices of the book in Britain were long and lukewarm. Reviewers sensed that his revulsion against the war had manoeuvred Shaw into metaphysics that would disturb most readers. 'I do intensely feel that *Back to Methuselah* is harmful to the soul of man,' protested Marie Stopes. His climax was the result of religious thought with 'hardly a gleam of religious emotion', wrote Desmond MacCarthy who, describing the play as 'a kind of Hegelian cosmology in pictures', judged it to be 'an extraordinary imaginative effort, but not an artistic success'. Almost everyone agreed with Shaw's own eventual view that 'I was too damned discursive.' In the critical opinion of T. S. Eliot such garrulity had been a product of the 'potent ju-ju of the Life Force [which] is a gross superstition'. This 'master of a lucid and witty dialogue prose hardly equalled since Congreve, and of a certain power of observation', wrote Eliot, was now 'squandering these gifts in the service of worn out home-made theories, as in the lamentable *Methuselah*'. Even those not religiously affronted were unsettled by the length of the play. 'Are you yourself quite happy with the notion of the Universe as an enormous theatre where one long Shaw play is being acted?' J. C. Squire asked readers of the *Observer*. 'I don't think Bibles are made this way.' Yet so vast a theme required length as well as weight.

Squire expressed the belief of most critics that the play in its entirety was 'no more actable than the second part of *Faust*', though adding: 'the first act and part of the last would be as effective in the theatre as anything that Mr Shaw has ever done'. Since then *Faust* itself has become actable. Shaw had not counted on a performance in the theatre. He had calculated, however, without the 'lunatic' founder of the American Theatre Guild, Lawrence Langner, who came to Shaw's apartment in Adelphi Terrace in the spring of 1921. He was examined, as Trebitsch had been, by Charlotte: 'a gentle gracious lady with plain, pleasant features', Langner observed, 'of medium height and comfortable build'. G.B.S. had introduced her 'in the grand manner' as if she were a *prima donna*, then ostentatiously seated her in a chair and stayed unfamiliarly quiet. Once her mystic scrutiny of Langner was over, Shaw sprang from his chair and dashed 'like a sprinter to the door' which he held open 'with a deep bow until she had passed into the hall'. Herself being favourably impressed, Himself was free to give Langner a brief synopsis of his play, lasting two hours, at the end of which Langner concluded that 'Shaw had more than a touch of the fanatic about him'. But between fanatic and lunatic (as Shaw called Langner in a spasm of affection) an oddly effective partnership developed. Shaw had been pleased by the reports and photographs he saw of the Theatre Guild's production of *Heartbreak House* which, he cautioned Langner, was like 'a musical comedy' compared with *Back to Methuselah*. But despite its eight changes of scene, a cast of forty-five characters, and a duration exceeding twelve hours and ending with the aridity of the Ancients, Langner decided it was 'just the kind of thing for the Theatre Guild to do'. He sailed back to New York, frothed up public interest, and at length persuaded his colleagues to stage the cycle of plays as a special Shaw Festival at the Garrick Theater.

'The Guild stands awed,' he reported back to Shaw. '... It has been a tremendous undertaking.' The rehearsals, which began early in 1922, called for a group of actors who were sufficiently talented to play several parts, and sufficiently flexible not only to play them on succeeding weeks but to rehearse them almost simultaneously – 'much as the Grand Central Station had to be built while the trains were run'. All manner of innovations were employed, such as a Linnebach projector which threw a coloured slide on the white backcloth and 'painted' the drop with living light – an aid both to theatrical illusion and to the economy of handling so many sets on a small stage. Eve's costume of pink tights threaded with hair of cloth-of-gold, which proved a brilliant compromise between naked realism and the requirements of the New York Police Department, successfully held the attention of the stage hands. Sheets of five tickets with perforated card divisions began to sell six months before the opening night, which only called for the arrival of Shaw himself in New York to guarantee its success. 'We would shield you from all publicity by every possible method,' Langner wrote. 'What suggests itself immediately is that you enter the country clean-shaven, so that nobody will recognize you.' His presence, Langner added, would do much to raise the prestige he had forfeited over his apparent prediction in the *New York American* that Georges Carpentier would beat Jack Dempsey in the World Heavyweight Boxing Championship ('he is not even a prophet out of his own country', remarked James Joyce). But Shaw, who increasingly kept his distance over things he cared about, sent only words of advice for the play's production, together with many more words of disingenuous exculpation of himself as a boxing authority.

Back to Methuselah opened in New York on 27 February 1922 with a matinée of Part I and evening performance of Part II. The cycle was completed over three weeks, Parts III and IV beginning on 6 March, and Part V on 13 March. '*The lunatic has prevailed!*' Langner signalled Shaw. The acting and production, including Lee Simonson's scenic designs, were highly praised: but not the play itself – which Shaw was persuaded to shorten for its subsequent performances. Over nine weeks, twenty-five performances of the complete cycle were given, at the end of which the financial loss had risen to $20,000. On the other hand, the Theatre Guild had nearly doubled its subscribers. 'We shall look for our reward in heaven,' Langner wrote. Apprehensive of Shaw's reaction, he went on to explain that 'the Garrick Theater was too small for us to make money out of the play. If we had had a theater twice the size, there would have been a profit instead of a loss.' But Shaw was steeled against disappointment. The production of his play was 'an exploit still unique, which so amazed me that I have hardly yet recovered my breath after it', he remarked to Langner. ' . . . It isn't likely that any other lunatic will want to produce *Back to Methuselah!*'

He had seriously underrated his attraction for lunatics. Going up to Birmingham in 1923 for a matinée of *Heartbreak House* he met for the first time another lunatic very much to his liking. This was Barry Jackson, christened after Shaw's actor-hero Barry Sullivan, and known locally as 'the Butter King' after the Birmingham Maypole Dairies founded by his father, from which he derived a large private income. Jackson's madness took the form of philanthropy: over a period of twenty-one years he was to spend more than £100,000 of his own money on the Birmingham Repertory

Theatre. He had founded it in 1913 and ten years later it was established as the leading regional theatre in England. Jackson loved the glittering history of the stage, but had been disenchanted by the fashion machine of the London West End theatre. His repertory was both what J. C. Trewin called a 'revolving mirror of the Drama across the centuries' and also a forum for modern plays with new actors and directors. It had affinities with Continental expressionist drama – he put on Georg Kaiser's *Gas* and the Čapeks' *Insect Play*.

Heartbreak House was the ninth of Shaw's plays to be produced there since its opening, and Jackson now proposed a tenth, the impossible *Methuselah*. 'I asked him was he mad,' Shaw remembered. '...I demanded further whether he wished his wife and children to die in the workhouse. He replied that he was not married. I began to scent a patron...'

Barry Jackson's patronage between the wars became the equivalent in England of Lawrence Langner's promotion of Shaw's plays through the Theatre Guild in the United States. Almost twenty-five years younger than G.B.S., Jackson inherited Granville-Barker's kinship of the stage. 'Elegant, urbane, unselfconsciously dominating, always seeming to be a head taller than his companions', he appeared like one of the superior long-lived among the short-lived inhabitants of Birmingham. According to John Drinkwater, his passion was 'to serve an art instead of making that art serve a commercial purpose'. He actually put on plays he liked, presenting himself more as the educator than the servant of the public. Though his theatre was one of the happiest places in which to work, it offended Birmingham's respect for profit-making and was disparaged as a rich man's plaything.

Jackson appealed to Shaw as someone whose speciality was to make the impossible take place: a conjuror converting dreams into reality. He therefore handed over *Back to Methuselah!* (which at that time ended with an exclamation mark) and saw it staged in the autumn of 1923, with sets by Paul Shelving, directed by H. K. Ayliff, and featuring a cast of 'provincial nobodies' that included Eileen Beldon, Gwen Ffrangçon-Davies, Cedric Hardwicke, Raymond Huntley and Edith Evans (who played the Serpent, the Oracle, and the She-Ancient). 'It is a mighty work,' Gwen Ffrangçon-Davies wrote during the rehearsals, '...But opinion is divided about it in the theatre...I do not myself know whether it will be as enthralling to see as it is to read.' There were rumours that Shaw himself was coming up to superintend rehearsals 'so we are all rather terrified!' But, except for a visit towards the end of the dress rehearsals ('an amazing stunt'), he preferred to stay away as a mark of trust in Barry Jackson, and confined most of his early advice to letters about the hiss and sway of Edith Evans's 'very fascinating' reptile. 'I have half a mind not to meddle with the rehearsals at all,' he wrote

57

to Edith Evans: 'I am rather afraid of upsetting you at the last moment and doing more harm than good. Authors are not really necessary evils.'

The Lord Chamberlain's office had licensed *Back to Methuselah* on condition that the puppet paraphrase of the Athanasian creed in Part V be omitted in performance, that Burge and Lubin should not be made up to look like Lloyd George and Asquith, and that Adam and Eve should observe the 'usual conventionalities of dress'. Shaw's response was a fine example of how to give way while appearing to carry off the battle honours. He agreed that Lloyd George and Asquith should be disguised but added that they 'will probably be disappointed and feel to some extent defrauded . . . neither of the two statesmen he [the Lord Chamberlain] names will thank us for our delicacy'. He also agreed with the censor over Adam and Eve – except to point out that the usual conventionalities of dress in the Garden of Eden were 'no dress at all'. But he absolutely refused to withdraw the words in which the puppet 'uses the Athanasian formula to express his horrible mechanistic creed'. They would continue to appear in the printed book, and be left out of the performance only 'if the licence is endorsed to the effect, making it clear that they are omitted under duress, and leaving me entirely free to throw the responsibility of their omission on the Lord Chamberlain', whom he suspected of being 'a bit of a Mechanist himself, as the creed is now quite fashionable'.

Four consecutively-played cycles were performed at Birmingham and produced a loss of around £2,500 (of which a little was recovered from a further four cycles put on at the Royal Court Theatre in Sloane Square early the following year). But Shaw was happy. 'This has been the most extraordinary experience of my life,' he declared after the first performance. It did not seem to trouble him that others disagreed. James Agate wrote in the *Sunday Times* that the composition and production were 'a mystery and a mistake'; and Arnold Bennett fell asleep during the performance, having to be woken up 'for fear a snore might be heard on the stage'.

But there were surprises – from the thrilling sequence of secrets and revelations in the Garden of Eden to the terrible cry of the Elderly Gentleman receding into the distance. Desmond MacCarthy, who had been told that, though marvellous, the play was rather boring, listened with riveted attention to the final part. He had already learnt that those of Shaw's ideas which 'first struck me as silliest were the ones which I subsequently found had modified my thoughts most', and he recognized that G.B.S. was placing his ghostly faith out of reach of human discouragement. This kind of drama, with its chords of inspiration, flashes of moral passion, and searching chaos, was rare in the theatre. 'The superb merit of the play is that it is the work of an artist who has asked himself, with far greater seriousness and courage than all but a few, what is the least he must believe and hope for if he is to feel life is worth living.'

[5]

What we need is not a new edition of rules of the ring but the substitution of law for violence as between nations. (1918)

In these first half dozen years following the war, the Shaws made five journeys into Ireland. Usually they spent some weeks bathing, boating, walking and writing at Parknasilla, which Charlotte had known as a child and which to her mind always rejuvenated G.B.S. Near the opposite coast, they would stay with Horace Plunkett of Foxrock outside Dublin – 'the kindest and most helpful of my Kilteragh guests', he called them.

Plunkett had been grateful to Shaw 'for your attempts to save this awful situation' after the failure of his Irish Convention. 'It is quite clear that nothing can be done at the moment,' he had written to Shaw in 1918, 'but no situation is hopeless and possibly there may be a reaction from the chaos and disorder Parliament has provoked.' He pressed G.B.S. to visit him again – 'remember, you are coming over to settle the affairs of Ireland!' – and Shaw had gone there in the autumn of 1918 on his way back to England after visiting Lady Gregory at Coole. It was then that he first heard of Plunkett's somewhat desperate scheme to invent an Irish Centre party after the British government had outlawed the Assembly of Ireland (Dáil Éireann). 'One reason that I am anxious to get him here,' Plunkett had told Charlotte, 'is that I feel it in my bones that the time has come for him to do his great service to Ireland.' It was difficult for Shaw to resist such unusual trust, and when Plunkett's new party, known as the Dominion League, was formed in 1919, he began making numerous contributions to its paper, the *Irish Statesman*, edited by AE. 'All the sane men in the country agree with Sir Horace Plunkett that it is the Centre, and not the marginal Impossibilism, that must formulate the demands of Ireland,' Shaw wrote in the summer of 1919. 'All the wise men would rather be associated with Sir Horace than with any other leading figure in Irish Politics.'

What appealed to Shaw about the Dominion League was its exaggerated moderation. In his imagination it became a forum for all extremists (except rigidly conservative Unionists) whose opposing views could be beguiled into a visionary Irish Bill that none of the extremist factions could obtain separately. To pull off this amazing trick 'the ace is the public opinion of the world', Shaw reckoned, 'especially the English-speaking world'. He

59

attempted to play this ace in the *Irish Statesman*, where he promoted the League as a sensible way forward for businessmen, an attractive vehicle for patriots, and an honourable solution for the British government. 'What the Irish want is the freedom of their country,' he declared. To this everyone agreed; yet no one could agree what freedom meant. Was it complete independence, or the gaining of a position similar to Australia and Canada, or the occupation of a place equal to England's within the British Commonwealth, or the beginning of a federated partnership of the United Kingdom?

While all this was being discussed, Ireland continued to exist under a virtual state of martial law. 'Laws are enforced, not by the police, but by the citizens who call the police when the law is broken,' Shaw argued. '... But in Ireland nobody will call the police, nobody will give away another Irishman to the policeman.' The result was a miserably weak British regime holding on to power through Black and Tan coercion. In Ireland 'you have every sort of liberty trampled on', Shaw told the Fabians. 'You have people in a state of the most furious hatred of this country [England]; all these petty persecutions, annoyance, these flingings of men into jail, putting down newspapers, charging political meetings with bayonet and baton charges have produced a condition of the most furious revolt against the British Government and, of course, you have the governing class in this country quite deliberately and unmistakeably going on with that in order to provoke revolts against them which will enable them to say it is impossible to give Ireland self-government.' Amid the raids, ambushes and weekly acts of terrorism, the attempted assassination at the end of 1919 of Lord French, the Lord Lieutenant of Ireland, which appeared to shock the English, came as no surprise to Shaw. 'The mischief of political coercion in a body like the British Empire is that the coercion cannot be organized so as to stop short of the extreme provocation at which bombs and pistols come up just as turnips and scarlet runners will when they are duly sown,' he wrote in the *Irish Statesman*.

But what did take him by surprise was the sudden action of Lloyd George who announced a Bill for the 'better government of Ireland', partitioning six of the nine Ulster counties from the twenty-six so-called 'southern' counties, north and south being provided with separate home rule and a local parliament. The proposal horrified Shaw. He was convinced that partition could not work. 'They wont want to make it work,' he wrote.

While Lloyd George's Bill progressed over various hurdles on its way to becoming law at the end of 1920, Plunkett's Dominion League continued to debate with itself and, following a large Irish Peace Conference in Dublin in the summer of 1920, presented its resolutions to Dublin Castle – which took no notice of them. It was once again the story of Plunkett's Irish Convention. 'The futility of the Irish gentry,' Shaw explained, 'despairing of the Castle and disaffected to Sinn Fein, beat him.' In truth, the political initiative had passed to Lloyd George's Bill which, brought into force in April 1921, led to the Anglo–Irish Treaty and was another step towards the partition of Ireland at the end of the year.

There remained a debate in the Dáil, ostensibly on the oath of association. 'There is no reason to fuss about the upshot of the Dáil debate,' Shaw advised his readers. He reckoned it to be just another example of Ireland's 'wonderful power of magnifying herself and her affairs in the eyes of the world'. The Dáil ratified the treaty, but the minority opposing it, led by Éamon de Valera, attracted the support of a majority of the Irish Republican Army. The Anglo–Irish war had ended: in June 1922 the Irish Civil War began.

'This is an impossible situation,' Shaw wrote in the *Irish Times* that summer. It was literally impossible in the sense that the men he had always called 'marginal impossibilists' had won the day. The IRA was flushed with success, though to Shaw's eyes it represented 'the stale romance that passes for politics in Ireland' and that 'I cannot stand'. So far as he could see, de Valera 'does not know how to play his hand', he wrote to the editor of the *Daily Express*; 'and as nothing is more dangerous than the messes into which unskilful players run international games, I had better play the hand for him'. But the game had changed, a new pack of cards was in play, and there were no longer any aces in Shaw's hand or up his sleeve. 'Words have lost all meaning.' His purpose throughout all these complicated Anglo–Irish troubles had been to promote any act of grace that could sweeten the atmosphere of this war-tortured country. 'We must all, at heavy disadvantages, do what we can to stop explosions of mere blind hatred,' he wrote. The heavy disadvantage was discouragement, the killer disease he had examined in *Back to Methuselah*. 'Victims always let you down if you take up their cause,' he remarked.

'I am an Irishman and need not mince matters.' Yet Shaw's proposals on how to restore order in Ireland have all the texture of prime Shavian mincemeat. Every citizen should be registered, he asserted, then armed with a gun and a supply of ammunition. Anyone found unarmed could be charged with neglect of duty; anyone who failed to respond to another citizen's cries for help would be liable to be shot for cowardice and desertion. Old Nationalists would be generously pensioned off by the State and every live Irishman automatically made a hero and heroine – a socialist, as opposed to an Irish, hero and heroine. It is an ironic Shavianizing of Larkin and Connolly's Irish Citizen Army.

Ireland's history had reduced the country to a rag-and-bottle shop of national junk, Shaw thought, glowing with the phosphorescence of romance. Once England had deserted Ireland as the chief customer for these romantic heroics, there was no other customer for such outdated stock-in-trade than the home market. Why else would they impose on themselves a Coercion Act (with a flogging clause) more savage than any coercion imposed by the English? It seemed to him they would be happy to die storming Dublin Castle, even though the Castle had already surrendered, and to go on dying after it had been as completely demolished as the Bastille. 'The rallying of the Irish against English tyranny has long since become a reflex action with them,' he wrote in the *Irish Statesman*, 'and they cannot control their reflexes.'

Shaw's literary purpose was to train these reflexes to make Ireland a country fit for civilized men and women, rather than heroes, to live in. After the ratification of the treaty, whatever skirmishes went on between IRA and Irish Free State Army troops, the country would have to govern itself, 'which means that her troubles are beginning, not ending'. He continued to visit Ireland, keeping himself up to date with political developments. On 19 and 20 August 1922 he and Charlotte stayed once more with Horace Plunkett at Kilteragh where they met Michael Collins, one of the most attractive of the Free State leaders. Collins had been a member of the Irish delegation that negotiated the Anglo–Irish Treaty and now, as Commander-in-Chief of the Free State Army, was leading the fight against some of his ex-comrades in the IRA which he had organized after 1916. A few days before this meeting, following the death of Arthur Griffith, he had been appointed head of the new government of the Irish Free State. To be dining with Michael Collins at Kilteragh seemed entirely appropriate to Shaw. With the political realignment between Irishmen, Collins had been moving from extremism to the moderate centre until he now occupied Plunkett's old role – the very change that Shaw had looked for, by non-violent means, in his sportsmanlike proposals for the Dominion League.

The Shaws left Kilteragh next day; and a day later Collins was shot dead in an ambush near Cork. 'How could a born soldier die better than at the victorious end of a good fight, falling to a shot of another Irishman – a damned fool, but all the same an Irishman who thought he was fighting for Ireland – "a Roman to a Roman"?' Shaw wrote to Michael Collins's sister. 'I met Michael for the first and last time on Saturday last, and am very glad I did. I rejoice in his memory . . .

'So tear up your mourning and hang up your brightest colors in his honor; and let us all praise God that he had not to die in a snuffy bed of a trumpery cough, weakened by age, and saddened by the disappointments that would have attended his work had he lived.'

It was a handsome letter, masking Shaw's own pessimism under its shining style. For in the Shavian perspective, Michael Collins was one of those descendants of Cain who still ruled the political world and would see Shaw himself weakened and saddened. 'I grow old apace,' he wrote a few days later to Beatrice Webb. ' . . . I am recovering the triviality and cynicism of my youth without its vitality. Probably I ought to die.'

Though de Valera ordered a ceasefire among all Republican commands at the end of April 1923, he himself refused to surrender, and sporadic acts of terrorism continued to erupt in the months leading to the general election that August. Shaw had returned with Charlotte to Ireland for a couple of months in mid-July, burning up the thirty miles of mountainous Cork and Kerry roads between Glengariff and Parknasilla 'in a new 23-60 h.p.'. Despite alarms in the papers, excursions across the south of Ireland were safer than anywhere else in Europe, he reported to *The Times*. There was, he allowed, some outdoor socialism-in-action – 'the loot from plundered houses has to be redistributed by rough methods for which the permanent law is too slow and contentious' – but none of this was exercised at the expense of the errant Englishman. 'The tourist's heart is in his mouth when he first crosses a repaired bridge on a 30 cwt. car, for the repairs are extremely unconvincing to the eye,' he wrote, 'but after crossing two or three in safety he thinks no more of them.

'Since I arrived I have wandered every night over the mountains, either alone or with a harmless companion or two, without molestation or incivility . . . there is not the smallest reason why Glengariff and Parknasilla should not be crowded this year with refugees from the turbulent sister island and the revolutionary Continent, as well as by connoisseurs in extraordinarily beautiful scenery and in air which makes breathing a luxury.'

On 12 September, following this assurance of safety, Shaw fell on some rocks along the Kerry coast, damaging two ribs and badly bruising himself where his camera had been driven into his back. He returned to England six days later, like an Irish hero himself, to be attended by an osteopath, a surgeon and a radiographer.

'A man who is a failure is always popular,' he had told Lady Gregory. Shaw himself had never quite won the hearts of his countrymen, though he presented his failures as feats of floating pre-eminence. This was his fourteenth visit to his country since he had emigrated from Dublin almost fifty years before, and he would not go back again. His last political hopes for

Ireland had appeared to go up in smoke when Horace Plunkett's house Kilteragh was burnt to the ground by the Republicans earlier that year. He had already written his valediction.

'I am returning to England because I can do no good here ... I was a Republican before Mr de Valera was born ... I objected to the old relations between England and Ireland as I object to the present ones, because they were not half intimate enough ... I must hurry back to London. The lunatics there are comparatively harmless.'

[6]

Nature must have a relief from any feeling, no matter how deep and sincere it is.
Jitta's Atonement

'The war is over,' Shaw wrote. '... All the literary, artistic and scientific institutions should be hard at work healing up the wounds of Europe.' When the Spa Conference on economic reparations was held in 1920, he gave his opinion to the German Society for Education in State Citizenship that it would be better 'not to have any conferences at all, and simply to accept the fact that each of the Powers, having indulged in the dissipation of a war, must pay its own damages as best it can'.

What he advocated as public policy he tried to implement in his private dealings, seeking to invest his German royalties in German industry. 'It is with great pleasure that I find myself able to correspond with my German friends again,' he had written to Carl Otto in the autumn of 1919. 'I need hardly say that the war did the most painful violence to my personal feelings, and that I was unable to make any distinction between the German casualties and those of the Allies in respect of the loss they inflicted on European civilization.'

He expressed this wish for healing Europe's wounds most tenderly over the case of his patient German translator, Siegfried Trebitsch. 'I shudder to think of what the blockade must have meant to you,' he sympathized. '... Charlotte's heart bled frightfully for you.' For much of the war they had hardly been able to communicate at all, and even during the long months of the Armistice Shaw had to obtain official authorization to write Trebitsch a letter, all his correspondence to Austria and Germany being inspected to make certain it was confined to business and 'expressed in terms suitable to the existing political relations between our respective countries'. When

64

Trebitsch moved for a time to Switzerland, Shaw vented his relief: 'At last I have got you in a country which I can write to without being shot at dawn.'

He attempted to help Trebitsch in various ways, acting as agent in the sale of his wife's jewellery, and appealing to the British Military Attaché in Vienna with a strongly-worded description of Trebitsch's services to English literature. But only by employing him again as his translator was he really able to give practical help. In the summer of 1919 he received permission from the Board of Trade to enter into new arrangements with Trebitsch for the performance and publication of his plays in Austria and Germany. Six days after its première in New York, *Heartbreak House* opened in Vienna. 'The whole work, from the beginning to the end, is filled with a faint tremor of melancholy leave-taking,' wrote Trebitsch.

Although Shaw was now allowed to receive money direct from Austria, and, through an Allied clearing-house scheme, from Germany, he instructed Trebitsch to hold on to all monies due and use them for himself and his wife. To dispatch money to England 'is to treat me as an enemy', he explained. 'Do not be so haughty: spend my money: *steal* it: do anything you like with it as if it were your own until you are in easy circumstances once more.' But Trebitsch could not get the hang of these economic reversals. Despite all Shaw's urgings and warnings – 'My head is in the lion's mouth; and I shall give him no excuse for snapping his jaws' – he would convey strange sums by dubious routes at odd intervals, imperilling their licence to trade. Partly because of this, and also because he was aware of Trebitsch's growing dismay at becoming principally known as 'Shaw's translator' (a 'horrible expression', Trebitsch called it. 'To the best of my knowledge there has never been a parallel case ... my name as a writer in my own right faded away'), he hit on the corrective paradox of translating his translator. 'I am going to translate a play of yours,' he had threatened before the war; and when Trebitsch sent him a copy of his latest play, *Frau Gittas Sühne*, shortly after the war, he accepted it as an opportunity to make a singular counter-reparationary gesture with *Jitta's Atonement*.

To Trebitsch himself such an extension of their relationship was both a surprise and the most natural thing in the world. It was natural for his friend Shaw to have been 'particularly interested in this work of mine after reading my letters about it', he accepted, 'before he knew the work itself'. It was blatantly natural that, the play having arrived, it should have made 'a deep impression on him and struck him as very characteristic both of the atmosphere of Vienna and of the author'. What was surprising, in these circumstances, was that Shaw had made his proposal understanding hardly a word of German.

More surprising still, according to Shaw, was that Trebitsch himself, whose knowledge of English was always suspect, did not seem to know any German, but to have invented a new language of his own: not even the word *Sühne* could he find. 'I have read Gitta,' he notified Trebitsch in May 1920, 'though most of your words are not in the dictionary.' Within this tangle of difficulties there opened a beautiful advantage for Shaw: 'I had to guess what it was all about by mere instinct.' The advantage to Trebitsch was political: following Shaw's instructions he could tell the Burgtheater in Vienna that *Heartbreak House* would not be available until they had produced *Frau Gittas Sühne*, which may have hastened what Trebitsch called the 'great success' of his play there and in Berlin.

Shaw took a year over the translation. Using 'some telepathic method of absorption', he wrote, 'I managed at last to divine, infer, guess, and co-invent the story of Gitta'. In his reports to Trebitsch he sometimes made light of this work, but according to Blanche Patch it had been a 'heroic decision' which engulfed him in much laborious fumbling and fingering through dictionaries. He had also asked Blanche Patch's German-speaking *locum tenens* to provide him with a literal translation of the play which served as a helpful departure guide. 'I hope my tricks wont make you furious,' he wrote uneasily to Trebitsch after completing the first act. The chief alterations to this act, which remained generally faithful to the original tragedy, were the addition of some directions providing a promising undercurrent to the sombre narrative. 'Charlotte says I have made it brutally realistic; but this is an unintended result of making the stage business more explicit for the sake of the actress,' he explained. ' . . . The stock joke of the London stage is a fabulous stage direction "Sir Henry turns his back to the audience and conveys that he has a son at Harrow".'

Sending him this first act, Shaw advised Trebitsch to 'tear the thing up if it is impossible', but not to do so 'merely because it is disappointing' since all translations were that. 'It is much better than the original,' gallantly responded Trebitsch, who had learnt Shaw's politeness without its component of irony. He eagerly exhorted Shaw to complete his version, which 'proves again your stage-genious', and to add his name as co-dramatist to increase its chances of production. 'I feel a childish delight reading Trebitsch in English,' he wrote happily. ' . . . Please handle that play like your own.'

This, increasingly, is what Shaw did. At the end of the first act, the fifty-year-old Professor Bruno Haldenstedt lies dead of a heart attack on the floor of an apartment where he has been keeping an assignation with his mistress, Jitta Lenkheim, the wife of a medical colleague. Following this convulsion of bliss, 'I was horribly tempted to make Haldenstedt sit up after

Jitta's departure, and make a comedy of the sequel,' Shaw warned Trebitsch. His struggle to resist these temptations weakened in the second act and was joyously abandoned in the third. The second act is still reasonably close to Trebitsch's event-plot, but changes its key so that actions tragically weighted in the German drama by internal destiny are made to look unnecessarily constrained – until in the final act, their constraints stripped off, the cast rejoices in 'the most wonderful difference' and, with 'a paroxysm of agonizing laughter', evolves into a hilarious troupe of Shavians. 'The real person always kills the imagined person,' announces Jitta as Trebitsch's characters die away; and the dead lover's daughter, Edith Haldenstedt, agrees that it is 'such a relief' to be acting sensibly at last. 'We havnt spoken naturally, nor walked naturally, nor breathed naturally, nor thought naturally,' she says, 'because we were all so determined to feel naturally.'

This transmutation of Trebitsch's play was a symbolic act of free will, releasing the characters from their ridiculous destinies and by theatrical intervention bestowing on them the humorous, sensible attitudes that Shaw had tried to introduce with his political interventions into Anglo-Irish and Anglo-German international affairs. Had he not been so unsuccessful at bringing 'natural history' into politics, he might have felt less strongly prompted to introduce 'realism' into this romantic melodrama.

Studying the typewritten transcription from Shaw's shorthand turned out to be a strange experience for Trebitsch. 'I was puzzeled very much reading your bold alterations,' he admitted. '... The III Akt is in your version almost a comedy!' Shaw was quick to provide healing explanations for liberties which, as Trebitsch later observed, he himself would scarcely have forgiven his own translator. It was true, he acknowledged, that he had not done justice to Trebitsch's poetry, and that the melancholic delicacy of the original had eluded his cheesemongering treatment. But Trebitsch would be overjoyed to discover that by making the characters less oppressively conventional, and then inserting a little mild fun into their lives, he had managed to rescue the hero and heroine from their dark fates of misery and malice, blackness and despair. 'That is the good news,' he confirmed. Then there were the commercial and sociological reasons to support this sunny uplift. He had been obliged to translate the audience as well as the play, Trebitsch must understand, replacing Vienna, which still lay in the romantic haze of Strauss waltzes, with London and New York, where the delicious anaesthetic of romance was only tolerated in Italian opera. 'Life is not like that here,' he explained. Trebitsch was surprised to learn that even with such artificial aids as black clothes, visits of condolence and retirement from society the British exercised a reaction against grief over death – an irresistible reaction into cheerfulness. Also 'nine tenths of the adulteries end in reconciliations', Shaw notified Trebitsch, 'and even at the connivance of the injured party at its continuation'.

The childish delight that had initially flowed through Trebitsch was by now rather confused with tributaries of more adult emotion. He wanted success abroad, and dreamed of regaining his reputation as an original creator of plays and novels, but to what degree was *Jitta's Atonement* his own work? The tragedy of his first act and the melodrama of the second had been dissolved in the comedy of Shaw's ending. It was true that he had been invited to refashion the play if he found those treacheries too unbearable, but he trusted Shaw's 'diabolical skill' and the play's increased chances of performance. So with an eye on future business relations with G.B.S., in spite of his qualms and because the authentic *Frau Gittas Sühne* was already printed in German, he gave his alleged translator the go-ahead to prepare an acting version of the text. 'What could I do but agree?'

'I am now postponing everything to it,' Shaw wrote consolingly in mid-May 1922. '... It is a devil of a job, but not at all uninteresting; and I hope I shall not spoil it.' A month later he received the prompt copies in typescript and forwarded one to Trebitsch. 'You will find that in this final acting edition of the play I have committed some fresh outrages,' Shaw added, '... Nothing has been lost by this except the characteristic Trebitschian brooding that is so deliciously sad and noble in your novels but that I could never reproduce ... My method of getting a play across the footlights is like revolver shooting: every line has a bullet in it and comes with an explosion ... so you must forgive me: I have done my best.' It was too late now for Trebitsch to protest at this final execution of his work. 'If this play,' he had written, '... will reach the English–American footlights I shall owe it to your genious.'

'I am cabling New York,' Shaw informed Trebitsch. He was anxious that its author should not see the play snatched from him altogether by a wave of fame-snobbery. 'Novelty is always valuable; and novelty is the one quality that I have lost hopelessly with the affirmation of my reputation,' he advised Lawrence Langner. 'The line to take is to boom Trebitsch in New York ... and to suggest that as what has been lacking in my plays is HEART, the combination of the emotional Trebitsch with the intellectual Shaw is ideal, and will make the most dramatic event of the season.' But Lee Schubert's production in Washington and New York, with Bertha Kalich as Jitta, lasted for only thirty-seven performances and 'did not succeed even as a comedy', Langner recorded.

For two years Shaw held up *Jitta* in England in the hope of getting a West End production, then he handed it to Violet Vanbrugh, 'who in her bloom was a leading London actress, and is still very handsome . . . she will try it at a rather nice suburban theatre at Putney Bridge, called the Grand Theatre . . .' Shaw was abroad for this first English production, but caught up with it two months later at Leicester, one of several towns where Violet Vanbrugh had arranged to give a few matinées during her provincial tour. 'The funniest thing about it is that I was very much struck with your play when I saw it on the stage,' he told Trebitsch. ' . . . Miss Vanbrugh was all wrong . . . she took the greatest pains to present Jitta as an unattractive *whore*, and succeeded only too well.'

In spite of careful instructions, Shaw's name had appeared in larger letters than that of Trebitsch. The reviews too were 'exasperating in their patriotic assumption that all the parts they didn't like were yours', Shaw specified, 'and all the parts they did like mine'. Most of the reviews made it clear that, as the *Daily Telegraph* reported, 'Mr Shaw conjugates the verb "to translate" very differently from most men'. But whenever the reviewers should have felt like 'holding up our hands in horror at the shameful way the original author has been manhandled', wrote the *Nation & Athenaeum* critic, 'we are laughing too loud to remember to do so . . . it cannot possibly have been better entertainment'.

One of those most deeply entertained was Arnold Bennett, who saw it at the Fulham Grand. 'A large audience. A feeling of vitality,' he wrote to Dorothy Cheston. ' . . . *The thing is simply masterly*, & contains a *lot* of the finest scenes that Shaw ever wrote.' In his diary Bennett recorded that the effect of re-engineering a machine-made drama with Shavian wit had been electrical: 'The mere idea of starting on a purely conventional 1st act and then guying it with realism and fun, shows genius.

'In the other acts there is some of the most brilliant work, some tender, some brutal, and lots of the most side-splitting fun that Shaw ever did – and he is now approaching seventy, I suppose. The "hysterics" scene of laughter between the widow and the mistress of the dead man is startlingly original. The confession scene between the mistress and the daughter of the dead man is really beautiful . . . And this in spite of very, very little good acting and a great deal of very bad acting.'

Dorothy Cheston Bennett was also impressed with *Jitta* and, having taken the Royal Court Theatre late in 1927 with Theodore Komisarjevsky as her producer, proposed to put it on with herself in the title role. But everything went wrong: Komisarjevsky was run down by an automobile; Dorothy decided she must stage Bennett's *Mr Prohack* first; Shaw discovered that Dorothy 'cannot act' and that the prosaic forty-five-year-old professor, Alfred Lenkheim, was to be played by a young low comedian from the Royal Academy of Dramatic Art – a born 'funny fat man, not a bit what we need' – called Charles Laughton. Shaw was apologetic – 'I have spoiled the play horribly' – but, though none of his fantasies of film versions and West End triumphs became facts, Trebitsch had already settled on success. 'The play was indeed a success,' he recorded, '... even greater than that at the Vienna Burgtheater and that at the Berlin Residenztheater.' In Shaw's view *Jitta* was now 'kyboshed' in the theatre. 'I hardly know what to do about the play,' he confessed. What he did was to pay Trebitsch £100 for a perpetual non-exclusive licence to translate and publish *Frau Gittas Sühne*, after which *Jitta's Atonement* became his own property, appearing in 1926 in *Translations and Tomfooleries* with several *jeux d'esprit* that Trebitsch had not translated.

Long before this Shaw had diverted Trebitsch's interests elsewhere. 'Did I tell you that I am working on a play about Joan of Arc?' he asked. There was, he supposed, 'no chance of your coming over here.' But Trebitsch reacted formidably. Not having seen Shaw now for some ten years, and feeling it was his 'destiny and privilege' to meet his friend again, he swore 'a vow that in spite of all difficulties and all qualms I would receive the master's new work only from his own hand', he declared. 'The work was there; *Saint Joan* summoned me, and I had to go and receive her.' Shaw's welcome was realistic and statistical. He provided information on the prices and standards of London hotels, made some comments about his own paralytic condition after his fall in Ireland, added an unglamorous assessment of Ayot – 'a village where nobody dreams of dressing' – and noted some of the house rules: 'If you smoke cigars, you will give Charlotte asthma.' All the same, he conceded, Trebitsch might find Ayot 'bearable', and 'I hope to be able to give you printed proofs of Joan.'

The trip was an 'outrageous extravagance in money' though a healthy change for Trebitsch. 'I still think the money the journey cost should have been spent on new clothes and a holiday for you,' Shaw wrote to Trebitsch's wife. The main obstacle to his visit was what Shaw called 'a disgraceful Aliens Act'. The British Embassy had cautioned Trebitsch against trusting to his visa alone. To avoid the risk of being sent straight back across the Channel, he would need an authoritative letter from a British citizen. The letter Shaw sent him admirably fulfilled its purpose, disarming 'the austere passport control officials' at Dover with 'considerable merriment'. Shaw met him at Victoria station, 'coming with long strides along the platform', Trebitsch remembered, '... a laughing giant ... I grasped the hand this long-missed man held out to me'. They drove to Ayot where, for the first time, Trebitsch heard Shaw read one of his own works aloud: the 'singularly effective' *Saint Joan*. 'Shaw read with tremendous intensity, bringing every word to life, brilliantly illuminating every smallest scene with the light of its own inevitability,' he recorded. '...From many scenes there rise undertones of a vainly combated despair of humanity's goodwill.'

Afterwards they spoke of the dreadful war years – experiences, moods and opinions that could never have been sent through the mail. 'My generation has passed away and I shall soon have to follow its example,' Shaw said, but despite this conviction, he was in high spirits and the days passed all too quickly for Trebitsch. When they said '*auf Wiedersehen*' it seemed to him that the additional unspoken phrase 'in a better world' was plainly implied. He carried with him the latest work. 'There is no other new play,' Shaw told him: 'Joan is *the* new play.'

CHAPTER II

[1]

We want a few mad people now.
See where the sane ones have landed us!
Saint Joan

It's done his art and heart good to get the doctrine
of Methuselah *off his breathing-works: and the poet in him is now going*
to have a little dance.
T. E. Lawrence to Charlotte Shaw (16 March 1924)

Shaw had been long familiar with Joan of Arc in the theatre. As a music critic he had listened unenthusiastically to Liszt's 'Joan of Arc at the Stake', had described as 'trashy melodrama' a version of Joan adapted by Jules Barbier for Gounod's self-imitative incidental music and had heard Moszkowski's symphonic poem *Johanna D'Arc* (based on Schiller's 'romantic flapdoodle' *Die Jungfrau von Orleans*), deciding that it contained 'nothing very fresh, and a good deal that is decidedly stale'.

To his mind Joan had been little better served in literature since making her appearance in Shakespeare's *Henry VI* as a 'trull', 'witch', 'strumpet' and

> 'foul fiend of France and hag of all despite
> Encompass'd with thy lustful paramours!'

Though rescued from this scurrility in the eighteenth century, and transformed by Schiller and Southey (as well as by Verdi and Tchaikovsky) from being an agent of foreign devils into a popular liberator and nationalist heroine, Joan had been allowed to languish for over a hundred years as the creature of romance and stagey melodrama. Even after Jules Quicherat made the facts of her trial and subsequent rehabilitation available in the 1870s, she persisted in people's hearts as a legendary rather than historical figure, partly because knowledge of the trial deepened so many of the problems it was intended to solve. Shaw had been in Dublin when Tom Taylor's heroic historical pageant play *Jeanne Darc* was performed there, but came away feeling that with such remorseless theatre-of-entertainment 'serious character study was impossible'.

72

By now Joan was public property: a voice that spoke to the imagination of the artist, and a symbol that represented the needs of successive historical periods. But Shaw felt she had been exploited: licentiously by Voltaire, who used her in his mock Homeric epic *La Pucelle* to kill with ridicule everything that he 'righteously hated in the institutions and fashions of his own day'; and misogynistically by Anatole France who was so disabled 'by a simple disbelief in the existence of *ability* (in the manly sense) in women' that he committed the anti-feminist gaffe of reducing her in his *Vie* to the puppet of soldiers and priests. She had been exploited romantically, too, by Mark Twain, whose fictionalized memoirs of Joan's page converted her into 'an unimpeachable American school teacher in armor', and sentimentally by Andrew Lang to whom she appeared as a 'beautiful and most ladylike Victorian'. 'I love the real Joan,' Shaw later wrote: 'but the conventional Joan of the stage makes me sick.'

In his Notes to *Caesar and Cleopatra* he had classed her with Nelson and Charles XII – all 'half-witted geniuses, enjoying the worship accorded by all races to certain forms of insanity'. Some ten years later, in the Preface to *Getting Married*, she is no longer a lunatic but a dangerously good person gifted with 'exceptional sanity'. In the interval, Quicherat's factual testimony had been translated and published in England, providing authentic evidence of the real Joan. Nevertheless it was the conventional heroine of second-rate opera who continued to appear on stage. 'In the theatre, the state of things would break your heart,' Shaw had written to Harley Granville-Barker in 1907, after witnessing Percy Mackaye's verse drama, *Jeanne d'Arc*. On hearing a rumour that Edmond Rostand, a playwright touched with 'a certain modern freedom of spirit', might be at work on a Joan play, he had exclaimed: 'For this be all his sins forgiven him!'

But Shaw does not seem to have considered adding to Joan literature himself until 1913 when, returning from Germany through the Vosges and 'pleasing myself as to my route', he remembered, 'I took Domremy on my way for the sake of St Joan of Arc.' He had often travelled through what he called 'Joan of Arc country', but never before visited Orléans. It was here, at the Musée Historique, that he saw the fifteenth-century sculptured head of St Maurice, traditionally believed by the inhabitants to have been modelled from Joan after her triumphant relief of their town from the English. Shaw was happy to embrace this belief. For the Gothic image, which was reproduced as the frontispiece to T. Douglas Murray's edited translation of Quicherat's *Procès de Jeanne d'Arc* (and later appeared on the programme of the first English production of Shaw's play), was large and strong and showed a remarkable face – 'evidently not an ideal face but a portrait, and yet so uncommon as to be unlike any real woman one has ever seen,' he wrote. '... It is a wonderful face ... the face of a born leader.' This was the image before Shaw ten years later when he presented Joan in the turret doorway of his play – *an able-bodied country girl of 17 or 18, respectably dressed in red, with an uncommon face: eyes very wide apart ... a long well-shaped nose ... resolute but full-lipped mouth, and handsome fighting chin'.*

From Orléans he wrote to Stella Campbell: 'I shall do a Joan play some day.' He imagined it beginning with the 'sweeping up of the cinders and orange peel *after* her martyrdom', and ending with Joan's arrival in heaven. 'I should have God about to damn the English for their share in her betrayal,' he wrote, 'and Joan producing an end of burnt stick in arrest of Judgment.'

'"What's that? Is it one of the faggots?" says God. "No," says Joan "it's what is left of the two sticks a common English soldier tied together and gave me as I went to the stake; for they wouldnt even give me a crucifix; and you cannot damn the common people of England, represented by that soldier[,] because a poor cowardly riff raff of barons and bishops were too futile to resist the devil" ... one of my scenes will be Voltaire and Shakespear running down bye streets in heaven to avoid meeting Joan...'

Commenting on this letter of 1913, Stanley Weintraub observed: 'Ten years later he wrote the play which was preface to that epilogue.' Other critics, echoing Shaw's defence of his epilogue (more than once threatened with excision) as 'the most earnest part of the play', have agreed that indeed it is, in the words of Dan H. Laurence, 'the most meaningful and indispensable part of the play'. This bedroom cabaret in Charles VII's dream has some affinities with Shaw's original fantasy, and features a 'saint from hell' who is the redeemed English soldier. But more significant is the change of surroundings in which Shaw places his 'adventurous impetuous masterful girl soldier' after the First World War, and the different task he assigns her. The chronicle play he wrote in 1923 is his 'one foray into popular myth-making', Irving Wardle has written, 'undefaced by his usual ironic graffiti'; while the epilogue is a Shavian revue sketch which does not remove Joan up to heaven, but brings her forward from the fifteenth into the twentieth century – a move implicit in the previous six scenes.

In this medieval visionary Shaw felt he recognized the simplicity of spirit needed for the regeneration of society in the modern world. Fleetingly he had turned his hopes towards President Wilson, who had soon been engulfed by the 'greed and rancor which abuse victory'. Shaw's St Joan possesses a superior power – what he had called in *Peace Conference Hints* 'the entirely mystic force of evolution applied through the sort of living engine we call the man of principle'.

Though St Joan is the latest model of this living engine, its design had been patented a quarter of a century earlier in *The Perfect Wagnerite*, where 'Siegfried as Protestant' anticipates Joan, the first Protestant. Siegfried and Joan both quell their fear of fire, and are transfigured by the flames. Describing Protestantism in the late fifteenth century as a 'wave of thought' that led 'the strongest-hearted peoples to affirm that every man's private judgement was a more trustworthy interpreter of God and revelation than the Church', Shaw concluded:

'The most inevitable dramatic conception, then, of the nineteenth century is that of a perfectly naïve hero upsetting religion, law and order in all directions, and establishing in their place the unfettered action of Humanity doing exactly what it likes, and producing order instead of confusion thereby because it likes to do what is necessary for the good of the race. This conception, already incipient in Adam Smith's Wealth of Nations, was certain at last to reach some great artist, and be embodied by him in a masterpiece.'

Saint Joan is Shaw's attempt at this masterpiece and the vehicle for a living dialogue between ancient and modern worlds. Being 'intensely interested, and to some extent conscience stricken, by the great historical case of Joan of Arc', he felt any demonstration as to how it happened was 'an act of justice for which the spirit of Joan, yet incarnate among us, is still calling'. But the proceedings of her trial had entangled politics with religion. If Joan's rehabilitation was an example of a modern show trial, the original court hearing seemed to Shaw one of history's secret trials – like those of the Star Chamber. 'Joan was killed by the Inquisition ... The Inquisition is not dead,' he wrote in 1931. '... you always will have a spiritual tribunal of some kind, and unless it is an organised and recognised thing, with a body of law behind it, it will become a secret thing, and a very terrible thing ... And when in modern times you fall behind-hand with your political institutions ... you get dictatorships ... and when you get your dictatorship you may take it from me that you will with the greatest certainty get a secret tribunal dealing with sedition, with political heresy, exactly like the Inquisition.' Such a passage makes clear Shaw's intention of rehearing the case in the theatre to answer not only the claim of a great spirit for justice, but also 'a world situation in which we see whole peoples perishing and dragging us towards the abyss which has swallowed them all for want of any grasp of the political forces that move civilizations'.

The hero as victim transformed into saviour had been in Shaw's mind as early as the *Passion Play* he had started to compose at the age of twenty-one. Like Jesus, Joan was an agent for change religiously inspired against the idealist *status quo* of the established Church. Cauchon's great cry – 'Must then a Christ perish in torment in every age to save those that have no imagination?' – makes the connection plain, and Joan herself endorses this connection when she tells the court: 'I am His child, and you are not fit that I should live among you.' So *Saint Joan* became Shaw's passion play and represents Joan's life as another coming of Christ to the world. G.B.S. came to feel that Joan's story was far better suited than Jesus's to his realist purpose. 'Joan's heresies and blasphemies are not heresies and blasphemies to us,' he wrote to Trebitsch: 'we sympathize with them. And she defends herself splendidly, wiping the floor with her accusers every time. Jesus is convicted for asserting that he is the Messiah, and that he will rise from the dead after three days and come again in glory to establish his kingdom on earth. To us that is the delusion of a madman.'

Joan's righteous fanaticism, reaching us through the perspective of five hundred years and then filtered through the sanity of Shaw's art, becomes the protest of plain-spoken individual conscience. 'What other judgment can I judge by but my own?' she asks. Shaw presents her as an evolutionary force whose miracles are, as Cauchon tells de Stogumber, 'capable of a natural explanation' but allowed to trail as legends behind her miraculous personality. The miracle of the eggs in the first scene, for example, is announced by the Steward only after Joan, having imposed her will on the bullying but indecisive Robert de Baudricourt, is on her way to Chinon, and it is used by Shaw to illustrate de Poulengey's belief that 'the girl herself is a bit of a miracle'.

As the critic Brian Tyson has observed, the second scene similarly contains an apparent and a real miracle. The ostensible miracle – Joan's identification of the Dauphin whose place on the dais has been theatrically taken by Gilles de Rais – is made a matter of intelligent observation. 'She will know what everybody in Chinon knows: that the Dauphin is the meanest-looking and worst-dressed figure in the Court,' predicts the Archbishop. The Archbishop is accustomed to miracles. They are, he explains, simple and innocent contrivances which create faith. When Joan enters the Throne Room everyone feels the thrill of the supernatural and senses the glory of God; even the Archbishop feels his faith confirmed by the simplicity of the Maid, and signals the miracle by blushing. It is the same effect that has been produced on Captain La Hire. He believes Joan to be an angel after she has told a drunken soldier not to swear when he was going to die – and the man is subsequently drowned. 'We are all going to die,

Captain,' the Archbishop reminds La Hire. 'I hope not,' answers the Captain, crossing himself. The final part of Joan's real miracle takes place at the end of the scene when she 'quickly puts her hand on Charles's shoulder' and imbues him with courage. His change from sickly coward to potential leader is a distant parallel of Sonny's conversion into G.B.S. and demonstrates the action of vicarious will that Shaw himself had vainly tried to exercise on Janet Achurch, Florence Farr and others.

The third stage miracle, signalled by the streaming pennon in Scene III, is the sudden change of wind at Orléans. Though this is accepted by everyone on stage (and possibly in the audience) as the work of 'God and the Maid!' Shaw arranges for it to take place before Joan has gone to church 'to pray for a west wind'; and he goes on to emphasize the ordinary climatic explanation by adding an everyday suggestion made by Lady Gregory. 'In Gort we often sneeze when the wind changes,' she told him. 'Why don't you use a Kiltartan sneeze in your play?' So he gave the Kiltartan sneeze to Dunois' page. But the real miracle, which happens off-stage, is Joan's reformation of the French army. 'There is a new spirit rising in men,' the Archbishop has observed: 'we are at the dawning of a wider epoch.' Joan represents the dawning of this new spirit of nationalism. Before she came, these soldiers had fought blindly and fearfully under any lord who was in the ascendency. 'Our soldiers are always beaten because they are fighting only to save their skins; and the shortest way to save your skin is to run away,' Joan says. She replaces their fear with a belief that they are led by someone inspired from heaven. The miracle is in the belief – which causes these soldiers to follow Joan and her doctrine of France for the French with fatalistic confidence – a belief that Shaw, in the dawning age of internationalism, mocks with de Stogumber's patriotic platitudes reminiscent of civilian bloodthirstiness during the Great War.

Shaw was to be accused of rationalizing Joan's voices; more accurately he Shavianized them. He interprets them as evidence of a living imagination – the 'inspirations and intuitions and unconsciously reasoned conclusions of genius' – which are miraculous not by virtue of their alleged source but because of exceptional consequences. These voices and visions, being the manifestations of Joan's instinct ('the voices come first', she explains, 'and I find the reasons after'), operate similarly to Shaw's own methods of writing. 'I am pushed by a natural need to set to work to write down the conversations that come into my head unaccountably,' he had explained ten years before. 'At first I hardly know the speakers and cannot find names for them. Then they become more and more familiar, and I learn their names. Finally I come to know them very well, and discover what it is they are driving at, and why they have said and done the things I have been moved to set down.' By this telepathic process of 'sane hallucination' Shaw hoped to attune himself to Joan, he echoing her when following the court testimony, she echoing him when he departs from it, and together collaborating in the miraculous creation of the play. He disclaimed the real authorship of Saint Joan. 'I have done nothing but arrange her for the stage ... Make your offerings at her altar, not at mine.'

But it seemed to many that the final miracle had been Saint Joan's transformation of G.B.S. She was 'the only woman who ever managed to wipe the smirk from Shaw's face', commented Bernard Levin over fifty years later; and Johan Huizinga claimed that she had brought Shaw 'to his knees'. Such reverence certainly looked like a conversion. 'G.B.S. – do you know that your old nurse didn't sprinkle you with Holy Water for nothing?' Laurence Alma Tadema wrote to him. 'If you live to be 90 St Joan herself will fish you up to Heaven ... '

More eloquent is the miraculous transmutation of the wretched innocent who had 'talked with angels and saints from the age of thirteen', Marina Warner reminds us, had defended the 'external and objective reality of those voices', had 'made a continual profession of her deep love for her feudal suzerain the king, and turned to the Pope for help in her long and appalling trial'. In Shaw's creation (still looking through Marina Warner's eyes) Joan reappears as a 'sharp-witted individualist, who attributes her motives and ideas to hard common sense, fights for a twentieth-century idea of the self-determined state ... [is a] protesting prophet, subverter, active agent of the Life Force, rational dresser'. To have succeeded in getting this Shavian 'pert spitfire' to enter English consciousness so positively as the true Joan was an authentic miracle.

'The first thing he invariably does when his setting is in the past, is to rub off his period the patina of time,' wrote Desmond MacCarthy; ' ... he will scrub and scrub till contemporary life begins to gleam through surface strangeness and oddities'. Shaw worked fast, filled with relief at having lifted himself free from the post-war débâcle and entered a previous century to fight another war against English imperialism. In the staging of this fifteenth-century campaign he translated his own assertion of style into Joan's inspired efficiency of action – 'She is so positive, sir,' Robert de Baudricourt's steward says to account for her effect on everyone. It is as if she goes into battle flourishing with her white banner a fluttering copy of *What I Really Wrote about the War*. Shaw presents her as the heroic example of an undiscovered modern leader, the warrior-saint he had sometimes thought of dramatizing as Cromwell and Mahomet, and had looked for in a play about the Unknown Soldier. But after *Saint Joan* he needed to write none of these works. 'It's a stupendous play,' Sybil Thorndike wrote to him, '& says all the things that the world needs to hear at the moment.'

*

Shaw had first seen Sybil Thorndike auditioning for a touring production of *Candida* in 1908. At the conclusion of her bouncing performance into which she put 'everything I'd got ... Lady Macbeth, Everyman, Beatrice, everything,' he had advised her to go home and, like Candida, 'have a husband and children and do the housekeeping' – after which she would be very good in the part. All the same, he engaged her as understudy and delighted her at rehearsals by saying that she possessed some qualities of Janet Achurch. Then, in Ireland on the first night of the tour, she went out front and watched a young man called Lewis Casson playing Trench in *Widowers' Houses*. She had found her husband. By the time Shaw went to see her as Hecuba in *The Trojan Women* her acting had been enriched by four children and a decade of housekeeping. But it was not until he saw her play Beatrice in the trial scene of *The Cenci* at the end of 1922 that he is alleged to have said: 'I have found my Joan.'

Sybil Thorndike had felt destined to act St Joan and in 1923 commissioned Laurence Binyon to write a play for her about the Maid. Shaw, too, after several months' reflection and research, had begun writing his *Saint Joan* in 1923 – on 29 April at Malvern, on his way to Stratford-upon-Avon. 'A good deal of it was written in rapidly moving trains between King's Cross and Hatfield on the London, Midland and Scottish railway,' he remembered. He seemed to work at it all the time, taking everything Blanche Patch had typed by 18 July to the Eccles Hotel at Glengariff, and pursuing it to the Great Southern Hotel at Parknasilla, where on 24 August he was able to write 'The End' on his manuscript. 'Saint Joan is finished (except for the polishing),' he announced three days later: ' ... and I thought I should never write another after Methuselah!'

It was not until he had finished the play, adding the stage business and preparing to write his Preface (which he started on 8 December 1923 at Adelphi Terrace and completed at Ayot St Lawrence on 28 January 1924) that Sybil Thorndike and Lewis Casson got to hear of it. In some consternation they wrote, telling him of Laurence Binyon's work-in-progress and asking what should be done. G.B.S. was flatteringly adamant: 'Sybil is to play my Joan; let someone else play Binyon's.' In the event, Binyon gracefully withdrew and the difficulty lifted.

In the various accounts of *Saint Joan*, the long gestation and rapid delivery seem hardly connected. 'I am the creature of circumstances,' Shaw remarked when asked why he had selected St Joan. ' ... sometimes the urge to write a play comes over me and I cannot think what to write about. That happened before I started *Saint Joan*.' This urge to write a play may partly have been aroused by a letter he had received from his old friend William Archer, a letter goading him for having so successfully discouraged the public from taking him seriously that his influence was less than it had been twenty years before. 'Let us for once, or twice, or thrice, have the gold without the slag,' Archer challenged him, 'working it into whatever artistic form you please. Say, for instance, a great play, realistic or symbolic, that should go to every city in the world and shake the souls of people...'

Charlotte seems to have been instrumental in Shaw's choice of subject. 'Yes, I sometimes find ideas for plays for the Genius,' she conceded. 'If we can find a good subject for a play, he usually writes it very quickly.' According to Shaw, as reported by his biographer Hesketh Pearson, Charlotte recommended St Joan to him one day and he readily agreed. According to Charlotte, as reported by Shaw's biographer St John Ervine, he was deaf to her suggestion and believed that he had come upon the idea himself after she had cunningly deposited books about the Maid in every place where he was certain to pick them up.

The same proposal, according to another of Shaw's biographers, Archibald Henderson, had also been made by the man he had named as his literary executor, Sydney Cockerell, curator of the Fitzwilliam Museum in Cambridge, to which, early in 1922, the Shaws had presented one of Augustus John's portraits of G.B.S. Cockerell had been stirred with excitement by the English translation of Quicherat, which he was to give to each of his children as well as to a number of his friends including Shaw early in 1923. 'I have always been under the impression that I was in a small way responsible for St Joan,' Cockerell wrote to Shaw twenty years later, 'by giving you or introducing you to Douglas Murray's book containing the full proceedings at her trial and rehabilitation and suggesting that you might do something with it...'

There was yet another begetter, a teacher at St Mary's College, Hammersmith, called Father Joseph Leonard, whom the Shaws had met in 1919 on holiday at Parknasilla. He, too, recommended the Douglas Murray volume when, in December 1922, Shaw sent him a letter asking where he could find a record of the proceedings of Joan's canonization. 'What I want to know is how the Church got over the fact, which must have been raised by the *advocatus diaboli* if he did his duty to his client, that Joan asserted a right of private judgment as against the Church,' he explained. '...I may write a play about her some day; and this is the only point on which I do not feel fully equipped.'

This letter initiated a long exchange between Shaw and the priest who became his 'technical adviser' on the play, though not all his advice was accepted. Father Leonard pointed out that Joan's trial by a local ecclesiastical tribunal had been illegal and unjust, since it was held without any reference to the Pope and its conviction carried out in defiance of her appeal to the head of the Church. This illegality was confirmed twenty-four years later by the annulment of her sentence. Shaw took this to mean that Joan's beatification and canonization were based on legal expedient rather than renewed examination of the actual testimony which contained Joan's heresy of preferring her 'voices' to the voice of the Church. 'A flaw in the procedure may be useful later on,' says the Inquisitor. Joan's canonization, several centuries later, appeared to Shaw based on technical flaws 'and though I do not see how the avoidance of these could have saved her', he wrote (echoing the Inquisitor), 'yet the fact that they were not avoided invalidates the excommunication'.

'... Now the Church stresses two qualifications for sanctity; heroic virtues and private revelations ... The Church does not recognize private judgment, but it does recognize inspiration. By holding that at the first trial the private revelations, now recognized as genuine, were mistaken for presumptuous private judgments, the Church puts itself in order in canonizing the one-time heretic.'

It had been the rehabilitation, staged so as to save the consecration of Charles VII from stigma, that was corrupt, and not the trial, says Ladvenu in the epilogue, and this was Shaw's view. He held Joan's private judgment to be inspired and the Church's judgment banal. He took the evidence from the court – often in Joan's words – and dramatized it in the theatre as the speeches of a natural rebel against the Church's authority. Father Leonard declared Joan's loyalty to the Pope to be of far greater significance than any number of eccentric voices, for 'the Church is large enough to contain all sorts of queer fish'. But to have made Joan a queer fish within the Catholic aquarium would have destroyed the Protestant purpose of Shaw's play, which was to bring a realist heroine before a perfectly-conducted court of idealists, and to leave his audience with a real view of the idealist world they still inhabited. 'Joan was persecuted essentially as she would be persecuted today.'

From Shaw's answer to Leonard that December it becomes clear that he had already studied the translation of Quicherat's *Procès* which Cockerell and Leonard were urging him to read; and from a letter to Middleton Murry a little later it appears that he went to some trouble to avoid the other Joan volumes that Charlotte was deviously depositing round the rooms of their house and flat. 'My Plutarch was the report of the trial and the rehabilitation: contemporary and largely verbatim,' he confirmed. 'I took particular care not to read a word of anything else until the play was finished.' Because the historical material was ready-made and so interesting, needing only his knack of dramatic reporting, the play seemed almost to write itself. More difficult was the revision, in which he eliminated many tempting digressions and incidents, though 'this drastic "cutting" was not new'. His unplanned way of working often led him to 'overwrite a play by as much as one third', he explained. His revision was well advanced and into the second set of proofs by the late autumn when Sybil Thorndike and Lewis Casson came down to Ayot to hear G.B.S. read his play. After lunch – 'chicken for us and all sorts of funny-looking things for him because he's a vegetarian' – they went through into the sitting-room, and he began. 'He read it beautifully – he ought to have been an actor really and from the moment he started we couldn't move!' Sybil Thorndike wrote to her son John. Though in a fever to play St Joan, she had also been apprehensive lest she would not like Shaw's version. 'But we needn't have worried. It's the most marvellous play . . . ' The reading lasted three hours and three minutes, following which Shaw made another gigantic effort at revision, cutting out the three minutes. 'When it came to the Epilogue Lewis and I were in tears,' Sybil Thorndike recalled.

*

Though Sybil Thorndike was the theatrical vehicle Shaw had in mind for the role, he had used another model as Joan's contemporary equivalent – the middle-aged Fabian Mary Hankinson. Hanky, as she was known, had been born in Cheshire, physically trained in Kent, employed as Head of a Sunday School and then put into front-line service by the Fabians. For thirty years she acted as Spartan hostess at the Fabian Summer Schools, captaining their cricket teams, drilling their country dancers and policing their morals. She was vividly remembered for teaching Shaw to waltz backwards. 'It was absolutely priceless,' one Fabian remembered. 'She was short and fat; he tall and thin – an unforgettable sight!' There was 'no panky with Hanky', as another Fabian put it, for she seemed entirely sexless, pouring her energies into gymnastics and flute-playing, and sharing her domestic life with her friend Ethel Moor. Shaw had attended the Summer School in 1919 at Penlee where Hanky had miraculously quenched a

82

Fabian uprising against her demanding programme. But though a rigid disciplinarian, this

> 'maid with silver hair
> With school-boy heart and skipper air'

as John Dover Wilson serenaded her, inspired much admiration, for she was a woman of 'unusual good sense', St John Ervine observed, 'a remarkably self-controlled woman, and so full of personal charm that people meeting her for the first time felt certain that there must be some terrible flaw in her character, since no human being could possibly be so devoid of disagreeable characteristics: only to learn, as they became better acquainted with her, that she was the one human being anybody knew who was so composed'.

It was to Mary Hankinson that Shaw wrote from Parknasilla in August 1923 explaining that he could not get to the Fabian Summer School that year because 'I must stay here until I finish my Joan of Arc play, and let everything else go smash.' When *Saint Joan* was published the following summer, he presented Hanky with a copy inscribed: 'To Mary Hankinson, the only woman I know who does not believe she was the model for Joan, and also the only woman who actually was.'

Rather stout, with straight hair and a resolutely pale complexion, she had great muscular strength and a legendary reputation. 'I have seen three average young men, struggling unsuccessfully to get a grand piano on to a platform,' one Fabian remembered; 'she swept them aside and did it single handed.' 'Hankinson and Moor Limited', as Shaw once addressed them, shared a cottage at Jordans, a village in Buckinghamshire founded in 1919 by the Quakers. Latterly 'a completely square figure, always dressed in immense tweed suits', she stiffened her Quaker villagers against the incursions of road builders and developers, her commanding Cheshire accent spreading awe, especially among the children. 'Her steely clear blue eyes always noticed the slightest untidiness or misdemeanour about the place,' one of them recorded. 'If a bluebell were missing from the woods she would notice it. It was she who organized the maypole on the green on May Day, and she was also responsible for afternoon games of netball, during which she stood on the sidelines fiercely blowing a whistle.' On Sundays she would sing buoyantly in the chapel choir and, according to her clergyman brother, was 'always devoted to her own church, though tolerant to all creeds and races and parties'. It was the Quaker ingredient, however, that appealed to Shaw. 'Joan was the spiritual mother of George Fox,' he wrote.

'It is difficult,' wrote the critic Maurice Valency, 'to understand in what way Miss Hankinson ... could have served as a model for Saint Joan.' But her feminism, which modulated Joan's speech to the extent that it sounded to Desmond MacCarthy like the voice of 'a suffragette and a cry from a garden city', was of particular service to Shaw who also gave Joan his own public-speaking skills. Hanky had been a member of the Fabian Women's Group since its foundation in 1906 and would remain a campaigner against women's wrongs all her career. It was to this influence that T. S. Eliot took exception when criticizing Shaw for having created 'perhaps the greatest sacrilege of all Joans' by turning 'her into a great middle-class reformer ... [whose] place is little higher than Mrs Pankhurst's'. Shaw might have accepted this criticism as an endorsement of his aim – indeed he almost did so (and may have had Eliot in mind) when, delivering a radio talk in 1931, he stated that although no modern feminist was exactly like St Joan, 'I believe every one of them did regard herself as, in a measure, repeating the experiences of St Joan. St Joan inspired that movement ... If you read Miss [Sylvia] Pankhurst, you will understand a great deal more about the psychology of Joan ...'

Shaw's play carries on the historical business of literature, which is to reconstruct the roles of past figures and to keep the dead in perpetual employment. He uses Joan's symbolic dimensions to add credentials to his vitalist philosophy, as Voltaire and Anatole France had used her for their purposes, and as Shaw's contemporaries were themselves using her for opposing ends. Not long before he had begun contemplating his play, Charles Péguy had recreated Joan as a socialistic mystic and martyr who found her equivalent in the government-persecuted figure of Dreyfus; and Charles Maurras had rediscovered her as a proto-fascist emblem of the Action Française, reinforcing military and national authority as Joan had reinforced the French army and the King.

Joan had become everyone's reflection. Shaw's Joan is the complete outsider who feels most lonely when she is in company with those who voice the opinions of the day. Her own timeless voices echo her unworldliness and establish her kinship with the man who felt a stranger on this planet and at ease only with the dead. But Joan is not, as some critics have asserted, a simple spawning of G.B.S.; Shaw's methods of composition were too oblique and multifaceted for straightforward self-portraiture. In the perspective of history, Joan's allies belong to that conglomeration of degenerates and incompetents for whose deliverance G.B.S. had crusaded with *The Sanity of Art*. But to help Joan 'pull me through', and to illustrate how the progress of humankind still depended on some people regarded by philistine society as sick, eccentric, wicked and even lunatic, Shaw enlisted more than one contemporary parallel. In addition to Mary Hankinson there was Lawrence of Arabia.

Shaw had been introduced to T. E. Lawrence in March 1922 when

Sydney Cockerell brought him along to help carry away the portrait by Augustus John. Shaw was one of Lawrence's heroes, and five months later he received a letter from Lawrence asking him to read 'or try to read, a book which I have written ... because it is history, and I'm ashamed for ever if I am the sole chronicler of an event, and fail to chronicle it: and yet unless what I've written can be made better I'll burn it'. In agreeing to give his opinion of the book G.B.S. assured Lawrence that he was 'a privileged soul, and can deal with both of us as with old friends'. By the middle of September one of the eight copies of Lawrence's *The Seven Pillars of Wisdom*, cumbersomely printed on a linotype machine by the *Oxford Times*, arrived at Ayot. 'I may profit by your reading it, if I have a chance to talk to you soon after, before you have got over it,' Lawrence had written. 'You see the war was, for us who were in it, an overwrought time, in which we lost our normal footing. I wrote this thing in the war atmosphere, and believe that it is stinking with it.'

This awkward and prodigious work, weighing nearly six pounds and 'about twice as long as the Bible', stood at the centre of Shaw's working life. Nobody but an Imam, he exclaimed, could have time to study it thoroughly – except Charlotte who took it up while G.B.S. was 'road tubthumping' round England on the general election campaign that autumn, and began ecstatically reading passages aloud on his return. To Lawrence himself this sounded 'dreadful news, for my builders'-yard of a book is most unfit for a lady's eyes ... please explain that I didn't ask her to read it', he petitioned G.B.S. from whom he was still 'mad keen' to hear. 'Patience, patience,' Shaw counselled at the start of December. '... The truth is, I haven't read it yet. I have sampled it.' But even from this sampling one thing was clear. 'You are evidently a very dangerous man: most men who are any good are,' he told Lawrence. '... I wonder what, after reading the book through, I will decide to do with you.'

The reading 'is now under weigh', he promised, but he had not promised to be quick – 'I shall read it sooner or later.' His detailed revisions (including virtuoso use of the semi-colon), which affected 'the spirit as well as the letter of the book', Lawrence acknowledged, and 'left not a paragraph without improvement', were not completed until some two years later. But Shaw had read the book 'to the last morsel' much sooner. By the time he started on *Saint Joan* he had only forty pages left to read, and when he finished it early in the summer he felt convinced that here was 'one of the great books of the world', he told Lady Gregory.

In the meantime he had found out some strange facts about this puzzling man. Lawrence had quitted his Arabian adventures, left the Colonial Office, erased his old name and, having been discharged from the RAF following his public identification as 'Private Ross', enlisted in the Royal Tank Corps in Dorset using as his new alias – of all names – Shaw. 'Lawrence is not normal in many ways,' his friend D. G. Hogarth advised G.B.S., 'and it is extraordinarily difficult to do anything for him.' G.B.S. had tried to do something for him that May by appealing to Stanley Baldwin a few days after he had become Prime Minister for 'a decent and indeed a handsome provision' to place Lawrence in the position of 'a pensioned commanding officer in dignified private circumstances'. But 'I'm afraid I'm rather a difficult person to help,' Lawrence confirmed.

Lady Gregory visited Ayot St Lawrence that May, and her diary records that the two people most on Shaw's mind were Joan of Arc and Lawrence of Arabia. To some degree *The Seven Pillars of Wisdom* may be read as a cross-referring work to *Saint Joan*: the two chronicles, Stanley Weintraub has suggested, providing a parallel between the saintly Maid and the ascetic Prince of the desert as well as a Shavian perspective on the historical recurrence of Joan's experience as an unconventional military leader brought down by politicians. Lawrence was what Shaw called 'a grown-up boy, without any idea of politics'. He had gone to the Paris Peace Conference expecting President Wilson to secure self-determination for the Arab peoples, and had come away full of the bitterness of defeat. 'I meant to make a new nation,' he wrote, 'to restore to the world a lost influence, to give twenty millions of Semites the foundation on which to build an inspired dream-palace of their national thoughts.' He had laid this foundation by organizing the Arab revolt against the Turks. His inspired leadership of their guerrilla campaign, which kept all the Arabs fighting for the Allies instead of among themselves, helped to redeem them from their Ottoman servitude. Like Joan, Lawrence had been 'in the grip of a nationalistic impulse to create a unified state from a feudal order, and to set a monarch representative of that unity upon the throne of the nation-state'. Joan had succeeded with the Dauphin and been martyred; Lawrence had failed with King Feisal and seemed, after Versailles, to be backing into oblivion. Shaw fixed on them both the same quotation from Marshal Foch, who remarked that Napoleon would have fought the First World War magnificently, but 'what on earth would we have done with him afterwards?' Had Joan escaped burning, she would have 'fought on until the English were gone', Shaw believed, 'and then had to shake the dust of the court off her feet, and retire to Domremy', seeking fulfilment in a convent. As for Lawrence, if he had lived in the Middle Ages, 'he would have gone into a monastery'.

As a man-of-letters in peacetime who became a man-of-action in war, Lawrence provided a living connection between G.B.S. and Joan that helped Shaw to bring his heroine 'close to the present day'. In the Preface to

1 Edith Evans as the Serpent in *Back to Methuselah*, Birmingham, 1923

2 Blanche Patch with Shaw

3 Charlotte photographed by Shaw

4 Sybil Thorndike as Saint Joan,

5 'A wonderful face'. Shaw's Saint Joan

6A The Ethical Movement, G.B.S. and Miss Hankinson at a Fabian Summer School;
B Prince Troubetzkoy working on his head of Shaw

7 Molly Tompkins

EQUAL INCOMES

GRADUS AD MILLENNIUM.

MR. BERNARD SHAW AS THE "INTELLIGENT WOMAN'S GUIDE."

(With apologies to G. F. Watts's "Love and Life.")

his play he examined 'Joan's immaturity and ignorance'; elsewhere, he pointed to Lawrence's political ignorance ('he showed no consciousness of the existence of Lenin or Stalin or Mussolini or Ataturk') and singled out his self-defining immaturity: 'powerful and capable as his mind was, I am not sure that it ever reached full maturity'. Lacking an adult sense of his identity, Lawrence invited his heroes to invade his character and associate it with their own, as if gathering from these feats of empathy some nucleus of self-confidence. Getting to know Shaw was 'a great adventure'. His choice of Shaw's name, the opening he gave G.B.S. to edit and amend his vast first-person chronicle of the Arabian campaign, and the visits he began making that summer to the Shaws' village, the name of which so coincidentally sanctified his own, were part of the mechanics by which G.B.S. became encouraged to merge their destinies.

Already, by the beginning of 1923, Shaw was advising Lawrence to 'get used to the limelight', as he himself had done. Later he came to realize that Lawrence was one of the most paradoxically conspicuous men of the century. The function of both their public personalities was to lose an old self and discover a new. Lawrence had been illegitimate; Shaw had doubted his legitimacy. Both were the sons of dominant mothers and experienced difficulties in establishing their masculinity. The Arab revolt, which gave Lawrence an ideal theatre of action, turned him into Colonel Lawrence, Luruns Bey, Prince of Damascus and most famously Lawrence of Arabia. 'I note that you have again moulded the world impossibly to your desire,' G.B.S. wrote to him. 'There is no end to your Protean tricks ... What is your game really?' It was natural to interpret it all as a Shavian game, and to see in the shy bird who had helped to carry the Augustus John portrait a version of Sonny. 'I was naturally a pitiably nervous, timid man, born with a whole plume of white feathers,' he confided to Lawrence; 'but nowadays this only gives a zest to the fun of swanking at every opportunity.'

But it is this swanking and fun, some modern critics say, that makes Shaw's Joan into the Principal Boy of a pantomime, and the play into a charade exhibiting 'all Shaw's most irritating stylistic habits', as Irving Wardle wrote: 'displays of false hair on the chest, garrulousness, flimsy poeticism, and thick-skinned flippancy'. Lost in this paraphernalia of emotional falsity Joan speaks with 'no recognizable voice of her own'. For against all propaganda to the contrary, hers is not a good star part, Walter Kerr has argued, because Shaw 'felt uncomfortable as a writer with the lyricism and melodrama of the Maid'. Finally, these critics for the prosecution conclude, Joan's congregation of voices and bells, kingfishers and larks and lambs in the sunshine produce that chorus of over-inflated sentimental rhetoric Shaw had relished pricking in Shakespeare's more indulgent sequences, and that only escape embarrassment in translation.

Shaw was to say that as he wrote, Joan 'guided my hand, and the words came tumbling out at such a speed that my pen rushed across the paper and I could barely write fast enough to put them down'. The air was full of voices, filling the wavelengths on which he was trying to make telepathic communication with Joan. Simultaneously he plotted vicarious diversions to find his way back to her while guiding her forward with a series of complicated instructions into the twentieth century. Like another of Pygmalion's experiments, he had constructed a likeness of Joan by grafting the eccentric muscle of Mary Hankinson, and framing her with the aura of 'an accomplished poseur with glittering eyes', as Beatrice Webb described Lawrence. With their missionary zeal to mould the world to their personal convictions, Joan and Lawrence were two small homeless figures elected by the *Zeitgeist* and picked out by the spotlight of history. This fascinated Shaw. He gave Lawrence several copies of *Saint Joan* – variously dedicated 'to Shaw from Shaw' and 'to Pte Shaw from Public Shaw' – but Lawrence, who prized these copies, also mislaid them, and was an unreliable chaperon for the rendezvous of G.B.S. with his saint. For all the Shavianizing of this 'very strange fellow' who was 'a born actor and up to all sorts of tricks', Lawrence remained as much of a mystery to Shaw as Joan herself whom, he conceded, 'I do not profess to understand'.

*

Shaw's own relation to the *Zeitgeist* was measured by the reception of his play. 'Mortal eyes cannot distinguish the saint from the heretic,' warns Cauchon in the Epilogue. *Saint Joan* puts the case for toleration; it is Joan's judges, the priests of the Church and the princes of the world, who are on trial. From the perspective of history it may be easy to see that Joan is inspired and that the other fanatic, de Stogumber, who throws himself into Joan's chair after her burning, is comically heretical. But there exists a more sophisticated fanatic in the Inquisitor, who gives a warning of where the toleration of fanaticism may lead. His words build up a fearful condemnation of change and are orchestrated with such idealistic sympathy that some critics have understood them to define G.B.S.'s own attitude to fascism. What Shaw intended to voice through this 'most infernal old scoundrel' was his audience's opinion of the Church and Empire, before demonstrating where such opinions led. The Inquisitor's crescendo of moral obloquy on Joan's masculine dress is also a denunciation of Shaw's rational Jaeger costume. Changes in fashion exhibit how easily the unorthodoxy of one time becomes the convention of another, a point dramatically made in the Epilogue by everyone's amusement at the appearance of the clerical-looking gentleman wearing 'a black frock-coat and trousers, and tall hat, in the fashion of the year 1920'. The Inquisitor's court has reduced justice to the dictatorship of fashion, but added to the intellectual poise and balance of the play with its hint that Joan's exasperating lack of compromise might itself be corruptible by power.

Saint Joan is a tragedy without villains. The tragedy exists in human nature where the mad credulity and intolerant incredulity of religious and secular forces meet and fix the *status quo*. Against this social structure Shaw's heroine gains no victory; she can win a battle as Shaw can win a debate, but she will never change the social order until the world truly becomes a fit place for heroes to live in.

The Epilogue, which reflects the flames of Joan's burning in the summer lightning against the windy curtains and brings us into the present century, gave Shaw the chance to step forward and 'talk the play over with the audience'. What he told them – and tells us – is that they and we too would burn Joan at the stake if we got the chance. It was not surprising that much of the hostile criticism of *Saint Joan* centred on this Epilogue, which 'shattered the historical illusion' of his play – and made way for Brecht.

The historical illusion was cherished by the public. In vain did the American critics protest after the play opened in New York that Shaw had made Joan 'a super-flapper' surrounded by puppets, that the play contained 'too little comedy' and 'a good deal of fustian', and was 'a mere historical scaffolding upon which the dramatist drapes the old Shavian gonfalons'. Alexander Woolcott warned readers of the *New York Herald* that 'certain scenes grow groggy for want of a blue pencil'; and in the *New Republic* Edmund Wilson was to complain that it had the characteristic over-explicitness of the social historian turned dramatist, giving the audience a sense 'that it is reading a book instead of witnessing a real event'.

On the opening night a number of these critics and some of the audience began leaving the theatre before the final curtain came down at 11.35 p.m., reviving fears in the Theatre Guild that the play would fail unless some repetitious matter was omitted. Lawrence Langner cabled urgently to Shaw stating that if he refused to shorten it, *Saint Joan* could not be successfully produced till after his death. Shaw cabled back:

'THE GUILD IS SENDING ME TELEGRAMS IN YOUR NAME. PAY NO ATTENTION TO THEM.'

He followed this up with a letter to the Theatre Guild declaring the press notices, which had so frightened them, to be 'magnificent'. For it was true that Alexander Woolcott had also called the play 'beautiful, engrossing and at times exciting', and Edmund Wilson described it as 'a work of extra-ordinary interest'; that the *New York Times* critic who found the play 'monotonous' had nevertheless thought it a 'great triumph', that the *New York Post* critic who found it 'exasperating' still thought it 'brilliant'. All these favourable points seemed to have been gathered together in a long eulogistic review for the *New York Times Magazine* by Luigi Pirandello. 'I have a strong impression that for some time past George Bernard Shaw has been growing more and more serious ... he seems to be believing less in himself, and more in what he is doing,' Pirandello wrote. '... In none of Shaw's work that I can think of have considerations of art been so thoroughly respected as in *Saint Joan* ... There is a truly great poet in Shaw.'

Shaw ranked Pirandello as 'first rate among playwrights', believing that he had 'never come across a play so *original* as Six Characters'. Realizing the worth of such a notice, he advised the Theatre Guild to recover its nerve. 'It is extremely annoying to have to admit that you are right,' Lawrence Langner replied the following January. 'People are coming in droves to see *Saint Joan*, and it is a great success.' The demand for seats increased to such an extent that the production had to be transferred from the Garrick to the larger Empire Theater, and ran for 214 performances before being sent on tour.

By this time the English production had opened in London. It was anticipated by a preview from A. B. Walkley who aired his misgivings in *The Times* over the probable disfigurements Shaw would make on his noble subject: 'the usual sort of "Shavian" pleasantry about this heroine would be unspeakably odious', he remarked. 'I can only hope my misgivings will prove to have done him an injustice.' Walkley's review of the play the following day attempted to reserve his position while making faint amends to the man whose work he had been reviewing for over a quarter of a century with little pleasure. Generally it was agreed that the play's faults belonged to Shaw, while its strengths derived from Sybil Thorndike's heroic acting and the wonderful costumes and designs by Charles Ricketts.

This production at the New Theatre in St Martin's Lane marked the culmination of Ricketts's discreet and largely anonymous partnership with Shaw which had begun in 1907 at the Court Theatre with his 'inscenation' of *Don Juan in Hell*. His costumes there, modelled on Velázquez, had stood blazing against a stage dowsed in black velvet and appeared magical to Shaw. 'If only we could get a few plays with invisible backgrounds and lovely costumes like that in a suitable theatre,' he had written, '... there would be no end to the delight of the thing.' He had again turned to Ricketts for *The Dark Lady of the Sonnets* in which Shakespeare, clothed in greys and russets, Queen Elizabeth in silver and black, and the Dark Lady, wearing crimson and black, appeared before an 'intense and abnormal starlit sky of a fabulous blue'. The following year Ricketts had attired the Venetian *père noble* Count

O'Dowda after Thomas Lawrence's portrait of George IV and given his daughter a strict Empire dress to lend her the look of a fillette 'depicted on elegant pre-revolution French crockery' in the successful run of *Fanny's First Play*. The 'gorgeous white uniform, half covered by an enormous green overcoat trimmed with black fur' he designed for Lillah McCarthy's role as *Annajanska* seven years later had been so successful that Margot Asquith copied the overcoat for her dressing-gown.

For *Saint Joan*, Ricketts created costumes designed to be an 'intelligent blend between Pol de Limbourg and the Van Eycks, avoiding the bright fourteenth-century colour of the first and the rather prosy phase in dress in the second'. He 'flung himself into the job', authenticating heraldry on the magnificent tapestries, tents and curtains, designing the stained glass for Rheims Cathedral, and basing the sunny stone chamber in the Castle of Vancouleurs on the kitchen of a Mormon keep at Chilham which he shared with Charles Shannon. In his history of British theatre design, George Sheringham was to describe the visual effect as being, within its conventions, 'one of the most beautiful things that has ever been seen on the London stage'.

Shaw had long recognized the importance of visual interest for his 'debates'. Partly perhaps as a heritage from William Morris and partly in response to Gordon Craig's influence, he had used artists such as Albert Rutherston and Ricketts to carry the theatre away from Victorian scene-painting into twentieth-century realms of stage design that could produce a unity of style to match the director's view of a play. This had gradually become accepted as part of a Shaw play-in-performance by the time Barry Jackson took over the Vedrenne-Barker tradition and appointed Paul Shelving as his regular designer.

Both Shelving and Ricketts designed productions of *Saint Joan*. The public's delight in the beauty and vitality of Ricketts's designs for the first production helped to establish it as Shaw's most successful play. At last he had done what Archer had been goading him to do: he had written a realistic or symbolic work that 'should go to every city in the world and shake the souls of people'. In Berlin and Vienna, Max Reinhardt's production, presenting Elizabeth Bergner as Joan, scored 'the greatest theatrical success that I have ever known', recorded Trebitsch. Before long, the play was being performed in Scandinavia, throughout Eastern Europe, and even in Paris where seven unsuccessful productions of his previous plays in the Hamons' impenetrable translations were thought to have established complete 'barriers of language, thought and feeling between Shaw and the French'.

This world triumph was seen by W. B. Yeats as 'the brilliant mirror of a shallow time, a time dominated through fatigue by the falsehood of a monist materialism'. But Shaw's relation to his time, which was distorted and oblique, conformed to the regenerative theme of his play and the lesson of its Epilogue, and was caricatured by his extraordinary success in Paris. The play's producer and star actress, George and Ludmilla Pitoëff, who were to revive it in Paris no less than a dozen times in ten years, had been appalled by the Hamons' version. In collaboration with Henri-René Lenormand they revised it so as to present a dreamlike vision suffused with religious mysticism upon which a miraculously sublimated Joan floated above Shaw's interpretation of her. Ludmilla Pitoëff's acclaim was even greater than Sybil Thorndike's and arose from the fact, Shaw believed, 'that her every gesture and intonation was directly contrary to the spirit and intention of the author'. For the first time, however, the French critics united in their praise of the Hamons' brilliant rendering; for the first time they praised Shaw for an innovative structure of hagiography that contrasted the saint with the farcical world of Shavian satire, and parodied the court in the manner of an Offenbach operetta, while leaving Joan spiritually uncontaminated. This original technique was hailed as an effective means of dramatizing the supernatural and liberating the subject from the stereotypes of traditional treatment. Shaw was credited with having invented a new type of historical drama. *'C'est du théâtre!'* cried André Rivoire enthusiastically in *Le Temps*. Yet for all this panegyric there was 'not a reference to a single specifically Shavian characteristic', an American drama critic observed. 'On the contrary, Shaw is commended for strictly subordinating himself to his material and keeping discreetly out of the way of Joan ... for the majority of critics, what was best about *Saint Joan* was what was least typical of Shaw.'

'Once more the formidable saint vanquishes the enemy,' exclaimed Martial Piéchaud in the *Revue hebdomadaire*, echoing the verdict of English and American playgoers. The critics' text in France was the audience's subtext in Britain where it had been incorporated by Shaw in Ricketts's designs. By linking his historical reconstruction to a vitalist view of history, Shaw had created an acceptable dramatization of the Life Force at work. But his ideas were so finely suspended in the event-plot that audiences found they could enjoy a strong dramatic narrative unhampered by central Shavian asides. It was as though, one critic noted, 'Joan herself were the real author of the play'.

'Woe unto me when all men praise me!' says St Joan in the Epilogue. Shaw greeted his own popularity with similar scepticism. He had sent out his play to rescue Joan from canonization and restore her heresy, but found it was to lead to his own canonization with the Nobel Prize for Literature. He had been put up, and turned down, for the Nobel Prize four or five times previously. But the literary adviser to the Swedish Academy, Per Hallström, who had found him unacceptable as a perverse genius and writer of prefaces, was converted by *Saint Joan*: 'even if the real Saint Joan was a different figure', he acknowledged, 'Shaw has created a great one'. Shaw was appalled. 'The Nobel Prize has been a hideous calamity for me,' he told Augustin Hamon. '... It was really almost as bad as my 70th birthday.'

He had never encouraged prizes. 'They eat up money; elicit a lot of trash; and invariably go to some second best composition. You cannot give examination paper marks to works of art,' he had written in 1918. Now that his views were to be tested in a practical court he decided, so he informed his Swedish translator Lady Ebba Low, that 'I will not accept the Nobel Prize; but I will not throw it back at their heads until the distracted Baron Palmstierna [a Swedish envoy in London] has had an opportunity of discussing the terms of my refusal with me.' He had not changed his mind on prizes. 'If the prizes are to be reserved on Safety First principles for old men whose warfare is accomplished,' he wrote to Ebba Low, 'the sooner they are confiscated and abolished by the Swedish Government the better.'

His response to the award was to be accomplished 'in my very grandest style', he promised H. G. Wells; 'but it shall be done very emphatically'. It was certainly a characteristically Shavian response, generous and ingenious, causing consternation and upheaval as well as good results. Following a description of the award as a reinforcement between British and Swedish culture that, especially after W. B. Yeats's prize two years earlier, would not be lost on his native Ireland, he went on to discriminate between the award, for which 'I have nothing but my best thanks', and the prize of some seven thousand pounds which 'I cannot persuade myself to accept'. His readers and audiences 'provide me with more than sufficient money for my needs', he explained, 'and as to my renown it is greater than is good for my spiritual health'. He therefore proposed that the Swedish Royal Academy confer on him the 'final honor of classing my works in that respect *hors concours*', and use the money to commission good English translations of Sweden's literature. But the Swedish Academy did not permit this use of the money which, if Shaw rejected it, would disappear back into the Nobel fund. To carry through his plan he was therefore obliged to accept the prize, then help in the creation of an Anglo–Swedish Literary Foundation, and finally hand over to its Trust Fund all his prize money.

When the news of the prize was announced, thousands of people all over Europe 'wrote to me for loans, mostly for the entire sum', Shaw told Hamon. 'When the further news came that I had refused it another million or so wrote to say that if I was rich enough to throw away money like that, I could afford to adopt their children, or pay off the mortgages on their houses ... or let them have £XXXX to be repaid punctually next May, or to publish a priceless book explaining the mystery of the universe. It says a good deal for female virtue that only two women proposed that I should take them on as mistresses.' To grapple with the emergency he began practising a complicated facial expression which combined universal benevolence with a savage determination to rescue no one from financial ruin.

'He is now the most famous author in the world,' one newspaper declared. The world saw his benevolence wonderfully enhanced by his generosity with the Nobel money. 'Such steps towards Mr Shaw's canonization are being made,' wrote an *Evening Standard* reporter, 'that people are forgetting that he was formerly almost always described as Mephistophelean.' Though the press announcement was made in 1926, he had officially been awarded the prize for the year 1925. 'I wrote nothing in 1925,' he told the newspapers, 'and that is probably why they gave it to me.' Of course this opened the way for Trebitsch to point out that *Jitta's Atonement* had been published that year. But everyone recognized that, as Shaw himself phrased it in a letter to Edith Evans, 'I am in the very odor of sanctity after St Joan.'

[2]

I can scarcely believe that the septuagenarian in the looking glass is really G.B.S. (1927)

'On the 26th we sail for Madeira,' Shaw notified William Archer in mid-December 1924. Charlotte had finally persuaded him to travel abroad again. 'My wife expects me to return in the middle of February; but my private intention is never to come back...'

Shaw was in his seventieth year, 'too old' he told his publisher Otto Kyllmann, who nevertheless prevailed upon him to prepare a collected edition of his writings for Constable. 'I ought to be retiring,' he protested; 'and my business is advancing instead. Only by being utterly conscienceless can I get on at all.' His passage to Madeira, with its 'flowers, sunshine, bathing, and no theatres' was not a retirement from business – he took with him a sack of correspondence. But since the war he had less desire for new experiences, and there were fewer people he liked to see. An exception was Archer. 'I don't know whether you are in England or not, and should be glad of a hail if you are,' he signalled him shortly before sailing. Earlier that year he had been invited to chair a lecture by his friend, enthusiastically entitled 'The Decay of Decency', and replied: 'As Archer and I are the same age

94

(though he doesn't look it) I think we should be meditating on the Decency of Decay ... ' But the truth was that when he and Archer got together and relived their old campaigning days, they felt quite startlingly young. Archer still saw in the extravagance of G.B.S. a deep menace to the exercise of his friend's talent. 'Like a hen with a duckling,' Max Beerbohm had observed, 'he is never free from the stress of nervous anxiety.' This anxiety had survived the war and went flourishing into the 1920s, for it was still not too late, Archer felt, to get Shaw on to the right lines. He never wearied of attempting this feat and, because his attempts were so vivacious, G.B.S. never wearied of responding to them. They had been at it now for forty years.

'Oblige me with a hammer, a saw, a beetle and a couple of wedges that I may operate on your all but impervious knowledge box,' Shaw had requested in the summer of 1923 after looking through Archer's new book, *The Old Drama and the New*. What lay between them was the name and nature of drama. Shaw believed that though Archer's taste in novels was for merciless realism, he treated the theatre as a tinted fairyland. Archer believed that for all Shaw's advanced sociological interests, he was a blatant fantasist whose dramatic constructions made no connection with the real world. Where then lay reality? There was a chance of settling the matter, Archer urged, if Shaw would simply amend his language: in short, use different words. As a professional translator, Archer felt well-qualified to change Shaw's language, and generously offered to do so. 'I say a cat is a quadruped, with a brain, a backbone, and (unless of the Manx variety) a tail,' he explained. 'You say, "Oh no – a cat is a round, mushy iridescent object with long streamers, usually observed on the shingle at low tide." "Why", I reply, "that is not a cat but a jelly-fish." '

'The alternatives are not a cat and a jelly-fish,' Shaw countered, 'but a clockwork cat and a live cat.'

'It won't do,' Archer wrote.

'You haven't got it yet,' Shaw wrote.

But there was still time. In December 1924 Archer changed his tactics and published in *The Bookman* a long exegesis entitled 'The Psychology of G.B.S.' This presented his friend as one of the most baffling characters to have appeared on the world stage, as well as 'the most uncompromising, not to say fanatical, idealist I have ever met'. Shaw's life had been devoted to 'a system of interwoven ideals to which he is immovably faithful'. Most readers, Archer believed, would be shocked to learn that G.B.S. was governed by a passionate sense of right and wrong. Though considering himself preternaturally skilful in the art of persuasion, he was 'so unique, so utterly unlike the overwhelming majority of his fellow-creatures, that he has never mastered the rudiments of that art'. So, though he had gained the ear of the public, he had never got at its will. Unlike Carlyle or Ruskin, he had influenced no one's motives, shaped no one's actions. 'Shaw, a professed revolutionist, will revolutionise nothing.'

Unless, that was, Archer could bring him into a more serious relationship with his public. For years he had struggled to reason G.B.S. out of his fantastic misreading of the public mind. Finally, he was appealing in his *Bookman* essay to the public itself. He invited his readers to overlook the irresponsible tic of Shaw's joking, forgive the Shavian blunders of tone. For in G.B.S. they had among them an original thinker and artist, and where Archer himself had benefited, so could they. 'There is no man for the fundamentals of whose character I have a more real respect,' he wrote. 'I own myself deeply indebted to him for many lessons taught me in the years of our early intimacy.'

Shaw read 'The Psychology of G.B.S.' that December. 'I never was offended by anything Archer ever said to me or wrote about me,' he later acknowledged. He knew Archer to be incapable of malice, knew how much affectionate sensitiveness lay beneath his reticence. Being emotionally reticent himself he sent off a letter simply asking for news of their friend Harley Granville-Barker, and whether, before sailing for Madeira, there was any chance of seeing Archer. For he was someone of whom Shaw had 'not a single unpleasant recollection, and whom I was never sorry to see or unready to talk to'.

'G.B.S. has taken like an angel to my article,' Archer reported to Granville-Barker. 'I am especially glad in view of this operation business.' Archer had been told he had to undergo an operation for the removal of a cancerous tumour 'one of these days' – in fact, he was going into hospital the following day. He refused to believe it was such a mighty matter – 'I feel as fit as a fiddle' – and treated it with the same sprightly reticence that had served all these years as an emotional code between himself and G.B.S. But because 'accidents will happen', for a few apologetic sentences, Archer suddenly broke this code. 'Though I may sometimes have played the part of the all-too candid mentor,' he wrote, 'I have never wavered in my admiration and affection for you, or ceased to feel that the Fates had treated me kindly in making me your contemporary and friend. I thank you from my heart for forty years of good comradeship.' It was said – and time to leap quickly back into a joke about the King of Norway.

Shaw played his part rather well: 'I was not seriously alarmed, and presently sailed for Madeira.' In fact, Archer had got through his operation and was recovering by the time Shaw and Charlotte sailed. On board G.B.S. soothed himself with writing, in particular an obituary of another incorruptible colleague, H. W. Massingham, the most exceptional editor of Shaw's career in journalism.

The Shaws arrived at Reid's Palace Hotel on 30 December, and saw as they entered the hall a news bulletin announcing Archer's death three days earlier. Now it was G.B.S.'s turn to break the code – but too late. There was nothing to be done. Each morning after breakfast he would work frantically, emptily, then smooth himself out by plunging into the Gulf Stream. In the afternoons, while others played roulette and tennis, he sat miserably in the glorious sunshine. 'This is one of those unnaturally lovely hells of places where you bathe amid innumerable blossoms in midwinter,' he wrote bitterly to William Rothenstein.

At first Shaw overrode his misery with 'a transport of fury'. He had never been able to regard a death caused by an operation as natural death. 'My rage may have been unjust to the surgeons; but it carried me over my first sense of bereavement.' Later he overcame this anger with a whimsical piece of therapy on the dance floor, which would surely have impressed Archer as quintessentially Shavian. Having heard that the wife of the hotel proprietor Max Rinder had been successfully operated on for cancer, he joined her as a dancing partner and together they learnt the tango. A photograph of them, correctly positioned, still hangs in the hotel. They are preparing to put their best foot forward under the watchful instruction of Max Rinder, 'the only man who taught me anything', the caption reads. But the lesson was symbolically Archer's. By recognizing the practice of modern operative surgery to be 'often more successful than its reasoning', Shaw was taking a step towards Archer's view that, outside the theoretical world of his own construction, a real world existed to which he should move in rhythm.

'All good wishes for 1925 – Ever yours, W.A.' These had been Archer's last words to him. But when Shaw returned on 16 February 1925 to an Archerless London, 'it seemed to me that the place had entered on a new age in which I was lagging superfluous'.

*

Shaw's last twenty-five years can be viewed in part as a rewriting of his first seventy years. He ghosted more biographies; he re-edited his collected works for their Standard Edition; he pursued obsessive themes in new plays as well as in the transposition of old plays on to radio and into films; and he set about re-casting friendships that had fallen vacant.

He still led and followed a dashing public life, giving some thirty lectures a year to local Labour parties, groups of feminists, gatherings of chief constables. He pitched into debates at the Smoke Abatement Society, the Art Workers' Guild, the British Drama Guild, or the London School of

Economics; and he would turn up for meetings at the Royal Academy of Dramatic Art, Stage Society Council, British Music Society and latterly the British Broadcasting Corporation's Spoken English Committee – a cacophony of Scottish, Welsh, Irish, crypto-American and purely academic sounds over which he waved the baton as 'a brisk, genial and dictatorial chairman', Alistair Cooke remembered. ' ... When he'd got his way, he'd jump up, stand like a ramrod, and say "that is the end of our business. Good day, gentlemen" and be off.'

He went fairly regularly to concerts, particularly Arnold Dolmetsch's revivals of early English instrumental music and the fine conducting of Eugene Goossens at the London Philharmonic, as well as to Rutland Boughton's compositions at Glastonbury and to hear the piano playing of Harriet Cohen, a new friend. Max Beerbohm had retired from the London theatre to Rapallo in north Italy, but Desmond MacCarthy still came to all his first nights and was joined by new critics such as James Agate and St John Ervine. He kept up with the theatre as best he could, seeing plays by Knut Hamsun, Pirandello, D. H. Lawrence, Sean O'Casey and later Eugene O'Neill. 'I have no doubt that you will succeed,' he wrote to Noël Coward after reading *The Young Idea* in 1921. But the play had borrowed his twins from *You Never Can Tell* rather too obviously, and Shaw advised him 'above all, never to see or read my plays. Unless you can get clean away from me you will begin as a back number, and be hopelessly out of it when you are forty.'

To some extent the routine of life continued as it had before the war. The Shaws often stayed with the Webbs at Passfield Corner and with Charlotte's sister and brother-in-law at Edstaston; and Lady Gregory, the 'charwoman of the Abbey', sometimes came and stayed with them at Ayot. In London, Charlotte continued to give her lunches for old friends and new acquaintances – Princess Bibesco, Lord Berners, Lady Colefax, Ebenezer Howard, Marie Stopes, Lytton Strachey. 'You can imagine how excited I was to be invited [to lunch] and how disappointed to find an old old gentleman and a cushiony wife,' wrote E. M. Forster in 1926. 'Shaw was pleasant and amusing, but I felt all the time that he'd forgotten what people are like ... She wanted to talk mysticism, and denounced "atheists" with the accents of a rural dean. I came away with the hump ... '

With the Trebitsches and the Hamons, Shaw maintained his literary-business correspondence and replaced other translators as they fell away in exhaustion with still more exaggerated figures, such as the impoverished Polish adventurer Floryan Sobieniowski, who had been the lover and blackmailer of Katherine Mansfield. 'You are in money matters the most incapable, incorrigible, impecunious, always-borrowing, never-paying victim of a craze for literature at present alive in London,' Shaw advised him in 1924. '...I wish somebody would endow you with a million or so; for I cannot afford to be your banker...God send you safely to Poland, and keep you there!' But despite such devastating farewells, Sobieniowski was to remain entrenched in Shaw's career until his death.

He remained in friendly communication with G. K. Chesterton and Gilbert Murray and continued to see Barrie, Arnold Bennett and Galsworthy (who had 'whitemailed' him into joining the writers' society PEN). But he could not easily forget those who had died. 'I still feel that when he went he took a piece of me with him.' Archer's death had also closed Shaw's best means of access to Granville-Barker. He had written to G.B.S. after seeing *Saint Joan*, and they were both to compose obituaries of Archer, after which there followed years of silence. No single person could understudy Harley, though Barry Jackson, Lawrence Langner and T. E. Lawrence between them filled part of the vacuum.

For Charlotte, T. E. Lawrence was to emerge as something more than a substitute. While G.B.S. put himself forward as editor of *The Seven Pillars of Wisdom*, Charlotte volunteered to be its proofreader. 'I devoured the book from cover to cover as soon as I got hold of it,' she told Lawrence. 'I could not stop. I drove G.B.S. almost mad by insisting upon reading him special bits when he was deep in something else.' It was an extraordinary experience, sending her back on a wave of excitement to her twenties when, 'reaching out for something that was beyond her understanding', she had become absorbed in Eastern religions. From the pages of his book, Charlotte had an impression of Lawrence as 'an Immense Personality soaring in the blue (of the Arabian skies)'. But following the irregular changes in his career and the simplicity of his letters to her, she began to see him as more human, an inexpressibly complicated person, of course, but also tragically sincere and 'the strangest contact of my life'. She sent him anonymous gifts from Gunter's and Fortnum & Mason's: honey and chocolates and *marrons glacés*, nectarines and peaches; records, particularly of Elgar's music, to play on the gramophone G.B.S. had given him; also books by Lady Gregory, Sean O'Casey, Yeats, Wells, Chesterton – and G.B.S. Usually 'a very grudging taker', and distrusting human affection, Lawrence defended himself from becoming an object of charity by giving her his manuscripts. But he accepted a motor-bicycle (from Charlotte and G.B.S. together) which he called Boanerges (a name he transferred from one bike to another), and would roar up in his goggles, gauntlets and peaked cap to arrive without warning at Ayot – Charlotte's Arabian Knight. Sometimes he stayed a weekend in what became known as 'the Lawrence room'. At other times the conspiring birds and flowers and quietude induced such a terrifying reluctance ever to leave that, after an hour or two, he would have to jump on his machine and hurtle back to barracks or on to another of his sanctuaries – to Max Gate to see Thomas and Florence Hardy, or to Alderney Manor and Fryern Court to visit Augustus and Dorelia John. 'When I'm at Ayot,' he told Charlotte, 'the serenity of the sky overhead, and the keen air and the intellectual delight of fencing with a real swordsman intoxicate me.' And Charlotte, seeing his gleams of happiness, felt that 'Ayot is justified – it lifts its head'.

They grew closer when further apart. When Lawrence went to India and they could start up a 'tennis game' of correspondence together, she wrote more frequently than he did. 'I want to tell you something about myself,' she wrote. She told him what she had once begun to tell G.B.S. about her parents and childhood, and after 'a fearful lot of cogitation' she told him about the 'teachings' and 'treatments', meditations and healings of her religion. They were 'such a help'. What chiefly impressed Lawrence was Charlotte's courage in entrusting him with 'so many life-lines'. He responded by confiding some of his own secrets – the emotional disturbances with his mother and his sexual trauma at Deraa. He sent her poems, his private anthology *Minorities*, and the unexpurgated text of *The Mint*. 'It *is* a wonderful book ... that no one but yourself could achieve,' she replied. '... *It is a splendid thing*. Heart searching in its depth and force, and ... has stirred me to the very depths of my being.' Her valuation of his work amazed him and made him feel guilty.

To no other woman could Lawrence write quite so frankly. 'You remain the solitary woman who lets me feel at ease with her, in spite of all the benefits you heap on me,' he acknowledged. It was their solitariness that seemed to have brought them together. They eavesdropped on each other's life. Lawrence felt untaxed by their relationship. By unburdening his emotions to this undemanding lady, anonymous wife to the celebrated G.B.S., he was also secretly communicating with posterity. Over thirteen years they were to exchange some six hundred letters in which Charlotte revealed to him things 'I have never told a soul'. She had never met anyone like him, though she had met all sorts of people, being now 'an old woman, old enough at any rate to be your mother'. This image, however, suddenly chilled Lawrence. 'Let me acquit you of all suspicion of "mothering me". With you I have no feeling or suspicion of that at all.' His mother was monumental – her inquisitorial letters 'always make me want to blow my brains out' – no trust 'ever existed between my mother and myself'. This was perfectly unlike his relationship with Charlotte. At Ayot he was on neutral ground. 'I do not wish to feel at home,' he warned her. '... Homes are ties, and with you I am quite free, somehow.'

'You know, it's a great privilege to keep company with G.B.S. – but difficult, difficult,' Lawrence admitted. He didn't feel he could offer him 'any pearl less good than one's best'. But in Charlotte's company he expanded. 'I have several times secured your agreement to the fact that I am not G.B.S.,' he teased her.

They were not disloyal to G.B.S. Lawrence felt genuinely grateful for all his help as literary agent and editor, genuinely curious also over what G.B.S. might try to make of him in future plays. He was determined to evade a Shavian take-over, though his letters to Charlotte teem with praise of her husband's strength, confidence and mastery. 'He has given himself out to his generation year by year, without reserve or grudge.' When Lawrence compares his own career, the advantages all seem to be with Shaw. 'Between the power and courage of G.B.S. & my weariness, how great a gap!' he exclaims. '. . . My exhaustion at 40 is quaint, in comparison . . . I wish I was as old as everybody I like: but sometimes I wish I was as young as G.B.S. He has it both ways.' It was curious how sympathetically Lawrence came out of comparisons so heavily weighted against himself ('he's great and I'm worthless . . . G.B.S. has brought forth twenty books; and I'm in a mess over one'). From Charlotte he had received a sense that 'there is something not right about your peace, or your circumstances'. It was 'sad' that public exposure kept such company with their marriage, dragging her into the footlights as an appendage. It was 'very hard' being a 'great man's wife', though she 'succeeds with it'. 'G.B.S. has become too famous any longer to be really great,' he suggests. 'His reputation is dwarfing him. However,' he adds with apparent tact, 'that will pass.'

The tone of these letters was perfectly judged. Charlotte was proud of her husband and his achievements, but hated the publicity that overflowed from these achievements and rose around their ordinary lives. Fame had been an emollient for G.B.S., soothing his vulnerabilities, but 'such sureness of success', Lawrence believed, 'has closed his pores'. And it was true, Charlotte had found, that G.B.S. was not 'interested in anything but his work'. In Lawrence she saw again the suffering and loneliness that had been exposed in her husband at the time of his physical breakdown and their marriage. Now, feeling sometimes stranded in this marriage, she gazed towards Lawrence as if into her own past. Once admitted within the circle of his integrity, she developed a half-undisclosed friendship that counterbalanced her husband's letter-writing relationships with women, and that Lawrence encouraged her to feel was unique. It was not difficult to divulge her own unconventional views to someone who confessed such scandalous urges and experiences. 'Marriage is not natural – but unnatural and disastrous,' she wrote to him. '. . . The idea [of having children] was physically repulsive to me in the highest degree.' Yet these revelations, which she felt unable to disclose to another soul, could have appeared in *Man and Superman* or *Getting Married*, so heavily impregnated were they with Shavian attitudes. Her lack of reticence, however, did surprise Shaw. 'I realize that there were many parts of her character that even I did not know,' he later owned to Hesketh Pearson, 'for she poured out her soul to Lawrence.' Perhaps he had once known them, and forgotten.

Lawrence had approached the Shaws' marriage like an undercover agent, the kindred spirit of each partner separately and the ally of both. Charlotte and G.B.S. 'mix like bacon and eggs into a quintessential dream', he eulogized. 'I would rather visit them than read any book or hear any music on earth.' He was at his best in their company 'for they loved and comprehended him', Osbert Sitwell observed; 'and there was, I noticed, a sort of audacity of mischief about his attitude and conversation when they were present, that was enchanting'. But the strange self-immolation, like a penal servitude, that Lawrence sought in order 'to keep sane' and bring peace to his bones painfully reminded Shaw of his own early obscurity. Their relationship became a teasing tug-of-war between Shavian possessiveness and assertion and Lawrentian waywardness and ambiguity. 'Do you ever do things because you know you must?' Lawrence asked. But G.B.S. had other imperatives. 'You and I,' he told Lawrence, 'are worse than characters: we are character-actors.' 'You have read too much of yourself into me,' Lawrence warned, and 'Your advice would sink my ship.' But this was how G.B.S. went into operation. His friendship was a form of patronage. He would make a second vain attempt to secure Lawrence a civil or military pension; then he applied, fortunately without success, to the Secretary of State for Air to include Lawrence on the maiden flight of the R101 airship that crashed in flames at Beauvais; he also ushered him, via Lady Astor ('a cocktail of a woman ... a whirling atom') into the Cliveden Set, and introduced him to his favourite English composer, Elgar. Finally he helped to elect him a Fellow of the Irish Academy of Letters, which pleased Lawrence 'because it is a gesture on my part that I am Irish'.

Lawrence's spasms of superiority and awkward self-denigration occasionally exasperated Charlotte. 'He always had one eye on the limelight,' she admitted. Perhaps that was why she sometimes suspected that she had been used as a messenger service between him and G.B.S. But as a vehicle for Shaw's theories of power, Lawrence proved 'a most troublesome chap': a man of marvellous dual abilities who pathologically failed to unite literature with action, believing he could 'never quit myself of the consequences of my past actions till I am dead'.

Another candidate for this romantic synthesis was Apsley Cherry-Garrard, a neighbour of the Shaws at Ayot, who had been one of the youngest members of Scott's last expedition to the Antarctic. Cherry, as he was known, won golden opinions from Scott for his pluck and popularity, especially on the 'weirdest bird-nesting expedition there has been or will ever be', gathering the eggs of the Emperor Penguin at Cape Crozier. Their zoological jaunt, involving 'the extremity of hardship and danger' to work out the embryology of 'a missing link in genetic theory', was a wonderful example to G.B.S. of the evolutionary appetite.

Cherry was approximately the same age as Lawrence – that is, some thirty years younger than G.B.S. His exploration of the Antarctic, with its awful outcome (he was one of the team that had found Scott dead in his tent on the Great Ice Barrier) marked the rest of his life, as the Arab campaign had marked Lawrence's. It had been a legendary exploit, the apotheosis of his career while still in his twenties. 'Nature would be merciful if she would end us at a climax and not in the decline,' Lawrence wrote. It was the same for Cherry-Garrard. 'To go through a terrible time of mental and physical stress and to write it down as honestly as possible is a good way of getting some of it off your nerves,' he stated in an essay on Lawrence, adding: 'I write from personal experience.' Lawrence had tried to back out of the race 'rather than be a half and half, a Cherry-Garrard'. For whatever Cherry-Garrard did from his thirties onwards seemed merely a postscript to his early heroic experiences – even the war appeared incidental. Invalided out of active service, he returned to Lamer Park, the country estate bordering Ayot, and passed his long convalescence attempting to exorcize the past. 'We have lately become intimate with him,' Shaw told Lillah McCarthy in September 1917, 'and as he took very warmly to Harley [Granville-Barker], the week ends are spent at Lamer when we are away.'

Cherry became a great favourite of Charlotte's too. She encouraged him to write a book, and when she told Lawrence in December 1922 that 'both G.B.S. and I have lots of experience about books and we would both *like* to put it at your service', the joint experience she had in mind was over Cherry-Garrard's *The Worst Journey in the World*. After the Shaws' editorial advice and textual emendations, the book had been published by Constable earlier that month. This account of the journey by a survivor was originally commissioned by the Captain Scott Antarctic Fund, but finding himself becoming critical of his leader, Cherry had withdrawn from his official commitment and produced an independent narrative on which, Shaw believed, 'the expedition will be finally judged'. Several passages were drafted or rewritten by G.B.S., who described himself as having saved

Amundsen from the part of 'a lubberly candle-eating Swedish second mate, who had meanly stolen a march on the heroic Scott'.

Shaw's presentation of Cherry took no account of the Lawrence-like agonies of self-doubt that had prompted his writing of the book. 'Lawrence had never escaped himself nor his nerves which drove his muscles,' Cherry was to write. 'He knew that he had shot his bolt . . . ' In similar circumstances his own readjustment was complicated by the death of his father, a rival spirit who had spurred him with initiative. He had travelled to the end of the earth to find a separate identity his father could admire, and made Scott a temporary replacement for his father. He had worshipped Scott but, after his father's death, came to resent his influence. To reconcile these feelings of worship and resentment he simply divided Scott in two. 'He considers Scott a schizophrenic,' Shaw later told Lord Kennet, 'two different persons.'

Like *Seven Pillars*, *The Worst Journey* was partly theatre, the open-air theatre of boyish adventure in which G.B.S. retrospectively took part and, with great delight, almost took command. The two books attracted him strongly. 'Why should not sand have the same appeal as snow?' he demanded after Lawrence had demurred over the public interest in his own work. When the abridged *Revolt in the Desert* was published in 1927, Shaw made a specific comparison. Each book was written by a man who had packed into the forepart of his life an exploit of epic bulk and intensity. Such a combination of opportunity, ability and motive power was extremely rare. 'Yet the combination occurs in this amazing age of ours in which we sit holding our breaths as we await wholesale destruction,' Shaw wrote.

'In Mr Apsley Cherry-Garrard's *Worst Journey in the World* we have a classic on Antarctic exploration written by a young man who endured it at its blackest. And within ten years of that we have "Colonel Lawrence" . . . emerging into clear definition as the author of one of the greatest histories of the world . . . '

Cherry-Garrard had described his life-and-death experiences so effectively 'that the reader forgets how comfortable he is in his armchair, and remembers the tale with a shiver as if he had been through it himself'. Lawrence too possessed this power of recreating action. He 'made you see the start of Feisal's motley legions as plainly as he saw it himself', and gave you a sense of the 'track underfoot, the mountains ahead and around, the vicissitudes of the weather, the night, the dawn, the sunset and the meridian [that] never leaves you for a moment'.

Shaw stole into these heroic landscapes but took care to conceal his literary stage management of them. 'It would be fatal to make any suggestion of collaboration on my part,' he advised Cherry-Garrard. 'The book would be reviewed on the assumption that I had written all the striking parts of it, and that they were "not serious". As my experience on the ice dates from the great frost of 1878 (or thereabouts) when I skated on the Serpentine, my intrusion into the Antarctic Circle would be extraordinarily ridiculous.'

There was another reason for minimizing Shaw's influence on *The Worst Journey in the World*. Increasingly in these last twenty-five years of his life he relished schoolmastering the English and promoting foreigners over them. But by recreating Amundsen as 'an explorer of genius' and the temperamental Scott as 'so unsuited to the job he insisted on undertaking that he ended as the most incompetent failure in the history of exploration', he risked losing the sympathy of Scott's widow Kathleen, 'a very special friend'. She had recently married Hilton Young who came to believe that Shaw denigrated Scott because Cherry-Garrard, 'an egotistical man, with a grievance against his leader', had worked his way into Charlotte's esteem and 'flattered Shaw by letting him rewrite [his] book, more or less'. To head Kathleen off from what he considered a false position, Shaw wrote as gently as possible to explain that 'bringing a hero to life always involves exhibiting his faults as well as his qualities', and on this occasion his tact successfully kept a friendship afloat.

Shaw's instinct about Scott and the need to 'debunk him frankly' was to be largely vindicated; but his evaluation of Cherry-Garrard was distorted by his need to see him as a superman. In his imagination the appalling conditions of the Antarctic became a metaphor for the moral climate of Britain between the wars, and Cherry-Garrard's survival a triumph of human will over social adversity. Like Lawrence, Cherry was converted into a Life Force investment in which G.B.S. banked his hopes. But he overestimated the evolutionary dividends. Though the idealized adolescence of both Lawrence and Cherry-Garrard answered his own parent-damaged emotions, 'experiences such as Lawrence had been through do not drop you', Cherry-Garrard was to write, 'they torture you'. Shaw believed that their literary talents might prove resurrectionary. Over twenty years later he reported Cherry as having 'recovered his health rather miraculously' and escaped his pessimistic destiny. This was a loyal and partial judgement. Meeting 'Charlotte's one neighbourhood friend' in the 1930s, Beatrice Webb was to describe Cherry as 'a semi-maniac in his hatred of the working-class...'

'He is at war with all his neighbours; he has closed footpaths, dismissed tenants, and cannot keep servants. Years ago he was personally attractive, a rather distinguished youth with artistic and intellectual gifts, today he is drab and desolate, looks as if he were drinking and drugging as well as hating. I should not be surprised to hear that a revolver shot had solved his problem.'

*

'On the very threshold of seventy I have fallen through with a crash into ninety,' Shaw told Kathleen Scott. '. . . I haven't had the slightest pain; I haven't had a stroke; I have nothing but temperatures and disablement and something wrong with my inside that doesn't hurt; so you must not weep for me.' As his vigour declined, so his need for vicarious exploits through younger men-of-action-and-letters intensified. Feeling as if 'I have left half of me behind', he replaced the missing half with a team of athletic candidates.

One of these was Cecil Lewis, a wartime flying ace with the Military Cross whose war memoirs, *Sagittarius Rising*, showed him also to be 'a thinker, a master of words, and a bit of a poet', Shaw reckoned. Lewis submitted some of his early writings to G.B.S. and came to count him 'one of the great influences of my life'. As a founding member of the British Broadcasting Corporation, he arranged for Shaw to give a reading of *O'Flaherty V.C.* (which was broadcast live on 20 November 1924) and fired his interest in radio technology. Before long, G.B.S. had bought a Burndept four-valve set with loudspeaker and was issuing the BBC with advice. Lewis was instructed to seek out good dramatic readers who, regardless of memory and appearance, were particular as to voice-characterization; to find a 'good uncle to read the necessary explanations and directions'; and to keep this 'company of wireless specialists' as a permanent dramatic staff.

The 'invisible play' was a phenomenon that fascinated G.B.S. Though seldom satisfied with BBC productions of his own plays, he gave permission for them to be broadcast from the late 1920s onwards, recognizing the unstoppable power of radio. In his view the 'British Mike' was a detective. By magnifying the symptoms of the speaker's condition, it would find out as never before the self-intoxicated windbag and the post-prandial humbug. It would enable those who could not bear the degradation of public speaking to address their fellow-countrymen in solitude and out of sight, 'using no art except that of giving each syllable its value, an art which to a poet is simple nature'. But the chief power of radio lay in the growing size of its audience. In the past, when there were 'no loud speakers except human ones', G.B.S. had been 'a public speaker without publicity'. Forty years later 'my voice reaches millions of people instead of hundreds'.

106

He asked no fees for his radio talks, regarding them as an extension of his political speaking in the 1880s and 1890s. After those little knots of people he had spoken to in the wind and rain and smoke, the vast size and variety of his audience delighted him. He celebrated it grandiloquently. 'Your Majesties, your Royal Highnesses, your Excellencies, your Graces and Reverences, my Lords, Ladies and Gentlemen, fellow citizens of all degrees,' he began a talk in the BBC series 'Points of View' on 14 October 1929; 'I am going to talk to you about Democracy...'

Cecil Lewis records that Shaw had 'impeccable verve and artistry' as a broadcaster, and that he 'set standards of conscience, integrity and professional craftsmanship I have never met elsewhere'. Lewis made it his business to see that this lonely writer 'quite outside the ordinary run of men' and over forty years older than himself should be given a modern platform. This was in the nature of a debt repaid. For years Shaw watched over his career 'with parental care and I grew to idolize him', Lewis was to write, 'for, in those days when I was part of the spearhead of the exploding mass media which were changing the whole shape of society and in touch with many of the leading figures of the day, he was the only man among them who appeared to have any social conscience or any practical suggestions to offer to combat the Dragon's Teeth which I felt were everywhere being sown among us'.

To push his political ideas into renewed life Shaw needed to make contact with younger men and women who might rule the future. By his contemporaries he was celebrated for his past, and usually for his literary rather than his political past. At a 'Complimentary Dinner' for his seventieth birthday he declared that he did not care a snap of the fingers for this literary success in comparison with his pioneering and constructive work as one of the Fabian founders of the Labour Party – but the BBC refused to broadcast the speech, 'Socialism at Seventy', on the grounds that it was politically controversial. 'The sole notice taken of my seventieth birthday by the British Government was its deliberate prohibition of the broadcasting of any words spoken by me on that occasion,' he notified the German ambassador who had delivered a note of congratulation. From his German publisher, too, arrived a 'gorgeous album' containing the autograph tributes of Einstein, Hauptmann, Thomas Mann, Schnitzler, Schönberg, Spengler, Richard Strauss and others; while in the United States his speech was printed in full by the *New York Times* – and pirated throughout the country.

Yet it was difficult wholly to please G.B.S. Did they imagine, he demanded, that he had time to gaze at albums or respond to congratulations from around the world? As for his celebratory dinner, such meals would have come in handy fifty years ago. 'The birthday nearly killed me,' he complained to William Maxwell. 'Killing a man with kindness is much more fatal than trying to kill him with abuse. When you are 69, skip to 71. Cut out the septuagenarian event.' According to the *Observer*, reaching the age of seventy was 'the only ordinary thing that Mr Shaw has ever done'.

Yet he was not displeased to have his celebratory dinner at the St James Room of the Hotel Metropole hosted by the Parliamentary Labour Party and chaired by Ramsay MacDonald. He had admired MacDonald's courage in resigning from the Labour Party leadership to oppose the war, and campaigned for him in the coupon election of 1918 at Leicester in which MacDonald lost his seat. To many it appeared as if MacDonald were politically destroyed. But, after the clouds of chauvinism had blown away taking Lloyd George with them, MacDonald emerged as a luminously popular figure. His glowing oratory, and the polished humour with which he had defended himself against attacks, added to his credentials and on his re-entry into Parliament in 1922 he became a natural choice as Labour leader. His brief premiership two years later established the Labour Party as a valid alternative government to the Conservatives and himself as the first socialist of national stature.

There seemed much in MacDonald to appeal to Shaw. He was a kindly man, an obsessively hard worker, a mystic who was also a tactician, and an evolutionary socialist who wanted to make the Labour Party independent of the trade unions. He believed that socialism would inevitably follow on from the success of capitalism, if in the meantime he could conciliate the warring factions within the Labour Party. Yet Shaw's attitude to MacDonald in the 1920s appeared perverse. He had been supportive in the days of his ostracism and seconded his ecstatic welcome of the Russian Revolution. But he grew suspicious following MacDonald's disillusionment with Lenin and his struggle to prevent Labour joining the Third International. MacDonald offered G.B.S. various honours which were refused on the grounds that such titles distinguished the mediocre, embarrassed the superior and were disgraced by the inferior – besides, he had already conferred them on himself. 'Still, it is just as well that my lack of official recognition should not be the fault of the Labor Party,' he wrote to MacDonald when refusing a knighthood in 1929.

When MacDonald first became Prime Minister in January 1924, with Sidney Webb as President of the Board of Trade, Shaw had optimistically hailed him as the 'ablest leader in England'. By the time he came to form his second Labour Cabinet in June 1929, with Webb now translated into Lord Passfield and Colonial and Dominions Secretary, Shaw like some others was already preparing to discard him. MacDonald's radicalism had subsided. All he had to offer the country was a substitute for socialism. He was a Liberal at heart and his position as leader of the Labour Party, legitimately won during his days as a rebel and an outcast, was now actually preventing the experiment of socialism from taking place. Behind the rhetoric were muddle and vacancy. Of course it should have been possible to permeate such a leader with ideas, except that, as Shaw admitted to Stanley Baldwin, 'MacDonald knows me too well to pay any attention to me.'

At the peak of his career MacDonald struck Shaw as being politically dead: his period as leader should be ended with retirement to the House of Lords. But who among the living should take his place in the Commons? Shaw backed someone forty years younger than himself, 'more able than either Napoleon III or Hitler at his age'. This man was Oswald Mosley.

Mosley's political career in the 1920s had the radicalism and unorthodoxy that Shaw admired. At the beginning of the decade Mosley had broken with the Conservative Party over its Irish policy – particularly the notorious Black and Tan reprisals – and exhibited his superiority to the party system by standing as an independent candidate, and winning. After MacDonald first came to power, Mosley joined the Labour Party and, following two years in the wilderness during Labour's opposition, became a junior minister in MacDonald's second administration. He was tipped by many as a future Prime Minister, an outsider ideally placed and increasingly fancied to overtake the tiring leader sometime in the 1930s.

Mosley was a wonderful manipulator of words. He sounded rational, he sounded omniscient, and when he vented his full powers of assertion it seemed as if heroic deeds were being performed. His air of certainty, deriving perhaps from maternal adoration unchecked by any paternal competition, and furthered by his wealth, social privilege and prominent looks, was marvellously appealing in a world of danger and confusion. He was athletic and quick-minded, part child and part strong man – could this be the superman whose advent Shaw had been prophesying?

Mosley certainly thought so himself. He had pored over *The Perfect Wagnerite* and in his own pamphlet *Wagner and Shaw* would envisage mankind rising through mists of ignorance to a transcendental conjunction of art and action. He had also investigated Shaw's ideals of leadership in *Caesar and Cleopatra*, and come to see himself, his biographer Robert Skidelsky writes, 'acting out in real life the central dramatic situation of Shaw's plays: the vital man, with ideas and impulses, confronting the inert creature of ideology and habits'. Since Mosley, unlike MacDonald, was eager to use other men's brains, it seemed that here was an opportunity for G.B.S. to speak with a voice from the past through a political adventurer with a brilliant future. Though hated by the Tories, Mosley was still an intruder into the Labour Party. Shaw tried to strengthen his socialist ideology – his diary reveals that he actually wrote one of his speeches in 1924 – and to illumine the picturesque myth-making which, for the time being, held Mosley in Labour politics. By the beginning of the new decade he had become an amalgam of Keynesian economics and Shavian political philosophy, and saw himself as the leader of an élite group of heroic technicians. 'Has MacDonald found his superseder in Oswald Mosley?' Beatrice Webb wondered in 1930.

In January that year Mosley made his move, bypassing his superior, the Lord Privy Seal J. H. Thomas, with a memorandum to MacDonald proposing public stimulants to the economy, a recovery plan that called for the mobilization of national resources to combat unemployment. This heterodox programme of state intervention and large-scale public works was casually turned down by a Cabinet committee and on 20 May Mosley resigned – a 'melodramatic defection from the Labour Party', Beatrice Webb called it, 'slamming the door with a bang to resound throughout the political world'. Using this memorandum as a political manifesto, in the spring of 1931 Mosley formed his New Party which was planned as a Labour ginger group but which evolved eighteen months later into the British Union of Fascists.

Shaw watched Mosley's operatic career with a mixture of emotions. 'Oh, if Oswald had only waited,' he wrote after the New Party had been created, '– if only he had known that MacDonald was contemplating political suicide!' To some extent Shaw preserved his loyalty to Mosley by blaming MacDonald for his rush of blood to the head and by attacking his 'new party', the National Coalition Government that came to power in the summer of 1931. This, rather than Mosley's splinter group, seemed to Shaw the real danger. Twice the Labour Party had been elected, and still there was no socialism in Britain. Shaw had praised MacDonald as 'the most imposing Parliamentary figurehead since Gladstone'. In London society he had been courted as a Highland chieftain and was 'inevitably pressed away from the Socialism which he knew to be impossible for *him* to prime ministership', Shaw wrote in a letter to St John Ervine. ' ... But he could not take his party with him: he could only throw it into the gutter to be counted out for five years and to rise up then in a fury against him, leaving him meanwhile in the air and partyless except for the Conservatives, which was by no means what he intended at his age and with its failing strength.'

Shaw believed that the implementation of Mosley's programme (similar to Roosevelt's New Deal) in 1930 would have gone some way to averting the financial crisis of 1931, which had been brought about partly by the cost of unemployment benefits. He also believed that the government should have abandoned free trade and the gold standard, and he blamed MacDonald for allowing one of his ministers, as late as the autumn of 1931, to 'make a speech in defence of the gold standard without warning him that its abandonment was already settled'. Finally he believed that MacDonald had been unnecessarily imposed upon by American bankers and unknowingly exploited by British politicians using the economic situation to split the Labour Party. MacDonald's 'clear course when the crisis came was to go into the Opposition and lead the Labour Party in a strenuous fight to balance the Budget at the expense of property instead of at the expense of Labour. That, at least, he could understand, if he could not understand the currency question,' Shaw wrote at the beginning of 1932. 'When he went over to the enemy and led the attack on wages and doles instead without ever mentioning the alternative, he was lost to Socialism for ever.'

Shaw interpreted the extraordinary rally to the Nationalist idea, which gave MacDonald his landslide victory in the autumn of 1931, as a sign that 'people are tired of the party system'. This was how he himself felt, though he knew that a coalition was the opposite of strong government. By his mid-seventies Shaw was disenchanted with the Fabian concept of weakness permeated by strength and the politician's empty head continually filled with other people's ideas. He had tried permeation all his life and it did not work – the ideas leaked away. 'The Fabian parliamentary program was a very plausible one,' he wrote in 1932, 'but, as MacDonald has found, parliament and the party system is no more capable of establishing Communism than two donkeys pulling different ways.'

Shaw struggled to be polite to MacDonald during the 1930s. 'He now sails the admiral's flag in the Tory fleet,' he wrote. 'There is no use in grudging him his triumph.' But every so often he was, in Charlotte's words, 'very naughty about Ramsay'. In an interview for the *Manchester Guardian* he declared that MacDonald had not said anything in public for several years that 'was not complete bunk'.

'He has been saying the sort of thing that people like, and he has said it very well, for he is a very taking man. His voice has three registers in it, and he uses it with great artistic skill. There is no need to condemn him for that. I do not say he is a man of evil intentions, and he will no doubt do what good he can with his new party, but he never will speak sincerely.'

But what of Mosley's intentions, and how sincerely did Shaw speak of them? While addressing an audience 'in praise of Guy Fawkes' at the Kingsway Hall in November 1932, he singled out Mosley as 'a very interesting man to read just now: one of the few people who is writing and thinking about real things and not about figments and phrases'. MacDonald was applauded by the people for his phrases; Mosley was feared because he represented change. Shaw translated the one into a Shavian idealist and the other into a realist who 'keeps hard down on the actual facts of the situation'. He ignored Mosley's layers of dissimulation and his uninhibited private ambition, and used his fascism ('the only visible practical alternative to Communism') as a stick with which to beat a philistine parliamentary system.

Shaw's speech, which lasted one and a half hours, was largely an attack on speech-making. The chief function of Parliament, he declared, had become the defeat of democracy through the art of fooling the public. What this 'painfully incoherent tirade' (as Beatrice Webb called it) most eloquently communicates is the despairing sense of impotence that Shaw could no longer hide. 'For fortyeight years I have been addressing speeches to the Fabian Society and to other assemblies in this country,' he told his audience. 'So far as I can make out, those speeches have not produced any effect whatever ... I have come to see at last that one of the most important things to be done in this country is to make public speaking a criminal offence.'

In which case Shaw himself was a major criminal. This indeed was how he had come to feel. All Tanner's revolutionary 'talking' from *Man and Superman* had merged with 'this continual talk, talk, talk in Parliament'. Words themselves were devalued. From this rise of pessimism emerged his tribute to Mosley. What could be more appropriate – or more pleasing – in a speech praising the man who 'saw that the first thing to enable the Government to do anything was to blow up Parliament', than to *threaten* people with Mosley? 'The moment things begin seriously to break up and something has to be done, quite a number of men like Mosley will come to the front ... ' he warned. 'Let me remind you that Mussolini began as a man with about twentyfive votes. It did not take him very many years to become the Dictator of Italy. I do not say that Sir Oswald Mosley is going to become Dictator of this country, though more improbable things have happened ... You will hear something more of Sir Oswald Mosley before you are through with him.'

What the public was to hear in the later 1930s was the stamp and chant of Mosley's Blackshirts. In Shaw's experience of British politics the only precedent for these rallies were the ineffectual marches and parades of Hyndman's Social Democratic Federation. A measure of Mosley's political invalidity in Shaw's mind after 1933 is his absence from both *The Intelligent Woman's Guide to Socialism, Capitalism, Sovietism and Fascism* in 1937 and *Everybody's Political What's What?* in 1944. Even his campaign for Mosley's release from prison in the Second World War was to be based on the assumption of his political insignificance. 'I think this Mosley panic shameful,' he told a newspaper in November 1943. '... even if Mosley were in rude health, it was high time to release him with apologies for having let him frighten us into scrapping the Habeas Corpus Act ... We have produced the ridiculous situation in which we may buy Hitler's "Mein Kampf" in any bookshop in Britain, but may not buy ten lines written by Mosley. The whole affair has become too silly for words.'

Shaw distanced himself from the unsavoury aspects of Mosley's British Union of Fascists. 'Anti-Semite propaganda has no logical connexion with Fascism,' he said. '... Anti-Semitism is the hatred of the lazy, ignorant, fat-headed Gentile for the pertinacious Jew who, schooled by adversity to use his brains to the utmost, outdoes him in business.' In 1933 he described fascism as 'anything from a mere blind reaction against the futility and anarchy of the British parliamentary system and its Continental and American imitations to the Corporate State as established in Italy'. A dozen years later he defined it as 'State fina₂₂ed private enterprise' or 'Socialism for the benefit of exploiters'. From the 1930s onwards Shaw chose to call himself a communist: 'that is, I advocate national control of land, capital, and industry for the benefit of us all. Fascists advocate it equally for the benefit of the landlords, capitalists and industrialists.'

It followed that, in so far as fascism or National Socialism made common cause with communism against the parliamentary system, Shaw was not unsympathetic, for this was part of his own 'blind reaction' against the 'futility and anarchy' of that system. He remained indulgent towards Mosley as if it had been a stroke of bad luck that directed him to Mussolini's Italy instead of Stalin's Russia.

Mosley believed himself to be the hero of a Shaw play. His outcast state did not cause Shaw to re-examine his own political mood for he was then nearing eighty. But why should he apparently advocate Mosley or Mussolini, Stalin or even Hitler as leaders to be followed? Putting this question to him in 1934 Beatrice Webb protested that Mosley, Mussolini and Hitler had 'no philosophy, no notion of any kind of social organization, except their own undisputed leadership instead of parliamentary self-government – what was the good of it all?' Admitting this lack of economic principle, Shaw asserted that they all had the *personality* to change the world and that Mosley was 'the only striking personality in British politics'. Though good at finding war leaders, Britain was in decline because she did not recognize that social progress also depended on great leadership. But Beatrice was not convinced. 'This strange admiration for the person who *imposes* his will on others, however ignorant and ugly and even cruel that will may be, is an obsession which has been growing on G.B.S.,' she reflected a year later.

'...As a young social reformer, he hated cruelty and oppression and pleaded for freedom. He idealized the rebel. Today he idealizes the dictator, whether he be a Mussolini, a Hitler or a Stalin, or even a faked-up pretence of a dictator like Mosley... And yet G.B.S. publicly proclaims that he is a Communist... What he really admires in Soviet Communism is the *forceful* activities of the Communist Party. He feels that this party has a powerful collective personality that imposes itself willy-nilly on the multitude of nonentities, thereby lifting the whole body of the people to a higher level of health and happiness.'

[3]

Man is the occupation of the idle woman.

'Hello, Bernard Shaw.'

'Hello,' he answered politely.

'We've come to see you.'

In the late summer of 1921 an American girl had accosted G.B.S. on the sidewalk outside Adelphi Terrace. She was twenty-four and blatantly attractive, with dark hair, eyes like muscatel grapes, 'and a fine shape'. Her name was Molly Tompkins. She had come from Atlanta, Georgia, with her husband Laurence, their two-year-old son Peter and a nurse, to 'find' him, she explained; they had got his address at Hatchards. 'Then where is Laurence?' asked Shaw. He was round the corner nervously drinking coffee. Leaving him there, and under the spell of her good looks, Shaw invited her to 'come upstairs and tell me all about it'. She came and, over buttered crumpets, unfolded their simple plan. Laurence was rich and had ambitions as a sculptor; Molly herself had paraded across the stage in Ziegfeld's *Follies*. Together they dreamed of creating a Shavian theatre, he carving in stone the story of Creative Evolution, she interpreting it on stage. As designer and actress, they would give Shaw to the people.

'What a monstrous idea!' But he had been touched by these two 'innocent infants' and felt moved to help them as he himself had never been helped in his twenties. He saw that Molly was 'as vain as a goldfinch', knew she was only 'pretending to have read all my books', and reckoned that 'poor Tompkins' had 'taken on a fine handful'. Yet her eagerness 'softened my stony heart a little', he admitted; 'and now I suppose I am in for taking some interest in you occasionally'. So began a bizarre compendium of all his previous love affairs.

They would need more than a nurse, he thought. So he put himself in charge of their education. 'Education in the ways of the world is a series of humiliations,' he wrote, 'like learning to skate.' He instructed Laurence to get a studio and arranged for Molly to take the written and oral examinations for the Royal Academy of Dramatic Art. He had been on the Council of RADA since W. S. Gilbert's death in 1911 and his bracing influence was largely responsible for broadening its constitution and liberalizing the students' education. By the time Molly began to attend, the value of this institution to actors and the theatre-going public had been recognized by Royal patronage. But Molly did not think much of it. The two houses which comprised the Gower Street part of the premises (and which, with the help of £5,000 from G.B.S., were later replaced by a larger building) impressed her as being 'dim and dingy'; the director Kenneth Barnes was 'pompous'; and she took an 'instant dislike' to her first teacher, the actor Claude Rains. Indeed, she behaved so badly that Claude Rains was soon saying he would prefer to resign rather than continue with her in his class, and Kenneth Barnes threatened to expel her. 'You are a disgrace to me,' Shaw admonished her. 'They lay all your sins on my shoulders ... and ask me despairingly what they are to do with you and why I didn't bring you up properly.' He continually had to scold her in this fatherly style. 'What you need is to become conscious of what you are doing ... you must take on all sorts of jobs until you are perfectly handy at doing anything you want to with your instrument, which is your face plus your figure plus your voice ... You must not abandon Barnes until you have completed your course and taken your diploma ... the work there, much as you despise it, has done you a lot of good; and you are not yet finished ... You don't exist as yet.'

Shaw could not help being tickled by his protégée's goings-on or conceal his entertainment at the *beaux gestes* with which, at the very last moment, she would regularly avoid their consequences. For every quality, she seemed to have some infamous defect. 'You are worse than the tragédienne who rehearsed Pygmalion in the upper division for me some years ago,' he told her. This, perhaps, was part of her appeal. She challenged him to re-embrace past sentiments, improving his old performances and rephrasing some painful scenes, this time painlessly – for surely he was beyond pain and humiliation now.

*

Recently Stella Campbell had been pressing Shaw to let her publish the 'dear letters' she had inspired him to write. 'What have you written?' he demanded. 'Your life or mine or both?' He referred to her forthcoming book as *The Autobiography of an Enchantress*; she called it *My Life and Some Letters*. There was nothing 'confidential' in it, she assured him. 'There's no such thing as falling in love. Joey don't be silly.' Knowing how much she needed the money ('the poor woman can hardly lay her hand on a hundred pound note') he wrote to her publisher stating that he had made a 'gentleman's agreement' with her not to raise the question of copyright over his correspondence. Then he left the matter to her judgement.

Gentleman's agreement! Her judgement! Had she enchanted him again? Awakened by Charlotte to the implications of what he had done, he asked Stella to send him the proofs: he might perhaps 'spot some dangers that you may not have thought of'. She did not dare let him see all her proofs, but had a copy made of the correspondence she proposed publishing. 'People talk carelessly, but nobody will *think* anything but what lovely letters and what a dear man you are,' she prompted him. 'I do not fancy that Charlotte will misjudge me, or that she will see that permitting the letters to be published is other than a *panache* in her bonnet.'

This 'terrible wadge of letters' arrived at Ayot St Lawrence shortly after Christmas 1921 and it appalled him. He dared not reveal its contents to Charlotte. 'Public exposure' of them would be as 'utterly impossible', he warned Stella, as for 'you to undress yourself (or me) in the street'. Their only chance was for him to edit them.

She had no alternative. 'I send you the letters in proof,' she replied. '...Please be young and give me my own way ... Tell Charlotte not to worry.' Advising her to sell the correspondence itself to an American millionaire, he set about cutting the text for publication. 'My treasure, my darling, my beloved, adored, ensainted friend of my very soul' was pared down to 'my adored ensainted friend', and his 'most agitating heart's darling' vanished altogether. What remained, he told himself, was ten times more than any publisher had the right to expect. 'Nobody can reproach you for publishing it as I have left it; and there is the requisite touch to set Charlotte right without which I would have seen the whole universe damned before consenting to the publication of a line,' he soothed Stella. 'It will be hard enough on her as it is to see her husband as the supreme ass of a drama of which you are the heroine.'

But Stella was not soothed. 'You have spoilt my book', she objected. 'You have spoilt the story ... Lustless Lions at play ... It is really sad: you creep on the ground, instead of flying in the air – through taking away those delicious letters.'

Shaw had wanted to calm Stella and avoid distressing Charlotte. 'You *must* have some more love letters,' he appealed desperately to Stella. 'You cannot appear as a famous beauty who had only one catch: an old idiot of 56. Will there be nobody to keep me in countenance?' The truth was that she had been more feared by men than loved, and Shaw's correspondence with her was unique. This was partly why she felt so angry. These 'massacred' letters in their 'murdered bundle', she let him know, had become 'the only insincere thing in the book', and no more like love letters 'than my hat'. And really he agreed with her. 'I hate the whole thing, because it is impossible to present it in its simple truth to the public,' he explained, 'and it is dishonest to disguise it, and disloyal to pretend that it was all play-acting. I felt a great deal more than you did; and I still feel a great deal more about it than you. You are doing – if you only knew it – a dreadful thing.'

Being unexpectedly hurt, Stella stretched forth her claws. 'You have ceased to amuse me. You have *revoked* – that's your game always . . . Next time you try and fascinate an actress, don't use her as a means of teasing Charlotte – *that* was the ugliest thing you did.' If Charlotte felt distressed, Stella was 'truly dreadfully sorry'. But 'I *am* going to publish exactly what I like . . . ' she threatened. Her book was to be serialized in May 1922 by the *New York Herald* to which the corrected proofs had been sent with the lines Shaw had excised still legible. 'Oh Joey – oh lor! oh Hell! I have just seen the *New York Herald*, they have put in all the letters uncut, this in spite of all their promises,' she apologized. ' . . . I feel *very* unhappy because I know how much you will mind.'

He did mind – because of Charlotte. As for himself, he considered the publication of a love letter as 'an indecent exposure'. But if Stella regarded it as 'a splendidly courageous declaration . . . I have no argument to oppose: it is instinct against instinct', he explained to G. K. Chesterton. 'She has a right to her view, and to her letters. I cannot call a policeman . . . I cannot control her. I cannot even contradict her . . . Besides, it was delightful while it lasted; one cannot refuse gratitude when it has absolutely no damned nonsense of merit about it; *and the money was very badly wanted*. Still, a dreadful thing to do.'

He had always loved Stella's dreadfulness. 'I forgive you the letters because there is a star somewhere on which you were right about them,' he wrote to her, 'and on that star we two should have been born.' Molly Tompkins too seemed to have arrived from that star. But perhaps he could teach her to live on this one. Then he need not hurt Charlotte. Molly reminded him of Stella when beautiful and, he hoped, would make him forget all their stupid conflicts. He would police their correspondence in exemplary fashion. 'I read your letters diligently,' he assured Molly. 'I even read them aloud to my wife (with an occasional skip).' And again: 'Your letters are extremely readable (my wife is quite keen on them) and they make me feel romantic at times, which is pleasant at my age.' Of course he knew these letters would not be so amusing 'if you had a scrap of prudence or foresight. I never do anything because I am prudent or foresee anything. My life lacks the imprevu.' Or so he hoped, for this time he meant to control his innocent infant of an actress, making it clear early on for example that he could never go to meet her after dark because 'my mate does not like to be left alone in the domestic cage in the evenings'. His friendship with Molly blossomed as the struggle over publication of Stella's love letters was warming up, and it appeared to offer him an opportunity for rewriting the past. 'If you knew the trouble those unlucky letters made for me you would understand a lot of things,' he later confessed to Stella. His exchange with Molly was intended as a simple series of letters between a 'delightful correspondent' and a 'useful bore' which would record a relationship as innocent as that of Higgins and Eliza. He had lost 'all *specific* interest in women', he told a disbelieving Stella in 1923. '... I can no longer tell myself love stories.'

*

Shaw was well aware that Molly Tompkins brought out qualities he shared with Professor Higgins. 'I exhort you (in the manner of Higgins) to remember that you are a human being with a soul and the divine gift of articulate speech,' he wrote, 'and not a confectioner's shop'. To help polish up some of her letters, drop certain provincialisms and generally acquire the English alphabet, he sent her twice a week for lessons in diction to Professor Daniel Jones, who taught phonetics at London University.

But principally he tutored her himself, and never had he luxuriated more gorgeously in good-advice-giving. 'You just do what I tell you,' he explained. He told her how to model her handwriting, address an envelope and stick stamps on it; when to use make-up, how to pronounce Spanish and order a vegetarian meal at a restaurant without risking early death. He described the correct manner of bargaining for white oxen when in Italy; went through the drill for curing a fear of bats; and strongly recommended parrots as preferable to dogs as pets for beautiful women: 'Parrots are amusing, and never die. You wish they did.' He instructed her in the art of having rows ('for heavens' sake make them as rowdy as possible: give them some tragi-comic acting') and of saying 'No!' with conviction ('It is the most useful accomplishment in the world'). Finally he provided hints on how to take all this advice: 'When you get a bit of advice, don't bolt it. Chew it fortyseven times; and then it will digest all right.'

'Besides the people who give advice,' he added, 'there are the people who take it.' That seemed fair and the casting obvious. Yet how curious it was that the more advice his 'Mollytompkins' heard, the more she appeared to need. 'That is why it is so useless to try to help people whom God does not mean to be helped,' he concluded. '... the old should not prevent the young making fools of themselves'. In this sense at least he was successful.

He went to see her perform at Gower Street, where she was learning elocution, eurhythmics and fencing as well as acting, and invited her to lunches at Adelphi Terrace where she met Barrie, Galsworthy and others who 'didn't register with me'. In the afternoons he sometimes gave her help with the lines she was learning. 'I was supposed to be able to go to Adelphi Terrace whenever I felt like it and make myself at home,' she remembered, 'but when Shaw wasn't there Charlotte was cool, and she could be very icy indeed ... so I just went when I was invited.'

Molly was invited to spend part of the spring at Stratford-upon-Avon with the Shaws in 1922, and Laurence (her husband) came too. Then, when RADA broke up for the summer and Charlotte went to Ireland, G.B.S. invited them both to meet him at a Fabian Summer School at Godalming and accompany him on a motor tour of English cathedral towns.

At Godalming Molly and Laurence acted as 'an admirable baffle' against some of the more pressing Fabian ladies, especially one fiery redhead. And then there was a moment in the garden at Godalming when Molly spoke her love for Shaw. 'You will grow out of your Shavian infatuation (alas! for I hope it is a great pleasure to you),' he had told her. But later on he explained 'why I was so shy at Godalming'. Whatever age they might be in fairyland, in prosaic society (and what could be more prosaic than a Fabian garden) they were an old man and a young thing. 'La Rochefoucauld says that the very old and the very young, if they desire to avoid making themselves ridiculous, should never allude to the garden at Godalming.' He did not mind making himself ridiculous – 'I play my part of pantaloon to your columbine with my usual histrionic skill.' What he minded was causing her physical disgust – 'I don't like to give young women cold shivers.'

They began the tour, bowling along the English lanes in Shaw's car, 'open, high, doorless, with gears outside, and painted a hideous brown, but it was enchanting', Laurence thought. '... We took turns sitting up front with the chauffeur or in the back with Shaw.' They went to the music festival at Glastonbury, to Salisbury Cathedral, to Wells in Somerset and then diagonally across the country up to Northumberland. Shaw dressed for this adventuring in what Molly called 'old-fashioned knickers with stockings and a Norfolk jacket with pleats down the front and belt'. At night, while Molly and Laurence changed into evening clothes, Shaw presented himself in a buttoned-up, double-breasted, blue outfit, 'like a sailor's reefer'.

None of this appeared to make Molly's flesh creep. She seemed intoxicated. But she was not an easy travelling companion, wanting to go off on expeditions with G.B.S. to less historical sites – such as the man-eating caves in the Cheddar cliffs – and objecting to being booked into a separate hotel with Laurence and not with Shaw. Their destination was Scarborough where another Fabian Summer School was taking place, and where they saw again the Fabian redhead who inflamed G.B.S. It was obviously she who had placed Molly in an annexe, sharing a cramped little room with Laurence far removed from Shaw. This arrangement was 'out of the question', so 'just before dawn we packed and walked out', Molly recorded, 'hired a car and went into Scarborough to catch a train to London'. But there were no London trains till the afternoon, so they took a room in a hotel and went out to 'a movie'.

Shaw came into Scarborough, searched the station, searched the hotels, and found them in the cinema. There were no explanations. They sat through the film to its end, then he took them to their train, promising to see them in London that autumn. Laurence had thought Shaw would never speak to them again after they had run away without leaving a word. It was curious, he remarked on the train going back to London, that their bad behaviour actually seemed to have made him more friendly.

*

After Molly returned to RADA, Shaw's stream of advice poured forth again. He wanted her to finish her course and win the Gold Medal. But, hearing that the Plymouth Repertory needed a leading lady on a year's contract and that Kenneth Barnes had the giving of it to a senior RADA student, she immediately caught a train to Plymouth where the hypnotized manager engaged her. Kenneth Barnes and Claude Rains breathed with relief, and Shaw wrote to congratulate her on this unsportsmanlike initiative. 'All this is first rate: you couldn't have done better.' Yet there remained a problem. Molly confused her liking for roles with her ability to act them. 'If you had a sense of humor . . .' Shaw began. But she hadn't and he was obliged to accept that this pretty well ruled her out of his own plays. She would have to succeed as a woman of sorrows 'drowning the stage with unshed tears instead of setting the table in a roar'.

Unfortunately the stock company at Plymouth wanted comedies and, in a spirit of high-strung protest, Molly's voice rang through the theatre almost always in top register. 'I do not think she's any good for the stage,' the Plymouth theatre manager notified Shaw. ' . . . it would be fatal to her chances to let her go sublimely on, thinking she was all right, when she was all wrong'.

Given the sack from Plymouth, she took to the road over the next fifteen months searching for a sufficiently tragic lead. Besides G.B.S., she had another theatrical champion in Johnston Forbes-Robertson, three years older than Shaw and soon to be knighted. Twenty-five years before there had been a romance between Shaw's handsome Caesar and the girl Shaw had wanted for his Cleopatra and who became his Eliza. Now, for the second time, playwright and actor were led away by similar good looks. 'It is very kind of you to encourage her. She could get no higher testimonial,' Shaw wrote to Forbes-Robertson. '. . . She has gorgeous nights of happiness when you take her to the theatre.' Forbes-Robertson 'seemed to ask me to every first night at the theatre', Molly noticed, 'and to lunch or supper whenever I had a free moment'. A shadow-rivalry soon developed between her two septuagenarian suitors. 'I envy Shaw being so near you at the play, and seeing you in your lovely green dress,' Forbes-Robertson lamented: 'Oh, he doesn't like your earrings, doesn't he? Well *I* do, and I must come first, so there.' And Shaw enquired reprovingly: 'I gather that another gentleman of my age, and famous for his good looks and charm, was bolder; and you see what happened to *him*!' Molly was always opening letters from these two fond old men. She felt embarrassed by some of Forbes-Robertson's 'outbursts'. It seemed that G.B.S. wrote 'every day and Forbes-Robertson two or three times a day'.

These letters were also read by a Plymouth drama critic called Mollie Little, who had taken on the role of secretary and housekeeper to the Tompkins family in London, and who in 1925 tried to use them to blackmail Molly's admirers. Miss Little 'asks me with extraordinary persistence for sums of money in three figures, undaunted by the dead silence into which her letters fall', Shaw told his Molly in the summer of that year. 'I hesitated to give her away to you when the letters poured in at first . . . but as I am pretty certainly not the only friend of yours she is trying, you had better know.' With Forbes-Robertson, whose knighthood might have been imperilled by such revelations, Miss Little appears to have had some success, but, following the publication of his correspondence to Stella Campbell, Shaw was unable to take the threats seriously.

With this episode, Molly's theatrical career ended. 'Suddenly I was sick of the whole business,' she wrote. '. . . I wasn't supposed to be an actress.' She tended to blame Laurence, whom she had been dragging from one provincial theatre to the next, for having persuaded her on to the stage, and turned to Shaw for further advice on what to do and where to go. 'I rather doubt whether the stage is really your job,' he agreed. But her acting might have been training for a career in literature 'for your literary faculty is unmistakable'. As for where she should start: 'I see no reason on earth why you should not go to Italy,' he volunteered. 'Everybody should go to Italy.'

So Molly went to Italy, taking Laurence and inviting G.B.S. to join them. 'I will not come to Italy to share the fate of Achilles,' Shaw replied. In England – at Godalming for example – he had been 'bound to behave very well indeed for the credit of the [Fabian] Society', he explained. But there were not the same constraints abroad. 'I am very nearly as bad as you; and if I were to drive all the women mad and you all the men we should [be] deported as undesirables.'

*

'I am not at all convinced that I shall never see you again,' he had prevaricated in a letter to Molly. During the late spring and early summer of 1925, his diary and letters record, he had been 'ill in bed' and 'crawling about a bit'; after which, between July and October, Charlotte raced him away on a bracing tour of the Orkneys and the Shetlands – 'up to our eyes in scenery', he cried. But by spring the following year his health had seriously collapsed. 'I had been ill for many months,' he later told Harriet Cohen, 'and had come to believe that it was all over with me. I could not do a stroke of work . . . ' It was this work, in particular a 'terrible book on Socialism', that Charlotte believed was dangerous: 'my great struggle has been to keep G.B.S. from working,' she confided to Beatrice Webb. ' . . . he is not *well*: not in the least himself or as he ought to be: and I do not think 70 years is enough to account for his state'. She was determined to take him away to recuperate, not round Scotland this time ('for the last six months in England he really *never was warm*'), but abroad, where he could get over his shivers. On 5 August 1926 they arrived at the Regina Palace Hotel at Stresa, overlooking Lake Maggiore.

It seemed an inspired choice. 'I am getting stronger, but I can't work in this climate,' Shaw signalled Blanche Patch, 'which is perhaps just as well.' Before starting out by train ('I am nearly dead, and the journey will probably finish me'), he had felt 'an obscure fire within me that craves for cold water'. At Lake Maggiore he was able to bathe every morning – '& I bathe sometimes', added Charlotte in a letter to Apsley Cherry-Garrard. 'Altogether I think we have fallen on our feet & GBS is far more bright and happy.' They were particularly lucky to have found 'some gay bright young friends here who adore him, & take him about, & amuse him'. She was referring to the conductor Albert Coates who owned a villa three miles from their hotel on the opposite side of the lake, 'a magnetically charming person', Charlotte described him, with a 'wife [Madelon] we like too', and a succession of interesting guests which included Cecil Lewis and his wife 'Dooshka', who turned out to be a 'Prima Donna from Moscow who has never sung (in public) outside Russia, & who GBS thinks the best singer he ever heard!'

When not listening to music and bathing 'on the clean side' of the lake, Shaw was at the other side near Pallanza sitting for a statuette by Prince Paul Troubetzkoy who had 'a big studio & an astonishing wife', Charlotte reported to Beatrice Webb. '. . . It has been splendid as it has kept GBS employed & amused going over day after day & sitting.' Altogether they were both 'getting on splendidly & *like* this place immensely . . . We are on the lake in motor boats most of the time . . .' One of the *Isole Borromee* round which they boated – the tiny luxuriant island of San Giovanni, once infested by serpents – was advertised in their hotel as being available for renting from an Italian prince. In fact, it had been taken by Molly and Laurence Tompkins.

Shaw knew this before setting out for Stresa. 'At last an address!' he had written to Molly the previous month. '. . . You must settle down somewhere. You have been living the life of a lost dog, and making Laurence live it . . .' But when he arrived, their palazzo was being renovated and Molly and Laurence were in Paris. 'I cannot tear myself away from the Isola Molli,' he wrote. 'I sailed round it again today . . .' On hearing this, Molly rushed down on the Orient Express, and arrived at the Regina Palace in a horse and carriage, the dust rising in the bright sunlight behind her.

She went bathing and picnicking with the Shaws' 'gay bright young friends', but could not enjoy herself. The presence of Charlotte, invariably dressed in black – sometimes in a black taffeta swimsuit with a stuffed canary on the shoulder – clouded her spirits. 'I like it best without Charlotte,' she stated. But when she did manage to serenade Shaw alone, she found that Charlotte had been watching them through powerful binoculars. 'You and Charlotte have got to come to some arrangement,' Shaw insisted. But they could not. Molly hated Charlotte's air of ladylike smugness, her acid superiority, and she resented her central position in the party. She could not understand why everyone else seemed to like her. Then, after Charlotte had accused her of having 'an evil mind', Molly fell silent, scuffing her feet in the white dust, kicking the stones, feeling sulky and hard inside and wondering as she lay in her lonely room that night what was making her so cross. Next morning she caught an early train back to Paris. Four postcards from Shaw pursued her: 'Your life seems to be one of considerable quite unnecessary friction,' he wrote. 'But I will not preach.' 'I didn't exactly want to leave,' Molly explained to Laurence. So, she despatched a telegram and let Laurence put her on the train for Italy.

Back at the Regina Palace, the concierge handed her a note from Shaw. They had not known when she was arriving, had stayed in till half-past two and were now on a previously arranged excursion to Orta, the silent green lake to the west, from which they would be back at dinner. The note gave details of the next day's programme: 'You can join on as you please. GBS.' But he had not detached himself and waited for her. 'Fury blazed up inside me,' Molly remembered. 'So sorry to miss you this trip. Returning to Paris immediately,' she scribbled on a Tiffany card, and caught the afternoon train back. 'Return immediately to hell,' Shaw replied to her that night, '…and never dare write to me or approach me or mention your poisonous island to me again as long as you live.'

All this crazy commuting had not made Molly popular; even Laurence, she observed, was 'almost beginning to lose patience'. There seemed only one thing to do. 'I suppose it's the only thing you *can* do,' Laurence agreed. So once more he put her back on the train, the same train, and she checked into the Bellevue Hotel at Baveno on the edge of the lake two and a half miles from Stresa. 'Driving along the road to Stresa, which Shaw called the road to Baveno, I promised myself this time I'd be good.' And she very nearly was. Whenever she began 'behaving like an idiot' she would receive a caution from Shaw 'to pull yourself together' or 'you will spoil everything', for by now they had come to share something that could be spoilt. After sun-filled days and quiet evenings, when they sat in a boat rowed by the leisurely stroke of the fishermen, Shaw would walk her back to Baveno, 'and then I would walk back with him halfway to Stresa and then he would return again to leave me at Baveno on the steps of the Bellevue, striding off into the night, the sound of his brogues fading into the lap-lap of wavelets from the lake'. On her last day, with autumn in the air, Molly accompanied the Shaws to a grand garden-party; then after they had taken Charlotte back to the hotel, Shaw 'came with me up to the station and put me on the train to Paris'.

*

He felt miraculously restored, 'better and much stronger than I had been for years before my illness'. This new vigour was 'partly you, I think', he wrote to Molly. She had confided her growing adoration of him in a 'bothersomely honest letter' at Stresa, and this adoration was now 'an indispensable Vitamin in my bread of life'.

'I have still two years of youth left,' he had assured her when retreating from their tête-à-tête at Godalming: 'so make the most of them.' Now that he was seventy and she not yet thirty, it was time for some advice: 'Find your own way,' he tried to tell her; 'never mind me'. She must also mind Laurence who 'will certainly be vamped, and elope', he warned. 'You have trained him to be imposed on.' Unless he found his roots back in America and got to work there, Laurence would never do anything: the Jamesian era for 'deserting America to live in Europe as an artistic vagabond (like the sculptor Story, whom Charlotte knew quite well) is gone by'. But after this direct exhortation to Laurence came the irresistible afterthought: 'By the way, you might leave Molly behind if you are tired of her.'

He tried again. No longer did Molly figure in his mind as an innocent infant: she was obviously a natural coquette 'and the sooner you realize that what is fun to you is heartbreak and homebreak to your victims, the better', he admonished her. 'Not that that will stop you; for the instinct which delights in dancing on the edge of a precipice when you have lured a giddy man there, knowing that your own head is sound and that you can get back in safety, is incurable.' In which case she had better leave all those young Italians she mentioned in her letters, and 'remain faithful to me, your ancient Shotover'.

Something had gone seriously wrong with the Shavian advice-machine. 'Love me as long as you can,' he wrote; 'but make young friends.' He felt some provident care for Molly; then a less agreeable voice, one that did not want to shield her or deny an old man his prey, would interrupt. 'You would get wearied if I were always nice and considerate of your feelings,' he wrote early in 1927. '...And anyhow, you must take me as I come ... I am beginning to let the mask slip occasionally and damn the consequences.'

The consequences rested largely with Charlotte. 'It always upsets me to find myself, helplessly innocent, between you and the other lady,' Shaw had written. Charlotte hugely disliked Molly, but for the sake of G.B.S. had made many stiff efforts to be nice to her. 'I think I shall have to bring him to live here!' she had joked with Molly that summer at Lake Maggiore. She was sure that their 'intercourse' was 'one-sided' and that G.B.S. must soon get bored with his impolite young admirer – there had already been signs of his impatience.

Early in 1927, when Shaw finished his book on socialism, Charlotte took him to Torquay, to Malvern, and to stay with the Webbs at Passfield Corner. Beatrice and Charlotte appeared to be on more affectionate terms as they grew older. Charlotte interested Beatrice. Her placidity, replacing the striving restlessness of earlier days, seemed obscurely nourished on mystical tracts published in Kensington by the School of Silence. Using meditation and self-hypnosis as a means to realizing 'wholeness' and 'God Power', Charlotte had become indifferent to the suffering of the poor, it appeared to Beatrice, and had risen above the vicissitudes of human relationships. 'Hence she wends her way through a luxurious existence, spending lavishly on clothes and self-beautifying, thinking of her own state of mind and of GBS's health,' Beatrice wrote in her diary: '...she has developed admirable manners and a pleasing and cheerful personality ... there is fascination in an exquisitely clothed and cared-for person, if those artifices are combined with personal dignity and graciousness. Certainly she holds fast GBS's respect and affection...'

In her analysis of the Shaws' married happiness, Beatrice took no account of Charlotte's incurable arthritis and the pain she sought to rise above, through religious meditation; nor did Beatrice sense the dangerous restlessness that took possession of G.B.S. whenever he relaxed from his writing. Now that his book was completed, the attraction of Molly on her magic island grew 'very strong'. He knew that 'it is a mistake to go back anywhere' and that if he did go back to Lake Maggiore 'my infatuation would be suspected at once'. All the same, he still dreamed of the Baveno Road. The decision lay with Charlotte.

To the Webbs, Charlotte had kept discreetly silent about Molly. Only to T.E. Lawrence did she show a glimmer of her feelings. 'She has no influence, but what she has is bad – you will understand.' Charlotte knew that G.B.S. wanted to return; she felt another holiday in Italy would benefit his health. He could listen to music again with Albert Coates, and pose for a full-length statue this time by Troubetzkoy. Charlotte was confident of having overcome her emotional anxieties. By the first week of July 1927 they were back in the same corner suite at the Regina Palace.

Laurence and Molly were now living in their palazzo on the Isolino San Giovanni, and each morning Shaw and Charlotte came over the Bay of Pallanza in a small motorboat to swim. After lunch all four of them would return to the mainland and go off by car into the Lombardy hills. As the summer progressed and the heat intensified, Charlotte more often preferred to stay on the secluded island during these afternoons: it was cooler to sit reading on one of the terraces under the trees in her black taffeta bathing dress than to bounce over the country roads at a mile a minute with Molly at the wheel. Laurence, too, was grateful to get back to his studio. So, while Charlotte read and Laurence worked, Shaw and Molly would drive off together into the mountains, sometimes staying late to eat supper at a trattoria or to watch movies in one of the towns round the lake, and coming home so late that Charlotte began to feel uneasy and 'even Laurence would frown'.

One day, as they were raising a cloud of white dust behind them, Molly turned off the road and bumped the Renault over the hollows and rough grasses of a field until they reached a copse of trees by a concrete emplacement 'just right for parking a car'. Not far from these trees flowed the river Toce, its smooth and pale green surface concealing strong currents and treacherous whirlpools. They walked to its low sandy banks, and sat down under the eucalyptus trees. 'For a long time we lay on the river bank looking down at the water, or up at the tree limbs and sky, content and with no need to talk,' Molly remembered. 'All the million things I had to say to Shaw were forgotten.' Later, in his 'curiously enchanting voice', he began talking of what was 'uppermost in both our minds', and at the end Molly turned to him 'so full of you, and the river, and trees, and sweetness' – but suddenly out of the landscape a uniformed soldier appeared and informed them that they were in a military zone, had perched their car on a gun emplacement and must remove it. *Subito!* He saluted and vanished.

This afternoon was the high point in their romance. Molly, who confessed to being 'dazed by the violence of my desire for you', went on to imply that there had been some sexual as well as spiritual liaison between them that 'gave my body and my mind and my heart peace when I lay by the side of a river'. Shaw, too, appears to suggest that he may have come near to celebrating his seventy-first birthday that July as he had celebrated his twenty-ninth. 'I hoarded my bodily possessions so penuriously than even at seventy I had some left,' he reminded Molly eighteen months later, 'but that remnant was stolen from me on the road to Baveno and on other roads to paradise through the same district. Now they are all dusty highways on which I am safe because nobody can rob a beggar.'

Whatever happened that afternoon, it led to different expectations. Shaw had stated his belief that love 'does not last, because it does not belong to this earth; and when you clasp the idol it turns out to be a rag doll like yourself; for the immortal part *must* elude you if you grab at it'. He was to warn Molly against her erotic romanticism because it could not make her happy. 'You thought that when you had secured your Ogygia and lured me to its shores you could play Calypso to my Odysseus and make a hog of me. Aren't you glad you didn't succeed ...' But Molly was not glad. She wanted a completely fulfilled love affair with Shaw, and in the after-vacancy she began looking at him 'with hatred in her eyes and speaking with it in her voice'. They all had a dreadful time of it that summer: Shaw falling ill and Charlotte feeling wretched, Laurence like a helpless prisoner on the island and Molly a 'predestinate damned soul, a Vamp fiend'. 'You will prowl round that lake, making men's wives miserable, tormenting yourself whenever their glances wander from you for a moment,' Shaw retaliated, 'until the lake water changes to fire and brimstone and rises up and scorches you into nothingness.'

During a sudden storm one night Molly and Laurence were almost drowned as they tried to reach Stresa in a canoe. The evening had been planned as a reconciliation. Arriving hours late at the hotel, Molly was still trembling with fear and cold. Shaw picked up her shipwrecked figure in his arms and put her in his bed upstairs. Why had she been so rude and unreasonable? Lying on his bed she told him she was pregnant, that she did not want another baby and was going to Milan for an abortion. 'Please don't go to Milano, Molly,' she remembered him saying. 'It will be my spiritual child at least.' But being in love with one man and apparently pregnant by another, Molly felt determined. Later she noticed that Shaw's eyes looked old and tired 'and for the first time I saw a hint of grey in his face ... and I felt I had committed a murder'. After this Shaw came every day to the island and would sit in the garden holding her hand. 'But there was little to say, and neither of us tried ... it was almost a relief when the last day came.'

Shaw and Charlotte took the Orient Express back to London on 6 October. It had been a troubling episode, and characteristic of earlier affairs. 'I must not think about you; for I cannot save you; I have done my best and only made matters worse,' he wrote to Molly, as he had written to Florence Farr and Janet Achurch. ' ... You are not a thing evil in itself, and it is impossible to believe that you *must* go to the devil by natural necessity, though my experience tells me that you will.'

'For Mephistopheles whispers to me as he did to Faust "She is not the first". Before you were born I have had to do with sirens as seductive as you. And now! You will go their way ...'

He asked Molly the same question he had asked Stella. 'Can you not learn how to live in the world?' But if he had taught them that, he would have destroyed what he loved in them. They could not relegate love affairs to occasional distractions. Isolated on her island, there seemed no future for Molly, though her future, like Stella's, was to stretch out as a long vexed sequel, shadowing their aborted romance. Molly's love-island, Shaw told her, was 'a place to spend six weeks a year in, but not a place to live in'. Yet it lingered like a sea fantasy over his last plays and continued to haunt his memory. 'Write oftener, far oftener, even if I cannot answer,' he appealed. 'The restless hands sometimes tire of the pen and remember the road to Baveno ... angels will always love you, including G.B.S.'

[4]

Such books are never written until mankind is horribly corrupted, not
by original sin but by inequality of income.
The Intelligent Woman's Guide to Socialism

'My dear GBS
  You will think me a dreadful bore when I tell you that I want you to send me a few of your ideas of Socialism. Unfortunately the Study Circle to

which I belong have got hold of the fact that you are my brother-in-law, so I promised I would write to you. We want to know so many things . . . Will you answer my questions *quite plainly* . . .'

'It would be easy, dear madam, to refer you to the many books on modern Socialism which have been published since it became a respectable constitutional question in this country in the eighteen-eighties. But I strongly advise you not to read a line of them until you and your friends have discussed for yourselves how wealth should be distributed in a respectable civilized country, and arrived at the best conclusion you can.

'For Socialism is nothing but an opinion held by some people on that point . . .'

So Shaw began his two-hundred-thousand-word riposte in 1924 to 'Mrs Chumly's' modest request. It was to extend over three years and cost 'more labor and thought than half a dozen plays'. When the going was good he welcomed the challenge 'to have to do a real hard literary job, all brains, instead of writing plays', he told Molly Tompkins. But in other moods he would admit to having 'nearly killed myself' over 'my confounded book for women on socialism!' Only by neglecting everything else over long stretches could he hope to finish it. 'I find as a matter of invariable experience that if I answer letters,' he answered Archibald Henderson, 'or relax in my desperate resolution to let everything else slide, it is out of the question.' By 7 March 1927 it was 'within a chapter of its end', he told T. E. Lawrence, and nine days later Charlotte wrote to Lawrence: 'The book – the Socialism book – is <u>finished</u>! Last words written this morning!'

There was a good deal more to follow these last words. He enlisted the co-operation of Graham Wallas and the Webbs that summer in correcting his proofs and his ideological waywardness; he entered complex business-aesthetic negotiations with his Edinburgh printers over the choice of paper, width of margin, the size and density of the Caslon typeface. He prepared two private copies of the *Guide* with special title pages: one for T. E. Lawrence and the other for his sister-in-law, Mary Cholmondeley, whose name he misspelt in the dedication. He took on the indexing of the first 213 pages until 'I can stand it no longer', after which he delegated the job to Beatrice White, an experienced indexer recommended by the Webbs and 'a terror for spotting faintly printed letters'. He was determined to make the original setting a 'masterpiece of printing' and the production a 'model to all future ages', even playing tricks with the text to avoid ending paragraphs with a short line. The four-colour dust-jacket was designed by Eric Kennington and showed a naked woman (actually Mrs Kennington) 'making a copious display of bare breasts and indolently scratching a swelling on her right forearm' protested a Dublin reader, as she peered in a well for the truth like a figure in a fairy story. The olive cloth binding had a woven-chain pattern by Douglas Cockerell in gilt and green; the laid paper was opaque and marked with wide vertical chains; there were green endpapers and a gilt top to the pages. Over 90,000 copies were published simultaneously on 1 June 1928 in Britain and America, costing 15s. and $3.00. 'The reception of The Guide has been overwhelming,' he reported four months later. 'I meant it to be.'

*

Shaw wanted his *Guide* to look beautiful because it celebrated a beautiful concept of moral fairness: that everyone is entitled to an equal share of the national wealth, regardless of occupation. 'Socialism means equality of income or nothing,' he insisted. His *Guide* reads like a sweeping preface to a play (with starring parts for women) he hopes to see performed on the political stage.

Though ranking his treatise as 'my magnum opus' and wanting it to become 'a standard work on Socialism', he nevertheless sensed it was untimely. It should have been the work on socialist economics that Havelock Ellis had tried to commission from him in the 1880s, and that he had himself prepared and failed to write each succeeding decade. In or about December 1910, when first advocating 'the abolition of class by the abolition of inequality of income', he had composed what was in effect the opening chapter of this book as an exploration of how to get the economic basis of society right in a civilized country – but stopped and broke it up into a lecture called 'Equality'. 'I have a book on Socialism to write – *the* book on Socialism,' he repeated to Edith Lyttelton two years later; and, when resigning from the *New Statesman* during the war, he wrote to Beatrice Webb: 'I have therefore to take my solution and my policy elsewhere. And there is nowhere else except in a book doing at long range what should be done by a journal at short range.'

In one form or another his *Guide* to Socialism had been waiting in the wings for forty years until he came to feel it was now making its appearance as his last will and testament. 'After a life of Socialist preaching it would be a pity to die without having a textbook that nobody else could write,' he told his publisher Otto Kyllmann. 'The only difficulty about it is that it ought to have been written at least 70 years ago, and then it would have been of some use.' But he was to welcome the plundering of his *Guide* for ammunition during the election campaign in May 1929. 'It would not do to make tracts of the chapters as such; but the compilers of your leaflets and pamphlets can quote as much as they like,' he wrote to the General Secretary of the

Independent Labour Party and editor of the *New Leader*, Fenner Brockway, who was to win the Labour seat at East Leyton.

Shaw himself hoped that 'it may affect the flapper vote'. Six weeks before the *Guide*'s publication an Act had been passed in Parliament lowering the voting age for women from thirty to twenty-one and giving them the same residence qualification as men. With the small exception of business and university franchises, the democratic equality of one adult one vote was finally reached in the 1929 general election. This extension of the franchise added five million newly-qualified women to the electoral register. Since Labour increased its support in the country by three million votes, it was popularly assumed that 'the flapper vote' had begun by helping socialism. In this sense Shaw's special appeal to women had been perfectly timed. For its fifth reprint in May 1929 his publisher brought out a five-shilling 'popular' edition, called by Lord Lothian 'a Manifesto for the election of 1929'.

But otherwise Shaw had delayed too long. 'He belongs to a generation which some will say is dying, thank Heaven, and best forgotten,' wrote Father Martin d'Arcy. '. . . the sources of his intellectual creed are the tenets of the late Victorian era'. His faith in government power and compulsory labour was unshadowed by any auguries of totalitarianism. 'When Mr Shaw studied economic and political theory, centralization and the expert were just emerging into fashion,' explained Harold Laski. '. . . I doubt whether he really cares very much about individual freedom.' Changes in economic principle and social organization brought about by the war appeared to have left little impression on him: the *Guide* contained more John Eliot Cairnes than John Maynard Keynes and was more or less exclusively addressed to women from his sister-in-law's class. His fascination with nineteenth- rather than twentieth-century writers was natural for someone who had 'spent the first forty-four years of my life in that benighted period'. He explicitly links his work to that of European authors who had been some years dead, and admits his lack of involvement with post-war society:

'Ibsen's women are all in revolt against Capitalist morality . . . The modern literature of male frustration, much less copious, is post-Strindberg. In neither branch are there any happy endings. They have the Capitalist horror without the Socialist hope.

'The post-Marxian, post-Ibsen psychology gave way in 1914–18 to the postwar psychology. It is very curious; but it is too young, and I too old for more than this bare mention of its existence and its literature.'

Aside from the newly enfranchised readers to whom it was offered, the *Guide*'s merits did not depend on topicality. Here was the summary of a lifetime's thought, a work of eloquent insight and fantasy, and Shaw's political autobiography in the form of a socialist Sermon on the Mount. As he marches forward on his pilgrimage the social landscape behind him grows brilliantly illuminated, while ahead the Promised Land (which, like Moses, he knows he will never reach) glows with an eerie light. Only the marching figure himself is lost in the midst of current confusions, so that we cannot see whether he has struck an original short-cut or is losing himself on a precipitous digression.

A number of economists refused to review the *Guide* as a serious contribution to their subject because it did not comply with the axioms of economic analysis. By making use of simple definitions, such as 'capital is spare money', Shaw had set out to demystify a subject that, like medicine, was increasingly viewed as being impenetrable to non-specialists. 'Economics is supposed to be an involved and abstruse subject,' acknowledged Martin d'Arcy, 'yet here we have the secrets of it set forth in a prose worthy of Platonic dialogue.' The *Guide* is a sustained act of teaching that aims at driving the reader back to the foundations of her own beliefs (Shaw uses throughout the feminine pronoun which in certain contexts, he points out, 'includes the masculine'). Most standard works on economics and political science had been addressed to a sort of abstract reader conceived as aridly male: 'You might read a score of them without ever discovering that such a creature as a woman had ever existed.'

To reveal economics as the everyday business of ordinary people, Shaw tied his examples to the likely experience of his women readers. 'Think of the whole country as a big household, and the whole nation as a big family, which is what they really are,' he invites us, in much the same manner as Britain's first woman Prime Minister would use sixty years later. But, though he argued from a similar premise, he came to an opposite conclusion about the morality of unpaid labour: 'because there is nothing to sell, there is a very general disposition to regard a married woman's work as no work at all, and to take it as a matter of course that she should not be paid for it'.

Anyone who can manage her domestic economy, Shaw maintains, can understand the political economy of twentieth-century capitalism. He further raises the self-esteem of his readers by attributing the greater success of men in business and the professions to their sexual inferiority, the jobs of accountants, barristers, doctors, managers, shopkeepers and so on being generally neuter. Since women have a natural monopoly in bearing children, he argued, it followed that, 'being as it is the most vital of all the functions of mankind, it gives women a power and importance that ... men cannot attain to at all. In so far as it is a slavery, it is a slavery to Nature and not to Man ... The only disadvantage the woman is at in competition with the man is that the man must either succeed in his business or fail completely in life, whilst the woman has a second string to her bow.'

Feminism was only one aspect of his general theory of equality; nevertheless, as Margaret Walters has written in the 1980s, the *Guide* 'remains an important feminist document'. Though it bored both Molly Tompkins and Beatrice Webb, who respectively knew too little and too much, it impressed an extraordinary variety of politicians, historians and intellectuals. 'After the Bible this is in my eyes the most important book that humanity possesses,' Ramsay MacDonald remarked, an aside that revealed him to be 'more of a wit than I suspected', Shaw granted. Albert Einstein, too, promoted the book as having 'great insight into human activity'. 'It is a very great book,' T. E. Lawrence wrote to Charlotte. ' ... It is like the aged Hardy writing poetry.'

The poetry is in the dogma. Shaw's Paradiso is a place where all citizens have as natural a right to equal incomes as they have to air and sunlight, justice and education. 'You would certainly think anyone mad,' he writes, 'if he claimed to own the air or the sunlight or the sea.' He examines seven ways of distributing wealth, pulling out the stops of his literary and debating skills to expose all but one of them as deadly sins. This logical annihilation, which appears to drive capitalism itself into its last ditch after a series of surrenders and retreats, is a bewitching display in the art of political pamphleteering. He surveys our national institutions, from the courts of justice and the institution of marriage to the usefulness of our schooling and the quality of our newspapers, and finds them all ingeniously bedevilled by the evil effects of dividing people into rich and poor.

Shaw's Purgatorio is here and now. His case against the existing order is its incisive severing of capitalist civilization from health-giving moral principles without which civilizations cannot survive. In this indictment he struggles free from his own respectability to retrieve the power of anger and sense of disgust that had so impressed William Morris during their street-campaigning days. 'His criticism of the modern capitalist muddle is so damaging, his style so trenchant, and so full of reserves of indignation and righteous scorn,' Morris had written, 'that I sometimes wonder that *guilty*, i.e. non-socialist, middle class people can sit and listen to him.' Now that he was addressing an audience of Conservative matrons and obliged to be charming, reasonable, elementary, Shaw wondered whether his old fires were failing. 'I miss from its babytalk the sweep of my ancient periods,' he confessed. But in his early chapters, and again in the peroration at the end, he rekindles these flames of his youth. They rise most brilliantly when swept by the disillusions and betrayals of political events he had lived through, and

133

when seen against the clouds of his own rising despair. 'At present nobody can be healthy, happy, or honorable: our standards are so low that when we call ourselves so we mean only that we are not sick nor crying or lying nor stealing (legally or illegally) oftener than we must agree to put up with under our Capitalist Constitution,' he writes. 'We have to confess it: Capitalist mankind in the lump is detestable . . . '

'The working classes, the business classes, the professional classes, the propertied classes, the ruling classes are each more odious than the other: they have no right to live: I should despair if I did not know that they will all die presently, and there is no need on earth why they should be replaced by people like themselves.'

When Shaw described William Morris's hatred of capitalism as being 'far deeper than that of persons of only ordinary mental capacity and sensibility', he was also referring to his own abhorrence. He writes as one whose normal affections have been gouged out by capitalism and whose politics have rushed in to fill the emotional void. 'I do not want any human child to be brought up as I was brought up . . . Life is made lonely and difficult for me in a hundred unnecessary ways.' In such passages he joins the company of Dr Johnson 'who described his life as one of wretchedness: Anatole France, who said he had never known a moment's happiness; [and] Dean Swift, who saw in himself and his fellowmen Yahoos far inferior to horses'. Shaw's peroration to the Intelligent Woman is similar to Swift's 'unanswerable' indictment of mankind as 'the wickedest of all known species'. He finds his redemption in a formula that, substituting inequality of income for original sin, provides him with an abstract optimism. If moral triumphs, like mechanical triumphs, are reached by trial and error, he reasons, then it is possible to despair of capitalism without despairing of human nature. Under more benign conditions we would discover human nature to be good enough for reasonable purposes and would come to read *Gulliver's Travels* as a vivid clinical lecture on extinct moral diseases 'which were formerly produced by inequality as smallpox and typhus were produced by dirt'.

Shaw had known enough good and generous individuals to support his trust in human nature. But they were exceptional people whose qualities operated in spite of a system that promoted property rights over human rights. In his view, capitalism diminished the collective well-being by creating an unenterprising slum mind and by directing so much of a nation's energies to maintaining the parasitic rich who lived by owning land and consumed without producing. Under these inequitable conditions we can see 'half-fed, badly clothed, abominably housed children all over the place;

and the money that should go to feed and clothe and house them properly being spent in millions on bottles of scent, pearl necklaces, pet dogs', he complained. '...[This] is a badly managed, silly, vain, stupid, ignorant nation, and will go to the bad in the long run no matter how hard it tries to conceal its real condition from itself by counting the pearl necklaces and Pekingese dogs as wealth.'

Shaw's socialism was a means of achieving social responsibility by active interference in the production and distribution of the nation's income – that is, by a bureaucratically-managed public service to replace the quarrelsome and divisive social effects of capitalism. The land and the great basic industries needed to be managed for the benefit of all, though not, he urged, until an efficient organization was in readiness to take over control from private hands whose insatiable drive for profit had shown no concern with the public interest. Agencies on which our common lives depend would, after generous compensation, be made community property – the railways, the mines, the cotton industry and, above all, the banks which were the chief factor in determining the level of prices and the use of capital for development over an expanding area of economic enterprise.

Shaw is at his most original when examining contemporary politics from the platform of 'my favourite plan'. The General Strike of 1926, for example, 'need not have alarmed a mouse' because the working class was necessarily its first victim. But a serious general strike, he believed, run by a stronger network of trade unions, could be a form of national suicide. Shaw represents strikes and lock-outs as battles in the civil war between labour and capital – natural eruptions in a country split between poor and rich. In his single economic state, however, they would be seen as acting against everyone's interests and so would 'pass away as duelling had passed away'.

His futurist plan depended upon equality of leisure and the imposition on all serviceable citizens of compulsory social service. He recognized that the most frantic opponents of a Compulsory Service Bill would be the trade unions, whose chief weapon was the strike, and which had no objection to the capitalist method of industry, provided labour got the lion's share of it. From the Shavian perspective, trade unionism was therefore the application of the capitalist principle to labour. As a defensive conspiracy against the public, trade union power would divide the Labour Party, Shaw predicted, and delay the introduction of socialism.

Placing himself ahead of contemporary events, Shaw looked back and saw most progressive movements wandering away from real progress. Such a peculiar focus gave the *Guide* some of its originality, but also explains its lack of political impact. Shaw is especially critical of Britain's complacent acceptance of democracy, with its parliamentary athletes and actors, as the best available type of government. 'If democracy is not to ruin us,' he warned, 'we must at all costs find some trustworthy method of testing the qualifications of candidates before we allow them to seek election.'

'When we have done that we may have great trouble in persuading the right people to come forward. We may even be driven to compel them; for those who fully understand how heavy are the responsibilities of government and how exhausting its labor are the least likely to shoulder them voluntarily. As Plato said, the ideal candidate is the reluctant one.'

Shaw's economic proposals were not so much methods for changing the present as fantasies for escaping from it. He wanted the world to be controlled by dreams rather than experience. But when he draws close to contemporary politics his pen takes on a self-destructive cunning, as if the boy once neglected by his mother has grown into a man convinced he is neglected by his adopted mother country. Nobody understood what was happening except 'here and there a prophet crying in the wilderness and being either ignored by the press or belittled as a crank'. He threatens smug British democracy with all sorts of bogeymen dictators who, by direct action, will avenge this treatment. In such recurring passages he invites the disrespect of which he is complaining. His tone wavers, his judgement narrows, and there is another symptom. 'To put the same thing in another way ... I could go on like this for years.' All this was 'too boring for the intelligent man, if I'm any sample', commented D. H. Lawrence. 'Too much gas-bag.'

Shaw was at his best when passionately defending his plan. To a journalist who asked him to calculate what everyone's equal share in the national income of England would be, he answered: 'All you have to depend on is the flat fact that every worker can produce enough for himself and several others as well. Stick to that; and it will not let you down.' When questioned as to what income would content him, he retorted: 'Who cares what I would or would not be content with? ... The question is not what we would be content with, but what there is for us to get. We shall have to be content with our share ... It is our public business to see that everyone shall have as much as possible, and not less or more than anyone else.' To a correspondent who had questioned the compatibility of socialism with foreign trade, he replied that difficulties arose from the false assumption that without commercial profit there could be no foreign trade. 'I need not remind you that trade, home or foreign, is something to be minimized, not maximized and regarded as an index to prosperity,' he wrote.

'...the garden of Eden was happy without trade. But to many of our statisticians it seems as if Eve, instead of handing Adam the apple, had sold it for a bunch of Algerian dates, and the purchaser had sold it for a pound of Italian olives, and the olive sellers sold it for some Spanish figs, and the fig merchant sent it to Ireland in payment for a blackthorn stick, and so on round the globe until it came round to Mesopotamia again and was purchased by Adam for an ostrich feather, both Adam and Eve would have been much more prosperous.'

Harold Laski objected that 'for a man to tell you that the desirable thing is equality of income without telling you how to get it is simply irritating'. But Shaw had argued that people would win socialism by desiring it, and his *Guide*, like an alchemy, had been written to create that desire. 'The difficulty of applying the constructive program of Socialism lies not in the practical but in the metaphysical part of the business; the will to equality,' he wrote.

He was sometimes accused of attempting to banish evil from the world. He would respond that his *Guide* simply traced certain specified evils to inequality and suggested that they would not occur under his plan. 'No woman would have to turn her back on a man she loved because he was poor, or be herself passed by for the same reason. All the disappointments would be natural and inevitable disappointments; and there would be plenty of alternatives and consolations.'

Shaw's economic solution for uniting people in a true democracy was the invention of a man who believed his own disunities to have arisen from the marriage of his parents made under economic dictatorship. By changing the economic basis of society, he hoped to change natural behaviour. His socialist millennium was one step towards a world of realists with whom his sense of strangeness would disappear and where he would feel at one with people. Such transcendental dimensions put his *Guide* beyond the limits of ordinary criticism. Beatrice Webb, who had thought it would 'be a marvel if it is not a bad book' came to marvel at its autobiographical sincerity and pathos. 'His acknowledged genius, his old age, the warmth and depth of his earnestness and his amazing literary brilliance have paralysed his would-be critics and opened the hearts of fellow-socialists, especially those on the left,' she wrote. 'He denounces society as it is, he gives no credit and no quarter, and he preaches a curiously abstract utopia, which eludes criticism because of its very unreality.'

CHAPTER III

*I have played the clown in so many harlequinades that it is perhaps
unfair for me to suddenly strike a serious attitude...*
(1926)

In fact all men are comic.
(1926)

Adelphi Terrace was scheduled for demolition. While G.B.S. and
Charlotte were in Stresa during the summer of 1927, the servants moved
their furniture and belongings to a service flat found for them by St John
Ervine in 4 Whitehall Court. This was a large and wonderfully turreted old
building, with pavilion roofs and loggias, facing the Thames at Westminster
between Charing Cross Bridge and Old Scotland Yard. Number 130,
which had been previously occupied by Countess Russell (author of
Elizabeth and her German Garden) was a corner flat with five rooms and a
surrounding balcony overlooking the Embankment and the river.

They moved in early that October. All was still unpainted and nothing
looked right. 'We are in a fearful crisis,' Shaw cried out from the middle of
their upheaval. He was determined not to like the place, but gradually
Charlotte rearranged the furniture, positioned her Chinese pottery around
it, and settled in the Dolmetsch clavichord, the Rodin bust, the Sartorio
watercolour landscapes, the print of William Morris and other treasures. It
was 'healthier' than Adelphi Terrace, she pointed out, and G.B.S.
acknowledged that it was indeed more comfortable. He had soon organized
his study – a dozen filing cabinets, hundreds of books, a big flat-topped desk
for himself opposite a smaller one for Blanche Patch, and between them a
typing table. They were in business again.

'G.B.S. was not fond of Whitehall Court,' observed St John Ervine who
was a neighbour there for the first year and a half, 'but Charlotte loved it.' It
was so 'convenient': there was positively nothing to do in the way of
housekeeping, except to study the menu which was discreetly slipped under
the door each morning from the restaurant downstairs. There were about
150 service flats in the eight-storey block as well as a selection of clubs – the
Junior Army and Navy, Golfers & Lady Golfers and, with its separate

entrance at the end of the building, the National Liberal Club. The ceilings were high, the floors of marble and the walls panelled. It was a world apart, a temple to the rich. There was little need to go out: almost every service was given to the wealthy residents who included tea-merchants, oil magnates and diplomats from around the world, as well as retired officers, the editor of *Punch* and various commuters to the House of Lords.

G.B.S. was always going out. He appeared to enjoy taking charge of the doors, handles and buttons of the lift, placing the liftman in the role of passenger. The young bookshop assistant in the foyer would watch him stride from this lift across the hall and out of the door. He was often followed, she noticed, by two women of contrasting appearance. The first, slightly behind him loaded with a bundle of papers and looking firmly ahead, was tall and austere; the second, who was older and more solid, wearing a squashy hat and carrying a travelling rug, smiled and nodded as she passed. One morning when G.B.S. was hurrying out alone, this young girl held the door open for him, but he deliberately walked through a side entrance. 'Never hold open any door for a man,' he said to her. 'It embarrasses him and belittles you.' He seemed to think this all the more important as she had only one arm. After this introduction, he would sometimes come over and chat to her at the bookstall. He was interested in how 'she spent her time, where she had her lunch and how much it cost and other everyday details of daily life', for his own life was far removed from such details. She also took on jobs for him – looking out for articles by G. K. Chesterton, selecting readable books for a journey, or ringing his bell when she saw newspaper reporters going up so that he could nip down the back stairs. Occasionally she went up and had tea in the flat and was surprised to find that the dumpier of the two ladies (whom she had guessed must be a housekeeper) was Shaw's wife, 'a very homey, comfortable person' who told her she was 'undernourished' and presented her with a tin of biscuits each month.

Though Shaw tried to avoid signing books for people, he signed one for this girl when she asked.

*

'I have seen very little of anyone who has not worked with me,' Shaw wrote early in 1928. 'Except with my wife I have no companionships: only occasional contacts, intense but brief. I spring to intimacy in a moment, and forget in half an hour.' One vital new companion for Charlotte and workmate for G.B.S. was Lady Astor. 'The inimitable Nancy has laid many snares for me, but never the right one,' he wrote in 1926. 'She thinks I want to meet people: I dont. But Charlotte sometimes does . . .' A year later, after their return from Stresa, Nancy Astor snared them both with an invitation to spend Christmas at Cliveden, which, rather to her surprise, Charlotte accepted. 'We have come to the conclusion that you asked us for Xmas in that delightful and friendly way in a fit of enthusiastic benevolence, & desire to be kind to two old crocks,' she replied. They had planned to go for a long weekend but were snowed up there for eighteen days. It was for both of them a surreal time – like floating in a Shavian play-world – and Charlotte marvelled at it all: 'we both agree that all that has occurred during the last 3 weeks is a wonderful & impossible dream', she wrote to Lady Astor. '. . . I feel as if I had known you and your husband all my life.'

Nancy Astor had acquired a taste for English country life in Virginia where it was assiduously imitated. With her father, a man of ringing confidence who rose from night-watchman to become a wealthy trader, she shared a determination to succeed. From her mother she inherited her good looks and lack of interest in sex – vaguely interrupted in her mother's case by the birth of eleven unwanted children. Nancy, the seventh child, had grown up a tomboy, a relentless baseball player and horsewoman. She was probably attracted to her first husband, Robert Shaw, by his spectacular polo: he had an uncanny knack of tumbling off his one-eyed pony without damaging his handsome features. Was he intoxicated? The teetotal Nancy left him several times, beginning on the second night of their marriage. Sex had come as a shock to her: it was so rude.

After the final break-up of her marriage and the death of her mother, Nancy had come to England, a politer country. Here she was courted by the aristocracy, and in 1906 married Waldorf Astor, a perfect gentleman of German origin with money made by his father from the fur trade and real estate in the United States. Waldorf had a bad heart and plenty of excellent racehorses, and had attached himself to what he called 'a V-2 rocket'. But Nancy's career belonged less to science fiction than to historical romance. She enters the history books as the first woman Member of Parliament to take her seat, though she achieved little in the House of Commons except a series of vivid back-bench interruptions.

'Charlotte is very fond of you,' Shaw wrote to Nancy. 'So am I. I don't know why.' Charlotte liked the feeling of security that enveloped Nancy's fairy-tale existence. Her devastating personality guarded a rather frail character but admitted others to her protection. Except in medical emergencies she was supported by a wilful belief in Christian Science and, unlike Beatrice Webb, was never derisive about Charlotte's mystical wanderings. Preferring to be loved from a distance, she did not dream of flirting with G.B.S. The liberties she took with him were spectacularly safe – and rather tickled Charlotte. Once, approaching his shed at Ayot, she pulled open the door and seeing G.B.S. at work on a manuscript barked out: 'Come out of there, you old fool. You've written enough nonsense in your life!' Charlotte knew, of course, that Nancy really worshipped G.B.S., and sometimes wished she herself had been able to interrupt his work so forthrightly.

The tone they took with each other was part of what Nancy Astor's biographer, Christopher Sykes, has called the 'freemasonry' of famous people. Nancy was a glorious mixture of combustible qualities – 'a violently radical Conservative, a recklessly unladylike Lady, a Prohibitionist member of the Trade Party, and all sorts of contradictory things, including . . . the most turbulent member of the Party of Order' – a 'volcano' Shaw called her. She appealed both to his sense of the exaggerated and his need to see such diversity harmoniously combined. What could be more diverse than their political views? 'Why not come and improve your just-beginning-to-grow mind?' he invited her. But he did not really expect to convert her to socialism. 'The papers may say "Lady Astor attended Mr Bernard Shaw's lecture last night at Kingsway Hall; and her attachment to him as she sat by his side on the platform was very obvious"; but they will not say that you have joined the Labor Party.' Occasionally he might rehearse her for an election, try to permeate a Private Member's Bill or influence an amendment to some clause in a government Bill, but what he chiefly wanted was to demonstrate how people of absolutely different ideological commitments could strike up a lasting friendship.

There was much in Nancy's weakness and strength to remind Shaw of his mother. He saluted her public spirit in a foreign land. Flourishing in the limelight rather than in sunlight, she seemed like a Shavian creation. Her politics expanded from her social life, and her social life was a theatrical arrangement. At Cliveden, a vast nineteenth-century Italianate mansion overlooking the Thames, she created a fantasy kingdom that surrendered to reality only under extreme pressure – such as the First World War, when it was converted into a hospital and convalescent home.

She invited G.B.S. to this amphitheatre in Berkshire as a new star, and provided him with a new audience. He responded in his most extreme style. 'I "peacock" here (Charlotte's expression) amid week end crowds of visitors,' he wrote to Molly Tompkins near the end of his first visit. 'The mutual liking of the Shaws and Astors grows apace,' Beatrice Webb noted disapprovingly in her diary, ' . . . G.B.S. will find himself in an atmosphere of adulation, lit up by his hostess's sparkling wit and the talk of good-to-look at, light-hearted and charmingly deferential youths and maidens.'

Shaw brought such celebrities as Lawrence of Arabia to Cliveden and performed before people who belonged neither to his Fabian nor to his theatre worlds. He would hold reading parties for one or two of his new political comedies there, going through the supporting guest list with Nancy. 'What about Balfour? ... what about Mosley & his Cynthia (to represent the Labor Party)? ... Are you on visiting terms with Ellen Wilkinson? Dare she – if you asked her? ... However, unless she would amuse *you*, disregard this suggestion, as I can easily get at her when I read for the Webbs and the Fabian lot.'

Cliveden appeared an ideal place for the presentation of Shaw's political extravaganzas: in the public imagination the 'Cliveden Set' was itself a political extravaganza. For G.B.S. it offered an Arcadian alternative to Parliament. He was at the centre of a hypothesis, the hypothesis of appeasement between the two world wars, for Cliveden became renowned as the headquarters of a conspiracy to make a second Western accord with Hitler. Shaw himself was contemptuous of this theory of secret intrigue. He conspired with no one, treated his own opinions as unique, and had never been secretive about them. 'Never has a more senseless fable got into the headlines,' he wrote. The fable had floated up from a series of ingenious articles by Claud Cockburn in his paper, *The Week*, recreating Cliveden as a castle of plot and machination. 'I could prove that Cliveden is a nest of Bolshevism, or indeed of any other bee in the world's bonnet,' Shaw countered in an article for the *Sunday Graphic*. He resented this extension of his own theatre being converted into a branch of the Foreign Office, and ridiculed 'the silly notion that big historic changes can be effected by the country-house clique of a wicked British aristocracy'. In the wake of these rumours, Nancy Astor was referred to in the House of Commons as 'the honourable member for Berlin', and all sorts of treacherous scandals were passed from paper to paper. Shaw went to her defence in the American magazine *Liberty*, pointing out in a letter that, far from being German fifth column agents, the Astors 'have become the representation of America in England; and any attack on them is in effect an attack on America'.

This defence of his friend – taken up after an uncharacteristic appeal from Nancy – was read by Beatrice Webb with a wry smile. The game was up. 'Alas! poor Shaw, you have succumbed to Charlotte,' she had written in her diary. Arnold Bennett had observed that Charlotte 'plays the role of the super-celebrity's wife with much tact'. This tact did not impress Beatrice. She acknowledged that the Astors were public-spirited and philanthropic, and that they might reinspire G.B.S. as his old friends, the Webbs, no longer could. Yet she disapproved of the Cliveden Set as she had disapproved of 'the Souls' before the First World War. Both were aspects of a world she had renounced in order to be a socialist. 'What troubles us is that this new intimacy will widen the estrangement of G.B.S. from the

Labour Movement,' she wrote, 'build higher the barrier between him and the young intellectuals who are working out the better way of life for the bulk of the people – and dishearten and discourage his old admirers.'

To Shaw's mind the Cliveden Set also thought they were working out a better way of life. It 'is really a Fascist set, originating with Milner in South Africa, and picking up Virginia on the way hither', he was to write to Nancy in 1943. 'Fascism is an attempt to moralize Capitalism and enrich it at the same time through Fabian State organization...' Democracy, Shaw believed, meant the trial and error of political experiment through representatives of opposing ideologies meeting and exchanging thoughts without party political whips. Cliveden, where a 'vociferous Marxist Communist' such as himself could meet Colonel Lindberg (the friend of Hitler's chief-of-staff), a dyed-in-the-wool Liberal Lord Lothian, and Charlie Chaplin, was fundamentally more democratic than Parliament. Shaw did not flatter himself that he had influenced Chamberlain's appeasement policy; he had no special knowledge of Lord Halifax's visit to Goering and Hitler late in 1937. But he believed that, if denied war, both Hitler and Mussolini would fall: 'Twopence worth of manners may make all the difference.' Such opinions were increasingly out of sympathy with the mood of the country which, suspended between Churchill and Chamberlain, wanted a violent war of words with Hitler and Mussolini, but no bloodshed – what Shaw called a foreign policy of virtuous indignation.

What discouraged young intellectual socialists and disheartened old Fabian admirers was Shaw's championing of Mussolini in the 1920s. Like Nancy Astor, Mussolini was a triumph of equality of opportunity. His father had been a blacksmith and he himself had grown up a revolutionary socialist. During the war he had served in the trenches (unusual for a political man of action), been invalided out and, returning to politics, mobilized a group of ex-servicemen into an aggressive party which wore black shirts, attacked the civilian-controlled trade unions, broke strikes and talked grandiloquently of marching on Rome. People 'are so tired of indiscipline and muddle and Parliamentary deadlock', Shaw wrote, 'that they feel the need of a strenuous tyranny, and think Mussolini the right sort of tyrant'. Certainly Mussolini's remarkable *coup de théâtre* could not have been brought off without some popular support. His blackshirts prompted so much street disturbance that he was summoned by the King to Rome and, emerging from the train in top hat and frock coat, was created Prime Minister.

'All dictators begin as reformers and are encouraged by all sensible people until they find that their subjects do not understand their reforms and respond to nothing but military glory,' Shaw was to write. 'I applauded both Hitler and Musso while they were in their reform phase, just as Churchill did.' For a couple of years Mussolini had played the parliamentary game; then, on the road to dictatorship, with the official title *Il Duce*, he had begun a campaign of beating up his opponents. The murder in June 1924 of Giacomo Matteoti, Secretary-General of Italy's Socialist Party, led to a reign of oppression lasting until his fall from power nineteen years later. Shaw had picked up some bits and pieces of information about Mussolini from one of the neighbours at Stresa, Carlo Emanuele Basile, a novelist, politician, and 'the best talker I know'. As a fascist bureaucrat, Basile had become Federal Secretary of the province of Novara in 1925, was to enter parliament in 1929 and would be condemned in 1945 to thirty years' imprisonment for war crimes. What Shaw learnt was that Mussolini was accepted as the only competent leader available, capable of making the Civil Service earn its pay, of getting the trains to run famously on time, and of clearing the Pontine Marshes, where his powerful body, stripped to the waist, was to be seen digging alongside the workers. He was a 'Big Simpleton', in Shaw's view, as well as a man of the people. These people 'know that what they need is not more paper liberty and democracy, but more discipline,' he told Ramsay MacDonald; 'and Mussolini's grip of this fact is the whole secret of his command.' He might have bluffed his way to power and be holding on to it by an illusion of military strength, but in the long term his fascists 'could no more stand against public disapproval than against the London Metropolitan police'.

Much of the antagonism of anti-fascist Italian exiles in England to Mussolini during the late 1920s was directed at Shaw. 'If you meet Basile,' he wrote to Molly Tompkins, 'tell him that I have got into hot water with the Liberals for defending Mussolini.' Some colleagues assumed that he was unaware of the assassination of Matteoti and other atrocities. He repudiated this: 'I knew about them,' he wrote, '... [but] our attitude towards a new regime cannot be determined by the means employed to establish it.' Acknowledging that the dictatorship of *Il Duce* had been established with 'all the usual villainies', he assured the Austrian socialist politician Friedrich Adler that such brutalities and retaliations 'which accompany the eternal struggle of government with anarchy ... disgust me as much as they disgust you'. But he considered these savageries so customary in history as to be hardly worth remarking. 'The only question for us is whether he [Mussolini] is doing his job well enough to induce the Italian nation to accept him *faute de mieux*,' he wrote. 'They do accept him, some of them *faute de mieux*, several of them with enthusiasm.' Shaw placed himself in the first category: 'I have no "enthusiasm for Mussolini",' he insisted; 'but I back every ruler until he goes wrong. The fact that he generally goes wrong under pressure of popular ignorance does not put me in the wrong.'

But Mussolini had gone wrong in the early 1920s, the anti-fascist historian Gaetano Salvemini argued, and Shaw had put himself in the wrong by openly accepting fascist Italy. Shaw replied that what he was accepting were facts: he would have preferred the Italian workers and liberals not to have been 'so hopelessly incompetent that Italy gave Mussolini *carte blanche* to extirpate them'. Italian exiles had the right to cry 'Tyranny! Murder!' British citizens, with no such *locus standi*, must insist on a practical foreign policy: 'let us remember that it did not pay to be uncivil to Cromwell while he lasted', he wrote in the *Daily News*, '... we had better treat him with distinguished consideration as a matter of policy, no less than of good manners'.

By the late 1920s, the blacksmith's son was being billed as the leading political statesman in Europe. Shaw handled him as a theatrical director might, removing him in his imagination from Italy and making him perform before a crowd of anxious British onlookers. Shaw's letters to the press, he told Ramsay MacDonald, 'were really written *at* our own people'. He wanted Mussolini to school those who had woundingly dismissed G.B.S. in politics and who had underrated Sidney Webb (who 'gets no grip in parliament because he is neither an actor nor an ambitious scoundrel'). Mussolini was the actor-scoundrel Britain would deserve, he implied, if it continued to neutralize socialism with the procrastinations of sham democracy.

What made socialists indignant was the lack of moral perspective in someone who had asserted that progress depends on changing moral sensibility. The social critic who once challenged rule by historical precedent now appeared to slot fascist Italy into an inevitably recurring historical pattern going back to Caesar and Antony. Where was the sense of proportion in giving precedence to diplomatic courtliness over physical barbarity, to train times over terror? Shaw's absolutism 'is merely a mental exercise in history', commented Friedrich Adler, 'but not a real experience'. Even if his history was academically sound, his politics had grown insensitive and he seemed to have moved dangerously near the point of view of the British ruling class. 'What G.B.S. has lost is any sympathy with the underdog,' Beatrice Webb was to comment after reading the 'Preface on Bosses' he wrote for *The Millionairess*. '... He feels the frustration of old age and resents it.'

Shaw's Mussolini was a product of this frustration and resentment, a figure of make-believe whom he could command to refight and conquer old enemies. When Mussolini invades Abyssinia, Shaw goes with him – and invades Ireland, imposing on her all Mussolini's hypothetical improvements ('policed and water-supplied roads for a savage or waste country'). So Mussolini remains a wandering and displaced phenomenon, satisfying many urges, appearing on picture postcards on which Sonny draws all sorts of absurd bubbles and balloons, while G.B.S. is simultaneously extolling *Il Duce* as an emblem of national efficiency. 'He is still obsessed about Mussolini,' Beatrice Webb wrote, 'and his obsession takes queer forms.'

[2]

What takes place in a theatre is not always a simple matter of you
please me and I'll pay you.
Malvern Festival Book (1935)

Sitting alone in Whitehall Court, his typewriter on his knees 'like a sailor with his lass', Shaw would sometimes wonder whether he had finally shot his bolt. He was now in his seventies. But at least his migraines had gone after *The Intelligent Woman's Guide*: 'I transferred them to my readers.' While still at work on this book he had got a notion of a play which continued germinating until the following autumn. 'I slept very well last night; and the morning was all sunshine,' he announced to his printer William Maxwell on 5 November 1928. '*Consequently I began a new play.*' He wrote it with extraordinary ease and swiftness partly because his *Guide*, which had brought him back to the political theatre, had dammed up his dramatic outflow; and partly because the subject matter and stimulus had been provided by Granville-Barker's long-maturing new tragicomedy *His Majesty*. His speed was a lesson to Barker. 'The play is hurling itself out in such a torrent after my long abstinence that I believe it will be shorter to let it rip,' he reported the following month to Maxwell who had felt anxious over this straying from the Collected Edition. 'I can hardly write shorthand fast enough to keep pace with it,' he told Cecil Lewis. In less than eight weeks he had a complete play 'in the rough' – just in time for it to be read to Nancy Astor's selected guests at Cliveden over the New Year. Having settled the stage directions and the revisions ('How I shall ever cut it down to $3^1/2$ hours I cannot imagine') and sent it to the printers, he had rehearsal copies ready by 22 March to dispatch to his translators. 'The name of the play is *The Apple Cart*,' he wrote, 'and it is as unlike St Joan as it possibly can be'.

*

The man who had fired the starting-pistol over *The Apple Cart* was Barry Jackson. Shortly after mounting the British première of *Back to Methuselah*, Jackson had announced that he was closing the Birmingham Repertory Theatre in Station Road. This ultimatum, which paradoxically saved the theatre, was a measure of how far local apathy had discouraged him. For three years he was to divide his work between Birmingham and London. But though his career appeared successful – bringing him a knighthood in 1925 during his Royal Court production of *Caesar and Cleopatra* – he was far from content. The stagnation of Birmingham was matched by the soaring prices of London. 'The condition of the English Theatre has moved steadily downward, and today it may be said to have touched its lowest level on record,' wrote the stage-director William Poel in 1920. '... The public has for so long seen theatrical amusements carried on as an industry, instead of an art, that ... the plays of Shaw, Galsworthy, Barker, Masefield, with those of all men who respect themselves and their calling, are put on one side as being impossible compositions, written by those who do not understand the needs of the public, meaning those who are not with the Stock Exchange financiers.' Shaftesbury Avenue had been taken over by Threadneedle Street, driving the majority of Shaw's London productions in the 1920s to a drill hall out in Hampstead converted by Norman Macdermot into the Everyman Theatre; while his touring rights in thirteen plays were leased to the successful Macdona Players led by Esmé Percy (a graduate of William Poel's productions) 'with whom I never meddle'. More than ever, Shaw believed, the arts and sciences would be kept alive not by the big fees of central London, but by the half-crowns, florins and sixpences of the suburbs and provinces.

Barry Jackson shared Shaw's dislike of the West End which had contaminated so much of the repertory movement in London. 'Where are we who love the theatre, and are of sincere endeavour, situate?' he asked him in July 1928. 'Is history going on repeating itself to the end of time, and is the Birmingham Repertory Theatre to go the way of the Horniman and Barker ventures?'

Jackson was tired of being an intruder in London. He cherished a dream of founding a pastoral theatre, similar to the Three Choirs Festival at Gloucester, staged in idyllic surroundings where he could renew his dramatic inspiration. It was while walking with Shaw one day near Jackson's home at Blackhill that the idea came to him of fulfilling this dream in Malvern. The place had everything to recommend it – accessibility, ample hotel accommodation and wonderful country from the Severn Valley on the east to the Welsh mountains on the west. Malvern was a spa town built on terraces along a steep range of hills, its spacious houses grouped round the priory. And it had a newly reconstructed theatre. Having bought the late-Victorian Assembly Rooms the previous year, the Malvern District Council had raked the auditorium floor, lowered the ceiling and added a circle; then they had widened the proscenium arch, erected a stage tower, and installed technical equipment with modern lighting. Barry Jackson proposed to rent this new theatre, which seated over 900 people, and make it the centre of a festival of drama dedicated to Shaw. He saw the Winter Gardens, Concert Hall and Pump Room attached to the theatre as natural rallying points for festival visitors. Every instinct told him that here was the ideal place for such a venture. In the socialist England of Shaw's dreams, Barry Jackson would have found himself manager of a national theatre. But without public endowment there was nothing for it but to leave London and make a fresh start in the country where rents were comparatively low. While London's West End had become one of the most depressing growths of capitalism, Jackson's private enterprise impressed Shaw as a fine challenge. So he made a pact. If Jackson went ahead with his scheme for a festival at Malvern, he would write a new play for it.

And Barry Jackson had gone ahead, assembling a company of more than sixty players who rehearsed for seven weeks at Lillian Baylis's Old Vic before the Malvern Festival opened. The pattern was to present a different play each evening for one week at Malvern and then to repeat this programme over a second week. Tickets were cheap and it was hoped that visitors would stay a whole week to enjoy the extra-theatrical enjoyments of morning lectures and concerts in the Winter Garden, donkey rides up the hills, gondoliering and night bathing in the pools. Afterwards the production would transfer to Birmingham and only after that would the more successful ones advance into London. 'The whole idea of the festival is that the modern city does not give great plays a chance,' Jackson was reported as saying in the *Observer*. 'In London or Birmingham the effect is dissipated by being pitched out into a noisy street, and then a tiring journey home. At Stratford and in Germany, where festivals of this kind are held, there are beautiful surroundings that conduce to a lasting appreciation. There is a sense of continuity among the audience and an opportunity for exchange of ideas.'

Jackson had made Shaw the figurehead of the festival because he realised that if this venture was to rise above the level of a local flower show it needed a dramatic patron – or 'patron saint', as Shaw called it. 'We gather here, among the hills, to perform an act of homage to our greatest living dramatist,' Jackson wrote, 'to be amused and quickened by his humour and wisdom.' Six thousand people were to visit the Bernard Shaw Exhibition over the fortnight, and the cycle of plays included *Back to Methuselah, Caesar and Cleopatra* and *Heartbreak House*, as well as what Shaw called, in his flyleaf dedication to Jackson, 'the play which owes its existence entirely to you'.

Having laid the foundation stone of the Shakespeare Memorial Theatre in Stratford the previous month, Shaw arrived in Malvern on 18 August 1929 and stayed until 12 September, doing all in his power to catch the tourists between Stratford and Gloucester and to change Malvern from 'a forgotten Victorian water-cure resort . . . to a focus of theatrical interest with a conspicuous place in all the London headlines'. No other dramatist could have shifted the attention of the newspapers to a small town in the west of England on a sweltering Sunday afternoon in August. It was not even a world première. (To Trebitsch's dismay that had taken place, using Floryan Sobieniowski's translation, two months previously, at Warsaw's Teatr Polski before an audience that included the President of the Polish Republic, Ignacy Moscicki who, *The Times* correspondent reported, 'was obviously delighted by many of the political witticisms'.) Nevertheless the first British production, inaugurating Jackson's 'Bayreuth', was treated as a lustrous international event. A special Sunday train was hired to carry down from London more than sixty drama critics who were delivered to the theatre doors in plain vans. Cedric Hardwicke was starring as a future King of England with Edith Evans as his mistress, and G.B.S. was able to assure everyone that, like the exciting new films beginning to fill the cinemas, his play was 'One hundred percent talking'.

*

The two acts of *The Apple Cart*, roughly equivalent in components and parallel in structure, are introduced by an overture and interrupted by an interlude. Technically this is an adroit Aristophonic burlesque of parliamentary governments in the form of *opéra bouffe*. 'This music is a music of ideas – or rather, perhaps, it is a music of moralities . . . in which moralities are used as the motifs,' wrote Edmund Wilson. The chief role, taken by the King of England, is played against a children's chorus of uniformed Cabinet Ministers dextrously led by the head boy or Prime Minister. Altogether it is a piece scored for nine male voices and four female: a Soubrette Chantante (the Princess Royal), a 'sepulchral contralto' (the Powermistress-General) who emerges from the chorus to complement the King, a musical comedienne (the Postmistress-General) and a brilliant Millamant (Orinthia, the beloved) who provides an operatic soprano. Edmund Wilson described the progress of the first act exclusively in musical terms. After the overture 'the urbane and intelligent King and the "bull-roarer Boanerges" play a duet against one another'.

'Then the King plays a single instrument against the whole nine of the cabinet. The themes emerge ... the development is lively: the music is tossed from one instrument to another ... The King's theme gets a full and splendid statement ... This silver voice of the King lifts the movement to a poignant climax; and now a dramatic reversal carries the climax further and rounds out and balances the harmony. Unexpectedly, one of the brasses of the ministry takes up the theme of the King and repeats it more passionately ... This ends on crashing chords, but immediately the music of the cabinet snarlingly reasserts itself. The act ends on the light note of the secretaries.'

Initially it is these two walking gentlemen who carry on the Mozartian overture which, Shaw told the playwright Alfred Sutro, had been part of a false start. 'I began with a notion of two great parties: the Ritualists and the Quakers, with the King balancing them one against the other and finally defeating a combination of them. But I discarded this, as there wasn't room for it.' What he retained was a duet that presents a decorative variation on the theme of Shavian idealism. It is a mocking celebration of a ritualism that artfully supports the philistine *status quo*, and this prepares us for an investigation into the appearance and reality of democratic power.

The Interlude, which precedes the second act and takes place in Orinthia's boudoir, is another exploration of power based on appearance. Shaw himself described this scene as 'a brief but intense sex interlude' and certainly it was intended to offer the audience an erotic interest absent elsewhere in the play. But it gave him a great deal of trouble. 'Orinthia, the proud, the aristocratic, the goddesslike, the woman of lofty enchantments and "strangely innocent relations" ' had been modelled on Stella Campbell: 'the magnificence of the picture is due to you', he was to tell her. But Stella these days no longer felt magnificent. She was in her middle sixties. 'I cannot stand up to life much longer,' she had written to him. '... I think I am going to die soon ... I was under the impression that the great battle of life was fought in our youth – not a bit of it – its when we are old, and our work not wanted, that it rages and goes on – and on – and on ...'

Nothing seemed to have gone right since her beloved son's death in the war; now her marriage to George Cornwallis-West had come unstuck, the roles she could take in the theatre were diminishing and, having paid her son's and her husband's debts, money was finally running out. 'Doesn't your conscience prick you – you with your daily fortune pouring in – and I a beggar – I cannot think how I can go on loving you as I do!' she chided Shaw. She had been forced to sell his wedding present to her – an inscribed edition of his works – but refused to part with his 'lovely letters' (those letters over which she had behaved so badly in her autobiography), despite Shaw's advice to put them on the market before their price tumbled. A better solution, it seemed to her, would be to play a special role in his new play.

'I wonder if you will come and read the new play to me,' she invited him on 12 February 1929, 'as you half promised you would.'

'I can't read plays to a starving woman,' he prevaricated – and offered instead to pay her telephone and electrical bills.

'Come and read your play to me,' she ordered him. '... You cannot dare to make my poverty an excuse!'

But he had another excuse. 'I have just been smitten with a frightful and probably infectious cold ... and I will not risk giving it to you this week, nor next ...'

'I wonder if you are ever coming to read your play to me,' she enquired despairingly on 26 March.

This time he confessed to being 'too shy to read you the only scene in that play that would interest you. Its scandalous climax is a reminiscence of Kensington Square.'

'I know why you feel shy,' she responded. Her friend Edith Lyttelton had by now told her something about the scene and how Shaw had explained that Stella could not play Orinthia because 'no one could play themselves'. From all she had pieced together it had become obvious that 'the scene isn't true, though it may amuse you to fancy it so'. He readily agreed with her: it was fiction, not fact – in short, a play. 'Of course the scene isn't true; but you will recognize bits and scraps.' Still she pressed him ('You *must* come and read the play tomorrow') and still he resisted ('I can't read it to you now because I do not possess a copy'). His procrastination, strung together in a chain of lacklustre excuses and evasions, persisted until 14 April, when he escaped for two months to the Continent.

In the interval Stella happened to encounter Edith Evans who 'gazed eagerly at me saying she was playing *me* in *The Apple Cart* at Malvern and in Birmingham and London'. She turned to her friends, and they all echoed and augmented her own conviction that this was an 'insult', an 'infamy', a 'natural calamity', perhaps an 'illegal act'.

When Shaw returned to Whitehall Court a letter from Stella was waiting for him. 'I am truly distressed about *The Apple Cart*,' she had written. At moments she felt tempted to try some legal injunction, but her most effective act was to give a dignified statement of the truth. 'You should have sent me your play to read,' she wrote on 8 July. 'You are out of tune with friendship and simple courtesy.'

He had put off this dreadful confrontation for five months – too long, he now realized. Cancelling a meeting at the London School of Economics, he at last went round to her flat in Pont Street on 11 July. Though they had kept in correspondence they had not met for the best part of fifteen years. He was conscious of no longer being her 'brilliant adorable Irish lad' but a white-haired pink-cheeked skeletal figure on the eve of his seventy-third birthday; she had expanded from his 'blessedest darling' gypsy child into a woman of 'magnificent bulk ... the chins luxuriant too ... [and] noxious little dogs yapping at her heels'.

They still had their famous voices – hers more throaty than ever, his lilting Irish tones like the shivering of a wind across a lake – and with these voices they set out to repeat their *Pygmalion* duet in Edith Lyttelton's drawing-room before the war. He began the Interlude, and she listened uncharmed but impassive until he came to the passage where Orinthia offers to give King Magnus 'beautiful, wonderful children' in order to win him from his wife and make herself Queen, and adds: 'have you ever seen a lovelier boy than my Basil?' Shaw then delivered the King's reply: 'Basil is a very good-looking young man, but he has the morals of a tramp.' This was too much for Stella. It was true that her pampered son had dissipated his life in gambling and affairs, but she loved him and felt she would never forgive Shaw for this traducement of his memory. 'You hit below the belt when you juggle with gossip picked up about my dead son,' she told him, insisting that he remove the reference to Orinthia's Basil from the play. But 'when it comes to the point I can't take Beo out,' Shaw answered, 'it's like killing him over again.' Nevertheless, though defending his portrait, he registered the depth of Stella's mortification and conceded: 'I will let him go as a beautiful child ... as he suffered for other people's sins, the balance of justice is struck.'

Stella also felt sensitive over references to her marriages – 'and why this lie "Both husbands ran away" is it necessary for your wit. Look to it.' This difficulty was partly solved outside the text by Shaw's promise to cease aiding and abetting George Cornwallis-West's plans for divorce. 'Not another word on the subject shall ever fall from my lips,' he lied. The struggle between them went on into August. 'How troublesome you are!' Shaw complained. With desperate tact he contended that some of the changes she had forced on him were improvements. 'I shall now be able to say that you revised it yourself, and dictated some of the best bits.' Yet, though he himself might feel better, these piecemeal revisions were no cure for the soreness in Stella's heart. 'Tear it up,' she commanded him, 'and re-write it with every scrap of the mischievous vulgarian omitted, and all suburban backchat against Charlotte and suggested harlotry against me, and the inference of your own superiority wiped out ... Please do as I say – you will feel strangely relieved.' But he would not give them this relief: 'I have made a superb picture of you, God forgive me! and you must play the game.'

Shaw's game was to charge Stella with wanting it both ways – of being furious when identified as Orinthia but objecting whenever he altered her likeness. He knew that her real objection sprang from the corrupted picture of their romance. 'My love for you was the love of a child who feels safe,' she wrote to him. Shaw echoes this sentiment when he makes King Magnus tell Orinthia that they were 'two children at play'. But there is nothing childlike in Orinthia and nothing 'innocent' about her relations with Magnus. She is a tyrant of the emotions who treats ordinary people as 'dull slaves' and sees their purpose as being to 'keep the streets swept for me'. She exploits the King's susceptibility to her beauty. 'Heaven is offering you a rose; and you cling to a cabbage,' she tells him. The cabbage is Magnus's wife, Queen Jemima. 'Oh, drown her: shoot her: tell your chauffeur to drive her into the Serpentine and leave her there. The woman makes you ridiculous.'

The previous year Granville-Barker had published *His Majesty*, a play in which the Queen, who is a snob and a political idiot, irresponsibly precipitates a crisis which can only be resolved by the abdication of the King. Shaw characteristically reverses the situation. Though described as 'romantically beautiful, and beautifully dressed', Orinthia is without charm, except perhaps the charm of a precocious child, and her enticing powers are simply handed over to the actress who plays her. Stella Campbell did not of course know how unhappily his recollections of her had been disturbed by Molly Tompkins, who also, like Orinthia, had used her sexual powers to keep him from returning to Charlotte. King Magnus, who stands for 'conscience and virtue' in his dealings with the Cabinet, admits to Orinthia that he has no conscience 'when you are concerned' – which is, in effect, what Shaw said to Stella about his writing of *The Apple Cart*: 'I am an artist and as such utterly unscrupulous when I find my model – or rather when she finds me.' This is the attitude of Louis Dubedat in *The Doctor's Dilemma* and it is ironic to see it used gainst a character in the play who embodies the unscrupulous.

Stella's complaint was that conscienceless art led to falsification. 'I think it right to tell you that I will never be able to bear in silence the implication of that scene in your play,' she told him, 'its mischevious [*sic*] vulgarity, and untruthfulness.' It was mischievous in that it took away her talent and occupation ('It is what I am, not what I do, that you must worship in me,' Orinthia proclaims); and vulgar in that it robbed her of all wit and sensitivity (the duty of a King, Orinthia states, is 'to wipe your boots on common people'); and untruthful in that it diminished her significance to an 'enormously amusing interlude' in the life of the Shavian Super-King ('what I come here for is to enjoy talking to you like this when I need an hour's respite from royalty'). By casting Orinthia as the King's platonic mistress, Shaw also negated Stella's sexuality. 'I ran away from you at Sandwich because I wanted to remain Queen of the Kingdom of my Heart,' Stella explained, ' – but I suppose you mustn't humble the King in your play like that.' 'Yes: you were right, Sandwich and all,' Shaw confirmed. In the fantasy of the play, which combined erotic suggestion with metaphysical platonism, the humiliating facts are reversed and it is the King who struggles free of Orinthia. 'You are so abominably strong that I cannot break loose without hurting you,' he says.

Orinthia is Shaw's attempt at creating a sex-goddess. '*I* tread the plains of Heaven. Common women cannot come where I am,' she declares. '. . . They cheer me in the streets. When I open one of the art exhibitions or launch a new ship they crowd the place out.' The King tells her that, like royalty, 'You belong to fairyland.' But Shaw was out of love with fairyland when he wrote the play and could summon up no dazzling enchantments. Orinthia is merely bad-tempered. She dismisses all politicians as 'frumps and busybodies' and describes the Cabinet as 'riffraff' in an 'overcrowded third class carriage'. Yet this thoroughbred in her first-class carriage is also a politician. For Orinthia's bedroom is no fairyland but a battlefield for sexual politics. And it is this theme, ending with its skirmish on the floor and reaching back beyond Stella to Shaw's memories of Jenny Patterson, that connects the structurally intrusive Interlude to the rest of the play.

Orinthia is one of three queens in *The Apple Cart*. 'Everyone knows that I am the real queen. Everyone treats me as the real queen,' she announces. '. . . I am one of Nature's queens.' By Nature's queens she means those who are naturally endowed with physical superiority, and by real she means the reality of romantic appearance: she speaks for the profundity of the superficial. What she offers the King is the exploitation of democratic popularity to establish a pop-star dictatorship of the masses by beautiful people. 'What you need to make you a real king is a real queen,' she tells him. '. . . We are meant for one another: it is written across the sky that you and I are queen and king. How can you hesitate?' But Shaw turns aside this temptation: 'you must be content to be my queen in fairyland' he has King Magnus reply.

Magnus's conventional Queen is Jemima who rules over a domestic kingdom. She is part of the King's 'real workaday self', but the role is simply that of the wife-mother, her job being what Orinthia calls that of a 'common housekeeper wife' who brings up 'common healthy jolly lumps of children'. Her limitations counter-balance those of her husband whom she treats as 'a good little boy' and whose public interests she prevents from growing into round-the-clock obsessions by the imposition of her own household priorities. 'You do not always know what is good for you,' she tells him. At the end of the play, when he has 'something really big to think about' – America's proposal to annex the British Commonwealth – Jemima interrupts and leads him off, making a 'grimace of hopeless tenderness', to dress for dinner, leaving the political problem unsolved.

The name Jemima was 'not satirical', Shaw wrote to Floryan Sobieniowski. 'But it is a slightly comic name, suitable to an old maid or a very respectable and domesticated old lady.' Jemima is not developed in the second act beyond a silhouette of Charlotte; nor, islanded in her Interlude like Molly Tompkins on her lake, does Orinthia grow 'full of magic', like 'The Pilgrim of Love' from whose song her name is taken. This is because the abstract climate of Shaw's political fable sustains neither the romantic nor the domestic sources of power they represent.

The third Queen of the play is Amanda, 'a merry lady in uniform like the men' and Postmistress-General in the Cabinet. She can mimic people, she can sing funny songs, 'and that – with all respect, sir – makes me the real queen of England', she tells the King. Amanda is a performer from the music-hall stage – 'You and I are a pair, sir,' she says to Magnus. Shaw uses his knowledge of what has happened to the London theatre to warn us what might happen to English society. Amanda's popularity – intermittently like Shaw's – arises from her gift for hilarious entertainment. Her comic songs and clever mimicry cover all their targets with ridicule: even Breakages Ltd, the capitalist conglomerate that governs the country, is powerless against her. She is truly a democratic Queen in the sense that she answers the public's demand to have everything trivialized and turned into a sport – 'And thats how England is governed by yours truly,' she concludes.

But there are limits to Amanda's queenly power: she can stop anything; she can start nothing. If the country were governed responsibly, then its Queen would be Lysistrata, the Powermistress-General. 'Here am I, the Powermistress Royal,' she announces herself, but she has neither power nor royalty in this democratic dystopia. Lysistrata is a thinker – 'a grave lady in academic clothes' – who combines Beatrice Webb's devotion to public service ('I love my department: I dream of nothing but its efficiency,' she says, 'with me it comes before every personal tie') with Lady Astor's old-fashioned and assertive patriotism – 'a regular old true blue Diehard', Amanda calls her. She is the 'studious' King's one supporter in the Cabinet, his intellectual equal who in their first-act duet responds to his long oratorio on the condition of England by letting herself go with an impassioned denunciation of capitalism. Lysistrata is very like the long-lived housemaid in *Back to Methuselah*. She is the Life Force hobbled by the economic force of Breakages Ltd, the capitalist monster 'with its millions and its newspapers and its fingers in every pie'. Power has moved from government by public servants to exploitation by profiteers: it is, she admits, 'heartbreaking'. Yet in the long view Lysistrata is still an optimist. 'It is not the most ignorant national crowd that will come out on top,' she believes, 'but the best power station.'

Shaw sets *The Apple Cart* towards the end of the twentieth century so as to reveal in an extreme and aggravated form – an extravaganza – the developing plutocracy of the late 1920s. The England to which he points his audiences is one that manufactures chocolate creams, Christmas crackers and tourist trophies, and that exports golf clubs and polo ponies. Hardship and poverty have largely been abolished by sending capital abroad to places where they still exist so that Englishmen can live in comfort on the imported profits of their investments in cheap labour. The country is little more than a staging post for the movement of foreign capital: the heart has gone out of politics and into moneymaking. Less than seven per cent of the electoral register bother to vote and almost no one of ability is attracted to the political life. 'Our work is no longer respected. It is looked down on by our men of genius as dirty work,' Magnus says to his Cabinet. ' ... All the talent and genius of the country is brought up by the flood of unearned money. On that poisoned wealth talent and genius live far more luxuriously in the service of the rich than we in the service of our country.'

In such a country politics has deteriorated to Shaw's kindergarten Cabinet of squabbling nonentities, caricatures of politicians he had known: the 'snaky and censorious' Foreign Secretary Nicobar is taken from Harry Quelch, a Social Democratic Federation leader; and the aggressively assertive President of the Board of Trade Boanerges is based on John Burns who had held that post before the war. Presiding over this tomfooling nursery school is Proteus, Shaw's cartoon version of Ramsay MacDonald. Proteus is 'good for nothing else' but being Prime Minister, though the job has brought him 'to the verge of a nervous breakdown'. 'My opinion of you is that no man knows better than you when to speak and when to let others speak for you,' Magnus tells him frankly, 'when to make scenes and threaten resignation; and when to be as cool as a cucumber.' Proteus starts off in 'conciliatory' mood, continues 'impatiently' and is soon 'flinging himself back into his chair in desperation'. His tantrums and hysterics are calculated to raise or lower the temper of his absurdist Cabinet: at one moment he dashes from the room in a fit of contrived rage, knowing that the King will follow him and that they can settle their business in private. These were the exaggerated manoeuvres of Ramsay MacDonald who, according to Sidney Webb, 'always had neuritis' when things got difficult. In the second act Shaw displays MacDonald's sentimental speechifying as another of his special prime ministerial skills.

The tussle between Cabinet and Crown as to whether England shall be seen to be ruled by democratic or monarchical government is really a trial of strength between the conventional politician and the Shavian Superman as to who is better fitted to oppose Breakages Ltd. Encumbered by his Cabinet, Proteus is no match for Magnus. In the first act he threatens to appeal to the country against the King by holding a general election; but in the second act the King steals this card from him and, by threatening to abdicate and form a new political party, plays it as his own ace of trumps. Shaw denied having 'packed the cards by making the King a wise man and the minister a fool'. Both, he wrote in his Preface, 'play with equal skill; and the King wins, not by greater astuteness, but because he has the ace of trumps in his hand and knows when to play it'. But it is G.B.S. who has slipped him this winning card. Later, when reproving critics for having called the game ill-matched, he attempted to conceal this trick, by describing Proteus as a 'very elaborate study of an able man', Magnus as a 'classical example of the governing type', and then throwing out the suggestion that their controversy demonstrated in stage terms female versus male methods of ruling.

Though they may be equally astute over political tactics, the Prime Minister and the King are philosophically rather than sexually opposed and have wholly different political perspectives. For Proteus the fight is between royalty and democracy, and his aim is to come out on top. For Magnus the enemy is plutocracy. In his Olympian declaration of principle he states, 'I stand for the great abstractions: for conscience and virtue; for the eternal against the expedient; for the evolutionary appetite against the dog's gluttony; for intellectual integrity, for humanity, for the rescue of industry from commercialism and of science from professionalism.' This is the voice of the Shavian realist raised against the arch-idealist Proteus.

Some people assumed that King Magnus was a veiled portrait of King George V. 'I have a lot in common with the present monarch,' Shaw conceded, 'we are both human beings and we were both christened George, and I dare say he dislikes the name as much as I do.' Others believed a Polish journalist's report that Magnus's personality was based on that of Marshal Pilsudski. 'I never dreamt of using him, or any other living person as a model,' Shaw announced in a press statement, 'though every living ruler in the world would find a melancholy resemblance between his predicament and that of King Magnus.' He is very like Granville-Barker's King in *His Majesty*; both are parts for an actor-manager. Shaw pointed to several historical precedents: 'Charles II had manners, tact, and a precise knowledge of the cards he had in his hand and how and when to play them. So had Henri Quatre.' But when cross-examined by his biographer Hesketh Pearson, he later admitted, 'The real King Magnus is sitting within a few feet of you. Never having been offered a throne, I have had to seize one and crown myself.'

King Magnus belongs to the Shavian family tree of strong beneficent rulers. He is Caesar transported through history from *Caesar and Cleopatra*, a man whose originality confers 'an air of frankness, generosity and magnanimity by enabling him to estimate the value of truth, money, or success in any particular instance quite independently of convention and moral generalization'; he is Napoleon from *The Man of Destiny*, 'imaginative without illusions and creative without religion, loyalty, patriotism or any of the common ideals'. He is Shaw's ideal realist not blind to romanticism, an artist-philosopher and modified man of action, the pragmatic visionary combining the heroism of William Morris with the calculation of Sidney Webb: he is Shaw's fantasy of himself.

'The Apple Cart is a warning to those who are still dreaming the old dreams and listening to the old speeches,' Shaw wrote to Trebitsch. His own dreams, which started in *Major Barbara* with Undershaft, were of power: the subversive power of comedy, the persuasive power of good humour, manners, flattery; the power of intellect, quick wits, and the strength of one person against groups of people; the diminishing power of sex before the empty but growing preoccupation with power for its own sake.

Shaw's charge against democracy was that it enlarged the opportunities for philistine exploitation of idealism. Democracy, as it existed, gave political leadership to adroit humbugs with a talent for oratory who were eventually blown aside by unprincipled strong men. There are no Hitlers, Mussolinis, Stalins or Mosleys in *The Apple Cart*, for this is a play about the dangers of powerlessness. We are shown the conditions that favour the popular promotion of dictators – political leadership without powerful leaders, talk without action. For the time being, power rests with Breakages Ltd which distributes accumulating wealth with capitalism's characteristic injustice. In Shaw's analysis, such inequality leads to a moral degeneration that can be cleared away only by violent social and ideological revolution. 'I dread revolution,' says Magnus. All the Cabinet, except the women, laugh at him, but it is this dread that brings the extravaganza to a halt. If democracy gives power, as Bunyan put it, to 'him that can get it', and if Magnus will 'top the poll' as 'Able Man, not as monarch', how can democracy be said to have failed? 'I look on myself as a man with a political future,' Magnus informs Proteus as he contemplates forming a government in the House of

Commons. But this is far from being the 'desperate bid for dictatorship' described in the Preface and assumed to be the only way of defeating Breakages Ltd. The King remains in his melancholy predicament as Shaw's fantasy peters out. 'I am too old fashioned,' Magnus tells Lysistrata. 'This is a farce that younger men must finish.' And the implication is that these younger men may have to finish it with violence.

*

Because of its direct political content *The Apple Cart* was greatly talked about and emerged as one of G.B.S.'s most controversial successes. 'I imagine that Shaw has made the sensation of his life,' W. B. Yeats wrote to Lady Gregory. The Conservative press and bourgeois audiences enthusiastically hailed the play. 'The wonder is that GBS and Charlotte have not been invited to Sandringham,' Beatrice Webb drily observed. Others were as shocked as if he had taken to gin-drinking. 'Those who have walked with Shaw through half a century must take leave of him here,' wrote one critic. It appeared as if he had executed a complete political *volte face*. 'All the tyrants in Europe will delight in the play,' warned H. W. Nevinson.

To such critics *The Apple Cart* seemed pernicious in its moral and badly constructed in its dramatic form. For the first time in his theatrical career Shaw refused to give an even distribution of argument to both sides of a conflict. His Cabinet of clowns 'stand up like ninepins for his dialectical bowling' complained Ivor Brown in the *Manchester Guardian* in 1929. '... To cartoon your elected persons until they are mere gargoyles and to idealize your unelected monarch is a pitiful approach to political philosophy.' Fundamentally the same objections were to be made fifty years later in the *Guardian* by the theatre critic Michael Billington, who found the play indefensible in theory – 'a snobbish endorsement of the inherent good breeding of royalty as against the bad manners of democracy' – and aggravating in performance – there was 'something dramatically unsatisfying about a play in which a clever king is allowed to run intellectual rings round a Cabinet ... seen as a collection of hare-brained boobies'.

'It is never safe to take my plays at their suburban face value,' Shaw had warned, 'it ends in your finding in them only what you bring to them, and so getting nothing for your money.' Theatre critics treated *The Apple Cart* as a naturalistic play rather than as a political extravaganza with personified abstractions set in a No Nonsense Court, an Otherworld of muted Offenbach extrapolated from twentieth-century England. It was 'good political fun' Shaw wrote to Elgar, 'but not rich in poetry'; though 'just rich enough to show up the superficiality of the treatment', Yeats judged. 'It was the Shaw who writes letters to the papers and gives interviews, not the man who creates.'

Though G.B.S. was more than ever a significant figure in the eyes of the general public, he no longer excited young intellectuals, who were turning to the new work of Eliot and Joyce, Pound and Proust, D. H. Lawrence and Aldous Huxley. Like Magnus, G.B.S. was 'old fashioned'. With *The Apple Cart*, it seemed to Desmond MacCarthy, he had ceased to be Shaw and resembled a more remote figure – his old adversary Hilaire Belloc. The play's points were 'precisely those at which Mr Belloc has been hammering for twenty years', wrote MacCarthy: 'the humbug of modern representative government; the unreality of party conflicts; the poor quality of the men attracted to public life; the helplessness of politicians in the hands of financiers and newspaper proprietors; ... the permeation of public life by indirect corruption; the Americanization and plutocratizing of old England' all leading to the same remedy: 'a real King'.

The modern literary periodicals of the 1920s and 1930s – T. S. Eliot's *Criterion* and F. R. Leavis's *Scrutiny* – had little interest in Shaw. Yet it was by writers and literary critics, rather than critics of the theatre, that *The Apple Cart* was later to be re-evaluated. In the judgement of Edmund Wilson 'the fact that Shaw is here working exclusively with economic and political materials has caused its art to be insufficiently appreciated'. Wilson's operatic analysis may not have particularly impressed the music critic who had once parsed *Hamlet*, or the dramatist who went to see his own play and pronounced it to be 'a frightful bag of stage tricks, as old as Sophocles'. But the contemporary view that Shaw was 'contemptuous as ever of shape and form' and that his play demonstrated, in the words of Ivor Brown, that 'pattern does not matter if the word be quick and the fancy fresh' has given way to an understanding of what Margery Morgan calls its 'deliberately dislocated structure' and 'meticulous patterning of detail' influenced by cinematic technique.

The Apple Cart was to be the last of Shaw's plays to win a regular place in the standard repertory. Desmond MacCarthy ascribed the immediate success to its topicality in the late 1920s: it was about things that people happened then to be discussing. But over twenty years later Thomas Mann was to describe it as a 'stunningly clairvoyant political satire'. Who could have predicted that within a few years several Labour Cabinet Ministers would have gone into the City; that in some electorates voting would drop as low as twenty-five per cent; that, when examining the abdication of Edward VIII, Lord Altringham would consider the strategy of King Magnus with his ministers; that Lord Strabolgi would actually advocate the return of the United States to the British Empire; and that an agreement would be made with the U.S. to exchange a lease of military ports as British bases? 'It is perhaps unfortunate that circumstances have not made the play date more,' complained a *Times* reviewer in 1965. In the opinion of the ex-Kaiser it qualified Shaw as 'the best democratic brain in Europe'. For sixty years it retained an acute contemporaneity. '*The Apple Cart* delivers an exasperated uppercut to the trade unions and forecasts the economic rebellion of the Third World, with glancing references to North Sea oil and the Poulson affair,' commented Irving Wardle in *The Times* after a revival in 1977. '. . . The crisis he is writing about is still our crisis.' Major revivals of the play were to come round each decade and 'each time it is rediscovered as a play for today', added Irving Wardle in 1986.

Beatrice Webb, who had dismissed *The Apple Cart* in 1929 as frivolous and annoying, was to write in her diary on 6 September 1940: 'GBS's brilliant satirical play, *The Apple Cart*, his last popular success, seems today an amusing forecast.'

*

The popular success of *The Apple Cart* was a good omen for the Malvern Festival. On reaching London the play ran for 258 performances which exceeded the first London productions of *Saint Joan* and *Pygmalion* and everything else of Shaw's except *Fanny's First Play*.

'I always avoid places where my plays are being performed,' he had told Sobieniowski. But for Barry Jackson's Malvern he made an exception. He liked the vertical green hills, the quiet light across the great plain towards the river, the air that 'would raise the dead' – though not the waters, 'one glass of which destroys my digestion for a week'. Over the 1930s he was to be seen almost every summer in the swimming pools, striding in his knickerbockers along the terraces and up the hills with his companions labouring after him, or planting before the cameras a municipal mulberry tree in Priory Park. He was constantly on view. 'I have . . . created a general impression that I was born there,' he wrote in the 1937 Malvern Festival Book. 'In course of time visitors will be shewn for sixpence the room in which my first cries were heard . . . As the festival habit grows from the seed down in Malvern I hope to plant many mulberry trees, and end by having as many birthplaces as Homer.'

Charlotte, who enjoyed the hydros and sanatoriums, found the people rather a nuisance. For this was no holiday. 'GBS sails along & is charming to everyone, & they worship in crowds,' she told Nancy Astor, '– but I have to plan & arrange & entertain & contrive meals & eliminate the worst undesirables! Oh!! . . . It is such a little place – and no refuge!' Nevertheless, she felt happy because 'it really is wonderful to hear the plays one after the

161

other – these big things set off one another like the pictures at a one-man show which never look so well separated'. She felt comfortable, too, at the Malvern Hotel, not a charabanc destination with raucous lounge and jazz band, but more of a boarding house with an automatic lift and suites of bed-and-sitting-rooms on every floor, each with a private bathroom. Its anonymity was safeguarded by a clientele of hypochondriacs sipping Malvern water. At the sound of the gong they would all rise up, like a *corps de ballet*, and rustle through to dinner 'as if they were going to the stake'. When Shaw strode in 'he was always clasping a travel book', Beverley Nichols noticed. 'Mrs Shaw, in her turn, clutched a volume of economics.'

Barry Jackson would rent for the summer a girls' school called Lawnside where many of his guests stayed. The atmosphere of the festival was that of an extended and overflowing country-house party. There were folk dances in the Assembly Rooms, people playing on the putting and bowling greens, garden parties at Lawnside, boating on the lake, Billy Gammon's syncopated band, starlight suppers and 'the scent and sounds from a thousand gardens'. Malvern became a 'non-stop twenty-four hour a day festival'. G.B.S. loved taking the cast for drives around the hills and sometimes on to Droitwich, where he ducked into the brine baths, motoring back with the salt still in his beard. He would read his plays to the actors before rehearsals which, when the stage was being used by technicians, took place in the town Gas Office and sometimes drifted past midnight. In the auditorium itself, the actors could see his illuminated pen flashing as he made notes. He was determined to make the Malvern experiment another chapter in the reform of the English theatre. By 1931 its scope was broadened by the inclusion of works from other dramatists; in 1934 it was prolonged into a four-week occasion; between 1929 and 1939 it established itself as the major off-season theatrical event in England and an international showcase for playwrights. Sixty-five plays by forty British and foreign playwrights (evenly distributed between the past and the present) were produced over that period. More than twenty of these plays were by Shaw, including world premières of *Geneva* (1938) and '*In Good King Charles's Golden Days*' (1939) and the first English productions of *The Apple Cart* (1929), *Too True to be Good* (1932), *The Simpleton of the Unexpected Isles* (1935) and *Buoyant Billions* (1949).

Though he described himself as a 'booster of festivals because they are the markets for my plays', Shaw would also support the festival in years when none of his plays were being performed. In 1936 he celebrated his eightieth birthday at Malvern accepting 'nothing over sixpence' from the cast – a razor blade, sealing wax, ink ('I gave him a coat-hanger from Woolworth's,' Wendy Hiller remembered. 'I gave him a pencil-sharpener,' remembered Mavis Walker, 'shaped like a globe of the world'). He continued visiting Malvern until the following year (the last time Barry Jackson directed the Festival) when he veered off to Sidmouth. 'I shall not come to Malvern this year if I can get in elsewhere,' he wrote to Will Rothenstein in 1939. 'I am tired of it.'

Though the Malvern Festival had effervesced into a national celebration, it was never popular locally. Resenting the invasion of theatre people, the natives of Malvern refused to celebrate their festival. The licensing hours in public houses were not extended and no restaurants stayed open after the evening performances. Despite added revenue, the Town Council contributed nothing until, after Barry Jackson's retirement, the future of the festival became uncertain.

Nevertheless the festival habit grew. Though the Malvern Festival itself was not revived with complete success after the Second World War, it had been the forerunner of an age of festivals that was to flourish forty and fifty years later and carry on the dramatic out-of-London development that Shaw and Barry Jackson had originally sought. G.B.S. had never wanted the festival to be a memorial to himself. When asked in the 1940s whether one of the aims of post-war Malvern should be the building of a Shaw Theatre, he replied: 'Even among the playwrights I was not the only pebble on the beach . . . The Festival was founded by Sir Barry Jackson and by nobody else . . . Malvern must look to its present and future, not dream of its past. I am only one of Ibsen's Ghosts.'

*

'One of the choicest attractions' of the Malvern Festival was Edward Elgar. During rehearsals of *The Apple Cart* Shaw had invited him over from his home near Worcester, adding that Barry Jackson was bent on getting from him an overture to the play. 'My own view was that six bars of yours would extinguish (or upset) the A.C. and turn the Shaw festival into an Elgar one,' he wrote, 'but that it would be a jolly good thing . . . ' Over twenty years earlier, and long before the playwright and composer had met, Shaw had responded in the *St James's Gazette* to a request for an opera libretto by invoking Elgar's name. 'I wonder whether Elgar would turn his hand to opera?' he enquired. 'I have always played a little with the idea of writing a libretto, but though I have had several offers nothing has come of it.' Shaw had not appreciated then what he called Elgar's 'hatred and contempt for singers'. Later they would discuss setting one of Shaw's plays to music, 'but I think we agreed to my view that he could do nothing with a play except what his Falstaff did with Shakespeare's', Shaw told the composer Rutland Boughton.

So there was no overture to *The Apple Cart*; but Elgar came to Malvern and, opening the Bernard Shaw Exhibition in the public library, told his audience that G.B.S. really knew more about music than he did. Shaw retaliated handsomely by admitting that 'although I am rather a conceited man I am quite sincerely and genuinely humble in the presence of Sir Edward Elgar. I recognize a greater art than my own and a greater man than I can ever hope to be'. Not to be outdone, Elgar warned the press that some people thought his friend Shaw rather fierce. 'Nothing could be farther from the truth. Shaw was a most remarkable man; he was the best friend to any artist, the kindest and possibly the dearest fellow on earth.'

These statements were more than reciprocal civilities for public consumption. They represented what each had come to feel about the other, and gave Elgar the chance to correct his initially hostile opinion of G.B.S. as 'hopelessly wrong, as all these fellows are, on fundamental things ... an amusing liar, but not much more'. That opinion, arrived at following an early performance of *Man and Superman*, had not softened much after he saw *The Devil's Disciple* which 'lacks conviction', he decided. 'Shaw is very *amateurish* in many ways.'

They had met in March 1919 at a lunch given by Lalla Vandervelde, wife of the Belgian socialist leader, which also included Roger Fry. Elgar's mind was so overloaded with his music ('which was quite inseparable from orchestration', Shaw observed) that he made nothing of other subjects. One subject he made nothing of that day was painting – 'Damned imitation' he called it – and turning with a growl from Fry's insignificant formulations, he appeared to make the wonderful discovery that Bernard Shaw and a music critic called 'Corno di Bassetto', who long ago had amused and fascinated him, were the same person. In fact he had praised Shaw's musical criticism in the *Star* and the *World* during a lecture on critics in 1905, but seems to have separated in his mind this combatant musicologist from the irreligious dramatist.

Shaw judged Elgar to be a great orchestral technician with as irresistible a vocation as Mozart's. Where English music was concerned, he had told readers of the *Morning Post* in 1911, 'the history of original music, broken off by the death of Purcell, begins again with Sir Edward Elgar'. After a century of imitation Handel, Mendelssohn and Spohr, Elgar's music had come as a new voice, free from the pedantry of Parry and Stanford, giving out a sound 'as characteristically English as a country house and stable are characteristically English'. All this had been written before their meeting in 1919.

A few days later Elgar invited the Shaws to Severn House, his home in Hampstead, to hear three of his chamber works including the Piano

Quintet. 'The Quintet knocked me over at once,' Shaw wrote the next day. '... There are some piano embroideries on a pedal point that didn't sound like a piano or anything else in the world, but quite beautiful ... they require a touch which is peculiar to yourself.' It was this peculiarity that Shaw sought to define and celebrate at the end of the year in a eulogistic essay which described Elgar as the man who was carrying on Beethoven's business. 'Elgar's Cockaigne overture combines every classic quality of a concert overture with every lyric and dramatic quality of the overture to Die Meistersinger,' he wrote. '... You may hear all sorts of footsteps in it, and it may tell you all sorts of stories; but it is classical music as Beethoven's Les Adieux sonata is classical music: it tells you no story external to itself and yourself.'

'... his range is so Handelian that he can give the people a universal melody or march with as sure a hand as he can give the Philharmonic Society a symphonic adagio ... Here [*Gerontius*] was no literary paper instrument-ation, no muddle and noise, but an absolutely new energy ...

'The enormous command of existing resources, which this orchestral skill of his exemplifies, extends over the whole musical field, and explains the fact that, though he has a most active and curious mind, he does not appear in music as an experimenter and explorer, like Scriabin and Schönberg. He took music where Beethoven left it, and where Schumann and Brahms found it.'

This tribute delighted Elgar's wife, hitherto suspicious of what she thought of as Shaw's atheism. Her death three months later, which finished Elgar as 'an oratoriowright', seems to have redoubled Shaw's championing of his work. In the summer of 1922, following a meagrely-attended performance of *The Apostles* by the Leeds Choral Union, he erupted in *The Daily News*:

'The Apostles is one of the glories of British music: indeed it is unique as a British work ...

'I distinctly saw six people in the stalls, probably with complimentary tickets ...

'The occasion was infinitely more important than the Derby, than Goodwood, than the Cup Finals, than the Carpentier fights, than any of the occasions on which the official leaders of society are photographed and cinematographed laboriously shaking hands ...

'The performance was none the less impressive, nor the music the less wonderful.

'... I apologize to posterity for living in a country where the capacity and tastes of schoolboys and sporting costermongers are the measure of metropolitan culture.'

Shaw's Irish disgust matched Elgar's English disappointment. Approximately the same age, they had both initially been 'discovered' in Germany, and were now beginning to go out of fashion in Britain, the audiences for Elgar's oratorios disappearing in the 1920s as they were to disappear in the 1930s for Shaw's extravaganzas. Shaw's pugnacious loyalty to Elgar was invigorated by a sense of cultural affinity. Though proudly unacademic, both of them seemed to have read whole libraries. But while they appeared to take their inspiration from the skies, they continued using structures perfected by their predecessors.

Their friendship ripened in old age when, after the Malvern Festivals began, they saw each other regularly. 'Shaw and Elgar dearly loved one another,' observed Harriet Cohen. 'The humility and outright admiration that G.B.S. showed to Elgar was a touching experience.' Like the artist Wilson Steer, Elgar was built on a model dear to most Englishmen. You would never guess that the one made up tunes or that the other muddled along with paint. Both resembled characteristic country gentlemen with, perhaps, some military connections. Wilson Steer actually carried his painting materials in a cricket bag ('I get better service that way'); Elgar, who could talk about every unmusical subject on earth, 'from pigs to Elizabethan literature', gave the impression of not knowing 'a fugue from a *fandango*'. And yet, Shaw wrote, 'Music was his religion and his intellect and almost his everything.' Elgar prided himself, however, on being a considerable playgoer. It was true that he had never stuck out *Romeo and Juliet* to the end (he used to leave when Mercutio was slain), but he would travel almost anywhere to see the comedian Jack Hulbert perform, and he came to relish the Shavian productions at Malvern. 'Can't you engineer that I sit with you for the first performance of *Too True to be Good* – my last chance,' he appealed to Shaw in the summer of 1932. 'I was old and remember the glory of being with you for *The Apple Cart*.' As Master of the King's Musick, he was a martyr to conventionality, insisting that Shaw and Charlotte were correctly dressed for these occasions and for his own musical performances at Gloucester, Hereford and Worcester. 'The Protestant Three Choirs were the centre of his musical activities, especially Worcester,' Shaw later remembered: 'to hear The Music Makers conducted there by him was a wonderful experience.' Shaw's letters to Elgar are full of music and reveal his knowledge and admiration of Elgar's work. In 1930 Elgar dedicated his Severn Suite to Shaw who, 'hugely flattered and touched', noted in his inscribed copy, 'so my name may last as long as his own'. After hearing the piece 'only eight times' at the Crystal Palace Band Competition in September that year, Shaw wrote to Elgar, 'Nobody could have guessed from looking at the score and thinking of the thing as a toccata for brass band how beautiful and serious the work is as abstract music.'

Shaw tried to get Elgar's co-operation when he rewrote (below right) the second verse of the National Anthem, for which Elgar had composed an orchestral arrangement in 1902.

O Lord our God arise!	O Lord our God Arise
Scatter his enemies,	All our salvation lies
And make them fall!	In! Thy! Great! Hand! (à la Elgar)
Confound their politics,	Centre his (her) thoughts on Thee
Frustrate their knavish tricks;	Let him (her) God's captain
On Thee our hopes we fix,	(handmaid) be
God save us all!	Thine to Eternity
	God save the King (Queen)

The war had 'killed Muscular Christianity' and created the opportunity for such a 'glaringly needed change'. This was the sort of brash Shavian statement that had upset Elgar in the old days. But after his wife's death, and as his religious faith faded, he began to respond to Shaw's bracing iconoclasm. 'G.B.S.'s politics are, to me, appalling, but he is the kindest-hearted, gentlest man I have met ... to young people he is kind,' he had written in 1921 to Sidney Colvin. But by the late 1920s, when they campaigned together against a restrictive new Music Copyright Bill, Elgar was beginning to look at Shaw's politics as a source of Shavian generosity, and the Shavian merging of art with sociology as the basis of his comradeship with all artists. 'If I were king, or Minister of Fine Arts,' Shaw had written, 'I would give Elgar an annuity of a thousand a year on condition that he produce a symphony every eighteen months.'

Elgar had opened himself up to a Shavian education by rather nervously enquiring what 'capital' was after the publication of *The Intelligent Woman's Guide*. By way of explanation, and turning the subject back to music, Shaw replied that Elgar's products were infinitely consumable without limitation or deterioration. He then proposed an Elgarian Financial Symphony: 'Allegro: Impending Disaster. Lento mesto: Stony Broke. Scherzo: Light Heart and Empty Pocket. Allo con brio: Clouds Clearing.'

Whenever Elgar needed the clouds to clear, the Shaws shone down on him. 'Don't let yourself think dark thoughts,' Charlotte urged him. And G.B.S., who made him a present of £1,000 early in the 1930s, persuaded the BBC to commission a Third Symphony for another £1,000.

'He [Elgar] does not know that I am meddling in his affairs and yours in this manner,' he wrote to John Reith, Director General of the BBC. '... but I do know that he has still a lot of stuff in him that could be released if he could sit down to it without risking his livelihood.' Welcoming this commission in a letter to *The Times* at the end of 1932, Shaw added: 'But is it not a pity that Sir Edward has had to wait so long for the advent of a public administrator capable of rising to the situation? The forthcoming symphony will be his third: it should be his ninth.'

The Third Symphony was never finished because of the collapse in Elgar's health. Shaw and Charlotte had tried to persuade him to go to an osteopath to manipulate his spine. A rumbustious American whose 'resemblance to an ophicleide would please you' was Shaw's choice, though Charlotte preferred a Chinese virtuoso from San Francisco who played expertly upon the bones. Alternatively, there was homeopathy in the person of Raphael Roche, a sensational unregistered practitioner from a well-known Jewish family of musicians (including Mendelssohn and Moscheles) who had a craze for healing which he successfully exercised on a hydrocele of Shaw's, using what appeared to be a grain or two of powdered sugar. In 'the depths of pain' Elgar seems to have felt that the Shaws were trying to cure him with laughter. In 1933 he entered a nursing home and Shaw, resisting an impulse to rush down and rescue him from the 'damn doctors', was left trusting to Elgar's mighty Life Force.

'Having friends like you,' Charlotte had written in 1932, 'is the one thing in life worth having when one arrives at the age of GBS & myself.' The following year Elgar returned the compliment: 'the world seems a cold place to me when you are both away'.

Shaw described his death from cancer on 23 February 1934 as 'world-shaking' and far too early. But there was still the music. At the Gloucester Three Choirs Festival in the summer of 1934, he and Charlotte heard *The Kingdom*. 'I cannot tell you how we all miss Edward Elgar,' Charlotte wrote afterwards to Nancy Astor. 'We loved him ... & when another man got up into the Conductor's Chair it was hard to bear.'

[3]

...I am honored and famous and rich, which is very good fun for the other people. But as I have to do all the hard work, and suffer an ever increasing multitude of fools gladly, it does not feel any better than being reviled, infamous, and poor, as I used to be.

Shaw to Frank Harris (7 April 1927)

Shaw's travels abroad at the end of the 1920s became a sequence of romantic flights and theatrical explorations. 'I want to retire; and I ought to retire, but I can't,' he complained to T. E. Lawrence. 'I shall be pressed to death under my reputation and my royalties.' In the summer of 1928 Charlotte arranged a long detour, almost seven weeks on the French Riviera. It was to be a holiday rigorously dedicated to 'sun baths and sea baths' and the banishment of work. From Agay they crawled into Cap d'Antibes at the crest of a heatwave, 'hotter than I have ever imagined any infernal regions', Charlotte objected. Once they had become acclimatized, they dragged themselves off on excursions to Menton, Monte Carlo, Nice and the mountainous hinterland of Haute Provence; and every day they plunged into the Mediterranean – 'even I can swim, swim, swim – & never tire', Charlotte discovered. 'You feel you cant sink in this sea. And when you get out you can lie – nuda veritas – on the rocks & bake. G.B.S. loves it – & that is why we stay.'

He loved it and hated it: 'one never knows whether the morning will find us smiling in a paradise', he wrote to Blanche Patch, 'or groaning in a purgatory'. The sea and mountains were a paradise; the people made it purgatory. Even Charlotte, with her experience of society, had never heard such blatherings. Their slang streamed along like helpless 'baby talk', and, she noticed, 'they wear no clothes'. G.B.S. appeared to her 'like a lamb among wolves – among all the legs, & (much too open) arms'. Defensively he began to reproach himself for spending half his time indulging in childish things and the other half going nearly mad. 'This Riviera is hell on earth with the scum of the earth stranded on the beach,' he burst out uncharacteristically in a letter to Trebitsch. '... I hate the whole human race. So does Charlotte mostly.'

What Charlotte called 'a slight amelioration' arrived with their various visitors. Lady Rhondda came, a 'real woman' properly clothed, a feminist and the proprietress of *Time and Tide* (for which Shaw wrote regularly in the 1920s and 1930s); and so did Troubetzkoy, devastated by the death of his Swedish wife and soon to turn from sculpture to the composition of music and a vegetarian stage melodrama. There were the Mosleys too, Oswald fresh from an International Congress in Brussels, Cynthia an Atalanta who 'queens it with the best' on the beaches, and both of them comically nervous of exposing themselves to press photographs. It was 'Dear Mr Mosley', Charlotte told Nancy Astor, who abetted her plot to carry G.B.S. off to Geneva, 'a decent, proper town', for twelve days early in September.

But the most significant meeting that summer was with Frank Harris, now living in Nice. While the reputation of G.B.S. was blazing forth ever more intensely, Harris's fortunes had gone crashing downhill. In England before the war he had been declared bankrupt and sent on a libel charge to Brixton gaol. During the war he had emigrated to the United States where he published *England or Germany?*, a series of anti-British articles that, unfortunately tipping Germany as the legitimate victor, had him ostracized in New York and branded a traitor in London. His decline as author and editor was accelerated by an erratic biography of Oscar Wilde that brought him nothing but trouble, and a series of apocryphal 'Contemporary Portraits' first published in his new American magazine, *Pearson's*, which, after threatening to fold each month, eventually did so.

'Your most interesting book will be your autobiography,' Shaw had predicted in 1915. After the war, Harris set about retrieving his bank balance and literary prestige by moving to France and acting on Shaw's advice. 'I long for peace, long to resume my life in France with a sort of maniacal intensity,' he divulged to Shaw. '...I am going to see if a man can tell truth naked and unashamed about himself and his amorous adventures in the world.' The first volume of his notorious *My Life and Loves* had been seized and burnt by customs officials; the second volume brought him to court on a charge of corrupting public morals. 'Il faut souffrir pour être Casanova,' Shaw reminded him.

G.B.S. was the one eminent contemporary in England who remained loyal to Harris. 'It is astonishing what bad company advanced views may get one into,' he observed. He believed that Harris had offended against an English class system that was his own enemy too. *England or Germany?* had presented a reasonably sound exposure of the pervasiveness of English snobbery and the power of the English oligarchy, but it had been devastatingly ill-timed. Shaw did not admire Harris, did not regard him as a fugleman for free speech, as he regarded Freud, Joyce, D. H. Lawrence and even Radclyffe Hall; he did not even like him, except for his humorous bathos. But he felt some kinship with Harris's sense of exile and did not want to see him penalized for his Anglophobia. The more that Harris was cold-shouldered by the British literati, the more G.B.S. assisted him – in his fashion. 'I always hate the people I have given money to,' he informed

Harris, 'and they – very properly – hate me.' So instead of handing him money, he provided him with words. 'For God's sake give me deathless words,' Harris had appealed from the United States. Shaw responded with numerous unpaid 'lines of rubbish' and pages of 'drivel' to fill up the columns of *Pearson's*, as well as with a fascinating account of his meetings with Wilde, which Harris was able to use in a cheap reissue of his biography. Then, when Harris sent over for correction a 'Contemporary Portrait' of Shaw, G.B.S. fired back as an alternative pen portrait a brilliant pastiche of Harris entitled 'How Frank Ought to Have Done It'. 'I cannot thank you enough for it,' Harris acknowledged. '...You are the first person I think in my journey through the world who has shown any wish to surpass me in generosity.'

To be thus surpassed troubled Harris who knew himself to be twice the man Shaw was and could not frankly conceal this knowledge. Surely his 'Contemporary Portraits' were 'about the best portraits of living men ever done', and his *Oscar Wilde* probably 'the best biography extant'? And yet, he accused Shaw, 'you have made more out of your worst play than I have made out of all my books put together'. How was this possible? They had, for example, both written plays about St Joan and yet for some reason Harris could not puzzle out, theatres round the world persisted in staging Shaw's *Saint Joan* and never his own *Joan la Romée*. It was worse than puzzling: it was inexplicable. Unless, of course, Shaw largely owed his reputation to Harris's proselytizing. 'I am doing my best to spread the true gospel about Bernard Shaw,' he had written, '...[and] make you more and more listened to in America as the highest voice in England.'

Harris counted on G.B.S. being persistent in his gratitude. As he grew more dependent, so his tone dived from the boastful into the pathetic. 'I have no country and no kin ... I lost caste in England and gradually everyone turned against me ... All the friends who would have helped me, are dead or out of my ken. I have no one I can turn to except you.' What he wanted from Shaw, he hardly knew. Of course he wanted more letters. 'If you only knew the pleasure I take in your letters you would write oftener,' he explained. '...You don't know what your letter has meant to me. I ventured to publish most of it without asking you because it was so interesting.' But there was a limit to what he could raise from publishing or selling Shaw's correspondence: 'Letters are unsatisfactory,' he concluded. He wanted Shaw's help with publishers. 'I could surely do an Edition of Shakespeare better than any living man,' he hazarded, '...you could get me this Shakespeare commission at once.' But Shaw calculated that such scholarly hack work 'would not keep you in bootlaces'. Harris also wanted to mine Shaw's good will and find some rich new vein. Shakespeare had failed him; Wilde had failed him; and in old age he was beginning to fail himself.

They met at Harris's villa in Nice in the second week of August 1928. Shaw came alone because Charlotte, he happily explained, could not be seen lunching with such a monster. Harris had no idea of the animosity his buccaneering manners and pornographic language provoked: 'his naïveté on such points is incredible'. Shaw came out of curiosity to observe someone whom, he now admitted, he had seriously misjudged: 'Like everyone else, I took you to be much more a man of the world than you really were.'

For Harris their day together was in the nature of a reconnaissance, just as their double-act over his 'Contemporary Portraits' had unwittingly been a dress-rehearsal ('I am certain I could do a readable book on you,' he had then notified Shaw). A little later he took off for New York. 'Your vogue in America is extraordinary, almost incredible,' he reported. 'The *New York Times* declares that you are the greatest Englishman since Shakespeare, and this is the opinion one hears on all sides.' To this reputation Harris now proposed hitching his wagon by getting himself appointed Shaw's biographer. 'Abstain from such a desperate enterprise,' Shaw hastily replied. '...I wont have you write my life on any terms: Nellie [Harris's wife] would do it far better.'

Harris signed up to write Shaw's life with far less enthusiasm than he had felt for his indecent masterwork, *My Life and Loves*. But he needed an old-age pension, and by 1929 was forced to accept the fact that only for a book about G.B.S., written with Shaw's co-operation, would any publisher give him a decent advance on royalties. Shaw's absolute refusal was a desperate blow. All this exaggerated success, he protested, had gone to Shaw's head. Such insults delighted G.B.S. who wanted to know to what other part of his body success should have travelled. 'You are honoured and famous and rich – I lie here crippled and condemned and poor,' Harris pleaded. But Shaw seemed briskly unaffected by Harris's threats and pleas. He could have resolved the matter by sending Harris a cheque, but he was committed to the habit of supporting him by his pen. 'I am never more generous than I can afford to be,' he had written. '...I can't manage the thousand dollars: I am far too rich.' He was to pay dearly for such jokes as the 'dreaded biography' advanced and began to encircle him. 'The truth is I have a horror of biographers,' he wrote. 'The Shaw legend had become so troublesome at one time that in self-defence I had to supply information enough to Archibald Henderson to enable him to produce his huge volume, which is only a colossally expanded extract from Who's Who? But I could not force myself to read the proofs for him; and to this day it remains mostly a sealed book to me ...'

'A book by you would be a very different affair, though, like Henderson you would find it enormously more troublesome than you think. And it is not your job. Every man has a blind side; and I should catch you just on it . . . my heart is never in the right – meaning the expected – place.

'Besides, it is premature. Only two of the ladies are dead.

'Think no more of it. And forgive me.'

But Harris could not afford to be forgiving. Henderson's twenty-year-old reference work was well out of date and, besides, 'there is hardly a gleam of Shaw in the whole tome'. This new biography was a matter of life and death – Shaw's life and Harris's death. 'If it were not for my wife I should make up my mind to end the silly pilgrimage from nowhere to nothing,' Harris had written. '. . . I want Shaw to live in my book from the first page till the last and I wish everyone to take a new interest in you.'

As he began to give ground, Shaw vicariously divided the problem between Charlotte's interests and those of Nellie Harris. To put his Life into the hands of a writer whose own memoirs (the opening volume voluptuously illustrated with naked girls) had been burnt by Charlotte, page by page 'so that not a comma should escape the flames', was surely too rich a paradox to swallow. In any event, Charlotte was a 'member of the firm' and would never permit such a Cyranesque gesture. But Nellie's interests were a different matter and Charlotte had no answer when Shaw echoed Charles II's deathbed appeal: 'Let not poor Nellie starve.'

For G.B.S. himself there was one further consideration. As they came to the end of the 1920s, he began to suspect that Harris might be better attuned than himself to the current interests of the reading public. And it was true that there had been many unsolved problems raised in 1911 by Henderson who had proposed putting together another biography for the 1930s. Then there was the tragic case of Demetrius O'Bolger.

*

Demetrius O'Bolger 'is an Irishman: a professor of literature at an American university', Shaw had told Harris. He had originally approached G.B.S. for advice on how to become a playwright, convincing him by his proposal to add an extra act to *Fanny's First Play* that he was fundamentally mad. His study of Shaw's own plays had begun in 1912 as a thesis for the Graduate Department of the University of Pennsylvania. 'He got Shaw-struck, and extracted a great deal of autobiographical information from me by sending me questionnaires,' Shaw explained to Harris. His policy was to follow up loose threads in the studies by Henderson, Chesterton and others, including Shaw's writings about himself. 'I determined to run out the thread of his home surroundings,' O'Bolger wrote. '...I thought I saw not a few reticences ... and I determined to penetrate them and systematize the results if Mr Shaw were willing to give me the necessary information.'

And Shaw was willing. After all, what could there be to fear from a madman? O'Bolger would send him a sheet of paper with a question typed at the top, and G.B.S. would fill up the rest of the page with an answer sometimes extending to five or six hundred words. 'O'Bolger got this solely through his diligence in study and his persistence in cross-examination,' Shaw instructed Harris. But it was Shaw's persistence in the witness-box that was really remarkable. His help swelled into a positive obstacle preventing his biographer from ever completing anything. Often and often O'Bolger believed he had completed his book, though never to anyone's satisfaction. He completed it, for example, in February 1916, only to receive a little later that month, twenty-nine closely typewritten pages from Shaw, describing the circumstances of his youth and the household in which he grew up. 'The death of my mother set me free to tell O'B. more than I could allow Henderson to publish in her lifetime,' Shaw revealed to Harris, who was then struggling with his 'Contemporary Portrait' of G.B.S. and feeling dismayed that he could not get 'what you have told O'Bolger and will not tell me'. But O'Bolger had drawn up his questionnaires from the sort of detailed examination of Henderson's *Life* and Shaw's work that was beyond Harris. He 'cast all delicacy to the winds, and asked me a heap of most intimate questions', Shaw wrote again to Harris. '...I once more sat down and spent a lot of valuable time answering these questions.' Never had G.B.S. been so forthcoming – but 'I do not send you the stuff for publication as it stands', he ominously added. '...You can avail yourself of the information, and quote a phrase on occasion ... subject to any correction that I may suggest when I read your MS.'

He felt obliged to read the manuscript so that he could eliminate any 'ridiculous constructions and surmises' that might arise from O'Bolger's inquisitiveness. 'Demetrius will presently slosh out what I have given him in what will be practically an appendix to Henderson,' he wearily predicted in a letter to Harris, 'and then, if you can stand it, and have any more questions to ask, I may gossip some more, as there are matters that would have a special prosperity in your ears.'

O'Bolger had celebrated the end of the First World War by completing his book for the third time. Receiving an offer a few months after Armistice Day from Harpers to publish a revised text, he notified Shaw and sat down to make a fourth draft, working 'till the nerves of neck and the back of my head could no longer stand the strain'. Harpers seemed delighted: but Shaw was not delighted. Having examined the contract, he declared that he would treat direct quotation as an infringement of copyright 'and hand the stuff over to Frank Harris', whereupon Harpers quickly cancelled their contract. Shaw had 'delivered a sound blow for principle's sake', O'Bolger observed. 'He had saved me from being fleeced by saving me from being published.' In a frantic begging-and-abusing letter, O'Bolger appealed to G.B.S. to change his mind. 'Dont be scared,' Shaw responded. 'You are suffering from a sort of delirium tremens brought on by overwork . . . Do not lose your head and try to drown your rescuer.' But when another American publisher, showing interest, asked for a Shavian Preface to the book, Shaw declined to authorize it in this way; after all, Archibald Henderson was his authorized biographer.

What had masqueraded as a question of contracts now settled on the matter of the text. As he indicated to Harris, Shaw felt a need after his mother died to gain control of his formative years, but he did not wish to see all he had spilled out immediately given away in print. So when O'Bolger sent him the yet-again-completed manuscript, he hung on to it, and it was still in his possession in the early 1920s. 'I somehow cannot make up my mind to send that blasted MS of yours back without another look at it.'

One difficulty was that this madman, Shaw discovered, was a complete duffer. And there was another factor that seemed to make the whole business more threatening. O'Bolger, he informed Harris, 'was the son of an Irish inspector of police; and he proceeded to investigate the case precisely as his father would have done'. His hereditary enquiries caused considerable offence to Charlotte – besides which, he also wrote like a policeman. This 'explains everything', Shaw informed O'Bolger. ' . . . your treatment of my mother and father as suspicious characters in custody, your rejection of all my statements as unsupported by evidence and coming from a tainted source &c &c.' 'I am not qualified to advise you medically,' he went on, before advancing a diagnosis. His biographer was suffering from something not uncommon in Ireland which could be identified as a Resentment Complex. He listed the symptoms. 'You have the resentment of the poor man against the rich man, of the Irish Catholic against the Irish Protestant,' he began, ' . . . and God knows how many private resentments unknown to me of which you have made me and my father the whipping boys and my mother the whipping girl . . . '

'You have, in particular, achieved a portrait of a most horrible woman whom you allege was my mother, with a sordid husband, and a disingenuous son, forming the sort of Irish interior which you most hate and despise as typifying every social injustice from which you and your people ever suffered.'

What this letter affirms is Shaw's genuine distress: O'Bolger had 'produced a book about me which began by describing my mother as an adulteress', he complained to Harris, 'and my father as a despicable fortune hunter'. O'Bolger's 'interior' had turned the Shavian paradoxes inside out and come up with an ugly picture of those Dublin years that Shaw himself had told Ellen Terry were 'frightful in realities'. The 'worst of it was', Shaw added in a letter to Harris, 'that I could not deny that the information I had given him bore [upon] his construction'.

So they reached deadlock. Shaw allowed that O'Bolger was entitled to his opinions, but not to Shaw's endorsement of them to the extent of gaining immunity from the copyright and libel laws. Under these conditions no publisher would agree to print the book until O'Bolger submitted to the process of exhaustive Shavian editing and emendation that Archibald Henderson accepted. 'Unfortunately this involved practically rewriting his book for him,' Shaw later pointed out; 'and for that it was impossible for me to find time.' So the manuscript, now in its fifth unpublished draft and entitled *The Real Shaw*, remained suspended: a great vexation to them both. 'You will certainly be the death of me,' Shaw cried out with one of his most lethal paradoxes. In the summer of 1923, O'Bolger suddenly died. 'I do not know whether to be glad or sorry,' Shaw commented. ' . . . The situation was a painful one for me . . . a great worry for him; and now it has helped to worry him into his grave . . . A tragic business; but he was unhelpable: one could only look on and be sorry one could not rescue him.'

But it was not too late to rescue Frank Harris. Had there ever been such a cautionary tale for a biographer? 'Harpers could not dare to publish this [biography] without my consent; and equally of course I could not consent,' he reported to Harris; 'so the unfortunate author died of disappointment, aided by pernicious anaemia, cursing me for ruining him.'

*

O'Bolger had made no startling discoveries about Shaw's early years in Ireland, but his enquiries had pressed on a bruise, disturbed G.B.S., and made him deftly rearrange some of the facts. 'And now you want me to start again,' he exclaimed to Harris. 'I had rather die misunderstood.' He knew that by making Harris his 'trumpeter' he risked multiplying such misunderstandings and directing everyone's attention to his 'personal history', which 'I have never admitted as more than the merest accident'. But Harris 'forced my hand'. Regretting the day when 'to avoid romantic misunderstandings' he had begun answering O'Bolger's questionnaires, and feeling like a 'dog returning to his vomit', he began early in 1930 to follow up his O'Bolger correspondence with a succession of auto-biographical letters to Harris.

While taking up Demetrius, Shaw had been careful not to let down Archibald, admitting him into a one-sided collaboration called *Table-Talk of G.B.S.* first published in 1925 by O'Bolger's would-be publisher, Harpers. This series of alleged 'Conversations on Things in General between Bernard Shaw and his Biographer' had actually been compiled from Shaw's written answers to questions submitted by Henderson, then augmented by a number of Shaw's own self-answered questions, all these 'dialogues' being comprehensively revised by Shaw in proof. Though the sole authorial credit for this fabrication was given on the title page to 'Archibald Henderson Ph.D., DCL, LL D', this did not prevent Shaw from paying over £100 in damages and costs for a technical libel Henderson had made on the Welsh novelist Caradoc Evans. 'You need not hesitate to let me have my own way in this matter,' he generously insisted, overriding his biographer's protests. '... it is quite intolerable that you should suffer in the matter.'

But there was no stopping Henderson from preparing a revised and expanded version of his *Who's Who* biography called, to Shaw's disgust, *Playboy and Prophet*. By 1930 over fifty works about G.B.S. had been published all over the world. The market was saturated, he protested, which accounted for their *Table-Talk* having been 'a complete flop'. Yet Henderson was not to be deterred. The best compromise Shaw could negotiate was a healthy delay until 1932, plus an agreement that he should thoroughly vet the text.

G.B.S.'s hand had been somewhat weakened in these negotiations by his involvement with Harris who 'is a sensitive creature (absurd as it sounds)', he apologized to Henderson. Harris was sensitive to the galling fact that there was more publisher's money in Shaw's tame life than in his own adventurings. His preparations for this last literary expedition were eccentric. He posted a letter to *The Times Literary Supplement* soliciting 'quips, inscriptions, autobiographs'. He also hired an editor by the name of Frank Scully, later an authority on how to spot flying saucers and have 'fun in bed'. According to Scully, it was Scully who actually wrote the book; certainly it is dedicated to him, and this part he may have written – he was a man, Shaw later learnt, 'incapable of making any precise statement whatever'. Nellie Harris noted in her diary on 17 January 1931 that 'Scully wants to employ labour – a competent man who knows how to write because now they have all the "material".' At the beginning of May, the two Franks had cobbled together over 100,000 words, a good fifteen per cent of which were by G.B.S. 'If you publish a word of mine I'll have the law on you,' Shaw threatened. Harris was panic-stricken. The lesson of O'Bolger had meant nothing to him – indeed, he had received an advance on royalties for the guarantee of Shaw's words rather than his own. And Shaw was obliged to relent, if only because Nellie and Frank 'were in rather desperate circumstances' he explained to Henderson. However, he cautioned Harris that 'if there is one expression in this book of yours that cannot be read aloud at a confirmation class, you are lost for ever. Your life and loves are just being forgotten,' he went on, 'and your old reputation as a considerable and respectable man of letters reviving. This book is your chance of recovering your tall hat ... So brush up your frock coat; buy a new tie; and remember that your life now depends on your being Francis Harris, Esquire ... '

In this way the subject put himself in charge of his biographer's reputation: the book had to be respectable for Harris's sake. Frank, the ruffian, must be removed. 'Bury him,' Shaw commanded in April 1931. 'If you dont the parish will.' Four months later, Frank Harris was buried in the British Cemetery at Caucade. Shaw sent the widow Nellie a cheque: and Nellie Harris arranged for G.B.S. to be sent the galley proofs.

'I have had to do many odd jobs in my time; but this one is quite the oddest,' Shaw wrote in a postscript to the book, where he gives the impression of having corrected the finished proof sheets. In a letter to Nellie he comes nearer to explaining what he had actually done: 'Frank knew hardly more about my life history than I knew about yours; and the mixture of his guesses with the few things I told him produced the wildest results.'

'I have had to fill in the prosaic facts in Frank's best style, and fit them to his comments as best I could; for I have most scrupulously preserved all his sallies at my expense ... You may, however, depend on it that the book is not any the worse for my doctoring ... '

In his postscript G.B.S. converts Harris into the sort of person most people believed Shaw to be. Harris, he explains, was really something of a prude and, despite the unwavering inconsistency of his views, rather intolerant. Of course he was impressionistically brilliant and hugely readable but, because he could never understand people, he simply made them into mouthpieces for himself. So Shaw does to Harris what he implies that Harris and others had done to him, undermining in his most sympathetic style the previous 387 pages of the book he had spent so much time preparing for the press. This postscript has something in common with his review of Chesterton's *Shaw*: he reinvents Harris and Chesterton as reflections of what he sees as their inventions of him. Frank Harris, he suggests, might be 'almost miraculously wrong in every particular', yet his biography was invaluable 'as a demonstration of my reactions on Harris'. This was part of Shaw's fifth-column tactics for disarming his biographers and neutralizing what, in a letter to Henderson, he referred to as 'the conventional biographer's game of trying to trace ideas to personal and particular influences when the whole air of the period was full of them'.

Shaw made certain that the galley-proofs of Harris's book were destroyed since he did not want his shadowing of Harris's style to be detected or confused with the autobiographical pages he was contributing as prefaces to some of the volumes in his Collected Edition. Yet it had amused him, under the camouflage of Harris's reputation for mendacity, to insert several authentic biographical passages, and even, as part of this strange collaboration, occasionally to slip the correcting pen over to Sonny:

'All through, from his very earliest childhood, he had lived a fictitious life through the exercise of his incessant imagination ... It was a secret life: its avowal would have made him ridiculous. It had one oddity. The fictitious Shaw was not a man of family. He had no relatives. He was not only a bastard, like Dunois or Falconbridge, who at least knew who their parents were: he was also a foundling.'

'Ought Mr Shaw to Have Done It?' demanded the reviewers. On the whole it was a pity, they judged, that he had allowed himself to be bullied by such a pugilist-of-letters. What they could not observe, since it was invisible, was the extent of Shaw's vicarious presentation of himself which by the 1930s was becoming part of his dramatic production.

Harris's book sold well – 27,000 copies, it was reported, on the day of publication. This was bad news for Henderson whose first biography had been so spectacularly outshone by Chesterton and whose second biography was to appear shortly in the wake of Harris. But the proofs of *Playboy and Prophet* were preserved, and they exhibit the cascading quantities of concealed rewriting done by G.B.S. in the persona of this friendly American mathematician who, without interest in politics or talent for writing, continued loyally to keep the pot boiling. Shaw, however, could not bring himself to write an endorsement of Henderson's biography. 'You must bear with my explosions of fury,' he consoled him. '...I make no apology: I am astonished by my own moderation. DAMN Bernard Shaw and his tedious doings and sayings!'

*

'For seven weeks I have been hiding within a day's ride ... I shall have left when this reaches you,' Shaw wrote to Molly Tompkins before moving on to Geneva; '...you should not drive me away to horrible hell-paradises like the Riviera by refusing to behave yourself tactfully.' His fortnight in Geneva, which prompted a long analysis of the League of Nations and

179

eventually a play, was enveloped in secrecy. 'Not a word of this to any living soul,' he cautioned one correspondent, 'or we shall be dogged by cameras, microphones and journalists.'

Searching for a paradise without hell in which to escape the repercussions of his own tactless behaviour with Stella Campbell, Shaw turned to the Adriatic in 1929, putting down on the Island of Brioni off the Istrian peninsula. 'A settled melancholy, peculiar to the place perhaps, devours us,' he wrote to Blanche Patch, and this, Charlotte sharply added, suited them both very well: 'The Island is dull, but that is good for us!'

From here they sailed to Dubrovnik ('a wonderful place'), then continued overland by way of Boka Kotorska to Cetinje, the capital of Montenegro, before going on to Split. 'I am treated here like a King,' Shaw wrote to Stella Campbell, 'nothing can be more exhausting.' The Royal Yugoslav Government, anxious to use his visit as an advertisement for tourism and as an endorsement of its political regime, had greeted him with a two-hour press conference at the Imperial Hotel in Dubrovnik. 'There are good reasons for me to be careful about my political statements,' Shaw announced. But he was angered by some of the misreporting of these statements and refused to meet the press a second time in Split. Instead he drafted a 'Program for Easing World Tensions' which he gave to Ivan Lupis-Vukić, one of the few Yugoslav journalists who spoke English. The provincial authorities, however, censored part of this statement in translation and Lupis-Vukić, not liking to print a mutilated text, withheld it during Shaw's lifetime.

Whatever Shaw seemed to give with one hand he appeared, like a conjuror, to steal away with the other. His praise of Dubrovnik was still being used by a Yugoslav Air brochure in 1985: 'Those who seek earthly paradise should come and see Dubrovnik.' This was perfect advertising copy, but Shaw had gone on to say:

'You seem to be of the opinion that everything should be sacrificed to the catering industry for foreigners since other kinds of industry can hardly be created in these bare mountainous regions. The same opinion was held in Italy until Mussolini starting pushing foreigners away which may be the best thing to do. You have the case in France where old olive groves are cut down to raise chrysanthemums for the benefit of American and English ladies.'

This mention of Mussolini was particularly embarrassing, since the Italian dictator had recently laid claim to Yugoslav territory. 'The feeling between Italy and Jugoslavia could hardly be worse,' Shaw discovered. The Kingdom of Serbs, Croats and Slovenes had been confirmed by the Treaty of Versailles and amended in 1920 by a supplementary Treaty of Trianon which added part of the lands previously owned by the Hungarian Crown of St Stephen to its border. Four months before the Shaws arrived, the constitutional monarch, King Alexander, had assumed dictatorial powers in order to suppress the various claims for autocracy that threatened to pull apart the multi-national state of Yugoslavia. Shaw seemed to be approving the King's 'statesmanlike decision' when he argued that a strong and large state, with a respected body of laws, was the necessary foundation for national democratic freedom. 'Small states are easy to overcome. If you were to be divided into Serbia, Montenegro and Croatia there would easily be someone somewhere who would swallow you. I dont say who that would be.'

Everyone understood that he was alluding to Mussolini, whose actions in unifying Italy he specifically likened to King Alexander's reinforcement of Yugoslavia's centralized government. He also described the Treaty of Trianon as 'a classic example of the Great British art of How Not to Do It' and pressed the Mayor of Cetinje with such searching questions over the feelings of Montenegrins on the integration of the Serbian people that official written answers had to be specially prepared. Individually complex, historically provocative, simultaneously humorous and in earnest, G.B.S. was politically impossible; and despite reports in the British and United States press that 'Shaw Upholds Dictatorship', the Yugoslav authorities never gained the international respectability they had been seeking from his visit.

The Shaws left Split on 27 May and sailed for Venice. 'The [Hotel] Danieli is palatial but frightfully exposed to noise,' G.B.S. reported. 'After three nights of it we can sleep through anything. We shall stay another week anyhow.' Travelling back on the Orient Express he saw Molly's Isola from the train window, and hurtled on to London where, a fortnight later, he finished a ten-thousand-word Preface, begun in Brioni, to his love letters with Ellen Terry.

Ellen had died the previous summer. For the last fourteen years of her life, since she played Lady Cicely Waynflete in *Captain Brassbound's Conversion*, they had not often corresponded. 'I wonder shall I ever act in a Play of yours again!' she had written to him in 1910, and then, more than two years later: 'I suppose an old woman would not attract as a centre piece in a play, and that you never could write such a thing for – *me*?' Her enquiries filled him with concern, with dismay. 'What am I to do or say?' he asked in a letter he was to exclude from their published correspondence. 'It's as if Queen Alexandra came to me and asked me to get her a place as cook-housekeeper...'

'Nobody dare have you in a cast: youd knock it all to pieces. A tiny yacht may throw its mast overboard and end its days quietly and serviceably as a ferry boat; but a battleship cant do that; and you are a battleship. What parts are there...? Matrons at £15 a week or less. And then the agony of learning a part, and being hustled by a producer, and finally overwhelming everyone on the stage by dwarfing them ... Can you wonder that we all recoil ... and then get some estimable mouse who would give no trouble and spread no terror?'

Later, he tried to ease her into the role of Mrs Higgins in a production of *Pygmalion* at the Duke of York's Theatre, but unknown to him the part had been promised to her younger sister, Marion Terry.

For Ellen, it was not simply a matter of money, as Shaw hoped, but of occupation and a sense of continuing usefulness. She was losing her eyesight, her memory for words, her stage confidence. 'Can you enlarge my prospect?' she had appealed to Shaw. '... I must work.' When very young she had enlarged her prospect by escaping from an imprisoning marriage to G. F. Watts and eloping with William Godwin, 'the greatest aesthete of them all', as Max Beerbohm called him. But having given birth to two illegitimate children, she found out what it was like to be a fallen and forgotten woman in nineteenth-century England. The partnership with Henry Irving had restored her reputation and the public happily identified her with the virtuous and sentimental roles Irving handed down to her. Shaw had then tried to enlarge their prospects together. But she had not wanted to risk public obloquy again by eloping with the follower of a Norwegian dramatist whom the English newspapers labelled a creator of unnatural plays 'of no use – as far as England's stage is concerned'. So she remained the jewel of the Lyceum and the First Lady of a vanishing theatre.

In the late nineteenth century every Victorian gentleman who came to the Lyceum had fallen in love with Ellen Terry, and no wife had objected because she was regarded not as a notorious seductress like Mrs Patrick Campbell, but as the ideal embodiment of motherhood. Shaw shared this fantasy; but he separated it from Ellen's career. Besides, he knew how ironically this image fitted someone who, unleashing a power denied to her in the theatre, had given her children such a difficult and divisive upbringing. In the early twentieth century, following Irving's death, 'Our Lady of the Lyceum' had faded into 'Our Lady of Sighs', fiercely fought over by her son, the legendary Gordon Craig, and by her lesbian daughter Edy Craig. Now Ellen turned to Shaw, but she was no longer his *femme inspiratrice*, and he could not rescue her. So her involvement in contemporary theatre, remaining largely vicarious and financial, continued to oscillate between her son's visionary stage designs and Edy's more modest if equally modernistic feminist experiments with the Actresses Franchise League. By the time Ellen died, she was financially and emotionally depleted.

G.B.S. was immediately pitched into the battle for possession of her memory. 'I scan the rising generations of women for another Ellen,' he had written to her; '... None of the wildest expressions I have ever addressed to you are to be considered in any way withdrawn.' Edy Craig had read these words when looking through the boxes of her mother's papers. At her request, Shaw sent her Ellen's letters, and she felt that both sides of the correspondence should be published in full. 'Do you want this correspondence between E.T. and G.B.S. to be published?' Gordon Craig enquired. In his reply, Shaw spelt out the moral, legal and financial alternatives facing the executors. That the correspondence would one day be published, he did not doubt. He therefore gave notice that he would draft 'an explanation for posterity' that would place Ellen in an intelligible theatrical context and could be used as a preface at whatever date the letters were given to the public. 'The rest lies practically with the executors,' he concluded.

Gordon Craig was not an executor. But Edy Craig was, and unknown to both men she had sold Shaw's letters to a publisher for £3,000. On learning this, Shaw immediately informed Gordon Craig. 'It is therefore no longer possible,' he wrote, 'to pretend that we are under any pecuniary pressure to publish the letters.' He proposed sending Ellen's letters 'to the British Museum (say) with a copy of the preface to be placed with them when they are put into the catalogue at some future date'. In the meantime he forwarded Gordon Craig a proof copy, marked 'Very Private', of his 'Preface to be attached to the Correspondence of Ellen Terry and Bernard Shaw should it ever be published', with the provocative request that he read it carefully because 'Edy tells me that you are at work on a memoir of Irving with incidental references to me'.

Gordon Craig had little intention of referring to G.B.S., whose part in Irving's career he believed to have been negligible. Irving was his hero, and he had now inherited the feud between 'my master', as he called him, and this 'literary gangster', as G.B.S. called himself. Goaded by Shaw's taunts of being an 'Imposter', a 'Thwarted Genius' and 'the Spoilt Child of Europe', he took the field under the banner of Shaw's old adversary. In the sallies and manoeuvrings of their war-games the familiar faded colours once more unfurl, and the dusty echoes stir, as that ancient jousting match between the Irish contender from the *Saturday Review* and the 'Ogre of the Lyceum' is rejoined. But on this occasion it is Irving's champion and not

G.B.S. who is banished from the arena of the commercial theatre. 'You were trying to make a picture frame of the proscenium to replace actors by figures, and drive the dramatic poet from the theatre,' Shaw accused Craig. 'And as I was doing precisely the reverse, and the Zeitgeist carried me to success, you felt that I was the arch enemy. So I was . . . the enemy who does not reciprocate your dislike – if you really dislike him.' But Gordon Craig, who opposed state-subsidised theatre, really did dislike Shaw as the man who had set out 'to damage my mother, Nelly Terry, my father, myself, my family, Irving, and a few more'.

Shaw had also sent a copy of his preface to Edy Craig whose desire to see the correspondence quickly published – with the preface attached – was revitalized. Calculating that it would advance this end, she sold the copyright in her mother's letters for another £3,000 to the same publisher who had bought Shaw's side of their correspondence, and who declared that if he could not induce Shaw to allow the publication of his own letters he would publish Ellen Terry's alone.

'I shall not allow my letters to be published,' Shaw stipulated to the publisher on 17 September 1929. As late as 8 April 1930 he repeated his refusal in the *Daily Express*: 'Certainly I won't give permission.' Since Edy Craig had now amassed £6,000 for the Ellen Terry Estate without the printing of a word, there seemed no need to 'do violence to our instinctive repugnance to any sort of publicity until we have all passed into history', he confided to Gordon Craig ' – or out of it'.

But by the summer of 1930 Shaw had swung round to Edy's opinion. 'At first I was almost as stupid as [Gordon] Craig,' he later explained. Except for a few hostile asides, he had been largely excluded from Craig's book on Irving and now he was threatened with complete exclusion from Ellen Terry's published correspondence. He was passing out of history. Reading straight through both sides of their exchange for the first time, he saw that 'the moral of the whole correspondence' would be the 'justice done to the great woman E.T. sacrificed to the egotistical man H.I.' Such a moral suited his own retrospective designs as well as the current feminist plans of Edy Craig and her lesbian lover 'Christopher St John' (with whom Shaw was silently to co-edit the volume). It also had the tactical advantage of forcing Gordon Craig to campaign simultaneously on two fronts.

Shaw's negotiations over the Ellen Terry correspondence were at once devious and honourable. He took care to omit all hurtful reference to living people, especially Gordon Craig himself; he gave all his own profits to the Ellen Terry Estate for the Memorial Museum that Edy was creating; and he agreed to the publication initially of a limited edition only, on the condition that Gordon Craig himself gave his consent – 'and he, swearing that he would ne'er consent, consented'.

Gordon Craig's consent took the form of a brief letter to Shaw in which he promised 'not to stand in the way' of the publication: 'you may rest assured that having said this I shall stick to it; and when the book containing my Mother's and your letters is published you can rely on me not to write about it in the papers or to give interviews'. Shaw was immediately generous in victory: 'I took it, and take it, that your consent to the publication is like mine, a very reluctant submission to circumstances over which we have no control ... you feel with me that we must stifle our natural repugnance and let the thing go through.' These circumstances had been imposed on them by Edy and her publisher. Trying to align himself with both brother and sister, however, Shaw was caught between the full incensed points of these mighty opposites. In his letter to Gordon Craig, he conceded, 'as to your complete liberty to write about those letters, about the Lyceum, about E.T. and G.B.S., you must continue to exercise that in all respects as before'. But when Gordon Craig did exercise this liberty in his book *Ellen Terry and Her Secret Self* the year after *Ellen Terry and Bernard Shaw. A Correspondence* was published, Shaw made devastating use of his earlier letter of consent.

'Here is his written consent to the publication of the letters ... He not only consents to the publication but explicitly gives his word not to do what he has done in his book. But do not get virtuously indignant: his consent was extorted by circumstances, and his heart was not in his promise. I do not blame him, for I knew my man; and my object was to make it impossible for him to attack his sister and denounce the publication of the letters as an outrage without putting himself helplessly in the wrong. I guessed that he would be unable to resist doing it; and I guessed right. But I shall not pretend to mount the moral high horse at his expense ... '

It was open to Gordon Craig to point out that technically he had stuck to his word by not writing about *A Correspondence* 'in the papers' or giving interviews; or he might have quoted Shaw's letters giving him 'complete liberty to write about those letters'; and he could have shown how G.B.S. was adroitly pretending not to mount a moral high horse while in fact doing so – as he had so frequently done in his crusades against Irving. Craig had given his consent to publication without seeing all the letters and his attitude, like Shaw's, changed after reading them through as a whole, though in the opposite direction. The only honourable course, he now felt, was for Shaw and Edy to have destroyed everything, posthumously releasing his mother from this awful entanglement. He had managed to avoid some of Shaw's traps (refusing, for example, the invitation to contribute an introduction on suddenly realizing it would be followed by Shaw's unmatchable preface). But after the publication of *A Correspondence*, he concentrated his anti-Shavian abuse in a curious pamphlet fitting into the back cover-pocket of *Ellen Terry and Her Secret Self*. 'Frankly, readers will suffer no irreparable loss if they leave it there' commented *The Times*.

In *Ellen Terry and Her Secret Self* Gordon Craig evokes the golden mother of his country childhood in place of the mortifyingly powerful woman who had looked on him as a weak little boy. 'What makes this book of his so tragically moving,' Shaw acknowledged, ' – for if you disregard the rubbish about me, which is neither here nor there, it is a poignant human document – is his desperate denial of the big woman he ran away from and his assertion of the "little mother" he loved.' *A Correspondence* had revealed the Ellen Terry her son resented, a woman who 'with all her charm and essential amiability, was an impetuous, overwhelming, absorbing personality', Shaw remembered. 'She could sweep a thousand people away in a big theatre; so you can imagine what she could do with a sensitive boy in a small house.' For this revelation, Shaw believed, Gordon Craig 'will never forgive me'.

When Edy Craig apologized for having brought down on Shaw's head her brother's 'spluttered spleen', G.B.S. waved it away as 'too babyish to do any harm'. Gordon Craig, however, had rightly observed that in regard to Ellen Terry, 'we are all of us just children – and the naughtiest is often preferable to the good'. To one side of this re-orchestrated battle over Irving's reputation raged a more intimate and childlike contest: a strange variation of sibling rivalry between the lost son, militant daughter, and claimant child from the theatre. In the marsupial annexe to his book, which is dedicated to Henry Irving and entitled 'A Plea for G.B.S.', Gordon Craig wrote as naughtily as he could, calling Shaw 'a very large, malicious, poke-nose old woman ... with an idle and vindictive tongue quite fussily spreading falsehoods ... up and down the street'. The 'falsehoods' were Shaw's claims to legitimacy with Ellen in a theatre world that had taken Craig's mother away and given her to everyone. He was an 'old woman' because he aligned himself with Edy's circle of feminists who had imprisoned Ellen after her retirement from the theatre. 'Mr Craig is under no obligation to like me,' Shaw acceded.

After *Ellen Terry and Bernard Shaw. A Correspondence* appeared in the autumn of 1931, everyone wanted their Shavian letters published. 'We have never had a correspondence in that sense,' Shaw explained to Frank Harris; and to Archibald Henderson he pointed out, 'After the Terry correspondence anything less romantic would be an anticlimax.' Only one body of correspondence had shadowed something more romantic. 'There is absolutely no comparison between Shaw's letters to Ellen Terry and his letters to me,' Mrs Patrick Campbell told American journalists when she arrived in New York that fall. 'I shall write my *own* preface to the edition, not Mr Shaw ... I do not intend to give him the opportunity to say the last word. I don't trust him enough.'

The Shaw–Ellen Terry correspondence prompted Stella to mount one last campaign over the publication of her own letters from Joey. For a year she persisted with her appeals. His letters to her had been valued at £10,000 but (aside from the odd misdemeanour) she had behaved herself 'like a gentleman' and guarded them for nineteen years. Now times were hard, 'almost unbearable', Shaw was psychologically incapable of giving her new parts, and she was gradually becoming unemployable in the theatre. She wanted this correspondence published for reasons of self-esteem as much as money. 'What objection can there be? Letters written so long ago, and all three of us on the verge of the grave!' But while Charlotte lived, Shaw could not agree: all other objections were as nothing compared to this. 'At all events for me you are an insoluble problem,' he admitted to Stella; 'and I have callously given it up, as there is no use making myself unhappy about it'.

These postscripts to his emotional life were strangely disturbing, almost as if he were already living posthumously. He felt unusually agitated, as Stella herself had felt over *The Apple Cart*. For both of them the past was growing clouded. 'I felt very apologetic indeed that day when I read Orinthia to you,' he wrote, 'and added to all your worries the shock of my senility.'

Still she persisted. 'Send me a telegram: "go ahead and be damned to you", [and] tell Miss Patch to send me what letters you have of mine.'

Still he refused: 'NO. The Fates, not I, decree it.'

For three years they recovered in silence. Then, in 1937, suddenly coming upon all Stella's correspondence, Shaw parcelled it up in six registered envelopes and sent it to her in New York. He made no copies, 'as I should certainly die of angina pectoris during the operation'. 'There's a clutch at my heart,' Stella rejoined, '... the desire to feel a child again will tempt me to read them.' Still nothing could be published while he and Charlotte remained alive, but 'as you are nine years younger than we are', Shaw calculated, 'your chances of surviving both of us are fairly good'.

But it was Stella who died first, in April 1940. 'AND IT IS MY DESIRE,' she had written in her will, '... that the Bernard Shaw letters and poems which are now in the custody of the Westminster Bank be published in their proper sequence and not cut or altered in any way, that they should be published in an independent volume to be entitled "The Love Letters of Bernard Shaw to Mrs Patrick Campbell" so all who may read them will realize that the friendship was "L'amitié amoureuse".' The copyright in her letters was to be held in trust until the income from their publication could be paid to her daughter and grandson, Stella and Patrick Beech, or their survivors.

Nothing more could happen until Charlotte's death three and a half years later. The month after she died, wishing to put his affairs in order, Shaw invited Patrick Beech to Whitehall Court. As a result of their discussions he gave authority in his new will for Stella Beech 'daughter of the late eminent actress professionally known as Mrs Patrick Campbell to print and publish after my death all or any of the letters written by me to the said eminent actress and in the event of Mrs Beech's death before publication to give such authority (which is a permission and not an assignment of copyright) to Mrs Patrick Campbell's grandson Patrick Beech'. The proceeds of this correspondence he reserved 'as far as possible' for the secondary education of Stella Campbell's grandchildren.

There was another pause until Shaw died. Two years afterwards, their leftover letters finally appeared. Against her mother's wishes Mrs Beech cut a few passages and published the volume more prosaically as *Bernard Shaw and Mrs Patrick Campbell: Their Correspondence*. G.B.S. had placed himself *in loco parentis* to Stella's family and made this the only volume of his correspondence to be removed from the control of his executors.

'You would not come out of it with a halo like Ellen's,' Shaw had warned Stella. But as Ellen had come out of *A Correspondence* far better than he imagined, so Stella would hold her own in *Their Correspondence*. 'Like a cushion, she baffles the incisive blade of Shavian argument,' commented *The Times* reviewer.

There was to be one more ironic revolution in this 'Comedy of Letters' when Jerome Kilty lifted it off the page and successfully transferred it into the theatre. '*Dear Liar* catches with remarkable theatrical assurance the spirit of the correspondence,' a critic in *The Times* wrote of the adaptation. '... it brings out rather surprisingly how sweetly reasonable the actress who was the terror of Tree, Alexander and other actor-managers proved to be in her letters to Joey.'

To its end the relationship had pulled Shaw painfully between comedy and tragedy without ever reconciling the two. 'I can laugh with the comedian,' he had written to her; 'but with the tragedian – oh my heart! ...

'Oh, Stella, Stella, Stella, Stella, *Stella!*'

Them and their Academy of Letters – all in all, and in spite of all.
Sean O'Casey to James Joyce (30 May 1939)

'The Works of Bernard Shaw', which G.B.S. had been preparing intermittently since 1921, began to appear in two editions early in the 1930s. This was recognized as an impressive record of his diversified career. 'We *must* give the purchasers something solid for their money – something that will make them feel they have the whole WORKS ... above all something that will bring in £20,000 net; and that means 20 volumes on the nail,' he wrote to Otto Kyllmann at Constable. '... Our broadside, when it *does* come, must be a thundering one; and I am slaving to that end.'

Twenty-one volumes of the Limited Collected Edition, bound in jade green Irish linen and with endpapers watermarked HOMERIC ANTI-QUARIAN came out in 1930. The broadside opened up on his seventy-fourth birthday, starting with the five novels, embellished with Forewords and Postscripts, at the head of which he delivered the first printing of *Immaturity*, slightly revised after its fifty-year wait, and given a long autobiographical Preface. Thirty-two plays and playlets, many with emendations, followed in eleven volumes; and to these he added *Major Critical Essays* (*The Quintessence of Ibsenism*, *The Perfect Wagnerite* and *The Sanity of Art*), *The Intelligent Woman's Guide to Socialism* and various compilations ranging from *What I Really Wrote about the War* to the more distant *Short Stories, Scraps and Shavings*. 'We are unearthing all sorts of forgotten masterpieces!' Charlotte exclaimed. But G.B.S. was subdued. 'It is all harrow and no rest for me now,' he wrote. '... I could not arrange the edition without appalling grave digging.' He continued to dig up dramatic, literary, musical and political essays as well as critical pieces on education and medicine; and he added half a dozen new plays in the 1930s, bringing the total number of volumes to thirty-three. Nevertheless, he told Kyllmann, 'I have conceived an extraordinary hatred to this particular edition, blast it!' and he later allowed it to be overtaken by what became known as Constable's 'Standard Edition' of his works, a cheaper set eventually rising to thirty-seven volumes uniformly bound in Venetian fadeless sail cloth. 'To the Standard Edition,' he wrote to Kyllmann, 'there is no limit but the grave'.

*

Rather unexpectedly, recognition also came from Ireland. G.B.S. had never felt easy with Irish writers. 'We put each other out frightfully,' he wrote, recalling his meetings with Oscar Wilde; 'and this odd difficulty persisted between us to the very last.' Though their parents had been married in the same church and Sonny and Oscar were born within two years and a couple of Irish miles of each other, no social contacts had been practicable in Victorian Dublin between families of such diverging histories. It was Charlotte's family that had lived opposite the Wildes in Merrion Square; while Shaw's father came to Sir William Wilde, 'Surgeon-Oculist in Ordinary to the Queen in Ireland', only as a patient. According to G.B.S., Sir William 'operated on my father to correct a squint, and overdid the corrections so much that my father squinted the other way all the rest of his life'.

In later years G.B.S. was seldom able to see Oscar Wilde as others saw him. He appeared to have two people in view: Oscar, the boyish romantic, chivalrously sympathetic to those less well-placed than himself and scrupulously well-mannered to others, such as Shaw, who were potentially his equals; and then Wilde, the arrogant Dublin snob encircled by acolytes. Shaw had first met Oscar at one of Lady Wilde's richly eccentric at homes in London to which he sometimes went in the 'desperate days' between 1879 and 1885. 'Lady Wilde was nice to me,' he remembered. Oscar too had come up and spoken 'with an evident intention of being specially kind to me'. Lady Wilde's position, 'literary, social and patriotic, is unique and unassailable', Shaw was to write in 1888 when reviewing her *Ancient Legends of Ireland* for the *Pall Mall Gazette*. 'If any reviewer finds the book dull, it is extremely unlikely that he will have the hardihood to say so ... '

'Lady Wilde can write scholarly English without pedantry and Irish-English without vulgarity or impracticable brogue phonetics. She has no difficulty in writing about leprechauns, phoukas and banshees, simply as an Irishwoman telling Irish stories, impelled by the same tradition-instinct, and with a nursery knowledge at first hand of all the characteristic moods of the Irish imagination. Probably no living writer could produce a better book of its kind.'

This was partly because, Shaw manages to imply, the book belonged to a literature and sociology that were now dead. He had cut loose from this culture when throwing himself out of Ireland and into socialism, and he seems to have attributed what he saw as Wilde's false start as an apostle of art to the pretentious influence of this dying tradition on the cult of aestheticism. Both Wilde, the complete dandy, and Shaw, the rational dress reformer, were showmen. The lilac puffs and frills, black silk stockings and tailored coats of braided velvet seen against backgrounds of lilies and sunflowers which made up Wilde's aesthetic presentation of himself were a 'coming out' of the superior cashmere combinations and other experimental underwear in which Shaw paradoxically showed off. Whenever these two noticeable figures met, they treated each other with elaborate courtesy, conscious that the British press resented their aberrations from ready-made Victorian behaviour. 'As far as I can ascertain, I am the only person in London who cannot sit down and write an Oscar Wilde play at will,' Shaw wrote in his *Saturday Review* notice of *An Ideal Husband*. ' ... In a certain sense Mr Wilde is to me our only thorough playwright. He plays with everything: with wit, with philosophy, with drama, with actors and audience, with the whole theatre ... '

'All the literary dignity of the play, all the imperturbable good sense and good manners with which Mr Wilde makes his wit pleasant to his comparatively stupid audience, cannot quite overcome the fact that Ireland is of all countries the most foreign to England, and that to the Irishman ... there is nothing in the world quite so exquisitely comic as an Englishman's seriousness.'

Wilde, too, made a point of treating Shaw's early work with true Irish seriousness. 'I like your superb confidence in the dramatic value of the mere facts of life,' he wrote after reading *Widowers' Houses*, ' ... and your preface is a masterpiece – a real masterpiece of trenchant writing and caustic wit and dramatic instinct.' He let it be known that Shaw's *Quintessence of Ibsenism* ('I constantly take it up, and always find it stimulating and refreshing') had led him to write *The Soul of Man under Socialism*; and he supported Shaw's campaign against the 'ridiculous institution' of stage censorship. 'England is the land of intellectual fogs but you have done much to clear the air,' he wrote to Shaw in 1893: 'we are both Celtic, and I like to think that we are friends'. But on another occasion, he was reported to have said: 'Shaw is an excellent man. He has not an enemy in the world, and none of his friends like him'; while Shaw wrote that Wilde 'was incapable of friendship, though not of the most touching kindness on occasion'.

They were compatriots rather than friends and, within the intellectual fogs of England, they were bright comrades-in-arms against a common enemy. Their diffidence with each other masked what was probably an apprehension of their respective powers. Wilde was the one man in London capable of making the young Shaw sound comparatively dull. 'I had not to talk myself,' Shaw acknowledged, 'but to listen to a man telling me stories better than I could have told them.' But Wilde appears to have been nervous of Shaw's combative spirit and that 'caustic wit' which could pierce his own protective charm.

Their ways parted, revealing real differences, once Wilde's social and literary aggrandizement seemed to implicate him in the very hypocrisies of Victorian society that his absurdist wit had mocked. In Shaw's view, success brought out the snob in Wilde. This was one explanation for his reaction against *The Importance of Being Earnest* – Wilde's 'first really heartless play'. He wanted to believe that Wilde's talent for puncturing morals and manners fitted him for a place in 'a large public life' as a fellow socialist. Instead, Wilde appeared to succumb to flattery. His unconventionality was the very pedantry of convention, Shaw was to write; 'never was there a man less an outlaw than he'.

In fact, as his trial, imprisonment and exile showed, Wilde formed no more solid social foundations in England than G.B.S. Remembering that Wilde had been the only writer in London to sign his memorial in the late 1880s asking for the reprieve of the Chicago anarchists, Shaw drafted a petition seeking a remission of Wilde's prison sentence, but finding that his signature would stand almost alone he gave up the idea, concluding that the support of a notorious socialist would 'do Oscar more harm than good'.

He was able, however, to find a more sophisticated way of defending Wilde. His major critical essay, 'The Sanity of Art', had been aimed at Max Nordau's thesis *Degeneration*, which included as part of its 'Ego-Mania' section a hostile analysis of Wilde in the chapter 'Decadents and Aesthetes'. Shaw's response, originally entitled 'A Degenerate's View of Nordau' and later subtitled 'An Exposure of the Current Nonsense about Artists being Degenerate', may be read as an intellectual rehabilitation of Wilde written during his second trial and published shortly after his sentence. In the happy days of the hugely successful *A Woman of No Importance*, which coincided with the shaky beginnings of *Widowers' Houses*, Wilde had paid Shaw the compliment of ranking their works together as dramatic literature; in the days of Wilde's disgrace Shaw returned the compliment by ranking himself as a fellow degenerate. He also went on favourably mentioning Wilde in his theatre reviews ('Mr Wilde has creative imagination, philosophic humor, and original wit, besides being a master of language') while Wilde was in prison; and six months after he was released, Shaw proposed his name – though that name was still taboo – as one of the 'Immortals' for an Academy of Letters. During the final period of Wilde's disgrace, they continued to send each other signed copies of their books, all works, as Oscar liked to say, of 'the great Celtic School' uniting socialism with aesthetics.

The great Celtic School had been held in place by its opposition to Victorian sexual and political ethics but, as the solid ground of Victorianism crumbled, it was to break up into two Hibernian tributaries. Shaw had rallied to Wilde in his misfortune, but switched off this support when he came to realize how tragedy was transforming him into a posthumous legend. Wilde's genius was for comedy, he declared, and having a negligible talent for unhappiness he had suffered little in prison: 'no other Irishman has yet produced as masterful a comedy as De Profundis'. By the 1930s Wilde was once again the more popular dramatist. 'My licence for the performance of my play Pygmalion ... did not include an authorisation to advertise it as "the brilliant comedy by Oscar Wilde",' Shaw wrote in 1938 to the Grand Theatre in Wolverhampton. 'Is Oscar's name a bigger draw than mine?' The manager of the theatre was disinclined to offer an apology, however, claiming that this substitution accounted for the play having attracted three times as much money as it did when billed as being written by Shaw. 'Beg him to continue the attribution, which was a most happy thought,' Shaw responded. 'I am not grumbling; I am rejoicing.'

Shaw's grumbles with Wilde arose less from personal rivalry than from their competing ideologies. By the 1920s and 1930s, Wilde's aesthetic creed had developed into the cult of personal relationships and the dogma of artistic significance practised by the Bloomsbury Group, and would later lead to the homosexual legislation, hedonism and pacifism of the 1960s. Shaw's alternative opposition to Victorianism, based on economic rather than sexual liberation, had concurrently developed its programme of socialist reforms towards the creation of a Welfare State, such as he was to see in the last decade of his life. He wanted egalitarian socialism to be accepted as the mainstream of twentieth-century culture in Britain. By giving his imprimatur to Frank Harris's inaccurate account of Wilde's life and by engaging for over a dozen years in a chastening correspondence with Alfred Douglas, Shaw sought to diminish the influence of a man whose memory was becoming an inspiration for the 'Artist Idolatry' he had attacked in the Preface to *Misalliance*, and whose ethics, with those of Beardsley, he had spotlighted in Dubedat, the amoral artist of *The Doctor's Dilemma*.

Shaw could accept Wilde as a writer of aphorisms that 'stood creditably on the library shelf with La Rochefoucauld's Maxims', and as a writer of plays that 'had a niche beside Congreve in the drama'. But Wilde was also 'an original moralist' and it was his moral force that Shaw held in suspicion. As presented by Shaw, Wilde becomes a weak man absurdly credited with omniscience, the voluptuary without a conscience who ended as an unproductive drunkard. 'What claim had Oscar on you or anyone else,' he demanded of Douglas, 'that it should be a reproach to us that we did not spend the rest of our lives holding his hand after he disgraced himself?' Such hostile rhetoric, which was false to Shaw's actual relations with Wilde while he was alive and ineffective as a means of discrediting him posthumously, gave currency to the view of G.B.S. as a 'certain notorious and clever, but cold-blooded Socialist' whom W. B. Yeats depicts anonymously in an essay on Wilde.

'It was the prerogative of youth to take sides,' Yeats wrote in his autobiography, 'and when Wilde said: "Mr Bernard Shaw has no enemies but is intensely disliked by all his friends", I knew it to be a phrase I should never forget, and felt revenged upon a notorious hater of romance, whose generosity and courage I could not fathom.' Like Wilde, Yeats valued Shaw's fighting qualities. His 'cold, explosive, detonating impartiality', which had made him 'the most formidable man in modern letters', was often used to 'hit my enemies'. Referring to his ballads on Roger Casement, Yeats was to tell Dorothy Wellesley in 1936: 'I am fighting in those ballads for what I have been fighting all my life, it is our Irish fight though it has nothing to do with this or that country. Bernard Shaw fights with the same object . . . I said when I started my movement in my 25th or 26th year "I am going to stiffen the backbone". Bernard Shaw may have said the same in his youth; it has been stiffened in Ireland with results.' Between Yeats's rejection of *John Bull's Other Island* (a work 'uncongenial to the whole spirit of the neo-Gaelic movement') and the later 1920s when, 'not sure I would know active life again', he listed Father Keegan's speeches from that play as among 'the events of life and art that had most [moved] me', the two writers had come to more accommodating positions.

Many years before, talking about G.B.S. as he walked back home in the evening with Florence Farr, the actress they both loved, Yeats had sometimes wondered 'whether the cock crowed for my blame or for my praise'. He praised Shaw for his 'logical, audacious and convincing' powers of argument, blamed him for his argumentative logic ('a logician is a fool when life, which is a thing of emotion, is in question'), and finally resolved the contradiction in a burst of Shavian-like humour: 'When a man is so outrageously in the wrong as Shaw he is indispensable.' He had accused Shaw of constructing plays like buildings 'made by science in an architect's office, and erected by joyless hands'; then he saw *Misalliance*, was delighted by the extravagant 'girl acrobat who read her Bible while tossing her balls in the air', and decided that her creator was 'irreverent, headlong, fantastic'.

But people lose their 'peace, their fineness in politics', Yeats said, so it was no surprise to him that, fighting the political barbarians, Shaw had become something of a barbarian himself. Yet in later years, the author of *Heartbreak House, Back to Methuselah* and *Too True to be Good* seemed to be, as George Russell wrote, 'coming back to Zion'. Yeats responded to the mystical vein in Shaw, without believing it would ever quieten the 'Shaw who writes letters to the papers and gives interviews' and who had written

The Apple Cart. 'He is haunted by the mystery he flouts,' Yeats wrote to Russell. 'He is an atheist who trembles in the haunted corridor.'

Yeats had also changed. 'At first he amused me because of Gilbert's entirely unsuccessful attempt to put Wilde on the stage as Bunthorne in *Patience,*' Shaw later wrote to Stephen Gwynn. 'Bunthorne was not a bit like Wilde; but he presently came to life in the person of W.B.Y., who out-Bunthorned him enough to make him seem commonplace.' But the romantic poet of the 1890s was to find a new language beyond modernism that absorbed his experience and gave out mysteriously timeless poetry. Shaw tended to regard him still as an Irish singer who had made his sad songs a coat

> Covered with embroideries
> Out of old mythologies
> From heel to throat;

He had not liked Yeats's allegorical plays which seemed to float, full of 'treading-on-air' roles, within the twilight Ireland of Lady Wilde's legends. He hardly had the patience to tease out Yeats's dense and studied symbolisms. He had felt 'quite touched' by *Cathleen ni Houlihan,* 'but Ireland meant something then that cut no ice outside the island of saints'. He had described *The Land of Heart's Desire* as 'an exquisite curtain raiser', but it had raised the curtain on *Arms and the Man,* a brisk modern comedy that Yeats likened to the hard-edged world of Epstein's *Rock Drill* and the Vorticism of Wyndham Lewis. He had singled out Yeats's *Where there is Nothing,* for which he helped to arrange a few performances at the Court Theatre, because it seemed to him a prophetic prose play of the Ibsen school centred round the figure of William Morris, at whose house they had met and discussed the political future. But Yeats's talent had not pointed in that direction, and when he came to revise the play he transformed it into the more fabulous *The Unicorn from the Stars.*

'I am a practical man,' Yeats protested. In the company of G.B.S. he was almost comically eager to appear a round-the-clock midday-man. After they stayed as fellow guests of Lady Gregory in the summer of 1910, Shaw had discovered 'what a penetrating critic and good talker he was, for he played none of his Bunthorne games, and saw no green elephants, at Coole'. He had also noticed the shrewdness with which Yeats, no mean swayer of crowds from the stage, handled the Abbey Theatre Company. 'The Abbey Players were enormously interesting, both technically and poetically,' he later wrote, 'and brought me into closer relations with him.'

Their relations were more professional than literary. 'I was always on very good terms with him personally,' Shaw made clear. In Chancery Lane one black night, he remembered, 'into a circle of light under an arc lamp there suddenly stepped, walking towards me, Yeats with his wing of raven black hair swinging across his forehead and Maud Gonne, dazzlingly beautiful in white silk, both of them in evening dress. The pair were quite beyond description. I was invisible in the dark as they passed on; and of course I did not intrude.'

This was the only time Shaw saw Maud Gonne. He had not intruded on Yeats's Irish Movement, though somewhere else he was campaigning in the same war. He did not invade that pool of light, though from his courtly dance with Ellen Terry to his troubadour's pursuit of Stella Campbell he circled hypnotically round it, while Yeats, despite 'that girl standing there', had stepped into the shadows of politics as an Irish senator.

Between the poet of the emotions who believed that 'we begin to live when we have conceived life as tragedy' and the playwright of the intellect who thought that 'all genuinely intellectual work is humorous' there had once seemed to be no sympathetic meeting ground. But as Shaw's thought dissolved more into the surreal, he came to accept Yeats's visionary energies as being valuable for Ireland; and as Yeats moved 'closer to the common world' he understood the complementary value of the artist as politician. Yeats used the Abbey Theatre to educate audiences much as Shaw had used the Court, and they now looked on the world as a theatre where they each dreamed of taking leading parts.

In his astrological system, Yeats sought Unity of Being through his occult imagination. On the Great Wheel of lunar phases round which he charts the twenty-eight categories of human nature and the evolution of the soul through these categories, he places Shaw alongside Wells in phase 21 where writers are 'great public men and they exist after death as historical monuments, for they are without meaning apart from time and circumstance'. Yeats positioned himself at phase 17, an ideal phase except that the world was at phase 22 of its historical cycle and he was consequently fated to be one of its 'tragic minority'. So when seeking a vehicle of contemporary time and circumstance, he turned to the man whose moon almost exactly coincided with the age.

The Irish Academy of Letters was Yeats's version of what Wilde had indicated with his *politesse* about the 'great Celtic School'. Yeats had discussed the concept with Lady Gregory before she died in May 1932 and written to Shaw outlining his plan for an organization with the character of the *Académie française* that would bring together those who had done creative work in Ireland, from the Celtic poet to the Cork realist, the Gaelic modernist and Big House novelist. He wanted a vigorous body capable of giving Ireland a renewed sense of her cultural heritage, which he believed to be as essential for the country's national self-esteem as political advancement. He knew that the proposal would chiefly recommend itself to G.B.S. as a strengthening of forces against the censorship of the Catholic Church in Ireland; and indeed Shaw's participation (on the understanding that he would have nothing to do with its management) was partly in acknowledgement of the help Yeats had given him in defeating British censorship at the Abbey with *The Shewing-up of Blanco Posnet*.

At the Academy's inaugural meeting in September 1932 Shaw was, in his absence, unanimously elected President. 'I am against myself as President,' he objected in a letter to Yeats. 'The President should be also Resident . . . I am really a London man . . . Anyhow if I am to be President there *must* be a resident Vice President, which is d——d nonsense.' In the event Yeats himself became Vice-President, and Shaw, despite his protests, remained President until succeeded by Yeats in 1935.

The letter sent to prospective academicians that September above the signatures of Shaw and Yeats emphasized the use of such an 'instrument' against official restrictions that made it impossible for writers 'to live by distinctive Irish literature'.

'Our sole defence lies in the authority of our utterance . . . for in Ireland there is still a deep respect for intellectual and poetic quality. In so far as we represent that quality we can count on a consideration beyond all proportion to our numbers . . . In making this claim upon you we have no authority or mandate beyond the fact that the initiative has to be taken by somebody, and our age and the publicity that attaches to our names makes it easier for us than for younger writers.'

Twenty founding members accepted nomination plus eleven associates whose work was classified in the rules as being 'less Irish'. Among the academicians was Shaw's biographer, St John Ervine; among the associates Yeats's biographer, Joseph Hone. Most of the names were suggested by Yeats, though Shaw proposed T. E. Lawrence and Eugene O'Neill as associate members.

One nominee who refused the invitation was Sean O'Casey. Yeats had been O'Casey's spiritual father in Ireland when the author of *The Plough and the Stars*, *The Shadow of a Gunman* and *Juno and the Paycock* had been happy to be enveloped by 'the great glory of the Abbey'. But after the Abbey's rejection of *The Silver Tassie* in 1928 he turned to Shaw as his new protector and made Yeats his enemy. Shaw, who wished to support O'Casey and his family without antagonizing Yeats, urged conciliation. But O'Casey needed enemies as much as he needed heroes. The influences of Yeats and Shaw mingled uneasily in his plays. He could find no rapprochement between the

Green Flag and the Red. But turning down the invitation to the Irish Academy was, he confessed, one of the hardest refusals of his life.

Another Irish exile, James Joyce, also refused the symbolic gesture, though warmly thanking Yeats through whom he also conveyed 'my thanks to Mr Shaw whom I have never met'. When reading parts of *Ulysses* in *The Little Review*, Shaw had been shudderingly reminded of the slack-jawed jackeens of his Dublin adolescence. 'I missed neither the realism of the book nor its poetry,' he later stated. Though admitting 'I could not write the words Mr Joyce uses', he acknowledged 'Joyce's literary power, which is of classic quality', adding, 'If Mr Joyce should ever desire a testimonial as the author of a literary masterpiece from me, it shall be given with all possible emphasis and with sincere enthusiasm.'

His purpose in publishing this encomium in the late 1930s was to quench the rumour that he had found the book so defiling as to have burnt his copy in the grate. In fact, he had defended its publication chiefly as a work of sociology rather than literature. '*Ulysses* is a document, the outcome of a passion for documentation that is as fundamental as the artistic passion – more so, in fact; for the document is the root and stem of which the artistic fancy-works are the flowers,' he commented in 1924. 'Joyce is driven by his documentary *daimon*.'

Shaw had received a prospectus for the Shakespeare and Company edition of *Ulysses* from Sylvia Beach who, believing he would relish the revolutionary aspect of the work, accepted Joyce's bet of a silk handkerchief to a box of cigars that Shaw's name would not be on the list of subscribers. But, though praising Joyce's 'literary genius', Shaw had gone on to explain that 'I am an elderly Irish gentleman, and that if you imagine that any Irishman, much less an elderly one, would pay 150 francs for a book, you little know my countrymen.'

After that it was the turn of Ezra Pound to bully him into a subscription. 'Am I bound to think in everything even as you do,' Shaw answered. '. . . I take care of the pence because the Pounds will not take care of themselves.' Though this helped to earn him Pound's rich condemnation as a 'ninth-rate coward', it delighted Joyce himself. Having eyed their 'letter fight over me' through his cigar smoke, he thought he spied how matters stood. Echoing Shaw, he cautioned Pound that if he thought G.B.S. had not 'subscribed anonymously for a copy of the revolting record through a bookseller you little know my countrymen'. And Pound had conceded: 'Dear old Shaw has amused us.'

Joyce also reckoned that he had seen ('with the one good eye I have') how matters stood over his play *Exiles*. The Stage Society had initially rejected this work during the war, then called it back, and held on to it until Joyce, exasperated by many months' waiting, withdrew it from them. He had been told that the play had got so far as being placed on the programme, but was removed on the grounds of obscenity 'owing to a veto of Mr Shaw's as I am informed'. Not until the last year of his life did Shaw come to hear this story, and then he refuted it. 'Joyce was misinformed about his early play Exiles,' he wrote.

'I at once spotted a considerable youthful talent; but as it contained a few words that were then tabooed as unmentionable, and still are; and as it was necessary to combat the current notion that the Stage Society existed for the performance of indecent plays, I reported that the unmentionable passages must be blue pencilled. I never said that the whole play was obscene.'

The evidence supports Shaw's memory. Two of the Stage Society's Reading Committee voted for producing Exiles, four voted against it. 'Reminiscent of Strindberg at his worst. Putrid' noted H. A. Hertz on the ballot paper. But Shaw, who was not a member of the Reading Committee and did not need to make a comment, wrote on the same sheet: 'Just the thing for the S[tage] S[ociety]. G.B.S.' With a few deletions Exiles was eventually produced by the Stage Society at the Regent Theatre in 1926. Shaw went to the performance on 15 February and was alleged to have spoken favourably at a public debate about the production two days later.

By 1920 Joyce's library contained thirteen volumes of Shaw, comprising seventeen works. In Zurich during the war he had become involved with the English Players' Company's presentation of The Dark Lady of the Sonnets (for which he wrote a darkly amusing programme note) and some unauthorized performances of the still-censored Mrs Warren's Profession. Shaw raised legal objections to this production, but although it was without benefit of royalties, Joyce may have thought he was engaged in defeating censorship as Yeats had done with The Shewing-up of Blanco Posnet.

Joyce's review of that play at the Abbey had been a 'shewing-up' of G.B.S. as a writer incapable of the 'noble and bare style appropriate to modern playwrighting'. In Joyce's eyes, Shaw was a preacher and a mountebank rather than a literary artist. This was the obverse of Shaw's view of Joyce as a literary genius in danger of dwindling into a limited edition belletrist. 'I shall not do anything that may encourage him to be a coterie author,' he had warned Pound: 'Irish talent, when it is serious, belongs to the big world...'

That the world would venerate a linguistic experimenter like Joyce as well as a supernatural speculator like Yeats said something to Shaw of literature's removal from the streets into the universities. He did not keep up with Joyce's later work any more than with Yeats's. 'I have tried to read

Finnegan but found it would take more time to decipher than it seemed worth,' he wrote in 1948. '... I might have persevered when I was 20; but at 93 time is precious and the days pass like flights of arrows.' He was divided from both Yeats and Joyce by a generation that had profoundly changed the discipline of literature.

Joyce and Yeats absorbed the world around them into their own myths; Shaw and Wilde, in becoming dramatists, had turned themselves into extroverts. 'The complexity of Shaw does not lie, as it does in Yeats, in the language itself, in cryptic allusions and symbols, or in the manifold connotations attached to names of people and places,' wrote the critic A. M. Gibbs. 'Shaw's complexity lies in the total organization of his plays, in the relations between the larger strands of theme and action.' Joyce, like Yeats, reacted strongly against the commonplaces of Shaw's plays. 'He found the frank vulgarity of the music hall less offensive than the falsity of most of the legitimate drama of his day,' Stanislas Joyce remembered: 'Jones, Pinero ... and, most of all, Shaw.'

This reaction was one of many eddies in the flowing crosscurrents of the Celtic School. 'Allow me to offer my felicitations to you on the honour you have received and to express my satisfaction that the award of the Nobel Prize for literature has gone once more to a distinguished fellow townsman,' Joyce wrote in 1926. This was the only letter of congratulation Shaw kept. Had he persisted with *Finnegans Wake*, he would have found within its overlapping contexts many Shavian echoes and allusions from 'Sainte Andrée's Undershift' and 'St Mumpledum' to the injunction 'Plays be honest!' and the disarming 'Candidately'. As Stanley Weintraub has discovered, even Blanche Patch takes a bow in *Finnegans Wake*.

'An Academy can only be an Academy, and nothing else,' O'Casey had written. Wilde's great Celtic School found a symbol but never a centre in Yeats's Academy. Like Shaw, Yeats had thought in terms of synthesis. But the Celtic School depended on antitheses. It was a school of truancy, thriving on a pressure that drove people outwards, and on the tension and reproach of exiles 'too conscious of intellectual power to belong to party', as Yeats wrote when describing Wilde and Shaw together. Joyce, whose imagination was lit up by a reference Shaw made to Wilde's gigantism, also coupled them in the Wildeshawshow of *Finnegans Wake* as brother opposites, like Sterne and Swift, of the same generation. From such half-admiring antipathies the Celtic–Hibernian School gained its positive capability.

This is the way with us ageing men. In the decay of our minds the later acquisitions go first.
H. G. Wells's obituary of Shaw

'And now I have come from the burial of Thomas Hardy's ashes in the Abbey...' Charlotte wrote to T. E. Lawrence.

Hardy had died aged eighty-nine on the evening of Wednesday 11 January 1928. 'It is rather a shock... He and I were on very friendly terms,' G.B.S. was reported as saying. '...I always liked his poetry better than his prose.' They had seldom met – a good arrangement for them both. Shaw's references to Hardy, though few (and sometimes parenthetical), were never less than respectful, for he acknowledged the 'high explosive' of his work. In Shavian ideology the novels seemed to represent a limbo between old and new religions where men and women were regarded as random victims of accident and Nature, and everywhere the intention of life was unfulfilled. But Shaw responded to the sobriety of the poems, where a fraction of will was admitted even ironically into the human equation, and he claimed them as 'literary implements for forming the mind of the perfect modern Socialist and Creative Evolutionist'. In this context, Hardy's three-part epic drama in verse, *The Dynasts*, particularly interested him. He recognized in the Immanent Will, moving our history towards an imperfectly realized purpose, Hardy's version of the Life Force. And he welcomed the glimpse of hope at the end (which Hardy himself came to regret), linking the play with the third act of *Man and Superman* as part of a growing philosophical nexus. 'Its metaphysics have been worked out by Bergson in his Creative Evolution,' Shaw wrote to a correspondent. 'It is implicit in Hardy's Dynasts, and is, in fact, coming into consciousness in all directions as the religion of the next epoch.'

Two days after Hardy's death, Shaw received a telegram inviting him to act as one of the pallbearers at Westminster Abbey. 'I desire to be buried in Stinsford Churchyard,' Hardy had written in his will; but according to Shaw he 'knew that he must ultimately come to the Abbey and he was quite reconciled to it'. As an extreme compromise his body was dismembered and the heart buried at Stinsford while the ashes were being laid to rest in the Abbey. Many people were horrified by this mutilation which, coming before the burning and the imposition of ceremonious splendour, they likened to the barbarous rites of a savage tribe. But G.B.S. reassured Florence Hardy that, since her husband belonged to the nation as well as to himself, she had had no choice in the matter. 'I think that the objections are quite unreasonable,' he stated in the *Daily News*. 'Everything that could be done has been done to meet national sentiment. Wessex has the heart, the nation has his ashes.'

It was snowing hard on the day of the funeral, but sprawling crowds had assembled and lots were being drawn for tickets of admission to Poets' Corner. Shaw felt uncharacteristically nervous. 'I havent any proper clothes.' But Charlotte saw that he was properly turned out. She watched him anxiously. 'It seemed absurd to have an immense bier and a great and splendid pall, white, embroidered with royal crowns and many other emblems enclose one small casket, but it made its effect,' she told T. E. Lawrence. '...I was terribly afraid G.B.S. would act: he did it perfectly.'

Barrie, Galsworthy, Edmund Gosse, A. E. Housman and Kipling were the other writers acting as pallbearers; there were Masters of two colleges that had made Hardy an Honorary Fellow, Queen's College, Oxford, and Magdalene College, Cambridge; as well as the Prime Minister and the Leader of the Opposition, Stanley Baldwin and Ramsay MacDonald. 'I was curiously impressed by Baldwin,' Charlotte noted. '...he is far stronger than I thought.' Ramsay MacDonald too was strongly cast and, being used to the Abbey by this time, could warn the others to 'look out when you come to the choir entrance or the bier will catch you in the side of the head'. A young biographer who had journeyed down from Cambridge for the funeral observed that, in startling contrast to the weight and texture of the other pallbearers, Shaw seemed an ethereal presence. 'I have never seen so *transparent* a complexion; a pallor, very slightly tinged with the freshest rose – such as any girl or child alone normally has ... His hair alone, still a glinting *gilt*, wire-like tangle of reddish threads, was material.'

Moving down the south transept 'they all looked pale and dignified', William Rothenstein noticed. No one looked more dignified than Shaw and Galsworthy, paired off because of their height on either side of the catafalque. Shaw attributed his success, despite almost falling over Kipling, to having posed for Troubetzkoy in a sublime attitude: 'I was in full practice,' he told Henry Salt. The service, ending with Handel's Dead March from *Saul*, was wonderfully sung. The clergy, full of worldly pomp and disdain, led the procession; and at the end, erect and calm, came Florence 'so completely swathed in crape that her face was invisible'. But as the chords of the organ music swelled and burst out and the procession passed back, she hung on Sydney Cockerell's arm, Charlotte observed, and appeared 'completely broken'.

It was 'a fine show', G.B.S. admitted, 'and I tried to look as solemn as possible; but I didn't feel solemn a bit,' he afterwards wrote to Florence Hardy.

'If you only knew how I wanted at the end to swoop on you; tear off all that villainous crape (you should have been like the lilies of the field); and make you come off, *with him*, to see a Charlie Chaplin film! But of course we wouldn't have dared. I had to be content with nudging Cockerell disrespectfully as I passed him.'

It was a relief to Charlotte that these perverse high spirits had carried G.B.S. no further out of bounds. In fact he had behaved with sensitivity, informing the press that Hardy 'had no enemies, at least that I know of', but in a letter to Florence Hardy revealing his awareness that her married life had not been easy: 'Just go to bed and stay there until all your arrears of sleep are made up and you feel the return of spring making you jolly and selfish and lazy. That may not seem possible yet; but it is inconceivable that Thomas Hardy's widow should be unhappy or unblest. Only, don't marry another genius: they are not all so sound at the core; and anyhow he would be an anti-climax. Marry somebody who has nothing else to do than to take care of *you*.'

In the public imagination Shaw was the most obvious candidate to fill Hardy's position as 'Grand Old Man of English Literature' during the 1930s. Kipling, who had 'fidgeted like the devil' when Gosse introduced them at Westminster Abbey, was another possibility. Politically they had seldom been in step, and when Kipling died at the beginning of 1936 Shaw's tribute to this 'great story-teller who never grew up' makes it clear that in his eyes Kipling never attained the contemporary maturity of H. G. Wells. 'A great figure in what may be called imperialistic literature,' he described him, '... [who] had very odd ways when he came face to face with the realities of war in South Africa ... I don't think the reading of Kipling has ever changed anybody's life very much, but you may well say the same of Sir Walter Scott...'

*

'I cannot sympathize about his death,' Shaw remarked on hearing that the actor Robert Loraine had died, 'because I am going to die myself shortly.' He took the same determined line when James Barrie died eighteen months later in 1937. Barrie hugged seclusion, craved affection. Far from being, as the public imagined, a genuine Peter Pan (like G. K. Chesterton) he had struck Shaw as having been born a thousand years old (like Max Beerbohm). He was one of the few people whom Shaw admitted to have been unhappy. 'Certainly he regretted that he had no children. Perhaps he ought to have had children...' But what was terrifying to Shaw was the way he had killed the child in himself. 'He gave you the impression that for all his playfulness he had hell in his soul.'

Barrie was 'a survival of the nineteenth century just as I am,' Shaw told one newspaper. 'I suppose I am now the last, and you will probably hear soon that I am dead. The sooner the better.' During the 1920s and 1930s his supporting cast was comprehensively changing. The deaths of Fabian comrades, colleagues in the theatre and those who had influenced his early intellectual life were regularly announced in the newspapers, often with some tribute from Shaw.

The Shaws were abroad when, in the early summer of 1935, they heard the news that T. E. Lawrence had been killed. Charlotte felt profoundly thankful to be away: the publicity would have been awful. G.B.S. limited himself in public to a simple statement that Lawrence deserved to be commemorated in Westminster Abbey. 'His country which refused him a small pension, owes him at least a stone.' They missed the funeral at the tiny cemetery at Moreton Church near Lawrence's Cloud's Hill home, but arriving back later became engulfed in the mystery and melodrama of his death. Some of the evidence at the inquest had been contradictory and afterwards a few people launched a rumour that he had committed suicide. Others were to repeat how he had been trailed by a big black car – and presumably murdered. One woman wrote to G.B.S., letting him into her secret that the accident had been faked, a view which was to amplify whisperings of Lawrence's undercover work in the Middle East during the Second World War. The facts, as the Shaws understood them, were that Lawrence had been racing home from Bovington Camp on his Brough Superior 'Boanerges', a motorcycle with the same name as the bull-roarer in *The Apple Cart*, that the Shaws had given him. He had swerved to avoid some boys on bicycles, gone into a skid, and been thrown over the handlebars. Charlotte and G.B.S. faced this news, Blanche Patch observed, like stoics. Lawrence had only been forty-six; but perhaps, Charlotte speculated, it was for the best. He had been the strangest contact of her life. But dreadfully lonely. 'He always dreaded pain and the idea of death (as a sort of sign of defeat!) and now, you see, he had got off without knowing anything about it.'

Worst of all had been the news in May 1927 that H. G. Wells's wife Jane was dying of cancer. It seemed particularly terrible since Jane 'is *valiant* & has been the gayest & pluckiest person I have ever known', Charlotte wrote to Wells. Shaw also sent him a letter the same day: 'Of course I am as helpless as everybody else ... I cannot express any feelings: the thing is quite beyond that. There it is, blast it!'

A few days later they motored over to Little Easton to see her. Shaw was appalled by the atmosphere of the house. Jane lay exhausted on a broad sofa in the drawing-room while H.G. darted anxiously in and out. He was desperate to do anything that might make these last months easier for her, for he knew she was doomed. 'The doctors and the nurse, having committed themselves to the opinion that Jane is a goner, are naturally creating an atmosphere calculated to produce that effect even on a perfectly healthy woman; and H.G.'s confounded scientific education makes him susceptible to such suggestions,' Shaw protested in a letter to Beatrice Webb. 'It makes me feel like Hercules tearing the wife of Admetus out of the grip of death; and I am trying to make her defy science and have a turn at all the empiricisms as aids to curing herself. Charlotte was rather distressed...'

They visited Jane again that summer, before leaving for Italy in the last week of July, and saw her getting weaker. Both Charlotte and G.B.S. felt lowered. It was, as Charlotte said, 'beyond words' and Shaw agreed. 'There it is,' he had written with a tone of finality. But he could not leave it there. Being unable to 'express any feelings', he was driven to try out more words on Wells – words to expel the pessimism from his mind – even when Charlotte entreated him to stop. He wrote to communicate his relief that the cancer was inoperable, advised Wells to take a gamble on anything from homeopathy to osteopathy rather than settle for the absurdities of orthodox medicine, went through his well-rehearsed anti-vivisectionist routine, and encouraged his old friend to 'grasp the horror of your own scientific education'. This repertoire was meant to help Wells 'watch and wait with an undarkened mind'. But, though it probably had something of this effect on G.B.S., it can only have pushed Wells himself nearer the end of his tether. 'Charlotte says I can do no good by worrying you, as you will only be made more miserable,' G.B.S. ended his letter that August. 'But I do not regard you as a miserable person ... it would be very jolly to hear that Jane is all right. Send us a bulletin, however brief.'

But no bulletin came. To Wells, in his distress, Charlotte's simple anxieties sounded far more sympathetic than these spasms of Shavian jollity. 'Please H.G. dont be angry with him,' she wrote privately that September. 'You know he is like that – he must sometimes let himself go in this aggravating way – & he means it all so more than well! ... Do – *do* – write a line – to *me*, even, & say you ar'nt angry.' So, within four weeks of his wife's death, Wells was obliged to comfort Charlotte over her husband. 'Your charming letter brought peace to me & a great deal of thankfulness,' Charlotte replied later that month '...We think of you & talk of you constantly. Perhaps now it will not be so very long before we meet...'

They met the following month for Jane's cremation at Golders Green. 'I haven't been so upset for a long time,' Charlotte wrote. The service was 'hideous – terrible and frightful'. Wells, dressed in a bottle-blue overcoat, came and sat with her and G.B.S. instead of with his family, and the organ started on an appalling dirge. Everyone stood for what seemed hours: at any second, Charlotte feared, G.B.S. might stride over and murder the organist in his loft. Beside them Wells, his handkerchief darting in and out of his pocket, 'began to cry like a child – tried to hide it at first and then let go'.

The funeral speech had been prepared by Wells and was delivered by T. E. Page, a classical scholar noted for his oratory. 'This oration was either not well done,' observed Arnold Bennett, 'or too well done.' Virginia Woolf, who had been looking forward to the outing ('What fun! How I love ceremonies.') thought the presentation somewhat nondescript. But one of Wells's statements, which reminded her of something her father Leslie Stephen had said after her mother's death, touched her: 'Some are set on a headland & their lives are a beacon to mankind. Others live retired & are hardly known; but their lives are the most precious.' This appeared to set Bloomsbury values in perspective against the Shavian style of life. Yet to Charlotte it sounded like grief curdled by guilty sentiment. 'He drowned us in a sea of misery and as we were gasping began a panegyric of Jane which made her appear as a delicate, flower-like, gentle being, surrounding itself with beauty and philanthropy and love,' she wrote. ' . . . Then there came a place where the address said "she never resented a slight; she never gave voice to a harsh judgement". At that point the audience, all more or less acquainted with many details of H.G.'s private life, thrilled, like corn under a wet north wind – and H.G. – H.G. positively howled.' It seemed all painfully wrong to Charlotte who knew Jane to be an exceptionally strong character.

At the end of the service the pale grey coffin with 'tassels like bell pulls' was 'shoved through the door into the furnace'. The chapel emptied. G.B.S. trotted out into the garden and encouraged Wells to take his boys into the furnace room. 'I saw my mother burnt there. You'll be glad if you go.' Wells did go, taking his two sons, saw the bright quivering flames, and was 'very grateful for it'.

Charlotte remained in the chapel: 'I took a little time to get quiet.' When she came out into the yard most of the congregation was still there. 'Number of really A.1 people present, very small,' noted Arnold Bennett who saw only one man in full mourning and observed that G.B.S. who had no overcoat was wearing an amber handkerchief. The great world was no longer interested in Wells. 'It was desperate to see what a dowdy shabby imperfect lot we looked,' Virginia Woolf remarked: 'how feeble; how ugly for the most part.'

The purpose of Wells's valediction, she judged, had been to emphasize how generous lives continue. 'We were doing our best to say something sincere about our great adventure (as Wells almost called it). And he had been adventurous & plunged about in his bath & splashed the waters, to give him his due.' But Charlotte felt Wells had got his due in quite another sense. 'I am an old woman and there is one thing I seem, at least, to have learned,' she wrote grimly. 'The way of transgressors is hard.' Many of the congregation were in tears. Looking 'stately and calm, and remote', Virginia Woolf disengaged the tiny sobbing figure of Lydia Lopokova from Charlotte's arms while G.B.S. consoled her. 'You mustnt cry,' he said. 'Jane is well – Jane is splendid.'

Then he began to 'behave badly' Charlotte noticed, firing off 'jokes to everyone, and finally – putting H.G. into his car – he actually got a sort of grin out of *him*'. But Wells had no wish to grin and resented being made to betray his grief in this way. G.B.S. was more useful to him as an opponent, someone tender-hearted, stimulating, but wrong-headed who 'hates infirmity' and 'hates the fear of death'. All Shaw's comedy and philosophy were marshalled against these fears. They were particularly acute at Jane Wells's cremation because the occasion let loose speculation of what life would be like for him if Charlotte were to die. Charlotte had written to Wells attributing her husband's vexing behaviour to a feeling of powerlessness – 'G.B.S. is really worrying about you both dreadfully just now, & would do anything in his power to help you.' But the reality was that he had no power: 'I am as helpless as everybody else.' Against this spirit of helplessness he summoned up 'all the empiricisms' of magical medicine to reach beyond reality at a time when 'I have had too many of my friends assassinated'. 'You go on, less & less propitiator to the public & more & more to yourself,' Wells was to warn him. ' . . . Pray the God of yours to chasten & enlighten you – & he will vanish as he answers your prayer.'

Their friendly antagonism extended into a macabre postscript. In 1945 the *New Statesman* asked Shaw to draft an obituary of Wells and this was published when Wells died in the summer of 1946. It was an even-handed recollection of a spoilt man of genius, temperamental yet 'without malice'. But, unknown to Shaw, Wells had been asked at approximately the same time to write an obituary of him for the *Daily Express*. In their correspondence Wells had often sent his 'salutations to Charlotte, without whom your errors might become at times excessive'; and he had assured Charlotte herself that 'I hate doing anything contrariwise to you.' But now he was free from all restraints. His obituary was published over four years after his own death and came, St John Ervine remembered, like 'a piercing scream from the grave'. It had been written at the beginning of the atomic age when 'the whole species is mad, that is to say mentally out of adjustment to its environment' and Wells was tethered in despair. Associating this despair with feelings that had overwhelmed him at Jane's cremation, he pointed – one prophet accusing another – to G.B.S. as the transgressor. Here was an example of the 'mental and moral consequences of prolonged virginity' on an imaginative, nervously active person. 'As a rule prolonged virginity means no real ascetic purity,' he had argued. ' . . . A furtive sexual system grows up detached from the general activities.' Needing to distance himself from reality, G.B.S. had grown forever out of adjustment to his environment. A secondary, vindictive personality took control whose method of self-assertion was 'to inflict pain'.

This was the danger of G.B.S.'s fantasies. He had been ruthless over Jane's death, 'impelled to write . . . that she would be much to blame if she died. There was no such thing as cancer . . . ' Charlotte, 'that most lovable of women', had tried to prevent such vanities, and that was 'more and more her role as life went on', Wells continued.

'She had married this perplexing being in a passion of admiration . . . and she found she had launched that incalculable, lop-sided, *enfant terrible*, a man of genius, upon the world.'

*

It had been a weather-beaten friendship, its ravaging storms first breaking out over Fabian politics forty years back. 'I tried to see H. G. Wells in his last year . . . We were very good friends . . . On paper he died in despair; but I cannot believe that his gaiety ever deserted him,' Shaw was to write in 1946 to Gene Tunney. Tunney, the world heavyweight boxing champion, was full of gaiety. A handsome man, more than forty years younger than Shaw, he was famously unmarked, a scholar of the ring. His fastidious and abstracted air suggested that he had won the world championship on his way to acquiring a good library. Americans were puzzled on being told that he had been found, shortly before his first contest with Jack Dempsey, poring over Samuel Butler's *The Way of All Flesh*. They laughed openly at his contention that each match was a problem of scientific analysis and that he would beat Dempsey by virtue of his superior mental training, and they never really forgave him for twice out-pointing their All-American Hero. For as Benny Green has written, 'he had contradicted the myth of an entire generation'.

Tunney's career was a Shavian romance. He regarded G.B.S. as 'the possessor of one of the greatest minds among living men – possibly the greatest', and some of his reasoning (such as attributing his lack of killer instinct to an invincible absence of fear) was quintessentially Shavian. Shaw himself was tremendously impressed by his victories over Dempsey. He had never seen anything so wonderful as Tunney's dance round the ring on Movietone News when he got up from the punch that put him on the canvas. 'His confidence in himself and his system amounts to something like contempt for his most famous adversaries,' Shaw wrote: 'reputations cannot frighten him: personalities cannot hypnotize him: he does not need to be a brilliant boxer like Carpentier or a terror like Dempsey; he wins by mental and moral superiority, combined with plenty of strength ... he most certainly is the most remarkable character; and it is on character that he has won. You might say that he wins because he has the good sense to win.'

Here was Shaw's fantasy of action made real, Cashel Byron come to life. The visionary prizefighter defeated the pugilist, the realist triumphed over the philistine, and Shavianism had its revenge on the capitalist champion. Others, too, had made the connection between Cashel Byron and Tunney, and one of them attempted to buy the motion picture rights in the story, providing Tunney agreed to star in it. But Tunney gravely let it be known that he viewed *Cashel Byron's Profession* as the product of Shaw's 'immature years'. Had G.B.S. written it forty years later, Cashel Byron 'would be a stronger, finer character', he stated, with more 'gentlemanly traits about him' – he would have been more like Tunney in the 1920s. Shaw agreed. 'Tunney is quite right in describing the work as immature,' he told the *New York Times* in 1926, 'but I am not quite sure he knows what boxers in the nineteenth century were like.' Had Tunney lived in those days he would inevitably have been more like Cashel Byron. Shaw had no objection to Tunney modernizing his novel. 'If Tunney said those things, he must have good taste. I'd like to meet the young man.'

They met in December 1928. Earlier that year Tunney had retired, like Cashel Byron, as undefeated heavyweight champion, after which he delivered a course of lectures on Shakespeare at Yale, accompanied Thornton Wilder on a walking trip round Europe and married a young gentlewoman from Greenwich, Connecticut. 'My great work now is to live quietly and simply,' he announced to the world, 'for this manner of living brings me most happiness.' His pursuit of culture led him, by the end of this year, to 'an extremely pleasant' luncheon at Whitehall Court.

He spoke of his travels over many countries and it was then that he introduced the Shaws to Brioni in the Adriatic, where they all met up the following year. The friendship began unpromisingly with a rather pointless practical joke. 'I sent him a case of cordials pretending they were wines, to get his reaction,' Tunney explained. 'I also sent a letter with the case, written in broken English explaining my devotion to him and not believing the report of his teetotalism.' Shaw's politeness having cleared this hurdle, their friendship bounded forward. Tunney was 'so handsome & gentle & babyish that it refreshes one to look at him', Charlotte wrote from Brioni to Nancy Astor. 'He takes G.B.S. for long walks (his boast is that you can walk 8 miles on the Island without repeating yourself!) & gazes at him, like a large dog at its master.'

This was a great boon to Charlotte who was in a state of nervous exhaustion following the death of her sister early that April. 'If Charlotte ever has more distress than I can pull her through I will send for you,' Shaw had written to Nancy Astor. In the event he had lightened Charlotte's ordeal with a little comic relief ('I think we all enjoyed ourselves,' he reported after the funeral). 'Mrs Chumly', who began as such an enemy of their marriage and ended as the dedicatee of *The Intelligent Woman's Guide*, had 'lived her life well out'.

On Brioni the Shaws passed many gentle days at the Tunneys' villa. 'He is a great resource in affliction,' Charlotte wrote. Even when she was well, Charlotte suspected G.B.S. of taking advantage of her siestas to press secretly ahead with his work. Now when she felt so tired, the knowledge that he was being actively prevented from working by Gene Tunney came as a tremendous relief to her as she ascended to her bedroom. 'Mr Tunney is a most wonderful help,' she reported to Blanche Patch. 'He takes Mr Shaw off to the polo ground, or the golf course, or sailing, or something, and so keeps him from writing, which is splendid.' Almost the only work G.B.S. was able to get down to on the island was a film scenario modernizing *Cashel Byron* and incorporating the actual Tunney-Dempsey fights – a silent dream that 'the advent of the talkies has upset . . . ' he afterwards told Tunney. 'I could not produce genuine American dialogue.'

When asked why he cultivated Tunney's friendship, G.B.S. was to reply: 'To plant my feet on solid ground.' Yet it was as airy a fantasy in its fashion as his island romance with Molly Tompkins – a magical relationship that enabled them to swap roles, G.B.S. being admitted as a champion boxing analyst in exchange for adopting Tunney as a very perfect literary gentleman. For Tunney this was 'one of the outstanding blessings of my life'. He met all manner of artists and writers at the Shaws' home, and they had to strain every nerve to match his sensitivity. 'You would never have guessed his profession from his conversation. It was so literary, you know,' remarked Max Beerbohm after dining with him there.

'The windows of G.B.S's flat looked out over the river, and the sun was setting . . . Mr Tunney took me by the arm and led me to the windows and compelled my attention to the beauties of the sunset . . . I had *never* before met anyone so militantly aesthetic.'

It was a shocking experience for a critic who, when reviewing *Cashel Byron's Profession* thirty years before, had stated categorically: 'Cashel does not credibly exist for us: he is the victim of a thesis.'

By the early 1930s Tunney had 'got into the book-writing field myself' with his memoirs of the ring, *A Man Must Fight*. Shaw refused to contribute a Preface, explaining that the publisher 'wants to trap my circulation on top of yours; but when you want a publisher for your next book on the strength of this one they will all declare that your first book does not count as it was the Shaw preface that sold it . . . if a publisher intimated to me that he would not touch a book of mine unless it had a preface by Gene Tunney, I should summon the last scrap of my failing strength and jump on him until we were both dead'. Besides, Tunney had his own public and was far more famous than any writer or artist. 'You may remember that at Brioni, when I was talking to Richard Strauss, nobody troubled about us until you joined us,' Shaw wrote to him; 'and then the cameras came with a rush.'

By the late 1930s, after Tunney had been retired for ten years, a change came over their relationship. G.B.S. was now the more famous of the two, and Tunney's confidence took a dive: 'I began to feel that I had no right to intrude on his time.' During the Second World War Tunney served as a United States Naval officer and 'was reluctant to write to him then'. But out of the blue a letter was to arrive from G.B.S. at the end of 1946. 'I feel I must give you a hail to shew that I have not forgotten our old happy contacts.' He had now passed his ninetieth birthday, 'have only some scraps of wit left and shall soon forget the alphabet and the multiplication table and be unable to walk more than a hundred yards without two sticks', he wrote. 'Still I am alive enough to drop you a line.'

Tunney being once more the stronger of the two, their friendship was resumed. 'I am not worth the journey,' Shaw warned him in 1948, but Tunney came to Ayot and noticed how keenly his friend was feeling his great age. G.B.S. was still eager to keep up-to-date and learn all there was to know about the new heavyweight wonder of the world, Joe Louis, who was reported as being anxious to exchange a few verbal rounds with him and the other champion of Britain, Winston Churchill: 'two comparatively unknown persons like myself and Mr Churchill could not but feel flattered by a visit from a world-famous head of his profession', Shaw said.

That summer, in his last letter to Tunney, Shaw signed off: 'I hold you in affectionate remembrance.' Afterwards Tunney wrote to Stanbrook Abbey that Shaw had been 'the saintliest man I have ever known'.

The Prioress of Stanbrook Abbey, Dame Laurentia McLachlan, was another of Shaw's new friends. Like Tunney, she was an island of confidence in a doubting world. She had been officially received into the

Order of St Benedict on the same day in 1884 that Shaw was enrolled in the Fabian Society. The Bishop had sheared off the long fair hair of the seventeen-year-old girl; and, dressed in a plain tunic of rough serge, she was symbolically clothed with a girdle, scapular and white veil. Then 'the great enclosure door swung open in answer to the novice's importunate knocking, and presently closed slowly again behind her, shutting out the world and its vanities for ever'. For almost seventy years behind high walls, church grilles and bolted doors, she was to follow the exacting codes and liturgical functions of the enclosed Benedictine discipline, devoting each day to prayer, scholarship and the ceremonial worship of God.

The Abbey of Stanbrook was a Victorian Gothic pile not far from Malvern. By the 1920s it had become a place of pilgrimage for Catholic savants and an oasis for many exotic travellers through 'the world and its vanities'. For some it was like revisiting their public school. One of these was Sydney Cockerell, the astringent antiquarian who had been a friend of Shaw's since his days as William Morris's secretary at Hammersmith. Cockerell first met Dame Laurentia in 1907, the year before he was appointed Director of the Fitzwilliam Museum at Cambridge. He had come to the Abbey to examine a thirteenth-century psalter and would continue to advise the Stanbrook Abbey Press. His curiosity was soon pricked by this nun with the beautiful voice in her 'rather nice cage' and he felt somewhat in awe of her great reputation among co-religionists as an authority on plainsong and liturgical ritual. The double grille through which they communicated seemed to simplify human relationships, and they quickly found a position of mutual scholarly assistance. He trusted her never to place a book she borrowed from him 'in the hands of anyone who does not know how to turn over the leaves or that the paint and gilding must not be touched'. She trusted him 'implicitly not to put before me anything that would be inconsistent in the least degree with the principles upon which our life is based and which you grasp and appreciate so fully'.

This was not easy. On one occasion Cockerell proffered some writings by Tolstoy whom he so admired that he had travelled all the way to Yasnaya Polyana to be in his company for half a day. But Tolstoy was unwelcome at Stanbrook Abbey: 'his works are not at all on the lines in which my reading lies', Dame Laurentia pronounced. After such a dismissal Cockerell sensed he must advance cautiously.

'Some I have to keep apart, others I wish to bring together,' he wrote to her. 'There are several I should very much like you to meet.' From the first, Shaw had been one of those Cockerell wanted her to meet. 'I wonder whether G.B.S's fame has got as far as Stanbrook,' he enquired in 1907, 'and whether he is there regarded as an imp of the devil – I have known him for many years and regard him not only as one of the cleverest (that is nothing) but as one of the best and honestest of living Englishmen.'

'I have never heard of Mr Bernard Shaw,' Dame Laurentia replied, '. . . I don't like to think that a person whom you regard with respect should be to us as a limb of the evil one!'

So Cockerell prudently held off until receiving an opening from Dame Laurentia seventeen years later. 'I hear Bernard Shaw has written a play about St Joan,' she wrote. 'I will lend you Shaw's play to read,' he offered. '. . . *Joan* is not yet published and mine is a very special copy . . . you may read it aloud to the nuns if you think it will edify them.'

He sent her his special copy; she thought it 'a wonderful play' and on returning it wrote: 'Joan herself is beautifully portrayed.' But it was not wholly edifying. On a number of historical and theological matters Shaw had gone astray. 'I should like to make some alterations . . . Mr Shaw's aspect of the trial does not please me.' Cockerell was sufficiently encouraged to show this letter to the Shaws themselves. Nine days later, on 24 April 1924, Dame Laurentia received a note from Charlotte enclosing two visiting cards: 'Our friend Sydney Cockerell has urged us very strongly to call upon you. We feel a little diffident about doing so, and hope you will not think us intrusive. But it would be a great pleasure to see you.'

After this formal opening came an impetuous rush as Charlotte and G.B.S. hurtled up to the Abbey a few hours later. Cockerell was as eager as a marriage-broker to find out how the hour between them had passed. He pressed Charlotte, who eventually revealed that 'we enjoyed our visit to her . . . We like her *very* much.' From Dame Laurentia he learnt that the Shaws were 'charming' and their conversation was 'very pleasant'. All this was highly frustrating for Cockerell, a 'born intriguer and puller of strings', but over the next six or seven years an enticing relationship began to shimmer before him.

It had the air of a flirtation. That was how Charlotte saw it: a chaste flirtation. Cockerell, she thought, 'gives the impression (sometimes) of restrained emotion, but I don't think he feels anything very deeply really'. What did G.B.S. really feel for Dame Laurentia? It was hard to muster much jealousy, but Charlotte tried. She seldom accompanied him on his jaunts to Stanbrook, preferring to take the opportunity while he was at these tête-à-têtes of 'tidying his writing table'. Sometimes she turned up all sorts of naughtinesses there. 'He went off this morning with Sydney Cockerell – who is as bad as himself – to flirt with an "enclosed" nun at Stanbrook Abbey,' she wrote in the summer of 1929 to Nancy Astor.

'It was an immense treat to see you and Shaw together,' Cockerell wrote deferentially to Dame Laurentia following this visit. 'You were both of you at your best & I think the encounter was a mutual tonic.' He was impressed by Shaw's manners. 'I never saw him so abashed by anyone but William Morris.'

Dame Laurentia agreed that 'Brother Bernard' was a 'delicious' tonic. She called him Brother Bernard ever since he had given her a copy of *Saint Joan* with the inscription: 'To Sister Laurentia from Brother Bernard.' He had taken the trouble to answer her objections to the play, explaining that in 'heathen literature like mine', it was necessary to present Joan's visions in such a way as to make them completely independent of the iconography attached to her religion: 'if I wrote in terms of this doctrine I should, from their own point of view, be calling, not sinners, but the righteous to salvation; and my book would reach no further than the penny lives of the saints which they sell in the Churches in Ireland. I want my sound to go out into all lands.'

This letter, Dame Laurentia acknowledged, 'pleases me greatly in spite of its heresies'. Immediately he seized upon and appropriated her pleasure: 'I am delighted to learn that my St Joan is yours also. It sets my mind completely at ease.' She had not meant to go quite so far as that, 'but when it comes to disagreeing, I find judgement very difficult', she confided to Cockerell. 'Brother Bernard has such a pretty knack of turning on you with a whimsical smile when you think you have caught him.' Yet this elusive and complex man continued to impress her with his 'absolute sincerity and simplicity'.

As Cockerell noticed, they complemented each other in various ways. 'I was greatly interested to meet such a famous man,' Dame Laurentia owned. She felt a special softness for famous people: they were a delightful disturbance in her seclusion. For Shaw her magic came from the opposite pole to that of Gene Tunney, 'another very special friend whose vocation was as widely different from yours as any two vocations on earth can be'. Tunney was 'a good man' imprisoned within the phenomenon of world publicity; Dame Laurentia seemed to hate publicity as much as Charlotte did ('there is nothing I should, or rather do, dislike more than advertisement or publicity of any kind', she explained to Shaw). She was, he hoped, an enclosed nun without an enclosed mind whose private world he could approach, 'shake your bars and look longingly at the freedom at the other side of them'. She appeared to represent an aspect of his own character he had eliminated during the creation of G.B.S. Her place in his life was really closer to that of the retiring Henry Salt than of William Morris who, with his 'robust conscience and healthy sensuality', had been a fighter in the world's campaigns. 'My pastime has been writing sermons in plays, sermons preaching what Salt practised,' Shaw wrote; and in much the same tone, he

9 Lady Astor with G.B.S. on his 73rd birthday

10 Shaw and Elgar at Malvern

11A G.B.S., Edith Evans and Cedric Hardwicke at the first Malvern Festival, 1929;
B Shaw in Moscow, 1931

12 'For much of this marriage Charlotte had remained unseen by the general public'.
They embark for their world tour, 1934

13 On the top of Table Mountain, January 1932

14A At the hot springs in Rotorua, New Zealand, 1934; B South Africa, January 1932

15A In Shanghai, 1933, l. to r. Agnes Smedley, Shaw, Madame Sun, Cai Yuan-pei,
Harold Isaacs (behind), Lin Yutang, Lu Hsun; B At a Hollywood lunch given by
Marion Davies with l. to r. Charlie Chaplin, Marion Davies, Louis B. Mayer,
Clark Gable.

16 With 'Grand Old Man' Sir Ho Tung in Hong Kong

confided to Dame Laurentia: 'you have lived the religious life: I have only talked and written about it'.

This attitude, Cockerell believed, accounted for Shaw's 'good behaviour' and seemed to admit 'that he was in the presence of a being superior to himself'. It came as no surprise to Dame Laurentia herself. She was, after all, in possession of the true creed. Of course she knew that other creeds and philosophies contained aspects of the truth heralding Christianity, but they were plainly riddled with Error. How perplexing then that intellectual aristocrats of the calibre of Cockerell and Shaw remained so wrong-headed, particularly Shaw who seemed to have a genuine understanding of the contemplative life. It was a 'sad puzzle' to her. Had they been born Catholics their minds would have thrived in a 'natural atmosphere'; as it was, they were 'very much to be pitied'. And very much to be prayed for too. 'You expose yourself to the danger of being prayed for very earnestly,' she warned Shaw, who welcomed this current of goodwill travelling towards him through the ether ('it would be shockingly unscientific to doubt it'). He could positively assert that he never felt any the worse for these prayers.

Though he put off the mantle of G.B.S., Shaw was still like a visiting jester at the Abbey. He enjoyed pretending to be bad. 'I shall begin by kicking my cloven hoof too obviously for your dignity and peace,' he admitted; 'but I mean well, and find great solace in writing to you . . . ' Such courtesy sounded like a call for guidance. Though Laurentia was equally available to the poor and unknown, these rich and celebrated visitors to Stanbrook could be of special benefit. 'Do you remember when you gave me one of your plays, you advised me to sell it?' she reminded Shaw. 'I have been tempted to take your advice, for I am in great need of money – just £5,000 would be a fortune to me – but I know that a seller would advertise the owner's name & I should not be able to endure that.' She valued Shaw's generosity and would sometimes tuck in a discreet financial reminder with her prayerful inveigling of his soul. 'I am more glad than ever not to have a millionairess in my monastic family,' she told him after he sent her his play *The Millionairess*, 'useful as her cash would be.'

Shaw valued Dame Laurentia for some of the same overpowering qualities she shared with the heroine of that play. He saw her as a millionairess of the spirit and a natural authoritarian. 'You would boss the establishment if you were only the scullery maid,' he told her. He relied on this strength like a child relying on his mother; indeed, she was more a Mother Superior to him than a Sister. He could be naughty and she would be wise. It was more than he expected. When Cockerell asked him after his first visit when he intended going again, he had been adamant: 'Never.' But then he suddenly enquired of Cockerell how long Dame Laurentia had been at Stanbrook, and being told it was the best part of fifty years, he reconsidered: 'Oh, that alters the case, I'll go whenever I can.' This story, which Cockerell delightedly passed on, gave Dame Laurentia the 'confidence to hope that God may use me for this soul's salvation'. But she had misunderstood the story. The centre of their relationship for her was the opportunity it offered for making a convert of G.B.S. to the divine spiritual and moral doctrine of Catholicism. But catholicity for him meant comprehensiveness and a collectivist universality of interests. The essence of their relationship lay in the unchangeableness of their positions and the complementary views and uses they could offer each other.

Shaw was an eye witness of the world providing visual confirmation for Dame Laurentia of what she already knew. She accepted all his impressions, jokes, reflections, books with simple interest. The most dramatic use of his eye came on a journey he made with Charlotte in March 1931 to the Holy Land. She had sent her blessing and asked him to 'bring me back some little trifle from Calvary'. But there was no credible Calvary, he discovered, and nothing removable, he wrote to Cockerell, 'except by a squad of engineers backed by a victorious army'. Rosaries and testaments bound in 'the wood of the Cross', together with all sorts of sham relics, were thrust at him by crowds of Jewish pedlars; and the only genuine souvenirs of Gethsemane he found to send her were some olive leaves, with which she was well pleased. Then, from the threshold of the Church of the Nativity in Bethlehem, he picked up a pebble, a chip of the limestone rock 'which certainly existed when the feet of Jesus pattered about on it and the feet of Mary pursued him ... '

'In fact I picked up two little stones: one to be thrown blindfold among the others in Stanbrook garden so that there may always be a stone from Bethlehem there, though nobody will know which it is and be tempted to steal it, and the other for your own self.'

This second stone, which he presented to Dame Laurentia later that year, was set in a silver medieval-style reliquary designed by Paul Cooper. Cockerell, who had recommended the work of Paul Cooper, suggested adding an inscription stating that it was from Shaw to Dame Laurentia and explaining its purpose. But Shaw refused: 'If we could explain its purpose we could explain the universe,' he appealed to Dame Laurentia, '... our finger prints are on it, and Heaven knows whose footprints may be on the stone. Isn't that enough?'

Besides, he had sent her enough words in his letters enabling her to bring alive what she had imagined of the Holy Land. 'I look forward to the promised account of your pilgrimage,' she had entreated him: and he told her of

'a region in which the miraculous is no longer miraculous but gigantically normal . . . with strange new constellations all over the sky and the old ones all topsy turvy, but with the stars soft and large and down quite close overhead in the sky which you feel to be of a deep and lovely blue. When the light comes you . . . are in a hilly country, with patches of cultivation wrested from the omnipresent stones, which you instantly recognize with a strange emotion which intensifies when you see a small boy coming down one of the patches, and presently, when he has passed away, a bigger boy of about thirteen, beginning to think, and at last, when he too has vanished, a young man, very grave and somewhat troubled, all three being dressed just as Christ dressed . . . The appearance of a woman with an infant in her arms takes on the quality of a vision . . . It gives you the feeling that here Christ lived and grew up, and that here Mary bore him and reared him, and that there is no land on earth quite like it.'

'You have made me feel that I have seen the Holy Land through your eyes,' Dame Laurentia answered, 'and have revealed a great deal more than I should have seen with my own. I . . . continue to view the world from my cell at Stanbrook.'

*

These long-distance friendships with a heavyweight boxer and an enclosed nun were characteristic of someone who picked up facts from everywhere and ran lines of communication between one discipline and another. 'Nowadays a Catholic who is ignorant of Einstein is as incomplete as a thirteenth-century Dominican ignorant of Aristotle,' Shaw wrote to Alfred Douglas in 1938. ' . . . Religion without science is mere smallmindedness.'

Science meant two things to Shaw. In its derogatory manifestation it was the algebraic hocus-pocus that had befuddled him at school and hypnotized so many adults. The codes and rituals of this superstitious system formed a second network of philistine defence after the Bible-smashing advance of Darwinism. There were scientists on both sides in this warfare, and the battle lines teemed with spies and fifth-column agents. Speedily replacing eternity with infinity, astrophysicists were flinging 'millions of eons about in the most lordly manner' or mystically descanting on the 'incredible smallness of the atom' and other fairy tales. Shaw viewed these priests of science as an élite corps of idealists who had corrupted physics and biology, and ingeniously substituted illusory progress for real progress. Using misplaced religious devotion, they had strengthened the philistine's citadel with inflexible scientific axioms and given it a brilliant technological façade.

Shaw classed these renegade scientists with clairvoyants, diviners, hand readers and slate writers – all 'marvel mongers whose credulity would have dissolved the Middle Ages in a roar of sceptical merriment'.

The Shaw who believed that scientific advancement would benefit society was the author of *The Irrational Knot* whose common-sense hero had been an electrical engineer. This same Shaw had subscribed to Karl Pearson's *Biometricka* and looked forward to seeing the statistical methods applied to biology widened at the London School of Economics so as to promote a 'scientifically civilized society'. He was also a life member of the Royal Astronomical Society and, in his nineties, would register his belief in the necessity of space travel by joining the British Interplanetary Society. This Shaw classed himself among scientific humanists and expected science to be used for the improvement of agriculture, labour conditions and sanitation. He looked forward to 'scientific suffrage' in our democratic evolution, and to a time when candidates for political office would need to master the mathematics underlying the economic theories of rent and exchange value as one of the tests of political capacity. 'The whole world has to be reorganized, has to be reset,' he stated during a speech early in 1920. 'That has to be done by thinkers, and men of science in the very best sense, and has to be done in the interests of humanity.'

This statement was made four months after *The Times* carried two articles on the verification of Einstein's General Theory of Relativity, explaining its revolutionary effect on scientific orthodoxy. 'Enough has been done to overthrow the certainty of ages,' *Times* readers were told, 'and to require a new philosophy of the universe, a philosophy that will sweep away nearly all that has hitherto been accepted as the axiomatic basis of physical thought.'

This was immensely exciting to Shaw. In *Back to Methuselah*, which was completed in May 1920, he made the scientist Pygmalion speak of children in the future possessing an innate 'sense of space time and quantity' and of knowing by instinct many things that the greatest physicists of the twentieth century 'could hardly arrive at by forty years of strenuous study'. For the first time in this play Shaw 'used mathematical speculation to characterize advanced intelligence', observed the critic Desmond McRory.

McRory argues that Shaw began writing futuristic plays after the First World War out of 'despair over the failure of his contemporaries and a desire to deal with a time distant enough to be hopeful'. He could use mathematics and the physical sciences to look beyond pessimism because Einstein had finally made nineteenth-century arguments obsolete. 'The universe of Isaac Newton, which has been an impregnable citadel of modern civilization for three hundred years,' says the Elder in *Too True to be Good*, 'has crumbled like the walls of Jericho before the criticism of Einstein.'

Shaw and Einstein first met at a dinner party early in June 1921 when Einstein was visiting London. In the nine years that passed before their second meeting in the autumn of 1930, their knowledge of each other had been advanced by Shaw's mathematical biographer Archibald Henderson. In 1923 Henderson published *Relativity. A Romance of Science* which Shaw sent to a number of his friends including Beerbohm, Belloc, Chesterton and Wells. At the end of that year Henderson had gone to the Institute of Physics at the University of Berlin to work with Einstein on relativity and atomic theory, and to instruct him on Shavian drama and politics in the evenings. On his return he resumed his schooling of Shaw on the latest advances in physics and the meaning of many scientific terms used by Einstein. 'I can't imagine why you take such interest in the Shavian drama when you could be devoting all your time to the study of Tensors,' Shaw wrote to him.

Henderson also facilitated a series of sympathetic exchanges between the two men. On being told that Shaw thought he looked more like a musician than a mathematician, Einstein had replied that 'the creative mathematician was always an artist, with a highly developed sense of form', an answer that delighted the artist-philosopher G.B.S. who told Henderson that it enabled him to 'take Einstein on trust'. By 1925 Shaw was speaking of Einstein as the great destroyer of scientific infallibility: 'he has upset the velocity of light, upset the ether, upset gravitation, and generally lit . . . a fire among the gods of the physicists'.

On Shaw's seventieth birthday Einstein published a tribute to G.B.S. describing his 'impersonal power of artistic expression' as having 'blessed and educated all of us'. Reading *The Intelligent Woman's Guide* two years later and feeling as a fellow socialist that he wanted to do 'something effective for the cause', he told the editor-in-chief of the *Berliner Tageblatt* that he found Shaw's book 'so excellent and so important for political enlightenment' that he would 'gladly permit the use of my name for the purpose of spreading his influence'.

Shaw and Einstein met again in October 1930 at a public dinner at the Savoy Hotel given by the Joint British Committee of Ort and Oze for promoting the economic and physical welfare of East European Jewry. Shaw's speech proposing Einstein's health, and Einstein's reply, were recorded by the BBC and broadcast to America. It was a singular moment for G.B.S. He could say exactly what he felt ('we have no suppressions to make, no hypocrisy to be guilty of') since his feelings, the polite occasion, and his ideological commitment to progress came naturally together. 'Suppose that I had to rise here tonight to propose the toast of Napoleon,' he said: 'undoubtedly I could say many flattering things about Napoleon, but the one thing which I should not be able to say about him would be . . . that perhaps it would have been better for the human race if he had never been born!'

Shaw classed Einstein as belonging to a different order of great men, a man of genius selected by Nature to carry on the work of building up an intellectual consciousness whose 'hands are unstained by the blood of any human being on earth'. He explained, too, the affinity he felt for this man who had recently spoken of his need for solitude. 'One may well understand that a man with faculties so much greater than ours must feel lonely on such occasions . . . we all have our little solitudes. My friend Mr Wells has spoken to us sometimes of the secret places of the heart. There are also the lonely places of the mind . . . our little solitude gives us something of a key to his solitude . . . his great and august solitude.'

Shaw represented Einstein's discoveries as arising from 'the intuitions of an artist, and I, as an artist, claim kinship with this great discoverer'.

' . . . I rejoice at the new universe to which he has introduced us. I rejoice in the fact that he has destroyed all the old sermons, all the old absolutes, all the old cut and dried conceptions, even of time and space, which were so discouraging because they seemed so complicated that you never could get any further. I want to get further and further. I always want more and more problems, and our visitor has raised endless and wonderful problems and has begun solving them.'

Shaw's toast – 'Health and length of days to the greatest of our contemporaries, Einstein' – is a salute to the ultimate realist of the twentieth century. In the plays and books of Shaw's last twenty years, Einstein was to become a symbol of human possibility, showing what mankind might be capable of within its existing framework. 'You are the only sort of man in whose existence I can see much hope for this deplorable world,' Shaw had written to Einstein.

In his reply at the Savoy, Einstein described what he believed Shaw's achievement to have been as a dramatist. 'From your box of tricks you have taken countless puppets which, whilst resembling men, are not of flesh and bone, but consist entirely of spirit, wit, and grace . . . '

'You make these gracious puppets dance in a little world guarded by the Graces who allow no resentment to enter in. Whoever has glanced into this little world, sees the world of our reality in a new light; he sees your puppets blending into real people . . . you have been able, as no other contemporary, to effect in us a liberation, and to take from us something of the heaviness of life.'

CHAPTER IV

[1]

I have just been in Russia – the oddest place you can imagine. They have thrown God out by the door; and he has come in again by all the windows in the shape of the most tremendous Catholicism.
Shaw to Dame Laurentia McLachlan (1931)

After exhausting the possible, he [Napoleon] had to attempt the impossible and go to Moscow. He failed; and from that moment he had better have been a Philadelphia Quaker ... his failure made him the enemy of the human race.
What I Really Wrote about the War

'Good news from Russia, eh?' Shaw had written to Frank Harris on learning the news of Kerensky's revolution in February 1917. 'Not quite what any of the belligerents intended ... but the Lord fulfils himself in many ways.'

In the early days of the war Sasha Kropotkin, daughter of the revolutionary anarchist Prince Peter Kropotkin, had prophesied that Holy Russia would come to save the soul of the world. It seemed a wild prediction. To the overwhelming mass of Russian peasants, the Tsar was still a god. But early in 1917 Shaw's hopes sprang up between two vast areas of political sterility.

One sterile plain had been Russian tsardom itself. 'It is our business,' he wrote in November 1914, 'not to help this abomination to hide itself under the mantle of Tolstoy.' He admitted to being strongly susceptible to the fascination of the Russian character as expressed in its music and literature; but 'when we fight for the Tsar we are not fighting for Tolstoy and Gorki, but for the forces that Tolstoy thundered against all his life ...'

In military terms he accepted the Allies' need for the steamroller of the Tsar's army. But this alliance with 'the most barbarous and bigoted autocracy in Europe' undermined our moral position. How could the cause of Russia, with its maintenance of a 'personal despotism which England got rid of by a revolution in the seventeenth century, France in the eighteenth, and Italy in the nineteenth', be part of 'the moral forces of humanity' for which Asquith proclaimed we were fighting? Their 'Bloody Sunday' in the Palace Square of St Petersburg on 9 January 1905 had resulted in two hundred peaceful demonstrators being shot. The language Shaw and others used to describe tsardom was to become familiar ten and twenty years later in Western reports of Stalinism. With its Siberian exiles, its pogroms, terrors, massacres, the Tsar's regime 'under which women spent years in dungeons for teaching children to read ... laborers lived in cellars and ... the dear princesses could hire a droschky to take them to the Opera for four pence', was the most inequitable society in Europe and should, Shaw recommended in 1915, be excommunicated from international society as 'the open enemy of every liberty we boast of'.

He made what efforts he could to find out what was happening in Russia during 1917. Early on, he had welcomed the turn of events, writing that spring in the *New York Times* of 'the enormous relief, triumph, and delight with which the news of the revolution in Russia was received in England'. The world was watching. There must be unity among communists everywhere. 'I regard the revolution as such a gain to humanity that it not only at last justifies the Franco-Anglo-Russian alliance (which in the days of the tsardom was a disgrace to western democracy), but justifies the whole war,' he wrote to Gorki in May 1917.

For most of this year Shaw found himself in unusual accord with liberal opinion in Britain. An incubus seemed to have been lifted from Eastern Europe. 'Hail! The Russian Revolution,' proclaimed Ramsay MacDonald when opening a Great Labour, Socialist and Democratic Convention held in Leeds that summer to 'Organize the British Democracy to follow Russia'. At the Albert Hall in London another joyful meeting was packed out and 20,000 people had to be refused tickets. 'Every person there was wanting a real absolute change in everything,' Bertrand Russell affirmed, 'not the sort of piecemeal niggling reforms that one is used to, but the sort of thing the Russians have done ... The Russians have really put a new spirit into the world, & it is going to be worth while to be alive.' Many felt as if they were living at the time of the French Revolution. It was 'a tremendous event for me', acknowledged Leonard Woolf 'and for all those whose beliefs and hopes had been moulded in the revolutionary fires of liberty, equality, fraternity'. People were filled with a sense of liberation. This 'giant stride from autocracy to republic-democracy astounded Western Europe', recorded H. G. Wells. '... Today Russia stands a gigantic challenge to every vestige of the dynastic system that has darkened, betrayed, and tormented Europe for unnumbered years.'

By the end of the year, however, what Wells called 'this banner of fiery hope' had been extinguished for many of these orators and idealists by Lenin's Bolshevik Revolution. There had been much in Kerensky's administration that was naturally appealing to Shaw. Kerensky's status as a lawyer and the presence in the provisional government of princes and historians gave these moderates a Fabian respectability. They had come to power by revolution, but it had been 'bloodless'. Shaw had felt the need to justify his revulsion from violence. Murder and arson, he argued, might clear the way for change but they brought the goals of socialism no nearer. Before 1917, he saw parliamentary action not as an alternative to physical force, but as its first stage. 'The mistake made by our wildcat barricades is not in believing that the revolution will be effected by force,' he had written, 'but in putting the fighting at the wrong end of the process.'

Kerensky's problems in uniting the ill-equipped masses mortally sick of fighting with the bourgeoisie who wanted to continue war against Germany to its victorious climax seemed familiar to someone who had used so much energy reconciling opposing Fabian factions as well as contradictory impulses in himself. Lenin described Kerensky as 'the boy braggart', which was exactly the sort of contemptuous dismissal people had flung at G.B.S. But everyone who saw him knew that Kerensky was a luminous orator: his 'words rose and fell in an inexhaustible, almost visible fountain of emotional sound', one of his audience wrote; and another, who heard him deliver an impassioned address from the stage at the Alexandrinsky Theatre in Petrograd (where *Saint Joan* was later to be performed), observed that the 'theatrical setting' had 'spurred him on in his acting, a rôle that was natural to him'.

Kerensky's overthrow by Lenin represented a defeat for the sort of political activity Shaw had so long been conducting. 'I have said all my life, the thing must rest on the will of the people. You have no right to introduce Socialism until you get a vote, until you get majorities throughout all the constituencies in favor of Socialism,' he told an audience at Kingsway Hall early in 1920.

'I have always said that my reason at bottom has been this, that I knew perfectly well as long as I waited for that I would never be asked to do anything but talk. I have talked all my life and I have managed to get beyond the age of sixty without ever having been called on to do anything really dangerous or important.'

In his study of fellow travellers, David Caute was to question when Shaw had 'ever torn up paving stones, hidden in the marshes, carried a gun, plotted a coup?' He concluded that the neighbours at Ayot who knew him as a 'gentle old man' were 'closer to the truth' than Shaw representing himself as a revolutionist 'in the light of the accomplished revolution in Russia', or than Lenin who described him as a figure 'far to the left of those around him' who would never be mistaken for a clown in revolutionary conditions.

But Shaw had made it plain that by the word revolutionist he did not mean 'a bloodstained man in shirt sleeves and a red cap of liberty' chopping aristo-crats to pieces 'with an axe'.

After Kerensky's fall and Lenin's rise to power, Shaw began to reassess his own political function. Engels had praised him as 'a most talented and witty writer'; Gorki acclaimed him as 'one of the most courageous thinkers in Europe'. But what were witty writing and courageous thinking worth in the historical process? Was he 'absolutely worthless as an economist and politician', as Trotsky seemed to think? Increasingly, as he grew older, Shaw came to share Dr Johnson's view in old age that 'every man thinks meanly of himself for not having been a soldier, or not having been at sea'. Once he had believed that artists and intellectuals formed the mind of a country which then gave politicians their mandate. But in the last period of his life this belief receded and he put his trust directly in men and women with a genius for action.

Shaw's confidence in these men of 'iron nerve and fanatical conviction' expanded and darkened as his own sense of political achievement shrank. 'I am tired of seeing Labor and Socialism rolling the stone up the hill with frightful labor only to have it rolled down again,' he complained in 1920. After forty years of political playwrighting, speech-making, pamphlet-eering, permeation, he looked round Britain and saw little to be admired. The House of Commons was full of what Stanley Baldwin described as 'hard-faced men who look as if they have done very well out of the war'. 'The higher ranks of the learned professions,' noted the Conservative Member of Parliament J. C. C. Davidson, 'are scarcely represented at all.' How could change be effected through such a philistine legislative body? It seemed to Shaw that a democratic system designed to prevent tyranny had been exploited so that it arrested progress. Here was the second area of political sterility.

Until now, with some dramatic hesitations, Shaw had clung to a belief in 'gradual modifications of existing systems' rather than revolution from which 'all humane men recoil with intense repugnance and dread'. He had dedicated himself to creating a socialist conscience and spreading the common morality of socialism through the country. He wanted others to share this craving for a new ethic; but all that had been going on through these long years was an attempt to gain the benefits of socialism under capitalism. He could no longer believe in the Fabians' waiting game. 'There is no use in waiting,' he declared in 1920. They would wait for ever to get the majority of votes from people who 'knew a little about football and very much less about politics', and whom the newspapers were continually 'bemusing and bewildering and bedevilling'. Legislation must create rather than succumb to public opinion because, if no political measure could be passed until everyone understood and demanded it, then nothing could be passed at all. Once democratic principles had been perverted by conservative idealists, then the time had come for realists to *impose* change. Lenin, the man of action, was such a realist; Kerensky, the man of speeches, had been another theatrical romantic, like Ramsay MacDonald. 'We Socialists when we are a little comfortable are perfectly willing to wait,' Shaw admitted, 'but the people who really want to have something done, like Lenin, do not wait.'

Shaw felt he really wanted to have something done: this was the only source of optimism available to him. 'I should very much like to see Communism tried for a while before we give up civilization as a purely pathological phenomenon,' he wrote. 'At any rate, it can hardly produce worse results than Capitalism.' Socialists in the West had lost too many of their propaganda battles not because of capitalism's economic merits, but because capitalism had been promoted as the 'glorification and idolization of the rich', he wrote in 1921. '. . . it gives to every poor man a gambling chance, at odds of a million to one or thereabouts, of becoming a rich one . . . no one is condemned by it to utter despair.' But in Shavian terms, capitalism remained the last refuge of the idealist and a paper utopia – 'the most unreal product of wishful thinking of all the Utopias'. Under assaults from socialists the system had been patched and plastered, and let in so much apparent change 'that superficial thinkers easily persuade themselves that it will finally progress into Socialism', he argued; 'but it can never do so without making a complete *volte face*. Slavery is always improving itself as a system.'

Shaw made his own *volte face*, switching his allegiance from Kerensky to Lenin, with the alacrity of one eager to abandon long-held lost causes and put himself in the vanguard of victory. In the summer of 1917 he had congratulated Kerensky's government on having a foreign enemy already provided by the Great War. He saw Germany fortifying the Russian Republic both by preventing ideological disruptions among the revolutionary comrades and by ruling out a civil war with the White Army, a reaction that was otherwise certain to occur if no Soviet Cromwell or Napoleon arose to establish a military dictatorship. 'If I were a Russian statesman I should say to my countrymen: "Do not fight one another, fight the Hohenzollern."' This was the very opposite of what Lenin actually did the following winter when making a separate treaty with Germany and transforming the imperialist war into a civil war. Nevertheless G.B.S. immediately took the salute of Lenin's troops in the British and American newspapers. He applauded the Russian soldiers for having finally acted on the Shavian remedy formulated in 1914 when he had advised both armies to 'shoot their officers and go home to gather in their harvests and make revolutions in the towns'. It was almost impossible for any revolutionary to fall out of step with G.B.S. since he had wavered, with momentary decisiveness, between so many alternative political tactics. 'Consistency is the enemy of enterprise,' he acknowledged, 'just as symmetry is the enemy of art.'

By the beginning of 1920 Shaw had settled on Lenin as the 'one really interesting statesman in Europe'. The following year he admitted Trotsky as a second world leader. 'They have had a terrific job to do,' he wrote; 'and the fact that after four years they are still holding Russia together shows that they are men of extraordinary quality.' By comparison Lloyd George was little more than 'a nurserymaid [who] leads her little convoy of children, by knowing her way about within a radius of half a mile or so, and being quick at guessing what promise or threat will fill them with childish hopes or terrors'.

Shaw could point to only one potential leader in Britain: Lloyd George's Minister for War and Air, Winston Churchill. But Churchill 'has lost his head over Bolshevism completely', he informed a Russian journalist in 1920, 'and raves incessantly against its leaders as murderers, thieves, libertines and what not'. At the turn of the century, when he began his political career as a Conservative, Churchill had felt G.B.S. to be one of his 'earliest antipathies'. But one day his mother took him to lunch with Shaw, and he was startled to find himself 'instantly attracted by the sparkle and gaiety of his conversation'.

Over the next couple of dozen years, while Churchill turned to the Liberals, the two men would occasionally meet, and enjoyed several 'pleasant' and 'memorable talks', Churchill recalled, 'on politics, particularly about Ireland and about Socialism'. Shaw considered Churchill to be a politician without an ideology. Such a man, whose popularity was enhanced by big cigars, genial romantic oratory and an adventurous sense of patriotism, should have been the perfect vehicle for Shavian permeation. Churchill liked literature too, relishing the novels of Wells and Bennett and believing Shaw himself to be 'the greatest living master of letters in the English-speaking world'. And yet their pleasant and memorable talks led nowhere. This was partly because, from his mid-forties onwards ('Every man over forty is a scoundrel'), Churchill moved to the right in politics, pursuing a policy of repression in Ireland, severing his connection with the Liberal Party and standing as an 'anti-socialist' or constitutionalist candidate before joining Baldwin's Conservative Cabinet in 1924 as Chancellor of the Exchequer. Nevertheless Shaw found it difficult to give Churchill up. 'You have never been a real Tory,' he informed him after he had been Conservative Prime Minister in the Second World War. The 'Blimps and Philistines and Stick-in-the-Muds' of the Conservative Establishment had 'never understood and always dreaded' him.

Churchill and Shaw responded to each other's high tidemarks and admired each other's buoyancy, but they grew disturbed whenever their interests seriously intermingled. Churchill compared G.B.S. to a 'continually erupting volcano' amid whose spouting smoke, mud, ashes and electrical flashes there occasionally appeared 'a piece of pure gold smelted from the central fires of truth'. But the gold was literary, not political. In Churchill's view, literature existed as a great verbal firework display above the artistic fairground whose colour and noise kept everyone's spirits up in those lulls following the waging of chivalrous wars and during the intervals between the gladiatorial contests of politics. At such peaceful pauses 'we are all the better for having had the Jester in our midst', he acknowledged. So G.B.S. continued to live in Churchill's imagination as a 'bright, nimble, fierce, and comprehending being, Jack Frost dancing bespangled in the sunshine, which I should be very sorry to lose'. But there were other times, serious times, when such an 'irresponsible Chatterbox' was well lost, and the fairground itself had to be folded away. 'Our British island has not had much help in its troubles from Mr Bernard Shaw,' Churchill was to write:

'When nations are fighting for life, when the Palace in which the Jester dwells not uncomfortably, is itself assailed, and everyone from Prince to groom is fighting on the battlements, the Jester's jokes echo only through deserted halls, and his witticisms and commendations, distributed evenly between friend and foe, jar the ears of hurrying messengers, of mourning women and wounded men.'

Churchill paid lip service to Shaw as a 'saint, sage' and 'thinker, original, suggestive, profound'; but after the curtain came down on his plays 'everything goes on the same as before'. It was as a 'brilliant intellectual clown' that he lived on the page, and it puzzled Churchill that he should try to struggle off those entertaining pages into a political world where he did not belong. 'The world has long watched with tolerance and amusement the nimble antics and gyrations of this unique and double-headed chameleon,' he wrote, 'while all the time the creature was eager to be taken seriously.'

This touched with lively contempt on the relationship between literature and politics that had been troubling Shaw. 'I think the country should be run by imbeciles like myself,' he was to write, 'and all the energetic, shoving, self-helping chaps shot.' He regarded himself and Wells not as fairground performers but as the 'world's family solicitors'. Politicians in Britain, however, were like magistrates who reached the Bench through their superior social connections rather than by any legal qualifications, and who appealed to the public simply as sportsmen might appeal to it. At his worst, Churchill exploited his popularity in much the same way as the fraudulent patriot Horatio Bottomley had done: 'by telling people with sufficient bombast just what they think themselves and therefore want to hear'. Instead of monkeying with politics Churchill would have been better employed, according to Wells, as 'a brilliant painter' or, according to Shaw, 'as a soldier'. They were agreed that as a politician leading the campaign against Bolshevism, he was a century out of date and represented what was most damaging in British foreign policy. The failure to support Kerensky had let in Lenin; the allied intervention had unintentionally provided the Red Army with British equipment and established Trotsky's credentials as a Napoleonic military campaigner; and the continuing refusal to trade with the Soviet Union helped to dig a deep moat of national paranoia round the country and establish it as another empire of conservatism.

Much of what Shaw wrote about the Soviet Union was designed to discredit Churchill's fearful picture of Bolshevism as a devouring cancer. He cites Churchill as a sad case of 'Russophobia' whose anti-communist ravings had about as much sense to them as the political statements of an 'extremely decayed gentlewoman in an inaccessibly remote village in a prehistorically backward district of rural Poland', he told readers of the *Sunday Chronicle* in 1924.

' ... What does Mr Churchill mean by it? He is not a brainless parasite like many politicians of his class: on the contrary, he is a conspicuously clever man, justly proud of being able to live by his wits ... Why then, does he, the moment Socialism or Russia is mentioned, lose his head, see scarlet, and become the most ridiculous tosh-merchant of his class in Europe? ... Try again, Winston.'

Recognizing that 'the whole Marxian vocabulary was alien to the Anglo-Saxon ear', Shaw used journalism to familiarize his audience with the word Bolshevism and, as the critic David Dunn has noted, 'change it from a term of frightening proportions into one of the most ordinary, unassuming words in the English language'. He mutilated 'Soviet concepts so that the British could look inside and see there was nothing to be afraid of'.

Lenin takes his bow in Shaw's pages as the Soviet counterpart to Churchill. It was an excellent double act and 'I take off my hat to both gentlemen'. Shaw grew adept at this game of humanizing Soviet leaders and taming their revolutionary language. What was totalitarianism after all but the State co-ordination of public welfare? The proletariat became a 'vast body of persons who have no other means of living except their labor', in contrast to the 'proprietariat' who lived 'by owning instead of by working' and were 'politically called the Capitalists'. He wanted Soviet Communism, like a good wine, to travel well. The Russian Bolsheviks arrived after their Shavian shipment behaving 'like our governing class in Britain', but thinking like our socialists. As a thinker, 'I am a Bolshevik', Shaw stated, 'as far as the word has any sense except what lawyers call vulgar abuse.' In *Common Sense about the War* he had predicted that there would be 'only two real flags in the world henceforth: the red flag of Democratic Socialism and the black flag of Capitalism'. After the war he told the Fabians that 'the Russian side is our side' and that Democratic Socialism now spelt Communism. 'There is now nothing but Communism, and in future it is quite futile to go about calling yourselves Fabians,' he said. '... I have always liked to call myself a Communist ... just as William Morris liked the name.'

Shaw let his imagination play round Lenin's revolution until it flowered into a thoroughgoing Fabian event. For if words did not have the power to initiate political change as simply as he had once believed, they could still encircle events and change them mythologically. The first things that should be changed in Russia, he decided, were the working-class origins and Marxist ideology of the Revolution.

Into his verbalizing against Marx, Shaw discharged much of his self-dissatisfaction. He remembered the shock of reading *Das Kapital*: it had been like lifting the lid off hell – capitalism would never recover. But, though a great prophet, Marx was hardly a competent guide (like Sidney Webb) to business affairs, and (unlike H. G. Wells) he knew less about 'working class psychology than the average office boy'. In their obedience to Marxist principles, the worker-revolutionaries in Russia disenfranchised the educated classes and denied their children common schooling; they criminalized the intelligentsia; abolished private trading for commercial profit; expelled all managers (even army officers) without replacement by qualified directors; handed over the farms from the landlords to the peasants and generally 'went through a hellgate of mistakes'. The result of this reaction against bourgeois habits was near starvation, ruinous waste and wreckage. 'Hordes of lost and deserted children, the aftermath of the war, wandered about Russia in little gangs, begging and stealing, following the seasons like migrating birds,' Shaw wrote in a chapter on Sovietism he added to *The Intelligent Woman's Guide*. '... Lifts ceased to work: electric light ceased to illuminate: sanitary arrangements were indescribable.' Made desperate by the country's anarchy and lack of government, Lenin was forced, under the title New Economic Policy, to introduce gas-and-water Fabianism. For what else was the electrification of Russia? Others might try to claim this New Economic Policy as a battle won for capitalism, but Lenin had simply adopted the Fabian device of allowing private enterprise to run the factories until their productive work could be taken over by public enterprise. 'That is to say,' Shaw concluded, 'Lenin was by the pressure of practical and immediate and imperative experience converted to what we call gradualism.'

For over a decade G.B.S. conducted an advanced Fabian course on Soviet Communism to counter the British and American 'Press campaign of calumny'. It was something like the rewriting of *Jitta's Atonement*. He told the Fabians that Lenin had candidly admitted his mistakes – or 'atrocities', as they were sometimes called – and frankly and effectively scrapped them. He had gently guided the Kulaks back at gunpoint to the farms from which they had been evicted; ushered the hordes of wandering thieves into well-appointed penal colonies; introduced compulsory labour to assist the unemployed; brought back ex-tsarist officers into the army to improve everyone's protection; and established the famous Cheka, a sort of Scotland Yard, 'which took over the necessary shooting'. Lenin had been able to reverse his engines and save the situation by using an administrative body called the 'Dictatorship of the Proletariat'. This select 'Cabinet of thinkers', which had been invited to take control of the country's political constitution, formed a middle-class élite at the head of the working-class body of the people. Not even Lenin himself had been brought up as a peasant – 'I have seen his hands,' Shaw was to witness, 'and they were not a peasant's hands.' The Fabians could easily recognize a system that was modelled on the political samurai Wells and Shaw had so often discussed at their meetings. But there was a difference. 'We are magnificent parasites,' Shaw told the Society. 'We grasp the whole thing. We know the history of it, but we cannot do it.' The Soviets had given up all these meetings and discussions, and 'nothing can stop them'.

But Shaw was critical of Soviet foreign policy which enmeshed itself in British domestic politics and was therefore of less abstract and more direct interest to him. He had emerged from the war a 'supranationalist', believing that disarmament was impossible until 'the world is effectively policed' and that the League of Nations should be developed to include international courts of law. 'Unless and until Europe is provided with a new organ for supernational [*sic*] action, provided with an effective police, all talk of making an end to war is a mere waste of breath,' he wrote in 1916 in a Preface to Leonard Woolf's *International Government*. When the League of Nations came into being in 1920 it was 'reduced to absurdity', he felt, 'by the fact that Russia, Germany and the United States are not in it'. By 1932 he regretfully concluded that the League had ballooned into another breathtaking example of windy political phrase-making. 'How are we to kill the killers: that is the real problem . . . ' he told the French internationalist writer Henri Barbusse.

Soviet Russia had transgressed against Shavian supranationalism by setting up the Third International dedicated to crusades and *coups d'état* abroad. The First International was an Old Testament with Marx as its Moses. The New Testament of World Socialism was the Second International, a catholic narrative that included, besides Shaw himself, figures as diverse as MacDonald and Mussolini. But the Third International, which was founded in 1919 and reached back for its inspiration to Marx, seemed to Shaw an apocrypha that had no place for evolutionary socialists such as himself. It reminded him of the extravagances of colonialism. From such a 'church', Shaw warned *Izvestia*, the Soviet government 'would do well to disassociate itself'. In Russia it must sooner or later come into conflict with the state; while its economic interferences abroad could lead to 'nothing but misunderstandings'. Shaw maintained that internationally 'the only objectionable Communist was the one who took his pay and orders from Moscow', David Dunn wrote. The British Communist Party, which had evolved from Hyndman's Social Democratic Federation, was losing public credibility by doing this, Shaw believed, as surely as he himself would have lost his integrity by accepting fees for his political speeches. For this reason he resigned in 1921 from the Labour Research Department, protesting that 'if the gaff is blown at the fatal time' about its banking of Russian funds, then 'the General Election will be wrecked for Labour'. The truth of this seemed to be borne out three years later when the authenticity of the notorious 'Zinoviev Letter', a forgery containing revolutionary instructions for a communist uprising in Britain, was largely credited by a British electorate who, reacting to the Bolshevik menace, brought Baldwin back for a second term as Conservative Prime Minister.

Shaw demonstrated his support for Soviet Russia in ways other than journalism. He encouraged Leonid Krassin's struggles as head of a Soviet delegation to conclude a trade treaty with Britain; he advertised the urgent needs of the Russian Famine Relief Fund; and he was photographed attending the first grand reception at the Soviet Embassy in London 'though wild horses would not drag me to such a thing ordinarily'. Another gesture in the same direction was his decision to go bail for William Gallacher, founder of the British Communist Party, who was being tried for sedition. 'I do not think it is possible to persist in a boycott of Communism as such; and I do not think it is wise to let ourselves be put in the position of an anti-Communist party from which Robert Owen and Morris would have been expelled, and in which I remain under false pretences,' he wrote to Ramsay MacDonald in 1925. '...[It] suggests hostility to the Russian Revolution.'

As a professed communist 'with a reputation as a frondeur and a man of extraordinary notions', Shaw recognized that his influence would often be discounted. He was careful to avoid impossible assignments. Refusing to be appointed chairman of the International Commission on Russia's Debit and Credit Relations with Europe, he commented: 'It would be like acting as chairman to lunatics.' Two years later he turned down an invitation to write a chapter on 'Communism in Russia' for the *Encyclopaedia Britannica* because 'I do not know what has happened in Russia, and cannot find out. Even if I were to visit Russia as I have been invited to do, I should come back not much wiser than I came as to the economic moral of the experiment. Besides, the experiment is not yet consummated.'

Between Lenin's death in 1924 and the economic débâcle of MacDonald's second Labour administration in 1931, Shaw added little to what he had already said about Soviet politics. He was in agreement with Sidney Webb's view that the job of the Fabians was 'simply waiting for Russia to prove its case' and then finding out how best to convey the consequences of this verdict into British life.

To Shaw's mind this was largely a matter of time. The work of organizing society would inevitably outgrow the capacity of private adventurers temporarily sustained by the superstition that an 'ability to acquire capital is identical with the ability to administer it competently'. Analysing capitalism's decline in a new preface to *Fabian Essays* in 1930, he wrote: 'the first symptom of excessive strain is an abnormal increase in unemployment accompanied by reconstructions and amalgamations of commercial business'. The slump of the early 1930s was therefore in Shaw's eyes a sign of capitalism's old age (it 'has passed its climax here, and is getting unsteady on its feet of clay') rather than evidence of the Marxist crash that was to end in world revolution. He could see no justification for the faith of an 'unteachable doctrinaire' like Trotsky in the concept of permanent revolutions abroad. He described Stalin's victory as 'a triumph of common sense' because it represented the principle of 'Socialism in a single country' over the interventionary excesses of the Third International. Instead of relying on military invasions, economic subversion or foreign concessions, Stalin's nationalism seemed to hand over to people like himself the vital missionary work of spreading communism 'to the rest of the world by permeation, example, and success'. As for Trotsky, exiled by Stalin in 1929, he should be 'warmly invited to favour us with his very interesting presence' in Britain.

Though a visit to Moscow would have given Shaw authority to carry out his missionary work, he held back until the chaos of the Revolution was over and the Communist state fairly launched. He feared what he might see. 'The Moscow Government may not be any fonder of really independent observers than other governments are,' he wrote in 1922. '...We want something from a capable observer and effective writer who is neither a fanatical Communist nor a scandalized bourgeois.' He could have joined a Labour Party delegation that had gone to study Lenin's government; or accompanied Gandhi and Tagore to the celebrations of Tolstoy's centenary; or even accepted handsome terms from the American newspaper owner William Randolph Hearst to report on events in Russia. 'I did not go because people were expecting miracles from Soviet Communism,' he told the communist composer Rutland Boughton in 1928. But three years later, when the Astors 'suddenly took it into their heads to see for themselves whether Russia is really the earthly paradise I had declared it to be ... [and] challenged me to go with them', Shaw finally agreed. 'I felt, at my age, that if I did not seize the opportunity, I should never see Russia at all,' he told Horace Plunkett. The expedition was 'a bit of an accident'. As Hesketh Pearson observed, he was 'curiously dependent on external pressures for any activity outside his daily routine': Charlotte's friend 'Lion' Phillimore described him as 'an old tramcar, always on the same set of rails'. But to many people's minds he was about to go wildly off the rails. 'I start for Moscow on Saturday, and expect to arrive there on Tuesday unless I am stopped by a revolution in Berlin,' he informed Horace Plunkett on 16 July 1931. '...if I am not despatched by the Soviet in the opposite direction to Siberia ... I shall be able to tell you all about that when I come back.'

*

'Might not so long a journey kill you?' a friend wrote to Charlotte. She had been unlucky lately with infections '(scarlet fever at Buxton and congestion of the lung in Paris)' and decided not to risk it. Of course she knew that G.B.S. must go and she sometimes 'got a frightened feeling' thinking of it all. It was a mercy he would be looked after by Nancy. 'But Nancy, I do trust you,' she wrote. 'You will take the right sort of care of him, & *not let him do too much!* It will be difficult: but if anyone can keep him in hand *you* can!'

Nancy Astor was additionally in charge of her own husband and their nineteen-year-old son David, and was accompanied by two Christian Scientists: Charles Tennant, who fell ill during the trip, and Philip Kerr, eleventh Marquis of Lothian, who had been Lloyd George's private secretary and was later to be appointed Britain's ambassador to the United

233

States. Also attached to the party were Sidney D. Gamble, a sociologist from Cincinnati, J. W. Mallin, head of Toynbee Hall Social Welfare Centre in London, and an old American friend of Nancy's, Gertrude Ely, who left them at Warsaw, having forgotten her entry visa. Her place was taken by the Russian-born, American-Jewish author Maurice Hindus, the only member of the party who spoke Russian. The Associated Press, however, tended to overlook these minor characters and regularly wrote of Charlotte's appearance at Russian art galleries, railway stations and collective farms – an example for G.B.S. of inaccurate reporting on all things Soviet.

Charlotte was careful to see that he took provisions of cereals and biscuits, though 'there are plenty of vegetarian restaurants in Moscow'. There were no single sleeping berths on Russian trains, so he paid double fares and secured compartments all to himself in which to stretch out during overnight journeys. He had asked the Soviet ambassador to rush through their papers, and he sent a telegram to Bela Illesh, General Secretary of the International Federation of Revolutionary Writers, stating that though his visit would be brief (he had a Summer School at Digswell Park to address in the first week of August), he was coming for 'serious business' and did not want to be 'burdened with parades, receptions or banquets'. Nevertheless, he warned Waldorf Astor, they could 'expect a salute of at least 101 guns on our arrival in Moscow'.

At eleven o'clock on the morning of 18 July, the party started out from Victoria Station, paused in Brussels for some sightseeing and, the following morning, arrived in Berlin. Amid general distraction and excitement, they were to be joined by Maxim Litvinov, Commissar of Foreign Affairs, who had timed his return from Geneva to coincide with their visit. That evening they all caught the night express to Warsaw, crossing the double frontier between Poland and the Soviet Union at 4 p.m. on 20 July. Armed guards mounted the train as they moved across the strip of no-man's-land, past flanks of sentries and fortifications, and under an arch inscribed 'Communism will do away with frontiers' to the areas of passport inspection, currency control and customs clearance. Here they were transferred to a wide-gauge Russian train. 'You are not hurried or fussed,' Shaw reported: 'the Moscow train will not start for ever so long.' During the three and a half hours it took to refuel this train and attach a sleeping car, he wandered into the railway buffet, followed deferentially by a deputation of publishers, novelists, and miscellaneous literary critics, and was introduced to a couple of young waitresses familiar, the interpreter emphasized, with a number of his plays. After pausing in wonderment, he rejoined his party and, there still being plenty of time, they strolled off into a village nearby

234

called Negoreloje. This was simply a line of human kennels made of unpainted ugly wood and spaced at wide intervals along both sides of a dirt track, a monument to the old Russia. 'Inside is a frowsy cupboard without a door, which is the family bed, and a kiln, politely called a stove, on the top of which you can sleep if you are chilly,' Shaw later wrote. 'The rest of the space is kept as free from furniture as possible for the accommodation of the live stock of the strip of land which the peasant cultivates.' With its bowing men, its careworn scantily-dressed women carrying heavyish sacks, the place reminded him of an impoverished Irish settlement. It was a veritable *sraidbhaile*, and he turned away to a vision of the comparative joys of collective farming. By replacing the obsequious peasant with a self-respecting, clean-shaven agricultural mechanic, and 'burning his kennel as soon as possible', it was 'obvious at first glance' Shaw concluded, that the Soviet Union was 'acting in the interests of civilization'.

Shaw's nine-day pilgrimage was studded with such split-second visionary glances. Walking back to the station they came across half a dozen bare-legged burly women with shovels – 'a piece of luck for Communism', Shaw judged, since these 'volunteers' provided him with the subject for his first ironically-tinted essay in adulation, as well as a choreographic contrast to the old-style women with their burdens.

'A bevy of girls were seated in two rows, one above the other, on some agricultural contraption that lent itself to this theatrically effective arrangement. They were armed with long-handled spades. There was neither stocking, sock, nor shoe among them; and their athletic freedom of limb and fearless air, which marked even the youthfully shy ones, had such a pleasant effect that we at once crowded round them ... They were doing railway work as holiday volunteers, and the spades were for unloading the freight trains.

'Whilst we were talking and chaffing, a freight train came in. Instantly these girls sprang to their feet and bounded to the train with a rhythmic grace and vigour that would have delighted Diaghileff. It was the only Russian ballet we saw in Russia.'

The train journey to Moscow took twelve hours and according to Waldorf Astor their arrival at 10.30 a.m. at Belorussko-Galtiyskiy Station was everything a film producer could have dreamed: 'I hear that the only two other people who had anything like a similar reception were Gorky and Fairbanks (with Mary Pickford).' They were welcomed by an official body of 'authors, artists, men of science, industrial managers and the like who', Shaw told readers in the West, 'with a little Savile Row or Conduit Street tailoring and here and there a touch of shaving cream, would have been at home in any of our West End bourgeois clubs'. Besides Karl Radek, a Jewish revolutionary with the aspect of a French Communard who was the leading commentator on foreign affairs, and the former Commissar of Enlightenment Anatoly Lunacharsky (who 'speaks six languages, looks like a university professor, and was one'), the delegation featured Artashes Khalatov, president of the State Publishing House, a swarthy cartoon figure in breeches, high boots and with a deep black beard. 'The Bolsheviks are queer chaps,' Shaw commented. 'They pick out a man to accompany me who knows no language but Russian, and they sew him up in black leather; the one thing they forgot was to put in his mouth a knife dripping with bourgeois blood.'

According to G.B.S. this assemblage of Soviet characters was knocked across the platform by an on-rushing American newspaperman, Henry Dana. Shaw was already getting used to this commotion. In each country, he claimed, 'the official or deputation advancing to receive me was shoved aside by an enthusiastic American, beaming with hospitality, and shouting genially, "Mr Shaw: welcome to France (or Poland or Russia or Germany, as the case might be): I am an American."' Henry Dana was clutching a genuine Dubliner called Verschoyle, apparently born in Synge Street ('a fellow Scotsman', *Izvestia* noted) who had come briefly to Moscow to work for the Writers' Union. 'If I were as young as you are I should move to Moscow altogether,' Shaw politely greeted him. Then he was whirled away into a monstrous mobbery of cheering and 'a salvo of fifty cameras'. Immaculately dressed in a freshly-pressed brown suit with brown cloth gloves and waving a soft brown hat above his head, his erect and elevated figure with its wise white beard spread admiration among the spectators as he glided through a corridor of Red Guards and out of the station. Walter Duranty of the *New York Times* caught an awed murmur through the crowd: 'What a noble old man!' The *Daily Herald* reporter conjured up 'wild applause' and shouts of 'Hail Shaw!' that could be heard, through the blaring of a brass band, from 'several thousands of people'. What was not clear from such accounts was that these crowds were football fans who had actually gathered at the station to welcome a team of foreign players travelling on the same train. The sudden popularity of Shaw's veteran figure has been attributed by the scholar David Dunn to 'hopes of some easy home wins'.

They were driven to the Hotel Metropole where Nancy Astor, 'desperately mothering me and assuring everyone that I must immediately be left alone to sleep in the hotel, found me utterly out of control', Shaw wrote happily to Charlotte. 'I insisted on sightseeing at express speed.' They hurried out to Lenin's mausoleum (Nancy and Shaw debating as to whether

Lenin was an aristocrat or an intellectual) and on to the Kremlin. In the Council Hall G.B.S. climbed the speaker's podium and experimented with the acoustics by yodelling. 'Nancy clamored for sending me home to bed, but finally gave way to her loudly expressed disgust at my playing to the gallery.' He was like a schoolboy, suddenly springing on to a bundle of cannonballs to be photographed at the base of the giant tsarist cannon, then jumping off and slipping into a little church where he found a priest officiating.

'The congregation was a very devout one: their worship was so fervently demonstrative as they knelt and smote the ground with their foreheads, punctuating the priest's intonations with moans of intense faith, that in Westminster Abbey they would have been handed over to the police and charged with "brawling"; but there were very few of them, not more than fifteen at the outside, including myself.'

Having registered this freedom to worship, Shaw allowed Nancy to lead him quietly back to their hotel. Everything seemed to suit him overflowingly well, and he could not resist showing off. 'You can't stop talking here,' he wrote to Charlotte. '. . . Health uproarious. Envy me . . . I get less and less tired everyday.'

Next day he started on an official programme of conducted visits, accompanied by Litvinov and Lunacharsky, to tourist points, Young Pioneer camps, Centres of Repose and Culture and various model institutions including the State Bank. Though eager for his commendation, the Soviet establishment was nervous of Shaw. In 1925 Lunacharsky had responded to his criticism of the Third International by deriding him for having set the hearts of bourgeois ladies aflutter in Britain 'without shaking to any serious extent the basis of the solid affluence of their lords & masters'. This agile belletrist had heaped condescending advice on the 'Moscow bandits' of the Revolution, picturing them as 'good chaps' who, by coming up with a 'hilarious paradox on a world scale' had unexpectedly found themselves in power and were in need of guidance. Shaw 'pats us on the back', objected Lunacharsky, '. . . telling us poor students . . . to replace Marx's work with the world-historical chatter of his friend Mr Wells'.

Six years later when Shaw arrives in Moscow, Lunacharsky has carefully modified his tone. In an article entitled 'Bernard Shaw is our Guest' he calls G.B.S. 'one of the freest-thinking minds of the civilized world', but cautions readers of *Izvestia* that 'people like Bernard Shaw – brilliant representatives of the intelligentsia, turn out to be too "free-thinking" . . . they start to get ironical'. The article is a skilful blend of welcome and warning, enabling his audiences to value Shaw's approval while discounting his eccentric criticism. The Soviet public is asked to remember that while Shaw's wit, 'like dazzling bursts of flame in the darkness, illuminates the dense twilight of the nightfall of capitalism', his jokes at the expense of communism are the peculiar reflexes of an individualist outside the Party who cannot help 'treating everything with semi-seriousness'. Though 'an unrestrained intellect', he was a limited political figure: for 'if it were left solely to people like Bernard Shaw to fight for the new world, then that new world would never be born'. Yet there was an important supplementary role for him. The Soviet people had a 'burning desire to achieve a closer understanding with this amazing old man', Lunacharsky concludes, because he was coming to test his suspicions 'that the bourgeois press lies, that it gives a distorted view of our socialist set-up, that our system has more meaning than is supposed in the west'. It was the job of Shaw's hosts in Soviet Russia to assist him to this conclusion.

Shaw's account of 'Touring in Russia' is as happy a fantasy as his 'Joy Riding at the Front' had been during the war. 'The reason why I talk so much,' he explained to nervous Soviet officials, 'is not to have to listen to what other people say.' He had grown so ingenious at manufacturing optimism that other people's paler ideological exercises merely stirred his ridicule. He likened the penal colony at Bolshevo to Battersea Park, salivating over its menus, applauding its entertainments and sympathizing with the criminals who 'will not leave at the expiration of their sentences'. He congratulated all Soviet citizens engaged in compulsory labour on working for the public service and not for the private profits of a few individuals: 'I wish we had forced labour in England,' he added, 'in which case we would not have 2,000,000 unemployed.' His imagination bleached away all signs of pain and horror. He looks forward to a good performance at 'the torture chamber of the Tcheka ... [with] a victim or two ready, so that we may witness the process'. It is as if his theatricalizing of reality has become a habit of mind. In place of 'shooting' he uses the word 'pistolling', a swashbuckling term such as might be used in *Arms and the Man* or *Annajanska*; he interprets the term 'liquidate' to mean unemployment occasioned by progressive technology; and he concludes: 'That is how the Communists get you every time. You think you have them convicted of the most monstrous crimes; and you find that the crimes are only very sensible arrangements which you resolve to advocate enthusiastically when you return to your own unhappy country.'

Below this parody of ideological engineering swarmed a mass of irregularities, as Lunacharsky had predicted. 'The interpreter groaned at the utter unexpectedness of my answers to questions,' Shaw noted. After visiting the Museum of Revolution he told nonplussed journalists that the government was 'mad' to allow such a dangerous exhibition. 'The moment a revolution becomes a government it necessarily sets to work to exterminate revolutionists ... For when the revolution triumphs revolution becomes counter-revolution. The young Russian fired with enthusiasm for the glorious old slayers of tsars, Grand Dukes, & chiefs of police, & finding their species as extinct as the buffalo, may try his hand on Stalin.'

Elsewhere he could not wholly suppress the impulse to denounce a group of prettily-dressed children singing about the glories of life in a farming commune as 'a parcel of insufferable little Marxian prigs'; or, after Nancy Astor had been heckled, resist exclaiming, 'the more I see of the proletarians the more I thank God I am not one'; or avoid calling for a 'Five-Year Aesthetic Plan' to remedy Moscow's temporary shabbiness. To one questioner who presumed too far on his sentimental loyalty to the Soviet people he objected, 'No! I am not the friend of any people as a whole. I reserve the right to criticize every people – including the Russians.' He was also to qualify his statement on compulsory labour by recommending a four-hour working day, and he inscribed the visitors' book at an electrical plant that was completing its five-year plan ahead of schedule with the words: 'My father drank too much. I have worked too much. Comrades push the 5 years Plan through in 3 years, and *then* TAKE IT EASY.'

Nancy Astor was soon causing Lunacharsky unusual problems too. 'Lady Astor is positively flirting with me,' he noted in his diary. 'Preaching Christian Science at me. Very odd.' Some of her outspoken announcements – 'I am a Conservative. I am a Capitalist. I am opposed to Communism. I think you are all terrible' – prostrated Lunacharsky with diabolical laughter but were greeted by others with acclaim owing to the kindly mistranslations of the interpreter. 'Nancy jollies them all until they do not know whether they are head up or heels,' Shaw wrote to Charlotte: 'her stock accusation being that they are all aristocrats, which does not wholly displease them.'

Shaw had been given a spacious suite at the Hotel Metropole – far grander rooms than those of the rest of the party – but the street noises outside were so terrific and the heat so hellish that he quickly closed the bedroom windows, flung off his eiderdown 'which would have been warm for the South Pole' – and overslept. Moscow struck him as a 'domestic sort of city ... frightfully overcrowded and under-trammed' and he was glad to get out of earshot of its 'slamming and tramming' and travel north to Leningrad. Soviet newsreels recorded a vast and welcoming crowd as the *Red Arrow* pulled into Moscovskiy Station on the morning of 24 July – not sports fans this time, but genuine airship enthusiasts eager to see the Graf Zeppelin on its way to the Arctic Circle.

Shaw's first impression of Leningrad (or St Petersburg, as the communist leaders absent-mindedly called it) was that it looked 'as if it had been built by Mansard to the order of Louis XIV and laid out by Haussmann for greater convenience in shooting down insurgent mobs'. He was lodged in an 'even more grand-ducal apartment' at the Hotel de l'Europe and over the next forty-eight hours conducted through an even more intense programme of ceremonies and receptions of the kind he had asked to be spared. He saw excerpts from Soviet films (including 'one of the very best films in existence', Eisenstein's *Battleship Potemkin*) and thought them all superior to Hollywood's 'sexual exploitations'; he was taken to an exhibition of anti-religious artefacts at the desecrated cathedral of St Isaak which, he said, 'would delight the soul of Martin Luther and all sturdy Protestants from Belfast to Philadelphia'; and he marched past several miles of pictures at the Hermitage until he confessed himself 'tired out by this gallery tramping'.

He seemed to treat this foreign country, David Astor noticed, as if it were an extension of his sitting-room. All his evidence appeared to come to him from reading rather than from observation. On train journeys he never looked out of the window at 'the light of the sky and the sight of the fields and flowers' without which his Saint Joan could not have continued to live.

At a home for retired people he met Stanislavsky, former director of the Moscow Arts Theatre; relaxed and animated, they chatted about Granville-Barker and were photographed over a glass of milk. He also met Gorki at his dacha outside Moscow. Shaw was fond of Gorki who was then ill and had written to him: 'the shattering blows your keen mind has dealt to conservatism and people's banality are beyond count'. Shaw later returned this compliment when he described Gorki as a sensitive 'hater of cruelty and injustice, the discoverer of touching virtues in the most impossible people', and added, 'to him the revolution has not brought the millennium, though he can forgive it as he can forgive worse things'. Another 'angel of the revolution' who had not been made happy by Stalin's Russia was Krupskaya, Lenin's widow. After protracted difficulties, due either to official disapproval or Krupskaya's own diffidence in meeting G.B.S., he was taken to her shooting lodge for tea. He admired her 'beautiful ugliness' and described her as 'a woman to be adored by children'. The story had reached him that 'she had given the Soviet a piece of her mind so roundly that Stalin had threatened that if she did it again he would appoint another widow for Lenin'.

G.B.S. had little problem in accounting for such people's difficulties in the USSR. 'They would be unhappy in the Garden of Eden because the cats played cruelly with the mice before devouring them.' Only the determination of his official hosts to honour and impress him seemed likely to cloud his enthusiasm. The interminable introductions, the endless laudatory greetings, the audiences that 'had been instructed to receive me with tumultuous applause', the tedium of 'faked meals' held up by long toasts and forced orations 'washed the virtue out of me'. 'I was exploited to the last inch', he complained after witnessing a production of the Brecht-Weill *Threepenny Opera* ('an amazing and at points disgusting perversion of the Beggar's Opera') at the Kamerny Theatre in Moscow. He was 'led to the middle of the front row of stalls, presented with a bouquet and a St Joan album [of Alexander Taïrov's production], confronted with a gigantic banner of welcome on the stage with the whole company assembled, tears cheers and laughter, gracious bows in all directions from the wretched G.B.S., and chuckles from Nancy ... Horrid!' Even worse was the special treat that had been prepared for his seventy-fifth birthday: a horse race entitled 'The Bernard Shaw Handicap' at a racetrack outside Moscow. 'I suppose there will be only one horse in the race,' he remarked, 'since there is no competition in a Socialist state.' Sitting in the sunlight in his grandstand box he fell quietly asleep, his chin on his chest, while the horses thundered past and Nancy Astor ostentatiously fanned the flies away from his face with a brilliantly coloured scarf.

'Of course they don't realise that he is an Irishman,' remarked the British ambassador Sir Esmond Overy, 'and he is growing more so every day since he has been here.' The British Embassy had given a reception for G.B.S. and his party on their arrival in Moscow. 'Noah's Ark had not a more varied and bizarre collection of creatures,' wrote one of the guests. 'The Soviet leaders of those days, who as a rule never entered those luxurious surroundings (Communism was still in its Puritan stage) have shelved their prejudices in order to meet the great playwright, and are sipping the dry Martinis and champagne cocktails presented to them on brilliantly polished silver plates ... Suddenly, Lady Astor's red foulard dress drops in a deep curtsey before Litvinov...'

Both Nancy Astor and Shaw had been handed 'a piteous volley of telegrams' from Dmitri Krynin, a professor of civil engineering at Yale University, asking them to intercede on behalf of his wife who had been refused an exit visa to join him and their son in America. Nancy went into action at once. 'As in days of yore, I present a petition to your government on bended knee,' she said. 'Most humbly I pray you in the name of humanity to save this suffering family.' But after a flustered glance at the telegram Litvinov brushed it aside: 'This matter is not within my jurisdiction.'

Shaw seemed more anxious over Nancy's distress than about the plight of the Krynin family. 'Dont worry about the sorrows and terrors of the poor things in Russia,' he tried to reassure her. But she could not leave it alone. Only with difficulty was she dissuaded from going directly to the police headquarters. Later she presented informal cables to the Soviet authorities at the Kremlin, while Waldorf Astor sought out Mrs Krynin, 'a pathetic sight terrified lest her husband or son should be induced to return to Russia, evidently afraid of what might happen to them if they did come', he wrote in his diary. 'It seems to me that he probably must have gone to America with a permit limited as to time and had not returned . . . I wrote to Khalatov telling him that the lady had no complaints to make against the authorities about her treatment but was merely anxious to join her husband in America.'

And Shaw did nothing. It is not easy to sympathize with such unresponsiveness, especially when set against the Astors' courage and persistence. In the years following the war G.B.S. had increasingly detached himself from such appeals, feeling that he would otherwise be overwhelmed. Besides, he believed he had learnt from the propaganda campaigns of the war itself that many horror stories were exaggerated, if not maliciously invented. Nancy's head 'is full of Bolshevik horrors', he comforted himself, 'in spite of what we see here'. Additionally, he suspected that telegrams delivered on such public occasions with newspapermen present were likely to be anti-Soviet stunts. The Western press had followed up the 'story', found Mrs Krynin, and reported the affair extensively. The Astors consoled themselves with the thought that, in the light of such publicity, the Soviet authorities were unlikely to contrive her 'disappearance'. Shaw reasoned differently. It was far easier to do harm with words than to do good; and in fact Mrs Krynin was secretly moved from her apartment. 'The notion that I am persona grata with the dictators is one of the Shaw myths,' he was to write to the novelist William Gerhardie who later appealed to him during the Stalinist purges on behalf of his brother-in-law, a mild expert in bee culture, who was imprisoned in Soviet Russia.

'I have a long experience of foreign agitations to procure the release of political prisoners in Italy, Germany, America and Russia: I am always asked to take a hand and assured that the word from me will do the trick. The result is always to make it worse for the unfortunate victim, as foreign interference is not only resented as such, but taken as additional evidence of disaffection . . .

'I am loth to pass by on the other side; but I do not see how I can act with any beneficial effect.

'Callously, alas!

G. Bernard Shaw'

Such a letter reveals the dark sense of reality that underlay Shaw's ideological make-believe and the spirit of pragmatism by which he reconciled reality with fantasy. During the last twenty years of his life this fantasy was to shine still more brightly. The assertive language he cultivated sprang from his need to affirm a faith rather than to decline into negative criticism. His violent words, which showed a widening disassociation of thought from feeling, followed a mode of phrase-making more commonly used by those in power (final solutions, acceptable losses), though sometimes echoed by academics prepared to sacrifice populations for libraries. Shaw tried to re-create himself through such language. In his early years he had looked for love but rejecting this as impractical for himself and perhaps only possible in the world of opera, he then attempted to replace it, through imaginative wordplay, with the exercise of beneficent political power. But here too he had been disappointed, and during the last period of his life he looked for illumination elsewhere. 'It is useless to criticize a blind reaction,' he wrote of fascism, 'one might as well criticize an explosion of dynamite.' Shaw's explosion of optimism, combining what the writer Lewis Coser was to call 'two apparently contradictory sentiments: rage for order and support for revolution', seemed to reunite Fabianism with the 'Fellowship of the New Life' and gave a surreal perspective to his political faith.

In his essay 'A Short View of Russia', Maynard Keynes had analysed Leninism as a combination of two factors usually kept separate, business economics and religious conviction. The economics, he argued, were destined to fail; only the religious power could survive. When Shaw travelled to Moscow he was chiefly interested in Soviet methods of social and economic reconstruction; by the time he left he had been converted to the religion of communism. Here was a creed, in practical operation and with a clear-cut code of morals, that could restore his homogeneity of thought and feeling. From Darwin to Einstein, the landscape of knowledge had been broken up during his lifetime, destroying many idealized and apparently absolute values that he had attacked, but leaving no solid ground of morality from which to survey the past and future. In their maze of anxieties people needed new rules of conduct. This was the appeal in the 1920s and 1930s of autocracies such as Mussolini's fascists and Hitler's Nazis whose dogmatic myths and parades of order gave Italy and Germany a sense of definite national purpose. 'I doubt whether the mass of men can live without a common metaphysic and a common scale of values,' Beatrice Webb wrote in 1926. Advancing across the continent like a medieval religion, Soviet communism appealed to her emotional needs and seemed to satisfy her intellectual beliefs. 'I wish Communism to succeed,' she wrote in 1932. And Shaw agreed. 'In all the prophesies of Russia's failure the wish is father to the thought,' he said. 'We have a lot of foolish people who want the experiment to fail.'

Shaw was eager, while in Russia, to meet Stalin. 'I want Stalin to become a living person for me before I leave Moscow,' he declared. He was granted an audience on the evening of 29 July and insisted on taking the Astors and Lord Lothian with him. 'We were just nobodies,' Nancy Astor recalled, 'he' was the great man; but he insisted on our full recognition and participation in every ceremony.' Litvinov accompanied them, and two interpreters were present. 'I expected to see a Russian working man and I found a Georgian gentleman,' Shaw wrote. During the interview, which lasted two and a half hours, the realities of Stalinist Russia were suspended and Shavian theatre prevailed. The set was simple: a large table and some chairs in an office. The costumes varied from Stalin's tunic and black top boots and Shaw's Norfolk jacket to Nancy Astor's spotted dress, Lord Lothian's lounge suit and the shirtsleeves of Litvinov. It was as if the encounter between Undershaft and Cusins from *Major Barbara* were being replayed in the Kremlin, with a remarkable transformation of the Soviet dictator into a frank, friendly and humorous character who 'was educated for the priesthood, and would pass with any western for a romantically dark eyed Georgian chieftain, or possibly the necessarily illegitimate son of an aristocratic cardinal'. Like Undershaft, Stalin is UNASHAMED. He also believes that the 'ballot paper that really governs is the paper that has a bullet wrapped up in it'. Shaw grants Stalin an 'extraordinary military ability and force of character' but cloaks these iron qualities with the pious toga of Fabian respectability: 'he is said to be a model of domesticity, virtue, and innocence'. This is the priggish endorsement of Cusins which itself becomes sinister in the light of Stalin's wife's suicide. Shaw's imagination clearly told him that this was someone who could 'kill the killers', but his imagination facetiously converted him into a smiling 'lady killer'. He was still no match during this Shavian scene for Lady Astor who described him as 'grim' and went for him 'like a steamroller', Shaw tells us, on education and humanitarianism.

In this staged seminar Stalin was also cast to play Shaw's Caesar opposite Nancy's spirited if elderly Cleopatra. 'The attempt to abash and silence Lady Astor was about as successful as an effort by a fly to make head against a whirlwind,' remembered Shaw, as though giving directions for their dialogue. Stalin is shown as 'able to say anything he pleased without giving the least offence, patient, assured, letting us talk back to our heart's content, and disarming us at every attack by a smile in which there is no malice but also no credulity'. But, to the audience beyond, it appeared that Shaw needed a creed; that Nancy Astor was never disarmed; and that though Stalin, like Undershaft, deceived others he was not self-deceived. 'The Russians have always been fond of circuses and travelling shows,' wrote Churchill. 'Since they had imprisoned, shot or starved most of their best comedians, their visitors might fill for a space a noticeable void. And here was the World's most famous intellectual Clown and Pantaloon in one, and the charming Columbine of the capitalist pantomime ... Arch Commissar Stalin, "the man of steel", flung open the closely-guarded sanctuaries of the Kremlin, and pushing aside his morning's budget of death warrants, and *lettres de cachet*, received his guests with smiles of overflowing comradeship.'

'The secret of Stalin is that he is entirely opportunist as to *means*,' Shaw was to tell Augustin Hamon, 'discarding all doctrinaire limitations, and confident that Russia is big enough to achieve Socialism by itself independently of the capitalist world, which can follow his example or go its own way to perdition'. But Shaw overlaid this realistic outline of Stalin with the image of 'Uncle Joe', head of the communist family. What he portrayed after their meeting was not the 'living person' he claimed to be seeking, and certainly no upstart proletarian, but an integration of priest and man of action. 'I scented the soldier and the ecclesiastic,' he wrote, 'certainly not the cobbler.'

For this brief period Shaw and Nancy Astor set the agenda and Stalin was obliged to respond agreeably. They romanced about Churchill visiting the USSR, discussed Lloyd George, alluded to Cromwell. 'When are you going to stop shooting people, like the Tzar,' Nancy Astor demanded. 'When peace comes we shall stop it,' replied Stalin who in turn wanted to know when the English were going to stop beating children as part of their education. He never lost his self-command, though in reality it was for him a most disagreeable experience, and he later complained to his daughter Svetlana that Shaw was an awful person. On their return to the Hotel Metropole reporters crowded round and Shaw agreed to make a short announcement to the press. He slowly mounted the marble staircase, turned at its summit, and crossed his arms. Everyone waited. 'Stalin,' he said, 'has splendid black moustaches.' Then he went to bed, leaving everyone seething below.

From Shaw's writings Stalin emerges as a Soviet icon. 'Stalin is not a dictator,' he was to explain using a comparison that Orwell also made. 'The nearest comparison you can get to Stalin is the Pope.' The religion is still Lenin's and the faith lies in collective immortality. Stalin becomes an instrument of the Life Force needed to implement Leninism and to break the pattern of collapsing civilizations – the concept that Shaw had absorbed from the work of the archaeologist Flinders Petrie. When invited, at the film studios in Leningrad, to give an impromptu speech in a film about Lenin, Shaw took the opportunity to affirm his belief in Lenin's significance for us all.

'We know from our recent historical researches that there have been many civilizations, that their history has been very like the history of our civilization, and that when they arrived at the point which Western capitalist civilization has reached, there began a rapid degeneracy, followed by a complete collapse of the entire system and something very near to a return to savagery by the human race. Over and over again the human race has tried to get round that corner and has always failed.

'Now, Lenin organized the method of getting round that corner . . . if this great communistic experiment spreads over the whole world, we shall have a new era in history. We shall not have the old collapse and failure, the beginning again, the going through the whole miserable story to the same miserable end . . .

'If the future is the future as Lenin foresaw it, then we may all smile and look forward to the future without fear. But if the experiment is overthrown and fails . . . then I shall have to take a very melancholy farewell of you, my friends.'

When asked how he would feel about living permanently in the Soviet Union, Shaw replied that he felt ill at ease among all people, but that his few days among the Soviet people had given him a rare and refreshing experience. In this beautiful country, for the first time anywhere, Shaw thought he saw the realists in command of the philistines. He was 'overwhelmed by the purposefulness and earnest conviction he met', Professor Arch Tait has written. When progressive ideas appeared in Soviet Russia 'the entire state apparatus, all its organs, the press and public opinion set about realizing these ideas', he said to Litvinov and Lunacharsky, 'whereas any progressive idea which appears in England is met not by sympathy, but by furious opposition from the powers that be and from the press'.

Shaw's pleasure at finding one of the forms of socialism he had preached almost fifty years before apparently coming to birth in Russia makes itself felt at the end of a speech he delivered on his seventy-fifth birthday at the Trade Union Central Hall (formerly the Hall of Nobles of the Nobleman's Club and later to be the showplace of Stalin's notorious treason trials). This celebration turned out to be 'a queer mixture of public meeting, snack-bar banquet and concert'. 'Tovarishchi,' he began, struggling to pronounce the only Russian word he knew, 'Comrades'. It came out as a meaningless blur of Slavonic sounds and was lost in the storm of laughter and applause.

246

Encouraged by the good humour, he went on to joke about his British 'valour' in making this journey into Communist Russia.

'Our weeping families clung to us, imploring us not to risk our lives on so dangerous a venture. And when our dear ones saw that we were still determined to set out on our journey they loaded us down with enormous baskets and parcels of food, so we wouldn't die here of hunger. They brought us bedding ... and some of them even brought us tents for fear that we would be without a roof over our heads. The railway from the frontier to Moscow is strewn with the things we threw out [of] our carriage windows as we saw with what comfort, attention and kindness the new regime in Russia surrounded us.'

He then neatly changed this extravaganza into an elegant tribute.

'We don't know how to adequately express our gratitude for all that your country's Communist government has done for us. We can only say that if the Soviet government succeeds in providing to all the peoples of the Union those same conditions which it has provided us – and we believe this is one of the Soviet government's goals – then Russia will become the most fortunate country on earth.'

Halfway through his speech 'my mind went blank suddenly', he wrote to Charlotte, 'and I had to frivol rather vulgarly'. He tried out one appalling pun: 'I have seen all the "terrors", and I was terribly pleased by them.' This was not the usual G.B.S. His wit had dried up. Then, suddenly, in a changed voice, he got going again. 'We shall carry profound impressions with us as we return to England,' he said. ' ... It is very difficult for me to end my speech. I can't talk to you as I generally do. As I look around I see in your eyes something I have never met in the audience of other countries ...' There was nothing left of the sardonic G.B.S. He was obviously moved.

'It is a real comfort to me, an old man, to be able to step into my grave with the knowledge that the civilization of the world will be saved ... It is here in Russia that I have actually been convinced that the new Communist system is capable of leading mankind out of its present crisis, and save it from complete anarchy and ruin ...'

He sat down disgusted at not having spread himself as imposingly as he wished. By his own oratorical standards his speech had been a 'bad effort', Waldorf Astor noted. Yet for some listeners its hesitant sincerity was more effective than his other brilliantly polished presentations.

On their last night in Moscow they handed to the hotel staff the biscuits, cereals and tins of food which G.B.S. had pretended were littering the

Russian railway tracks, and caught the night train to Warsaw and 'our Western countries of despair'. Shaw had warned Charlotte that 'I am at least 20 years younger' and he was soon busy denying rumours that his rejuvenation was due to a sexual gland transplant by the Soviet surgeon Serge Voronoff.

Charlotte was overjoyed to see G.B.S. so bronzed and well when he arrived back at Adelphi Terrace on the morning of 2 August. Nancy had obviously taken tremendous care of him: 'he never got a bite, or saw any sign of insects or infection', Charlotte told a friend. And he was so evidently enchanted with Russia it was wonderful to hear him talk of it all. 'He says,' she wrote, 'it all seems like a "splendid, sunny dream".'

*

The Webbs were particularly keen to question G.B.S. on his return. The newspapers had been full of his extravagant homage to the Soviet Union. 'Were I only 18 years of age,' he told journalists at the Silesian Station in Berlin, 'I would settle in Moscow tomorrow.' 'But surely you didn't find Russia pleasanter than Ireland?' an innocent *Star* reporter enquired, at which, with a cry of 'Good God!', Shaw remounted the train and continued his journey home. Arriving back in London, he announced in the *New York American* that the 'Soviet Leads in World Race'. In Shavian terms it was a race between the millennium and extinction. A few days later both *The Times* and the *New Leader* carried accounts of his speech to the Independent Labour Party National Summer School at Digswell Park.

'I have been preaching Socialism all my political life and here at last is a country which has established Socialism, made it the basis of its political system, definitely thrown over private property, and turned its back on Capitalism.'

After delivering this speech Shaw went on with Charlotte to stay with the Webbs at Passfield Corner, their home in Hampshire. 'He was tired and excited by his visit to Russia; carried away by the newness and the violence of the changes wrought,' Beatrice wrote in her diary for 8 August. 'Here is tragedy – comedy – melodrama, all magnificently staged on a huge scale. It *must* be right!'

But *was* it right? Beatrice could not yet decide. In 1927 she had thought that 'the Russian revolution, and especially the propaganda of it in Great Britain, has been the greatest disaster in the history of the British Labour movement'. G.B.S. was one of the chief agents for this British propaganda. It struck her as extraordinary that so great an objector to existing creeds and codes could have come to approve a dictatorship that 'liquidated' its objectors. She felt sceptical, too, of his religious confirmation, if such it was, after 'ten days' inspection of show institutions, surrounded with admiring crowds'.

Shaw's adaptation of Soviet Russia into the Webbs' magical conception of the threefold state ('citizens, consumers and producers' organization') did little to persuade Beatrice. She saw it as a gesture characteristic of her friend's charm in old age, for he was 'a supreme charmer', she reflected as she listened to him weaving his spell over the Fabians: 'appearance, voice, manner, gesture, outlook on other human beings, build up a perfect old man to be adored by the multitude'. But away from the multitude, over the next two days at Passfield Corner, she came to realize that he was in earnest about Soviet communism. Its egalitarian principles, which aimed to do away with the disastrous motive of pecuniary self-interest and replace it with a way of life based on common property, were the Webbs' principles too; and Soviet brutalities, he argued, though represented in the West as if Moscow had suddenly sprung up in the middle of the Home Counties, were manifestations of a backward country with a barbarous history. By the beginning of 1931 Stalin had not yet introduced any methods that would have raised an eyebrow during the tsarist regime; what he had done, Shaw said, was to build on Lenin's work in revolutionizing the purpose of government and the motives of human beings. This was the great adventure of transforming the environment that Don Juan had spoken of in *Man and Superman*. The only hope for the world was to change human nature – and that, Shaw claimed, was what the Russians were achieving.

'Putty is exactly like human nature. You cannot change it, no matter what you do. You cannot eat it, nor grow apples in it, nor mend clothes with it. But you can twist it and pat it and model it into any shape you like; and when you have shaped it, it will set so hard that you would suppose that it could never take any other shape on earth ... the Soviet Government has shaped the Russian putty very carefully ... and it has set hard and produced quite a different sort of animal.'

Shaw wanted to believe that the Soviet government was producing a new kind of human being, Communist Man. Soon there would be two different human species on the planet, and the capitalist species would die out. What becomes lost in this vision is the Devil's warning from *Man and Superman* that when we grow over-ambitious on behalf of the human race we threaten to destroy ourselves. Beatrice was aware of this danger. Yet she felt more inclined, after the fall of the Labour government later that August, to place her faith in Soviet social engineering than in the haphazard ways of Western democracy. The economic depression signalled to many people the breaking-up of capitalism, and it was difficult for disillusioned socialists to place much hope in the capacity of the Labour Party to reform a decaying society.

Shaw's challenge to Sidney and Beatrice was made at a critical moment in their lives. When lunching with them later that August, Philip Snowden described Shaw's speech as 'wickedly mischievous' and denounced the Soviet system as a 'cruel slave state' rather than the 'beneficent experiment in organizing production and consumption for the common good' that Shaw wanted them to believe. Snowden was then Chancellor of the Exchequer in Ramsay MacDonald's Labour Cabinet. A fortnight later he held the same post in MacDonald's compromising National Cabinet, and by November he had been created Viscount and made Lord Privy Seal in MacDonald's Conservative-dominated second National coalition; while Sidney Webb, who had been Secretary for the Colonies in early August, was stranded in the House of Lords without a job. For many on the left the choice seemed to be between Snowden's and Shaw's ways forward. 'The tension between those who accept and those who denounce the USSR increases day by day,' Beatrice was to write. The Webbs could agree with the political diagnosis Shaw made when he pictured MacDonald as having 'led his flagship, on the eve of Trafalgar, into the enemy's line, and hoisted the enemy's colors'. They also began to accept his prognosis: 'When the enemy finds that his fleet will not follow him he will be only a negligible prisoner of war ... For really intelligent and longsighted leaders there is nothing hopeful now except a new departure to the left of the Labor Party to begin scientific communism with the experience of Russia to profit by.' When Snowden denounced the influence of communism on the Labour Party, much as Beatrice had done in 1927, Shaw responded by saying that if the Labour Party was not communist it was nothing at all. This was more than a confusion of tongues. 'I had always given my friends MacDonald and Snowden credit for not only occasionally declaring themselves Socialists, but really knowing what Socialism was and really meaning it,' he said at the Kingsway Hall shortly after the formation of MacDonald's second National Government. 'It was a little bit of a shock to find that when it came to the point, they discovered they were not Socialists at all.' Six weeks later, in a letter to Augustin Hamon, he put it most succinctly: 'we are henceforth either scientific Communists or – whatever MacDonald and Snowden (I might have added Kerensky) now are'.

In his old age, G.B.S. seemed 'to hanker for some credo to be *enforced* from birth onwards on the whole population', Beatrice noted in her diary. She shared with him a susceptibility to the religious discipline of communism. When he spoke of the Russian people as being 'filled with a purely spiritual impulse' and embodying 'a wonderful new power in the world' which 'grows on you amazingly after a day or two', she felt instinctively attracted to a transformation of men and women 'in *this* world and not in a mystical afterlife'. 'There is hope everywhere in Russia,' Shaw proclaimed. What other hope was there at the end of 1931 in Britain?

Beatrice was converted – and so was Sidney. The choice for Sidney in his early seventies was between retirement and a new chapter in his political career. Shaw's tailoring of the Soviet Union into an inside-out community, showing public interests over 'private selfishness and vulgar ambition', was perfectly fitted to Sidney's self-denying personality. In such a place you could happily work 'for things outside yourself'. Sidney's was the negative and Beatrice's the positive charge in the Webbs' conversion.

'Everybody who can possibly do so should go to Russia,' Shaw had said at Digswell Park. The following year Sidney and Beatrice made the first of their own expeditions to 'the Russian show'. Shaw's reconnaissance had given him an impression based on instinct: their visit would be an investigation ostensibly based on facts. On 21 May 1932 Shaw came down to Hay's Wharf to see them off. Their voyage had a special value for him. In the 1931 reissue of *Fabian Essays* he had depicted the Russian Revolution as a European convulsion that 'has changed the world more in four years than Fabian constitutional action seemed likely to do in four hundred'. He concluded that it 'is not so certain today as it seemed in the eighties that Morris was not right'. For over forty years Shaw had been looking for a way of bringing together the two heralds of his political career – Webb, the constitutionalist, who 'made no mistake' and Morris, the revolutionist, who was 'right after all' – on the same territory. That territory was to be the Soviet Union and the synthesis between his opposing political mentors, the Saint and the Genius, would be formed by the alchemy of magic idealism. Taking on the posthumous mantle of Morris, G.B.S. transformed himself into a revolutionist after the event. Also after the event he persuaded Sidney Webb to underpin this new castle of civilization with a detailed social survey. That was the meaning of his coded paradox that 'the Russian Revolution was pure Fabianism' and the USSR a Union of Fabian Republics.

The Webbs were Shaw's pre-eminent converts to Soviet communism. But numerous fellow travellers in the 1930s heard his crusader's cry 'Vive Stalin!' and took their inspiration from him.

'You happen to be the man who, nearly thirty years ago, gave me my first ideas of socialism, and ... I am hoping that you will find a little of the thrill which I myself find in living here, and that it will draw you back again to see for a longer time ... one of the forms in which the things you fifty-years ago prophesied, are coming to birth,'

wrote a young American journalist, Anna Louise Strong, whom David Caute depicts as thriving 'like a cactus in the desert, devoting her whole life to Russia and China during the most punishing phases of socialist construction'. Edgar Snow, whom Caute calls 'America's most widely read advocate of Chinese Communism', revealed the influence of G.B.S. on many left-wing intellectuals.

'It was Shaw who convinced me that the advancement of mankind beyond the predatory stage of human development and the replacement of existing systems of economic cannibalism by planned co-operation for the common good ... were attainable and good ends and inevitable if men were to survive.'

   Shaw's political position was aligned with that of Theodore Dreiser and Upton Sinclair in the United States, with Anatole France, Romain Rolland and with Ernst Toller on the European continent. In Britain he appeared to converge with a new literary movement that caught up Stephen Spender, Edward Upward, and other poets and novelists in their twenties, in a eulogistic chorus over what Shaw called 'the gigantic Russian experiment'. Big was beautiful and distance opened vistas of romance: electrification from the steppes was seen as a futuristic construct and the drumming of Soviet machinery heard as the sound of modernism. 'Beauty breaks ground, oh, in strange places,' C. Day Lewis wrote in celebration of the 'grain-Elevator in the Ukraine plain'; and Charles Madge bowed down before the spectacle when 'Power and the factories break flaming into flower'. Shaw formed no personal attachment with this new generation of writers who hardly heard his footfall just ahead of them on the stair. 'He's a kind of concierge in the house of literature,' Katherine Mansfield had written to Middleton Murry, ' – sits in a glass case – sees everything, knows everything, examines the letters, *cleans the stairs*, but has no part – no part in the life that is going on.'

   Shaw had a more direct influence on such political ideologists and philosophers as John Strachey, the Labour Member of Parliament who published his polemical *The Coming Struggle for Power* in 1932; on R. Palme Dutt, the communist editor of *Labour Monthly*; on the zoologist and film-maker Ivor Montagu; and on C. E. M. Joad, the naturist civil servant and professional expositor of Shavian thinking for whom G.B.S. became 'a kind of God'. For the uncommitted newspaper-reading public his appeal was erratic. 'He is writing *at* and not *with* them,' Katherine Mansfield observed.

It had still been possible in the summer of 1931 to go to Moscow and see some evidence of an enthusiastic socialist country. But as the 1930s ticked away, the Shavian wonderland of Sovietism appeared more fanciful – a chimera that Beatrice Webb's nephew Malcolm Muggeridge was to label 'Fabian Fairyland'. Shaw was obliged to force his political views by way of letters, speeches, articles and interviews into a hostile press that, he believed, had become an organ of the acquisitive society and shared its fundamental corruption. 'Its business is to hold a candle to the devil,' he wrote, 'by flattering predacity and representing constitutional honesty as execrable villainy.' He knew, as the American journalist Henry Dana admitted, that 'if he said nine things favorable to the Soviet Union and one thing hostile, the reporters would cable over to America the one hostile comment and suppress the nine favorable'. To combat this 'most insanely dangerous feature of our foreign policy during the last twenty years', he outwitted the press by saying 'ten favorable and not one thing hostile'. Such absolutism appeared to lead readers into politics of the absurd, so 'airily detached' (in Churchill's words) had he become from reality. Yet who can say whether Churchill's anti-Soviet obsession was not a factor in setting off reactionary Stalinism?

The Life Force seemed in league with the politics of death. Increasingly, as he grew older, Shaw's imagination flirted pleasurably with death and, in more extreme fantasies, killing. Yet people like himself, who became 'revolutionaries' because they could not endure the injustices of 'capital in pursuit of surplus value', were temperamentally unfitted for signing death warrants. 'There is a mawkish hesitation to shoot me,' he acknowledged, 'which is reflected in an equally mawkish hesitation on my part to be shot.' He found a solution to this problem in the principle of copyright. 'Why should not the limitation that applies to my literary property apply to all my property?' he asked. '... I do not greatly mind being shot fifty years after my death. I dont think anybody would.' In other words, the final solution should be left to biographers.

Though Shaw wrote for instantaneous effect, he added a historical perspective to his journalism that magnifies the sense of his remoteness from contemporary events and heightens his air of insensitivity. 'Our question is not to kill or not to kill, but how to select the right people to kill,' he wrote in 1932. '... the essential difference between the Russian liquidator with his pistol (or whatever his humane killer may be) and the British hangman is that they do not operate on the same sort of person.'

There is a misanthropic relish in his tone when he writes about such things. As he told Henry Salt at the end of 1934, he believed that 'really the human race is beyond redemption'. He knew well enough that the dark side of Soviet Russia – the OGPU, for example was 'an Inquisition pure and simple'. But he made light of it. 'All that will happen to you is that when you have made yourself quite clear, you will suddenly find yourself in the next world.' He realized that the Soviet Constitution of 1936 could properly be 'dismissed as a feat of window dressing to conciliate Liberal opinion in Europe and America'. Though lacking first-hand news, he described Stalin's show trials that same year as 'another witch burning epidemic'; and, although he refused to join the committee for Trotsky's defence, he dismissed the accusations against him as politically malicious, adding: 'I hope that Trotsky will not allow himself to be brought before a narrower tribunal than his reading public where his accusers are at his mercy.' In 1937 he went out of his way to salute André Gide's *Retour de l'URSS* as 'a really superfine criticism of Soviet Russia', praising Gide's 'complete originality and sincerity', and perhaps reflecting on his own wisdom in not returning. There were 'too many fools in Russia to be trusted', he explained in a letter to Rutland Boughton, 'without a pretty sensitive and vigilant criticism'.

G.B.S. in his eighties was not the man for such sensitivity or criticism. 'Charlotte and I are old and in our second childhood. We can no longer feel things [except little things] as you do,' he wrote to Trebitsch in 1940, 'which is very fortunate for us, because human misery is so appalling nowadays that if we allowed ourselves to dwell on it we should only add imaginary miseries of our own to the real miseries of others without doing them any good.' They raised themselves above the facts of human misery, which had subdued both their childhoods, and ascended into the rarer make-believe of this second childhood. Beatrice Webb sometimes wondered whether the gathering unpopularity of G.B.S.'s Sovietism would trouble Charlotte – but she seemed perfectly sealed in her extraordinary mystical envelope. As for G.B.S., Sovietism was now a fundamentalist religion untouched by ordinary criticism.

Shaw's journey to Russia had been in the nature of a revelation – a revelation, some said, inspired by an hallucination. In 1932 he set out to bear witness to Soviet Communism from the Revolution of 1917 using 'the famous execution on Calvary' as a metaphysical basis. The Crucifixion 'has never been challenged in respect of the two thieves who suffered on that occasion along with the Communist', he wrote in this work which he was never to finish.

'The principle of the execution is fully admitted. All the controversies have arisen on the point whether the execution of the Communist was not a mistake – whether he was not rather the sort of person who should be encouraged rather than liquidated. Was he really an enemy of mankind or was he a saviour? Our general conclusion so far seems to be that, whether or no, we are well rid of him.

'I think we go to the opposite extreme ourselves in glorifying thieves, provided their booty is big enough and they play the game according to the rules they have themselves made, meanwhile holding up that particular Communist as the prince of such thieves.'

'You must not expect a paradise,' Shaw would tell travellers to the Soviet Union. Yet his book, called *The Rationalization of Russia*, was an attempt to rationalize an ideal. 'The Russians have "got religion",' he wrote, which meant that he had got the glass eyes of religion himself and could see Russian children in the future being born without the original sin of inequality. He also confided to the Reverend Ensor Walters, with whom he had worked on the St Pancras Vestry, that the blessed absence of social and religious castes, which had so complicated his Dublin childhood, and of competitive commercial friction, which had harmed his early years in London, was 'indescribable' in Moscow. He could not put into words the wonder of this equality; or describe how it uplifted and enchanted him during the Depression, the Second World War, and his old age. He wanted to transform this governmental practice into a science of happiness to rid human beings of 'the miserable delusion that we can achieve it by becoming richer than our neighbours'. His writing glows and fades as it circles round this romance, then hesitates, repeats, and peters out. For what he feels is not directly communicable, but will find its way obliquely into memories, dreams, reflections: the fables, spells, extravaganzas, visions, miracles and marvellous history lessons of his final period.

[2]

There is something fantastic about them, something unreal and perverse, something profoundly unsatisfactory. They are too absurd to be believed in: yet they are not fictions . . .
Too True to be Good

Shaw began his first play of the 1930s as he and Charlotte left the coast of Marseilles on 5 March 1931 for a month's tour of the Mediterranean. It was to 'take precedence over all other work'. By the end of May, Charlotte was writing to Nancy Astor that 'so far it is unlike anything I ever have read . . . only the 1st Act is done'. But it was 'progressing by leaps & bounds', she added, and a week later Shaw was more than halfway through the dialogue. 'It is up to date and a little beyond,' he notified his British publisher Otto Kyllmann, ' ... I call it provisionally Too True to Be Good.' He completed the first draft on 30 June, two and a half weeks before setting off for Soviet Russia, which appears like a mirage as the Utopian 'Union of Federated Sensible Societies' named Boetia where 'everybody wants to go'. He decided to keep the provisional title *Too True to be Good*, explaining to Trebitsch that it was based on 'a popular locution to express incredulity as to good news'. Shaw's reversal of this locution in a play that exploits reversals, reflects the bad news of living in a 'phase of disillusion after the war'. Boetia, or the UFSS, offers escape into a land of illusion which really is too good to be true.

After returning from Russia he tried out the play on various friends – Nancy Astor, Barry Jackson, Lady Rhondda, and the Dean of St Paul's, W.R. Inge, who had accompanied Charlotte and himself on their Hellenic Travellers' Club tour and was (Charlotte whispered to Nancy) 'so deaf that he cannot hear in a theatre'. To Beatrice Webb, who heard Shaw read the first act at Passfield Corner that summer, the play seemed 'a fantasy or farce – on the thesis of the present chaotic state of morals and the futility of self-expression and self-indulgence. Amusing, suggestive, brilliant, but leading nowhere, a characteristic in itself representative of the present lack of purpose ... ' T. E. Lawrence, to whom Shaw read it at Ayot, had felt that 'parts were authentic, & other parts felt long', but unlike Beatrice Webb, he preferred the sermons (it was 'all long sermons relieved by childish music hall turns' Shaw had told Kyllmann). As for Charlotte, 'I call it a Super Farce,' she confided in Nancy.

Since Barry Jackson wanted to stage the first British presentation at Malvern in August 1932, there was plenty of time for Shaw to allow changes to occur and to let the third act find its shape – the peroration at the end, with its pentecostal flame and echo from the Lord's Prayer, was not added until two days after the opening performance at Malvern. Working from unconscious impulses, he had used one idea to summon up another in an apparently random sequence of impressions, like fiery islands emerging from an ocean of fantasy. In this dreamscape of land and sea Shaw places his apocalyptic vision of humanity poised between drowning in despair and making an awakening ascent. 'G.B.S. is like a Gulf-Stream: and I wondered where he would bring up,' T. E. Lawrence had written to Charlotte. Reading an acting proof which Blanche Patch sent him early in 1932, Lawrence felt that the loose threads had mysteriously drawn together through the play's three diverse movements into an overwhelming climax. 'I get up from reading dumb struck and rather scared,' he wrote to Charlotte.

Shaw had drafted a paragraph for *The Times*. 'It is not a sequel to the *Apple Cart*, and it is not a historical play like *Saint Joan*. Its main theme is the dissolution of established morals by the shock of the war; but the examples may prove unexpected.' The play was to develop the contrapuntal style and anarchic comedy of *Misalliance*. It is like a sequel to *Heartbreak House*. The echoes and associations bring a transcendental air to these last plays, comparable in its heightened quality to Ibsen's *When We Dead Awaken* or Shakespeare's *The Tempest*, carrying audiences far from their familiar shores and out of sight of naturalism. It is the supernatural, gained from preparatory shipboard-reading on cruises round the world, that Shaw exotically sets against the tropical jungles, islands, deserts, temples, and seas of these final period plays. 'I, too, have found in the east a quality of religion which is lacking in these islands,' he was to write to the traveller and mystic Sir Francis Younghusband in 1934. His cast of aspiring souls fly from the calculable world into a realm of dream and actuality which is Shaw's synthesis of east and west.

*

When the curtain goes up on *Too True to be Good* it is night in 'one of the best bedrooms in one of the best suburban villas in one of the richest cities in England'. The class system still operates in post-war England, but though financially underpinned it is not secure. For this is a sickroom. The bedside table is congested with medicine bottles, thermometers and pill boxes; and the young lady with an unhealthy complexion smothered under blankets and eiderdowns is an invalid. She is heavily asleep. Near her, reclining on an easy chair, sits a Monster made of 'luminous jelly with a visible skeleton of short black rods'. Nobody who enters the room will be able to see this Monster: it is a phantasm of the young lady's, and this is her dream that we are witnessing.

The Monster, who proclaims itself 'a poor innocent microbe', soliloquizes futuristically on the Rights of Microbes ('I suppose it never occurs to you that a bacillus can be sick like anyone else'). It is in 'the last degree wretched' because the young lady's spoilt and sedentary life, her stuffy room and lethal diet (plenty of under-cooked meat washed down with glasses of port and champagne) are killing it. This is the first of the play's many reversals. 'These humans are full of horrid diseases,' the unfortunate bacillus complains in the presence of an expensive doctor looking after the Patient: 'they infect us poor microbes with them; and you doctors pretend that it is we that infect them.' Throughout this act the Monster keeps up a subversive commentary on the common-sense that kills.

The repository of this conventional common sense is the Patient's elderly mother, a 'maddening woman' named Mrs Mopply whose rule is Safety First and Last. She has already killed her other children by dense overprotection and is now spending a fortune on her daughter's illness. Her neurotic attitude to this daughter – who throughout the play is called 'the Patient' – brings to mind Charlotte's nervous attitude to health. 'The patient is happily convalescent,' Shaw had written of Charlotte to Blanche Patch from Paris at the beginning of May 1931 while working on his play; 'but she has had a full dress illness, with doctor, nurse, and all complete, and is still in bed.'

This, in a less happy climate, is the condition of the play's Patient for whom her mother has just hired a new and highly-recommended night nurse. Left alone with her charge, this young nurse begins behaving very oddly, opening the blinds and windows, switching on and off the lights, and throwing the bell cord with its button out of reach of the Patient. She is signalling to her 'gentleman friend', a well-dressed, disarmingly pleasant man in his early thirties, who, like Bluntschli in *Arms and the Man*, clambers through the window. But this is not an amorous tryst, as the Patient indignantly assumes. Far from being a qualified nurse, the young woman is actually the business partner of the gentleman who, wearing rubber gloves and a small white mask, politely introduces himself as a burglar somewhat in the fashion of E. W. Hornung's amateur cracksman, Raffles. Together 'Popsy' and 'Sweetie', as these Bright Young Things call each other, are after the Patient's celebrated pearl necklace. The Patient, however, springs from her bed and, defending her jewel case with unexpected athleticism, scatters the burglars, before fainting from the exertion.

'Then I awoke and dreamed again.' After the Patient has fainted, the play reaches into more optimistic realms of fantasy. A circus of bewildering Shavian paradoxes, proliferating identities, shifting illusions and inversions springs up. The Burglar peels off his mask and, revealing himself to be a clergyman, explains that he was secretly ordained while up at Oxford. 'But I must ask you to keep it a dead secret,' he appeals to the Patient as she comes round: 'my father, who is an atheist, would disinherit me if he knew.' Instead of tying up the Patient, he hands her back the bell. 'I am utterly at your mercy,' he volunteers. And instead of stealing her necklace, he proposes that the Patient steal it herself and divide the proceeds (which as payment for honestly sold jewellery will be far larger) among the three of them. 'Sell it; and have a glorious spree with the price. See life. Live. You dont call being an invalid living do you? ... You think you are in a state of illness. Youre not: youre in a state of sin. Sell the necklace and buy your salvation with the proceeds.' If the Patient can fight for her property like a champion heavyweight, he argues, she can also fight to emancipate herself from this wretched hospital of a home. His proposal 'may make another woman of you', he adds, 'and change your entire destiny'. As he continues speaking, the Burglar's ideas grow more dazzling. 'Lets stage a kidnap,' he suggests. '...We shall pretend to be brigands.' Mrs Mopply will then pay a ransom and her daughter 'will realize not only the value of the pearls, but of yourself'.

The Patient knows that she is dreaming. 'But it's delicious, because I'm dreaming that I'm perfectly well ... Let nobody wake me. I'm in heaven.' She feels herself falling in love with the Burglar ('a perfect film hero, only more like an English gentleman'). While he declaims with romantic eloquence on the thematic plot so far, she jumps out of bed and actually dresses herself without a maid. They kiss, and accompanied by Sweetie, rush out into the dawn (the Patient at the last moment remembering to carry off the necklace).

The stage is finally left to the Monster. Miraculously cured, it has been luminously bounding about, perching on pillows and even getting into bed beside the Patient. The Patient has attributed her wonderful hallucination to the doctor's new sleeping draught, but the Monster attributes its cure to the unusual exercise involved in 'that scrap for the jewels'. It is transformed from a 'bloated moribund Caliban', the stage directions tell us, into 'a dainty Ariel'. Just as Ariel obeys Prospero's (and therefore Shakespeare's) commands, and Caliban represents Shakespeare's audiences, so Shaw uses this preposterous creature to speak for the most monstrous members of his own audiences: the critics. 'The play is now virtually over,' the Monster says, anticipating their notices; 'but the characters will discuss it at great length for two acts more. The exit doors are all in order. Goodnight.' As a respectable critic the Monster cannot leave, but prepares itself professionally for the rest of the play: '*It draws up the bedclothes round its neck and goes to sleep.*'

Shaw created Sweetie, the Burglar, and the Patient as the trinity of the capitalist religion: sex, intelligence and money. 'In our firm I am the brains: you are the hand,' the Burglar reminds Sweetie. But their partnership needs the muscle of hard cash provided by the Patient who 'will be an invaluable bodyguard for us two weaklings'. The Burglar's capitalist dream conjures up an enchanting adventure: 'in dreamland generosity costs nothing', the Patient reflects. '...I'm going to make the most of this dream.' So her pilgrimage begins.

It begins in a capitalist nirvana which the Patient has imagined in Act I as an eternity in 'the loveliest earthly paradise we can find' and which in Act II opens up before us as 'a sea beach in a mountainous country' – perhaps not far from the Moorish castle where Lady Cicely Waynflete was once held in *Captain Brassbound's Conversion*. Also occupying these glaring sand dunes, and registering the colonial aspect of capitalism, is a British military cantonment. Here we are introduced to a couple of new characters, Colonel Tallboys VC DSO, and Private Meek, who present another reversal of categories illustrating the topsy-turvy values of the capitalist hierarchy. For the insignificant private, with the figure of a seventeen-year-old boy and a dismaying smile, is a far more skilled soldier than the head of the British expeditionary force whose real talent (possibly like Churchill's) is for watercolours.

Private Meek is famously modelled on Lawrence of Arabia. 'Perhaps I shall put you into a play, if my play-writing days are not over,' Shaw had written to Lawrence on 1 December 1922. And in a letter to G.B.S. six years later, Lawrence wrote from India: 'I do what I am told to do, and rewrite the drafts [of routine orders] given to me, meekly.' Meekly, too, Lawrence persuaded G.B.S. to add almost two dozen 'squalid accuracies' to his play, strengthening the farce with authentic military detail and guiding Private Meek between the dangers of servility and impudence.

Meek is a Shavian notion of genius, someone fulfilling his vocation and finding himself perfectly attuned to his environment. He is 'never at a loss': an omnicompetent, omnipresent, complete human being who appears whenever the Colonel calls for an interpreter, quartermaster's clerk or intelligence orderly. Colonel Tallboys believes that the other men 'put everything on the poor fellow because he is not quite all there'. It takes an attack by local tribesmen, which Meek repulses with irresistible authority, to show the Colonel that the man whom he has persistently called a 'half witted creature', and whom it is socially correct to address as 'a very distant inferior', is in fact the commanding spirit among them. In a letter to St John Ervine, Shaw claimed that he had taken 'advantage of the amazing case of Lawrence' to solve the conundrum of how impossible colonels and mad admirals functioned so competently. 'The secret of command, in the army and elsewhere,' explains Colonel Tallboys, 'is never to waste a moment doing anything that can be delegated to a subordinate.' The Colonel rather than the Private is actually the halfwit because, until the next stage of his pilgrimage is reached in Act III, he has never followed his own vocation. 'I have a passion of sketching in watercolours,' he tells the others. 'Hitherto the work of commanding my regiment has interfered very seriously with its gratification. Henceforth I shall devote myself almost entirely to sketching, and leave the command of the expedition to Private Meek.' Only by following their vocations singlemindedly, Shaw implies, will his characters arrive at the kingdom of heaven on earth – or Boetia, for which Colonel

Tallboys, in his capacity as an English watercolourist, is finally offered a visa: 'theyll make him head of their centres of repose and culture if he'll settle there'. In the event, he cannot settle there because, being married, he is not singleminded. 'But my wife,' he exclaims. '...there is nothing for it but to return to our own country.' In such split-second asides, Shaw glances at the what-might-have-been of his own life which underscores this make-believe play.

The British expeditionary force has been sent to this nameless country to rescue Miss Mopply from the brigands who have kidnapped her and demanded a ransom. It is not wholly the Colonel's fault that the three English tourists who have put themselves under his protection are actually the people he is supposed to be seeking, for they have altered their appearances and identities spectacularly. As in Barrie's *The Admirable Crichton*, the employer and employee switch roles. Sweetie has been changed from a nurse into a flamboyantly unconvincing foreign aristocrat, the Countess Valbrioni, 'brilliantly undressed for bathing under a variegated silk wrap'; while the Patient, who accompanies her carrying a parasol and rug, is 'disguised *en belle sauvage* by headdress, wig, ornaments and girdle proper to no locality on earth except perhaps the Russian ballet'. The Burglar too has changed. He now uses, for the purposes of concealment, his real name, the Honourable Aubrey Bagot, and emerges from a bathing tent 'very elegant in black and white bathing costume and black silken wrap with white silk lapels: a clerical touch'.

The parts played by Shaw's characters multiply rapidly as their adventures proceed. While they are adjusting masks, confusing ranks, assembling disguises, aliases, nicknames, they gradually expose layers of biographical origins. Sweetie and Aubrey, for example, reveal themselves as having been lovers back in England. 'I was in love with this woman: madly in love,' Aubrey says, '...there was an extraordinary sympathy between our lower centres.' Sweetie, who had been a love child, was trained as a hotel chambermaid and now 'gets so used to new faces that at last they become a necessity'. She has developed 'such amazing mobility of the affections' that, according to the Patient, she is 'always trying to get the better of somebody or to get hold of a man'.

Sweetie owes something to Molly Tompkins. She has soon become bored with this capitalist utopia. 'I am so lonely. The place is so dull ... Nothing to do but be ladylike,' she complains. Acting the Countess has actually removed her further from her 'lower centres', which indicate her true vocation, than playing the nurse-accomplice to a burglar. Aubrey, too, is without occupation in this sunny place. Before the play began he had employed his divine gift – 'a gift of lucidity as well as of eloquence' – to make

Sweetie fall in love with him and to convert her 'on principle' from chambermaid to criminal. But his 'most glorious achievement' has been the audacious rescue of the Patient from respectability and their elopement into a paradise where 'every day is a day of adventure'.

The Patient is transformed: 'I have forgotten what illness means,' she says. But she is also disillusioned: 'I am free; I am healthy; I am happy; and I am utterly miserable.' When she declares that 'the glories of nature dont last any decently active person a week' – about half the time that any indecently active man lasts Sweetie who 'wants a new face every fortnight' – it is ostensibly because the three adventurers are passing through a symbolic landscape rather than the natural world. Shaw uses this second act of his play to demonstrate how even the rich in a capitalist society have to drug themselves with 'cocktails and cocaine' into pretending they are happy when in fact they are maddened with boredom. Sweetie and the Patient both embody Don Juan's argument in *Man and Superman* to the effect that the direct pursuit of happiness leads to misery, and that happiness must be a by-product of other endeavours. Aubrey has taken on the role of capitalism's conscienceless idealist. 'The first lesson a crook has to learn, darling, is that nothing succeeds like lying,' he reminds Sweetie. The Patient, too, recognizes him as 'a liar'. 'I want something sensible to do,' she cries. But there is nothing sensible to do in capitalism's dream world, where all change – like the succession of Sweetie's lovers – is illusory. This is the Devil's hell, 'the home of the unreal', as Don Juan has described it, 'and of the seekers for happiness'. Shaw's theme in *Too True to be Good* is the journey of a post-war generation in its search for reality. 'Lets go and have a bit of real life somewhere,' urges Sweetie; and the Patient exclaims: 'Real life! I wonder where thats to be found!'

It may be found not far off in this surrealistic waste land. Passing through a narrow gap between two grottoes and down a meandering path to the beach, they all assemble for Act III. Over the more gothic-looking of the grottoes soldiers have scrawled ST PAUL'S; over the wider grotto, which is illuminated rosily with bulbs wrapped in pink paper and contains a bench long enough to accommodate two people, is carved AGAPEMONE in Greek characters beneath which has been chalked in red THE ABODE OF LOVE to which is added in white chalk NO NEED TO WASTE THE ELECTRIC LIGHT. These two grottoes recall the preceding two scenes of the play: the house of decaying superstitions and the fairyland of sexual pleasure.

As in Act II we are introduced to two new characters. St Paul's is occupied by a 'very tall gaunt elder' through whom Shaw presents the evolution of the fanatical Old Testament prophet into an imposing

Victorian intellectual. This Elder has replaced religious fundamentalism with a puritanical faith in scientific absolutes, but his moral authority has suddenly collapsed with the coming of Einstein's relativity. 'He is in the deepest mourning; and his attitude is one of hopeless dejection.' These stage directions emphasize the Elder's resemblance to W.R. Inge, the most famous clergyman in the Church of England between the wars, and popularly known as 'the Gloomy Dean'. The inscription 'St Paul's' seems to put a label on this identification, since Inge was Dean of St Paul's for over twenty years until his retirement in 1934. Classical scholar, diehard Tory, deaf to all music, Inge 'detested the twentieth century', A. N. Wilson has written approvingly; and yet Shaw admired him in much the same way as he admired Almroth Wright who had inspired *The Doctor's Dilemma*. The Elder is not a portrait of Inge, but takes life from one idea associated with him. Dean Inge 'is 700 years out of date with his terrible bringing-up and schooling; and yet he lives', Shaw wrote to Hesketh Pearson. '... When he is on his job he is easily one of the first minds in England.' The Elder employs this mind to trace the knot of his pessimism. 'Newton's universe was the stronghold of rational Determinism,' he says.

'... Everything was calculable: everything happened because it must: the commandments were erased from the tables of the law; and in their place came the cosmic algebra: the equations of mathematicians. Here was my faith: here I found my dogma of infallibility ... And now – now – what is left of it? The orbit of the electron obeys no law ... All is caprice: the calculable world has become incalculable ... Nothing can save us from a perpetual headlong fall into a bottomless abyss but a solid footing of dogma; and we no sooner agree to that than we find that the only trustworthy dogma is that there is no dogma.'

Though Dean Inge serves as a figurehead for the Elder, this philosophical position belongs more accurately to Beatrice Webb. 'How can the human mind acclimatize itself to the insecurity and uncertainty of this terrible doctrine of relativity, latent in all modern science long before Einstein applied it to the astronomical universe?' she had asked in her diary. 'It is a most disconcerting conclusion, that there is no absolute truth; and that the thoughts of the man are no more and no less valid than the analogous brain activities of the dog or the bee! What becomes of existing standards of morality or capacity? ... Like so many other poor souls I have the consciousness of being a spiritual outcast. I have no home for my religious faculty, I wander about disconsolate ...'

As another wanderer of this lost generation Shaw used the experimental plays of these last years to find a new home for his religious faculty. With an upbringing and schooling no less terrible in its fashion than his friend Inge's, he had prided himself as a young man on being 'up to my chin' in the contemporary world; but pessimism kept advancing until, in old age, he accelerated some '700 years' ahead of his time – the opposite direction from Dean Inge – to escape imprisonment by the Giant Despair.

Shaw's own position in the play is surprisingly represented by Sergeant Fielding, the occupant of THE ABODE OF LOVE. As a sergeant, he is halfway between the numskull Colonel and the genius Private, a man of talent and inquiry who 'is completely absorbed in two books, comparing them with rapt attention'. 'I myself was trained,' Shaw was to write, 'by reading the Bible *and* Bunyan.' The Bible and Bunyan's *The Pilgrim's Progress* are the two books that are absorbing the Sergeant. 'I carry them with me wherever I go,' he tells Sweetie who joins him in THE ABODE OF LOVE. 'I put the problems they raise for me to every woman I meet.'

Shaw's dream play is a version of Bunyan's fable 'delivered under the similitude of a dream'. It is the pilgrimage of Hopeful rather than of Christian and pushes Shaw's spiritual autobiography into a land of allegory and abstraction as he works his way out of a hostile world into futuristic spheres of optimism, his Boetia (unwittingly called the land of stupidity in the West) being an equivalent of Bunyan's Beulah, the illuminated country this side of death, near the Celestial City. His pilgrims all start from a point of certainty that has been destroyed. Even the Sergeant's religious faith is threatened with obliterating pessimism after the horror of a world war. 'I used to be a religious man; but I'm not so clear about it as I was,' he admits. Before this war the Bible and *The Pilgrim's Progress* had given him answers; now they raise questions. 'I used to believe every word of them because they seemed to have nothing to do with real life. But war brought those old stories home quite real ... here we are waiting in the City of Destruction like so many sheep for the wrath to come.'

The Sergeant's criticism of the Bible is that it is soaked in what Bunyan called 'revenging justice', which Shaw himself believed to be an obsolete guide to conduct. 'Revenge is not Justice', he was to write in the margin of *The Life and Death of Mr Badman*. 'But "action and reaction are equal and opposite", which is a different matter, and nearer the truth.'

The Sergeant also criticizes *The Pilgrim's Progress*. 'This uneducated tinker tells me the way is straight before us and so narrow that we cant miss it,' he says. 'But he starts by calling the place the wilderness of this world. Well, theres no road in a wilderness: you have to make one. All the straight roads are made by soldiers; and the soldiers didnt get to heaven along them. A lot of them landed up in the other place.' Shaw also provides a 'narrow gap' between the grottoes, but his path is far from straight: it is an expressionist convolution. He has renounced the well-made play as he renounces well-made Western civilization, and given up conventional structure as he gives up conventional morals. He is responding to the challenge of Freud's world, which was becoming known to the English-speaking community through James Strachey's translations, and to the advent of Adler and Jung. The profusion of mishearings, coincidences, accidents, illusions all suggest that dreams and the unconscious mind are as much aspects of reality as the familiar outlines of the known world. Our guide to reality is not the straight line of logical thought but an instinct that communicates, sometimes with crazy seriousness, from our buried selves.

This is the instinct that has brought Sweetie and the Sergeant together in THE ABODE OF LOVE. Sweetie has already decided in Act II that the Sergeant is 'my sort . . . and the one really lovable man . . . I know just what he'll say and what he'll do. I just want him to do it.' The Sergeant too knows he needs Sweetie's 'animal warmth'. To the intelligent eye they look an extraordinarily ill-matched pair. 'If I'd thought you were religious I'd have given you a wide berth,' Sweetie tells him; ' . . . God help the woman that marries you.' Shaw's joke is that God will help Sweetie when she marries the Sergeant since theirs is a truly instinctive merging of complementary natures ('a top story as well as ground floor'). The Sergeant concludes that in this world of vanities neither the Bible nor Bunyan sufficiently values sexual love. 'That's a hard fact of human nature,' he says after kissing Sweetie; 'and its one of the facts that religion has to make room for.' The implication for G.B.S. himself is that Talkative and Mr Head-mind have had rather too much control over his career. The criticism he makes of Bunyan's *The Life and Death of Mr Badman* is the same criticism that would be made by critics of his own political ideology in old age. 'It was the patent fact that John [Bunyan] was so entirely well-intentioned in wielding his trenchant literary weapon that he was a dangerous man when he was wrong or ignorant or both.'

When young G.B.S. had boasted that he never gave up a political evening for a romantic assignation. But in his seventies he makes his alter-ego Sergeant turn his back on 'our Government chaps' and take up with Sweetie just at an age – 'getting on for forty' – when he himself met Charlotte and settled down in a *mariage blanc*. 'Though there is a point at which I'd rather kiss a woman than do anything else in the world,' the Sergeant confesses, 'yet I'd rather be shot than let anyone see me doing it.' Shaw had reached this point with Jenny Patterson and Florence Farr, but seldom let anyone see him doing it again. With the enchantress Stella Campbell, and on Molly Tompkins's magical island, he had come to the frontier of this heartland; and in *Too True to be Good* he explored it through his disassociated sensibilities.

The Patient's road to salvation is very different. In Act II, which has been played with all three adventurers largely unclothed, she has gained physical health as a step towards reality. But Act II belongs to Sweetie. The Patient is disgusted by Sweetie's sexual frankness and herself repels Sweetie by a Swiftian eschatology that reduces these glorious adventurers to 'just three inefficient fertilizers' who 'do nothing but convert good food into bad manure'. Unlike Sweetie she has enjoyed only an *affaire* of words with Aubrey who seems (as G.B.S. had seemed to so many women) too well satisfied with verbal intercourse. From Aubrey's point of view, the climax of their relationship has been reached by her getting out of bed rather than his getting into it, a priority of word-power over the sex-act. No wonder the Patient concluded that 'men are not real: theyre all talk, talk, talk – '.

Sweetie is real. 'Her lower centres speak,' says Aubrey. 'Since the war the lower centres have become vocal.' But these lower centres never actually speak in *Too True to be Good* because G.B.S., the great pre-war vocalist, does not have the language of D. H. Lawrence or James Joyce. Sweetie's sexuality appears unreal; and this suits Shaw's technical purpose, which was to create phantasms – 'like his shadows falling or flickering across a broken wall', as T. E. Lawrence described them – that cannot find their reality in moneymaking or sexual games. Until she uncovers one more authentic biographical fact – that her name is really Susan Simpkins – Sweetie has been held back from approaching the Sergeant by her fictional identity as a Countess. The Patient has meanwhile cast her looks in the direction of Private Meek. But, rather like Vivie Warren at the end of *Mrs Warren's Profession*, the paradoxically-named Meek represents salvation through self-sufficiency: he is not a partner but an example. In Act III, which attempts to convert physical into mental and spiritual stripping, the Patient finds her own vocational self-sufficiency in the prospect of a feminist commune. 'There should be only women, strong women able to stand by themselves,' she fiercely predicts. ' ... I shall found a sisterhood ... I want to have every woman in my sisterhood, and to have all the others strangled ... No more lovers for me.'

The continuing process of biographical disclosure in Act III lights up Sweetie and Aubrey more clearly as war-casualties. 'During the war it was found that sex appeal was as necessary for wounded or shellshocked soldiers as skilled nursing,' Aubrey says; 'so pretty girls were allowed to pose as nurses because they could sit on beds and prevent the men from going mad.' This has been Sweetie's war training and the reason why, in Act I, she was still posing as a night nurse. In peacetime, however, values are reversed and Sweetie's sexual provocation drives men mad – 'she drove me mad', Aubrey confesses.

Aubrey himself is one of the wounded war-shocked. 'I was hardly more than a boy when I first dropped a bomb on a sleeping village . . . swooped into a street and sent machine gun bullets into a crowd of civilians: women, children, and all,' he says. After being wounded and losing his nerve, he became an army chaplain obliged to blaspheme by telling men who were about to die that they were going straight to heaven when actually he believed they were dying in mortal sin.

Aubrey's moral position has become like that of Mrs Warren: someone who proceeds from being victimized to victimizing others – what the Elder unsympathetically calls making 'your military crimes an excuse for your civilian ones'. But what is the theft of a pearl necklace, Aubrey demands, in comparison with all that war-killing? The damaged flying ace has become a hero of the post-war era, a symbol of a cynical age and the agent for an undiscriminating Life Force. 'My gift of preaching is not confined to what I believe: I can preach anything, true or false. I am like a violin, on which you can play all sorts of music . . . if I can get a moving dramatic effect out of it, and preach a really splendid sermon about it, my gift takes possession of me and obliges me to sail in and do it.' Aubrey's contact with his own guiding instinct has been fractured by the war and he has bound the wound with rhetorical indulgence.

Only two characters in the play seem damned: the empty Aubrey and the unadaptable Elder. Shaw uses one of his more casual coincidences to make them father and son ('Hello, father, is it really you? I thought I heard the old trombone: I couldnt mistake it'). It is as unlikely, Shaw suggests, for someone with an extinct mental frame of reference to find reality as it is to experience a miraculous conversion on the road to Damascus. But Mrs Mopply who, dressed in black like the Elder, distractedly re-enters the play in Act III to urge on the rescue party, undergoes such a miracle when she interrupts the Colonel's painting and so exasperates him that he whacks her sun-helmeted head with his umbrella – and literally knocks some sense into her. Suddenly she becomes 'my real self', and the encasing lies of her life fall away. 'My mother told me lies. My nurse told me lies. My governess told me lies . . . How was I to behave in a world thats just the opposite of everything I was told about it?'

'Oh, if only someone had done that to her twenty years ago,' sighs the Patient, applauding the Colonel's miraculous blow, 'how different my childhood would have been!' Escaping from her home in Act I she has announced: 'A woman's future is not with her mother.' But Mrs Mopply no longer recognizes her daughter ('a horrid selfish girl, always ill and complaining') and will find her real future in their liberating sister-hood.

At the end of the play, like a different species of Monster, Aubrey is left alone. 'I am by nature and destiny a preacher,' he declaims as the others hurry away. '. . . I must have affirmations to preach . . . I have lost my nerve and am intimidated: all I know is that I must find the way of life, for myself and all of us, or we shall surely perish.' He has helped others; himself he cannot help. He has indeed lost his way while all but his father have begun to find theirs. But the pathos lies in the fact that they are finding their various ways without the guidance of his gift for preaching.

*

'The people will not like it so well as the Applecart, I think: but it is far finer,' T. E. Lawrence had written to Charlotte. '. . . It leaves you to go off down the street with a question mark in your stomach.'

'EXPECT THE WORST', Shaw cheerfully cabled the New York Theatre Guild which was to produce the world première in Boston at the end of February 1932. After touring Washington, Pittsburg and Buffalo, the play was brought into New York early in April and ran for fifty-seven performances. Though it contained 'some of the funniest lines and situations Shaw ever wrote', observed Lawrence Langner, for the most part it 'fell on indifferent ears in the depths of the depression period'. T. E. Lawrence had judged this play to be 'probably the finest acting thing G.B.S. has ever made', and what success it achieved in America was largely attributed to the acting of Beatrice Lillie as Sweetie: it was a case, not of gilding the lily, Alexander Woolcott wrote, but of 'Lillie-ing the Guild'.

Shaw had written *Too True to be Good* for the Malvern Festival where it opened on 6 August. 'We live in a whirl here,' Charlotte wrote from the Malvern Hotel, ' – plays, rehearsals, parties, crowds of people.' Barry Jackson had assembled a fine cast. Ernest Thesiger, who had created the Dauphin in *Saint Joan*, became the Monster; Cedric Hardwicke, a successful King Magnus in the first British production of *The Apple Cart*, entered as the Burglar; and Ralph Richardson, who had recently played Zozim and Pygmalion as well as Bluntschli in revivals of *Back to Methuselah* and *Arms and the Man*, created the role of Sergeant Fielding with (James Agate wrote) 'medieval forthrightness and controlled passion beyond all praise'.

Barry Jackson chartered 'a sumptuous aeroplane' to carry London critics to the opening matinée. Soaring through the heavens towards the scene of action, they were each handed a printed letter from G.B.S. describing 'the moral of the play, or rather the position illustrated by it'. But it was a bumpy flight. The pilot lost his way in the mist and, overshooting their destination, deposited everyone at Hereford. From here they arrived by charabanc over an hour late, pale and disgruntled, one of them collapsing dramatically in the auditorium at the start of the second act.

'My new play will not, I am afraid, please everybody,' Shaw had promised. 'It is not meant to.' But H. W. Nevinson, who hated *The Apple Cart*, found *Too True to be Good* 'one of his greatest and more unpopular plays'; and a few others, such as Lady Rhondda, felt they had experienced 'a divine revelation'. 'I have always thought of it as highly suitable for revival by the *avant-garde*,' wrote Lawrence Langner. Only a public familiar with Samuel Beckett was to feel at home with some of its strange puritan images.

Shaw sensed among critics 'an unusual intensity of resentment, as if I had hit them in some new and unbearably sore spot'. Charles Morgan scolded him in *The Times* for the 'fantastic irrelevance' and 'ugly frivolity' of his 'leaky farce'; and even the sympathetic Desmond MacCarthy complained of his complete indifference to form: 'Here am I, an attentive playgoer, yet I can't tell you what the play I have just seen at the Malvern Festival is about.'

Never, it seemed to Charlotte, had there been such a discrepancy between the general public and critics. 'The PLAY has been an immense excitement,' she reported from Malvern to Nancy Astor ' ... every time it is done it seems to come out with more force ... The press has been too lamentable ... a torrent of vulgar abuse & drivel!' Charlotte saw audiences *wriggling* with pleasure, and was convinced that this play was 'Deeper & more searching – & incidentally, much more amusing!' than *Heartbreak House*. Somehow she felt personally implicated as if G.B.S. had merged some of her own mystical beliefs into this play. It was all 'new & strange'. She recognized that for an assured popular success G.B.S. needed 'a plot or situation provided for him as he had in *St Joan*', but prayed for a triumphal entry into London's West End once the cast got 'more accustomed to it and less terrified!' Meanwhile G.B.S. seemed buoyant. 'My new play, so deformed by the Press (bar Lady Rhondda) is, so far, a fantastic Feminist success,' he wrote to Christopher St John on 21 August.

After three crowded weeks in Birmingham and with Donald Wolfit taking over from Barry Livesey as the young doctor, *Too True* opened at the New Theatre in London during the second week of September. It ran for forty-seven performances and marked Ralph Richardson's first attempt to establish himself in the West End. Shaw protested against its withdrawal. It had closed in London while drawing £1,000 a week, he pointed out, and in New York while drawing $6,500 a week – in the full tide, that is, of what would have been a delirious success at the Court Theatre under the Vedrenne-Barker management. But the gap had widened between the profits of popular entertainment and serious drama. '*Too True* filled the cheaper seats and moved people as no play of mine has moved them before,'

269

he wrote. '... Thus the case for a National Theatre grows stronger as the commercial theatres and cinemas flourish more and more and raise the standard of expenditure to a pitch undreamt of at the beginning of the century.'

He especially resented the description of his play as a pessimistic work that showed him 'finishing my life in a condition of pitiable but theatrically very tiresome disillusion and despair...'

'if you hint that there is not a paradise they call you a pessimist... I have not recanted, renounced, abandoned, nor demolished anything whatever.'

Beatrice Webb had thought the play despairing. 'There is not the remotest hint as to how human beings are going to improve themselves or be improved by an inner spirit or outside force. There is no redeemer,' she wrote. It is true that there is no redeemer for the Elder. But is there for Aubrey? And to what extent does Aubrey mirror Shaw's temperament? In his review of the London production, St John Ervine assumed the worst. 'What right has an old man to throw up his hands and surrender every belief he holds?' he demanded.

'That game soldier, Shaw, who has hitherto valiantly put up his fists and been the foremost in every fight, is now whimpering in corners and assuring his followers ... that they had better all lie down and die ... Better indeed that [he] should have died a dozen years ago than live to write this whining play.'

This attack drew from Charlotte an instant rebuttal. 'It is a play of *revolt*,' she countered.

'... Everything in the play points to the fact that there *is* a "way of life", & that all these people, some consciously some unconsciously, are struggling to find it ... it will be understood that this is among G.B.S.'s *big* plays. The voice of one crying in the wilderness!'

This was uncharacteristic of Charlotte, but she felt strongly the injustice of Ervine's criticism and may also have feared that G.B.S. could be hurt. Even so 'the voice of one crying in the wilderness' does not obviously reverberate with optimism, and many, like Desmond MacCarthy, who knew Shaw's work well and found Aubrey's peroration 'an astonishing and moving feat' in the theatre, sensed that they were responding to G.B.S.'s own predicament. When the American critic Joseph Wood Krutch identified Aubrey with his creator, he gave Shaw the opportunity for issuing an explicit denial. 'I affirm, on the contrary, that never before during my lifetime has the lot of mankind seemed more hopeful, and the beginnings of a new civilization more advanced.' But still people wondered whether this was not one more illustration of Aubrey's 'I must have affirmations to preach.'

In the shell-shocked-young-gentleman-burglar-clergyman Shaw had created an omen of capitalism whose spending-without-earning was leading to a moral bankruptcy not to be identified with someone who had placed his capital in the bank of communism. Aubrey is the obverse of Meek and, as Stanley Weintraub has ingeniously argued, portrays the post-war situation of T. E. Lawrence – a man who, removed from his vocation and suffering from the afflictions of war, sees himself falling into a void. Even so, as Weintraub adds, 'there is more than a little of G.B.S. himself in Aubrey'. Shaw had scattered aspects of himself through most of his characters. 'I made him a good preacher,' he fluently explained, 'to warn the world against mere fluency.' So Aubrey becomes a capitalistic version of G.B.S. who actually paraphrases Shaw's speeches ('as a wellknown author has said') in his own orations.

But this warning against fluency remains like a distant protest from Sonny against the pilgrimage of G.B.S.; and the law of equal action and reaction, which Shaw cites, tells us from what dark centre he had to call forth his affirmations.

[3]

I am myself a missionary.

Unlike his earlier flights and explorations, Shaw's travels in the 1930s were planned as a series of evangelical missions. No longer was he a solitary theorist; he journeyed as one who believed he had seen his conception of the good society being born. In the 1920s he was ready to dream of literary retirement; now in his late seventies he once more had affirmations to preach as he set out to bring the light of the Soviet Church to new audiences round the world.

After the poetic prophecy of *Heartbreak House*, the visionary testament of *Back to Methuselah*, the illuminated landscape of *Saint Joan*, the legend of G.B.S. as a powerful and benign seer had gradually spread overseas. He was determined to put his international fame to use.

'English writers are not revolutionaries,' Shaw said while visiting South Africa. 'I, on the other hand, am.' In his round-the-world promotion of communism, he was to employ all his powers of creative fantasy. 'Civilization is like a tree,' he told a journalist from the *Cape Times*. 'It grows to a point and then perishes.' But he could imagine a future civilization, nourished by new capillary action, where dreams and ideas grew naturally into deeds. This Tree of Life, which overlooked the sunlit glades in the last cycle of *Back to Methuselah*, must be cultivated everywhere.

Shaw and Charlotte had discussed going to South Africa in the late 1920s, postponed a decision, and then 'in a moment of insanity' booked their passage on the *Carnarvon Castle* which sailed on Christmas Eve 1931. 'Charlotte wants sunshine,' Shaw explained. As for himself 'I undertook this long voyage solely to get away from my work, having no more business in S. Africa than at the South Pole.' But since he carried with him bundles of unanswered correspondence and occupied each morning of the seventeen-day voyage working on *The Rationalization of Russia*, 'I have done an extra long days writing every day since we sailed.'

Their mail boat steamed into Cape Town on Monday 11 January 1932. It docked and they were immediately encircled by crowds of journalists, photographers and Cape Fabians as well as a movie camera crew which persuaded G.B.S. to perform an on-the-spot 'talkie' up on deck ('Good Morning, South Africa ... Now that you have seen my face, I shall show you my left profile ... and the back of my distinguished head'), while Charlotte waited below in her cabin. 'Only the advent of Don Bradman or Mahatma Gandhi would have aroused greater interest,' commented the *Cape Argus*, while the *Cape Times* was impatient to find out 'What Will G.B.S. Say to South Africa?'

This became clear the next day following an interview with the *Cape Times*. 'Our religious codes are obsolete in many ways,' he was reported as saying. 'The average modern business man is not a Christian, even though he may call himself a Fundamentalist.'

'Where will you get genuine religious fanaticism? You get it in Russia. They have a religion and they believe in it ... [The Russian] carries out the Christian doctrine that "all are equal" ... No one believes here that the black man is equal of the white, that the professional man is the equal of the retail shopkeeper ... but the Russians do believe it ... Historical Christianity is largely a spent force ... Jesus Christ has come down to earth. He is no longer an idol. People are gaining some sort of idea of what would happen if He lived now.'

To the objection that such a transformation from individual Christianity to collective communism might lead to an unjust tyranny such as was rumoured to be developing in Soviet Russia, Shaw answered that the Russian people had been hardened by tsarist persecution and needed to go to greater lengths than people in the West. 'There is some urge in men towards development. In pursuit of knowledge and power men will suffer the most appalling sacrifices and endure terrible hardships.'

What were his plans? 'Seeing South Africa and saying nothing,' he replied. Yet he soon found himself saying something to Generals Hertzog and Smuts (the present, past and future Prime Ministers); something else in the City Hall; and something more on national radio. He criticized the University of Cape Town for excluding women from its dining-club and advised students at the University of Stellenbosch to believe nothing they were told. In place of lectures, he recommended Faculties to hold debates between professors of violently opposing views. 'Controversy should be applied to all subjects, even mathematics, which seemed such an exact science.' The proper social function of the university system, he said, was to create a civilized mentality. But universities in most parts of the world turned out people who, though qualified technically, remained 'schoolboy savages'.

In his public speeches Shaw struggled towards the rationalization of South Africa. Addressing a huge audience at the City Hall on behalf of the Fabians, he spoke of the example set by the Soviet march to prosperity through the pit of revolution, and described the Russian five-year plan as the 'Salvation Army's self-denial plan extended from a fortnight'. Under the headline 'Soviet Lesson to Union', the *Cape Times* reported him describing communism as

'the absence of a competitive commercial system ... The Russians, because they were advancing towards this ideal, were the most formidable people in the world today. There would be no greater crime, he declared, than to attempt to thrust Russia back to the conditions which existed in the majority of capitalist countries today. Your business is to study the experiment in Russia.'

'I did a stupendous lecture on Russia,' Shaw wrote afterwards to Nancy Astor, 'speaking for an hour and three quarters without turning a hair.' But judging from contemporary accounts the occasion was not wholly a success. 'Shaw failed himself and his audience,' wrote Leon Hugo, a professor of English at the University of South Africa. He had gone on too long and he had left people confused and wondering whether the confusion was his or theirs.

Nevertheless he remained popular in South Africa. Over his four weeks in Cape Town the newspapers put together an identikit picture of him: a 'charming old gentleman', with 'the fresh complexion of a child', the 'springiness of an athlete' and a 'gurgling chuckle that is irresistible'. Readers liked to see him sitting on top of a famous escapologist's box at the

Opera House declaring himself mystified; or advancing with his parasol from the tearoom and leaping among the rocks at the summit of Table Mountain. 'At my time of life, young man, you are beyond the youthful delusion of enjoying things,' he told a reporter. 'You are only too pleased if nothing unpleasant happens.'

With its fruit gardens and its vineyards, hot and cold oceans, mountains, sunshine, Cape Town seemed enveloped by pleasantness. Charlotte bloomed in the climate like an autumn rose and Shaw made use of a special room set aside for him at the pavilion on the beach to swim frequently, allowing some children to duck him for a bet. 'For sunshine, scenery, bathing, and motoring, the place is unbeatable,' he wrote to Nancy Astor.

They had put themselves under the charge of Commander C. P. Newton of the Cape Town Publicity Bureau, and the publicity continued to roll jauntily along, with just a hint of menace to come. 'On the whole Cape Town has been extremely polite to Mr Shaw and has respected his wish for a restful holiday,' commented the *Cape Argus* after he had been there a week. 'Mr Shaw, for his part, has been quite exceptionally polite to Cape Town – so far.'

Though complaining desperately that 'my failing hands are overfull; and there are only 24 hours in the day', Shaw tried his best to answer the large local mail he received each day, drafting replies in shorthand to be typed by Commander Newton's secretary. 'On the whole, I sincerely desire to say the best I can of it,' he pleaded after lengthy cross-examination by the press. Rumours of his wit and audacity breezed spicily through Cape Town society. When General Smuts was retelling stories of his guerrilla exploits at lunch one day and happened to mention T. E. Lawrence, Shaw brought him to a confusing halt by mentioning D. H. Lawrence: 'Every schoolgirl of sixteen should read *Lady Chatterley's Lover*.' Smuts, suddenly outflanked, found himself agreeing: 'Of course, of course.'

What South Africans particularly relished was Shaw's apparent enjoyment of their country. They seemed to share in his adventures. Topping everything was a flight over the Cape Peninsula in a Junker monoplane. G.B.S. had taken to the air earlier in his life – most remarkably in a balloon from Wandsworth in 1911. He had also circled Hendon Aerodrome in a biplane during an ascent in 1916 arranged by the aviation pioneer Claude Graham-White, though he derived little sense of flying on that occasion, despite the engine roaring behind him and no pro-tection in front, because his whole attention was fixed on the woman seated next to him whose wig he was expecting to see blow into the propeller. 'I took him up to about a thousand feet, circled over the flying-ground, did a few minor stunts, opened the throttle full out to show him a turn of speed, and came down again,' remembered the pilot H. C. Biard in his book *Wings*.

'He stood the display without turning a hair. He seemed chiefly interested in the fact that, when one is flying upside-down in the loop, there is no particular sensation of invertedness. Mr Shaw commented on this as he climbed out of his seat. "The world is like that, young man!" he remarked gravely.'

'It was one of the most thrilling experiences I have had,' he said to the waiting South African journalists at Wingfield Aerodrome. He longed to pilot a machine himself.

Charlotte too had reached for the skies and was heard saying out of the blue that she 'wouldn't mind flying to the north of Africa'. 'It was glorious!' she wrote to Blanche Patch in London. 'A perfect day. We flew over two oceans, and back over a chain of mountains ... we went about 120 miles an hour ... I believe I shall be very sorry to leave!'

They accumulated much goodwill at Cape Town, and on the eve of their departure Shaw exorbitantly spent it all. 'Hullo, South Africa. Bernard Shaw speaking from Cape Town.' He was the first person to be given a simultaneous broadcast from all five stations in South Africa. 'I have been asked to say some nice things to you ... But you must excuse me. Saying nice things is not my business.' Fifteen hundred miles of telephone wire carried his voice out of Cape Town to stations at Bloemfontein, Durban, Johannesburg and Pretoria. 'All the nice things have already been said by the Prince of Wales [who had visited South Africa in 1925] ... His Royal Highness pointed out very truly that the most important source of Cape Town's income is its sunshine. He said nothing about its moonshine ...'

This was not the beginning listeners had expected. The advantage of having the finest sun trap in the world, they heard, 'depends altogether on what you catch in it'.

'Sun traps have a powerful attraction for people with plenty of money and nothing to do; and you can prosper on the money they fling about – as long as it lasts.

'You may easily, if you are short-sighted enough, become dependent on their expenditure, and put all your capital into splendid hotels, golf links, polo grounds and the rest of the elaborate and expensive machinery for fleecing them.

'And you can devote all your skilled labour and professional resources into the arts of amusing them, doctoring them and burying them when they die of six meals and 20 cocktails a day.'

But at the first sign of trouble, Shaw warned, these unproductive plutocrats would collect their money and sail away. He could hardly keep the joy from his voice as he imagined the hotels taken over by people from the slums and the golf links covered by playing children. 'Do not hesitate to fill your suburbs with delightful dwellings, which only the rich can now afford,' he urged. 'They will be wanted as much as ever when the rich of all lands have gone the way of the Russian grand dukes. What you have to do is to abolish your slums, for which, let me tell you, Cape Town deserves to be destroyed by fire from Heaven.'

This was appalling – and there was worse to come. 'One of the first things I noticed when I landed was that I immediately became dependent on the services of men and women who are not of my own colour. I felt that I was in a Slave State, and that, too, the very worst sort of Slave State.'

He had asked on landing whether the indigenous population was admitted to trade unions (the answer was generally no – some legislation was introduced in 1978). What he had seen in Cape Town during these four weeks had disturbed him. 'Darkies do all the work,' he wrote privately to his friend Emery Walker. ' ... but the social problems ... are insoluble.' The race war between blacks and whites was complicated by the other race war between Dutch and English. Thousands of Afrikaners had been forced off their farming lands and, migrating to the cities, became 'poor whites', in competition for jobs with the unskilled black population.

'The slaves are not owned by masters who are responsible for their welfare, nor protected by stringent laws from ill treatment,' Shaw said in his broadcast; ' ... they are nominally free, like white people, and can be thrown into the streets to starve, without pensions or public relief, when nobody happens to need their services or when they are old and are displaced by the young.'

He knew that the affluent white population was uneasy, that it had examined the danger of a violent uprising, and calculated that for the next half-century at least it had the power to suppress any such rebellion easily enough, with the help of black men if necessary. So he avoided making the usual threats of black revolution. Instead he claimed that South Africa had already started on a moral revolution and that the black community was proving itself superior. 'If you let other people do everything for you you soon become incapable of doing anything for yourself,' he told his predominantly white listeners.

'You become an idler and a parasite, a weakling and an imbecile; and though you may also become a very pretty lady or gentleman you will be helpless in the hands of your slaves, who will have all the strength and knowledge and character that come from working and from nothing else.

'The coloured man is terribly dangerous in this way. He can reduce you to a condition in which you cannot open a door for yourself or carry a parcel...

'He actually dictates your ideas of right and wrong, respectable and disreputable, until you are his mental as well as his bodily slave, while all the time you flatter yourself that you are his lord and master...

'If white civilisation breaks down through idleness and loafing based on slavery ... then, as likely as not, the next great civilisation will be a negro civilisation.'

Though this moral rebuke was deeply insulting to the rich whites, Shaw had not been rude. He took care to remind his audience that he frequently criticized England's politics, adding that he would not like to accuse South Africans, 'who have heaped hospitality, distinction and the most generous personal cordialities of all sorts on me', of being as 'fat-headed' as English people. Then, having 'said as much of what the Prince of Wales did not like to say as I have time for this evening ... I broadcast my thanks to you from a heart full of gratitude and a stomach full of peaches. Good-night and good luck.'

Following his disappointing lecture at City Hall, the *Cape Argus* had commented: 'We want to know much more about moral values.' Shaw advocated 'such control of the production and distribution of wealth as will ensure equality of opportunity to every member of the community regardless of race, colour, sex or creed'. Lacking any such economic basis, he believed that the South African regime was heading for moral degeneration. It was a widely unpopular message. Many white South Africans wrote angrily to the newspapers. But none of these protests, nor the ripples of reaction in the British press against Shaw's 'rudeness to his hosts', answered his indictment of the slave state. As Leon Hugo was to write: 'Only Shaw could have said this – could have eschewed the platitude and seen the disturbing paradox in the master-servant, white-black relationship.'

Having exploded this bombshell, Shaw left Cape Town with Charlotte the next morning and, accompanied by Commander Newton, motored along the Garden Route towards Port Elizabeth. There they planned to board a ship for Durban and then sail back up the east coast of Africa. Shaw, who took a driving test in Cape Town, had hired a car and shared the motoring with Newton while Charlotte arranged herself comfortably in the back. After three days they reached a pretty seaside place called Wilderness and were travelling rapidly towards Knysna with G.B.S. at the wheel. 'I negotiated several mountain tracks and gorges in a masterly manner,' he later told Nancy Astor. Then he came upon half a mile of smooth road, 'and I let the car rip'.

'Suddenly she twisted violently to the left over a bump. I twisted her violently to the right, and rising with all my energy to the sudden peril, stood on the gas hard as I held the wheel in a grip of iron. The car responded nobly. She charged and cleared a bank with a fence of five lines of barbed wire; carried the wires to a bunker (a sunken path) three feet deep; banged her way through; and was thrashing down a steep place to perdition when at last I transferred my straining sole from the accelerator to the brake and stopped her with the last strand of barbed wire still holding, though drawn out for miles.'

It was really the fault of the De Dietrich that he had bought back in 1908 which had its 'loud pedal' on the left. Shaw never lost the trick of stamping on the right pedal to arrest his vehicle. Having failed to keep the accident out of the newspapers, he was soon taking what credit he could for their 'sensational exploit'.

> 'I cleared
> a ditch;
> a hedge;
> a fence;
> a formidable bunker;
> and several cross-country obstacles...'

The Commander had received a few negligible knocks and Shaw 'a clout on the jaw and a clip on the knee'. But 'oh! poor Charlotte! When we extricated her crumpled remains from the pile of luggage which had avalanched her I feared I was a widower,' Shaw wrote to Nancy Astor, 'until she asked were we hurt.'

'Her head was broken; her spectacle rims were driven into her blackened eyes; her left wrist was agonizingly sprained; her back was fearfully bruised; and she had a hole in her right shin which something had pierced to the bone.'

They entered Knysna, fifteen miles away, and the Shaws took up quarters at the Royal Hotel. For once Charlotte was in the spotlight, while G.B.S. sat in the corner looking downcast. 'She is still flat on her back with the shin hole giving no end of trouble,' he wrote a week later. 'She put up a temperature of 103 yesterday (my heart jumped into my mouth) but today the wound took a favorable turn ... She is very miserable.' To relieve her mind, Shaw cancelled all his arrangements, and engaged a nurse to come in every day while he himself sometimes accompanied the doctor on his car-journeys to patients in the country districts. Early each morning he would go swimming in the lagoon; and then, at 9 a.m., he settled down at a hard bench on the stoep of the hotel annexe to work until lunchtime. Cars hooted and screeched round him, people came up close to stare, but as one resident noticed 'he seemed to be in a dream'.

It was an opportunity to get ahead with his Soviet book. But during these weeks in South Africa he had become disengaged, as if discovering that his dream was only a dream, a sort of metaphor by which he had striven to express the real thing, but which was 'not itself the real thing'. Instead, he found himself beginning a fairy tale: *The Adventures of the Black Girl in Her Search for God*.

He had been set thinking about the contact of 'black minds with white religions' five years before by some correspondence he was shown from a missionary in Northern Rhodesia called Mabel Shaw. 'She makes it clear that a Negro girl is much less of a savage than an average post-war flapper,' he wrote. 'But I feel pretty angry with her for putting up that cross. When will people learn to introduce Christ as a teacher and not as a figure from the Chamber of Horrors?' In 1928 he had corresponded with this woman at the London Mission Station in Mbereshi, and met her a couple of years later while she was on vacation in London, describing her as 'a woman with a craze for self torture, who broke off her engagement with a clergyman (he died of it) to bury herself in the wilds of Africa and lead Negro children to Christ'.

This is the starting point of Shaw's fable. The black girl, 'a fine creature, whose satin skin and shining muscles made the white missionary folk seem like ashen ghosts by contrast', does not share the masochistic excitement of her teacher who 'found in the horrors of the crucifixion the same strange joy she had found in breaking her own heart and those of her lovers'. She is as 'interesting but unsatisfactory' a convert as Lueli in *Mr Fortune's Maggot*, the novel which Sylvia Townsend Warner (another 1930s Stalinist) had written 'in a very advanced stage of hallucination' five years earlier. 'Where is God?' the black girl demands. And when the missionary tells her, 'He has said "Seek and ye shall find me",' she accepts this literally and strides off into the African forest in search of God. Each god she meets in the jungle of Old and New Testaments – the gods of Noah and Job, the Preacher Ecclesiastes and the Prophet Micah – marks the Ascent of Man to a nobler conception of Nature, until she reaches Jesus's concept of a godhead that incorporates itself in man.

The black girl is guided on her travels less by the terrors of the Bible than by an instinctive good sense. She passes by the political figure of Mahomet, ignores our modern scientific gods ('fundamentalists with a top dressing of science') represented by Shaw's *bête blanche* the myopic vivisectionist Pavlov, and also the 'heathens & savages' of a disintegrating white civilization who form a 'Caravan of the Curious, like the Vanity Fair jury in the Pilgrim's Progress'. In the context of South African society, Christ is portrayed as 'a poor white' teacher who is obliged to play the conjuror (as Shaw played G.B.S.) in order to attract a following 'as they wont listen to his preaching but like his miracles'. Shaw removes Christ from the missionary's Chamber of Horrors to a more cheerful room in Madame Tussaud's. Lying on a big wooden cross with his arms stretched out, he is being skilfully carved by a sculptor because, he tells the black girl, 'I am so utterly rejected of men that my only means of livelihood is to sit as a model to this compassionate artist.' It is this economic motive, Shaw suggests, reinforced by aesthetic power and exploiting something dark in human nature, that has perverted Christianity into 'Crostianity' and made the instrument of torture a symbol of faith. 'Christ's clean water of life is befouled by the dirtiest of dirty water from the idolatries of his savage forefathers,' Shaw wrote in an epilogue. Using the method of Voltaire's *Candide*, he attempted to repurify the water in this fable, and replace the doped wine of religion with his own sparkling bottle of *élan vital*.

There is nothing new in Shavian religious thought here, except the form, which generates an unexpected ending. Christ's message that we should love one another is unsatisfactory to the black girl: 'our souls need solitude as much as our bodies need love', she says. ' ... We need the help of one another's bodies and the help of one another's minds; but our souls need to be alone with God.' Shaw reasoned that Christ's commandment was intended for his disciples and not the whole world which was far from lovable. He makes Jesus say to the black girl that to find God 'you must go past me'.

Her pilgrimage leads to the garden cultivated by Candide, where she comes across a red-bearded, potato-digging Irishman who proclaims himself a socialist and explains God as an eternal but as yet unfulfilled purpose. If G.B.S. looks something of a trespasser here, it is because he had cultivated a communal garden, believing that an author's proper business was to mind everybody else's business. Yet he drew Archibald Henderson's attention to the 'remarkable parallels between my career and Voltaire's' and concluded that 'Voltaire, Swift, Shaw make almost a special literary category'. Elsewhere he likened Voltaire to Bunyan as one of the 'would-be saviors' of the world, unlike Jesus 'who was strongly anti-missionary'. Then, in his epilogue to *The Black Girl*, he places Jesus in the same category as Swift. 'Jesus himself, shaken by the despair which unsettled the reason of Swift and Ruskin and many others at the spectacle of human cruelty, injustice, misery, folly, and apparently hopeless political incapacity, and perhaps also by the worship of his disciples and of the multitude, had allowed Peter to persuade him that he was the Messiah.'

What Shaw shared with these 'many others' was the threat of despair. Jesus says: 'I am the poorest of poor whites; yet I have thought of myself as a king. But that was when the wickedness of men had driven me crazy.' Shaw's craziness was his Soviet communism which rose, like a magic carpet, lifting him above the darkness. In a letter to Mabel Shaw, he had written: 'we all have our superstitions and our complexes, the difference between a rather mad writer like Saint Paul and a rather sane one like Voltaire being only one of degree'.

'One can only say it would have been better for the world if Paul had never been born, and that it would have been a great misfortune – a religious misfortune – to have missed Voltaire ... as the wickedness which he exposed and which he called on the world's conscience to renounce were too frightful to be contemplated without some sort of anaesthetic, he used his sense of fun to make people come to scoff, knowing that that was the only chance of getting them to remain to pray.'

Shaw was both 'a rather mad writer' and 'a rather sane one'. In a work modelled on *Candide*, which Voltaire had ironically subtitled *Optimism*, he could not risk exposing the complex superstitious roots of a political ideology that protected him from Swift's despair but that could too easily be linked within his fable to Christ's exalted megalomania. Had he conducted his black girl to a collective farm, what readers would not have scoffed at such a Panglossian finale?

Instead, Shaw made use of a device he had tried out with Sergeant Fielding in *Too True to be Good*. On Voltaire's urging, the black girl cuts off the fleeing Irishman at the garden gate and marries him. From then on her search for God as a complete explanation of life is crowded out of her head by the job of managing this Irishman and their 'charmingly coffee-coloured' children.

'Life is a flame that is always burning itself out; but it catches fire again every time a child is born.' Shaw's fable plants a series of prophecies: that 'the next great civilization will be a black civilization'; that future gods may be female rather than male; and that the biological solution to the race war between black and white is intermarriage. As he was writing *The Black Girl* he saw round Knysna a far more impoverished and exploitative society than in Cape Town. There were a few inbred poor whites, mainly forest-dwellers, who worked as wood-choppers. Otherwise the community was divided almost equally between Cape Coloureds and Blacks, the latter having no rights and being treated as slaves. 'If I told you the whole truth about it you would never publish it,' he cautioned a reporter. His final interview gave an indication of how these weeks in the Eastern Cape had darkened his spirits and influenced the adventures of his black girl. The Afrikaners around Knysna seemed to him untouched by a century of outside events. 'The French Revolution and other great developments in Europe have passed them by,' he told the *Cape Argus*. 'All they need is education ... above all, ban the Bible ... They depend too much on it.'

'I do not think your natives are psychologically more interesting than the white races. But they are more intelligent ... and they have far better manners.

'You ask me whether South Africa will ever "go native". I think the question should be: "Will the native ever go South African?" He seems to get little opportunity of doing so.

'... This country does not need a five-year plan. You have too much self-denial already. There are thousands of people in the country starving – thousands of natives with scarcely enough food to keep them alive ...

'What you want to do is to shoot your poor whites – every one of them. You should also shoot many of your rich whites.'

Shaw wrote *The Black Girl* over seventeen days, giving his shorthand draft by instalments to a local stenographer, Dorothy Smith. 'He writes so correctly and clearly,' she recorded, 'using very few contractions and only the more common grammalogues, so the transcription soon became quite plain-sailing.' Like many white Knysnaites, Dorothy Smith had imagined G.B.S. to be 'a terrible cynic'. She was surprised by his soft voice and considerate manner. 'He was always spick and span and looked as if he had just come from his bath, his hands beautifully manicured and his silver hair and beard trim and well-kept.' During the five weeks Charlotte was laid up for repairs, Shaw got to know a number of the rich whites whom he wanted shot, and they found him charming. 'He never made me feel he was the great G.B.S., but always thanked me as if I were doing him a favour,' remembered Dorothy Smith. 'I must confess I liked him exceedingly.'

Since Charlotte had triumphantly overcome her dread of flying machines, Shaw chartered a Union Airways Junker and on 18 March they flew back to Cape Town, the first passengers to make this three-hour journey by air. 'The flight was wonderful – splendid!' Charlotte wrote to her doctor. ' ... We were met at the Aerodrome – taken to the ship [the *Warwick Castle*] where we lunched & then there arrived such a crowd as I never saw.'

'There is a possibility that he will come back to South Africa,' reported the *Cape Times*, 'and learn rather more at first hand than he has had time to do on this trip of the white, poor white and native questions.' Shaw and Charlotte did return to South Africa three years later, 'rolling down' the Red Sea and along the east coast until they disembarked at Durban at the end of April 1935. Shaw made it clear on arrival that, since his last visit, he had retired from public speaking and was looking forward to a holiday. He was soon drafting interviews with himself, making broadcasts, and exploring what the *Natal Witness* called 'the less vaunted parts of our town'. In celebration of King George V's Silver Jubilee, he appeared as guest of honour at an Indian sports event between two celebrated wrestlers, the Masked Marvel and the Terrible Turk. He also escorted Charlotte to a Zulu war dance, joining in with a few ecstatic steps, chanting and clapping and delighting in the music which, he said, had probably inspired Wagner's *The Flying Dutchman*. 'All attempts to keep them [Zulus] in an inferior position,' he concluded, 'seem to break down before the fact that they are not inferior.'

On this second voyage he carried with him proofs of the Webbs' *Soviet Communism: A New Civilization?* which, like a prophetic text, took the place of his own aborted book on Russia and seemed to refuel his missionary fire. At a press conference on his arrival at Durban he spoke of Russia as a bulwark for peace which could be depended on to restrain the territorial expansion of Japan and, to some extent, Germany; and on his departure a month later from Cape Town he proposed the introduction of collective farms which, operating like open-air universities, would contribute to a fusion of the races. 'I believe in fusion. The more fusion the better. All that talk of Hitler's about pure race is all nonsense.'

Shaw's ideas on racial fusion, which transported his coffee-coloured children from the end of *The Black Girl* on to the front pages of many newspapers, brought him notoriety round the world. While in Durban he had heard the pro-Nazi Minister of Transport and Defence, Oswald Pirow, make a public appeal to immigrants to keep up the white population, and it occurred to him, following a discussion with a doctor there, that the effect of excessive sunshine on white skins might have something to do with white sterility. 'If so,' he reasoned, 'the remedy is clearly pigmentation, which can be brought about most easily by interbreeding with the colored races.' On his arrival back in England he announced himself to be 'an advocate of intermarriage between the white and black inhabitants' of South Africa. This was now his final solution to the racial problem.

'Marriages of White and Black', ran a *Daily Telegraph* headline. 'Startling Plan by Mr Shaw'. The South African press reported that Shaw's 'notorious' views were regarded in Britain as a bad joke. But in Germany they were described as 'blasphemy'. The *Deutsche Allgemeine Zeitung* reassured its readers that there was no danger of Germans on the African continent losing their political hold for want of reproductive vigour. Shaw was accused of misrepresenting Oswald Pirow who had been encouraging Germans to emigrate to South Africa where they had given proof of their prolific capacity.

G.B.S. was unrepentant. To the end of his life he continued to believe that 'the "Ghetto" legislation' of South Africa 'is flat persecution like that of the Jews by the Nazis'. In a letter to Trebitsch he claimed that many Germans in South Africa did not object to interbreeding: 'there are plenty of half breeds in what used to be German Africa ... '

'The white man, however "Nordic" cannot resist the very attractive native women ... We may live to see a Reichskanzler [German chancellor] with a Zulu, Bantu or Hawaiian wife ... The future is to the mongrel, not to the Junker. I, Bernard Shaw, have said it.'

*

'Religion is a great force: the only real motive force in the world,' says St John Hotchkiss, the young gentleman known as Sonny, addressing the rest of the cast in *Getting Married*; 'but what you fellows dont understand is that you must get at a man through his own religion and not through yours ... You are all missionaries and proselytizers trying to uproot the native religion from your neighbors flowerbeds and plant your own in its place.'

The army of missionaries which had moved across the world during Shaw's lifetime travelled in step to the march of imperial expansion. In place of ethnic cultures, they offered a strange trinity of Christian God, modern medicine, and market capitalism. For the road to a new heaven and a new earth led unexpectedly through a jungle of business civilization. When Stalin asked his visitors how they accounted for 'England getting possession of so much of the earth', Shaw had merely waved his Irish alibi, but Nancy Astor replied: 'I believe the translations of the Bible we distributed did it.' Stalin answered: 'If we don't do that we fail.'

In his preface to *Major Barbara*, Shaw had made reference to the 'part played by Christian missionaries in reconciling the black races of Africa to their subjugation by European Capitalism'. During the 1930s he travelled as a counter-missionary armed with an opposing set of coercive myths and texts. He was to glance ironically at such crosscurrents in *Geneva*, the political extravaganza he wrote during the late 1930s. In this play the Soviet Commissar complains of 'a most dangerous organization' called the Society for the Propagation of the Gospel in Foreign Parts. 'It has agents everywhere,' he complains. 'They call themselves missionaries.' But the British Foreign Secretary makes a similar complaint against Russian propaganda: 'surely you dont expect us to allow your missionaries to preach Bolshevism, do you?'

Unlike these messengers of the apocalypse who reached into the last redoubts of primitive tribes, Shaw brought his message to mass-circulation newspapers, students at universities and politicians. The most ambitious of these proselytizing tours was a four-month world cruise on a Canadian Pacific liner, the *Empress of Britain*, sailing from Monaco in the middle of December 1932.

'I'm like a tree – I should prefer to stay in one place,' he admitted. But Charlotte had 'taken it into her head that she must go round the world before she dies', he explained; 'and I shall have to go with her.'

They travelled in a suite of two staterooms, carrying Shaw's vegetarian menus typed out by Blanche Patch which Charlotte would hand the chief steward and head waiter, and sometimes forward to their hotels. They did not join the Captain's table, but sat at a small one of their own in a corner, reading from a large bookbag of recent publications and, except for breakfast, never missing a meal together. While Charlotte stayed late in bed, Shaw would rise early, complete several laps of the outdoor pool and orbits of the deck and, after a breakfast of oatmeal porridge, grapefruit and refreshing 'Instant Postum', take up his position in an isolated chair on the lounge deck, wearing a biscuit-coloured cap with a large flap to protect his neck against the trade winds. There being nothing else to do but gamble, play deck games and drink cocktails, 'all of which violate one of my cardinal rules of life, which is never to pretend to enjoy myself when I am being bored, worried and poisoned', he got through a heap of writing. 'All the time we have been on the ship he has done his mornings' work and there is a lot to show for it,' Charlotte reported back to Blanche Patch. 'As it is in Shorthand, I am not able to say what the quality is.' He would hand his correspondence to the ship's stenographer for transliteration. But he was also writing plays again: 'you have to work or go mad'.

Though they travelled comfortably, Charlotte was often fretted by foreign suns and bugs; while Shaw, despite his years of practice and the protective camera he sometimes brought into action, had never taken to the interruptions of sightseeing. 'We are alive; but that is all,' he acknowledged in a letter to Nancy Astor after four weeks' voyaging. '... this ship keeps stopping in ports where the water is too filthy to bathe in and shooting us ashore for impossible excursions to see the insides of railway carriages, and be let out, like little dogs, for a few minutes exercise and a glimpse of a temple or a hotel meal or a cobra–mongoose fight'.

All aboard at Monte Carlo; first stop Naples. They gazed down the crater of Vesuvius, glanced at Pompeii, then sailed on to Athens where they were assailed by journalists. 'If you are ever tempted to go to Athens, I advise you not to bother,' Shaw had counselled. 'Just buy a few second hand columns, and explode a pound or two of dynamite amongst them, and there you are.' They plunged into Egypt under a blanket of heat and among the snake charmers. 'I did some *awful* journies,' Charlotte admitted. On New Year's Day 1933 they sailed from Suez and a week later came to Bombay where the ship put in to replenish its tanks and Shaw braced himself to embark on his missionary work.

It had been widely reported in the Indian newspapers that he might be visiting Gandhi, then in Yeravda Jail at Pune. When asked by reporters what he thought of Gandhi, he replied: 'the second greatest man in the world!' They had met in November 1931 while Gandhi was in London attending the Second Round Table Conference on India. Though Shaw believed he was wasting his time keeping company with conference playactors, he saw in Gandhi a natural leader ('Superman = Mahatma') whose 'tactics like all tactics are subject to error and readjustment' but whose 'strategy is sound'. The two of them had taken an instant liking to each other ('Now look here, Gandhi, wouldn't you be comfortable on the floor'). Gandhi emerged from their interview in London paying tribute to G.B.S. as 'a Puck-like spirit and a generous ever young heart, the Arch Jester of Europe', adding later (after having read *The Black Girl*): 'In everything of his that I have read there has been a religious centre.' Shaw told Gandhi during their meeting that 'I knew something about you and felt something in you of a kindred spirit. We belong to a very small community on earth.' It was this kinship he stressed when later chiding Nancy Astor for occasionally reverting to the Churchillian view of Gandhi as a dangerous charlatan. 'Mahatma G. is not a crook: he is a saint, and as such under the covenant of grace,' he wrote, trying to open her to the catholicity of all religions, '... Just like Mrs Eddy, or Mahatma G.B.S.'

Churchill considered sympathy with Gandhi tantamount to treason and opposed any constitutional reform in India. Shaw viewed India as being in much the same political state as Ireland had been earlier in his life. 'India should be free to manage her own affairs,' he was to write. 'If she chooses to divide herself into fifty Pakistans and fight it out in fifty civil wars that is her business: not ours.' An editorial in the *Star of India* had warned Shaw to beware of Indian politics: 'there is nothing so dangerous as a sarcastic philosopher who tries to get a rise out of politicians'. Shaw concurred: 'the present situation in India will not bear being talked about,' he wrote to Rabindranath Tagore. 'I understand it only too well.' He understood it as part of a world-historical narrative, with each country poised at a different moment in the story. In his press interviews he levered information out of the journalists about conditions in India and refused to make statements about untouchability except when referring back to Britain: 'we have untouchability in England. Ask the labourer who wants to marry the duchess's daughter.' There was every likelihood, he believed, that a purely Indian government would be more tyrannical than an English one. But this did not weaken his support for Home Rule: as with the Russian Revolution, violence might be the historical route forwards.

Not everyone in Bombay was like Gandhi. 'He is, of course, the sort of man who occurs once in several centuries.' But his existence was encouraging to Shaw because 'there might come a future when the whole population of India would be much more like Gandhi than they were at present'. Was this optimism? A pessimist is someone who lives with an optimist. In this respect Shaw lived with himself. His pessimistic strain rises in the compliment he paid Gandhi on arriving in Bombay: 'Mr Gandhi is the clearest-headed man in India,' he was reported as saying, 'and he is so tired of you all that he goes on a "fast unto death".' From someone who was himself beginning to suffer from anorexia the kinship is transparent. After their meeting in 1931, Gandhi had said of Shaw: 'I think he is a very good man.' When Gandhi was assassinated in 1948, Shaw was to say: 'It shows how dangerous it is to be too good.'

While other passengers scurried across the country for five days and nights in crowded trains, Shaw and Charlotte remained on board. 'I am too old a traveller to be taken by such baits,' he told Tagore. '... My only regret is that I shall be unable to visit you.'

Nor could he visit Annie Besant, now in her mid-eighties and living near Madras, but was visited himself by Annie's adopted son, the handsome Jeddu Krishnamurti. Shaw had kept intermittently in communication with Annie on her infrequent trips back to England, sending her inscribed copies of some of his books (*Saint Joan* 'with love') and supporting her work for Indian Home Rule. 'Do you consider me an intelligent or an unintelligent woman?' she had asked rhetorically on receiving a copy of *The Intelligent Woman's Guide*. 'Whichever I may be, I keep a corner for an old friend. I am ever a fighting Home Ruler and Socialist.' But she was so many other things besides. 'What a forcing house of religious leaders the old atheists proved,' Henry Salt had written to Shaw: 'Annie Besant is now the leader of the Theosophists and looks, in her white robes, as though she sits on the right hand of God; [and] you, who insist on sitting on the right hand of the Devil to give him moral support.' It was difficult for Shaw, contending with a world of superstition, to sympathize with Annie's idealistic aspirations, and he applauded Krishnamurti's dignified refusal to be put forward as a new Messiah, the Star of the East. 'Do you ever see Mrs Besant now?' he asked.

'Every day,' Krishnamurti equivocated.

'How is she?'

'Very well; but at her great age she cannot think consecutively.'

'She never could,' whispered Shaw, and Krishnamurti smiled.

Later that year Annie Besant died. She had been in Shaw's estimate both intelligent and unintelligent – like himself – like everyone.

'I have been hung with flowers in the temples and drenched with rose-water and dabbed with vermilion in the houses; and the ship is infested with pilgrims to my shrine,' he wrote after five days at Bombay. According to Nirad Chaudhuri he had become 'almost an idol of educated Indians'. Though travelling with a political message, he was also, like his Black Girl, searching for something, and during his eight days at Bombay he appeared to find it unexpectedly in the Jain temples.

Of all the religious denominations he had felt nearest to the Quakers, by temperament if not by faith. During the Great War he was touched and impressed by their refusal to fight and willingness to serve as ambulance staff. He had looked into their history and shortly after the war mentioned to Hesketh Pearson that he was thinking of writing a play on a religious theme involving the seventeenth-century founder of the Quakers, George Fox. What seems to have appealed to him was the historical development from their fanatical origins of ecstatic prophecy and group mysticism to the 'morally mighty' spirit of community service in the Society of Friends. He responded to this 'great Cult of Friendship' because it reflected the historical and biological fact that all nations, and individuals, were interdependent. He also liked their lack of ritual. 'When we want to talk with God,' he was to write, 'we use the same language that we ordinarily use, not prayers composed for us by other people, and we do not need a church to hold communion with him.' By the late 1920s he declared himself to be 'more nearly a Quaker than anything else that has a denomination'. But by the end of the 1930s, when he did write a play ('In Good King Charles's Golden Days') that introduced George Fox on to the stage, he used it partly to chart the limitations of seventeenth-century Quakerism. These limitations, which are presented as an historical challenge, persisted in the twentieth century as the Quakers' denial of access to religion through music and the arts. The appeal of the Jains was that they allowed no such exclusion zone. Near the end of his life Shaw 'ceased to reply that my nearest to an established religion is the Society of Friends, and while calling myself a Creative Evolutionist, might also call myself a Jainist Tirthankava of eight thousand years ago'.

The ancient Jain religion, which emphasized the oneness of life and recognized God as human-being-and-animal as well as man-and-woman, black-and-white, provided the presuppositions for Shaw's prophecies in *The Black Girl*, as well as the sublime Shavian double paradox of a temple that contained all the gods and a temple containing none. After visiting these Jain temples he came to believe that Hinduism must be 'the most tolerant religion in the world' because, he wrote to the Reverend Ensor Walters as he sailed away from India, 'its one transcendent God includes all possible Gods, from elephant Gods, bird Gods, and snake Gods, right up to the great trinity of Brahma, Vishnu and Shiva, which makes room for the Virgin Mary and modern Feminism by making Shiva a woman as well as a man'.

'Christ is there as Krishna, who might also be Dionysos. In fact Hinduism is so elastic and so subtle that the profoundest Methodist and the crudest idolator are equally at home in it...

'There is actually a great Hindu sect, the Jains, with Temples of amazing magnificence, which excludes God, not on materialistic atheist considerations, but as unspeakable and unknowable, transcending all human comprehension.'

Creative Evolution remained Shaw's philosophy, communism his political ideology: and both could be accommodated within a religion that assumed the unity of God. Shaw the worshipper and Shaw the iconoclast were joined in the Jainist understanding of all gods and no gods. Bergson, Butler, Lamarck, and later perhaps Teilhard de Chardin share the Shavian temple with William Morris and Sidney Webb, Marx and Lenin. The Life Force had been Shaw's guarantee of a future and he saw communism as the route for human beings towards that future.

Increasingly as the shadow of his past lengthened Shaw stretched out towards a far-fetched future. He had eradicated determinism by releasing it into a fantasy where dreams were prophecies. All this intellectual technology, extending the circumference of what could be cured in contemporary society by 'laws or kings', had been designed to keep his spirit expectantly vibrating. But it was the unexpected that appeared to answer his wishes.

The Jains' integrity was a theoretical conclusion to Shaw's lifetime quest for synthesis. In place of the Shavian machinery which turned things inside out, Jainism seemed to hold internal and external forces in equilibrium.

Shaw had always accepted that religion was based on need and not dependent on evidence or reason, and that it must be feeling which set people thinking and not thought which set them feeling. He would refer to the Jains often in conjunction with Protestants and Catholics, indicating what he felt to be the Jain potential for healing. 'It is in these temples that you escape from the frightful parochiality of our little sects of Protestants and Catholics,' he wrote to Dame Laurentia McLachlan, 'and recognize the idea of God everywhere.'

Going round these temples with his guide he was struck by the corruption of Jainism into idolatry. To govern the multitudinous average person, all religions were reduced to his capacity by idols and miracles. The ancient Jainists had carried religion 'to the utmost reach of the human mind', he was to write in his preface to *Farfetched Fables*. They had 'renounced idolatry and blood sacrifice long before Micah, and repudiated every pretence to know the will of God, forbidding even the mention of his name in the magnificent temples they built for their faith'.

'But go into a Jainist temple to-day: what do you find? Idols everywhere. Not even anthropomorphic idols but horse idols, cat idols, elephant idols and what not? The statues of Jainist sages and saints, far from being contemplated as great seers, are worshipped as gods.'

Shaw's affinity with the Jains was reflected in the 'extraordinary beauty and purity of design' of the images he saw in these temple shrines around Bombay. They 'throw you into an ecstasy of prayer and a trance of peace when they look at you', he wrote to Laurentia McLachlan, 'as no Christian iconography can'. But why were such animal images in a Jain temple? Shaw received no satisfactory answer to this question until, in 1949, the Indian Prime Minister Jawaharlal Nehru came to Ayot and told him that they had been 'made by Greek refugees in order that they might worship the images they had in their own country'.

Shaw liked to say that all his 'globe-trotting' left little mark on his later plays except for *The Simpleton of the Unexpected Isles* which he wrote in 1934. 'I could not have written it exactly as it is,' he told Hesketh Pearson, 'if I had not been in India and the Far East.' The Preface to that play, which called for 'greatly increased intolerance of socially injurious conduct' was strongly pro-Soviet, while the play itself was imbued with Jainism, 'the most tolerant religion in the world'. Shaw subtitled *The Simpleton* 'A Vision of Judgement', but the vision and the judgement, thesis and antithesis, are not reconciled. Only in its corruption could the history of Indian Jainism be made to reinforce his view of contemporary Soviet communism as the newest and therefore least human-contaminated world religion. Otherwise, as the critic Valli Rao suggested, 'the pervasive Indian influence' of *The Simpleton* 'counteracts Shaw's Russian infatuation' by implying that he should 'wake up to the folly of idolatry' in his own life.

*

Leaving Bombay, the *Empress of Britain* steamed south-east, via Ceylon and Singapore, into the Pacific area that was already a testing ground for the Second World War. The whole Pacific was afraid of Japan since she had invaded Manchuria, claiming to liberate the region from the curse of Chinese banditry. China had appealed to the League of Nations. An international Disarmament Conference held in 1932 was ingeniously turned into a modified rearmament conference and, in the hope that it was becoming possible to fight more cheaply, the British government decided in principle to strengthen its defences while providing less money with which to do so. 'The greatest satisfaction to us,' commented Shaw, 'is that in the next war we will be knocked by a ten inch shell and not a sixteen inch shell.' Britain did send troops to Shanghai when the Japanese extended the conflict, though at the same time urging conciliation through the League of Nations at Geneva. A League of Nations commission had laboriously toured the Far East and on the basis of its report Japan was rebuked early in 1933 for using force to restore peaceful conditions to the province before trying all other means – whereupon Japan resigned from the League.

The League of Nations had been the creation of a pre-war generation. 'There was no living man to whom the generations which came to maturity between 1900 and 1914 owed as much as to Mr Shaw,' Leonard Woolf was to write in 1934. '... Nothing less than a world war could have prevented [him] from winning the minds of succeeding generations ... ever since [the war] the barbarians have naturally been on top.' Shaw supported the work done by Woolf, which by 1920 helped to set up the League of Nations. He also watched his friend Gilbert Murray's involvement with the League and was to witness his optimism change to disillusion. 'It seems to me clearer than ever,' Murray wrote in 1932, 'that public opinion is the real weapon of the League of Nations.' Shaw wanted to win militant public opinion and the minds of the post-war generation to the League. He believed that collective security could only be achieved if its members pooled their military resources. For what could the League do otherwise except secure its own moral legitimacy – and let the stronger nations destroy and murder wherever their ambitions led them?

On arriving in Hong Kong on 11 February, Shaw told the crowds of reporters who came scrambling on board that

'Japan is going to take Manchuria ... But hasn't she behaved very correctly over it all? She pledged herself to the League of Nations that she would not declare war on anyone. Consequently she has not declared war on China, but has contented herself with fighting ... the League has funked the issues. And now it is gradually ceasing to exist ... Japan has called the League's bluff.'

He was to give one public speech in Hong Kong as the guest of Sir Robert Ho Tung, a picturesque Eurasian millionaire. 'Grand Old Man' Ho Tung, as he was popularly known, had come from obscure origins and risen dramatically to be 'Manager of the Chinese Department of Jardine, Matheson and Company, erstwhile purveyors of opiates, now mightiest of hongs'. The Shaws arrived at the house of this entrepreneur on Monday 13 February and were taken upstairs to a domestic temple that G.B.S. was later to incorporate into the third act of *Buoyant Billions*. 'It was a radiant miniature temple with an altar of Chinese vermilion and gold, and cushioned divan seats round the walls for the worshippers,' he remembered. 'Everything was in such perfect Chinese taste that to sit there and look was a quiet delight.'

'A robed priest and his acolyte stole in and went through a service. When it was over I told Sir Robert that I had found it extraordinarily soothing and happy though I had not understood a word of it. "Neither have I", he said, "but it soothes me too". It was part of the art of life for Chinaman and Irishman alike, and purely esthetic.'

The experience raised an old quandary in a novel way. Was there some dislocation in human nature that divided the 'great force of religion' which 'I dont understand' from politics which he understood 'only too well'? On these world pilgrimages Shaw was trying to combine the long and short views of politics into a stereoscopic political vision. Such a combination would be the categorical imperative of his foreign-policy thinking. But his occasional dream of transforming the International Committee of Intellectual Co-operation at the League of Nations into an imaginative power base looked like Utopian moonshine to the eyes of professional politicians – until perhaps the development of UNESCO.

It also looked potentially dangerous: in dreams begin irresponsibilities. The Hong Kong government could not prevent Shaw from saying what he wanted, but it did try to prevent the Chinese press from reporting what he said. 'You do not look very much like Chinese,' he welcomed a group of local journalists waiting to interview him, but even this remark was to smuggle its way into the *North China Herald*.

The Great Hall of the University where Shaw was to give his speech was overflowing as he arrived. This was a piquant moment. He came from contemplative devotions with an industrialist who was a prominent benefactor of this 'British University on Chinese soil', and who supported Chiang Kai-shek's campaign to suppress communism throughout China. But, as in South Africa, Shaw's political opinions were not affected by hospitality or vested interests. He had been described in newspaper editorials as 'the greatest man ever' to visit Hong Kong, and he was determined to make some use of his reputation.

He began, as he had begun at the University of Stellenbosch in Cape Town, by exhorting the students to argue with their teachers, form their own opinions and read none of the books they were assigned. He was himself about to read Trotsky's *History of the Russian Revolution*.

'If you read, read real books and steep yourself in revolutionary books. Go up to your neck in Communism, because if you are not a red revolutionist at 20, you will be at 50 a most impossible fossil. If you are a red revolutionist at 20, you have some chance of being up-to-date at 40.'

From the prolonged applause they gave Shaw's peroration the students were 'clearly overwhelmed by the brio, the iconoclast gaiety ... the metaphysical defiance of the man', wrote a Senior Lecturer at Hong Kong University, Piers Grey. But, Grey went on to ask: 'How far can we see a real political gesture in it?'

In a welter of correspondence to the press the British community in Hong Kong made it known that 'few people in Britain take Shaw's social or political views seriously and it is unfortunate that any of the British in Hong Kong should have done so'. In fact Shaw had dismayed the British in Hong Kong by ignoring them and directing his words at the Chinese. The *South China Morning Post* reported that in his 'brilliant address' he 'advises university students to be communists'. But the *Hong Kong Telegraph* accused him of endangering the lives of his student audience at a time when Chiang Kai-shek's nationalists were shooting and beheading communists in the streets. Shaw answered this charge in neo-Fabian style during a talk to the PEN club in Shanghai four days later. 'I urged the students to start revolutions,' he explained. 'But please don't misunderstand.'

'I didn't ask them to go to the streets and fight the police. When the police come to suppress revolutionaries with their clubs, the safest way is to run ... for policemen are like the gun in a robber's hand ... those with guns in their hands should still be beaten down. But this takes time and you cannot make it by sheer force.'

Despite tight censorship over the local Chinese press, a number of correspondents from the larger newspapers in China had slipped into his audience at Hong Kong University and telegraphed inflammatory accounts back to Shanghai and Peking. When the luxury liner with its dangerous cargo docked there was 'such a scare among the Shanghai respectable society', according to the historian and editor of *Lun Yu*, Lin Yutang, 'that the entire Shanghai foreign press was in hiding that morning for fear of coming into contact with him'.

Shaw had planned to stay on board with Charlotte during their short stop at Shanghai, but changed his plan on receiving an invitation from Soong Ching Ling ('Madame Sun'), the sister of Madame Chiang Kai-shek and widow of the revolutionary leader Sun Yat-sen. This was a risky initiative. Shanghai was then bursting into medieval turmoil with many contending warlords – nationalists, communists, Japanese imperialists and European colonialists – all in barbaric struggle. Spies and conspirators, opium traffickers, gangsters and their victims jostled together. At no distance from the nightclubs, banks and luxury restaurants were the prison-factories, miserable refugee camps, and dead babies in the gutters. Into this 'feast of human flesh' Madame Sun secretly brought the notorious *agent provocateur* G.B.S., conveying him by tender from the *Empress of Britain* at five o'clock in the morning of 17 February to her house in the rue Molière.

He was officially the guest of the Chinese League for the Protection of Human Rights, co-founded by Madame Sun and Cai Yuan-pei, a radical ex-Chancellor of Peking National University. Apart from these two, with their assistant Yang Xingfo and Lin Yutang (who was to publish a 'Special Issue on Bernard Shaw' in *Lun Yu*), the guests included Lu Hsun, China's celebrated short-story writer and essayist, the political historian Harold Isaacs, and a remarkable pro-communist war correspondent, Agnes Smedley, whose career was to range from promoting birth-control clinics in Germany (from where she had recently arrived) and the raising of funds for the Indian revolutionary movement against the British, to nursing wounded guerrillas in the Chinese Red Army and, at the end of her life, opposing McCarthyism in the United States.

All of them wanted something special from G.B.S.. Harold Isaacs wanted him 'to denounce Kuomintang [nationalist] repression and make a worldwide propaganda score'; others wanted him to warn the world against the International Settlement under which they believed China was being handed over to the Japanese; Madame Sun herself pointed to Soviet infiltration into Jiangxi Province as a greater menace and wanted Shaw to point there too. 'So everybody hopes for different things,' wrote Lu Hsun observing them all close in on G.B.S. 'The lame hope he will advocate using crutches ... those who use rouge hope he will taunt sallow-faced matrons, and the writers of nationalist literature are counting on him to crush the Japanese troops ... You can tell the result is not too satisfactory by the great number of people who are complaining.'

But Lu Hsun was not complaining. He admired the composure with which, while perfecting his use of chopsticks, Shaw fielded crowds of questions, and also his absolute refusal to please. He was able to make all the subgroups of Chinese intellectuals equally uncomfortable, and therein 'lies Shaw's greatness', Lu Hsun concluded. G.B.S. was 'a great mirror' and 'from the antics of those who want to look in it or do not want to look in it, men's hidden selves are revealed'. Watching him being interviewed by journalists after lunch, Lu Hsun noticed that when Shaw spoke frankly, people roared as though he had made a satirical thrust; when he joked about not being infallible (at least not always), they insisted on treating him as an encyclopaedia; and when he excused himself as being on holiday, they besieged him the more earnestly to expound his political principles.

By reflecting in his own mirror a world comedian who forced paradox on to others, Lu Hsun was declaring his fellow-status with the legendary G.B.S. This was important. His 'prestige as China's foremost writer', wrote Harold Isaacs, 'protected him from arrest'. Harold Isaacs himself and Lin Yutang were later removed from the commemorative photograph taken in Madame Sun's garden that afternoon; Agnes Smedley's reputation was clouded by accusations of her involvement in a Soviet spy ring at Shanghai; Yang Xingfo was shot dead by a group of unidentified gunmen three months after this lunch; and Qu Quibai, the Marxist poet who compiled a book, *Bernard Shaw in Shanghai*, was executed by Chinese nationalists in 1935.

Shaw's day-trip into this nightmare was 'very jovial', Agnes Smedley recalled, 'filled with thought-provoking and witty remarks and Soong Ching Ling's [Madame Sun's] laughter'.

'But, as the situation outside was getting extremely tense, we were getting ready to be jailed by the Chinese fascists ... Shaw said his Fabianism would probably collapse and he would become a revolutionary if he were tried by Chinese law and jailed in a feudal prison ... Soong Ching Ling laughed so hard she cried and had to wipe away her tears with a handkerchief.'

This was Shaw's role: to add the solvent of fantastic humour and to subdue divisive detail wherever he went. 'Socialism will surely be implemented in every country sooner or later,' he told the 'matrons and debutants' of the PEN club later that afternoon. 'The means and process of the revolution may appear in different forms in each country, but as all roads lead to Rome so all countries will be on the same path and the same level in the end.'

The Shaws' journey northwards over the next week was a return from politics to art and religion. Near Peking the *Empress of Britain* became ice-bound and they had to transfer to a heavy ice-breaking steamer and slowly smash their way to shore. Inland all the lakes and rivers were frozen hard. 'I have fallen in love with China,' Charlotte wrote to Nancy Astor. '. . . China is wonderful. I felt *at home* there – I belonged there!' Shaw attended his first classical Chinese theatre in Peking and later told a baffled Chinese novelist how deeply impressed he had been by 'the throwing and the catching of bundles and hot towels deftly performed from great distances in the auditorium by the ushers'. But to an English composer, he wrote:

'When there is a speech to be delivered, the first (and only) fiddler fiddles at the speaker as if he were lifting a horse over the Grand National jumps; an ear splitting gong clangs at him; a maddening castanet clacks at him; and finally the audience joins in and incites the fiddler to redouble his efforts. You at once perceive that this is the true function of the orchestra in the theatre and that the Wagnerian score is only gas and gaiters.'

In matters of art, Shaw felt, the Chinese had an instinct for doing things right. He listened to a choir at a lama temple sitting in rows round a golden Buddha fifty feet tall and singing in unison, mostly without changing the note, and 'I have never had my ears so super-satisfied. The basses are stupendous.' At Tientsin a Chinese band revealed to him the secret of opera. There was 'a most lovely toned gong, a few flageolets (I don't know what else to call them) which specialized in pitch without tone, and a magnificent row of straight brass instruments reaching to the ground', he wrote. '. . . They all played the same note, and played it all the time, like the E flat in the Rheingold prelude; but it was rich in harmonics, like the note of the basses in the temple.'

'At the first pause I demanded that they should play some other notes to display all the possibilities of the instrument. This atheistic proposal stunned them. They pleaded that they had never played any other note . . . and that to assert that there was more than one note was to imply that there is more than one god. But the man with the gong rose to the occasion and proved that in China as in Europe the drummer is always the most intelligent person in the band. He snatched one of the trumpets, waved it in the air like a mail coach guard with a posthorn, and filled the air with flourishes and fanfares and Nothung motifs. We must make the BBC import a dozen of these trumpets to reinforce our piffling basses.'

As a prelude to their next destination, Shaw and Charlotte ended the expedition in a Chinese air-marshal's biplane, its seats open to the skies as they soared high over the Great Wall where the Chinese and Japanese armies were fighting, and higher still on its flight back, so high they could see neither the Great Wall nor the fighting because 'the Chinese do not study identification marks before they fire'.

*

They arrived in Japan showing signs of exhaustion. Though the *Empress of Britain* made stops at Beppu, Kobe and Yokohama, Charlotte was feeling too ill to see almost anything of the country and withdrew into her cabin like a snail in its shell. Shaw, who had slipped on deck while throwing off a chill, was using a walking-stick, but could still fence with up to fifty journalists for an hour or so – and according to *The Times* he 'conquered them by kindness'. Dazzled by his pink cheeks and keen eyes 'like an airplane pilot', they conveyed to readers the wonder of his straight back, white tennis shoes, and all the other cheerful features of his seventy-seven-year-old boyishness.

One advantage of age, Shaw informed everyone, was that it made you recklessly candid. His visit had been heralded by the first eruption for more than a century of Mount Aso, the world's largest active volcano, and coincided with an earthquake. To the Japanese authorities this seemed an ominous introduction and accompaniment. They had been looking forward to his first coming with unease. 'Foreigners with technical knowledge have always been welcome here, foreigners with ideas much less welcome,' explained a British resident in Tokyo. 'Now Mr Shaw is the "foreigner with ideas" par excellence, and from the Japanese point of view the worst possible ideas at that.' For a month the newspapers had been filled with explanatory and emollient articles about him. Now he spoke to them direct.

Turning his back on the beautiful Bay of Beppu, Japan's Inland Sea, he began what was to lengthen into a ten-day press conference, uttering seismic criticisms round a country where, as he later wrote in the Preface to *On the Rocks*, 'it is a crime to have "dangerous thoughts"'. He was referring to Japan's Peace Preservation Law under which the harbouring of 'dangerous thoughts' (which might range from communism to liberalism) was punishable by imprisonment. The knowledge that he was speaking for those who could not freely speak for themselves charged his words with extra force.

He started by trying to weaken the heroic central spring of Japan's militaristic foreign policy. The conflict in Manchuria 'won't be won by courage and Bushido', he warned; 'it will be won by machinery'. Like all wars it was being fought in 'self-defence', but of what value was such an

297

alibi, he asked, when more women could be killed by bombs in modern warfare than soldiers by shells? All thinking people had learnt from the Great War that no one could control or predict the consequences of war in the twentieth century: even the victors risked revolution and bankruptcy. Though careful not to involve the Imperial Family in his criticisms, he trained his guns on imperialistic patriotism as a force that, though temporarily uniting Japan, must ultimately destroy it.

After a few days' reconnaissance and enquiry at Kobe, Osaka, Nara and Kyoto, he switched his offensive to Japan's social and economic policies which were as much feared abroad, he said, as her militarism. The exploitation of men, women and children who were willing to work twice as long as people in other countries for half the wages made Japan the deadly enemy of workers throughout the rest of the world. 'The real danger of Japan is cheap labour and foreign trade,' he later wrote. She had come to depend on goods of horrible and wicked cheapness, 'measuring her prosperity by the magnitude of her exports instead of the well-being of her people'.

At Osaka he felt he was entering 'a huge industrial hell'. He had resented not being allowed into the factories there. He noticed the dirty women and children, saw their squalid huts and breathed in the acrid fumes of the place, recognizing that 'Japanese cities are like our cities one hundred years ago.' They had abandoned their own feudal system and having been converted to Victorian values were 'busy making fortunes for half a dozen people'. In consequence the country was partly uninhabited, partly uninhabitable. The Shavian solution was to reverse foreign and domestic policies by bringing some of the heavy guns back from Manchuria and using them on these slums. But was Japan ready to take a step beyond Western plutocracy? 'It is silly to go on pretending that Communism is a criminal horror in the face of the great Russian experiment ... In future Japan and all other Powers will have to compete with Russia in promoting the welfare of their people. If you shut your eyes to this you may live to see a statue of Lenin and a bust of Marx in every Shinto temple.'

Shaw emphasized that he had 'no feeling against Japan where I was treated extremely well'. Though his 'preposterous statements' had spread a rash of irritated embarrassment among ambassadors, consuls, cultural attachés and high commissioners in British embassies round the world, his popularity abroad was rising dizzily. 'The interest taken in Mr Shaw was really remarkable,' reported a British consular official, G. B. Sansom. 'I have never seen anything quite like it.' Diplomatically it was baffling, and what was worse G.B.S. seemed to have set up an international contest to find which country could inspire his most heady flights. 'The more ruthless

298

his statements, the more the public loved him,' G. B. Sansom reported in an embassy memorandum.

'When, instead of praising the cherry blossom and the samurai spirit, he said that he didn't care twopence for Japan, and that Japanese cities were slums that ought to be blown up, and that the Japanese theatre was horrible, everybody was delighted. In fact, one prominent journalist complained to me that Mr Shaw had been far too mild ... On the other hand, a secretary in the Chinese Legation told me with great pride, that Mr Shaw had said far more awful things about China than about Japan.'

George Sansom was deputed to look after Shaw and arrange his programme in Tokyo. Arriving at Yokohama, his wife Katharine discovered 'an old man wandering with a slightly lost look on the deck of the ship' who became rejuvenated in conversation. A steward took her down to Charlotte's cabin. 'G.B.S. will love to go with you,' Charlotte instructed her. 'But don't let him talk too much; he always does. And please, make him rest after lunch.' He talked throughout the car drive to Tokyo and during lunch at the Sansoms' house in the British Embassy compound, performing such 'gorgeously funny' antics while demonstrating points of musical instrumentation that the elderly butler and two maids 'gave up the struggle for correct deportment and fled from the room'. Protesting at being made to rest after lunch, he immediately fell asleep.

His appearance in the streets of Tokyo on his way to theatres, museums, Waseda University and the Upper House of the Diet (where he brought all business to a halt) was like the progress of a hero, interrupted yard by yard with 'old countrywomen climbing into buses, children, old men, chic girls, shop assistants – you could see each and every one with excited gaze and gaping mouth saying, "Shaw San!"'

George Sansom had arranged for him to meet a delegation from the Japanese Federation of Labour. They courteously assured him that they studied *Fabian Essays in Socialism* (1889); he informed them that he was now the author of *The Intelligent Woman's Guide*, and that his ideas might still change any day. 'It is like trying to be a disciple of a whirlwind!' one of them cried out admiringly. They seemed to Shaw exactly like old-fashioned trade union men in Britain; he appeared to them, especially when lighting up his vision of communism, 'essentially an artist and not a social and political leader at all'.

Sansom had also arranged for him to have a private meeting with the Prime Minister, Admiral Makoto Saito. A reporter in the next room overheard them laughing exuberantly as they discussed old age. Afterwards

Shaw remarked to Sansom that he did not understand how state affairs could be conducted by such an 'amiable old nincompoop'.

'Above all,' he said to one of his Japanese audiences, 'I am a man of the theatre.' His encounter with the fanatical Minister of War, General Araki, was even more theatrical than his meeting with Stalin. The playwright and General introduced themselves in a grand waiting-room watched by some splendidly bemedalled officers. Suddenly large double doors sprang open and a pack of thirty snapping press photographers poured in, driving back the soldiers and encircling the two protagonists. The air filled with the explosions and smoke, and there was tumult as the chorus of cameramen 'grinning and snarling like wild beasts . . . mauled the general and Mr Shaw . . . It was an awful scene,' George Sansom later recalled. ' . . . The all-powerful militarist leader was quite unable to control this pack of ruffians.'

Meanwhile the full cast assembled round a table: G. B. Sansom seconding G.B.S., a Japanese Colonel shadowing the General, and somewhat in the manner of Pamphilius and Simpronius, the Private Secretaries to the King in *The Apple Cart*, 'two ridiculously earnest young officers taking notes'. Each time their conversation started up, they were tantalisingly interrupted by a *soubrette* in the shape of the General's daughter, a pretty girl 'who kept on bringing cakes and tea and sandwiches at inconvenient moments'.

The comedy gave way to philosophy as General Araki strove to convert G.B.S. to his own mystical ideas. Did Shaw, he demanded, have 'a philosophy of earthquakes?' The General believed that earthquakes were good for Japan. They bolstered the character, encouraged self-control, and prevented people from becoming too attached to their possessions. They were deeper, the General ventured, than air-raids. It was a pity that Shaw had not regularly experienced earthquakes in England.

In his reply, Shaw conceded that England was unhappily deficient in moral advantages of this kind. It was true that Englishmen were unable to conceive that the solid ground could move and possibly General Araki would favour the planting of dynamite by the British War Minister to provide artificial earthquakes periodically. 'But we have our earthquakes in England,' Shaw added. 'When people think that their institutions, their religions, their beliefs are firm and immutable, some disagreeable fellow like me comes along and upsets their cherished convictions. Now you need that kind of earthquake in Japan!'

In his conversation with Madame Sun, Shaw had described Stalin as 'a practical man' who paid 'little attention to theory' and was 'unscrupulous in trying to reach his goal'. Now, after listening to a discourse on the reasons why materialistic communism was abhorrent to the spiritual culture of the

Japanese, he reflected how closely General Araki resembled Stalin and assured him that were he to visit Moscow for a month he would return to Tokyo a devout communist. Already the Japanese army, which found little incentive in moneymaking, exemplified the spirit of pure communism. He offered the General a military tip: give priority to octogenarians, followed by septuagenarians then sexagenarians, when conscripting men for the army and sending them to the front.

Shaw brought the act to an end by declaring that he would have liked 'to stay talking to you until the Chinese troops get to Tokyo'. In a memorandum sent by the British ambassador to the Foreign Secretary in London the occasion was judged to be 'a great success'. General Araki praised the refinement of Shaw's jokes and his epigrammatic 'life view'. But he still did not think Englishmen understood earthquakes: one 'does not just experience an earthquake and then forget about it'.

Besides shaking the earth of a country fortified against criticism, Shaw had also been going about the quieter business of collecting religions. He visited Buddhist temples and Shinto shrines, tapping bells ('much better than Big Ben') and offering some devastating proposals: 'Why don't you worship your descendants?' The artist, he said, 'no matter how old, always has something to learn'. He learnt 'what can be done in the way of producing atmosphere with one banjo string pizzicato and a bicycle bell' in Noh theatre music. He had read some articles by his Japanese translator Yonejirō Noguchi on Noh theory and was quoted as saying: 'I understand though I don't understand.' In particular he was struck by some of the contrasts in technique, such as the deployment of ghosts, use of chorus, and the sense of continuity suggested by the passageway of the thrust stage as opposed to the picture-frame of the proscenium stage in Western theatre.

A special performance in his honour had been arranged at the Kudan Noh Theatre. At the end of the first work, a warrior-ghost play of the Komparu school called *Tomoe*, he rose to give a short speech of thanks saying he had comprehended the 'artistic intention' of what he had seen. Artists and poets of the theatre would always do their work out of the necessity to follow a sincere impulse, he said, even if doing it meant destroying the human race – an outcome that might cause 'some of us' to follow it more enthusiastically. He seemed overcome by a sudden revulsion against all his trekking through the insincerities of international politics. In this theatre and among these actors he felt at home. 'I belong to it and it belongs to me.' But he did not belong to the world outside where people were cutting one another's throats. 'Let us artists follow our sacred mission,' he concluded, 'and make the best of our art regardless of consequences.'

The climax of this world tour in March 1933 was Shaw's first visit to North America. 'I can't face America,' he had admitted early in the century when invited to go lecturing there. These invitations, sugared with huge financial enticements, would come in 'at the rate of 60 per minute all the time' and every year the newspapers reported that he was finally on his way. But 'I am as far as ever from seriously contemplating it', he wrote when refusing another offer in 1921. 'If I go to America, I think I shall speak in the open air for nothing, if the police will allow me.'

His facetious refusals, attributed to fear of being made President or of the effect of his fatal good looks on American women, masked a real and complicated fear. He was in some ways a natural American ('I'm like New York. It's hell and damnation for me to be doing nothing') who carried on a life-long quarrel with the United States very much in the manner of Charles Dickens. He would remind Archibald Henderson that, after the publication of *Martin Chuzzlewit*, Dickens 'never retracted a syllable of Scadder (the realtor), Chollop, Mrs Horning and Jefferson Brick, all of whom are the mildest of pleasantries compared to the latest realtors, gangsters and highbrows. The truth of the matter is that writers like Dickens are privileged to tell the truth without malice or partiality.'

Like Dickens, Shaw seems to have believed that for historical reasons there was a natural antipathy between the English and Americans and that, since some of the causes for Anglo–American dislike were not of a fundamental nature, it was better to carry on abusing one another than simulate an affection that was not felt. 'This pretence of being affectionate cousins is pure poison,' he wrote. '. . . Better, where there is volcanic activity under the lid to lift the lid once in a while than sit on it until it blows off!' He had made a speciality of baiting the hundred per cent American as a ninety-nine per cent idiot. 'I do not want to see the Statue of Liberty,' he said. '. . . I am a master of comic irony. But even my appetite for irony does not go as far as that!'

Many of the Americans in his plays appear to represent a nation that is riven with money-materialism. There are the two women in *The Devil's Disciple*, Judith Anderson, who is 'petted into an opinion of herself sufficiently favorable to give her a self-assurance which serves her instead of strength', and the exceedingly disagreeable mother of Dick Dudgeon whose face is 'grimly entrenched by the channels into which the barren forms and observances of a dead Puritanism can pen a bitter temper and a fierce pride'; there is the vituperating lynch mob that fills the court during *The Shewing-up of Blanco Posnet*; and there are the Americans who turn up in

Europe, such as the baffled-looking, bullet-cheeked millionaire Hector Malone Senior 'whose social position needs constant and scrupulous affirmation' in *Man and Superman*, and the blandly effusive Ambassador Vanhatten who strides onto the terrace of the Royal Palace in the second act of *The Apple Cart* 'like a man assured of an enthusiastic welcome' and vigorously shakes the Queen up and down with his prolonged handshake.

In his twenties, when the Land of the Free had seemed a natural fatherland for him, Shaw had momentarily thought of emigrating there. 'I could have come when I was young and beautiful,' he wrote when in his sixties he turned down an invitation from the New York chapter of the Drama League of America. 'I could have come when I was mature and capable.' But in his seventies, 'I cannot help asking myself whether it is not now too late'. He almost denied that he would be landing at all – he was merely looking in and out again. The *Empress of Britain* 'is calling at Los Angeles for five minutes, and then calling at New York for five minutes', he told reporters. 'That is not my fault. I may meet a few friends . . .'

He had kept on friendly terms with a surprising number of native and adopted Americans – actors, anarchists, politicians, publishers. There was his special 'lunatic' friend Lawrence Langner and the directors, designers and performers of the Theatre Guild of New York; writers, too, such as the pro-Soviet novelist Upton Sinclair and the pro-German poet George Sylvester Viereck, as well as his continuous biographer Archibald Henderson; and a generous lobby of correspondents including Henry Neil, a Chicago judge, who regularly published Shaw's answers to his unusual queries (What would he do if he were a woman? What difference would being hatched in an incubator have made to his life?) until, his excitement rising in this year of Shaw's arrival, he was confined to a mental institute. 'That is the worst of you Americans,' Shaw had complained to the theatrical producer George Tyler: 'you are uncommonly nice people personally; but you have no notion of practical affairs.'

Americans had been impractical over many of Shaw's own affairs. They had pirated his early books and called him an 'Irish Smut Dealer' when issuing arrest warrants for disorderly conduct to the entire cast of his 'illuminated gangrene' *Mrs Warren's Profession* after its opening performance in New York. They had also removed *Man and Superman* and other volumes from the shelves of the New York Public Library; and actually imprisoned a man in Detroit for reading *An Unsocial Socialist* in a streetcar.

'Personally I do not take the matter so lightly,' Shaw had written to the *New York Times* when asked for his reaction to the withdrawal of his books from the state's libraries. 'American civilization is enormously interesting and important to me, if only as a colossal social experiment, and I shall make no pretence of treating a public and official insult from the American people with indifference.'

The resentment he felt at having his moral authority impugned, income cut, and early illusions extinguished sharpened his criticisms and gave them a vindictive edge. He could hardly dig up insults enough to pile upon the childishness of Americans 'which enables them to remain simple New England villagers in the complicated hustle of New York and Chicago, never revising their ideas, never enlarging their consciousness, never losing their interest in the ideals of the Pilgrim Fathers'.

Shaw argued that the anarchical plan of letting everyone mind his own business and do the best he could for himself was only practicable in a country newly-cleared and settled by ambitious colonists without any common industrial tradition or body of custom. North America had been incapable of developing beyond this village stage. 'Every social development, however beneficial and inevitable from the public point of view, is met, not by an intelligent adaptation of the social structure to its novelties,' he wrote, 'but by a panic and a cry of Go Back.'

Before the Soviet Revolution Shaw had accepted that American politics had to be co-ordinated with the collective interest of civilization round the world. He took issue with revolutionaries who threatened the United States with the breakdown of capitalism for want of markets and who prophesied that socialism would build on its ruins. He preferred a more inviting evolutionary scenario. 'Socialism is only possible in the consummation of successful Capitalism,' he wrote, ' . . . only possible where Individualism is developed to the point at which the individual can see beyond himself and works to perfect his city and his nation instead of to furnish his own house better than his neighbor's.'

Shaw's gestures of political diplomacy confusingly punctuated the joyous stream of his Dickensian invective, and once the only European power bigger than the United States had been transformed into a federation of communist republics, he gave up these diplomatic contortions with relief. 'I am not an American,' he admitted, 'but I am the next worst thing – an Irishman.' His tirades against Americans were partly self-inflicted criticisms – an involuntary response to the damage he sometimes felt he had done himself by manufacturing an ostentatious G.B.S., designed to travel in a world increasingly governed by the culture of the USA. 'For what has been happening during my lifetime,' he had written in 1912, 'is the American-ization of the whole world.' He struck back as one in danger of being classed an enemy of the whole world.

After his return from the Soviet Union he had used a special broadcast from Savoy Hill to give 'A little Talk on America', heaping up his abuse to giddier, more ecstatic heights. The event was recorded by Movietone with G.B.S. at his most child-devilish encircled by immense lights like furnaces welcoming Americans into hell.

'Hello, America! Hello, all my friends in America! Hello, all you dear old boobs who have been telling one another for a month past that I have gone dotty about Russia . . .'

Even Charlotte had to laugh. 'I wish you could have heard G.B.S. broadcast to America about Russia,' she wrote to Nancy Astor. 'My dear! All the insults he sent over! Too bad – but so funny.'

Yet it was not all so funny. Lifting the lid on the volcanic activity within himself, he covered this 'most awful country' with the ashes of colossal contempt. Sometimes in the past he had singled out the coast-to-coast desire for money as the most encouraging social aspect of American life. But since the accepted method of acquiring this money in the United States was theft, he liked to add, the country had grown rich only in paper dollars that were no protection against a real financial crash. He comes near to crowing over the predicament of President Hoover 'who became famous by feeding the starving millions of war devastated Europe, [but] cannot feed his own people in time of peace', and castigates American 'business incompetence, political helplessness and financial insolvency' with an animosity that defies any listener to dismiss what he is saying as a Shavian joke.

'That is what makes you so popular all over the world,' he persisted, moving into rare sarcasm: 'you make yourself at home everywhere; and you always have the first word.' Shaw wanted the last word. With his long-range artillery he aimed to smash the glitter of Western plutocracy and laugh the American in Europe out of countenance. 'You cannot persuade an American that he can fail to talk you into doing something foolish,' he wrote to St John Ervine. On the other hand you might arm an infatuated British public against surrendering to such foolishness. When he lets off his word-fire at the United States he often has a Britain of the future in his sights.

He was happiest at long range and somewhat uneasy at the prospect of having to divide and subdivide his attitude after he came ashore and began mixing with these 'uncommonly nice people personally'. His few preliminary exercises in tact – 'Americans are conceited enough to believe they are the only fools in the world' – show his diplomatic skills to have been somewhat rusted. Equally ineffective was his pretence that Americans loved his wisecracks ('they just adore me') and that he was following the example of Dickens in rousing their devotion by holding them up to ridicule as 'windbags, swindlers and assassins'. In fact it took Dickens quarter of a century to atone for his *American Notes* and *Martin Chuzzlewit*; and, as the actor Maurice Colbourne noted, America was also 'long sensitive to the Shavian sting'.

'Indeed no,' Shaw had replied when asked in Honolulu whether he was still a socialist. 'I'm a communist. And tell that to your government.' Free love and anarchism had given way after the war to alcohol and communism as the most dreaded social perils in the United States, enabling G.B.S. to use his awkward status as a prim, teetotal red communist to challenge American orthodoxy. He looked forward to obliging the immigration authorities with answers of the utmost frankness and representing himself throughout this country of immigrants as a dangerous alien. 'I have my passport for the U.S.; and all the world knows I am a more thoroughgoing Communist than Lenin.'

In matters involving others he was more careful. He answered the appeal of Thomas Mooney, a militant American labour leader wrongly imprisoned more than fifteen years before in connection with a bomb explosion, by explaining that the interference of a 'Communist foreign celebrity' would do more harm than good. 'I do not consider it humane to use you as a stick to beat Capitalism,' he wrote to him in San Quentin prison. He would try to remain as non-committal with Mooney as he had over the Krynin family in Moscow, but 'I cannot pretend that I am not shocked at having any person put into a vault for 16 or 17 years', he told reporters on landing at San Francisco. And he made it clear that his own political views were far more extreme than those of this fifty-year-old American who was to wait several years more for a pardon.

Leaving the *Empress of Britain* at San Francisco, Shaw and Charlotte were flown to San Simeon to stay with 'a personal friend, and a first rate paymaster', the millionaire newspaper owner William Randolph Hearst. 'I do not write for the people intelligent and instructed enough to share my views,' Shaw would later explain, '. . . but to startle and wake up the readers of the H[earst] P[ress]'. For four days they put up at his prodigious castle-ranch with the seventy-year-old Hearst and his young mistress, Marion Davies, together with more than forty other guests – starlets, sirens and swells of all sorts, as well as the apes, eagles and zebras that occupied the grounds outside.

Afterwards they flew by plane from Hearst's vivarium, swooping down as if 'to catch a fish' below a sudden thunderstorm and making a forced landing on the beach near Malibu. There they were picked up by a college sophomore who rattled them into Malibu Airport for a number of official handshakes. Then, in a dignified cavalcade, they entered the MGM studio-village of Culver City – to be welcomed, as in a nightmare, by the people they had so recently left, William Hearst and Marion Davies.

Charlotte felt 'a little nervy' in this jungle of Hollywood fantasy and startled everyone by calling for a glass of whisky. She knew that G.B.S. had been careful never to say a civil word about the place and had so far refused all American offers to film his plays. He had gone out of his way to praise Eisenstein at the expense of Hollywood, offering him the film rights in *Arms and the Man* after meeting him in London in 1929, though refusing Mary Pickford the film rights to *Caesar and Cleopatra* in 1930. Eisenstein's disastrous experiences in Hollywood during the very early 1930s only strengthened Shaw's hostility.

At her ornate Hollywood bungalow Marion Davies had prepared a splendid lunch party for G.B.S., who found there was nothing (except a sprig of decorative parsley) any vegetarian could eat. On the film sets afterwards, they met a sprinkling of stars, but 'no performer they encountered that afternoon had a kind remark to make about G.B.S.', records Dan H. Laurence. Shaw's most widely-reported encounter took place with the actress Ann Harding. She told him she would soon be playing Lady Cicely again in *Captain Brassbound's Conversion* whose film rights she wanted, and was taken aback to hear that Shaw had not known of her previous performance at the Hedgerow Theatre, near Philadelphia. 'I'm sure it must have been a piratical performance,' he volunteered – at which 'Ann's pretty toy balloon popped', an observer wrote, she rushed to her dressing-room and according to one report 'wept for hours afterward' and according to another 'went into hysterics and said she wouldn't work any longer'. What no one reported, as the critic Bernard Dukore explains, was that Shaw's quip had been a harmless pun about a play whose title character was a pirate. When asked later on to comment on the Hollywood actress's famous tears, he replied: 'Everyone there had forgotten how to cry.'

Charlotte and G.B.S. were in Hollywood only two and a half hours, but 'bitterness and rancor of a kind hovered in their wake' and years afterwards Marion Davies (who had wanted the film rights to *Pygmalion*) described Shaw as having 'that caustic Irish wit which is very detestable'. Though RKO Studios was also seeking the rights to *The Devil's Disciple* for John Barrymore and *Saint Joan* for Katharine Hepburn, 'I don't believe that Hollywood is within ten years of tackling my stuff, Shaw wrote shortly after leaving. His relations with the United States film industry were commemorated by the 'caustic Irish wit' of his reply to Samuel Goldwyn who tried to flatter him into signing a contract for the screen rights of his plays: 'The trouble is, Mr Goldwyn, you are interested in art, whereas I am interested in money.'

They rejoined the *Empress of Britain* at Los Angeles, sailed down the Pacific coast to Panama, and up the Atlantic coast towards New York. Shaw had agreed to give one public lecture in the States – for the Academy of Political Science at the Metropolitan Opera House in New York. He was anxious for it to be known that 'I shall not take a cent out of America on this visit' and so avoid the charges thrust at Dickens of grabbing as many dollars as he could from audiences of whom he was contemptuous. 'I wish to make as much money as possible for the Academy,' he wrote. This wish was somewhat frustrated by the non-profit status of the Academy and by the publication of a pirated edition of his lecture three months before the appearance of the authorized version whose royalties were assigned to the Academy.

Another reason why he had agreed to give this formal lecture was to produce an authentic record of what he was saying. The press coverage trailing behind his world pilgrimage had been growing chaotic. 'I have been misquoted everywhere,' he was quoted as saying, 'and the inaccuracies are chasing me round the world.' The American freedom to tell lies worked like an ingenious form of censorship. The country was a vast Hot Air Volcano spouting superlatives – or so it looked to Shaw after his dip into Hollywood. Like children, Americans called their lies 'stories'. Their newspapermen did not even know they were guilty of malicious invention when they told the story of him insulting the blind and deaf writer Helen Keller, whom he had met in England with Nancy Astor, by saying 'all Americans are blind and deaf – and dumb'. Charlotte reassured Nancy Astor that G.B.S. 'does not mind one scrap about Helen Keller'. In fact it was obvious that he did mind, though not so much as he minded the lies wrapped round his political statements. 'When I say anything silly, or am reported as saying anything reactionary, it runs like wildfire through the Press of the whole world,' he wrote later this year in his Preface to *On the Rocks*. 'When I say anything that could break the carefully inculcated popular faith in Capitalism the silence is so profound as to be almost audible.' He was dreading 'what the reporters will do to me' in New York and had forewarned them that he would not be interviewed to death before his lecture. But when the *Empress of Britain* docked, 200 reporters and photographers swarmed on deck in search of him. They found a message pinned to his cabin door which was guarded by the ship's master at arms:

'The New York press may return to its firesides and nurse the baby until tomorrow morning, except the enterprising section which came on board at

Havana, and discussed everything with me for an hour and forty minutes. Today I am in training for the Metropolitan Opera House tonight, and may be regarded as deaf and dumb for the moment. With regrets and apologies. GBS.'

But they would not leave. After a couple of hours under pounding siege, Shaw sent out his biographer Archibald Henderson, like a dove from the Ark, with a message that he would pose for photographs but say nothing. 'It was a terrible business for me,' he wrote afterwards to the actress Constance Collier. 'On the day of our arrival I had to fight off a raging press to get some sleep and quiet before my big effort.' Eventually he was spirited away through the throng by his new American publisher, Howard Lewis, of Dodd, Mead. 'I can think of no private citizen with the exception of Lindbergh who had been greeted by more reporters and publicity than Mr Shaw,' he wrote to the British publisher Otto Kyllmann. Lewis drove Shaw and Charlotte through New York to a quiet restaurant overlooking the Hudson River, and afterwards to the Theatre Guild. 'The press conducted a frantic search for him all over the city,' Lewis reported, 'and it rather tickled me to be able to give them the slip.'

Charlotte had been getting increasingly worried over Shaw's 'big effort' at the Metropolitan Opera House. 'I do not feel he is up to it. It will be a terrible strain after all the exertions & fatigues of this amazing journey,' she had written to Nancy Astor. '... Of course he will "get through" – But I cannot believe he will do himself justice.' It was to be what he later called 'the most hectic day of my entire life'.

They arrived at the Metropolitan Opera House a little after 8.00 and were steered by police through the fast-flowing crowds. With 'the lithe step, all but prancing, of a cavalier', Shaw walked on to the platform led by his chairman – the President of the First National Bank – at 8.35. He had agreed to a national radio broadcast of his lecture on condition that it was not edited, and was now obliged to wait ten minutes, clasping his 'long tapering hands around his knee', for the National Broadcasting Company's schedule, while a standing ovation from the audience of more than 3,500 people changed into an impatient stamping of feet. Among this audience was Edmund Wilson, observing the 'arms folded of the schoolmaster' and 'the reddish nose of the old Irishmen' dressed formally in his 'double-breasted black coat buttoned up high under the collar with an austere effect almost clerical so that it sets off the whiteness of his beard as his eyebrows against his pink skin look like cotton on a department-store Santa Claus'. Shaw stood up, a dark arrowy figure, slim and straight; and then his caressing Rathmines accent began to permeate the huge auditorium, blending courtesy with irony, touching the imagination with a peculiar enchantment.

'Finding myself in an opera house with such a magnificent and responsive audience,' he began, 'I feel an irresistible temptation to sing.' But it soon became clear that he was not there to sing America's praises. 'You guessed that I should not hand you the usual visitor's bouquets.' He told them he had visited 'two plague spots' in the United States, Hollywood and New York. Behind the growing international power of the film industry, Hollywood was everywhere bringing public and private morals under its influence. But its philosophical answer to every challenge was a sock in the jaw. 'When shall we see a film issuing from Hollywood,' Shaw asked, 'in which the hero acts like a civilized man?' And he concluded: 'Hollywood is the most immoral place in the world.'

The 'vast dumb audience', likened by Edmund Wilson to a 'demoralising aquarium of blind deep-sea creatures', received this dismissal of the macho style coldly and was no better pleased by Shaw's picture of New York 'under the thumbs of your private racketeers, from the humble gunman to the great financial magnate'. His main target was the money kingdom of Wall Street whose power was 'so irresistible that it becomes a political and industrial power, not to say a religious power'. Under this rule of the 'neurotic gambler with the insoluble complex', he warned, the United States had grown into 'a wonderful night clubby sort of nation; but there is nothing so helpless as a raided night club'.

Ostensibly Shaw's lecture was an examination of American government. He accurately predicted that private financiers would not allow Franklin Roosevelt to carry through his National Recovery Program, and that if necessary they would use the American Constitution to stop him. This Constitution had become a paradoxical symbol of Shaw's own frustration: 'a great protest against the tyranny of law and order', representing the struggle of his early career, that had been turned into a Charter of Anarchism guaranteeing 'to the whole American nation that it never should be governed at all', shadowing his sense of powerlessness in late middle age.

The United States did not want to be governed, Shaw reasoned, because it did not trust its own political election system which, like Hollywood film-making, only appealed to children. Read aloud his sentences and you will hear the revulsion still throbbing through the language he used to describe 'those scandalous and disgusting spectacles that are called election meetings, at which sane and sober men yell senselessly until any dispassionate stranger looking at them would believe that he was in a lunatic asylum for exceptionally dreadful cases of mental derangement'. But Shaw is not a dispassionate stranger. He is painfully involved. 'I have never spoken nor listened at an election meeting without being ashamed of the whole sham democratic routine. The older I grow the more I feel such exhibitions to be, as part of the serious business of a nation, entirely intolerable and disgraceful to human nature and civic decency.'

This was the largest audience he had ever addressed. His speech was less an essay in persuasion than a statement from the confessional. Behind the outrage to civic decency lay the outrage to human nature. In private he admitted to telling people 'all sorts of things that I do not believe, because I think it will please them'. But 'speeches made through the microphone to millions of listeners', he later said, '. . . take on a necessary sincerity'. His ringing warfare against the United States sounds like an echo from within his disunited self. It was as if the microphone could pick up a peculiar Shavian chord, and we can hear again the voice of Sonny using this climax to Shaw's missionary travels to make his objection heard to the fêted progress of G.B.S. around the world. Was not the spell of money on G.B.S. an American spell; his trick of overstatement 'an American trick; his gift for monologue, an American gift', as Blanche Patch was to suggest? Playing with these spells and tricks and gifts like sparks in the air, translating the child who had never grown up into the country that remained so juvenile, Shaw blinds and illuminates, angers and amuses his audience with this variety show of his dissatisfaction: 'An American has no sense of privacy,' he protests. Such lines, carrying his protest through a commotion of feeling and motive, show his inability to tread the dry route to power. For this was not the controlled politics of the ballot-box, but the politics of estrangement, alienation, where the undercurrent of everything is passionate and personal.

He was attempting to bring some of the principles of his plays directly into current politics. The 'wonderful night clubby sort of nation' in the United States and the moral gymnasium of Soviet industrial society where all 'pulled through because all pulled together' were manifestations of the hell and heaven over which the Devil and Don Juan contended in *Man and Superman*. When he appealed for his audience to be thankful that Russia was not a capitalist competitor for world markets and 'to appreciate the benefit to America of having other countries Communistic', he was responding to the same promptings that in *John Bull's Other Island* had made him try to reconcile the dreams and realities of Ireland's and England's political histories and national characteristics. But now he was exasperated. In his urgent warning to Western civilization that it had 'reached the edge of the precipice' over which previous civilizations 'fell and were dashed to pieces' rose the anguish and relief of someone nearing the end of his own life.

'Mr Roosevelt, by a happy chance, got photographed with a baby. The baby was a success: Mr Roosevelt went to the White House in its arms.'

There is a charm in such passages where the voices of Sonny and G.B.S. seem to blend, and a peculiar insight where they combine against a common enemy such as the financiers who 'live in a world of illusion'. Circling this illusory world Shaw presents a stereoscopic vision of the planet manoeuvred by the calculations of exchange value judgements from one great war towards another. The system of civilization he views and maps is dependent on countries weighing their prosperity by simple excess of exports over imports which, from the Shavian perspective, is 'incompatible with international peace and domestic prosperity'. The financier's sock in the jaw was to 'levy a colossal tribute on a defeated and penniless population', he exclaimed, 'and prove their ability to pay by lending them the money to do it with!' All the gold in the world was being shipped to the United States – but what use was it? 'Ask your armies of the unemployed.' This question and command mirror Shaw's own position as someone financially successful, continuously at work, but who felt politically 'unemployed' in the modern world.

'Whenever in the search for truth I hit the nail exactly on the head, there is always a laugh at first.' But in several places where he expected laughter in the Metropolitan Opera House there was a 'curious dead silence'. It was evident to Edmund Wilson that he had not been able to sense what kind of audience he was up against and in the end 'found himself trying to talk to two different and irreconcilable elements ... conventional after-dinner dodos, and ... a certain number of radicals'. He navigated this course with difficulty. 'Somehow I felt he had let us down,' wrote the American publisher William H. Wise. He seemed to have entangled himself in his own words: accusing the United States of being as incapable as England of doing anything but 'talk, talk, talk' and then delaying the broadcast of a concert by talking himself for an hour and forty minutes.

Looking through the transcript he acknowledged that, as Charlotte feared, he had not really done himself justice: 'I'm afraid I bungled a great deal of it.' His need for self-dramatization had delivered him into the hands of modern publicity, making the effect a little compromising, as if he were having to 'handle like hot potatoes convictions which were once incandescent', Edmund Wilson judged. And yet 'he can still thrill us from time to time as he is able to make the timbre of the old daring, the old piercing intellectual clarity, ring out ... in the pompous opera house ... he continues to stand for something which makes us see audience and theatre as we have never quite seen them before'.

He had invited several people to come and see him next morning on board the *Empress of Britain* before it sailed, but they were quickly rushed aside by a 'riot of reporters and camera men all over the ship', he told

Constance Collier. 'The crowd pressed after us like a tidal wave,' wrote William Wise; and Howard Lewis was embarrassed by the banality of the journalists' questions and the 'rude and persistent importunities' of the photographers. A 'gang of hoodlums' began to take movies. 'Evidently under instructions to "get Shaw's goat", they did everything possible to irritate and disconcert him,' Lawrence Langner observed. 'In one instance, a lout set off a flashlight bulb almost in his face, amid loud guffaws, and took advantage of Shaw's shocked surprise to snap an absurd picture of him which was later published in a New York journal. Not one of these hoodlums showed the slightest respect for the man . . .' Langner went up to a steward and asked whether some gangway could be made for Shaw. 'You'd need fixed bayonets, sir,' he was told. Eventually Shaw reached his cabin and, as William Wise described, 'literally had to throw his weight against his stateroom door'. 'We left the boat sadly,' recorded Lawrence Langner, 'wishing that GBS might have taken away with him a better impression of our national manners.'

As soon as the ship sailed, Shaw re-entered the world of his plays, and Charlotte was left reflecting on the 'very mixed business' of their wanderings: 'it is a sort of worthlessness that comes over one in this vagabond life'. On 19 April the *Empress of Britain* steamed up Southampton Water, her bunting flying, and the sirens hooting from the shore. Two days later they were 'off the map' back at Ayot. 'I do not say I will never go to America again,' Shaw told a reporter from the *Sunday Chronicle*. 'I found everyone extraordinarily hospitable. It is a kind of lunacy with them there.'

They were to have another brief look at the United States early in 1936 as part of a second world tour – this one from west to east aboard the *S.S. Arandora Star*. Before starting out they lunched at the London School of Economics and dined at the Russian Embassy, both lunch and dinner in celebration of the Webbs' *Soviet Communism: A New Civilization?* 'Two most agreeable gatherings,' Beatrice wrote in her diary, ' . . . somewhat too reverential of the old Webbs, but very pleasant for us to experience in our old age.' Charlotte, who had invited them to lunch the following day at Whitehall Court, noticed that both Sidney and Beatrice 'look 10 years younger since they got the book off their hands!' She looked for a similar shedding of years from G.B.S. following their cruise. On 20 January she brought her will up to date, and two days later they set off again from Southampton.

Shaw was now in his eightieth year and 'cannot do what he used to do', Charlotte wrote. This, their last voyage abroad, was a postscript to G.B.S.'s missionary travels. He gave a 'low-keyed' interview to jostling crowds of reporters at Miami ('you should greet visitors in respectable silence') and kept the rest of his trip as private as he could. Across a stormy Atlantic, between spasms of sickness, he wrote prefaces; along the Gulf of Panama, in temperatures of almost 90°F, 'I try to write plays falling asleep between every sentence'. At Honolulu they had lunch in a Chinese restaurant with Charlie Chaplin. At the Grand Canyon, startlingly covered with snow, they met J. B. Priestley. Wearing his plus-fours and Norfolk jacket, G.B.S. 'refused to wonder and exclaim at the Grand Canyon, muttering something about Cheddar Gorge', Priestley later complained. '...It is only fair, however, to add that he was then about eighty and had probably been travelling too long and seeing too many sights.'

The cruise lasted seventy-five days, during which Shaw completed his last political play, *Geneva*. 'We have seen some glorious places & made some delightful friends & learned quite a lot of things,' Charlotte had written to Nancy Astor. Shaw would remember best the natives in Equatorial countries. They were the originals of our Smiths and Browns, still unsmudged by the hands of commerce, and always looking carefree. But in the developed countries he had found people worried and anxious. Civilization was dying of fundamental bad manners called religion, politics, patriotism and other fine names. The world was not yet fit for decent people to live in, and those who thought otherwise were living in a fool's paradise. Was it any wonder that he had paused to ask his audience at the Metropolitan Opera House: 'What is wrong with us?'

*

Between these two world cruises Shaw made his last evangelical venture, and the most far-flung of all his sea-voyages, to New Zealand. By now he had perfected his boat drill. After early morning exercises on his back (during which Charlotte miraculously 'lost my backache!!'), he would search the promenade deck for an 'unprotected lady who is ripe for a friendship with a celebrity'. He had an unerring eye. 'I plant my deck chair beside hers and ask her whether she minds my working at a new play instead of talking,' he had told William Rothenstein. 'She is so delighted at being given the role of protector of G.B.S. that whenever anyone comes near she makes agitated signs to warn him off, whispering that *Mr Shaw is at work on a new play*. So I make a new friend and get perfect peace during the entire voyage.'

At the end of this trip he was able to present Blanche Patch, who had as usual remained on duty at Whitehall Court, with shorthand drafts of three completed new plays: *The Simpleton of the Unexpected Isles*, *The Millionairess* and *The Six of Calais*.

New Zealand had passed a law enabling the government to refuse landing to 'persons who have recently visited Communist countries'. A few people had advocated that Shaw be disbarred from entry and there was 'some lively press discussion as to what would happen to me' before his arrival.

As he and Charlotte came down the gangway the dockers began cheering – and so began 'a sort of Royal progress'. In Auckland there was 'a continual whirl of people and entertaining and sightseeing and journalists'. They drank tea with the Prime Minster, G. W. Forbes, and ate lunch with the Governor-General, Viscount Bledisloe. 'G.B.S. is marvellous!' Charlotte wrote. 'The amount of interviews, talking, public speaking he can do!'

'I shan't do it again,' he had promised after his lecture at the Metropolitan Opera House: 'I am too old for these feats of endurance.' But he could not quite hold to this resolution. From the *RMS Rangitane* he had written to R. M. Campbell, Secretary to the New Zealand Ministry of Finance: 'I cannot yet say what I shall do when I land . . .'

'As to taking on a big meeting at the Town Hall . . . though I can still carry a lecture through with apparent ease as I did in New York last April I pay for it a day or two afterward, and resolve, with good reason, never to do it again. Broadcasting for half an hour is what I prefer now. I get a much larger audience and suffer much less.'

In the event he gave one lecture to the hastily-formed Wellington Fabian Society and a national broadcast, also relayed to Australia, entitled 'Shaw speaks to the Universe'. His address to the Wellington Fabians was a cheerful demolition of parliamentary democracy. In Britain, he told them, the House of Commons had become a House of Hypocrisy, which seemed to suit Ramsay MacDonald 'who soon picked up all those tricks', was himself tricked into being leader of the Conservatives, 'and so became no use to us at all'. But such trickery had confounded a 'fine man' like Keir Hardie.

'Keir Hardie kept the flag flying to the very last . . . he was the finest gentleman in Parliament. But that meant that he never understood that an English gentleman could get up in Parliament and tell a lie, or, still worse, convict him who never told a lie anywhere, of telling a lie in Parliament.'

Shaw appealed to New Zealand socialists to free themselves from this lying model of government based on Westminster. What the country needed, he said, was a Cromwell: 'a politician with sufficient courage to rise up, and, instead of talking about democracy, say, "Damn democracy! Down with democracy!"' He drew back the curtains and in this beaming Shavian sunlight exposed the night demons of dictatorship as insubstantial phantoms. For if the sublime virtue of democracy was a mirage so also was the black vice of totalitarianism. All law had to be totalitarian and everyone lived under a dictatorship of the proletariat or a dictatorship of the plutocracy. 'Your landlord comes and citates to you that you pay your rent to him for the land which he bought for twopence from the Maori. But the question is: are you going to be dictated to by a Government of the farmers and landowners, or are you going to be dictated to by a Socialist Government.' Shaw's advice was categorical: stick to socialism and let it dictate, rather than a clique of wealthy businessmen.

When asked whether he intended submitting a text of his speech to the Broadcasting Board, he answered: 'I should have no objection if I could foresee what I shall say...' In the event the New Zealand government waived its broadcasting regulations which barred all controversial statements and allowed Shaw to say whatever he wanted. He was seeing a number of socialist politicians during his visit, including two future Labour Prime Ministers, Peter Fraser and Walter Nash, and he had briefed himself carefully before making an original proposal. 'You have in Wellington a remarkable milk supply, which is the envy of the whole world,' he said.

'... But your milk I think costs too much. I just want to ask, why not distribute milk freely? That is very important in New Zealand. A little loss on milk does not matter ... when you have distributed free milk, which is just as possible as free water, I would then suggest that you should go on from free milk to free bread ... [then] such a thing as a hungry child will be impossible in New Zealand.'

Shaw was the first to recommend this scheme in public and it became one of his successes. The first Labour government that came to power at the end of 1935 distributed half a pint of free pasteurized milk each school day to all schoolchildren. Later in the thirties he would receive grateful letters from New Zealand mothers (children themselves grew up feeling less grateful) but replied that the credit lay with the New Zealand government for implementing his suggestion. The scheme lasted for thirty years and was expanded in 1941, not by free bread, but by free apples once the war had cut New Zealand's export market to Britain. This was therefore less of a socialist initiative than a borrowed solution to the problem of an unsaleable agricultural surplus.

To writers of a younger generation watching him stalk across the international scene like one of 'those big heads on stilts in carnival processions', it was astonishing how G.B.S. got away with his polemical feats. Fame was his passport. He had no job to lose and he exploited the world's fame-snobbery in order to break the conventions that harnessed other people. He aired unspeakable opinions vital to a democracy. With a prophetic eye on the German Olympic Games, he pointed to competitive sport as creating 'more bad feeling, bad manners and international hatred than any other popular movement'; he criticized the exclusivity of New Zealand's immigration laws which let in only Scandinavians, British and a few other people from north-west Europe; and he described as 'non-sensical' a system of employment that encouraged overtime from some workers and left others without jobs.

Above all, he begged New Zealand to stop acting as a dairy for the rest of the world (which was learning how to milk its own cows) and, once everyone in the country had plenty of cheese, cream, and butter on their bread, for pity's sake to 'produce something else'. Foreseeing something of what would happen with the European Common Market, he attacked the illusions of imperial-patriotic 'En-Zeds' who called England 'Home' and relied on this special relationship for trade protection to the end of the century:

'Keep your wool on your own backs; harness your own water power; get your fertilising nitrates from your own air; develop your own manufacturers and eat your own food; and you can snap your fingers at Britain's follies.'

Shaw's watchword to New Zealand was self-sufficiency. Happy the country that would not be dependent on trade in the years to come, for she would not be dominated by interfering foreign capitalists. He predicted the utilization of thermal power from the subterranean forces of New Zealand's geysers; he recommended the creation of a New Zealand film industry 'or you will lose your souls without even getting American ones'; and, after a reminder that 'all tourists are not exemplary characters like myself', he warned people against too much reliance on tourist traffic: 'If New Zealand wants to develop a big tourist industry it means that New Zealanders are to become hotel-keepers, waiters, cooks . . . the attractions of New Zealand are better kept for the recreation of New Zealanders themselves.'

After five exhausting days in Auckland ('bright, clean, sunny and happy; all gay bungalows with brilliant little gardens – a garden city') Shaw and Charlotte hired a guide, philosopher and chauffeur and sped off on a three-week motor tour of the North and South Islands. 'We are going to spend nearly our whole time in the country,' Charlotte wrote to Nancy Astor. 'First a week at Rotorua, where are the geysers . . . ' Charlotte was fearful that 'G.B.S. will get the bit in his teeth and drag me about travelling'. By travelling she meant walking. Herself, she 'never walks a yard when there is a vehicle – even a wheelbarrow – to be had for love or money', G.B.S. had told Lady Gregory. Himself, he loved walking and, according to their breathless Maori guide at Rotorua, was the fastest walker in the Antipodes. Charlotte however could usually catch up by car, and together they stared into streams and lakes at thousands of small fishes 'so clear that their whole life has to be lived exposed to view'. They examined strange thermal peaks, craters, and sulphurous steam holes reeking of brimstone like Hades – 'pure and boiling & bubbling & making the most absurd faces at one' – over which Charlotte could not help laughing ('but it is malevolent too') and which Shaw complimented as being the most damnable spot he had ever visited, adding admiringly that he would have willingly paid £10 not to have seen it. They floated through the wonderful glow-worm cave at Waitomo, a firmament of blue shimmering lights that, since noise would extinguish them, completely silenced G.B.S. They motored beside the sub-tropical vegetation of the bush, climbed high up to the national park at Chateau Tongariro, and saw the sacred mountains covered in snow. 'All goes excellently well with us,' Charlotte reported. At a civic reception in Christchurch towards the end of their tour, Shaw told everyone: 'I will make the admission that New Zealand is rather a desirable place to live in.'

Wherever he went he had to combat a tendency to assume that he had come to New Zealand to study the Maoris. Travelling as a political medicine man, he could see nothing wrong with the Maoris – except that, knowing how to live in harmony with their surroundings, they were probably better off, he thought, before the Europeans arrived. It was a pity that everyone had to study a pedantic treaty in differing versions from the last century to find out how to behave to one another rather than consult their own best instincts. 'I have never seen a Maori unhappy,' he told a journalist from the *Dominion*, 'in spite of our endeavours to make them religiously miserable.' He listened to Maori workmen singing and went to hear some formal Maori music. It 'is what we call Gregorian chanting', he wrote. 'It is not primitive: it is rather music refined upon to the verge of effeteness, like Highland pibroch or the ornamentation in the Book of Kells . . . the Maoris now care for nothing musical but the sentimental German waltz tunes of the early nineteenth century, and the best rhythmical jazz.'

They ended their tour in Wellington and, shortly before leaving, called on 'the greatest man in New Zealand . . . a strange old genius, Sir Truby King' who had founded the Royal New Zealand Society for the health of women and children and brought down the infant mortality rate to '*less than half* the English rate'. At the Truby King Karitane Hospital, G.B.S. spoke with the matron, mothers and nurses but unlike a politician, reporters observed, took little notice of the babies all out in front of the nursery doors in the sun. Afterwards he was driven round to meet Sir Truby King who received him 'on a couch in his living-room, where the windows were all open and the sun pouring in'. This pre-Spock revolutionary of infant care appealed to many facets of G.B.S. The socialist warmly approved the New Zealand system of free clinics for mothers; the adolescent who had been so impressed by Vandeleur Lee could recognize in Truby King's insistence on the health-giving properties of 'fresh air, light, warmth, proper food' eccentricity vindicated and made common-sense; and the boy who had suffered from the neglect of his mother and later transferred his loyalty to the adopted mother country responded sympathetically to a reformer who placed more importance on nurse-educators than on motherly instinct ('We must remember that in the rearing of children ignorance tempered by kindness is not sufficient').

Bouquets of flowers were passed through their portholes as the *Rangitane* cast off from Wellington on 14 April, and Shaw and Charlotte carried with them tikis, bars of greenstone, ear pieces and a copy of John Lee's remarkable *Children of the Poor*. Legendary stories were already floating in their wake: how G.B.S. had borrowed a lady's scarlet bathing-suit and plunged into the breakers at Mount Maunganui; how at Auckland he had presented Adolf Hitler's *My Struggle*, together with twenty-two other books he had read on the voyage out, to the Turnbull Library which he described as a 'treasure house' that 'would even make the Bodleian sit up'. It had been a carefree month – even the journalists were amiable. Though some editorials commented critically on his political speeches, the newspapers generally presented this 'old elf in the zip-fastened jersey' as a brilliant social diagnostician, gifted educator and advocate of national welfare. 'I seem to be the most popular stranger to visit the Southern Hemisphere,' he remarked. 'I had no idea that New Zealanders were such good Shavians.'

He had sensed that the country was on the verge of a political shift to socialism. It was like looking at 'a growing child', he said, and wondering what it was 'going to look like in years to come'. On his arrival at Auckland he had announced that 'I have been in Russia. It is a very remarkable place. I want to see if New Zealand is any better.' In one respect he did find it better. 'Changes which have been made peacefully and reasonably in New Zealand have been made violently and even ferociously in other parts of the Empire.' One observer in Wellington noticed that 'Mrs Shaw, quietly knitting in the far corner of their Midland hotel sitting-room, stirred uneasily' as she heard her husband embark on a long eulogium of the Soviet system and that she 'ordered a mug of cocoa' to comfort herself. But as Charlotte later told a journalist: 'I only appear conventional on the surface ... underneath I am the most unconventional of persons.'

'When you see the name "NEW ZEALAND" what does it suggest? What vision rises at its name?' an interviewer had asked Shaw at the end of the 1920s. 'It suggests New Zealand,' he answered. But after crossing the world to what Mark Twain had called 'Junior England', he experienced something of what Trollope had found the previous century – 'You are, as it were, next door to your own house.' So New Zealand came to suggest an idealized Ireland. 'If I were beginning life, I am not sure that I would not start in New Zealand,' he said. '. . . I, being an old Victorian, am much more at home here than in London. You are quite natural to me . . .' Such tributes suggest a mirage reflecting what his life might have been like in another Ireland without a tearful childhood and the divisive violence of Irish politics. 'If I showed my true feelings I would cry,' he told a photographer on board the *Rangitane* who had asked him to give his brightest smile on leaving New Zealand: 'it's the best country I've been in.'

[4]

I feel apologetic for my existence now that all decent men of my age are
committing suicide . . . But I can still write to some purpose,
and so must brazen it out until some assassin saves me the trouble of
shooting myself. (1932)

'All modern and revolutionary movements are at bottom attacks on private property,' Shaw wrote in the Preface to his play *On the Rocks*. The prefaces he wrote in these years of travel are his missionary tracts and have their origins in the private property of Synge Street and Hatch Street and in the uncontrollable break-up of that private world. But now he has put himself in charge of its final destruction.

It is a loveless territory these writings of the early 1930s illuminate, the inhabitants 'so demoralized by the notion that they would be happy if only they were rich, that they make themselves poorer'. His prefaces to *On the Rocks* and *Too True to be Good*, the 'Preface on Bosses' and the 'Preface on Days of Judgment' that precede *The Millionairess* and *The Simpleton of the Unexpected Isles* parade the history of the knout, the cat, the axe, the stake, the wheel, the guillotine, garotte, electric chair, the disembowellings, floggings, burnings, hangings, lynchings, batterings to death – all the barbarities that, disguised under religious aliases, infest our landscape. He writes as one maddened by the organization of all this savagery round the world into popular spectacles: 'Cruelty is so infectious that the very compassion it rouses is infuriated to take revenge by still viler cruelties.' His own revenge is insistently presented as compassionate. It was not true that it took all sorts to make a world, 'for there are some sorts that would destroy

320

any world very soon if they were suffered to live and have their way'. Therefore, he asks: 'Is there really nothing to be done with such men but submit to them until, having risen by their specialities, they ruin themselves by their vulgarities?' In practice there was nothing more he could do. But on the page he recommends treating these people 'as we treat mad dogs or adders'. There was obviously nothing foreign to human nature in this proposal: he is seeking merely to upgrade the joyous habit of extermination to 'a humane science'. And who can say that those granted premature retirement from the appalling misery of life would not be better off? 'People with any tenderness of conscience will feel the deepest misgivings as to whether they are really worth keeping alive in a highly civilized community.'

The problem of who should earn promotion into oblivion leads Shaw to a treatise on dictatorship. Dictators were thriving in the 1930s, he believed, because parliaments had removed themselves from the needs and feelings of the people. The capitalistic system, with 'its golden exceptions of idle richery and its leaden rule of anxious poverty', was a desperate failure. Any society that maintained a belief in the harmony between self-regarding activities and the collective interest benefited exploiters, encouraged the fabricators of falsehoods, and impelled even the honest ruler to become a tyrant. To minimize the dangers of despotism Shaw called for a new social creed and legal code, an economic Reformation in which the nobler coinage would drive out the baser currency. He wanted to take his readers to the bar for an investigation of our social values, draw up a set of conditions fundamental to human society and commission a new work of social philosophy to bring Mill's essay *On Liberty* into the twentieth century. 'We all live in glass houses ... Is it wise to throw stones at all?'

Shaw had put his heart into politics. His hope of a Reformation, 'now long and perilously overdue', to ease the pain of a cruelly mismanaged world was aptly directed to the phenomenon of dictatorship in a decade of what he calls 'glaring contemporary examples'. But he has grown obsessed with dictators and by death. The peculiar tension of these prefaces arises from this relish and his recoil from it. He cannot resolve the contention. Dividing himself into two voices, the old Shaw insists on the political necessity of killing people who are in his view already pretty well dying from underwork and too much luxury; while the young Shaw raises the banner of tolerance and argues that there may be good biological reasons for the workshy. The old Shaw declares that no hostile critic of the existing social order should behave as if he were living in his own particular utopia: 'Not until the criticism changes the law can the magistrate allow the critic to give effect to it.' The young Shaw answers that 'civilization cannot progress without criticism, and must therefore, to save itself from stagnation and putrefaction, declare impunity for criticism'. The old Shaw writes that 'the community must drive a much harder bargain for the privilege of citizenship than it now does'. The young Shaw reminds us of Morris's saying that 'no man is good enough to be another man's master' and warns us that most 'autocrats go more or less mad'. The old Shaw points to 'the final reality of inequality'; the young Shaw insists that 'rulers must be as poor as the ruled so that they can raise themselves only by raising their people'.

So irreconcilable are Shaw's two voices that in his Preface to *On the Rocks* he separates them in a dialogue between Pontius Pilate and Jesus. This experiment of a play-within-a-preface underscores the imaginative voice of the young Shaw which sounds clearer in the plays. The prefaces, which were published in omnibus editions in the 1930s, tend to be increasingly dominated by the will of the old Shaw.

'Terror drives men mad: hope and faith give them divine wisdom,' Shaw has Jesus tell Pontius Pilate. Driven sometimes to feelings of madness himself, Shaw was aware that he might do ordinary people 'the mischief against which Jesus vainly warned our missionaries'. But once he had 'satisfied himself that he was justified', Jesus admitted that his word would bring not peace but the sword. Despite Soviet 'sideslips', Shaw too felt satisfied over his justification of communism based on 'the hierarchy of the Catholic Church'. Whenever in ill thoughts, he would tell himself to buck up and preach the Revolution. This was the Shavian 'Vril' – a nectar that gave him visions of the coming race among whom his two voices could be sublimely joined. He saw communism as the political manifestation of a Christianity that for almost 2,000 years had remained 'paradoxical and impracticable' to 'all Governments'. In the 'deluded' nineteenth century, he could remember the 'dream' of democracy appearing as a political ascent into Christian ethics. 'That was the golden age of democracy; the phantom was a real and beneficent force,' he wrote. 'Many delusions are.' Communism might prove a phantom of the twentieth century, but Shaw's hope and faith lay in its beneficent force.

*

Nowhere is this hope and faith more visible than in the publication of *The Adventures of the Black Girl in Her Search for God*. 'I don't know what I shall do with this Black Girl story,' he had written to his Edinburgh printers. But when William Maxwell suggested that, with the addition of some good illustrations, it might make an attractive little book, Shaw began to see possibilities. 'I want something as simple and serious as Holbein's Bible pictures but with modern beauty,' he wrote to Trebitsch who had proposed the 'hideously clever work' of Georg Grosz. '...I want a *religious* artist, not an anti-clerical satirist.' After seeing a trial drawing, he picked a then unknown draughtsman and wood-engraver in his early thirties called John Farleigh who had been recommended by Maxwell. 'The idea is that you and I and Maxwell should co-operate in turning out a good-looking little volume,' Shaw wrote to Farleigh. He wanted pictures designed as part of the book, not 'illustrations' stuck into it. His explanations were so clear, his primitive drawings so observant and the tale itself so filled with word-pictures that 'I discovered I was learning the business of illustration from the best master possible,' Farleigh later acknowledged. Shaw was perpetually encouraging. 'I think you can make a real job of it,' he wrote, '. . . let yourself rip.'

He was seeking to do something new in publishing that anticipated the Penguin paperback revolution of the later 1930s and carried the Shavian gospel to a wider book-buying public. 'The disease of high prices is curing itself,' he prophesied in a letter to Michael Sadleir at Constable. 'We must all turn honest, however ruefully.' As he had reacted against the ever-increasing cost of West End theatre, so he wanted to experiment with lower book prices, making a feature of the volume's slenderness. 'Half a crown is the extreme limit,' he wrote explaining his tactics to Otto Kyllmann.

'I should much prefer sixpence or at least a shilling; but I think that the book may tempt the people I want to get at to indulge in the extravagance (for them) of two and six . . . I am utterly sick of the futile handful of plutocrats to whom five shillings is nothing.'

By lowering the price, concealing his 'preface' at the end of the story, choosing an alluring title, then publishing the book on 5 December 1932 got up to look like a Christmas card embellished with twenty sensuous wood-cuts that made 'the story clear to the blankest intelligence', Shaw was scheming to enter thousands of Christian homes with a fable that chal-lenged the Church's assumptions and exposed the contemporary state of religion. Describing G.B.S. as a wonderful 'weedkiller' and his *Black Girl* as an 'illustrated tract for the times', Beatrice Webb judged it to be a courageous indictment of a creed 'which is no longer practised or believed in by the majority of the citizens, rich or poor, enlightened or ignorant'.

'I should like to sell 250,000 in the first five minutes of publication,' Shaw had told Kyllmann. In its black paper boards with illustrations in white, 'Shaw's Strange Book About God' darkened the windows of bookshops and swept through the Christmas trade like the Black Girl through the jungle. A first printing of 25,000 copies was followed by five additional impressions before the end of the year, and in a letter to one of his translators the following summer Shaw reported sales as being 'roughly 100,000' – in addition to more than 50,000 copies brought out early in 1933 by his new American publisher, 'an old firm of unchallenged piety and respectability', Dodd, Mead & Company.

'If it were not for the author's prestige,' Beatrice Webb wrote in her diary, 'it would be considered blasphemous by all churchmen, conventional or genuine.' Shaw wanted it to be considered blasphemous. 'Tell the Vatican that something must be done about the Bible,' he wrote to G. K. Chesterton when sending him an early copy. 'It is like the burden on Christian's back at present; only it won't come off.'

Reviewers were divided, calling it an innocent *jeu d'esprit*, an old-fashioned parable, or a modernist Christian exegesis. But some ordinary readers (such as the old lady who publicly burnt it and the enraged beekeeper who wanted Shaw stripped of his life-membership of the Wexford Bee-Keepers Association) were quicker to see the danger of this 'deadly dart – disguised as a fascinating Xmas card'. 'I am still a highly esteemed member of the W.B.A.,' Shaw rallied his Polish translator. But six months after publication, the Irish government banned all sales of the *Black Girl*, alleging its 'general tendency' to be 'indecent and obscene'. Shaw was curious to know whether the ban would be lifted if he issued a special Irish edition with the women draped in long skirts. 'The reverend censors are not nudists, and probably regard a nude negress as the last extremity of obscenity,' he wrote to W. B. Yeats who was marshalling the Irish Academy of Letters to challenge this censorship. Fifteen years later, in January 1948, the Censorship of Publication Appeal Board finally revoked this order on the *Black Girl* together with those on Hemingway's *For Whom the Bell Tolls* (1941) and Arthur Koestler's *Arrival and Departure* (1944).

'I shall not protest,' Shaw had written to Yeats, 'if the Churchmen think my book subversive they are quite right from their point of view.' But he was 'ridiculously surprised' by the violent hostility of Laurentia McLachlan. 'The story is absolutely blasphemous, as it goes beyond all the Churches and all the gods,' he had written to her when sending his early typescript to the printer. 'I forgot all about you, or I should never have dared . . .'

'The truth is, dear Sister Laurentia, I have finished with all these deities, who seem to me more or less grotesque signboards announcing that the Holy Ghost is lodged within . . . Perhaps I should not disturb the peace of Stanbrook with my turbulent spirit . . . Shall I send you the story or not? It is very irreverent and iconoclastic but I dont think *you* will think it fundamentally irreligious.'

Dame Laurentia, recently elected Abbess of Stanbrook, 'demanded to see the book'. Shaw sent her a proof inscribed on the flyleaf: 'An Inspiration which came in response to the prayers of the nuns at Stanbrook Abbey and in particular to the prayers of his dear Sister Laurentia for Bernard Shaw.' She had not finished reading the proof when she received a tiny playlet from him set in 'God's office in heaven' where God and the Archangel Gabriel are discussing the impasse between Dame Laurentia and G.B.S. Though the interrupted dialogue reflects Shaw's initial uncertainty as to how he should proceed ('it will come out in the Standard Edition Short Story volume sooner or later' he had told his printers) it is God who represents Shaw's view ('I gave him a first class job in his own line') and merely the Archangel ('You'd better let her have her way') who speaks for the Abbess. Nevertheless Dame Laurentia took this to mean that Shaw was withdrawing the book. 'You have made me happy again by your nice little play and I thank you from my heart for listening to me,' she wrote ominously. 'I have read most of the book and I agree with many of your ideas, but if you had published it I could never have forgiven you . . .'

Nine days after its publication, and just as he was setting out on his world cruise, Shaw sent her a copy. 'This black girl has broken out in spite of everything,' he wrote in it. 'I was afraid to present myself at Stanbrook in September. Forgive me.'

It was as if he had thrown a bomb. 'The effect of the book on Dame Laurentia is difficult to describe,' records Dame Felicitas Corrigan. 'To the end of her life she could hardly bring herself to mention it.' As a natural authoritarian ('faithful servants are the worst of tyrants', Shaw has God tell the Archangel Gabriel), Dame Laurentia was used to deference from her famous admirers. Indignation welled up in her at Shaw's incredible stubbornness. At the same time she felt humiliated. She had prayed that God might use her for the salvation of his soul, and now had to bear witness to a revolting profanity. Even her beloved crucifix had been twisted into the symbol of a neurosis. It grieved her too that someone she regarded as a dear friend had broken trust and fractured their 'brother-and-sister relationship'.

Deeply displeased, she wrote to upbraid him. Her letter reached Shaw in Bangkok. He tried several times to reply from aboard the *Empress of Britain* but, fearing that his letters might wound her further, tore them up. 'I innocently took [it] to be a valuable contribution to the purification of religion from horrible old Jewish superstitions; and even my callousness was pierced by finding that it had shocked and distressed you,' he pleaded on 29 June 1933 after returning to Whitehall Court. '. . . I am afraid of upsetting your faith, which is still entangled in those old stories.'

This was additionally insulting to the Abbess. It was not her faith but her susceptibilities Shaw had upset. He had preferred his own wrong-headedness to the divinity of Christ; he had tried to analyse an experience that surpassed human understanding and reduced God to abstraction. 'The only way to comfort me would be for you to withdraw the Black Girl from circulation,' she answered, 'and make a public act of reparation for the dishonour it does to Almighty God.'

This was obviously impossible. Shaw had hoped she might readmit him to her grace, but her mind was not 'unenclosed' after all. She was another of those worthy people who had no intimation of Christianity as a revolutionary political idea. He wished to conciliate her, but could not falsify his own hope and faith. 'Laurentia: has it never occurred to you that I might possibly have a more exalted notion of divinity,' he appealed. Then he went on to counterattack.

'. . . You think you are a better Catholic than I; but my view of the Bible is the view of the Fathers of the Church; and yours is that of a Belfast Protestant to whom the Bible is a fetish and religion entirely irrational. You think you believe that God did not know what he was about when he made me and inspired me to write The Black Girl . . . I leave you to settle it with God and his Son as best you can; but you must go on praying for me, however surprising the results may be.'

She did not answer. What was the point? Their opinions were not negotiable. After more than nine years their friendship was at an end, and when Shaw went to the Malvern Festival in the summers of 1933 and 1934, he did not visit her. 'I never passed through Stanbrook without a really heartfelt pang because I might not call and see her as of old,' he later confessed. Then, in the autumn of 1934, after returning from Malvern via Ayot to Whitehall Court, he found, among the correspondence waiting for him, a card.

IN MEMORY OF SEPT 6
1884–1934
DAME LAURENTIA MCLACHLAN
ABBESS OF STANBROOK

He wrote at once to 'the Ladies of Stanbrook Abbey' telling them that he had had no knowledge of Dame Laurentia's state of health 'and no suspicion that I should never see her again in this world'. He had not dared to show his face at the Abbey, he explained, until she had forgiven him for his little book.

'She has, I am sure, forgiven me now; but I wish she could tell me so. In the outside world from which you have escaped it is necessary to shock people violently to make them think seriously about religion; and my ways were too rough.'

This letter of condolence was answered by Dame Laurentia herself. 'My dear Brother Bernard, As you see, I am not dead,' she wrote. The card had been a souvenir of her Golden Jubilee. She did not tell him that she had been advised to send it by her archbishop. 'When next you are in the neighbourhood you must come and see me again ... You have my daily prayers. I hope they will have nothing but good results in future.'

It was a miracle, a friendship resurrected. Shaw's 'superhowler' had made it supernatural. 'Laurentia! Alive!!' he exclaimed. '...I thought you were in heaven, happy and blessed. And you were only laughing at me. It is your revenge for that Black Girl.' They were back on terms of equal superiority. What is implicit in his letter to her is made explicit in a letter he sent Sydney Cockerell ten days later. 'But I felt as if a soul had been dragged back from felicity,' he wrote. 'Which is queer, as of course I dont believe anything of the sort.'

It was more a matter of feeling than belief. 'I am not sufficiently fond of myself to wish for immortality,' he had told Virginia Woolf and Maynard Keynes. 'I should like to be different.' Being himself, he would have liked, he sometimes felt, to be dead. There had been a number of exemplary deaths recently. 'Cockerell's friend Sir Emery Walker made a good end on Saturday – was apparently mending comfortably when he just gave a couple of gulps and died,' he had written to Dame Laurentia in the summer of 1933. '...Walker was a most amiable man; but he had lived his life; and it was time for him to die. And for me also...'

This sense of having missed his exit cue gained on him whenever another of his near-contemporaries died. At least four times by the 1930s he positively made his Last Will and Testament, and still he lived on. 'It seems the most ridiculous thing in the world that I, 18 years older than Gilbert, should be heartlessly surviving him,' he was to write to G. K. Chesterton's widow. '...The trumpets are sounding for him.'

No trumpets had sounded for Shaw's fellow playwright Pinero whose death on 23 November 1934 'passed almost unnoticed'. Few people noticed either when the following day, in the middle of a telephone conversation, Shaw himself suddenly dropped down dead...

CHAPTER V

[I]

Didnt you know that English politics wont bear thinking about?
On the Rocks

It had always been a relief to get back to Ayot. The staff there were fiercely loyal. According to Mrs Bilton, the Norwegian housekeeper, Mr Shaw was a 'Christ-like man'; and, as Henry and Clara Higgs were to testify, he had never spoken a cross word to them in forty years. No one was afraid of him. The new young Irish parlourmaid, Margaret Cashin, soon learnt that 'Mr Shaw did many unknown kindnesses ... He had no violent dislikes for anybody.' She often came upon him slipping money into envelopes and he always paid for her trips back to Ireland. He was a thorough gentleman. When she married he lent her the Rolls-Royce. 'It was grand.'

Out-of-doors he still looked spry and active. Chopping wood, making bonfires, sawing logs, collecting acorns, eyeing the strawberries while patrolling up and down with his notebook, camera, and special secateurs, he appeared to one neighbour 'like a magic gardener in a fairy story'. He would write in the garden too, stepping out from a veranda at the back of the house ('my Riviera') and hurrying past the flowers and trees to a small revolving hut, like a monk's cell, with its desk and chair and bunk. Here, in what some visitors mistook for a toolshed, he was conveniently out of the staff's way and the world's reach.

As for Mrs Shaw, she was 'one of the best', the assistant gardener Fred Drury reckoned. 'Mrs Shaw *made* Mr Shaw. She used to help him a lot with his work.' The two gardeners often speculated over what was going on between Mr and Mrs Shaw as they circumnavigated the lawn together. 'They had a special route round the garden which was just about a mile, and they put one stone down every time they passed,' Fred Drury observed. Henry Higgs noticed these stones too, and how they 'used to take them off the window sill on the way back, one by one'. In this way several balanced miles would be measured out.

Such symmetry was particularly characteristic of Mr Shaw. Indoors he was a very tidy man. 'He always put chairs back in place, and his pyjamas on his bed in his room, neatly folded,' Margaret Cashin noted. '...[He] was very particular about his erectness and appearance – proud of his person and figure ... He always changed for the evening meal regardless of whether anyone was coming to see him or not.' Sometimes there were famous guests: heavyweight boxers, film actresses, war-heroes, prime ministers – those sorts of person. But that didn't bother the staff who saw one of their prime jobs as protecting Mr Shaw from the outside world: by which they meant the villagers.

This became easier when, after his eightieth birthday, he more or less gave up driving. In recent years he had grown more reckless and Fred Day, his chauffeur, was often obliged to pull the wheel out of his hand or cry out 'Brake, sir!' and 'Stop! That will do sir'. It was an anxious time. 'I was fully occupied trying to keep him out of trouble,' Day admitted. In other ways he was no trouble. 'I don't know why on earth they let me have a driving licence at my age. I'm not safe,' he complained one day after plunging into some hot water pipes at a garage. 'Besides, I think too much of you, Day, to risk your life by taking the wheel – you're a married man with children.'

As a pedestrian he went on into his mid-eighties disappearing downhill and updale for walks of up to six miles. He was supremely noticeable as he sailed by in his knee breeches, brown shoes, wide-brimmed hat and cape or Norfolk jacket. For wood-chopping, to the delight of local children, he sometimes appeared helmeted. In the street, clipping the hedge, he could be spotted wearing a battered panama hat, a darned tussore suit, white shirt and a collar and tie in conflicting shades of beige. A bright macintosh sometimes illuminated him at night.

He had some funny ideas too. When invited to present a prize at the village school for the best-conducted boy or girl, he suggested starting a rival prize for the worst-conducted boy or girl, 'and we will watch their careers and then find out which really turns out best'. After returning from South Africa, he came up with a notion that all the villagers should dance to the hymns in Church 'as the black people do' and add to their repertoire 'O, You Must be a Lover of the Lord' and other African songs: he actually gave a demonstration of them in the street. Then there was his 'Plan for Ayot'. This featured a 'glorious' eighty-foot colonnaded water tower to be erected in the Church meadow and to stand as an ornament to the village. 'I believe it was meant to be funny,' grumbled Mrs Harding, wife of the licensee of the Brocket Arms, 'and we were all very serious.'

But there was little doubt that he was serious about the rubbish dump a mile or so south of his house where the Wheathampstead refuse was deposited from the early 1920s. His campaign to reclaim this acreage, which vented its poisonous gases at full blast through a layer of old trays, perambulators, bicycle wheels, umbrella frames and hovering flies, was sustained over ten years. In 1931 he informed the District Council that he had recently been cruising in the Mediterranean 'where I was very strongly reminded of the dump by the fumes of the island volcano of Stromboli, which is believed by the islanders to communicate directly with hell, and to be, in fact, one of the chimneys of that establishment. I was able to assure them that this could not be the case, as our Wheathampstead volcano, which has no crater, is a much greater nuisance.' Eventually, in 1932, changes were made and four years later Shaw received a single enormous green apple that had grown from a tree on the site. 'I swallowed some of it before I was told what it was,' he wrote. 'I shall never be the same man again; but Mrs Shaw rather liked it.'

This was the bitter taste of success – success delayed too long. Would it have tasted sweeter, could he have achieved more, had he been capable of campaigning differently? The trouble was he seemed so strange to ordinary people. He had 'a funny way of expressing himself', a fellow villager objected after hearing him lecture for the local Women's Institute on 'How to Quarrel Properly'. It didn't sound like proper quarrelling at all. He was so unpredictable too. It was disconcerting for the chemist to be invited to 'try out' some of his bottles of medicines on himself first so that his customers could witness how they worked; or for other villagers when greeting him in the street with a 'How are you?' to be answered: 'At my age, Sir, you are either well or dead.' You never knew where you were with such a person.

He had been living at Ayot now some thirty years. He was invariably courteous, but 'remote as a god'. And, like a god, he seemed made of mystifying contradictions. Why would someone rumoured to be an atheist contribute so generously to the cost of repairing the roof of the Parish Church, pay for the renovation of the organ, and keep up what he called his 'pew-rent' to the Church's funds? And why would someone who attacked standard education for children arrange at his own expense to put Vitaglass into the school's windows? Finally, why did he keep so quiet about these things when he was well-known to be a colossal publicity seeker?

There were various answers. According to the apiarist, a diffident man who came to give a hand with the bees, he seemed 'nervous and shy if anything'. To a local joker he appeared 'the greatest leg-puller the world has ever known'. And it was obvious to the Conservative Party Agent that he was no more a socialist than the man in the moon. 'Politics was not in his line,' the barber who cut his hair found out.

But on one point there was general agreement: he had natural good manners. He 'made you feel you were his equal', said the organist; he was 'prepared to engage in conversation on my level', said the oculist; 'he always put you completely at your ease', said the landowner. But few of them would really claim to know him. 'If you ignored Mr Shaw he took more notice of you than if you didn't,' recalled Mrs Harding. And Mr Williams observed that 'he seemed on guard. He wouldn't, or couldn't, let himself go.' He was easier with children and animals. 'He always stopped and spoke to my little dog, Judy,' said Mrs Hinton to whom he did not speak much. 'He always talked to my children as an equal,' said another villager, 'so they liked him and looked upon him as a favourite uncle.' Each year he sent the headmistress of the school a cheque to be spent on sweets. She would pass the money over to the village shop and the children were allowed to get their sweets, without paying, to a maximum of one shilling each.

'He never talked about his plays or anything like that,' one villager gratefully remembered. This was a mercy because, though they all accepted him as a great playwright, practically no one had actually seen his plays. It was a wonder he continued writing them. 'I shall have to stop sometime or other,' he told his chauffeur. At the rate he was going he would soon ruin what reputation he had left. But he gave no sign of stopping. He was up and ready for work before eight o'clock each morning, but latterly took a couple of hours over lunch, during which he might tune into the wireless and go through his correspondence. There followed a siesta which began with a book and ended, rather guiltily, with a nap. Then more work and, in the evenings, he would listen to the wireless again, play the piano and sing to Mrs Shaw. He was last to bed and, sometimes still singing, liked to go into the garden before, forgetting to lock up, he would wander upstairs nicely before midnight.

It must have been the love of moneymaking, people thought, that kept him working. His hairdresser did not think much of him as a dramatist; there was no response from his head gardener Henry Higgs at having had his name mismanaged in *Pygmalion*; and in the view of Jisbella Lyth, the village postmistress, some of his work 'lacked suspense'.

Mrs Lyth was a widow. She had started her career as a kennel-maid, then spent a dozen years teaching in Hong Kong, followed this up by working as a nurse in the United States and, after some adventurous travelling, returned to England where in 1931 she and her husband took over the post office at Ayot. Almost immediately Mr Lyth had died of a heart attack in the garden. When Shaw and Charlotte called on the widow, she told them her story. 'Oh! What a glorious death to die,' G.B.S. vicariously complimented her. 'I hope I die like that in my garden underneath the stars.' 'Yes sir,' Mrs Lyth replied, 'but not at fifty-four, surely.' On leaving Shaw said: 'I hope we shall have you here in Ayot for many years.'

And they did. 'Mr Shaw wrote personally to me for every batch of stamps he needed,' Mrs Lyth recorded over twenty years later. 'He wrote every request in his own hand ...'

331

'Some would say, I suppose, that it was eccentric of him to order all his stamps from me by letter, but I prefer to regard it as simple kindness, I've sold almost all those letters . . . I believe he meant them to be a sort of legacy to me.'

Shaw let his imagination play on this relationship. During January 1933, while steaming along between the Red Sea and the Indian Ocean, he wrote the first draft of an 'Unladylike Comedietta for Two Voices in Three Conversations' which he initially called *The Red Sea*. He had developed a habit of labelling his characters with sequences of letters, from *A* onwards for the males, and *Z* backwards for the females. He needed only two letters, *A* and *Z*, for this short play and when he completed the last draft that summer, changing its title to *Village Wooing*, he kept these letters in place of names.

'I do not see myself as the Man,' he told Lillah McCarthy: 'he is intended as a posthumous portrait of Lytton Strachey.' But *Village Wooing* is not a sophisticated Bloomsbury *pas de deux*. *A* represents the side of Shaw that most closely approximated to Strachey – a man of letters as opposed to a political writer. Consequently the play held little interest for Shaw's political friends: 'clever and amusing', Beatrice Webb noted, 'but nothing in it'. As for *Z*, she is not Charlotte but an approximation of Jisbella Lyth. Many's the time he's helped me with my crossword puzzles,' she said. Shaw's alphabetical characters may derive in part from the lettering of these puzzles, but the effect is to give general application to their ordinariness. They are any one and every one of us. 'Part of him was quite ordinary,' a local journalist at Ayot said of Shaw, 'and wanted to behave and be treated as an ordinary person.'

In the First Conversation on board the pleasure ship *Empress of Patagonia*, 'a literary looking pale gentleman under forty in green spectacles, a limp black beard, and a tropical suit of white silk' is crustily anxious not to be disturbed by *Z*, 'a young woman, presentable but not aristocratic, who is bored with her book'. *A* is an isolated intellectual obliged for financial reasons to write the popular 'Marco Polo' series of guidebooks; *Z*, who insists on interrupting his work with her life story, is the daughter of a 'man of letters' – a postman – who is using the money she has won in a newspaper competition to see the world. The Second Conversation takes place in a village shop and post office on the Wiltshire Downs where *Z* is putting through telephone messages. *A* enters as a customer on a hiking holiday, but does not recognize *Z*. She describes their cruise as having destroyed her romantic illusions of the world (partly created by *A*'s books). 'Give me this village,' she says. But in half an hour it is *A* who has surprisingly been persuaded to give up the occupation of literary gentleman and buy the village shop. In the Third Conversation *A* has been the shop's proprietor for three months and learnt more, he realizes, than he had over three years at Oxford. *Z*, who is working as his assistant, replies that he still has more to learn since the shop does not earn enough to keep three. The play ends with the Rector's wife, telephoning for vegetables, being asked by *Z* to fetch the Rector as she wants to put up the marriage banns.

Village Wooing is a celebration of change. The first conversation is ostensibly between an intellectual and an idiot (who, we later learn, has made a bet that she can get him into conversation); the second is between a gentleman and a villager; and the third between an employer and employee. In all three scenes Shaw is demonstrating the need to break down these academic, class and economic barriers to change.

He is also speculating on change within himself. What might have happened had he been unable to protect himself so unerringly and if he had married, worked and lived differently: in short, if 'some habits [that] lie too deep to be changed' could be changed after all and, unlike Professor Higgins, he was able to 'change my nature'?

This Shavian romance shadows the more commonplace romantic story and gives charm to this rare piece of chamber music. At the climax, *A*'s outpouring on the magical relation of the sexes, which is his proposal of marriage to *Z*, was described by the actress Siobhan McKenna as 'intensely poetic and moving'. Yet it is an overwritten speech and most moving when played as pathos – as the overreaching of a 'Complete Outsider' trying to feel at home with ordinary living people.

*

Village Wooing encapsulates many Shavian themes and obsessions from phonetics to the Life Force, and forms a miniature pendant to *Man and Superman* and *Pygmalion*. The other play he composed at this time and called *On the Rocks* is a political fable 'rather in *The Apple Cart* line, but contemporary', Shaw notified Blanche Patch; but it is also, as the critic Frederick P. W. McDowell noted, 'a coda to *Heartbreak House*'. The ship of state was adrift and heading 'on the rocks' in *Heartbreak House*, and only an ingenious King among captains enabled her to drift clear in *The Apple Cart*. But the violence with which *On the Rocks* opens and closes – defiant crowds of unemployed confronted by armed police – is the sound of this ship of fools finally breaking up.

The time is 'The Present' – still the Depression. Shaw takes us to the centre of the political madhouse, the Cabinet Room at 10 Downing Street, and keeps us there throughout the two long acts of his play. The powerhouse is full of hot air producing a merry-go-round of lies and illusions. 'This is not the time to talk about economic difficulties,' says the genial Prime Minister, Sir Arthur Chavender, 'we're up to the neck in them.' He has a 'hopelessly parliamentary mind', in the opinion of his wife, and lives 'in fairyland'. Governing 'within democratic limits' he presides over a dictatorship of democracy. 'I cannot go faster than our voters will let me,' he explains. The result is that the 'country isn't governed' his wife points out: 'it just slummocks along anyhow.'

Sir Arthur Chavender is an addict and a trafficker in the drug of oratory, an empty cavernous man who echoes Shaw's idea of what parliamentary life had done to Ramsay MacDonald and what, he feared, had happened to himself. 'I make speeches,' he says: 'that is the business of a politician.' In the Shavian analysis, orators had once been powerful because, in their inspired utterances, they caught the spirit of the times. But the introduction of adult suffrage revealed the frivolity of public opinion and turned these men and women of words either into the exploiters of people's fears and prejudices or into entertainers trained to meet every crisis with a diversion.

Sir Arthur is responding to the unemployment crisis by preparing a soothing oration about the sanctity of family life. Shaw accompanies the rhetorical composition of this speech with interruptions from the Prime Minister's own family whose uncontrollable bickering (like the uncaring sounds from Sonny's Dublin home) gives the lie to every melodious phrase. 'Treat the House to a brief description of this family,' says his son David, 'and you will get the laugh of your life.' Even Sir Arthur himself, underscoring this domestic analogy to the political situation, remarks to his secretary: 'Has it occurred to you, Miss Hanways, that the prospect of Socialism destroying the family may not be altogether unattractive?'

Sir Arthur is an emblem of the times. He has piloted not only England but himself on to the rocks. 'My brain is overworked: my mental grasp is stretched and strained to breaking point. I shall go mad,' he cries, before going on to explain, 'Thirty years in Parliament and ten on the Front Bench would drive any man dotty.' His wife, who sees that he will soon 'have a nervous breakdown if you go on like this', makes him promise to see a strange lady doctor who then mysteriously appears, in ghostly grey robes, near the end of the first act. This Lady Oracle, who was modelled by Shaw on the founder of Christian Science, Mary Baker Eddy, and influenced by Lady Astor, is a ghost from the future, a healer as well as a messenger of death. She half-hypnotizes Sir Arthur before giving him her diagnosis: 'You are dying of an acute want of mental exercise . . . You are suffering from that very common English complaint, an underworked brain . . . a bad case of frivolity, possibly incurable.'

In the unwritten interlude between the two acts, Sir Arthur passes three or four months at this lady's sanatorium in the Welsh mountains, drinking nothing but barley water and reading the works of Marx, Lenin and Trotsky. 'It's amazing,' exclaims the Chief Commissioner of Police Sir Broadfoot Basham at the beginning of the second act. 'I could have sworn that if there was a safe man in England that could be trusted to talk and say nothing, to thump the table and do nothing, Arthur Chavender was that man. Whats happened to him?' What has happened is that he has passed through a form of death and been resurrected as a born-again Shavian. *On the Rocks* is Shaw's version of Malory's *Morte D'Arthur*, with Avalon (the Celtic Isle of the Blest) transposed into the Welsh sanatorium and the legendary Round Table remodelled as an imposing Cabinet table. Sir Arthur himself is a Once and Future Prime Minister and the second act his promised second coming in the hour of England's need. To lift the country off the rocks he brings with him a programme of regeneration which gathers together many of the political remedies G.B.S. had been picking up and putting out during his world travels – the nationalization of banks, transport and ground rents; the municipalization of urban land and the building trade; the extinction of rates, abolition of tariffs and the prohibition of private foreign trade in protected industries; a doubling of surtax on unearned income and a removal of death duties; compulsory civilian or military service irrespective of income; collective farming; and the use of natural resources (nitrogen from the air and power from the tides) to make Britain self-supporting and blockade-proof.

The Foreign Secretary strongly objects to this Shavian effort to 'stand the country on its head' and is confident that 'free Englishmen' will never tolerate such a monstrous 'outburst of Bolshevism'. But the Prime Minister's 'dose of boiling Socialism' contains subtle ingredients to appeal to each section of English society. The Admiral looks forward to a larger navy and the Chief Commissioner to a better-paid police force; the President of the Board of Trade likes the panic-proof national and municipal banks because they will support the small traders in his constituency; the City financier welcomes land nationalization because lower land prices will lead to lower wages and arrest the exploitation of the entrepreneur by the predatory landed class; and the property baron sees the removal of death duties as saving his class from extinction in three generations.

Since everyone approves the items which favour his own interests and regards all other items as fictional caprices that will never be implemented, there seems to be some chance that the National Government will be able to introduce this programme by means of parliamentary democracy. But the plan is shipwrecked by the coming together of two political extremes: the bedrock of the far left and the rocklike uncompromising right.

The extreme left is represented by some members of a Labour deputation from the Isle of Cats which arrived in the first act to protest against the unemployment crisis and which arrives in the second act to protest against the Prime Minister's solution to the unemployment crisis. 'You dont know how I feel; and you never will,' says the eloquent Alderwoman Aloysia Brollikins (an umbrella name partly covering the identity of Ellen Wilkinson, the fiery trade unionist and Member of Parliament who was to lead the Jarrow March on London, and partly recalling the voice of Annie Besant). 'We are going to save ourselves and not be saved by you and your class.' She and other far left members of the deputation object to compulsory labour, the no strike agreement and compensation for land nationalization. They are in love with the class war because they feel they are winning it and will soon be masters of the country. They look forward to oppressing the landowners who have for centuries oppressed them. 'Labor is coming to its own; and it is your turn now to get off the earth.'

'I am glad we have arrived at the same conclusion from our opposite points of view,' the explosive leader of the Conservatives, Sir Dexter Rightside, tells the leader of the Labour deputation. Sir Dexter is a 'regular old diehard' (meaning that he is pretty well incapable of going through the death-transformation of Sir Arthur) and his job is 'to prevent the world from moving'. As the archetypal Shavian idealist he heads a country that does not want change. 'The Country never has wanted change. The Country never will want change,' he tells the Prime Minister. '...I will resist change while I have breath in my body.'

The symmetry of *On the Rocks* comes from the attraction of opposites. The Duke is attracted to the factory girl; the Prime Minister's son is determined to marry a trade unionist and his daughter has sworn to marry a poor man (though she actually becomes engaged to an aristocrat who, as a member of the Labour deputation, dresses and talks as she imagines poor men dress and talk). The Prime Minister himself is married to a shadowy woman who apparently has no enthusiasm either for politics or for her children: her boredom with public life and inability to 'take an interest in people' derive from Lucinda Elizabeth Shaw's indifference to both Sonny and G.B.S. She is a complex woman nevertheless, with insight into the other characters, capable of manipulating the plot and preparing the way for her husband's political illumination.

The political programme Shaw gives the Prime Minister is his attempt at a watertight synthesis that will buoyantly unite these opposing interests, and the irony of the play centres on the alliance of 'opposite points of view' that splits apart this unity and sinks it. In the manner of Sir Oswald Mosley after his failure with Ramsay MacDonald's Labour Cabinet, Sir Dexter Rightside threatens to put 'fifty thousand patriotic young Londoners into Union Jack shirts ... My party has the flag, the traditions, the glory that is England, the pluck, the breed, the fighting spirit.' Unable to carry through his programme democratically, the Prime Minister threatens, in the style of Cromwell, 'to prorogue Parliament and then do it'. In a decade of dictators Shaw can find no escape from slow economic decay between these two dictatorships.

The dramatic opinions that fill the Cabinet Room are the voices that reverberate in Shaw's mind – what he hears others say and what he tells himself. At its best, the 'vigour and pace of the whole exchange', writes Margery Morgan, 'the orchestration of the dialogue for such a collection of voices, temperaments, manners and viewpoints, are not surpassed anywhere in Shavian drama'. The case for fascism is put with the same lucidity as the case for socialism; the seductive strengths and parochial limitations of Western intellect confront the criticisms of Oriental culture (eloquently expressed by the Sinhalese plutocrat Sir Jaffna Pandranath). The play exhibits Shaw's 'anarchic comic gift doing spirited battle with his authoritarian opinions', the critic Irving Wardle has observed, 'and the separate factions are orchestrated with effortless fluency and the ability to spring surprises'. The virtues of law and order match themselves against the vices of a police power state. 'I wonder should I find any bombs in your house if I searched it,' the Chief Commissioner of Police asks the elderly East End socialist, Hipney, who knowingly answers: 'You would if you put them there first, Sir Broadfoot. What good would a police chief be if he couldnt find anything he wanted to find?' The paradox of power, according to Shaw, is that *anciens régimes* are defended by oppressed and oppressors alike. 'Chained dogs are the fiercest guardians of property; and those who attempt to unchain them are the first to get bitten.'

On the Rocks was to achieve the peculiar Shavian feat of eventually offending almost everyone. After its American première in 1938, Professor Richard Nickson recalls, 'critics to the Left called it "Fascist", while critics to the Right called it "Communist" '. There was a similar division in Britain. Such reactions appeared to endorse the experiences of Shaw's Prime Minister.

After its opening in London Shaw reported a 'unanimously good press (for once)'. The *Morning Post* praised him for having 'made politics amusing' and achieving a 'sparkling farce of ideas'; *The Times* applauded his refusal to be canonized after *Saint Joan* or to let his audiences fall asleep; and Kingsley

Martin in the *New Statesman & Nation* made the crucial observation that G.B.S. 'warns rather than advocates. Make up your mind, he says, that Parliament, as you know it, cannot be the instrument of salvation. Devise a constitution which gives scope to personal and national loyalty, but do not imagine that it can succeed without transformation of the social order.'

Despite the initially favourable reviews, Beatrice Webb predicted that 'critics of future generations, if they notice *On the Rocks*, will cite it as a picture of British society in catastrophic decadence, portrayed by an aged cynic who had outlived his genius'. Yet the play, which mirrors the mass unemployment of the 1930s and the quandaries of a National Government waiting for what politicians called 'natural recovery' in trade as it slowly drifts towards the rocks of war, was to retain and renew its topicality. 'The political situations are now so alike in all countries that the points will carry everywhere,' Shaw wrote to Theresa Helburn at the Theatre Guild of New York near the end of 1933. When the play was revived at the Mermaid Theatre in the 1970s, Robert Cushman in the *Observer* called it 'quite the most topical play in London'; J. W. Lambert in the *Sunday Times* wrote of his 'astonishment at how little things, and people, have changed since 1933'; Irving Wardle in *The Times* pointed in detail to 'the numerous parallels between the Depression years and the economic ills of the 1970s'; and the critic J. C. Trewin summed up: 'What appeals to us now is the prophetic quality. The date is 1933, yet the dramatist could well have been thinking of 1975.' Again, when it was brought back at Chichester during the Falklands War in the 1980s, these same critics remarked on the play's continuous contemporaneity – as if time had stopped and was pointing for ever at 'the Present'. *On the Rocks* seemed 'topical when I read it 10 years ago', wrote Robert Cushman in the summer of 1982, 'prescient when the Mermaid staged it a couple of years after that, and positively uncanny at Chichester now'.

Shaw deployed his disputatious Cabinet Ministers, blustering Labour deputation and the Prime Minister's nagging family so as to present a multi-layered view of disintegrating Western society. His thoughts flow in after the deputations go out and a dialogue starts up between the Prime Minister and Mr Hipney, the 'sunny comfortable old chap in his Sunday best' who has stayed behind. Like the two scenes between Rosmer and Ulric Brendel in *Rosmersholm*, their conversations arrest the action, but prove to be moral turning points. They have the air of '*beginning the business instead of ending it*', the stage directions tell us. 'Now we can talk a bit,' Hipney remarks as he makes himself comfortable in the Cabinet Room.

Hipney, a convincing portrait of an older, shrewder, working-class politician, represents the young Shaw who put his heart into politics; and

338

the Prime Minister comes to represent the old Shaw who uses his head. Yet Hipney's words, which give utterance to Chavender's unformed thoughts, mark the stages of awareness in the Prime Minister. In the first act it is Hipney who recommends the Prime Minister to read Marx: 'Youll realize that your college conceit is up against a Marxist conceit that beats anything you ever felt for cocksureness,' he says. He hasn't actually studied Marx himself but has felt his power and seen his effect on 'them as had read him'. 'Turned their heads, eh?' queries the Prime Minister and Hipney concurs: 'Turned their heads. Turned them right round the other way to yours.'

This is the turned-about figure the Prime Minister becomes in the second act. His parliamentary career is 'a very arduous and trying one', he tells Hipney: 'I might almost say a heartbreaking one.' As for Hipney himself, his 'heart is in the revolution', but following the political develop-ments of the twentieth century has, he admits, taken 'the heart out of old Hipney'.

This heartlessness is at the centre of what the writer James Fenton has called the 'crazed and insidious' Preface to *On the Rocks*, and hostility to this Preface has carried over to the play itself. The critic Benedict Nightingale, after referring to the 'peculiarly bloodthirsty' Preface, described a performance of the play in 1982 as being 'precisely the sort of thing decent people should *not* have resurrected at a time like this, when unemployment is once again rife, party alignments confused, and parliamentary democracy itself under attack from both right and left'.

But the writer of the play subverts the writer of the Preface. Shaw is like de Stogumber clamouring for the burning of St Joan and, only after seeing her burnt, having his eyes opened to what he has done: 'I meant no harm. I did not know what it would be like ... it is so easy to talk when you dont know. You madden yourself with words...' This is the same reaction as that of the Prime Minister's secretary who rushes out to join the crowds of unemployed after seeing them trampled and beaten by the police. 'It's all right when you only read about it in the papers; but when you actually see it you want to throw stones at the police.' It is as if the artist in Shaw cannot accept the Shavian polemicist. He cannot abandon conscience for efficient action. 'I'm not the man for the job,' Chavender admits. '... And I shall hate the man who will carry it through for his cruelty and the desolation he will bring on us and our like.'

But why should such desolation be necessary? Shaw believed that though Britain might be good at finding leaders in wartime when socialism advanced, her politicians were uninspired in peacetime, and the country instinctively felt the need for a peacetime fighter, whatever party she might lead. The Cabinet meetings in both *The Apple Cart* and *On the Rocks* 'are something Shaw *had* to give us some day', wrote Eric Bentley, '– a rounded picture of the political madhouse which directs our destinies'. These two plays are less surreal than his other plays of this period. The crash of breaking windows at the end of *On the Rocks*, like the bomb explosion near the end of *Heartbreak House* (or the Day of Judgment in *The Simpleton of the Unexpected Isles* and the planetary disaster in the last act of *Geneva*), are all symbols, as Eric Bentley indicates, of the atomic age and the global threat to our environment, as well as the anticipation of Hitler's Germany.

In the proofs Shaw subtitled the play 'A Political Fantasy' but he reduced this to 'A Political Comedy' when it was published, perhaps because he could find no plausible way of carrying through the Prime Minister's fantastical programme. 'With the eruption of the uprising we should be plunged into a situation which could no longer be appropriately handled by the characteristic methods of his comedy,' wrote Edmund Wilson.

'He is still splendid when he is showing the bewilderment of the liberal governing-class minister: it is surprising how he is still able to summon his old flickering and piercing wit, his old skill at juggling points of view, to illuminate a new social situation ... But with the shouts and the broken glass, we are made to take account of the fact that Shaw's comedy, for all its greater freedom in dealing with social conditions, is almost as much dependent on a cultivated and stable society as the comedy of Molière.'

Shaw's comic mask seldom appears in *On the Rocks*. Behind the play is a lifetime's work for socialism – come to what? The basic two-act construction of his late plays (*The Apple Cart*, *On the Rocks*, *The Simpleton of the Unexpected Isles*, *The Millionairess*, '*In Good King Charles's Golden Days*') suggests that the synthesis in Shaw's political thought had disappeared. A clash of revolution might be necessary after all. The emergence of suicidal images and themes shows the personal effect of this change. In the after-vacancy it occurs to Chavender that he would 'make a hole in the river with his wife' rather than do what Hipney has come to think is politically necessary in this world between the wars.

Playwriting is becoming a Platonic exercise with me.
Shaw to Leonora Ervine (12 May 1934)

'When in doubt, play Shaw,' Lawrence Langner had said in the late 1920s. But, though the Theatre Guild was to stage more than twenty of Shaw's full-length plays in New York during his lifetime, neither *Village Wooing* nor *On the Rocks* was among them. By the mid-1930s Shaw seemed to have lost his stage-worthiness and become again what he had been in the 1890s: an extravagantly versatile composer of play-texts.

The productions of these latest works were often unorthodox, suggesting that he had also regained his status as an experimental dramatist. *Village Wooing* received its world première at the Little Theater in Dallas, Texas, and was first presented in Britain by his fellow-dramatist Christopher Fry at the Pump Room in Tunbridge Wells. *On the Rocks* waited until the summer of 1938 before reaching New York when it was brought in by the government-sponsored Federal Theater which took over Shaw's plays from the Theatre Guild. In Britain the play was given its world première at the unfashionable Winter Garden Theatre in London where it was presented by Charles Macdona.

The Macdona Players, with Esmé Percy as their director, had 'led the forlorn hope of advanced drama in England' between the wars and toured many of Shaw's plays through Britain, round the Continent (staging the long-banned *Mrs Warren's Profession* in Paris in 1925) and in South Africa, India and the Far East. In the late 1920s they had begun taking a London theatre for a season – the Chelsea Palace, Kingsway, Garrick or Embassy – and would regularly put on Shaw revivals in repertory. Between 1929 and 1931 they staged nine of Shaw's works (including *Man and Superman* in its 'frightful' entirety) at the Royal Court Theatre in Sloane Square where many of them had received their first public presentation a quarter of a century before.

On the Rocks was the only world première produced by Charles Macdona. Shaw had wanted Esmé Percy to direct the play, 'but now there is a nice man, a man G.B.S. likes nearly as well', Charlotte wrote, '& I hope, later, G.B.S. will throw a good deal of work on to him'.

This 'nice man' was Lewis Casson. He had worked with Shaw when directing the London production of *Village Wooing* which starred Casson's wife, Sybil Thorndike, as *Z*. 'I look back on the few days when you and I and Sybil worked together on Village Wooing . . . with a quite special pleasure,' Shaw wrote to Arthur Wontner who played *A*. Lewis Casson's son

Christopher Casson remembered the rehearsals of *Village Wooing* and *On the Rocks*. Shaw 'always acted all the parts and directed the performances too. My father had to smooth the way and perhaps pick up the pieces.'

Shaw enjoyed interfering with his own plays. He 'had a disgraceful appetite for "getting the laughs"', recalled Stephen Murray who played the part of the Prime Minister in the Malvern production of *On the Rocks* in 1936.

'I remember exactly his voice exhorting me, with monstrous overacting and over-inflexion, to get a separate laugh on almost every word in one speech: "The Family? What family? (laugh), the *Holy* Family (laugh), The *Royal* Family? (laugh). The SWISS FAMILY ROBINSON? (laugh)." It couldn't work of course. I had learnt to take his direction with more than a pinch of salt, and on the first night I ran the whole speech in one to get the laugh at the end. I can still hear him, from his seat in the stalls, laughing loudly and happily long after the audience had finished. "That's the way to do it – I told you!" he said to me shamelessly after the show.'

He appeared a more dictatorial figure than in the Vedrenne-Barker days, talking more and listening less. He had been 'all eyes and ears', remembered Cedric Hardwicke when rehearsing *Back to Methuselah*. Now his eyes and ears had dimmed, but not his opinions. According to Edith Evans, he was getting old-fashioned. 'The Shavian "method" of rehearsal was the precise opposite of Stanislavsky's,' recalled one of the Macdona Players. 'He made no attempt to help one to gain an imaginative feeling for the character and situations. Instead he went through the part line by line instructing me how he wanted every sentence emphasized and pronounced in his own, idiosyncratic Anglo-Irish accent.' He insisted on placing his dominant speaking character well up-stage to get absolute clarity, grouped the other actors decoratively round and gave a highly-coloured orchestration to the vocal tempo and pitch. 'You've got to go from line to line, quickly and swiftly, never stop the flow of the lines, never stop,' he told Ralph Richardson when rehearsing *Arms and the Man* at the Old Vic. 'It's one joke after another, it's a firecracker. Always reserve the acting for underneath the spoken word. It's a musical play, a knockabout musical comedy.' Richardson remembered him as 'a wonderfully courteous, wonderfully polite man, I think perhaps the most polite man I've met in my life'. And John Gielgud, who played the Emperor in *Androcles and the Lion* 'with a red wig, a lecherous red mouth, and a large emerald through which I peered lasciviously', remembered that the cast was 'so amused that we forgot to be alarmed' when G.B.S. turned up to read his play to them. And there were still characteristic outbursts of generosity. 'I dare say your words

17 John Farleigh's title page to the first edition, 1932

18　The opening scene of *Too True to be Good*, London, 1932

19A At Cap d'Antibes; B Watching the rehearsal of *The Six of Calais*,
Regent's Park, 1934

Chapter II.

Alone in Ireland

George Bernard Shaw, ~~as he has frequently informed the world,~~ was born in Dublin, July 26, 1856, *in a seven roomed house, with two sisters older than himself, an Irish nurse and an Irish "thorough servant" or maid of all work. Solitude there was out of the question.* ~~From his early youth, Shaw was a lonely and solitary child. Although he~~ *The child Shaw, of imagination all compact, was born (he decides) able to read without effort. He read* ~~was shy and sensitively aloof from others, he had no real sense of inferior-~~ *every book he could lay his hands on; used the longest words he could find or them with Johnsonian* ~~ity. On the contrary, his inner sense of importance was even more pronounced~~ *gravity; and whilst still in the infantile stage of arrant cowardice lied like fifty Bobadils about his* ~~than his superficial lack of self-assurance in company. Yet he was not con-~~ *personal prowess and fearlessness, with most humiliating consequences when he was put to the test. He was not con-* scious of his *powers any more than, as he once put it, "I was conscious of* the taste of saliva that was always in my mouth." *Assuming that anybody was like himself, he made* ~~A sense of strangeness and~~ *many ridiculous miscalculations, and sometimes felt, that* ~~isolation was always his:~~ like Einstein, he ~~has always felt as if~~ he had wander- *Henever thought of himself as an impudent and voluble boy, deplorable* ~~ed into a strange and alien world, which he was only visiting for a time. It~~ *careless of his dress and person, which is how he must have struck other people. He was uncontrolled and unquestioned* ~~Life, for Shaw, was an abyss between two Eternities, it was a curious and~~ *and uncounselled and unstructured to a very unusual extent, learning how to live by, as* ~~provocative abyss which from the first he was determined to explore. In this~~ *he says "breaking my shins over everything". He was frightfully sensitive to trifling rebuffs and failures, and yet so* ~~abyss he has found much to amuse him, much to anger him, much to make him in-~~ *strongminded that he often produced an impression of being extremely unfeeling. He soon found this out, and amused* ~~patient with the entire human race. Even to-day, although he observes the~~ *himself by shocking his elders. In this and other ways the future playwright began early to act a part in public, or* ~~mundane scene from the lofty eminence of philosophy, he has always enjoyed~~ *to hide his real personality behind it. Like his most famous predecessor he* ~~was~~ *was an actor to whom all the world* ~~mingling with people, whom he has found the most provoking and intriguing set~~ *a stage. In the language he was "a character actor" who never "played straight". In "character" he was impudent and* ~~of creatures in the world.~~ *audacious: in himself he was mortally diffident and shy. What is called his development is nothing but the gradual*

As a child, Bernard had an air of quiet superiority and self-contained *discovery of a very* assurance, feeling entirely sufficient unto himself and not leading upon the *unexpected re person behind* strength of other people. He was never bored, for he held limitless reserves *all the fonts and intriguing* within himself. *Theatrically* Imaginative to an exceptional degree, he covered the walls *playboy of the western world*

CHAPTER II

ALONE IN IRELAND

GEORGE BERNARD SHAW was born in Dublin, July 26, 1856, in a seven roomed house, No. 3, afterwards re-numbered 33, Synge Street, with two sisters older than himself, an Irish nurse and an Irish "thorough servant" or maid of all work. Solitude there was out of the question.

The child Shaw, of imagination all compact, was born (he declares) able to read without effort. He read every book he could lay his hands on; used the longest words he could find in them with Johnsonian gravity; and whilst still in the infantile stage of arrant cowardice lied like fifty Bobadils about his personal prowess and fearlessness, with most humiliating consequences when he was put to the test. He was not conscious of his real powers any more than, as he once put it, "I was conscious of the taste of saliva that was always in my mouth." Assuming that everybody was like himself, he made many ridiculous miscalculations, and sometimes felt, like Einstein, that he had wandered into a strange and alien world. He never thought of himself as an impudent and voluble boy, deplorably careless of his dress and person, which is how he must have struck other people. He was uncontrolled and unquestioned and uncounselled and uninstructed to a very unusual extent, learning how to live by, as he says, "breaking my shins over everything." He was frightfully sensitive to trifling rebuffs and failures, and yet so strongminded that he often produced an impression of being extremely unfeeling. He soon found this out, and amused himself by shocking his elders. In this and other ways the future playwright began early to act a part in public, and to hide his real personality behind it. Like his most famous predecessor he was an actor to whom all the world's a stage. In the language of the stage he was "a character actor" who never "played straight." In "character" he was impudent and audacious: in himself he was mortally diffident and shy. What is called his development is nothing but the

[9]

22 Gabriel Pascal...

23 …'G.B.S. had never met a human being who entertained him more'

24 Programme cover by John Farleigh for Macdona's 1933 production

are as good as mine,' he told Phyllis Nielson-Terry who kept fluffing her lines during a revival of *Candida*.

'There won't be any dress rehearsal,' Shaw had written to the actress Gertrude Kingston. 'It [*On the Rocks*] is one of those abominable plays in which there is one part which needs six weeks work, and sixteen others which could be over-rehearsed in a fortnight.' On the day of the final rehearsal he came into his own. 'We had what was supposed to be a "word-rehearsal" in the morning, but it turned into a full-scale rehearsal by Shaw which lasted till 3 p.m.,' wrote Stephen Murray.

'There was a photo-call at six, which Shaw insisted on attending. Dress-rehearsal at eight, and the curtain went up on it with Shaw on-stage. He never sat down for four hours, turning everything upside down and this way and that. At midnight he gave us vigorous notes for twenty minutes and then walked home. He had his eightieth birthday that week.

' ... Shaw battered and hammered away at me throughout that evening. At the end I was limp and exhausted. And then he came to me and said "Of course, Stephen, you'll go to London after this, and I don't suppose I'll be able to get you in one of my plays again". I was at his feet.'

As the opening night of *On the Rocks* approached, a current of excitement went through the Winter Garden Theatre. It was like the old days. 'An extraordinary evening,' Charlotte wrote. 'The way that enormous audience took the points and flung themselves into the whole thing was startling. I never met anything like it before. It does not necessarily prove that the play will run. It was a special G.B.S. audience. I expect the whole Fabian Society was there.'

Macdona and Shaw had experimented by charging 'popular prices' – between one and five shillings a seat, which was half the regular cost – to fit the new distribution of income and culture in society. They needed to fill the large, uncomfortable and out-of-the-way theatre to keep the play profitably running – and after the huge first night success and excellent notices it seemed they might succeed. The congregation of fans came over and over again, but the general playgoing public seemed to agree with Shaw's Prime Minister – 'This is not the time to talk about economic difficulties: we're up to the neck in them' – and stayed away. Beatrice Webb, who went to the theatre a fortnight after the play had opened, reported 'Unrelieved ugliness, scenic and psychological ... the hall cold and cheerless, the cheap stalls not completely occupied, the gallery practically empty, a badly tuned gramophone playing during the one interval, did not constitute an attractive setting.'

After forty-one performances the shutters went up towards the end of January 1935. 'My popularity does not increase,' Shaw wrote to his publisher. But then he had never counted on the commercial success of either *On the Rocks* or *Village Wooing*: 'I shall not take any trouble to have them performed,' he had assured Trebitsch, 'but publish them in the same volume as Too True.' Early in 1934, 27,000 copies of this book were published in Britain and America, and two years later it was joined in the Standard Edition by another volume, *The Simpleton, the Six, and the Millionairess*, containing the last three plays from his world travels.

*

'The greatest fact of your lifetime is that nothing has happened in the twentieth century except the impossible,' Shaw wrote to St John Ervine in 1932. '...nothing has succeeded like impossibility'. *The Simpleton of the Unexpected Isles* is Shaw's enhancement of 'impossibility' far-advanced into the twenty-first century – or at least to some unspecified time he calls 'Approaching Judgment Day'.

The Unexpected Isles have recently risen out of the Pacific Ocean (where Shaw completed the play) and been occupied as a Crown Colony of the British Empire. In the three short scenes of the Prologue, past, present and future are brought together as in the third part of *Back to Methuselah*, 'The Thing Happens'. Some of the characters belong recognizably to the contemporary Western world: for example, the modern young woman, a dynamo of outspokenness, who arrives at the emigration office without her papers but with the catch-phrase (which becomes a theme of the play) 'Let life come to you'; and also the Emigration Officer, 'an unsatisfactory young man of unhealthy habits ' who vents his frustrations in bureaucratic bad temper. The Young Woman, who spends her life 'making up other people's minds for them', marches the Emigration Officer out of his office to show her round the island, leaving his clerk alone there. This shabby clerk is also recognizable – partly as Shaw's father. Life has never come to him. He has apparently thrown away his luck when he flung a dead cat over the garden wall, and nothing has gone right since. Once upon a time he dreamed of becoming another Cecil Rhodes; now he has settled into being an indispensable servant of a shortly-to-be-dispensed-with British Empire. There is nothing for him to do but join this vanishing past and so, the stage directions instruct us, he begins singing 'Rule Britannia', *blows his brains out and falls dead* – the fifth such suicide that month.

Meanwhile the Young Woman and Emigration Officer have progressed to Scene II – 'a grassy cliff top overhanging the sea' reminiscent of the Dover Cliffs in Act IV scene vi of *King Lear* where Gloucester, Edgar and the King himself meet within a foot of the extreme verge, and trifle with despair. The Emigration Officer too has reached despair: 'If you hadnt come in this morning I'd have done myself in,' he tells the Young Woman who is amazed that he should feel so wretched in this 'earthly paradise'. The explanation is given by a dark native Priest who rises into view up a concealed cliff path, rather as the islands themselves have risen. The Emigration Officer, he says, comes from a 'strange mad Country' whose inhabitants 'die from their own hands to escape what they call the horrors' when 'in the midst of life and loveliness' they feel that only man is vile. Despair again overcomes the Emigration Officer who is determined to go over the fearful cliffs. He bends and continues bending tremendously on the edge – until the Priest shoots out a foot against his posterior and with a prodigious splash he is sent catapulting into the sea. The Young Woman is appalled, but, as in *King Lear*, the cliffs are not simply what we have been led to expect; they mark the line of redemption as well as the abyss of death. 'There are nets below,' the Priest explains to the Young Woman as they advance into the third scene.

This is set in a temple made out of a shelf of rock halfway down the cliff, reminiscent of the arches, spires and pinnacles of the Skelligs off the southwest coast of Ireland. Upon this Gothic cathedral of the sea, and representing the coming together of East and West, Shaw imposed the gigantic images of Oriental deities he had seen on Elephanta Island, off the coast of Bombay. This temple belongs to holy people who are not recognizable to us, but who unite Shaw's impressions from the East with his concepts of evolutionary ascent. The Priest and the Priestess are perfectly attuned to their paradisaical surroundings. They treat visitors from the old country with something of the backward-looking contempt that British imperialists have treated natives of their annexed territories. 'I find these heathen idolaters very trying,' sighs the Priestess after encountering an affected English lady tourist, guidebook in hand. This turns out to be Lady Farwaters, the wife of Sir Charles Farwaters, a man of pleasant aristocratic appearance on the young side of middle age, who owes a little to Shaw's Fabian friend Sydney Olivier.

What is to be done with such specimens? The Priest and Priestess decide they might be used – for who would wish to be entirely useless? – in a eugenic experiment blending the flesh and spirit of East and West, and they all retire into a magical cavern (like the Abode of Love from *Too True to be Good*).

The alternative method of fulfilling what Don Juan has called 'Life's incessant aspiration to higher organization, wider, deeper, intenser self-consciousness, and clearer self-understanding' is enacted by the

Emigration Officer's plunge into the baptismal flood. 'I brought up my immortal soul,' he says after he *rises into view in a spotless white robe* looking *pale* but *regenerated*. '... Theres nothing of the man you met this morning left except skin and bones. You may regard me as to all intents and purposes born again.' Writing of Shaw in the 1920s T. E. Lawrence had noticed 'some sea-change [that] has come over G.B.S. in the last ten years'. It is a cleansing sea-change, compressed into ten minutes, that Shaw has granted his Emigration Officer. He is redeemed because, unlike his clerk, he did not feel himself indispensable in an office of the past and allowed himself to be rescued by the vital Young Woman. To that extent life came to him. But now 'the tables are turned', and just when the Young Woman thinks that life is 'coming a bit too thick for me', he rushes her screaming to the edge of the rock shelf and hurls her over. So ends a Prologue remarkable for its surplus of action over talk.

In a letter to Trebitsch, Shaw called *The Simpleton* 'an ultra-fantastic oriental modern (or futurist) play ... contents indescribable'. With a peculiar blend of fantasy and satire, the two acts of the play survey the delights and drawbacks of the pantomime Utopia that arise from the Prologue. The first act takes up the story about twenty years later and carries it on through the experiences of an accidental traveller to this Otherworld: a young, highly credulous clergyman who, like the Elderly Gentleman in *Back to Methuselah*, gives an ironic view of Shaw's own pilgrim's progress from the perspective of the future. This simpleton has been kidnapped by pirates at Weston Super Mare and forced to sail round the world, making them ill with laughter by giving Church of England sermons and services. 'They were crooks, racketeers, smugglers, pirates, anything that paid them,' he says as if recalling the ex-criminals of Captain Brassbound's crew. 'They used me to make people believe that they were respectable.' And Shaw uses them, the stock-in-trade crew of island literature, to echo Captain Shotover's warning in *Heartbreak House* against capitalism's ship of fools and to remind us of its stranded destination in *On the Rocks*.

Suddenly released and set ashore, the simpleton wanders through the Unexpected Isles 'with the air of a stranger who is trespassing' and comes to a terraced garden overlooking the port of Good Adventure. He is lost in enchantment. 'It's like the Garden of Eden: I should like to stay here forever.' The garden is given a hieratic aspect by four Oriental shrines at the corners of a raised flowerbed. As he gazes at the two magically beautiful girl-goddesses and two wonderful boy-gods, the simpleton's heart is filled with longing. 'How I wish you were alive and I could kiss your living lips instead of the paint on a hard wooden image,' he addresses the fair goddess. But in this wonderland wishes come true. 'I must kiss you,' he says, and the stage directions tell us what then happens: '*He does so and finds that she is alive. She smiles as her eyes turn bewitchingly towards him.*' In this variation of the Pygmalion legend, both the two goddesses and the two gods reveal themselves as four children from the Prologue.

'We formed a family of six parents,' explains Sir Charles Farwaters, who is now Governor of the Isles. His wife has changed from an affected tourist to a bland and matronly silhouette of Charlotte Shaw; while the Emigration Officer is transformed into a '*very different man, disciplined, responsible and well groomed*' – and married (a distant image of the Webbs' marriage) to the Young Woman who is '*still very much her old self*'. The other two parents are Pra and Prola, the Priest and Priestess.

'We are making a little domestic experiment,' says Lady Farwaters. This Wellsian experiment 'has been a little disappointing from the point of view of numbers', Sir Charles continues. There is something lacking in the constitution of these four superchildren. They are all, like Hitler's Aryan ideal, physically perfect, and have 'artistic consciences' of the highest order, but they cannot muster 'between the whole four of them a scrap of moral conscience'. They are the embodiment of art for art's sake.

Providence seems to have brought them a clergyman who is 'suffering from a morbid excess of conscience'. Besides, he too is the result of an experiment, being 'a nitrogen baby' whose father, a madly famous biochemist, raised him on nitrate products and christened him 'Phosphor'. But there is a hint that the experiment may have miscarried, since the child was nicknamed Iddy, short for idiot. 'I am weak-minded and lose my head very easily,' he warns everyone.

From the idea of loving one another the superchildren have advanced to the ideal of being one another. 'Perfect love casteth out choice,' says the dark goddess Vashti. '... Your lives and ours are one life.' And the fair goddess Maya refuses to have sexual intercourse with Iddy 'in this Kingdom of Love' until he agrees to make love to her sister also. He barricades himself round with all the thou-shalt-nots of his religion but, being weak-minded and losing his head so easily, he cannot resist either Vashti or Maya, and the act ends as '*the three embrace with interlaced arms and vanish in black darkness*'.

Shaw's Garden of Eden is unclouded by any evil. No serpent slides through the undergrowth, no original sin flowers in the grounds: this is a paradise without demons below. We are shown a pure fairy story, like an adolescent's daydream, that joins Oriental fable to allegorical romance, and reflects Shaw's view of Edgar Allan Poe's poetic principle. 'His kingdom is not of this world,' he had written of Poe. '... Life cannot give you what he gives you except through fine art.' Shaw's Unexpected Isles, which give us something of Annabel Lee's kingdom by the sea, are located near *Eureka*, the prose poem in which Poe sought to relate poetic intuition to scientific thought. The first act is perhaps the nearest Shaw came to writing what is apparently art for art's sake in the theatre. In this Utopia to end all Utopias, the mood is celestially light – until the ominous ending in *black darkness*.

In a letter to an American osteopath, Shaw later wrote: 'Too much nitrogen is killing the human race.' The *black darkness* into which the nitrogenous simpleton and his two phantom goddesses disappear, interlaced as three-in-one, is the phosphorescent light of Lucifer – an idea that reappears in the second act when, after the Dissolution of the British Empire, the Day of Judgment arrives and the simpleton turns again home. 'England's next war will be a war with heaven,' Pra and his children prophesy, recalling the Devil's rebellion against God. '...The most splendid of all her wars! ... To overcome the angels! To plant the flag of England on the ramparts of Heaven itself! that is the final glory.'

Throughout this play, the British Empire is seen as doing the Devil's work by exploiting the weaknesses of human nature. But in Shaw's myth Iddy is not evil, any more than Lucifer is Satan. He appears as the 'shining one', whose glowing credulity and unshadowed faith make him an 'impotent simpleton' who cannot assist the millennial dream beyond 'a single little household with four children, wonderful and beautiful, but sterile'.

But the experiment profoundly agitates the rest of the world whose fleets sail from the east and from the west and crowd the port, thundering out their apocalyptic threats and counter-threats. For, as their name suggests, the Unexpected Isles are islands of relativity, and the theory of relative values once formulated in Poe's *Eureka* and now perfected by Einstein, is violently opposed by the fundamentalist forces of the contending mainlands – until they are suddenly scattered by an adept foreign-policy statement from Pra that the Isles are full of smallpox.

Though the simpleton cannot change anything, he can learn. 'Respect the wisdom of the fool,' Prola counsels her children. The simpleton learns what Shaw himself has learnt from his early search for love. 'It is a terrible thing to be loved,' he says. '... But there's not so much in it as people say...'

'It is my belief that some day we'll have to try something else. If we dont we'll come to hate one another ... the discovery I have made is that we were commanded to love our enemies because loving is good for us and dreadfully bad for them ... Nothing human is good enough to be loved. But every decent human creature has some capacity for loving ... I cannot bear being loved, because ... nobody could love me unless they were completely deluded...'

A fortnight after finishing *The Simpleton*, Shaw wrote to Leonora Ervine: 'As my playwright faculty still goes on with the impetus of 30 years vital activity, I shoot into the air more and more extravagantly without any premeditation whatever – *advienne que pourra.*' What arrives is the Day of Judgment; and it comes with startling lack of premeditation, heralded by what appears to be an albatross, but which is correctly identified by the simpleton as an Angel. This is the most extravagant entrance in the Shavian theatre since a Polish acrobat shot out of the air and crashed into a glass pavilion in *Misalliance*.

The set of Act II is the same as for Act I but, as Margery Morgan observes, 'the imagery transforms it from a Garden of Creation to the landscape of Apocalypse'. The trumpet rings out from the sky and the Angel (peppered with bullets) descends. But Judgment Day is 'hardly what we were led to expect'. The Angel, which has some difficulty in flying, apologizes: 'I am afraid you will find it very dull.' For it is, after all, 'not the end of the world, but the end of its childhood and the beginning of its responsible maturity'. Judgment turns out to be the valuation of what the Young Woman and the clerk had discussed in the Emigration office: 'Dispensables and indispensables'. But that discussion had been in the context of the British Empire and its past. Those who wish to emigrate to God's Empire must be of value to the future. Others, with no possible future, the Angel offhandedly remarks, 'will simply disappear'. It is *Surrealpolitik*.

In his essay on Poe some twenty-five years before, Shaw had written: 'His poems always have the universe in the background.' *The Simpleton* has the world in its background. As Judgment Day spreads round the world he charts with exhilarating relish the widespread disappearances of what *The Times* calls 'our most important people'. The critic Frederick McDowell notes that Shaw's satirical newspaper reports have the flavour of the clownish Lord High Executioner's song from the first act of *The Mikado*: 'And they'll none of 'em be missed – they'll none of 'em be missed!'

The simpleton finally learns what Shaw wants his audience to learn: that we create a fool's paradise by falling in love with our ideals. In the second act, the quartet of exquisite superchildren, chanting like an antiphonal choir, perform as a mechanical stage chorus. 'They declaim, their speech is musical, rhythmical, artificial in the last degree,' Shaw told his Polish translator, Floryan Sobieniowski. They recall the self-destructing puppets created by the fanatical scientist Pygmalion in *Back to Methuselah*. As the disenchanted simpleton can now see, they have been the illusory ideals of Love, Pride, Heroism and Empire. 'When Maya is making love she coos like a dove,' Shaw directed. She is love itself, an emanation and an apparition: the emanation of Shaw's young actress 'Mollytompkins' on her enchanted

Isola, and the apparition created by the simpleton's inexpressible longing. 'I held Maya in my arms. She promised to endure for ever; and suddenly there was nothing in my arms.' When the simpleton ceases to believe in them, these ideals vanish so completely that no one can remember their names or even how many of them there seemed to be.

The simpleton too, once idealized by these superchildren as the Vision in a dream who 'on honey-dew hath fed, And drunk the milk of Paradise', vanishes back into his real self, an apprehensive clergyman nicknamed Iddy. Released from the island spell, he will go homing back to England.

The world advances to the foreground of the play at its conclusion. 'There is no Country of the Expected. The Unexpected Isles are the whole world.' It is a world of miracles but not of ideological Utopias and Millennia. 'We are not here to fulfil prophecies and fit ourselves into puzzles,' says Prola. The heaven on earth that Shaw has raised at the beginning has dissolved at the end but there is no despair. Left alone on stage Pra and Prola unite in a hymn to unexpectedness: 'Let it come.' Turning their backs on romantic fairylands, Pra acknowledges that even wars can be justified 'because only under the strain of war are we capable of changing the world'. And Prola pledges herself 'to strive for more knowledge and more power'.

The Simpleton is the deepest and happiest of Shaw's fantasies, 'openly oriental, hieratic and insane' as he called it himself. This magical gathering on an island, with its dreams and illusions, its spectacular aesthetic rather than dramatic air, and its departure to the real world after the political lessons have been delivered, is reminiscent of *The Tempest*. Reading it in New York, Lawrence Langner instinctively sensed that here was a 'magnificent' allegory containing 'some of Shaw's most inspired writing'. Yet with its extraordinary range of musical, mannered and comic acting styles, as well as its use of film techniques and cartoon effects, the play sets its director enormous problems – and opportunities. 'The Theatre Guild's hero-worshipping of Shaw was nowhere better demonstrated than on our production of *The Simpleton of the Unexpected Isles*,' wrote Langner. The first director to whom he gave the play 'could not understand it' and it was then handed to a specialist in the choreography of farce. The world première in New York bemused and discomforted the critics. 'Like a dignified monkey,' wrote Percy Hammond in the *New York Herald Tribune*, 'he climbs a tree and pelts us with edifying coconuts.' A month later, examining photographs of the production, Shaw realized that, though lavish and earnest, it had been 'all wrong'. The leading part of Prola, for example, which was inspired by a vision of Stella Campbell's beauty recollected in tranquillity, had been played by the sultry Russian actress Nazimova who, like some Javanese dancer, appeared 'as a slinking sinuous odalisque', Shaw complained.

'She should have been straight as a ramrod; an Egyptian goddess. My four wonderful young Indian deities, clothed to the wrists and ankles in silks and bangles, and full of mystery and enchantment, came out simply as a naked cabaret troup in the latest Parisian undress.'

As a result, the play 'flopped completely' in New York and came off after forty performances. In Warsaw, where a number of Shaw's recent plays had been successfully staged in Sobieniowski's translations, the press reported on 'The Unexpected Failure of an Aged Simpleton'; and in Britain 'G.B.S's Queer New Play', as the *Daily Mirror* called it, was put on by Barry Jackson at Malvern but did not reach London.

Though there were plenty of literary signposts in these Unexpected Isles (to Coleridge, W. S. Gilbert, Goethe, Voltaire, and the Book of Revelations among others), though it drew on the prodigious literature of Utopias 'outside the domain of economics' as well as on those romances and adventures which had taught Shaw how to dream as a boy, and though there were connections also with the popular Oriental extravaganzas that had played in Dublin and London theatres during the late nineteenth century, as well as with the fabulous *Chu-Chin-Chow* in the First World War, drama critics reacted to *The Simpleton* as if it were like nothing else. In the United States, the critic Joseph Wood Krutch described it as a divertingly reckless theatrical departure in which no serious meaning could be discerned; in Australia, the reviewer of *The Bulletin* in Sydney treated it as a uniquely Shavian vaudeville revue, 'a magnificent confusion'.

Part of this confusion arose from the publication of Shaw's disconcerting Preface to the play, and from what *The Times* judged to be the difficulty of 'keeping up with Mr Shaw'. On one side there was his 'finality of assertion', and on the other his 'life-long capacity for growth and change of mind'. But there were other difficulties too. Some of the sexual scenes had shocked American audiences 'even in these days of theatrical improprieties'. In Austria, the play's strange divinities and eugenic impurities worried the censors, and it was banned. In Germany, where audiences burst spontaneously into cheering at such statements as Vashti's 'Obedience is freedom from the intolerable fatigue of thought,' the Nazi newspaper *Hamburger Tageblatt* commented that 'the applause of those eternally behind the times neither surprised nor frightened us ... And just as little can Shaw upset us.'

But he had upset Stanbrook Abbey. Plainly the play was tinged with heresy. Sometimes Sister Laurentia wondered whether Brother Bernard really knew the difference between Truth and Error; then she would recollect that of course he must do. She had instructed him herself. So when his own Day of Judgment came round 'you will not be able to plead ignorance as the excuse of the evil that your books may do', she warned him. Shaw pretended to be puzzled. Why 'in the name of all the saints' did she 'fly out at me when I devoutly insist that the Godhead must contain the Mother as well as the Father?' He knew that Catholic theology did not class the Immaculate Mother as a goddess (as Prola implied in the Prologue). But 'she is the people's goddess, and will be worshipped by them as such as long as they worship any personification of divinity'. Their resurrected friendship survived the duel. 'I wish we could take Laurentia to the east,' he confided to Sydney Cockerell, 'and make her pray in all the Divine Mother's temples.'

Shaw wished he could take all the directors and designers of his play to the East. 'I should have made you send [Lee] Simonson to Bombay for a month,' he wrote to the Theatre Guild, 'not only to see the Elephanta caves, but to feel the sex appeal of the women, especially the Parsee ladies, and the enchantment of the temple gods, especially Jain no-gods.' In the West, the confidence of theatre directors was to be long undermined by Edmund Wilson's influential judgement, delivered in the late 1930s: '*The Simpleton of the Unexpected Isles* is the only play of the author's which has ever struck me as silly.' It *is* silly; but in such 'silliness', though it may be traced to a psychological weakness, lies Shaw's genius. 'Why don't you do "The Simpleton of the Unexpected Isles"?' he asked William Armstrong at the Liverpool Repertory Theatre in 1937. 'It is a lovely play; and you can let yourself go on the production.' But repertory theatres had settled into a well-tried routine of some dozen Shavian comedies, histories and pleasant plays.

Not until the 1980s, and Denise Coffey's staging in the Shaw Theatre at Niagara-on-the-lake – 'happily mating everything from vaudeville turns to anguished soliloquies' – was Lawrence Langner's original instinct vindicated. After unisex styles and hippy ashrams had become familiar, the dramatic possibilities of a play long regarded as unproducible began to reveal themselves.

*

The Six of Calais is another illustration, by means of history being dramatically propelled forwards, of how much better we could all have behaved if Judgment Day had arrived a little sooner. As the simpleton discovers that human beings were commanded to love their enemies because loving was 'dreadfully bad for them', so Shaw's King Edward III comes to realize that charitable forgiveness is the most satisfying means of revenge. Like *Caesar and Cleopatra*, *Great Catherine*, and *Androcles and the*

Lion (with which it shared the grassy stage of the Open Air Theatre in Regent's Park at its première), this one-act play washes away bloodshed with a douche of juvenile farce.

Early in 1917, while joy-riding in France, Shaw had filled his 'last evening stretch of the journey by inventing a play on the Rodin theme of The Burgesses of Calais, which', he told readers of the *Daily Chronicle*, 'like the play about the Rheims Virgin, I have never written down and perhaps never will'. What Quicherat's *Procès* supplied for his *Saint Joan*, Froissart's *Chronicles* now provided for *The Six of Calais*. In Froissart's story, Edward III agreed to lift the eleven-month Siege of Calais by the English in 1347 on condition that six starving hostages surrendered themselves to be hanged, wearing sackcloth and halters and carrying the keys of the town. Rodin's sculpture group (a duplicate of which stood at the Victoria Tower Gardens, Westminster) 'commemorates the bravery and selflessness – and misery – of the six burgesses who submitted themselves to Edward's humiliating conditions', wrote Stanley Weintraub, 'and immortalizes the wretched men, half-naked and wearing halters at the moment of their surrender'.

But Froissart was an 'absurd old snob' and had 'got it all wrong'. Shaw's play, according to an explanatory subtitle on the proof copy, was 'A Medieval War Story Told by Froissart and Now Retold with Certain Necessary Improvements by a Fellow of the Royal Society of Literature'. In a Prefatory Note to the published edition, Shaw claimed that it had been written 'to provide an exhibition of the art of acting' and had 'no moral whatever'. Rodin had cast one of the burghers in an attitude that suggested a diehard even more extreme than the King. All that remained for Shaw to do was 'to correct Froissart's follies and translate Rodin into words'. In his comic strip version of history, the mulish burgher and the donkey of a King ('Neddy') confront each other, sense an animal bond between them; and the play ends with a bray of hilarious laughter in which everyone joins.

'I care nothing for historical accuracy if I can get a handsome pictorial effect,' Shaw replied to a specialist in historical pageantry who wanted to see the play correctly equipped and accoutred. At such a distance, he believed history had passed into the public domain, and was in urgent need of improvements. He also wanted to get a handsome moral effect, creating a nursery world where cruelties arose, not from evil, but from the whims and reflexes of bored and frightened children. Like an imaginary entry in a child's encyclopaedia, complete with a King from A. A. Milne, this painless lesson shows us that the first step towards maturity is to cease playing at being adults and admit our childhood status.

*

'I was like a princess in a fairy tale,' exclaims Shaw's athletic millionairess, Epifania Ognisanti di Parerga. In a capitalist reversal of Portia's test from *The Merchant of Venice*, Epifania's late father, 'the greatest man in the world', had made her promise that whenever a man proposed marriage to her, she was to 'give him one hundred and fifty pounds, and tell him that if within six months he had turned that hundred and fifty pounds into fifty thousand, I was his'. But it had slipped the old man's memory that 'ninety per cent of our self-made millionaires are criminals'. Or fools. Epifania has been led into an unsatisfactory marriage with a magnificent empty-headed sportsman, Alastair Fitzfassenden, who won her by a mixture of pure luck and criminal 'kiting' – thieves' slang for a system of speedily raising money on false credit (later to be recycled from Shaw's play into Salman Rushdie's novel *The Satanic Verses*).

In Act I Epifania is making her will before committing suicide. She recounts this story to her solicitor whose office, as if activated by the sheer force of her magnetism, becomes filled with the dramatis personae – her estranged husband and his demure girlfriend as well as Epifania's own bland admirer – while the smart young solicitor vainly attempts to take instructions. His attitude to these clients is Shaw's attitude to the world: an incredulous striving to discover what advice he should give.

In the second act, which takes place that evening at a dismal riverside inn, the Pig and Whistle, Epifania throws her parasitical admirer over (over her shoulder, downstairs, and into hospital) and sets her cap at a serious-looking, middle-aged Egyptian doctor who, caring nothing for money ('I care for knowledge ... knowledge is no man's property') keeps a clinic for penniless Mahometan refugees. 'I have a mother fixation,' he announces. He has made his mother a solemn financial promise that forms the counterpart to Epifania's vow to her father. So a contract is struck between them: Epifania, 'the plutocrat of plutocrats', sets out to live for six months on his 35 shillings, while the doctor resigns himself to losing her £150.

Shaw subtitled his play 'A Jonsonian Comedy in Four Acts'. All the characters have their humours, and the first two acts are crowded with much disorderly and indecorous knockabout – as if Shaw had decided to blow one of his farcical skits into a full-length work of comic bravura. Though 'commonplace in form' and with a 'stuffily matrimonial' theme, he told Leonora Ervine, 'the dialogue is raving lunacy from beginning to end'.

Shaw's fairy tale is a treasure hunt which begins next morning at a basement sweatshop along the Commercial Road where Epifania sets out to remake her fortune. This short sober third act is a variation of the Jonsonian antithetical prelude or anti-masque – a realistic interlude to highlight the extravaganza. 'The sweater and his wife speak Whitechapel Cockney,' Shaw wrote to the producer Matthew Forsyth in 1936. '. . . There is not a gleam of fun in these two poor devils.' This scene is unique in Shaw's plays and at the end, when Epifania has used her managerial genius to take over the business, the stupefied sweater rubs his eyes. 'It seems to me like a sort of dream,' he says – and we are about to re-enter Shaw's dream world.

His Cinderella soon wins her Egyptian Prince. Like the miller's daughter, she has learnt Rumpelstiltskin's secret of how to spin straw into gold; like King Midas she can turn everything, even her emotions, into money. 'My stories are the old stories,' Shaw had written in his Preface to *Three Plays for Puritans*, but he gave these ancient legends and folk tales ironically happy endings. Beginning as a scullery maid at the Pig and Whistle, Epifania has transformed the place within five months into an attractive riverside inn and appointed herself its new proprietor. 'It was cruel for us; but we couldnt deny that she was always right,' acknowledges the son of the previous owner, who is now its manager. '. . . My father had a stroke and wont last long, I'm afraid. And my mother has gone a bit silly. Still, it was best for them; and they have all the comforts they care for.'

As in the first act, the characters assemble on stage round Epifania. The Egyptian doctor has given away his £150 to a widow whose husband had omitted to patent a successful invention – but this is interpreted by Epifania as a profitable retrospective investment, which meets her father's stipulation (and provides a nice example of Shaw's belief that logic is merely a device for getting what you want). The doctor too gets what he wants. He has fallen in love with Epifania's pulse. 'Ooooh! I have never felt such a pulse. It is like a slow sledge hammer,' he exclaims. '. . . it is a pulse in a hundred thousand. I love it: I cannot give it up.' The play ends with the solicitor finally taking instructions.

Epifania is a monetarist heroine and the genius of capitalism. 'I think Allah loves those who make money,' she says. She sweeps everyone before her with this gospel of money and dominates the play much as Undershaft dominated the action of *Major Barbara*. Shaw had been forced to rework the last act of *Major Barbara* and, for similar reasons, he offered a highly implausible alternative ending to *The Millionairess*. Here the happy couple contemplate going to Russia but decide instead to 'make the British Empire a Soviet republic'. Shaw was following the advice he had fathered on Henry James over his play *The Saloon*, as well as responding to those Marxist critics who 'since virtually the beginning of his career', the critic Bernard Dukore wrote, had been urging him to 'provide an upbeat ending'. In Shaw's version for 'countries with Communist sympathies', Epifania's assets (not her life) will be liquidated, and her abilities converted into worthwhile social and political power. It is also a brief golden romance spun around Shaw's hypothetical career in a communist country. 'I shall not be a millionairess,' Epifania predicts; 'but I shall be in the Sovnarkom within six months and in the Politbureau before the end of the year ... such scope for my natural powers!' In this never-performed alternative Shaw abandons the last illusion of reality and smilingly floats his make-believe like a fragile soap-bubble in the air – without trying to satisfy his reader's credulity or appease his scepticism.

Epifania can trace her lineage back to Lydia Carew, the lady who had won the prizefighter in Shaw's novel *Cashel Byron's Profession* and provoked R. L. Stevenson's admiring exclamation: 'My God, what women!' She is instantly recognizable, the biographer Margot Peters reminds us, as the quintessential Shavian heroine. 'She has Blanche Sartorius's temper, Vivie Warren's athletic grip, Ann Whitefield's "bounding pulse", Saint Joan's bossiness and Orinthia's arrogance – compounded daily.'

Epifania takes centre stage and commands all eyes. She is an amalgam of every powerful woman Shaw had known – a 'female Cecil Rhodes' he called her, who believed that 'Men are a different and very inferior species.' Though the cocks may crow, it is the hens that lay the eggs. 'People will say you are the millionairess,' he had written to Nancy Astor, '– an awful, impossible woman.' The short third act in the Commercial Road uses some of Beatrice Webb's experiences in a tailor's sweatshop in London's East End ('Beatrice will have to revise the Millionairess,' Shaw wrote to Sidney, 'as she has a scene in a sweater's den'); and the title itself is a reference to his ironic description of Charlotte at the time of their courtship and marriage – 'my Irish millionairess'.

Shaw's attitude to this superwoman is conveyed by his Egyptian doctor: 'You are a terrible woman; but I love your pulse.' Here is the irresistible beat of the Life Force reduced by capitalism to the rhythmic rise and fall of market forces. 'I have to take the world as I find it,' Epifania claims. To which the doctor replies: 'The wrath of Allah shall overtake those who leave the world no better than they found it.'

Shaw's provisional title for the play had been *His Tragic Clients* and he advised the Birmingham Theatre's stage-director Herbert Prentice that Epifania 'is exotic and essentially tragic all through. She should speak perfect English ... but with the tragic rhythm of Mrs Siddons.' In *The Millionairess* a great princess in prison lies. 'Epifania is essentially tragic and volcanic,' Shaw told Edith Evans: 'she has no sense of humor. Except the solicitor, who is mildly amused at the follies of the others, everyone in the play is intensely in earnest.' Her tragedy lies both in the dissipation of her natural powers into pointless money-making and also in the fortress-like personality she shares with Shaw's mother which bars emotional relationships. G.B.S. knew her tragedy well. She is a person 'that no one can live with'.

Epifania has been disliked by generations of theatre critics. 'What makes the play rabidly distasteful is Shaw's patent admiration for the eroticism of wealth and power,' wrote Michael Billington in the *Guardian* after a revival of the play in 1988. This is much the same distaste felt by Beatrice Webb when she read the play in 1935 and saw in it a representation of her friend's 'admiration of what is *forceful*, however ugly and silly'. Unlike Shylock, humiliated at the end of *The Merchant of Venice*, or Volpone cast in irons at the end of Jonson's comedy, Epifania begins on the verge of suicide and ends triumphant. 'The heroine Epifania is sexy *because* rich,' wrote Robert Cushman after seeing Penelope Keith play the role in 1979. '... She is cold and challenging: so is the play.' Shaw makes his dictator an 'awful, impossible woman', then aligns his own 'mother-fixation' with the prevailing spirit of the mid-1930s. 'No; you don't want a Mussolini,' he had written in 1933. 'But if you are not very careful you will get one.'

'My third manner is going to be more trying than my second,' Shaw had predicted in a letter to J. C. Squire after the Great War; 'but then third manners always are.' His digressions and lapses into buffoonery had grown more frequent, his flights from reality more extreme. 'There is no time for silences or pauses: the actor must play on the line and not between the lines, and must do nine-tenths of his acting with his voice,' he had written to John Barrymore in 1925. Two years later, in a letter to the *New York Times*, he explained that even in his *Plays Unpleasant* he had never been a representationist or (except in the Platonic sense) a realist in the theatre. 'I was always in the classic tradition, recognizing that stage characters must be endowed by the author with a conscious self-knowledge and power of expression, and ... a freedom from inhibitions,' he explained. '... My plays require a special technique of acting, and, in particular, great virtuosity in sudden transitions of mood that seem to the ordinary actor to be transitions from one "line" of character to another. But, after all, this is only fully accomplished acting.'

Shaw's string of tricks and turns often depend for their effects upon what he called 'drunken, stagey, brassbowelled barnstormers' and the gargantuan acting tradition he had witnessed as a boy in nineteenth-century melodramas and music-hall entertainments. All his plays, with their emphasis on vocal contrast, bear the marks of his musical knowledge. 'Opera taught me to shape my plays into recitatives, arias, duets, trios, ensemble finales, and bravura pieces,' he was to write towards the end of his life, 'to display the technical accomplishments of the executants.'

357

The executant he wanted for *The Millionairess* was Edith Evans. 'It is not really a difficult play,' he wrote to her in 1935. 'It all depends on your part and not on any great nicety of production: either you can do it or you cannot; and I think you can.' But Edith Evans felt uncertain: the part was unsympathetic and called for a type of big acting that had gone out of fashion.

After its world première in Vienna *The Millionairess* was performed in Munich and Berlin, and there were also successful productions in Poland and Italy. The first English-language presentation was put on in March 1936 by the McMahon Players in Melbourne who had skilfully produced *The Simpleton* and were becoming famous for introducing good foreign plays into Australia. In Britain it 'is having hole-and-corner performances all over the place, [and] will be played at the Malvern Festival, by whom God knows', Shaw wrote dispiritedly to Sybil Thorndike in April 1937. 'Whether it will ever get any further not even God knows.'

After more than four years Edith Evans relented, but a London production starring her as Epifania at the Globe Theatre was prevented from opening in the autumn of 1940 by the Blitz.

It seemed an unlucky play for Shaw, but he continued to keep his eye out for the 'very vigorous actress' who could take on Epifania. 'The part requires just such a personality as Miss [Katharine] Hepburn,' he wrote to Lawrence Langner in 1940. 'Has she ever read the play?' In fact she had read it but decided she did not like it enough; then she read it again ten years later and persuaded the Theatre Guild in New York and Binkie Beaumont of Tennant Productions in London to produce it with her in the title role. Shaw had been dead for two years but, just as he 'had prophesied, Hepburn was superb in the part', recalled Lawrence Langner. This was the last new Shaw production by the Theatre Guild in New York and it played to packed houses. In London, too, it was welcomed with enthusiastic notices by critics unfamiliar with such prodigious acting. Shaw had always insisted that the play would 'not bear underplaying or half-playing'. A young critic, Kenneth Tynan, describing it as 'that terrible hybrid, a didactic farce ... written in the twilight of a civilization and of its author's life', and believing the part of Epifania to be 'nearly unactable', found himself carried away.

'Miss Hepburn took it, acted it, and found a triumph in it. She glittered like a bracelet thrown up at the sun; she was metallic, yet reminded us that metals shine and can also melt. Epifania clove to her, and she bestowed on the role a riotous elegance and a gift of tears ... *The Millionairess* scores a bull's-eye on the target of her talents ... in her last long speech, a defence of marriage and all the risks it implies, an urchin quaver invades the determination of her voice and coaxes the heart.'

[3]

I cannot tell you the exact date of my death. It has not yet been settled.
Shaw to Hannen Swaffer (26 February 1938)

'...I dropped dead on the 24th Nov,' G.B.S. notified John Reith on 3 December 1934. The doctor had diagnosed a 'not serious' heart attack and Shaw slept continuously for almost three days and nights. It was 'the greatest pity', he told his old friend Henry Salt, that his heart had officiously started again and 'that I revived like Lazarus. I was literally tired to death...'

Though feeling very incompetent, it was a matter of Shavian pride to be sending Maynard Keynes within a week of his attack what Virginia Woolf was to call 'a long magnificently spry & juicy letter' done in his most breathtaking style with 'the whole of economics twiddled round on his finger'. Keynes, recognizing that 'the old gentleman is weak and ill', wondered why the great men of that generation went in for such stunts. It was difficult to treat them seriously. A man such as Shaw could never understand the revolution in economic thinking that Keynes was shortly to set off with his *General Theory*. So were these Shavian stage effects simply a box of cosmetics for colouring up morale as 'the old gentleman' grew further out of date, or some acoustical gesture for catching the ear of the young? In the mid-1920s Virginia Woolf had sighed over her teenage nephews, Julian and Quentin Bell, for believing 'Bernard Shaw greater than Shakespeare'. By the mid-1930s Keynes was deploring the students' zeal for communism at universities. He had an 'unmitigated contempt', Beatrice Webb noticed 'for the Communist undergraduates'.

Beatrice and Sidney went up to London in the second week of January 1935 and found G.B.S. much recovered ('I cannot pretend that there is anything wrong with me'). But Charlotte lay ill in bed. Three doctors attended her, with a day nurse, a night nurse and a maid – 'yet she lives!' Shaw rejoiced. What would have happened to her had he died? Only Sidney, she confided, (and of course Beatrice) could have helped her. 'The two old couples are each other's oldest friends,' Beatrice wrote in her diary, 'and we all dread the death of anyone of the quartet, and would feel responsible for the remaining partner.'

Watching each other anxiously, Shaw and Charlotte reported their ups and downs to the Astors and the Webbs, and a few other remaining friends such as Cockerell and Trebitsch, Gilbert Murray and Henry Salt. 'She is

359

decisively convalescent now,' Shaw informed Sydney Cockerell in the second week of February; 'but it was quite a near thing.' He wished she were happier, but then 'we are both slightly dotty with age'.

From the middle of the 1930s onwards Shaw struggled to reduce his volume of work. 'I do not practise now as a journalist unless there is something I want badly to say,' he explained to the editor of the *Morning Post* in the summer of 1936. '... my experience of octogenarians who imagine themselves as good as ever when they are actually outmoded bores is rather intimidating.' 'I Have Retired,' he insisted during a speech the same month at the People's Theatre, Newcastle. He did retire from the drudgery of directing his plays ('I am too old for such games,' he told Binkie Beaumont), but the bibliography of his writings lists thirty-seven contributions to the press in 1936; fifty-five in 1937; fifty-nine in 1938; and sixty-three in 1939. 'We cant take G.B.S. away from all his business & papers & interviews & usual occupations,' Charlotte admitted to Nancy Astor. '... He works – writes – as well as ever, but the result is he sits over his jobs too long.'

But was he really writing as well as ever? 'Give him a good situation, like Edward VIII's abdication, or the coronation of George VI, and his literary response is brilliant and wise, witty and worthwhile,' Beatrice Webb wrote in her diary. But she could not endure his late plays with all their irritating slapstick and knockabout. He seemed unable now to visualize complicated social institutions and their reactions on individuals. 'But how can G.B.S. get through this last spell of life without his daily stint of thinking and writing?' she wondered.

'Without this daily task life would be meaningless ... There is no remedy for the defects of old age – whether they take the form of continuous discomfort or poor quality of output – or both.'

But sometimes, as he reasserted the poise and agility of a young man, G.B.S. seemed to have found a remedy. The actress Irene Hentschel saw him entering the Globe Theatre in London at the end of 1936 'with the vigour of a hurricane'. Virginia Woolf too marvelled at his wires, his spring. 'What an efficient, adept, trained arch & darter!' she exclaimed. '... And the hands flung out in gesture: he has the power to make the world his shape.' Visiting him in Whitehall Court, the Irish writer John Stewart Collis noticed how 'easy and ungrand' his manner still was. But he had grown terribly thin, his body supporting a white-bearded head 'like a long stem holding up a large flower'. Another Irish writer, the poet Brendan O'Byrne, watched him 'awesomely bearded and erect' advancing along Pall Mall

> 'one long leg placed
> Before the other as if he could – if he wished – so
> Bestride the earth, his stout ash walking-stick
> Striking the pavement before him as if
> To teach it a lesson.'

Recently come over from Dublin and sleeping rough in the London streets, the young man

> 'had a hat I remember, and that
> Is most important, for the whole point of this story is
> That I raised my hat to Bernard Shaw, and he
> Raised his hat to me.'

In such ways, for as long as possible, G.B.S. kept in touch with his own youth. 'But alas! we are *old*.' Old age brought the Shaws renewed problems. 'The tropics cannot be too hot for Charlotte; the equator suits her to perfection,' G.B.S. wrote to Sydney Cockerell; but Charlotte confided to Nancy Astor that 'Sea life does not agree with him [G.B.S.], & the climate of the tropics knocks him to pieces.' After 1936 they did not travel abroad or go to the Malvern Festivals. 'It's like that: up & down: but alas! the downs tend to come round too soon,' Charlotte noted in 1938; and Shaw reckoned that 'the only way I can keep Charlotte up at present is by deciding that we are NOT going to do something'. Even so, she still fretted over his work and her own weakening ability to interrupt it. He 'does not get enough changes of scene ... We are really getting immovable!' Nevertheless each summer they would move to a country town hotel, usually by the sea, and declare themselves the better for it. 'This hotel is a success for us,' Shaw reported to Blanche Patch from the Impney Hotel at Droitwich. 'We sleep like anything ...'

At Droitwich Shaw had his portrait painted again. 'I am not the man you read about in the papers,' he said to the artist Vincent Moody. Beatrice Webb had also remarked on the widening contrast between his world fame and the intimate charm of his personality. She resented the fame. But though he no longer stimulated her on world events, he was far more fascinating now, she felt, than he had been as a young man. Then he was merely *impish*; old age had made him statuesque – 'he is always lovable and exciting to look at and listen to'.

When Beatrice had fallen ill earlier in the 1930s and the Webbs' finances during the slump had become depleted by over-expenditure on travel and research, Shaw arranged for £1,000 to be credited to Sidney's account at the Soviet Bank in London. 'We need, I think, have no scruple in accepting this most generous gift from my oldest friend,' Sidney reassured Beatrice who was then recovering from a kidney complaint in a nursing home. In Sidney's letter to Shaw himself there is an unusual tremor of emotion. 'I am overwhelmed ... It comes most timely to remove our anxieties [and] ... as an immense relief to me,' he wrote.

'It is a long time since we first met at the Zetetical Society ... It led to nearly half a century of a friendship and companionship, which has been most fruitful to me. I look back on it with wonder at the advantage, and indeed, the beauty of that prolonged friendship. Apart from marriage, it has certainly been the biggest thing in my life; which without it would have been poor indeed.'

The Webbs and the Shaws continued their annual visits to each other's houses through most of the 1930s. 'Two nights with the Shaws: GBS failing, Charlotte still going strong, Sidney well and I ailing,' Beatrice noted in the autumn of 1936 after a visit to Ayot. 'Shall we four meet again here or at Passfield? I have my doubts ...' In the summer of 1937 the Shaws went to Passfield and G.B.S. helped the Webbs with the proofs of their revised edition of *Soviet Communism* while Sidney helped the Shaws to redraft their wills. 'So continues the old unbroken comradeship in work, started forty-five years ago, between GBS and the Webbs,' observed Beatrice.

Though these were affectionate meetings, each one seemed to mark another stage on a downward journey. Early in the New Year, a few days after Beatrice's eightieth birthday (celebrated by Shaw with two columns in the *Spectator*), Sidney had a stroke. 'The inevitable has come, one of the partners has fallen on the way, the youngest and the strongest,' Beatrice wrote in her diary. 'He may lie there for a while, but we shall never march together again in work and recreation. I cannot march alone ... So there he is lying in the bed ... He will have care and love so long as I am strong enough to give it.'

Shaw was too deaf these days to use the telephone with ease. He tried, and later wrote: 'Sidney has given us rather a fright ... we shouldnt do such things ... we should arrange to die quietly in our beds of heart failure.'

Though he made a recovery, and was able to read and follow conversations, Sidney remained a semi-invalid at Passfield, partially paralysed and with his speech impaired. 'I suppose it is best for you to be alone at Passfield with nobody to bother you, except your invalid,' Shaw wrote to Beatrice; 'but somehow it does not feel that way to us: the impulse to stand by is so strong that it needs an exercise of conscious reasoning to stifle it.'

'I dare say it's time for all us nineteenth century writers to clear out,' he was reported as saying when he learnt of Maxim Gorki's death. 'You'd better prepare my obituary,' he instructed the *New York Times*. Actuarially he was dead already, or so it sometimes felt. 'My number is up,' he told the British journalist Hannen Swaffer at the end of February 1938.

Three months later, he suddenly collapsed again, fainting under Charlotte's eyes. Sidney managed to send him one of his first short letters since his own illness. 'What a long life you and I have had, and done so much in it, with the aid of wifes!' But G.B.S. was such a 'naughty patient' that Charlotte found it almost impossible to aid him – she even called in her eighty-year-old ex-inamorato Dr Axel Munthe for a lunchtime consultation. Shaw lay on a sofa claiming that he was curing himself of all his disablements, from angina pectoris to locomotor ataxy, by prolonged relaxation. 'He scoffs at doctors & we were going on & he is getting weaker & yellower until I nearly went mad!' Charlotte protested. '*Then* he consented, & our dear American osteopath [William Cooper] found him just the right doctor!'

The right doctor was Geoffrey Evans, a pathologist from Bart's, who diagnosed pernicious anaemia. Until recently the treatment for pernicious anaemia had been 'swallowing pounds of raw liver', as Gilbert Murray confirmed to Shaw, 'but I think perhaps death is preferable to that, and evidently you have a superior way of your own'. The new remedy consisted of fifteen monthly injections of liver extract which he allowed the doctors 'to squirt' into 'my lumbar regions'. Almost at once the *Daily Express* reported 'G.B.S. Takes Meat'. 'I do not,' he answered, and he went on to reassure the *Vegetarian News* that 'My diet remains unchanged.'

All this looked like the same battle he had fought with orthodox medicine over forty years ago when Charlotte, cursing his obstinate diet, had carried him off and married him. With her team of general practitioners, pathologists, osteopaths and consultants she was now rescuing him again. 'G.B.S. seems to be responding to their treatment in a wonderful way,' she wrote to their Ayot neighbour Apsley Cherry-Garrard on 20 June. 'He seems a different man already.' Though he soon changed from yellow to pink, Shaw was not entirely happy. The liver extract had apparently set up a rejuvenated supply of red corpuscles, but 'my own view is that I am by nature a white-blooded man', he confided to Henry Salt.

The weapons in Shaw's armoury were still bright from the last century and he took out all the old and glittering arguments. But the battleground was changing and he found himself having to combat not only Charlotte's anxieties and the doctors' conventionalities, but also the new militancy of vegetarians themselves. They bombarded him with queries and complaints.

'Poor G.B.S. just returned from death's door,' wrote Charlotte, '... forced to write letter after letter when he could hardly hold the pen.'

His miraculous recovery had seemed complete when, in the first week of December, he suddenly collapsed again. In a letter to Nancy Astor, he explained what had happened. 'I went out to lunch with the Londonderries too soon after the operation [his monthly injection]. I felt queer in the cab; and when I had given up my hat and things in the hall in Park Lane I flopped bang on the flags, and upset the whole luncheon party.' Remaining unconscious for quite a long time, '[I] gave Charlotte a considerable fright before I spontaneously resurrected.' This fright restored his moral authority over Charlotte and he was able to replace the liver injections with tiny grains, clean and tasteless, of a naturist's concoction called Hepamalt. 'Of this I have consumed tons to please the doctors and redden my blood counts, without as far as I can make out, producing any effect whatever,' he told Kathleen Kennet several years later. 'But the anaemia and all its symptoms are gone. The liver gets the credit, though I suspect I have cured myself. I believe in the Nature Cure.'

By the end of January 1939 G.B.S. was calling for research into vegetable hormones and developing a theory of protein poisoning which he later added to a new Vegetarian Diet postcard. But this was not good enough for vegetarian fundamentalists and Shaw was stung by their hostility. 'Liver extract you would take if you developed pernicious anaemia,' he answered one subscriber to *The American Vegetarian*. 'If you were diabetic you would take insulin. If you had edema you would take thyroid. You may think you wouldn't; but you would if your diet failed to cure you. You would try any of the gland extracts, the mineral drugs, the so-called vaccines, if it were that or your death...' Shaw's anger was partly political. He believed that his own aesthetic and economic arguments were more honest than the claims of disease-free longevity made by radical vegetarians, and he felt convinced he was the better public advocate for vegetarianism. But privately he was in sympathy with some of their extreme views. Though he was to claim that 'I had no more scruple about trying it [liver extract] than I have eggs and butter,' the truth was that he had felt 'intense disgust' at being filled with such 'loathsome stuff'. Having studied the subject during his convalescence he had made the unpleasant discovery that 'modern hormones have been arrived at by thousands of experiments on dogs, and that many of them are extracted from unappetizing materials which', he wrote to Henry Salt, 'I shall not nauseate you by particularizing'. He was greatly relieved when he could bring 'this repulsive story' to an end and replace the hormones with yeast. 'We are now so damnably old,' he wrote to Lady Londonderry a few days before his collapse at her house, 'that we have to regard ourselves as morally dead.' His response to militant vegetarians was to seek an official assurance early in the Second World War that, when rationing began, special provision would be made for them. It was a fighting diet. 'For some unexplained natural cause vegetarians are the most ferocious class we have; and any underfeeding of them would produce a reduction of our national fighting spirit out of all proportion to their numbers.'

Charlotte was the reason why Shaw consented to live. 'My most distressing complaint is Anorexia, or dislike of food,' he told Henry Salt: '...if I were not a married man and could do as I pleased, [I] would not lift a finger to survive.' This was how Beatrice felt about Sidney. If he died, 'I would gladly sleep and rise no more', she had written. But since his illness she slept less, rose earlier, and felt a greater stimulus to keep going. Visiting the Shaws during G.B.S.'s illness she had found him a 'white-skinned shadow' with Charlotte 'bending over him with motherly affection'. He was so delighted to see her that they 'actually embraced, and for the first time I kissed GBS!'

'Are you both bearing it well?' Shaw asked Beatrice as the Second World War began. '...Charlotte is not yet well enough to write.'

'Sidney remains calm and happy,' Beatrice replied. 'Meanwhile love to you both – as you say "we are too old to love" in such tragic times – but we should miss each other.'

The war was to make travelling difficult, but in the early summer of 1940 Sidney prevailed on Beatrice to take him up to London for one last meeting with G.B.S. and Charlotte. 'Yesterday we drove up to lunch with the Shaws at Whitehall Court. Sidney insisted on doing so: he had not seen them for two and a half years and wanted badly to see them "once again",' Beatrice wrote in her diary on 24 May. Old people, she sometimes thought, were either obsessed or scatterbrained. She had become obsessed with Soviet Russia; Shaw's eclectic mind, always singling out the unexpected, was brilliantly scatterbrained. She envied him his unquenchable interest in the future. 'Of the four I think I am the most willing to sink into nothingness and GBS least so.' If she felt resentment, it was quickly dissolved, as it always had been, by his admiration for Sidney and his wonderful kindness to them both. She felt more warmly now towards Charlotte too. Her stamina and loyalty were extraordinary. At lunch they spoke about the Fabian Society (of which Beatrice had been made honorary President) and the London School of Economics (to which Charlotte had given another £1,000) and about contemporary politics which for fifty years had been the fabric of their friendship. 'They were delightfully affectionate,' Beatrice wrote. But 'Why have we lived so long', Shaw asked her. 'One war was enough.'

*

Others would just escape the war: W. B. Yeats, who died at the precocious age of seventy-three; Troubetzkoy, who had fallen into a fire and burnt to death (it did not bear thinking about); and also 'one of my most intimate and valued friends', Henry Salt. 'He was, and I am, too old to desire reasonably to live any longer; but you will miss him for a while before you benefit by the release,' Shaw wrote to Salt's wife Catherine, with his own and Charlotte's death in mind.

As his life lengthened so the *Lives* continued to multiply and spiral around it. By 1939 over eighty works had been published about him. There were critical as well as biographical studies springing up everywhere – Canada, China, Denmark, Finland, France, Germany, Holland, Hungary, India, Italy, Japan, Norway, Poland, Russia, Switzerland, Yugoslavia...

Frank Harris's 'unauthorized biography' had been first published in Britain in 1931, the year before Archibald Henderson's authorized *Playboy and Prophet* came out in the United States. These books, largely ghosted by G.B.S. himself and supporting in different ways his commitment to socialism, represent the aspects of his personality and career he was prepared to make visible to the public. But the public was not wholly satisfied and by the mid-1930s St John Ervine was preparing to show them how Harris and Henderson should have done it.

Shaw tried to head him off. He had known Ervine for twenty years and recognized him to be an aggressively independent man-of-letters. He was less likely to allow his book to be taken over and rewritten than Henderson had been; and he could not be humorously disparaged like Harris. 'Dont,' Shaw advised him. 'When you have had as many biographies written about you as I have, you will learn that there is only one way to flatten out their distorting mirrors, and that is to write an autobiography or else get at the proof sheets of the biographers and rewrite them.'

Besides it would take infinite patience, pitiless time.

Having outlined what he hoped were unacceptable working conditions, Shaw disparaged the project itself. When his autobiographical writings and volumes of correspondence were added to the shelves of works about him, it became obvious that the market was glutted. Perhaps Ervine could splash around instead with a harmless critical compendium – like Chesterton he was bound to get 'a splash or two in on the right spot'. Some day 'I shall have to write The Quintessence of Shavianism', he added – 'probably in the form of a catechism – unless you do it first'.

But Ervine was obstinate: 'I began to write it.' So Shaw was obliged to redouble his disparagement. He gave Ervine particulars as to why he was quite the wrong sort of chap – he would put an almost Webbian mass and intensity of research into the job, but none of his talent. 'You seem interested not in individuals but only in their classes,' he was to write to him. '... Sociology is not biography. Genius abolishes it. If I am not a genius I am not worth a biography. If I am a genius you must keep your spotlight on me and your ambers only on Protestant Dublin.' This ran contrary to the instructions he had issued Archibald Henderson to 'make me a mere peg on which to hang a study of the last quarter of the XIX century'. And it omitted the sociological reminder he had given James Elroy Flecker: 'For Heaven's sake remember that there are plenty of geniuses about.'

But as he began warming to this exposition of his friend's shortcomings, so he started to dig out some of the essential material Ervine needed for his book. It took Shaw until 1942 to abort this biography; and it took St John Ervine until 1956 to resurrect it for publication with a Foreword revealing how G.B.S. had 'hoped that I would one day finish what I had begun'.

Shaw's method of postponing this biography until after his death was peculiarly exasperating to Ervine. He made absolutely certain that the market was glutted by publishing at the Gregynog Press an autobiographical miscellany misleadingly entitled *Shaw Gives Himself Away* and then by helping into print another biography which he felt more confident of controlling: the celebrated *Life* by Hesketh Pearson.

Pearson, like Ervine, had known Shaw for many years. Before taking up biography he had been an actor and created the part of Metellus in the first production of *Androcles and the Lion*. Like Ervine, too, he was a professional writer. His *Lives* of Hazlitt, Labouchère, Tom Paine and Gilbert and Sullivan were establishing him as the most popular British biographer of the 1930s. But he cared little for Lenin and Marx, and hinted that he would rather die than read *Das Kapital*.

Why then did Shaw prefer Pearson to Ervine? Perhaps one reason was that Pearson had the advantage of not being an Ulster man. The collaboration between a native of Belfast and a native of Dublin could be explosive: 'You will understand the Irish side of me better than anybody who is not Irish,' St John Ervine was later to quote Shaw as saying to him. But perhaps he did not want the Irish side of him 'understood': Demetrius O'Bolger's 'understanding' of his Irish years was a daunting precedent. Shaw needed to dissolve his Irish past into international socialism. Ervine, whose unreconstituted socialism was without ideological foundations, would make a horrid mess of his politics, Shaw appears to have believed, and would get his Soviet faith unalterably wrong, whereas Pearson would cover it skimpily and let G.B.S. augment it with his own version. Indeed Pearson, it seemed, was in the line of previous biographers. G. K. Chesterton had written a friendly Introduction to his Life of Sydney Smith; Frank Harris had been his youthful literary hero. So it was really the old game all over again and a good way, in the last decade of Shaw's life, of forestalling any other game.

In his first book, a volume of essays called *Modern Men and Mummers* published in 1921, Pearson's opening sentence read: 'We moderns are the products of Bernard Shaw.' Since then modernism had moved elsewhere and modern biography was reputed to be growing increasingly inquisitive. But Pearson was not of the Strachey school and G.B.S. knew roughly what to expect. He tested his biographer with the customary shot across the bows and when in 1938 Pearson sent him a proposal for his book, replied simply 'Dont.' Then, as if conducting one of his early philanderings, he added: 'I shall dissuade you personally any time you like to see me.' Pearson called at Whitehall Court that autumn and over a long conversation, he tells us, demolished Shaw's innumerable objections. 'So you may go ahead with my blessing,' Shaw wrote to him at the beginning of December. 'There is no one else in the field' – which effectively edged out St John Ervine.

'If you want to be debunked with a loving hand, I'm your man,' Pearson had said. And Shaw answered: 'I need inbunking, not debunking, having debunked myself like a born clown.' Shaw liked Pearson. He liked his lack of formal education, his cheerfulness, his robust opinions – all Shavian attributes. 'It is far better to know nothing like me,' Pearson told him, 'than to know everything and get it all wrong like you.' Here was a man with whom Shaw could work. 'I find your company both restful and invigorating,' he wrote.

He was 'increasingly generous with help and advice', Pearson remembered. 'Though the busiest writer of his time, he never failed to see me when I wanted an interview, and he dealt with all my letters fully, mostly by return of post.' He also sent letters of introduction to his friends. 'Hesketh Pearson, a littérateur who specializes in biography and has been commissioned by the publishing firm of Collins to operate on me, is very anxious to get from you some account of our Russian elopement,' he wrote to Nancy Astor. But Charlotte felt uneasy. She thought Pearson was rather too assertively good-looking and suspected him of being a 'cad'. G.B.S. however assured her she would be omitted from the book. He quickly assumed command. 'The biography is the usual thing,' he notified Beatrice Webb. ' ... As he and I are old acquaintances since the days of Frank Harris I have promised to tell him anything he wants to know, and to recommend him to you, which I do accordingly, as anything is better than to leave biographers to their imagination and to press gossip.'

With this breezy assistance Pearson sailed along fast. 'My wife did most of the research work ... and I took about a year to write it.' At the end of 1939 he had pretty well completed the course but before sending off his typescript to the publisher he enquired whether Shaw would care to glance at it. 'His reply convinced me that it could not go to the printer until he had seen it.'

Over the next year Blanche Patch would come across chapters strewn all over the place as Shaw went to work altering, amplifying, editing and embellishing the biography. He worked 'to the confusion of my own affairs' under constant pressure from his biographer and would respond, when this pressure became too strong, by forecasting that it would occupy him another five years or that he looked forward to finishing it before Easter 2040. This revision of Pearson's text 'took me rather longer than writing the book myself', he told Beatrice Webb who noted in her diary: 'G.B.S. insisted on correcting it – much to H.P.'s disgust.' That was in the summer of 1942 but still it 'has not yet been published'.

At first the corrections were fairly light and made in pencil. But as Shaw grew more interested in his *Life* so he turned to ink using (as with Archibald Henderson) red ink for unpublishable outbursts: 'This is all poppycock . . . You jumping idiot.' Pearson had derived his technique as a biographer from his earlier career on the stage. To some degree he acted his characters on the page. Shaw's method of ghostwriting his Lives involved borrowing something of the character of his biographer. As Pearson's 'uninvited collaborator', he was faced with an intriguing linguistic exercise of impersonating someone who was Pearsonifying him. He saw in Pearson's stage career an opportunity to dramatize himself. He placed Charlotte out of bounds, revised the Fabian chapters heavily, and in two other areas suppressed or contradicted what Pearson had written.

'From the many hints that he dropped during the writing and revising of the biography,' Pearson later recorded, 'I came to the conclusion that the one event in his personal life that had brought him regret almost amounting to sorrow was his estrangement from Granville Barker . . . this break in their friendship was his most keenly felt loss . . . it was the only important matter about which he asked me to be reticent.'

But there was another important matter on which G.B.S. overrode Pearson, obliterating most traces of his original narrative. This was the chapter entitled 'Retreat to Moscow'. In his autobiography Pearson was to write: 'I gave his own account of his attitude to Communism and his trip to Russia, but I led up to it with some of those anti-institutional quotations which he thought beside the point.' In the original typescript Pearson had distanced himself from Shaw's Stalinism, given an ironic description largely based on Nancy Astor's evidence of their 'Russian elopement', and traced a vein of insensitivity to suffering in Shaw's character. Here, momentarily, was a man who shifted the centre of gravity from the individual to the state, filled his emptiness with facts, and let collectivism come like a curtain between himself and reality. 'He praised and upheld the Russian dictatorship, which suppressed free speech, murdered its political opponents, starved its recalcitrant peasants to death,' Pearson wrote.

'... The study of Marx, he believed, had made a man of him. But he was wrong ... not man but the masses engaged his attention and just as brooding too much on one's wrongs produces an indifference to other people's, so brooding too much on other people's wrongs produces an indifference to individuals ...

'... Though he had fought all his life for freedom of thought, though he had opposed persecution and oppression to the utmost of his ability, though he had ceaselessly preached the gospel of toleration, reason and humanity, he was able to shut his eyes to the cruelties of a government that appeared to him progressive ... '

To Shaw's mind the danger of Stalin and the Russian Revolution to Britain was similar to the danger of Napoleon and the French Revolution at the beginning of the previous century. Reacting to bloodshed that had stained originally noble causes, the British became more cautious, insular, resistant to all experimentation and change. As Hazlitt and Shelley held to their vision of *Liberté, Egalité, Fraternité*, so Shaw clung to his belief in pure communism as the dayspring of a new era. Affecting less emotion than he felt, he treated Soviet atrocities as unnecessary boulders stopping the passage of fresh ideas in Britain, and simply rolled them away. This was why the anti-institutional quotations that Hesketh Pearson used – 'Civic education does not mean education in blind obedience to authority, but education in controversy and liberty ... in scepticism, in discontent and betterment' – seemed to him beside his biographer's anti-totalitarian point. For it was primarily among the British that Shaw wished to promote controversy, discontent and betterment.

Shaw condensed Pearson's objections into a single paragraph and allowed a transitional passage ending with the sentence: 'But we must make an effort to see what happened from his own angle.' Then he eliminated the rest of Pearson's account and substituted more than 4,000 words of his own, painting a harmless yet exhilarating picture of the Soviet political landscape. 'To Shaw it was better than he expected, and full of novelty and promise,' he wrote.

By the end he had given so much of what he called his 'unique private history' to the book that Pearson, a most open and honest writer, suggested that his contributions should be shown in the text between square brackets or by indentation. But Shaw was horrified at the thought of his collaboration being exposed. His reply to Pearson is a revealing description of his semi-autobiographical technique. 'Not on your life, Hesketh,' he wrote. 'What I have written I have written in your character, not in my own.'

'As an autobiographer I should have written quite differently. There are things that you may quite properly say which would come less gracefully from me. I have carefully avoided altering your opinions except where you had not known the facts . . .

'. . . But if a word is said to connect me with the authorship of the book or its first proposal or its commercial profits I shall be driven to the most desperate steps to disclaim it. It must appear as Harris's book did . . .

'. . . Dont run away with the notion that your readers – least of all the critics – will spot any difference between your stuff and mine: they wont. In the Harris book they didnt. If the story carries them along they will not start detective work . . . I strongly advise you to do what I did in the Harris case. When the book is safely in print, take the copy and burn every scrap of it. It will then be forever impossible for either of us to lay a finger on any page or passage and say "This is Pearson's copyright, & this Shaw's".'

This copyright argument, which by implication holds a financial menace, is invalid because the third-person narrative was copyrighted by the publisher in Pearson's name, and in any case it was open to Shaw specifically to hand over the copyright in his contributions. In fact Pearson did not burn the typescript. It is now in the Humanities Research Center at the University of Texas at Austin and betrays a similar quantity of rewriting to the Henderson proofs at the University of North Carolina at Chapel Hill.

But Pearson's biography was far more entertaining than Henderson's. 'The success of your book has driven the whole trade mad,' Shaw congratulated him in January 1943, three months after its publication in the United States and Britain. To the end of his life he would refer readers to this biography ('there is nothing better than Hesketh Pearson'), using this recommendation as a deterrent to other potential biographers ('they are the plagues of my life') and as a protection against a third blockbuster from Henderson ('Drop it . . . are there not other geniuses . . . much less written-to-rags than I?'). Though this was not the best of Hesketh Pearson's biographies, it was the best biography of G.B.S. who felt so pleased by its success that, having warned Pearson never to reveal his co-authorship, he afterwards began speaking openly of his involvement. In Pearson's own copy, under the biographer's signature, Shaw added his own name: 'Also his humble collaborator G. Bernard Shaw.'

I want large circulations at low prices.
Shaw to Allen Lane

These accursed films are complicating life beyond endurance.
Shaw to Siegfried Trebitsch

When planning to launch the *New Statesman* before the war Shaw had written to Beatrice Webb: 'I have no faith in the success of any sixpenny journal that cannot be bought by the casual railway traveller with the certainty that there will be something in it to while away an hour of his journey in a pleasant and amusing way.' It was a casual railway traveller, searching Exeter railway station one weekend for a pleasant and amusing book on his way back to London, who went on to create the sixpenny paperback book revolution of the 1930s. Publishers had long known that a new reading public had been growing up since 1918. But this was being catered for, they generally agreed, by the twopenny libraries such as Boots specializing in 'family stories' and the 'yellowback' publishing of cheap crime and light romance available at Woolworth's. Some publishers had brought out a few long-running backlist titles (often Victorian novels) in paperback, but Allen Lane's idea of mass-producing reprints of good contemporary writing in 'strong paper covers' and selling them for the price of ten cigarettes seemed to his cautious rivals a formula for bankruptcy. 'The steady cheapening of books is in my opinion a great danger in the trade,' the managing director of Chatto & Windus warned him at the end of 1934: '... it is this lowering of prices which is one of the chief reasons why our trade is finding it so hard to recover from the slump.'

In Lane's experience it was the expensive case-bound volumes that were difficult to sell. The Bodley Head, of which he was Chairman, was almost insolvent, and since his fellow directors refused to finance this rash new venture he was forced to start Penguin Books as a private operation. Nine of the first twenty Penguins appearing in the summer of 1935 had been published in hardback by Jonathan Cape. 'Like everybody else in the trade I thought you were bound to go bust,' Jonathan Cape later told him, 'and I thought I'd take four hundred quid off you before you did.'

Many of these bookmen came to regard Allen Lane as the man who ruined their occupation. They applauded a financial *fatwa* from the great Forsyte figure of Stanley Unwin, a gentleman guru of publishing, condemning him to eventual failure. But to Shaw, Lane appeared as the saviour of a moribund trade. 'Our prices are too high for people with less than £1,000 a year,' he was to complain to his hardback publisher Constable. Lane's business sense and lack of literary pretensions appealed to him. Indeed, in several ways he was rather a Shavian character: leaving school at sixteen, puzzling many employees with his superior claims to near-illiteracy, pursuing his vision on Exeter railway station in opposition to all the experts, and then rising to become (as the publishing historian Ian Norrie called him) 'a man of action in the world of words'.

Shaw bought many of these early Penguins – the novels in their orange covers, biography in blue and detective fiction in green – and in August 1936 he wrote to Lane recommending his friend Apsley Cherry-Garrard's *The Worst Journey in the World*. Lane replied that the book he really wanted was *The Intelligent Woman's Guide to Socialism*. According to his biographer, he 'seldom missed a new Shaw play and became remarkably knowledgeable about the Shaw canon'. He offered G.B.S. the same terms as other Penguin authors and G.B.S. did not quibble: he was eager to be part of this new paperback movement. 'Prepare for a shock,' he wrote to his printer William Maxwell on 20 October 1936. 'The Penguin Press wants the Intelligent Woman's Guide. A sixpenny edition would be the salvation of mankind.' Having arranged for his paperback to be set by his Edinburgh printer, R. & R. Clark, 'who is accustomed to my ways', Shaw added two new chapters 'dealing with events that have occurred since its first publication in 1928', enlarged the index and extended the title to *The Intelligent Woman's Guide to Socialism, Capitalism, Sovietism and Fascism*, and drafted a note explaining that 'the present edition is in fact a better bargain than the first edition was, though the price is so much more modest'.

The Intelligent Woman's Guide, appearing in two pale blue volumes at sixpence each, heralded a parallel series of paperbacks called Pelicans. This was an even more radical enterprise than the Penguin list, breaking the convention of reprinting only books already published by other houses, and aiming to extend adult education by making serious works on politics, economics, the social sciences, literature, the natural sciences and the visual arts cheaply available to 'the intelligent layman'. *The Mysterious Universe* by Sir James Jeans, *The Inequality of Man* by J. B. S. Haldane, Sigmund Freud's *Psychopathology of Everyday Life* and H. G. Wells's *A Short History of the World* were among the early Pelican titles, as well as works by Julian Huxley, R. H. Tawney, the Fabian economist G. D. H. Cole and Beatrice Webb. The future of this ambitious list, to which Clement Attlee credited the Labour Party victory in 1945, was guaranteed by the success of Shaw's two opening volumes which came out to a fanfare of publicity in the summer of 1937.

This success also guaranteed his own future as a Penguin author which was to be celebrated on his ninetieth birthday by the 'Shaw Million' – simultaneous publication in Britain of ten titles in editions of 100,000 copies each. It was Allen Lane's most risky speculation yet: 'no venture which I have undertaken in thirty years of publishing has given me so much pleasure', he later wrote. Nearly all the staff were involved in the project and they were in the office by eight o'clock on 26 July 1946. The first telephone call came from the manager of W. H. Smith's in Baker Street. He had been surprised by the length of the bus queue that morning outside his shop. Surprise swelled to amazement as he realized that these were members of a rare – perhaps dying – species, the general reader, lining up for the Shaw Million. Soon booksellers were calling from all over the country to order replenishments of their stocks. In six weeks the Shaw Million was sold out.

*

This paperback readership was one of the two new markets Shaw was to gain in the last dozen years of his life. Apart from the plays and non-dramatic works, his Penguins included 'screen versions' of *Pygmalion* (with illustrations by Feliks Topolski) and *Major Barbara*. These editions, which consisted of the original plays broken up by scenes from Shaw's film scripts, were offshoots of his new career in the cinema.

From the early years of the century he had loved silent films. He could not keep away from them. And the new motion picture companies could not keep away from G.B.S. 'I am overwhelmed with proposals from film firms,' he wrote in 1916. He liked to recommend his work as being in the market for movie-makers everywhere (a Czechoslovakian film called *Roman Boxera*, for example, was made in 1921 from his novel *Cashel Byron's Profession*). The offers flowed in – from $50,000 for one play to $1 million early in 1920 for the rights to all his plays. 'I am replying to all inquiries "Thanks; but nothing doing at present",' he wrote that year. He gave a variety of reasons for these refusals: that he could not afford the supertax; that he was too old a dog to learn new tricks; that he had no wish to become a 'dumb dramatist'; that films killed plays and 'my plays are still alive'. At the same time 'I recognized from the first the enormous importance both artistically and morally of the film.'

During the 1920s, films were suspected of being a threat to the work of novelists and playwrights in much the same way as photographers in the late nineteenth century had been seen as the enemies of Victorian painters. Shaw's enthusiasm for films was a development of his interest in photography and his advocacy of the non-fictional realism of the camera against the 'idle fancies' of the artist. 'Photography comes up against a real antipathy in human nature to the truth,' he had written. 'One may attribute the hatred of photography which is felt by many artists to the fact that photography is a little too uncompromising.'

He welcomed movies as having a similar purging effect on the theatre. Audiences which deserted theatres for the picture houses to gaze at the gorgeous Mary Pickford were moved there by the blessed certainty that she would never say a word – and theatre managements were consequently forced to put on plays that did have something to say.

He predicted that the cinema would be an invention of even more revolutionary significance than printing. Films told their stories to the illiterate as much as to the literate – 'that is why the cinema is going to produce effects that all the cheap books in the world could never produce'. He foresaw a time when motion pictures would 'form the mind of England. The national conscience, the national ideals and tests of conduct,' he had written in 1914, 'will be those of the film.' One day pictures would be 'brought to my home for me' and it was in this direction, he told a journalist, 'that you must look for the most important changes'.

His cat and mouse tactics with the movie moguls partly reflected his sense of a film world in transition. As early as 1908, in a letter to his fellow playwright Pinero, he had speculated that once the gramophone was synchronized with cinematography a new career might open for them both. The screen's silence had been 'the only reason I did not permit the filming of my plays, because their greatest strength was in their dialogue'. Meanwhile he did not want to sell his rights and lose control of his property.

In the end came the spoken word. The day he had long awaited began with *The Jazz Singer*, shown in the United States by Warner Brothers in the fall of 1927. Shaw had already conducted a studio experiment that summer at the DeForest Phonofilm Company employing Sybil Thorndike and Lewis Casson to test five minutes of the Cathedral Scene from *Saint Joan*, and in the next two years he made several appearances himself on Movietone newsreels and in screen interviews. 'They were made to satisfy my curiosity and enable me to acquaint myself with the technique of the lens and microphone,' he wrote in 1930, 'as I believe that acting and drama can be portrayed far more effectively as well as lucratively from the screen than from the stage.' There seemed nothing to prevent his plays burgeoning into films. Yet he hesitated, did not proceed with the filming of *Saint Joan*, and three years later turned instead to his one-act skit, *How He Lied to Her Husband*.

The choice was significant. This *pièce d'occasion* had originally been composed in 1904 as a curtain-raiser 'to satirize those who took Candida to be a sentimental glorification of eroticism' and now came to serve its turn again, illustrating Shaw's contention that 'the whole history of the "movies" showed that "sex-appeal" was a thing that could be neglected almost altogether'. Where else lay the secret of Charlie Chaplin's success? Or Buster Keaton's or Harold Lloyd's? The heroine of Shaw's play is 'a very ordinary South Kensington female of about 37', and there are only two other people: her thick-necked City husband and a dreamy young admirer. The action, which revolves round a missing bundle of love poems (signifying the missing sex-appeal), takes place in a curtained room on the Cromwell Road and its shadowy simplicity reflects Shaw's view of the technical limitations of British films in 1930. These limitations also affected his opinion of the proper role of picture houses.

The question Shaw was examining with the film version of *How He Lied* was whether the best use of the medium lay in recording a perfect production of a play for showing round the world. He chose Cecil Lewis, the wartime flying ace who had been so helpful with his wireless career, to direct it, and persuaded British International Pictures to accept this 'absolutely unknown, untried man as director'. It was shot 'without transpositions interpolations omissions or any alterations misrepresenting the Author whether for better or worse except such as the Author may consent to or himself suggest' – a standard clause in Shaw's later contracts. According to Vera Lennox, who played the very ordinary South Kensington female, Cecil Lewis 'was as frightened as I was of changing one word'. He rehearsed the cast of three, none of whom had acted in a talkie before, until they were word and action perfect, worked out some camera angles for a cameraman who had never recorded a sound picture, and completed the film in four days. But he later admitted that it 'was as much like a movie as a cow is like a pianola'. When it came to be shown in London in January 1931 *The Times* commented on 'the folly of those who suppose that the right use, and the commercial use, of the talkie invention is direct transference from stage to screen', and the *New York Times* described it as 'an amateurish specimen of animated photography'.

Shaw defended this trial film as part of his campaign to encourage in Britain a more literary tradition of film-making than the 'children's picture book' story-telling of Hollywood. The acting in Hollywood was good, the photography excellent and the expenditure one of the wonders of the world. But when it came to the script, Shaw liked to imagine, they called in the office boy. 'I perhaps should have said the bell boy,' he later amended.

'The bell boy's vision of life is a continual arriving in motor-cars and going upstairs and disappearing through doors that immediately close and leave

376

life a blank ... 95 per cent of a film must consist of going up and down stairs and getting in and out of motor-cars ... My plays do not depend on staircases for their interest. I am therefore told that I do not understand the art of the screen.'

Shaw's guerrilla warfare against the big Hollywood corporations and movie moguls is a reminder of his embattled days fighting the West End theatre managements and actor-managers of the Victorian stage. Both were his enemies because they were happy to mutilate texts to suit their star performers. The dialogue of *How He Lied* was continuous, he pointed out, and the entire action took place in the same room. 'The usual changes from New York to the Rocky Mountains, from Marseilles to the Sahara, from Mayfair to Monte Carlo, are replaced by changes from the piano to the sideboard, from the window to the door, from the hearth rug to the carpet. When the husband arrives he is not shewn paying his taxi, taking out his latchkey, hanging up his hat, and mounting the stairs. There is no time for that sort of baby padding when the action of a real play is hastening to its climax.'

In film technique *How He Lied* explores similar ground to the experiment Alfred Hitchcock was to make in 1948 with Patrick Hamilton's claustrophobic stage-thriller *Rope*, shot to resemble a single eighty-minute sequence. According to Cecil Lewis, 'Shaw was delighted with the result.' But privately he had misgivings and professionally he had learnt some lessons.

Lewis's next film with Shaw was *Arms and the Man*, chosen by G.B.S. partly to forestall film adaptations abroad of the unauthorized musical taken from that play, *The Chocolate Soldier*. Shaw had also received an offer from Sam Goldwyn who 'wants to cut the play down to forty minutes'. He trusted Lewis to make a full-length version of his work. 'You may go ahead without any misgivings. I have none,' he wrote to Lewis in April 1932. 'I can leave the business in your hands with complete confidence – but mind! in *your* hands and not in those of the business staff or the callboy or the expert from Hollywood.'

The filming of *Arms and the Man* was a dismal experience. 'We were a little like a pilotless ship,' remembered Barry Jones who played Bluntschli. The actor cast in the part of Nicola, the manservant, died of a heart attack; and the prolonged attempts to recreate Bulgaria in North Wales were wonderfully unconvincing. All this was compounded by the economic anxieties of British International Pictures which finally decided to cut their losses by making it a second feature. In the end Lewis surrendered the film into the hands of what Shaw had called 'the business staff' who, no less philistine than their colleagues in the United States, deformed it with inept cutting.

Working with Lewis's scenario, Shaw had this time made a real attempt to adapt his play into a film, agreeing to many cuts and changes, suggesting others and only vetoing those that seemed to weaken the dramatic effect or confuse the thematic content. His alterations to the script show that he was beginning to develop a film technique, and had come to accept that, though the dramatic principles of stage and screen might be the same, the literary methods must differ. 'Get drama and picture making separate in your mind, or you may make ruinous mistakes,' he was to advise Cecil Lewis. The mistakes of *How He Lied* had taught him this. In April 1930, before *How He Lied* was made, he had written to Trebitsch about the desirability of making a film of *Arms and the Man* 'at full length *exactly as it stands* – NOT of a scenario founded on it'. Two years later, in April 1932, before the shooting of *Arms and the Man* began, he is writing to Cecil Lewis: 'I find this [scenario] game rather fascinating. If I had the time I would half rewrite the play and invent at least fifty more changes of scene.'

In his carefully drafted commentary accompanying the uncut film's first showing at Malvern in the summer of 1932, he wrote of it being 'a mere sketch, in which the talent of the actors has produced a few happy moments under difficulties not yet, but presently to be, triumphantly overcome'. Looking forward to the 'advantages' and 'possibilities' of the picture houses 'later on', he admitted that 'the films, in spite of all their splendors and enchantments, are still in their infancy'.

More significant in the context of Shaw's understanding of film is his comparison with the physical limitations of the theatre. 'The whole action of the play has to be confined to three scenes, two of them indoors,' he wrote.

'In the picture the battle is shewn, and the flight of the fugitive whom the heroine shelters. There is no pinning of the characters to one spot: they pass in and out of doors, upstairs and downstairs, into the gardens and across mountain country, with the freedom and variety impossible in the room with three walls which, however scene-painters may disguise it, is always the same old stage.'

This statement, contradicting what he had written after *How He Lied*, is Shaw's commitment to future film-making. 'My mind is always changing – it is not only a woman's privilege,' he said when asked in January 1933 to comment on his decision to allow RKO Studios in the United States to film *The Devil's Disciple* starring John Barrymore. In the absence of a more robust champion than Cecil Lewis to direct his films in Europe, he had decided to risk placing his work in the United States. British films were hopeless because 'they have no money', he wrote that April to Kenneth MacGowan, an associate producer at RKO, 'and want to put in minutes (mostly wasted) where months are needed'.

The script by Lester Cohen arrived at Ayot St Lawrence in January 1934. A glance through the opening pages convinced Shaw that he would have to put in about a month's work on it. A month later, the script now scrawled with 'comments which do more justice to my own feelings than to the work of my fellow-playwright Mr Cohen', Shaw called the deal off. 'I cannot be expected to lend a hand to my own murder.' Cohen's script was so deeply illiterate, so flounderingly primitive in its technique ('like the old dioramas of my youth') as to be beyond rescue. The Americans 'deal with a famous author for his publicity without the faintest sense of the quality of his work', Shaw complained. The critic Bernard Dukore confirms that 'an examination of the R.K.O. Script demonstrates the soundness of Shaw's judgement'. Hollywood's ways were not his ways. 'We are hopeless incompatibles artistically,' Shaw concluded.

This episode, which seemed to rule out collaboration with the United States, left G.B.S. curiously stranded: too Victorian to enter this brave new film world, yet too advanced for its spectacular hokum and sobstuff. He had come away from Culver City early in 1933 with the feeling that its picture studios were not 'within ten years' of tackling his work. After the fiasco of *The Devil's Disciple*, things moved backwards; 'Hollywood is not within half a century of knowing how to handle my stuff,' he wrote to Theresa Helburn. '. . . I contemplate the popular Hollywood productions in despair.'

But he did not despair of the future of films. They had been born and taught to speak in the United States, and would soon be old enough to travel abroad. 'Until lately the film work done here was not as good as at Hollywood,' he wrote to John Barrymore at the end of 1933.

'It is better now, and will be better still later on, as it is the English way to do nothing until others have made all the experiments and found out the way, and then go ahead with it strongly. And it may be that the development of the movie into the international talkie may operate in favor of the studios which are within easy reach of Paris, Rome, Berlin etc. as against remote Hollywood.'

His optimism soon appeared justified. By the summer of 1934 he was considering proposals from both Paris and Berlin for the filming of *Pygmalion*. These proposals differed in one crucial matter: the French proposal carried with it a competent screenplay already written by Albert Rièra. Shaw's French translator, Augustin Hamon, who sent it to him, argued that what G.B.S. needed was not script approval in his contract (more honoured in the breach than the observance), but a film adapter whom he could trust. Rièra was a trustworthy technician and his version could be filmed simultaneously in French and Italian as well as given accurate subtitles in other languages to provide an authentic *Pygmalion* with worldwide distribution. In Hitler's Germany, Hamon continued, no one could be trusted. Shaw's translator and chief interpreters there were all Jewish, and Shavian drama was generally antipathetic to the current regime.

This was a strong case and Shaw took a long time to answer it. Nevertheless, in February 1935 he signed an agreement with Eberhard Klagemann, head of a Berlin film company. 'France is not for me the centre of the universe,' he wrote that month to Hamon. He owed more to German culture than to French. Helping Trebitsch, his finances and morale, was one of his incentives. He bought Trebitsch's half-share in the German language rights of *Pygmalion*, and confirmed that he was prepared to deal with Klagemann 'if you can assure me that K. is a solid firm'. One of the tests of this solidity was that Klagemann should use Shaw's own screenplay ('I am cutting *Pygmalion* to bits'); another was that it should employ Trebitsch to translate it, for which the translator would be paid an extra fee.

There was one further reason why Shaw rejected Hamon's proposal. The habit of selling world rights in films (usually to Hollywood) was, he believed, a relic of the silent movie days. 'Now that we have talkies I am inclined to deal with the different countries separately,' he explained to Trebitsch. And to Hamon he wrote: 'As Holland has started making films I have a contract in hand with a Dutch firm ... The nationalisation of the talkie gives a lot of trouble; but it has the advantage in the case of a failure that the eggs are not all in one basket.' He aimed to strengthen his position and unite everyone's long-term interests by limiting the licence to five years and sharing his profits equally with his translators.

The German film of *Pygmalion* (first shown in Berlin in September 1935) and the Dutch *Pygmalion* (first shown in Amsterdam in March 1937) were commercially successful: and Shaw loathed them. 'I don't know what they did with my scenario, but they certainly did not use it for the film,' he said after seeing the German version at the beginning of 1936. In fact Shaw was not credited with the screenplay and Trebitsch not listed as translator. Shaw felt disappointed in Trebitsch, not for having agreed to the changes – as a Jew banned from Germany's film industry he would have had little chance of rejecting them – but for not having 'given me the smallest hint' that his scenario was not being faithfully followed. But this was not specifically a quarrel with Hitler's Germany: the trivial Dutch film was worse.

There was one last chance to get what he wanted. Almost immediately after finishing the *Pygmalion* script, he had started on one of *Saint Joan*. 'I had to make the scenario for that,' he told Theresa Helburn; 'for nobody could cut the dialogue and write the new scenes except myself.' It took him a fortnight and at the end of November 1934 he handed it to the Viennese actress Elizabeth Bergner who had created the role of Joan ten years earlier in Max Reinhardt's Berlin production. Bergner had recently married the Hungarian producer-director Paul Czinner who planned to form a syndicate including Twentieth Century-Fox and produce a film of *Saint Joan* starring his wife. By the summer of 1935, after discussions with Czinner and Bergner, Shaw had revised the script (which originally struck them as rigid) and the way was clear. But Czinner, who professed himself delighted with this revised screenplay, then sent it without consulting G.B.S. to the Scottish dramatist James Bridie for further rewriting; and Bridie contacted Shaw to ascertain whether this was being done with his approval. The cat was out of the bag.

This was Czinner's second initiative. Worried that Twentieth Century-Fox would not put up money if there was a risk of *Saint Joan* being subjected to a Catholic boycott, he had submitted Shaw's scenario to a newly created organization at the Vatican, called Catholic Action, which monitored the lay activities of the Church. Their report condemned the film as 'a satire against Church and State', and an 'attack to the R.C.C.' by the 'mocking Irishman'. On learning this, Shaw compared himself to someone run over by a car without a number plate. 'I cannot accept the pretension of the Catholic Action to represent the Vatican,' he wrote. But although Catholic Action was not an official body, no one doubted that its judgement carried the authentic Vatican voice. Unless the film script was substantially altered, the film would be met by a Catholic veto.

Here was the same doctrinaire censorship against which Shaw had campaigned in the British theatre. He knew that during the Depression film speculators in the United States traded in near-pornography and that there had been a reaction against 'vile and unwholesome pictures' from such organizations as the Legion of Decency. To regain control of their industry, American movie producers formed a Production Code Administration in 1934 which was already leading to what Shaw called 'an epidemic of censorships ... raging through the United States as a protest against the very licentious anarchy which has hitherto prevailed'. He saw Hollywood as being in a pitiable condition, as terrorized by its own policing as by the meddling of 'amateur busybodies who do not know that the work of censorship requires any qualification beyond Catholic baptism'. In much the same way as he had recommended a municipal solution, combining freedom with responsibility, to the problem of theatre censorship, he now urged the film corporations in the United States to 'pluck up enough courage and public spirit to insist on the control of film morality being made a federal matter, independent of prudes, of parochial busybodies, and doctrinaire enemies of the theatre as such'.

Shaw tried to free his film script from Catholic entanglements. 'I make it an absolute condition that the Catholic Action shall be entirely ignored, and the film made in complete disregard of these understrappers of the Church,' he was to write. '...The Hollywood simpletons say that none of the twenty million American Catholics will go to see it. When the Catholic Action can keep these Americans out of the saloons and gambling casinos and Ziegfeld Follies I shall believe in its power to keep them away from St Joan...' But no film of *Saint Joan* was to be made during Shaw's lifetime; he had been dead for six years when United Artists finally commissioned a script from Graham Greene. On being interviewed, the director of this film, Otto Preminger, said that he had never heard of Shaw's original screenplay.

'I have now cried off the film, and excommunicated Czinner with bell, book, and candle,' Shaw informed James Bridie in the summer of 1935. '...it is clear that he does not see the play as I see it, and that puts him out of the question as a director.' Like Cecil Lewis, Czinner had let him down. How long would he have to wait for an independent director who would carry his films to victory over these 'goddams' of Hollywood?

*

After more than fifteen years with G.B.S., Blanche Patch was an expert at fobbing off pests. The mail bulged with petitions from burglars, chemists, coffin makers, nurses, sailors, schoolboys, all of them 'howling to be answered'; and Miss Patch typed out the answers. What Shaw called 'unsportsmanlike requests by strangers to forge his own signature' were among her greatest afflictions. Sometimes, when a letter took her fancy and she had a spare signature nearby, she would snip it out and gum it on to her reply. At other times she would rather enjoy seizing on an indecipherable signature from some bank manager, osteopath or miscellaneous foreigner and pasting it on to Shaw's uncompromising rejection.

Those who wanted money were tiresome. They would demand anything from £2 to £20,000 and for all sorts of far-flung reasons: to save fifteen repertory theatres; help thousands of refugees; to fund a man's passage back to Jamaica; marry off an Indian gentleman's six daughters – or at the very least to provoke an insulting postcard. It vexed Miss Patch to see the amounts of money her employer simply handed away – often, she thought, to the most undeserving. Such people were 'greedy for a flicker from the flame' and trying to 'poach on his reputation'. It was difficult for her to accept that G.B.S. reigned as an international guru. At a distance he seemed all things to all people, a father – and eventually a grandfather confessor to the whole world.

Everyone turned to him: men who were thinking of entering the priesthood or taking up carpentry; women wondering whether to risk a divorce or send their daughters on the stage; children who wanted to name a pig or hedgehog after him. There were explorers needing radio apparatus for an Antarctic whaling expedition; importers eager to bring a Russian frost-resistant potato into Britain; inventors seeking Shaw's endorsement to promote schemes for causing clouds to dissolve and distilled water to consolidate into stone, or his testimonial to prevent cures for cancer, lunacy and hallucinations being stolen.

'I believe you have always had a warm corner in your heart for women and fanatics,' wrote a woman. 'I am a non-entity, you an entity,' wrote a man. G.B.S. was peculiarly the saint of the isolated, the odd, drowning women, desperate men – 'a doctor of the human soul', one correspondent called him. 'The total absence in your face, clothes & furniture of anything suggesting vice, extravagance or vulgarity; all made one feel in the presence of nature's aristocrat,' wrote a private in the army. Like Sherlock Holmes, he had a reputation for solving people's problems. They wrote to enquire where they should live, what they should do in retirement, how they should get out of jail. A number of people on the verge of murder or suicide tried him as their penultimate resort. 'I felt a little lonely,' admitted a twenty-one-year-old girl from New York, '...I love you very dearly.' 'I am rather stout and ugly,' explained a boy in South Africa, '...how should I go about getting friends.' 'I think your patronage was the greatest pleasure my poor father ever had,' claimed the son of a Colchester newsagent after his father's death. 'God love you, dont die, just beat the sordidness of the selfish,' pleaded eighty-year-old Ben Tillet, Shaw's socialist colleague, a dock-worker, who had been Chairman of the General Council of the Trades Union Conference.

All of them received immaculately typed responses. 'Irresponsible nonsense had an attraction for Shaw,' Miss Patch observed, 'which would lure him into correspondence of the most futile sort.' She found herself conveying his views on world slaughter, the fourth dimension, the existence of fairies. 'Why are you silent on public affairs?' demanded one man. That was a tricky one to answer. So was the woman who wrote regarding the forceps inside her, and the London busman who objected to Shaw's lack of interest in King George V and threatened to run him over with his bus.

Though it was all water off a duck's back to Miss Patch, much of what she fingered on to the paper and sealed into envelopes had that mixture of rare sense and inspired nonsense that the world had learnt to call Shavian. A cheque for £400 to a poet whose clothes had gone up in smoke was accompanied by a note saying how much Shaw had always disliked his poems. Someone in search of shock therapy was recommended to shave her head, put on a white wig and stand in front of a mirror. One fan who wanted a lock of his hair was advised to 'cut a wisp off the nearest white dog'. A family called Shaw who had christened their son George Bernard was accused of perpetrating a 'shocking outrage on a defenceless infant'.

Some of Miss Patch's typed replies were to gain fame. When he was asked 'Have we Lost Faith?', she sent back: 'Certainly not, but we have transferred it from God to the General Medical Council.' One day Shaw had come across one of his works in a second-hand bookshop with his handwritten inscription on the flyleaf, and Miss Patch was able to pack it up carrying Shaw's postscript – 'With the author's renewed compliments. G.B.S.' – and post it back to the original dedicatee. She rather relished some of their point-blank rebuffs. To a hostess who sent a card stating that on a certain day she would be 'At Home', the succinct reply had been: 'So will G. Bernard Shaw.' Then there was the matter of the Prime Minister: 'Absence from town and a strong sense of humor,' she typed 'will prevent me from accepting your invitation to dine in acknowledgement of the political eminence of Ramsay MacDonald.'

Over the worst period Miss Patch had to cope with up to three proposals of marriage a week. She helped to see off an actress from Zurich who claimed that since she had the greatest body in the world and Shaw had the greatest brain, they ought to produce the most perfect child, with a celebrated transposition: 'What if the child inherits my body and your brains?' But not all the famous stories were true. For example she had never sent Winston Churchill two tickets for the first night of a Shaw play inviting him to bring a friend 'if you have one'; and she had never received an answer from Churchill saying that he could come to the second night 'if there was one'. That was a journalistic invention.

Among Miss Patch's skills was the making of parcels. People liked to send things to Whitehall Court and, if they were not mislaid, she could send them back. 'I hate presents,' Shaw had said and on the whole she agreed with him, because they received such silly presents. The good wishes sent over by the Czechoslovakian army didn't exercise them; and artists who delivered poems, pictures, plays, operas and plans for the regeneration of the world had to take pot luck. A few presents, such as the rather handy axe, she could see he actually liked; but the bits of coal garnished with ivy, the individually-knitted socks, the seaweed, bison-foot inkstand and enamel washing-bowl with its base deeply registering the G.B.S. profile were nothing but trouble.

More often people wanted things from Whitehall Court – hats, handkerchiefs, trousers, really anything at all. One man of the streets demanded G.B.S.'s boots, and despite the awkwardness of packing them up, Miss Patch was actually obliged to post them off to him. But they had not reckoned on this pedestrian returning them whenever they were in need of repairs. Finally he sent the boots for auction and got over thirty times what they had originally cost. Such episodes, Miss Patch noticed, seemed to amuse G.B.S.

But she was not so easily amused, particularly by the hordes of time-wasters who made the telephone buzz with senseless questions, or who, despite their reputation for being more difficult to see than the King and Queen of England, still arrived at the door. Right up to the end they came. She didn't mind Charlotte's lunch guests – Dean Inge, Barry Jackson, Apsley Cherry-Garrard, the aviator Amy Johnson, the actress Ellen Pollock, though Lady Astor rather overrated herself, she was inclined to think. She quite liked some of the more casual visitors, such as Maurice Chevalier who seemed 'exceedingly nervous' in her company, or even Charlie Chaplin who was 'quiet and serious' when she took him round the flat. She could feel that 'visitors rather liked their flat'. It was a happy place, Lady Rhondda thought. 'The sun always seemed to shine there. Six or eight people would come to eat a good luncheon around a small table in a narrow little slip of a room overlooking the Thames. The people one met there were always interesting.' Blanche Patch herself wouldn't have gone that far. When people were separated from her and got stuck with G.B.S., they had to take their chances. 'Shaw talked knowledgeably about Kemal Atatürk,' remembered the Hungarian actress Zsa Zsa Gabor who had been invited to London by the British Council. Of course there was no accounting for tastes and all tastes seemed to be catered for at Whitehall Court. 'There was such a wonderfully free atmosphere about, you were sure that nothing you said or did would shock or surprise them,' D. H. Lawrence's widow Frieda declared. 'If you had suddenly turned a somersault they would have taken it along with the rest.' Blanche Patch was rather glad she hadn't. Though nothing surprised her, she thought the atmosphere was a bit too free. 'You have no notion,' she typed, 'of the hosts of people who knock at my door every day: beggars, sightseers, people who claim to be my cousins because my picture in the papers resembles their grandfathers ... all the nuisances on earth.' For example, there was the young man who had been directed in a *séance* to make off with the doormat in case 'some benefit might accrue to me' and landed up in an asylum; and the moon-struck scientist who wanted to discuss his theory of institutionalism and the planetary movement of the Earth; and, perhaps worst of all, the climbing American who, after publishing letters to them in the personal columns of *The Times*, scaled his way into the flat and had to be arrested by Scotland Yard.

After all this it was hardly a great surprise for Miss Patch to find on the doorstep one day towards the end of 1935 a swarthy Transylvanian gentleman commanding her to 'go and tell your master' that the film producer from Rome he had once met at Cap d'Antibes was here. 'Tell him,' he added, 'the young man with the brown buttocks.' How did he get past Miss Patch? 'He had no appointment, and we knew nothing of this caller who was obviously a foreigner,' she objected. Despite these disadvantages there was something appealing about him like 'a Puck who would Othello be'. At any rate, perhaps because 'his name made Shaw curious' too, he agreed to see this stranger and she ushered Gabriel Pascal into the study.

*

'The man is a genius,' Shaw announced ten years later. Like Vandeleur Lee, Pascal was a charlatan genius 'quite outside all ordinary rules'. He made Shaw laugh with his whole body, throwing his shoulders about 'while the laughter ran up his long legs and threatened to shake his head off'. As Blanche Patch saw, 'G.B.S. never met a human being who entertained him more.'

Pascal was a short, powerful-looking man with broad shoulders, high cheekbones, a strong head and dense black hair. His hypnotic eyes were set far apart. When he smiled he gave an enormous grin with a gap at the centre of his front teeth. He entered Shaw's study like an engaging gorilla.

Their previous meeting had apparently been 'one of those flitting social introductions and did not mean anything' – something Pascal would have shrugged off had it not already entered the repertoire of his legendary past. One blue and golden summer morning, his story went, he had been swimming naked in the Mediterranean and, coming across G.B.S. treading water far out from shore, made himself known as the Tsar of the film world whose destiny it was to make wonderful pictures from the Shavian playground. As he swam away, revealing his buttocks, Shaw had called out: 'When you are utterly broke … come and call on me … and I will let you make one of my plays into a film.' So here he was. He spoke in low solemn tones and with a strong Central European accent – then cracked open his enormous grin like an urchin. It was impossible to resist him.

'He reminds me of Frank Harris,' Shaw wrote to Trebitsch. Perhaps the mention of Cap d'Antibes where he had last seen Harris and allegedly first met Pascal prompted this happy comparison. Pascal was to gain a reputation

386

in films similar to Harris's in journalism: that of a Svengali who discovered new stars while remaining curiously in need of discovery himself. In the opinion of George Moore, Harris had been 'the most brilliant conversationalist who ever lived'. Pascal, according to Shaw, was 'an extraordinarily clever and dramatic talker' – also one of the very few people who could actually silence G.B.S. Like Harris too, Pascal was mesmerically attractive to many women, one of whom likened him to the Angel Gabriel ('a fallen angel, yearning for a lost heaven'). Charlotte liked him. Even Miss Patch liked him. But, more often than not, men saw only a colossal impostor whose surname should have begun with an R.

In fact his name was not Pascal any more than Harris's name had been Frank. He was born Gabor Lehöl, yet 'Gabriel Pascal' was not so much an invention as a mutation – as Samuel Goldwyn was a mutation of Schmuel Gelbfisz.

When Pascal recalled his early years, the air would fill with fleeting images and sounds – the bright crackling flames of a burning house, the despairing cries of women, a ramshackle gypsy caravan sauntering across the Alps; then cut to the life of a poor shepherd boy deeply attached to the earth; and afterwards to a daring circus acrobat who miraculously defied gravity, a rebel cadet at a famous military academy, a prodigy at the Imperial Hofburg Theatre in Vienna . . . and behind all these sets and scenes hovered the mysterious Jesuit priest who was his patron. Did Royal Blood course through his veins? Had he been kidnapped? Was he illegitimately descended from Metternich or Talleyrand? Everything depended on the translation, the direction, and the rewrites.

From this magic carpet of his past, Pascal showed G.B.S. many 'lovely episodes'. He knew he had been born – whether an orphan or a foundling – for great things but (again like Frank Harris) might be stopped from reaching them by his lack of height. 'Someday,' he promised, 'I shall try to figure out why this incomprehensible world confuses heroism with height.' He gained in mythical stature from his tall stories. To Shaw, who knew so well the springs of self-dramatization, there was a gallantry about adventures that could turn failure, poverty, obscurity and the ostracism and contempt which these invite, into such gorgeous entertainment. Pascal's morals might be those of the unscrupulous artist Louis Dubedat from *The Doctor's Dilemma*, but he was a man of wonderful naïvety and when he spoke of his wartime escapades either as a cavalry officer advancing along the Italian Front accompanied by two dachshunds, or hosting sumptuous banquets for his prisoners on the Russian Front, he brought back the innocent world of *Arms and the Man*. His favourite play was Shaw's melodrama *The Devil's Disciple* with its picturesque and fanatical hero; but the talk in Shaw's study turned to the filming of his Cinderella romance, *Pygmalion*.

'I threw myself with full energy into the films,' Pascal confided. 'I was happy once more ... ' But there had been little in Pascal's career since the war, except perhaps his production of Franz Lehar's operetta *Friederika* in Germany, to raise confidence. 'I believe that the prospect of too much success frightened me,' he explained, 'and therefore handicapped my work.' Around the time of Hitler's rise to power he had left Germany (for he could have been a Jew as well as a Catholic and a Jesuit) and began roaming the world. Several times he went to the United States. 'I loved the California climate, but I did not like the coldness of Hollywood, where they called me the hobo producer.' He went to India and squatted on a tiger skin with his 'awakener' Meher Baba who, having made a vow of silence, would communicate in faultless English on an alphabet board and, whenever Pascal came near, would moan with allowable soft laughter. But though he was presented with Baba's magic sandals, Pascal could not find his way to the oriental film he longed to make on reincarnation. At last this Tsar of the film world had been reduced to the penniless wanderer whose vagrant path led to Whitehall Court.

He claimed that 'only a foreigner could translate Shaw into films'. But Shaw had received plenty of these proposals from foreigners – Samuel Goldwyn, Alexander Korda, Louis B. Mayer, Harry Warner – all immigrants or the children of immigrants from Eastern Europe, now creating from gangster and horror movies, musicals and westerns, a vast national fantasy for native-born Americans. Pascal, the 'hobo producer' rejected of Hollywood, was the joker in this pack. People were to ask themselves how such an exorbitant fabulist could have hypnotized G.B.S. But Goldwyn and Korda were fabulists too. Pascal was driven by a similar need to bury his unstable past under an empire made from other people's myths and by fulfilling other people's dreams. Only this time it should be an empire of Shavian myths and dreams:

'Until he descended on me out of the clouds I could find nobody who wanted to do anything with my plays on the screen but mutilate them, murder them, give their cadavers to the nearest scrivener ... The result was to be presented to the public with my name attached, and an assurance that nobody need fear that it had any Shavian quality whatever, and was real genuine Hollywood.'

In Shaw's dramatic treatment 'When Pascal appeared out of the blue, I just looked at him, and handed him *Pygmalion* to experiment with.' In his equally dramatic rewrite, Pascal gave Shaw until four o'clock on Friday

13 December to make up his mind about *Pygmalion* and was packing for a journey to China when 'at the stroke of four' the contract from G.B.S. arrived in an enormous envelope.

At their first interview on 8 December Shaw had asked Pascal what capital he had – 'How are you fixed for money?' – and Pascal, emptying his pockets, cracking open his smile, pointed to one or two small coins. In the following week Shaw made what enquiries he could, but nobody appeared able or willing to say anything. Yet he was impressed. At their second meeting at Whitehall Court, he decided to take a big chance. 'I have disposed of the English film of *Pygmalion* to Gabriel Pascal,' he wrote to Trebitsch two days later.

As for Pascal, 'I was the happiest man in the world.'

'I have had to forbid Pascal to kiss me,' Shaw wrote again to Trebitsch, 'as he did at first to the scandal of the village.'

*

It was said of Pascal that he 'poured his orphaned love on Shaw'. He had nothing as yet to give G.B.S. but his own ambitions: 'I promise I will make you even more famous and very rich,' he declared. It was a pity that money was his second priority. When other moguls and tycoons consulted their accountants Pascal looked to the divinations of an Egyptian palmist. In fact he was 'essentially indifferent to money', the playwright S. N. Behrman noticed, which was to say he acted with great generosity when in the money and was 'even more generous when out of it'.

Shaw estimated that his *Pygmalion* contract was worth £60,000 to Pascal. But although there 'wasn't a studio in the world that wouldn't have given its gold teeth for the rights to Shaw's plays', Behrman continued, ' . . . Pascal found it seemingly impossible to get the money to screen them'. His headlong optimism carried him over two miserable years during which his gift for lighting up people's enthusiasms was regularly quenched by what one of his wives was to call 'Gabriel's genius for messing up anything'. He was transparently guileless and, like Shaw's early publisher Grant Richards, had 'hardly any sense'. 'The truth is, he needs nursing,' Shaw concluded.

Shaw's nursing made Pascal's clean bill of financial health all the more difficult to attain. His letters of agreement, which were always confined to one play at a time, gave Pascal only restricted rights to produce the film and retained for himself the contractual rights with all those clauses (five year licence, author's control of script and a royalty of ten percent of the gross receipts) to which film companies objected. 'Film work, or anything else of a theatrical nature, is fatal to business habits,' Shaw insisted. He was anxious not to leave Pascal, after whatever success they might achieve, penniless. But Pascal felt corralled by Shaw's bristling business habits. He was in something of the same predicament as Demetrius O'Bolger had been: protected from himself by being protected from doing his work. But to all his appeals and remonstrations Shaw presented a mind like granite. He did not want extra fame and money. He wanted victory over Hollywood and had chosen Pascal as his champion. Filmland was to him a mirage with occasional windfalls and 'there must be a rock somewhere in the shifting sands ... I have decided to be that rock'.

Urged on by G.B.S., yet weighed down with this rocklike handicap, Pascal rode desperately off. But he appeared to be permanently riding into a setting sun. His head blazed with visions of a dozen simultaneous schemes and whenever he was on the verge of roping one of them, he would utter his jubilant refrain: 'I go now see the old man to talk cast.' After a year of galloping activity he had got nowhere. 'He has no studio and is a pure adventurer,' Shaw wrote to Hamon; 'but he may be able to carry the effort through for me. In the film world they are all adventurers more or less.' As one studio after another turned him down, Pascal looked shabbier and shabbier. 'Vee go see Bernashaw,' he would tell everyone. He kept visiting Shaw and one day brought with him a financial backer who had made his fortune in flour. This was Joseph Arthur Rank. Suddenly he had the beginnings of a syndicate.

Pygmalion was finally scheduled for production at Pinewood Studios on 11 March 1938. Shaw attended the gala press luncheon at Pinewood, ostensibly to celebrate the first day's shooting though in reality to encourage investors to pay up, but he did not return to see the making of the film. 'I do not propose to interfere in the direction of the picture,' he notified Pascal, 'since I cannot, at my age, undertake it myself.'

He interfered as much as possible from a distance and whenever Pascal came 'to talk cast'. Wendy Hiller had been Shaw's choice for Eliza and he predicted that she would be 'the film sensation of the next five years'. He had wanted Charles Laughton to play Higgins and felt that Pascal's choice of Leslie Howard was 'fatally wrong' – 'the trouble with Leslie Howard is he thinks he's Romeo'. In his screenplay Shaw had tried to strengthen the role of Freddy Eynsford-Hill to make him a romantic second lead, but he suspected that the public would still love Leslie Howard 'and probably want him to marry Eliza, which is just what I don't want'.

Pascal had a flair for attracting names that were later to grow famous. Anthony Quayle played a hairdresser. Leo Genn a Grand Old Lady's son and the script editor was David Lean. But the cast of *Pygmalion* was chiefly remarkable for the names it gathered in from past productions of Shaw's plays. O. B. Clarence, who had created the Inquisitor in *Saint Joan*, became a vicar; Wilfred Lawson and Esmé Percy who had performed most major Shaw roles in Macdona repertory tours took on Alfred Doolittle and a new character, Count Astrid Karpathy; Scott Sunderland, a member of Barry Jackson's Birmingham Repertory Theatre, who had been seen as Britannus in *Caesar and Cleopatra*, appeared as Colonel Pickering; Cecil Trouncer, whom Shaw called 'the best heavy lead on the English stage', and Stephen Murray came from Malvern Festivals to put on the uniforms of first and second constables; Violet Vanbrugh, who created Jitta Lenkheim in *Jitta's Atonement*, was an Ambassadress and completed this invasion from Shaw's theatreland into the new film world.

There were other, stranger echoes from Shaw's past. Henry Irving's grandson, Laurence Irving, was the set designer; Beerbohm Tree's daughter Viola came to the ball as a character called Perfide, and his grandson David Tree played Freddy Eynsford-Hill; and Shaw loyally brought in Cecil Lewis as one of the script adaptors. The director was Anthony Asquith, son of the late Prime Minister, also brother of Elizabeth Asquith, for whom Shaw had written *The Fascinating Foundling*, and half-brother of 'Beb' Asquith who had called for G.B.S. to be shot at the beginning of the First World War.

It was Anthony Asquith who made *Pygmalion* a success. Pascal as producer was a whirlwind, stimulating, disruptive, unpredictable. There was 'a terrible row and throughout the whole shooting of the picture we were never on speaking terms', remembered Wendy Hiller. 'But as the direction was in the expert hands of Anthony Asquith we managed remarkably well.'

Shaw's scenario cut down the dialogue and opened up the play for the screen. He also added some extra scenes at Pascal and Asquith's suggestion, but did not accept all their proposals for giving the film more exteriors, greater movement and visual variety. It was then modified by various unseen hands which came together to sweeten the story and glamorize Higgins. Nevertheless, by Hollywood standards and compared with the Dutch and German versions of *Pygmalion*, it was faithful to Shaw's work.

And Charlotte liked it. Two days before the première she and G.B.S. came to a preview and at the end Charlotte told everyone: 'This is the finest presentation of my husband's work.' It was a tremendous relief. Pascal had been trembling with nerves, clutching Charlotte's hand and almost wringing these favourable words from her. He had shot three alternative endings to the film and chosen the romantic one anticipating the marriage of Higgins and Eliza. Later, when questioned about this ready-made happy ending, Shaw answered that apparently some '20 directors seem to have turned up there and spent their time trying to sidetrack me and Mr Gabriel Pascal, who does really know chalk from cheese. They devised a scene to give a lovelorn complexion at the end to Mr Leslie Howard: but it is too inconclusive to be worth making a fuss about.'

Shaw wanted to believe whatever Pascal told him. He enveloped him in the same atmosphere of gratitude and loyalty with which he had encircled Trebitsch and Hamon. The success of *Pygmalion* was to shoot many hostile arrows in Pascal's direction, but G.B.S. deflected them all on to those twenty nameless 'directors' who had invaded the studio, tried to spoil their film and presented themselves 'in the bills as presiding geniuses of the production'. He also gestured towards Leslie Howard as the source of all added romanticism and relegated Anthony Asquith to 'a talented and inventive youth [who] ... doesnt know the difference between the end of a play and the beginning'.

Pygmalion went on to break all box-office records and, as Lawrence Langner wrote, 'won the hearts of audiences and the plaudits of critics all over the world'. At the Venice Film Festival it was awarded the Volpi Cup and in the United States, where a censored version had to be shown to meet the Protection Code Administration's objections to 'comedy treatment of illicit sex', it was nevertheless given two Academy Awards. Shaw happily described his Oscar for the year's best-written screenplay as 'an insult', by which he meant that *Pygmalion* should be advertised as an 'all British film made by British methods without interference by American script writers, no spurious dialogue but every word by the author, a revolution in the presentation of drama on the film'. This Shavian exaggeration served well in his propaganda war, and *Pygmalion* was soon being spoken of as having 'lifted movie-making from "illiteracy" to "literacy", thus compelling Hollywood, at long last, to take on real writers'.

Pascal had won a famous victory and brought Shaw his revenge. For years 'I was supposed to know nothing about the cinema', he wrote to Lawrence Langner. Now the sensational film success of *Pygmalion* 'has suddenly brought me into vogue as a screen expert'.

Against most odds, and on Shavian terms, his adventurer had carried him through the celluloid jungle and to the top of the most powerful myth-making empire in the twentieth century. It was 'a tremendous triumph'. He felt as if Pascal had opened an Aladdin's cave, and the effect was spectacular. 'You, in your abandoning energy and reckless disregard of costs, persist in making plans for me on the assumption I am 35; but actually speaking I am a dead man; and a grasshopper is a burden,' he tried to complain. 'I discovered you ten years too late.' But as Charlotte saw,

Pascal's extraordinary vitality had rejuvenated her husband so that he was 'twenty-five years younger'.

'I am Cagliostro to Shaw,' Pascal boasted, '– I keep him alive fifteen years more.'

[5]

'Does it matter?'
My reply is that it does.

If it had been the love of moneymaking that kept him at work, as some neighbours at Ayot suspected, Shaw would have moved more whole-heartedly into films. 'It would pay me better to turn my old plays into scenarios,' he wrote to Trebitsch who was growing increasingly dependent on his Shavian income. But 'I cannot do this'. He still had new work to do, whatever its commercial prospects, and 'the very few effective years which remain to me must not be squandered in studios'.

In the late 1930s he composed a pleasant and an unpleasant play, began a 'Comedy of No Manners' and completed a variant ending to a Shake-spearean romance.

Cymbeline Refinished was conceived at a Governors' meeting at the Stratford-upon-Avon Shakespeare Memorial Theatre where a proposal to revive *Cymbeline* met with the objection that on stage the play always 'goes to pieces in the last act'. Shaw remarked that they had better let him rewrite this last act and 'to my surprise this blasphemy was received with acclamation; and as this applause, like the proposal, was not wholly jocular, the fancy began to haunt me ...'

The business of improving on Shakespeare had been going on since Colly Cibber's popular adaptation of *Richard III* and the 'happy' version of *King Lear* by Nahum Tate. As a drama critic Shaw had often ridiculed the acting versions put on by Henry Irving and other actor-managers of the Victorian theatre which he now saw as precursors to the sentimentalities of Hollywood. But, by perpetrating 'a spurious fifth act to *Cymbeline*' was he not joining this optimistic band of saboteurs himself?

Shaw's battles were fought against the surrender of power from composers to performers. In principle he had as little objection to a 'collaboration' between authors as to one between musicians. 'I stand in the same time relation to Shakespear as Mozart to Handel, or Wagner to Beethoven,' he was to plead in the Foreword to *Cymbeline Refinished*. His original title had been *Cymbeline Up to Date. A Happy Ending*. He regarded this happy operation of updating a post-Marlowe play across the centuries into a post-Ibsen play as equivalent to the process of translation. Certainly it did not involve any contradiction with his past beliefs. Forty years before, when coaching Ellen Terry in her role as Imogen, he had seen 'no objection whatever to an intelligent cutting out of the dead & false bits of Shakespeare'.

It was while preparing Ellen for her part in Irving's mutilated production at the Lyceum that he had become involved with the text of *Cymbeline*. His flights of invective against 'this silly old "Cymbeline"' were largely improvised to raise Ellen's spirits and get her over the difficulties of giving a convincing performance. But it had fixed the last act in his mind as a hopeless mess. Now, while preparing to tie the dangling ends into a neat Shavian knot, he found that Shakespeare's last act was not after all the *pasticcio* he had remembered, but full of verbal workmanship and theatrical entertainment.

This change of view was partly due to the play having floated free from the old entanglements of Ellen and Irving. But Shaw was also looking for the first time at a work of Shakespeare's final period from the perspective of his own final period.

Biographical criticism has treated *Cymbeline* as the dream-work of a man in the sunset of his life, too exhausted to invent new devices and so filling it with echoes from *Othello, King Lear, As You Like It*. In this interpretation the contortions of the plot, grandiloquences of speech, emotional disorientation, wanderings, vagaries all become symptoms of Shakespeare's second childhood and signposts in a world of fairy tales which 'complete existence for the young, and replace it for the old'. But in the context of historical criticism Shakespeare's change of mood reflects a change of mood in the country under a new monarch, King James I, a generous patron of Shakespeare's company, who claimed descent from the mythical King Arthur and encouraged the arts to draw their inspiration from ancient English history. The extraordinary last act, with its profusion of dénouements leading to the King's final speech, 'Publish we this peace to all our subjects', becomes in this historical context a commentary on King James's intricate policy of appeasement – with a flattering masque served up to appeal to the new Court's love of pageant. Later, in post-modernist criticism, *Cymbeline* was to be transformed into a post-Shakespearean romance that deconstructs the forms of Elizabethan tragedy.

What Shaw does is to replace Shakespeare's fairytale with his own, substitute a number of contemporary political comments, and continue the work of deconstruction with a parody of diplomatic realism. He makes short work of the 'ludicrous' battle sequences, jettisons the masque, banishes all apparitions, gods, soothsayers, and, condensing five scenes into one, straightens out Shakespeare's tortuous meanderings in little more than twenty minutes ('Are there more plots to unravel?' demands Cymbeline impatiently). He also uses the English victory over the Romans as a history lesson for Neville Chamberlain, advocating the preparedness of military training and rearmament. Finally, in the dismayed reactions of Guiderius and Arviragus to the discovery that they are the King's sons ('Not free to wed the woman of my choice ... I abdicate and pass the throne to Polydore,' cries Guiderius to which Arviragus objects, 'Do you, by heavens? Thank you for nothing, brother'), Shaw makes an approving reference to the abdication of Edward VIII which was announced while he was writing the play.

Cymbeline Refinished retains eighty-nine of Shakespeare's lines, but Shaw gives none of them to Imogen whom he converts, as if she were a posthumous gift for Ellen Terry, into the incipient New Woman he always believed Ellen to have been and whom she might have played with more conviction. Though some beautiful lines are forfeited, there is more than one '*hilarious sensation*' in the best Shavian manner and fleeting moments of beauty, such as Imogen's plea to the smiling Iachimo (who is made cleverer at the expense of Posthumus) and his response to her:

IMOGEN   Oh, do not make me laugh.
        Laughter dissolves too many just resentments
        Pardons too many sins.
IACHIMO   And saves the world
        A many thousand murders.

Shaw refinished *Cymbeline* in December 1936 but the Shakespeare Memorial Theatre, fearing a hostile reaction from tourists, fell back on the orthodox fifth act. One person who saw this production was Ronald Adam, who had taken over the Embassy Theatre in Swiss Cottage five years before and given it a reputation for adventurous work. Visiting the cast afterwards he heard them talking about Shaw's variant ending and later wrote to G.B.S. asking if he could put it on at the Embassy. Shaw agreed and in due course 'sent me a privately printed copy of his last act plus an Introduction for me to read', remembered Ronald Adam. '...He attended some rehearsals at the Embassy, literally leaping about on the stage while his wife sat in the stalls.' When Adam asked for a formal agreement, he received the usual Shaw contract with an addendum: 'In consideration of Shakespeare's collaboration the above royalties are reduced by 50 per cent.'

Cymbeline, by William Shakespeare and Bernard Shaw opened at the Embassy Theatre for a three-week run on 16 November 1937, the day before Chamberlain began his policy of appeasement with Lord Halifax's visit to Hitler. Joyce Bland, who had played Imogen at Stratford, again took the part. 'The performance, intrinsically interesting, left the impression that the actors were saving themselves up for Shaw at the expense of Shakespeare,' wrote *The Times*. '... [They] visibly thrilled to a brand new challenge when the fifth act began.' But the general public, worried by the news of the Japanese capture of Shanghai, General Franco's blockade of the Spanish coast, and the riots in Sudeten Czechoslovakia, were in no mind to enter fairyland. They wanted something that spoke to the formidable problems of the present – which is what Shaw, in his next play, tried to give them.

*

'Geneva is a title that speaks for itself.'

Shaw's expedition to the League of Nations Palace in September 1928 had been made towards the end of its ascendant phase. In this age of early tanks and aeroplanes, poison gas, and new guns and bombs, people looked to the League to quell their anxieties. Yet they knew that 'the big Powers have not, and never have had, any intention of relinquishing any jot of their sovereignty,' Shaw wrote, 'or depending on any sort of strength and security other than military.'

He had visited this 'temple of the winds' like a political weather expert, and the next year issued his report in Fabian Tract No. 226. The ripples Shaw set dancing at Geneva were similar to those he made round the Malvern Festival. 'I see again Mr Bernard Shaw stalking out of the dining-room of the Residence,' wrote the diplomatist Bruce Lockhart, 'an object of greater hero-worship and reverence to the throng of League visitors than any political delegate.'

Shaw was vividly aware of his starring role and responsive to the dramatic potential of the League from his seat in the Assembly gallery. 'Fortunately, the young ladies of the Secretariat, who have plenty of theatrical instinct, arrange the platform in such a way that the president, the speakers, and the bureau are packed low down before a broad tableau curtain which, being in three pieces, provides most effective dramatic entrances right and left of the centre,' he wrote.

'When a young lady secretary has a new dress, or for any other reason feels that she is looking her best, she waits until the speaker – possibly a Chinese gentleman carefully plodding through a paper written in his best French – has reduced half the public galleries to listless distraction and the other half to stertorous slumber. Then she suddenly, but gracefully, snatches the

396

curtains apart and stands revealed, a captivating mannequin, whilst she pretends to look round with a pair of sparkling eyes for her principal on the bureau. The effect is electric: the audience wakes up and passes with a flash from listless desperation to tense fascination, to the great encouragement of the speaker, who, with his back to the vision beautiful, believes he has won over the meeting at last.'

Next to the Assembly, which met in the erstwhile Victoria Hotel, worked the Secretariat, an international civil service, permanently in residence at the former National Hotel. Swarms of journalists circled through its whispering atmosphere, plunging after gobbets of scandal, as the politicians, like monsters from the past, grappled clumsily for personal advantage. Among these relics of what seemed like a species already extinct, G.B.S. saw his first spark of hope. The smaller states had sent to Geneva their 'heaviest champions' to hold the fort for sane internationalism against the cabinets of big Powers seeking to reduce the League to impotence. In such a situation the Whitehall socialite 'soon suffers a Lake change', Shaw noticed.

'In the atmosphere of Geneva patriotism perishes: a patriot there is simply a spy who cannot be shot ... In short, the League is a school for the new international statesmanship as against the old Foreign Office diplomacy.'

The social, economic and humanitarian work of the League was carried out by a third institution, the International Labour Organization, whose offices occupied a newly designed building where Labour was glorified in stained glass and muscular statuary. 'I have never been in a modern business building more handsomely equipped,' Shaw wrote. '... And here the air is quite fresh: no flavor of Whitehall leather and prunella can be sniffed anywhere. These neo-Carthusians are of a new order...' To his eyes they were genuine internationalists working at what he had regarded all his Fabian life as the realities of politics: improving labour conditions (mainly in Egypt, India, Japan and Persia); fighting epidemic diseases such as cholera, plague and typhus (particularly in China and Yugoslavia); finding accommodation and work for displaced people (more than a million refugees from Asia Minor were resettled mainly in Northern Greece); controlling the traffic in opium; establishing the rights of women; caring for children, protecting strangers, welcoming sojourners like Shaw himself, and generally forcing up the moral standards of the big Powers.

The danger to the League was that its failure to secure even a pretence of peace might lead to its starvation and even its abandonment. Shaw's Fabian

Tract had put the question: 'What do all these people do besides pretending that the League can prevent war?' He gave as his answer that Geneva could justify its existence ten times over through this work of the International Labour Organization.

'The really great thing that is happening at Geneva is the growth of a genuinely international public service, the chiefs of which are ministers in a coalition which is, in effect, an incipient international Government.'

His play, *Geneva*, written mainly in the late 1930s, when the League was diminished by the Japanese invasion of Chinese Manchuria, the Italian invasion of Abyssinia and the German invasion of the demilitarized Rhineland, was a make-believe – what Shaw originally called 'a fancied page of history' – about what might have happened if the Geneva Idea had spread. In fact the big Powers had escaped the Covenant of the League by means of disingenuous external treaties such as the Kellogg Pact which allowed nations to go to war 'in self-defence' – which meant they could go to war whenever they wanted. 'Now that Mussolini has run up the black flag frankly broadside on to the League of Nations,' Shaw had written to Beatrice Webb late in 1923, 'Europe will have to consider whether she means anything by that heavily whitewashed *papier mâché* institution.' His tract had been an attempt to dispel the public's natural scepticism. The League's roots, he claimed, 'had struck deep before it appeared above ground in 1919'. In his play he pretends that there is no veto to make the League sterile, that the Idea has flowered and blown a fresh moral climate into the political atmosphere.

There were to be no vamping episodes from the Assembly or intrigues at the Secretariat in Shaw's *Geneva*. He converts the natural theatre of the League's Palace into a Platonic forum for international opinion, using none of the three institutions at its centre, but two of its satellites: the International Court at the Hague and the International Institute of Intellectual Co-operation in Paris.

Of all the functions of the League, the permanent Court of International Justice at the Hague was the most widely understood. 'The League is still too uncertain of its powers to call the offenders to account,' Shaw wrote in 1930. Six years later he gives his Judge in *Geneva* this certainty – 'Its assumption is only a matter of nerve' – and makes the Hague Court, not the Geneva Assembly, the League's operative organ.

This Judge, who presides over the last act of the play, has been called forth by applications for warrants against the dictators of Europe issued in Act I from the office of the International Institute for Intellectual Co-operation. So little known was this organization that many of Shaw's audiences believed he invented it. In fact he had merely invented its usefulness.

Shaw reasoned that intellectuals could not legitimately criticize nations for failing to refer international questions to the League if they did not use it themselves. 'I do not know whether you have noticed that we treat the League of Nations just as the bellicose Powers do,' he wrote to Henri Barbusse who in 1932 had invited him to join Einstein, Dreiser, Gorki, Mme Sun Yat-sen and others on the organizing committee of a Congress against War. 'Whenever a serious international difficulty arises the Powers act precisely as if the League of Nations did not exist. We do the same. The League of Nations has a Committee for Intellectual Co-operation. It is impotent and almost useless because nobody takes any notice of it.'

Three years later, when E. M. Forster invited him to join a Permanent Bureau of international writers on the left, he tried again. 'Have you ever thought of the Committee for Intellectual Co-operation of the League of Nations as a possible instrument lying ready to our hands and quite neglected by us?' he asked Forster. 'I am too old to start on it; but if I were a beginner I should certainly organize an attempt to capture it. It is just dying to be taken notice of.'

But he was not too old to capture it in his imagination. The first chairman had been Henri Bergson, but it was not until Gilbert Murray took over the chairmanship in 1928 that Shaw began to grow interested in its possibilities. Murray himself had shied away from this 'beastly Intellectual Travail ... that bores me stiff'. It seemed clogged with fruitless discussions on lofty themes, 'almost a joke', attracting what Arthur Koestler called the intellectual 'Call Girls' of the world to its conferences. 'It was rather like a Shaw play,' Murray decided after one of these bureaucratic comedies. Yet in spite of himself 'I find that I am getting interested in the wretched business, from having to explain and defend it!' By the end of 1933 Murray had come to see its meetings as 'a record – fragmentary indeed and imperfect – of the unseen process which creates and maintains human progress; a process which seldom gets into the front page of any popular newspaper, because it does not consist of explosions or spectacular triumphs; only of the steady growth, and amid much discouragement, of the activity that will save civilisation, if civilisation is to be saved'.

Gilbert Murray 'believes in telepathy', Shaw later wrote. In other words they were thinking along similar lines – that human survival might one day depend upon some new environmental code of international law. This could only come about through world opinion – and the shaping of world opinion G.B.S. believed to be his speciality.

Gilbert Murray was godparent to Shaw's *Geneva*. After he became chairman of the Committee of Intellectual Co-operation, he invited Shaw to correspond with the League and for once G.B.S. was nonplussed: 'for what on earth was I to correspond about?' The content might be telepathically provided, but what should be the mode? This question too was answered implicitly by Murray who in 1933 published a study of Aristophanes which he dedicated to Shaw, 'lover of ideas and hater of cruelty, who has filled many lands with laughter and whose courage has never failed'.

'Thanks mainly to Gilbert Murray, I know as much as anyone need know of the ancient Greek drama,' Shaw later wrote. In *Geneva* he went back to the Old Comedy of Aristophanes, satirizing contemporary politicians to illustrate recurring historical processes. 'The play is a lampoon with Hitler and Mussolini unmistakably on the stage,' he told the theatrical producer H. K. Ayliff. Technically the shape, development and balance between talk and action are sound and the long last act, writes Maurice Colbourne, 'is composed and manipulated with a mastery that makes it an unexcelled example of what is meant by the symphonic quality of Shavian drama'. Though still making fun of Murray's committee, Shaw gives it something to do at last.

The first act opens in its invented Geneva office, a 'rotten little room' meagrely equipped with second-hand furniture, on the third floor of a 'tumbledown old house full of rats'. With her heels on the dingy table, facing an old typewriter, sits a good-looking self-satisfied young Englishwoman smoking and reading an illustrated magazine. Her name is Begonia Brown and she is the entire uninterrupted staff of the place. 'Nobody ever comes in here,' she says. But that May morning near the end of the 1930s she is astonished to be called on by five claimants in succession, 'each with a grievance which they expect her to remedy'. The first is a distinguished-looking Jew seeking to issue a warrant against the political tyrant who has tormented and exiled him. Her second visitor is an obstinate man known simply as the Newcomer who wants the British Prime Minister arrested for violating the Constitution. He is followed by the widow of a Central American President, recently assassinated by his successor, whom she is seeking to avenge, though she has herself been 'compelled by etiquette' to shoot her best friend for having engaged her late husband's affections. An elderly English Bishop arrives next, complaining that his footman has been brainwashed into joining a communist cell, but he suddenly drops dead on learning that the Conservative gentleman he had dined with the previous evening was a Soviet Commissar – the very man who also turns up at the office to protest against the anti-communist propaganda of a Society for the Propagation of the Gospel.

Not knowing what to do amid this disarray, Begonia Brown accepts the Jew's suggestion that she refer all grievances to the International Court at The Hague. Since one plaintiff has died of shock, however, there will be no warrant issued against the Soviet dictator. The Bishop's place in Court will be somewhat arbitrarily taken by a voluble middle-aged Deaconess who is a prototype of Britain's Mrs Mary Whitehouse and represents the new Christian force of moral rearmament – as well as revealing something of James Porter Mills's energetic influence on Charlotte Shaw.

All the plaintiffs represent in satirical form currents of political energy. The Jew speaks for persecuted minorities throughout history; the Newcomer, an old-fashioned supporter of the extreme left of Liberalism, is now a proponent of constitutional democracy expressed through adult suffrage, the House of Commons and the party system; Commissar Posky is the obedient servant of Bolshevism; and the revolver-carrying Widow proclaims: 'My name is Revenge. My name is Jealousy. My name is the unwritten law that is no law.' She is part of the endless vendetta of human history.

As the play proceeds into and beyond the second act we are introduced to the Spirit of Geneva in the person of the League's Secretary, a dogged ex-idealist disillusioned after innumerable interviews with 'distinguished statesmen of different nations ... each with a national axe to grind'. This refined but careworn official is Shaw's portrait of the permanent British Secretary General Sir Eric Drummond, and to him Shaw grants the 'Lake change' he referred to in his Fabian Tract. 'When I came here I was a patriot, a Nationalist, regarding my appointment as a win for my own country in the diplomatic game. But the atmosphere of Geneva changed me,' the Secretary will tell the others. '... When it comes to the point you are all cut-throats. But Geneva will beat you yet. Not in my time, perhaps. But the Geneva spirit is a fact; and a spirit is a fact that cannot be killed.'

Opposing this spirit of the future is the British Foreign Secretary, Sir Orpheus Midlander, 'a very well-dressed gentleman of fifty or thereabouts, genial in manner, quick-witted in conversation, altogether a pleasant and popular personality' – a damning Shavian description. He presents 'a very good symbol' of the Foreign Office, Gilbert Murray acknowledged, 'though I should say that of late years it has rather lost its traditional grace of manner'. On a wider scale he represents time present – 'Nothing wrong with the world: nothing whatever,' he tells the League of Nations Secretary in the manner of Tom Broadbent cheering up the disfrocked Irish priest Peter Keegan in *John Bull's Other Island*; and he prescribes 'a cup of tea' to cure despair rather as Broadbent recommends phosphorous pills to brighten up Keegan's view of the world as 'a place of torment and penance'.

As a trained parliamentary debater Sir Orpheus will score astute verbal points against the dictators, but he is opposed to change and believes that politics should be left to professional politicians ('we cant have literary people interfering in foreign affairs'). He is Shaw's portrait to the life of Sir Austen Chamberlain (Secretary of State for Foreign Affairs between 1924 and 1929) whose naïve English patriotism had been a standing joke at Geneva, 'so outrageous that only a man with a single eyeglass could have got away with it' Shaw recalled in his Fabian Tract. Yet Shaw is careful not to make Sir Orpheus a hypocrite: 'the Chamberlains are the most absurdly and naively sincere statesmen on the face of the globe', he later wrote. The choice of Chamberlain (who died in 1937) as his model for the Foreign Secretary is evidence that Shaw wanted to focus his view beyond specific topicalities to a more general political landscape.

More extreme than Sir Orpheus's restricted vision is the political blindness of Begonia Brown. We know more of her than we know of the other characters, both from her biographical narrative within the play and from Shaw's comments elsewhere. Her unprecedented action creates European chaos and a war, in consequence of which she grows so popular in Britain that the government is obliged to make her a Dame of the British Empire. Like Sir Orpheus she is a patriot – Shaw tightens their relationship by making her fiancé the Foreign Secretary's nephew, a Conservative candidate for Camberwell who has stood down in favour of Begonia. But she is far more pugnacious and parochial than the Foreign Secretary, treating all 'foreigners as her inferiors, especially when they differ in colour' – the sort of last-refuge patriot whom Shaw had called 'simply a spy who cannot be shot'. She represents the spirit of the past, and its aggressive resurgence into the present. 'If you want to know what real English public opinion is, keep your eye on me,' she tells the League's Secretary. 'I'm not a bit afraid of war...' She threatens the peace of the world because even dictators cannot ignore the strength of her primitive conviction. But she is more dangerous in a democracy. Though everyone agrees she is a political ignoramus, 'she has courage, sincerity, good looks, and big publicity', Sir Orpheus acknowledges. '...Everything that our voters love.' She is also intensely ambitious and knows that 'victory in war is the key to fame and glory'. This Boadicea is to become 'the first female Prime Minister, too late for inclusion in the play', Shaw was to tell readers of *Everybody's Political What's What?*. Here is his prophetic warning against the backward-looking culture of a nation in decline that will raise from its legendary depths a Warrior Queen to relive its heroic days.

Shaw wrote the part of Begonia Brown, the most common of his vital young women, for 'a capable and pushing comedian' who serves as a catalyst in the play's farcical plot, stirring the International Court to action. 'All that was needed was a *cause célèbre*; and Miss Begonia Brown has found several for us very opportunely,' says the Senior Judge. This severe young Dutchman, 'very grave and every inch a judge', is the spirit of ideal Shavian justice. 'Justice is an ideal; and I am a judge,' he says simply. There are no policemen in this Court and its judgements are followed by no executions. The only power is the Judge's perceived moral authority and his one punishment amounts to excommunication by world opinion.

It is to gain the good opinion of the world that the three dictators present themselves at his court – 'if the Hague becomes the centre of the European stage all the soldiers and police in the world will not keep them away', the Judge predicts. '...Where the spotlight is, there will the despots be gathered.'

Signor Bardo Bombardone, 'a man of destiny' got up in the British première as a Roman emperor, has had previous reincarnations as Nero and Napoleon; Herr Battler with his 'resolutely dissatisfied expression' and attired as Lohengrin suggests Hitler's permanent place in German medieval romance; and the name General Flanco de Fortinbras connects the contemporary Spanish leader to the Prince of Norway who calls for 'Soldiers' music and the rites of war' over Hamlet's body at the end of Shakespeare's play.

'What an actor!' exclaims Battler in admiration of Bombardone. He is indeed a wonderfully bumptious presence, with a flight of words for every occasion. He has risen by personal gravitation to the leadership of his country. From him, rather than from any character in *Man and Superman*, we can hear the doctrine of power, the praise of war, the belief in will and impulse that belong to Nietzsche.

Bombardone is somewhat contemptuous of Flanco, a limited archetypal gentleman-soldier from the old school; but he feels wary of Battler whom he sees on a razor's edge between inspiration and the megalomania that is a recurrent theme in Shaw's later work. Both of them make the connection between political power and the theatre. Bombardone is a star performer, Battler a compelling orator to whom 'the object of public speaking is to propagate a burning conviction of truth and importance, and thus produce immediate action and enthusiastic faith and obedience'.

Hitler had turned out to be 'a very difficult character to dramatize'. It was not easy for Shaw to get 'any credible account of the man'. He had struggled a little with an abridged translation of *Mein Kampf* before leaving his copy in New Zealand and was to study James Murphy's first complete translation into English, published later in 1939, only during 1942 when it impressed him as being 'one of the world's bibles', like Calvin's *Institution* and Adam

Smith's *Wealth of Nations*, which 'changed the mind of the reading world'. He distrusted the newspaper stories he read and in 1936 and 1937 there was little else to go on, apart from Goebbels's *My Part in Germany's Fight* (1935) and Rudolf Olden's *Hitler the Pawn* (1936). Some people he questioned, such as the German biographer Emil Ludwig, described Hitler as 'an illiterate semi-idiot'. However a book called *I Knew Hitler* (1938) by Kurt Ludecke, an early Nazi who had left the party and gone into exile, gave Shaw a picture he could recognize – that of a patient learner determined to rise above his obscurity. He supplemented this with some later first-hand impressions: from Lloyd George, for example, who in the autumn of 1936 wrote of Hitler as being 'unquestionably a great leader' and far from the 'mechanical moron' others liked to claim. Here again was something Shaw's imagination could use. 'I think I made Hitler give a better account of himself than he has ever done in real life,' he wrote in 1940.

In trying to explain the phenomenon of Hitler, Shaw involves everyone. His Battler has been born a nobody, grown up in a humiliated country and matched his life to Germany's history. He shares something of the Jew's grievance, Begonia Brown's political ambition, the mystical faith of the Deaconess and above all the vengeful spirit of the Widow. This is no freakish homuncule accidentally visited upon an unfortunate world, but a terrible combination of us all, and it is we who have created him and called him forth. He bears witness to having been carried forward by 'a mighty movement in the history of the world'.

'Impelled by it I have stretched out my hand and lifted my country from the gutter into which you and your allies were trampling it, and made it once more the terror of Europe, though the danger is in your own guilty souls and not in any malice of mine ... You must all come my way, because I march with the times, and march as pioneer ...'

But for those who expected him to prove the most sinister and ominous of the dictators, bringing extra intensity to the last act, Battler is a disappointment. To Beatrice Webb, who saw the London production, he appeared little more than a 'sentimental posturing mystic', and to the pro-Nazi writer George Sylvester Viereck, who saw the New York production, he was 'simply a maniacal braggart, unredeemed by reason or wit'. Partly it may have been that Hitler was beyond Shaw's range: he had chosen a brief period when he played 'understudy' to Mussolini. Partly it may be that his interest in power had declined in old age: many of Battler's lines lack bite and he is given no confrontation with his chief accuser, the Jew, to match the confrontation between Warwick and Cauchon in *Saint*

Joan. Partly, too, Shaw may have been worried by the consequences on Trebitsch of a horrifying stage presentation of proto-fascism ('I could not involve you in such a controversy,' he had written earlier, '. . . you would run all the risks and I none').

Shaw tried to develop the character of Battler through the many revisions of *Geneva*. The first draft had been written between the second week of February and the first week of April 1936. The following month he had taken it with him on his annual visit to Passfield Corner where he read it to the Webbs. From Beatrice it drew a horrified reaction similar to that produced on Shaw by the Brecht–Weill *Threepenny Opera*: it seemed ugly, built out of distortions, with every character depraved in morals and manners. 'Sidney felt obliged to be critical,' she wrote; 'we feared for G.B.S.'s reputation if the play be performed or even published in its present form.'

'I think I shall be able to turn Geneva into a presentable play after all,' Shaw wrote to her that May. But after his next annual visit, in the early summer of 1937, Beatrice observed that he was 'distressed that he can no longer write his plays'. On the bright side she added: '*Geneva*, I am glad to say, has been definitely laid on one side.'

Then, arriving at Ayot late in October, Beatrice found that G.B.S., 'looking frail, with uncertainty in his glance and gait, as if he did not know his way about in thought or expression', had again taken up *Geneva*. 'If he would only give up working at that play about the League of Nations,' Charlotte sighed. 'He can't get it right.' But 'I have to write plays like *Geneva*,' he insisted. 'It is not that I want to.'

Seven months later, now nearing his eighty-second birthday, he announced: 'Geneva is finished. So am I – very nearly.' Both statements were untrue. The world première, however, took place in Warsaw on 25 July 1938 while Germany was preparing to mobilize. The British première opened at Malvern on 1 August in a last-minute revised version that with further modifications was then transferred to London towards the end of November. The *Daily Herald* reported the new anti-semitic legislation in Italy under the heading: 'Mussolini Makes Shaw Re-Write Play'.

Shaw's alterations to *Geneva* were of three kinds: changes 'to cut it to the bone', changes to keep it up to date, and changes to appease Jewish feelings. None was perceived as being successful.

The fashionable length for a play in the 1930s was a little over two hours – 18,000 words. Shaw's plays were from a third to half as long again. 'I now overwrite to such an extent,' he had said at the end of 1933, 'that I have to cut the play down by a full third to pull it properly together and bring it within possible limits of time.' Yet they were still too long – and when he added a new penultimate act in 1945 the length of *Geneva* was extended to nearly three and a half hours.

'All plays with topical gags (and there is nothing else in Geneva) must have been altered almost from night to night in pantomimes and burlesques,' Shaw wrote to the producer, H. K. Ayliff. The most substantial of his topical changes was to be the 600-word scene he added in September 1939 bringing the event plot up to date. 'The declaration of war is the making of Geneva which has always lacked a substantial climax,' he told the theatrical presenter Roy Limbert. '...I have written a new scene – the arrival of the news of Battler's attack – which will just do the trick.' In the last weeks of 1938 and during the first eight months of 1939 *Geneva* had scored a spectacular success, playing for 237 performances in London before going on tour. 'When do you sail?' Shaw asked Maurice Colbourne on 17 September 1939. 'I can let you have the new version by the end of the week.' But Colbourne, who with Barry Jones was to give it an adventurous tour through Canada and the United States, believed that 'Hitler worked too fast ... the play was out of date before its ink was dry.' By the time *Geneva* opened at the Henry Miller Theater in New York on 30 January 1940, the League of Nations was moribund and Shaw's courtroom proceedings sounded 'extraordinarily futile' to Brooks Atkinson and other leading critics.

Yet one day something would have to take the place of the League of Nations. Though 'weak and slow and helpless and confused' as Gilbert Murray acknowledged, it had been a first tentative step towards Shaw's court of pure justice now being dismissed by critics as a midsummer night's dream. Shaw had wanted to use his audiences as juries who would evaluate this Platonic investigation into public morals and hear the case for open government where 'no walls can hide you, and no distance deaden your lightest whisper'; he wanted to show them the enormous pains that dictators will take to win public opinion – their opinion; he wanted them to attend another Shavian Judgment Day and see in the false apocalypse the falsity of despair.

Geneva was played and printed in at least eight different versions. 'You may now put the copy I sent you in the fire as useless,' Shaw had written to Lawrence Langner after the Malvern production. Langner had been deeply hurt by Battler's speech justifying everything that had taken place in Germany. 'I do not believe that you will want future generations of Jew-baiters to quote you as part authority for a program of torturing, starving and driving to suicide of Jews all over the world,' he wrote.

'... I do most sincerely ask you to reconsider the position you have given the character of the Jew in this play. Shakespeare, by the character of Shylock, and Dickens, by the character of Fagin, have added greatly to the cross of hatred which future generations of Jews must bear ... You have made him a pitifully inferior mouthpiece to express his case, thus playing into the hands of the breeders of racial hatred by ranging yourself unconsciously on their side.'

'To please you, I have written up the part a bit,' Shaw replied two months before the London opening. Yet he did not deeply reconsider the Jew's position in the play. In *The Millionairess* he had 'carefully avoided any suggestion' of the 'two poor devils' in the basement sweatshop being Jewish 'as it would drag in current politics'. But *Geneva* is all current politics. The plaintiffs present themselves as stereotypes; the accused stand as archetypes; and they all depend on one another for their roles. The British public wanted to see the terrifying spectres of Hitler and Mussolini ridiculed, and were convinced that this was what they were seeing. '*Geneva* was a great success judging by the packed house and continuous laughter,' reported Beatrice Webb at the end of 1938, as the thunderclouds of fascism and Nazism were darkening. 'The play has come at the best possible occasion: it relieves the terrible tension that we all feel about foreign affairs by laughing at every one concerned.'

But many critics disliked it. They had hoped to see a grand Shavian paradox with the tyrants tumbled from their thrones and the victims raised up into high places. Where audiences laughed, these critics felt uneasy. Shaw had admitted that his play 'flatters them [the dictators] enormously'. This embarrassed many Shavians, though they had approved the general principle Shaw set out in his Preface to *Plays Pleasant* forty years before:

'The obvious conflicts of unmistakable good with unmistakable evil can only supply the crude drama of villain and hero, in which some absolute point of view is taken, and the dissentients are treated by the dramatist as enemies to be piously glorified or indignantly vilified. In such cheap wares I do not deal. Even in my unpleasant propagandist plays I have allowed every person his or her own point of view ... '

But had the plaintiffs received a fair hearing? Reviewing the London production, Desmond MacCarthy objected: 'In this disputatious extravaganza, which Mr Shaw calls "A Play of the Moment", the case for the Jew ought of course to have been vigorously put. It was not. Nor was the case of the democrat...

'[Shaw] has been false to his mission in life. Until recent years one of the things I have admired most in him has been a spontaneous chivalry ...

Speaking for myself, it [*Geneva*] made me ask if it were possible that I had been a fool about Bernard Shaw all my writing life.'

Shaw's extra act, which takes place in the lounge of a fashionable restaurant overlooking the Lake of Geneva and which resembles a third farcical 'ante-chamber' before the Hague court, is an attempt to give a technical answer to MacCarthy's and Langner's objections without destroying the genre in which he was working. The act defines the 'Lake change' that has turned the League Secretary away from the philistine mainland towards the rich and strange figure of the Judge. It also separates everyone into their political and biological components by allowing them a few minutes' privacy in this public play. As political beings they have come to Geneva to air their grievances and push their interests. 'I never hear you talking politics without wanting to shoot you,' exclaims the Secretary; and the Judge concludes that 'None of you seem to have any idea of the sort of world you are living in.' In this political aspect they are all 'enemies of the human race,' in other words their own worst enemies. Their ideological hostility to each other is political death (the English Bishop has literally died of his contact with Soviet ideas); but biologically their differences are life-enhancing. Begonia Brown pairs off with the Judge; the Jew dines with the Widow; and Sir Orpheus spends his evening with the Soviet Commissar. All this supports the Judge's statement in the last act that even the dictators themselves seem 'personally harmless human beings' though their political deeds call for 'nothing short of your immediate execution'.

Shaw believed that critics were reacting to his characters as if they were real people rather than political abstractions. As public symptoms of human nature they are part of one another and all are satirized. The critics had wanted him to take sides and, as Gilbert Murray observed, 'did not see that you were flinging your satire impartially all round'. The result was that Shaw's play was equally unpopular with pro- and anti-Nazis – the proper fate, perhaps, for an unpleasant play.

The question remains as to whether he was justified in putting 'real plums into an imaginary pudding' and whether his use of Aristophanic comedy was appropriate in presenting part of history that would culminate in the killing of six million Jews in concentration camps. *Lysistrata* had been written to stop a war and *Geneva* was written in the hope of helping to prevent one. It is a piece of stage diplomacy, a variant to Neville Chamberlain's appeasement policy, by someone who remembered the horror and futility of the first war against Germany and refused to be drawn into popular confusion between reality and myth. All that a playwright can do, Shaw wrote, 'is to extract comedy and tragedy from the existing situation and wait and see what will become of it'. The tragedy is implicit in his play, the comedy broad and explicit. Battler protests to the Judge that the court is 'making fun of us', and the Deaconess gives Shaw's answer: 'God has ordained that when men are childish enough to fancy that they are gods they become what you call funny. We cannot help laughing at them.'

It was not easy to laugh in the 1940s and *Geneva* was to become Shaw's 'most frequently disparaged play'. He disparaged it himself. 'What a horrible play! Why had I to write it?' he asked H. K. Ayliff at the end of 1938. 'To hear those poor devils spouting the most exalted sentiments they were capable of, and not one of them fit to manage a coffee stall, sent me home ready to die.' It is clear that Shaw thought the effective way of exposing his dictators was not to falsify historical fact by allowing their accusers to dominate the court, but to let us see the authentic miming of their dramaturgical tricks, their bluster and defiance, mystical flights and neurotic fears, and the face-saving gestures that reveal the emptiness of their authority.

'Authority is a sort of genius: either you have it or you have not,' Bombardone tells the court. The nature of authority is the theme of *Geneva*. 'Your objective is domination,' the Judge replies to the dictators. His own objective is to create a code of justice that serves the desire for harmony underlying the discord of our lives. The dictators' authority stands on Will, is violent, and artificially imposes order; the Judge's authority proceeds from the imagination, is settled, and stands on faith. When the future of the world appears to be threatened by a science fiction disaster, the dictators are suddenly reduced from archetypes to stereotypes, like their accusers, and seen in much the same light as Isabella sees Angelo in *Measure for Measure*:

> 'but man, proud man,
> Drest in a little brief authority
> Most ignorant of what he's most assur'd,
> His glassy essence, like an angry ape,
> Plays such fantastic tricks before high heaven
> As make the angels weep.'

'A moment ago we were important persons: the fate of Europe seemed to depend on us. What are we now?' asks the Judge. Only he and the Secretary retain their stature. Only they, at the final curtain, can still tell truth from falsehood and know that the end of the world is not in fact at hand.

*

Shortly before the opening of *Geneva* in London, Shaw began 'In Good King Charles's Golden Days'. Moving his emphasis back towards the personal imagination, he turned over his 'Fancied Page of History' and opened his last pleasant play subtitled 'A True History that Never Happened'.

'It's about the time of Charles II,' Charlotte wrote. 'Such a lot of interesting people lived then & he is throwing them all in together to sink or swim. I am rather pleased about it.' Beatrice Webb also felt pleased that G.B.S. had moved from his unpleasant mode: 'unexpectedly he is writing a new play, which promises well', she wrote on 11 January 1939. '...I read the first scene – brilliant dialogue. Isaac Newton, George Fox, Charles and his ladies and James. If he can bring in some sort of striking incident into the play and not limit himself to sparkling talk, it may turn out A.1.'

Written in the aftermath of *Pygmalion*'s cinema triumph, '*In Good King Charles's Golden Days*' was begun as an 'educational history film' for Gabriel Pascal. The cast were to be sumptuously clothed in seventeenth-century costumes 'regardless of expense, numbers and salaries' – and far beyond the resources of most theatre managements. 'I never know what a play is going to be until it is finished,' he wrote on Christmas Eve 1938. By the time he had completed it on 3 May 1939 it had turned into a Shavian Restoration comedy. Either because he now lacked the vitality or else because he had no interest left in the devices and excitements of dramatic action, the play lacks the 'striking incident' that Beatrice Webb believed characterized his best work. It is a conversation piece, diversified by moments of burlesque, recitation and vaudeville, and alive with anachronisms that anticipate the future. 'Playwrights have their just privileges,' wrote Maynard Keynes, celebrating 'the proleptic quality' of these anachronisms.

'If one were asked to choose a date for the beginning of the modern world, probably July 15, 1662, would be the best to fix upon,' Lytton Strachey had written in 1928. 'For on that day the Royal Society was founded, and the place of Science in civilisation became a definite and recognized thing.' For similar reasons Shaw takes the year 1680 to mark his modern genesis. The two continuous scenes of the long first act are set in the cheerful library of a large house he invents for Isaac Newton at Cambridge. Here, one golden day, Newton's calculations into the future and the past are creatively interrupted by a procession of unheralded visitors. Charles II (travelling incognito as Mr Rowley) and a big man dressed in leather with bright eyes and a powerful voice who turns out to be George Fox arrive together ('the spiritual powers before the temporal' says Charles ushering in Fox before him). They are pursued by Charles's brother James, an obtuse and bigoted Catholic; and three of the King's Ladies, vivacious Nell Gwynn, Barbara Villiers, the jealous Duchess of Cleveland, and the 'baby-faced' Louise de Kéroualle, Duchess of Portsmouth, who has called on Isaac Newton for a love philtre. Finally the portrait painter Godfrey Kneller turns up in search of the King. All of them stay to lunch.

'You find yourself dining with all sorts,' Begonia Brown had remarked in the extra act to *Geneva*. There are several cross-references between the two plays. In Charles, whose education was completed 'at the Hague', the Geneva spirit lives on through this pleasant play. 'The riddle of how to choose a ruler is still unanswered; and it is the riddle of civilization,' he says. But Shaw has now turned from the riddle of authority to the mysterious process of learning. *Good King Charles* is a profoundly democratic play, its verbal choreography designed to show us that education depends upon the coming together of us all. 'I have made eight new friends. But has the Lord sent them to me? Such friends! ... What manner of world is this that I have come into?' exclaims George Fox in perplexity. From the blends and clashes of this diverse group everyone learns something. 'You unsettle my mind,' Fox tells James, Duke of York. 'I find your company agreeable to me, but very unsettling,' he tells Nell Gwynn. Charles encourages this unsettling process: 'The settled mind stagnates, Pastor.' Though Fox is dumbfounded by all the ungodly talk, wondering if he is 'dreaming that I am in hell', his imagination acknowledges that 'Divine grace takes many strange forms' – and he goes in to lunch arm-in-arm with 'the player woman' Nell Gwynn. 'You remind me that where my Master went I must follow.'

As religion bends to the attraction of human nature so science employs the perception of art. The meeting Shaw arranges in his play between Newton and Kneller had its origin in his own meeting with Einstein and the speech he delivered at the Savoy in 1930. Here he coupled Einstein's name with Newton's as great 'makers of universes' (as opposed to the 'makers of empires' who populate *Geneva*) and commented on the delusion of Newton's single vision which restricted one of the most wonderful minds of all time. 'Newton invented a straight line,' he said.

' ... he invented the force which would make the straight line fit the straight lines of his universe – and bend them – and that was the force of gravitation. And when he had invented this force, he had created a universe which was wonderful and consistent in itself and ... when he had completed the book of that universe ... it was not a magical marvellous thing like a Bible. It was a matter-of-fact British thing like a Bradshaw ... Then an amazing thing happened. A young professor got up in the middle of Europe and [said] ... "The world is not a British rectilinear world. It is a curvilinear world, and the heavenly bodies go in curves because that is the natural way for them to go." ... These are not results worked out by a mathematician, the results of equations marked out on paper, they are the intuitions of an artist ... I reminded myself that Leonardo da Vinci, the artist, born twenty-one years before Copernicus, wrote down in his notebook ... "The earth is a moon of the sun." And later on the English artist, William Hogarth, a contemporary of Newton – their lives overlapped by thirty years – ... said "The line of nature is a curve." He anticipated our guest.'

When he came to write *Good King Charles*, Shaw found that Hogarth's life had overlapped with Newton's by only twenty-two years and could not by any marvellous magic be fitted into the year 1680 (seventeen years short of his birth). So he fell back on Kneller, whose dates just fitted in, granting him Hogarth's intellect and a paraphrase of Hogarth's 'the line of beauty is a curve'. When the artist's 'different kind of understanding' joins issue with the scientist's, Newton suddenly wakes from his dream of a rectilinear universe (so visibly contradicted by the three curvilinear ladies) and is endowed with the foresight of an Einstein. 'I have made Newton aware of something wrong with the perihelion of Mercury,' Shaw gleefully explained in his Preface. 'Not since Shakespeare made Hector of Troy quote Aristotle has the stage perpetrated a more staggering anachronism.'

'You presume to teach me my profession,' objects the arrogant Kneller in his first speech of the play. *Good King Charles* is a demonstration of how, in an enlightened atmosphere, every professional can learn something from the amateur. This atmosphere, over which the King presides rather like the Waiter in *You Never Can Tell*, is largely created by Charles's mistresses – it is, for example, Louise de Kéroualle who sees that 'Mr Kneller and Mr Newton seem to mean exactly the same thing; only one calls it beauty and the other gravitation.' If these women do not often occupy the forefront of the stage it is because women were so seldom in the foreground of political life.

The arch-amateur is Shaw himself. In previous plays he had pressed his claims as amateur sociologist, philosopher, doctor, bishop ... During his Einstein speech he spoke as a scientist, and for *Good King Charles*, the proofs of which he subtitled 'A History Lesson by A Fellow of the Royal Society of Literature', he became 'a historian myself'.

As an adolescent Shaw had taken his history from the novels of Walter Scott and the plays of Shakespeare. 'Records of fact are not history,' he was to write. 'They are only annals.' He believed that ideas rather than these blocks of facts were the essence of history and that historical writing depended upon the cutting edge of imaginative interpretation. In his Programme Note to *Caesar and Cleopatra* he had mentioned an impressive list of sources, then added: 'Many of these authorities have consulted their imaginations, more or less. The author has done the same.' The evidence of history might teach us to be pessimists, but the human spirit demands optimism. Since our roots lie in the past and our hopes reach towards the future, it followed that by changing our concepts of the past we could ordain our future. 'As I can neither witness the past nor foresee the future,' he was to have the teacher say in the last of his *Farfetched Fables*, 'I must take such history as there is as part of my framework of thought.'

Only after the failure of his novels had Shaw seriously questioned whether 'in presenting the facts in the guise of fiction, you have, in spite of yourself, shewn them in a false light'. As he achieved success in the theatre, he became convinced that 'it is only through fiction that facts can be made instructive or even intelligible'. In a letter to the American novelist Upton Sinclair written in the early 1940s he argued that facts could not become significantly historical until a novelist or playwright, musician or painter 'rescues them from the unintelligible chaos of their actual occurrence and arranges them in works of art ... Until this is done, history does not exist.'

The two most influential historians in Shaw's lifetime had been Macaulay and Carlyle – one a natural optimist buoyed up with his belief in inevitable progress, the other a prophet seeking to unravel the divine principle. In his play Shaw gives a picture of George Fox that more closely resembles the man in leather from Carlyle's *Sartor Resartus* ('one of those to whom, under ruder or purer form, the Divine Idea of the Universe is pleased to manifest itself') than the wandering busybody, 'shaking like an aspen leaf in his paroxysms of fanatical excitement', who appears in Macaulay's *History of England*. His recreation of Charles II is, as the critic J. L. Wisenthal shows, 'a clear rejection of Macaulay's account of him'; indeed, in his letter to Upton Sinclair, Shaw was to write of his wish to teach 'the spectator more of the history of the year 1680 than Macaulay at his best taught in a thousand pages'.

He appears to have consulted G. M. Trevelyan's *History of England* as well as Macaulay's; and besides Carlyle he consulted Pepys, Belloc, Fox's *Journal* and Arthur Bryant's *King Charles II* which had been published in 1931. He also consulted two astronomers, Sir James Jeans and Sir Arthur Eddington. Then he consulted his own imagination. 'Charles I have to invent all over again,' he wrote to Beatrice Webb early in 1939. 'Newton and Fox I have only put on the stage, as they are strangers there, and are far too little known.'

Charles II's regular business on the stage had been to act the principal lover in historical romances featuring Nell Gwynn. He would stride on as a gorgeously costumed walking gentleman and from time to time sit down so that Moll Davis and Sweet Nell could nest on his knee. Shaw transforms the Merry Monarch who lived so badly and died so well, who never said a foolish thing nor ever did a wise one, into a version of King Magnus from *The Apple Cart*, a man with natural talent for life and an astute grasp of politics whose reputation has been warped by official histories.

Good King Charles is both the culmination of Shaw's work as a historical dramatist, which had begun in 1895 with the 'Fictitious Paragraph of History' about Napoleon he called *The Man of Destiny*, and a merging of the chronicle play into allegorical fable and extravaganza – which, the critic Martin Meisel argues, was the best medium for the Shavian drama of ideas. The third scene, which takes the form of a short second act, reads like an epilogue to the play – but it does not resemble the Epilogue to *Saint Joan*; it is a companion piece to the Interlude from *The Apple Cart*.

In the 'late afternoon' the Shavian King has returned from Orinthia's romantic boudoir (which he entered at about 3.15 p.m. in *The Apple Cart*) to the untidy boudoir of his wife, Catherine of Braganza, in *Good King Charles*. He has left 'one of Nature's queens' and come home to his domestic queen, who is 'guiltless of sex appeal'. He has left the hurly-burly of 'a large settee' for the deep peace of 'a couch', where his wife finds him sleeping.

They talk and the fifty-year-old Charles sighs: 'In the end one learns to leave the body out.' Then he asks: 'can anything I can ever do make up to you for my unfaithfulness?' Shaw allows Catherine to answer: 'People think of nothing but that, as if that were the whole of life. What care I about your women? ... They have set me free to be something more to you than they are or can ever be. You have never been really unfaithful to me.' Though this reads like a sentimental gloss on what Charlotte had once felt, it may approximate to her retrospective view, at the age of eighty, of G.B.S.'s flirtations. But Shaw has the honesty to hold some balance still between the two women 'I was born to love'. Charles admits to one real unfaithfulness, with the beautiful childish Frances Theresa Stuart, whose portrait as Minerva by Sir Peter Lely he insisted should figure on the coinage of the realm. By making the woman who represents Stella Campbell no longer a Queen of Nature with an act to herself, but merely one of the Queen's Maids of Honour, La Belle Stuart, who does not actually have a part in *Good King Charles*, Shaw was making amends to Charlotte for *The Apple Cart* Interlude. 'I never touched her,' Charles tells his wife. 'But she had some magic that scattered my wits: she made me listen for a moment to those who were always pressing me to divorce my patient wife and take a Protestant queen. But I could never have done it, though I was furious when she ran away from me and married Richmond.' And Catherine admits: 'it was the only time I ever was jealous'.

But they had come through: 'we are grown-up now', Charles hopes. The play exhibits Charles as 'the best of husbands', and the message he is sending to Charlotte is that theirs had been the best of marriages made on earth. The 'hopeless tenderness' that attaches the King to the Queen at the end of *The Apple Cart* unites the King and Queen throughout this second act of *Good King Charles*. There is only one fear that falls between them, and that is a fear of the other's death. 'Long live the King!' cries Catherine. 'May the Queen live for ever!' exclaims Charles.

And the curtain descends on them both.

Reviewers loved '*In Good King Charles's Golden Days*' as much as they had hated *Geneva*. Reviewing the crowded opening night at Malvern on 12 August 1939, James Agate observed that the characters were all good up-to-the-minute Shavians and that the play itself was the best to have 'come from the Shavian loom since *Methuselah*'. In Hesketh Pearson's opinion it was 'the most satisfying thing he had done since *Saint Joan*'. And in a letter to Shaw, Sydney Cockerell wrote 'if the G.B.S. of "John Bull's Other Island" is dead, there is a sweetness, a mellowness, an intense kindness, a wisdom, an absence of cleverness, and a mature perfection that pleases me as much as ever and that will make this play survive'.

Its production in London during the late spring and early summer of 1940 was badly affected by the war; but when it was eventually staged in the United States at the small Downtown Theater on New York's East 4th Street in 1957 it was to get excellent notices ('Shaw in his most stimulating form as a dramatist of abstract ideas', wrote Brooks Atkinson) and ran for nearly two years ('one of the longest runs of any Shaw play in the U.S.A.', recorded Lawrence Langner).

Many critics had taken the opportunity offered by *Good King Charles* to pay a farewell tribute to Shaw in the theatre. It was his fiftieth work for the stage (give or take one or two). 'This play embodies the reaffirmations of a great man,' wrote James Agate, 'of one who, in our theatre, has been and will remain a giant.' It was an ideal last play, Maurice Colbourne judged, 'ending the long career with a cosmic query, a challenge to human knowledge . . .'

I am tired of the way in which the newspapers ... continue to make it
appear that I am an admirer of dictatorship.
All my work shows the truth to be otherwise.
'G.B.S. Replies to the Man in the Street',
The Star (4 August 1938)

The strange fate of Shaw's reputation in Germany between the wars traces an ironic commentary over the rise of the Nazi regime. 'I thought that with my endeavours for Shaw I was adding a plus to my own work, but, alas, it was a minus,' Siegfried Trebitsch sadly reflected. 'It was incomprehensible!'

During the 1920s every play Trebitsch translated had opened to vast plaudits in Austria and Germany. Yet Shaw's reactions to this triumphal progress were strange. The gravest nuances arose over Max Reinhardt's versions of *Saint Joan* and *The Apple Cart*. These productions had to be seen to be believed: and blessed were those that did not see, Shaw signified, and still believed in G.B.S.

The high repute of both plays heightened Trebitsch's awful sense of responsibility. He was determinedly present from the first rehearsal of *Saint Joan*. Though it never did for a translator to talk big, he could hardly deny what he had done: which was to help transform Elizabeth Bergner into the most sensational actress of her day, cause the spectacular return of Max Reinhardt to the post-war German theatre, and occasion the award of Shaw's Nobel Prize for Literature. His success was almost too dizzying – indeed something of an embarrassment, not to say an impediment. Sometimes he longed for the profound peace of his own work. Besides, everyone in the theatrical world of Germany was imploring G.B.S. never to write another play 'because another play must infallibly fall far below the heights on which *Saint Joan* towered'.

Curiously 'Shaw did not have any qualms in this direction' and since Reinhardt was now taking acute interest in his new work, Trebitsch went straight to him with *The Apple Cart*. To his delight Reinhardt 'remained silent with approval' after listening to the reading. 'I was then very richly rewarded for my valiant trust in the play,' Trebitsch recorded. 'The first night turned out to be one of the greatest successes I have ever known ... it was the most progressive and modern play of our time ... Shaw had reached the highest limits of what was possible in the German language.'

And it was true that by the end of the 1920s Shaw had acquired the status of a German classic. His plays were studied and performed all over the provinces as well as in the capitals of German-speaking countries. While

'Sudermann has long disappeared from the stage ... while even Hauptmann occupies a very limited space', wrote Leon Feuchtwanger in 1928, '... Bernard Shaw since the war reigns supreme'.

Such was Trebitsch's achievement, and he was crestfallen when Shaw and Charlotte refused to come over and join in his celebrations. G.B.S. tried not to act the spoilsport. 'It must be a case of "Trebitsch, Trebitsch über alles",' he wrote. 'So do not step an inch out of the limelight under the mistaken impression that I desire your effacement.'

The truth was that Shaw found himself somewhat awkwardly placed between gratitude and dismay. Despite the record run of *Saint Joan* he was alarmed by what he began to learn of Reinhardt's production. Scenes had been scissored, speeches superimposed, and Joan herself played throughout as petite and pathetic. And Trebitsch had been a wide-eyed collaborator in this 'monstrous misrepresentation', exulting in their triumph and representing Max Reinhardt as a German edition of Barry Jackson.

When they met in 1927 Shaw rather took to Reinhardt. 'He looked extraordinarily well and open-airy, as if he had never been near a theatre in his life,' he wrote. 'I never saw a man less spoilt by his profession.'

But *The Apple Cart* was an even greater travesty than *Saint Joan*. Reinhardt had sandwiched his political comedy between episodes of jazzed-up Bach and Chopin, and served it to German audiences as a racy operetta. Boanerges, attired like a racegoer's bookie and talking like a 'dirty bargee', appeared as a Jew; Proteus was collapsed into a 'bilious fool'; and the goddess Orinthia prostituted as an 'unscrupulous little kiosk-mamselle'. 'Why have you not challenged him [Reinhardt], shot him, sabred him, buried him in unconsecrated ground', Shaw demanded of Trebitsch. '... you must either quarrel with Reinhardt or quarrel with me. Clearly you must quarrel with Reinhardt.'

Alas, it was almost impossible to quarrel with Trebitsch. He was as sensitive as a child and full of innocent happiness. For what neither he nor Reinhardt realized at the time was that their versions of these plays fed the atmosphere that, substituting one sort of pornography for another, was lifting the Nazi regime into power. No wonder Hitler was to declare that St Joan was portrayed 'much more faithfully by Shaw than by Schiller' when the German version emphasized the mystical nature of power vested in someone physically so unimpressive yet gifted with the oratorical magic of patriotic 'voices'. It was this version of Shaw's play that prompted William Mackenzie King, Prime Minister of Canada, to express the conviction that spiritually Hitler 'will one day rank with Joan of Arc'. The lonely genius of power was again underscored by Reinhardt's King Magnus in *The Apple Cart*. The King's 'strangely innocent relations' with the flapper-cocotte

Orinthia were presented as the sexual recreations of a Nietzschian Superman whose political inspiration rose clear above the poisoned well of anti-German Jewish democracy. What had been intended by Shaw as a warning against dreaming the old dreams became the inducement to a new nightmare, in short 'a pornographic Jew baiting farce', he told Trebitsch.

'How can I ever expect a decent German to speak to me again? ... Rheinhardt [*sic*] must find other authors to drag through the mud ... I have been kinder with him than he deserves (merely for your sake) ... I cannot afford another such disgrace, nor can you.'

A colleague of Reinhardt's, Robert Klein, directed *Too True to be Good*. The reviews, Trebitsch admitted, were 'confusing'. According to Professor Samuel Weiss, they 'reflected the sharpened ideological splits in Germany' at the end of 1932. The liberal press welcomed Shaw as 'a great souled Prospero' who had created a 'wise comedy'; but conservative and anti-liberal critics accused him of nihilism and issued a warning that the new Germany would no longer tolerate attacks on the family. When the play moved to Mannheim early in 1933, it was disrupted by Nazi shouts of 'Jew Shaw!' until the police came to restore order. 'Can it be possible that my vogue in Germany, of which I have been so proud, has been all a mistake?' Shaw had asked.

At the beginning of 1933, when Hitler became Chancellor, Shaw's reputation seemed to be on the turn. In March Reinhardt left Germany for Austria and that summer ceded his theatres via the government to the German people. By 1937 he was safely unemployed in the United States. 'In all he had introduced nine of Shaw's plays to Berlin, produced another five and added two others in Vienna for over 1,300 performances,' Professor Weiss notes, 'second only to Shakespeare in Reinhardt's repertory.'

Being an Austrian rather than a German Jew, Trebitsch felt less directly threatened. Until Hitler entered Austria early in 1938, he experienced the Nazi phenomenon chiefly as an economic setback. The new Germany did not want foreign playwrights: 'snobbish trifles' as Shaw and Pirandello were described. Undoubtedly, too, some of Shaw's later plays were rather 'dry and difficult', though also, Trebitsch hastened to add, 'most profound and imperishable'. G.B.S. had given him 'great moral strength for the future', but what he needed now was money. He came from a wealthy family and was married to the widow of a Russian Grand Duke. Expensive habits were ingrained. During the 1930s he looked towards Shaw's films to buoy him up. But G.B.S. was oddly unhelpful, indeed sometimes positively useless, not to say an obstacle. He refused to license a German film of *The Chocolate*

Soldier (the musical version of *Arms and the Man*), he was downright discouraging about the Hollywood prospects of *Jitta's Atonement* and he accused Trebitsch of conscienceless deception over his German-language film of *Pygmalion*. 'You would sell my soul for gold,' he remonstrated. Rather than be a party to such bargains, he preferred to give or 'advance' him money. 'Shall I lend you £500 on account pending some transaction between us for your translation rights?' he asked at the end of 1935. 'If so, send me a wire with the single word Yes, and I will remit.' Such sums were small in comparison with Trebitsch's enchanting dreams of a movie fortune. It seemed that Shaw simply could not take their status as distressed gentlefolk seriously. 'I know quite well that everybody in Vienna is stony broke, and that you and Tina are desperately trying to live on a mere million or two of Schillings per month,' he wrote. '... I am haunted by the thought of her starving on the top floor of the Park Hotel instead of wearing all her diamonds on the *piano nobile*.'

Shaw was still fond of Trebitsch, still hopeful that he would behave honourably and prove a true medium for his work. 'We shall be delighted to see you always, no matter how long you stay,' he wrote to him in 1933. 'The sooner we see you the better we shall be pleased,' he wrote again in 1938. Most years, right up to 1939, Trebitsch would come over to England and every time Shaw would amaze him by picking up the conversation exactly where they had left it twelve months previously 'as though the earth had not, after all, travelled once around the sun since we had last been face to face with each other'.

'I had come to know what English hospitality meant,' Trebitsch wrote afterwards. At Ayot it meant sessions round the piano while G.B.S. sang Tristan to Tina's Isolde, periods of tranquillity while he disappeared into 'his tent at the bottom of the garden', and when they all came together again there were 'the blessings of vegetarian cookery'. There were also regular walks in the 'hilly' countryside. Keeping up with Shaw's long joyful strides had from the beginning put a terrible strain on the seams of Trebitsch's suits. With the passing years, as his own panting figure solidified and slowed, G.B.S. appeared to be sprinting into the future, his arms swinging, nostrils eagerly extended.

Shaw used their meetings to dissolve the tensions and misunderstandings that arose between them in these difficult times. For Trebitsch, the crowning moment naturally came when his friend and master handed him the typescript of a new play; yet his genial spirits were equally lifted by Charlotte's benign company. He saw her as a great lady who lived as though condemned to silence. But he experienced no trouble translating these silences. She had little ways of showing her attachment to him that he appreciated better than words. 'Her presence in itself was something convincing. How rarely did she practise criticism!'

To mitigate the rigours of English hospitality, they would book Trebitsch into a first-class London hotel and take him to premières of Shaw's plays to show him how they should be performed. They also encouraged him to bring German friends to lunch at Whitehall Court – often refugees like Stefan Zweig – so that they could learn more of what was going on in Germany. It was difficult learning much from Trebitsch himself, though G.B.S. could pick up something from the fate of his translations. *The Black Girl* remained unpublished because 'it would have been banned by the German censorship' (it was eventually brought out in 1948). In 1934 *On the Rocks* 'was a very great success', Trebitsch insisted, yet he had been obliged to give it the subtitle 'England, Arise!' which was taken as a summons to follow Germany's example. *The Simpleton*, which was banned in Austria, and in Germany did not transfer from Leipzig to Berlin, was the last of Shaw's plays 'I was to translate into German while still living in my native country', Trebitsch recalled, 'and the last German première of which (at the Leipzig Stadttheater) I was able to attend'.

Joseph Goebbels attended the Berlin première of *The Millionairess* in December 1936, but the play had to be published without its 'Preface on Bosses' speculating on Hitler's Jewish ancestry and diagnosing Judophobia as 'one of those lesions which sometimes prove fatal'. Shaw's reputation in Nazi Germany was by now full of anomalies. Whatever he wrote for the British press was, to Trebitsch's bewilderment, carefully edited in the German newspapers. Hitler himself went to a revival of *Caesar and Cleopatra* in 1939, but *Geneva* was forbidden to be either published or performed that year and the actor who had played Battler at Warsaw's Teatr Polski was imprisoned after the annexation of Poland. The Nazi ideologist Alfred Rosenberg placed Shaw among the 'army of half-breed "artists"' opposing the 'revived racial spirit'; yet tributes were still paid to him in *Germania*, *Berliner Tageblatt*, and *Deutsche Allgemeine Zeitung* on his eightieth birthday. Even during the war, his work was protected from wholesale censorship and he was classified by Goebbels as a satirical, anti-plutocratic Irishman: a case on his own.

As the 1930s advanced, Shaw felt increasingly responsible for Trebitsch. Hitler's name is not mentioned in their correspondence until May 1933 when, condemning the Nazi Judenhetze, Shaw advised him to 'keep out of the mêlée as much as possible'.

'If you are pressed as to why you translate me, who am a notorious Communist . . . you must say that you are not concerned with all that – that you have introduced me to Germany as a great artist ... But you are not committed to my opinions.'

For much of this time Shaw treated Hitler as if he were a fellow playwright under vulgar attack from foreign critics whose mindless animosity was driving the Nazi national theatre crazy. Certainly the Nazis were mad on the Jewish question. 'It is idle to argue against this sort of insanity,' he wrote in 1933. 'Judophobia is as pathological as hydrophobia ... The Nazis are suffering from an epidemic of a very malignant disease.' Despite the idleness of argument, and in the belief that 'propaganda is a necessary means of achieving any political purpose that is fit for publication', he used his own influence in the press during the 1930s to counterbalance the schoolboy abuse of 'Herr Schicklgruber'. Setting aside the Jewish question, he took care to be 'scrupulously polite and just to Hitler (which nobody else in England is)'. He welcomed the incorporation of the German trade unions into a state-directed Labour Front, as well as the introduction of a compulsory labour service. In 1935 he wrote to Trebitsch: 'Tell Colonel Goering with my compliments that I have backed his regime in England to the point of making myself unpopular.'

Shaw recognized that there was a human instinct called nationalism that made people 'dissatisfied unless they think they are governed by themselves and not by foreigners'. He believed that the Treaty of Versailles, which placed Germany in an inferior position, was an affront to that instinct, and that Hitler had been hoisted to power by the force of national resentment. Such was the outcome of an abuse of victory. He had urged the Allies to dismantle the military frontiers imposed by the Treaty, and when they failed to take this initiative he applauded Hitler for 'the political sagacity and courage with which he has rescued Germany from the gutter and placed her once more at the head of Central Europe'. He believed that the weak liberal parliamentarianism of western democracies had produced a 'Four Power Funk' that was positively encouraging Nazi expansionism. He saw the best hope of peace in a formidable rearmament programme by the Allies and an unlikely pact between Britain, France, the United States and Soviet Russia which would banish the communist taboo and hold a broad equilibrium until Germany and Italy inevitably split apart and Hitler's supremacy came to its natural end. 'A lasting peace is a dream,' he wrote. Such dreaming was beyond national politics and floated among the supranational spires of the League of Nations whose reality depended upon the visionary strength of many countries' foreign policies. Had they exercised this strength during the 1930s, Poland would have been 'the business of the League of Nations' before the end of the decade.

Every country, Shaw believed, was entitled to its civil wars without foreign interference. He looked on the Spanish Civil War as an internal class war with Franco standing for property, privilege and 'everything we are all taught to consider respectable', and though his sympathies were generally on the left, he distanced himself from other British intellectuals. 'Spain must choose for itself,' he wrote: 'it is really not our business.' As Stanley Weintraub concluded: 'For Shaw, a victory for the wrong side in Spain was preferable to a general European war, which the internationalizing of the Civil War seemed to be making inevitable.'

'My slogan is "Africa for the Africans!"', Shaw wrote in 1938. His most extreme expression of this principle came in a letter to Beatrice Webb where he admitted 'the right of States to make eugenic experiments by weeding out any strains that they think undesirable'. This was written when, wishing himself to 'intervene' over Sidney Webb's stroke, he was obliged to stifle the impulse by 'an exercise of conscious reasoning'. Though he had called the Nazis 'a mentally bankrupt party', his conscious political reasoning led him to conclude that, since national feelings of superiority were always dangerous, we must not feel superior to Germany. By describing Hitler in 1933 as a reincarnation of Torquemada, he had meant to convey that he was not uniquely beyond historical processes but part of a pattern in human behaviour that, at some time or another, had infected all nations. 'In every country you can find rabid people who have a phobia against Jews, Jesuits, Armenians, Negroes, Freemasons, Irishmen, or simply foreigners as such,' he had written in the *Jewish Chronicle* in 1932. '... Political parties are not above exploiting these fears and jealousies...' When asked by a journalist in 1938 whether Hitler had solved the Jewish problem, he replied: 'He has created it.' But no single nation could tackle this problem with clean hands. G.B.S. persisted in reminding readers of unfortunate facts (such as England's treatment of the Irish or the Ku-Klux-Klan's lynchings of Negroes) in case the itch to intervene grew virtuously irresistible. But although making the miscalculation that Hitler 'shrinks from the massacre which the logic of his phobia demands', he recognized that by the late 1930s this had become a world problem.

'The League of Nations should at once appoint a committee, assisted by an international staff of expert psychiatrists, to determine whether the anti-Semite measures taken by Germany and Italy are legitimate legislation or pathological phobia. If the report of the Committee and the subsequent decision of the League is for phobia, the Führer and the Duce will have either to cancel the measures or stand before Europe as certified lunatics...

'Here is at last something that the League of Nations can do, and is meant to do ... something easily within its powers and precisely appropriate to its purpose.'

In much that he wrote about Germany in the 1930s Shaw had Siegfried and Tina Trebitsch in the back of his mind. On 13 March 1938, the day after Hitler's troops entered Austria, their car had been commandeered by the Nazis and their chauffeur beaten up. Three days later, having obtained Czech passports, they left Vienna, travelling to Prague and some time later to Zurich. 'We had lost our country,' Trebitsch wrote. '... A new and dubious life was to begin.'

'I dare not write a line frankly to anyone in Germany,' Shaw had explained. The day after Hitler announced Austria's annexation, he sent a card to Trebitsch in Vienna welcoming the 'glorious news' and suggesting that 'if Tina's health obliges you to travel, why not come to England, where we are having an extraordinarily fine spring?' This card was forwarded to Prague. It upset Trebitsch. He could not crack its code. 'And now you reproach me because I did not write letters pointing out that you are a Jew marked out for Nazi persecution,' Shaw explained.

But even after this escape, Shaw refused to take the terrible verbal revenge on Hitler that Trebitsch longed to translate. 'What good does it do? It only makes the mischief worse,' Shaw wrote.

'Nothing is more dangerous than to underrate your adversary ... If I joined in the vituperation I should do no good to you or anyone else, and I might do you a great deal of harm.'

They were still far from safe in Czechoslovakia. Shaw had immediately dispatched almost £1,000 and advised them to 'keep very quiet within reach of Zurich until the atmosphere is a little less electric'. He also tried to give Trebitsch some political coaching, explaining the benefits of having his name unjustly omitted from German programmes. After reading a report by the Berlin correspondent of the *Observer* stating that his translator was a Jew, he wrote to the paper describing him as 'an uncircumsized and baptized Lutheran German who has never as far as I know, set foot in a synagogue in his life, married to a lady of unquestioned Christian authenticity' – a description puzzling to Trebitsch, who wanted to know what uncircumcized meant.

Visiting the Shaws the month after his escape, Trebitsch explained that, though living in exile, they did not regard themselves as refugees. In fact they were to pass little of the next year in Switzerland, but resided at rather grand hotels in Nice and Paris. They had plans to become French citizens, after which Trebitsch hoped he could take over from the Hamons as Shaw's official translator in France. From time to time their chauffeur and housekeeper (who later married) would smuggle out some of their possessions. Otherwise they lived on what they had taken with them (including Tina's jewels) supplemented by what Shaw gave them (another £1,000 in April 1939).

'I am still very sceptical as to the likelihood of war,' Shaw wrote in March 1939. Raising Trebitsch's morale was a method of keeping up his own spirits. He was an ever-ingenious optimist, basing his predictions not on what he feared but on what he hoped would happen. He had come to see Hitler as an adroit political tactician who knew exactly how far he could push people without pushing everyone into war. But he feared that Hitler did not understand Chamberlain's mind and might have his head turned by the incompetence of the Allies. Having urged the Allies to make a pact with Soviet Russia, he represented Germany's non-aggression pact with the USSR as the next best thing because now 'Hitler is under the powerful thumb of Stalin, whose interest in peace is overwhelming.' Everyone else seemed terrified. 'Why? Am I mad?' he asked in *The Times*. A week later Britain and Germany were at war and the verdict was that G.B.S. had indeed been madly optimistic.

Such optimism had become a necessary bond between Shaw and his German translator. At Whitehall Court that year they had both experienced what Trebitsch called 'the justifiable premonition that this would have to be my last visit for a long time'. Despite everything, Shaw still 'refused to believe that the whole world would soon be in flames again'. However, before parting, they took special care to ask whether they had not forgotten anything, since it might be years before they saw each other. 'If only I could stop the war there would be no difficulty about your coming over as usual,' Shaw wrote that November. 'As it is – !!!!!'

But, he added: 'We shall both survive this bloody business.'

CHAPTER VI

[1]

History always repeats itself and yet never repeats itself.
April 1940

A young boy on holiday at Frinton-on-Sea saw them walking along the parade the day war was declared. They were arm-in-arm: he measuring his springy pace to hers and looking grave; she very slow and in tears.

They were to remain at Frinton till the last days of September. 'This is a pleasant place,' Shaw wrote to Beatrice Webb from the Hotel Esplanade; 'but we have had a terrible time...' It had been particularly terrible for Charlotte. After the shocks of G.B.S.'s illnesses this news of a second world war in her lifetime produced a painful relapse – a sort of nervous breakdown, G.B.S. believed, which took the form of crippling lumbago and arthritis. She retreated miserably to her bed, while Frinton filled up with evacuee children carrying gas masks and paddling like ducks in the sea ('they are having the time of their lives'). G.B.S. strove to lift everyone's spirits with displays of bravado. ' "War is Over", Shaw Says', announced the *New York Journal-American* in the first week of October 1939; and the following week the *Daily Worker* carried more Shavian optimism across its front page: 'Cease Fire, Turn up the Lights'.

All over the country false alarms were rising and carrying their single note of warning through the air. 'I was wakened and urged to get up and crowd with the other people downstairs,' Shaw wrote from Frinton to Blanche Patch who had taken refuge in Sussex. '...I absolutely refused to budge... there are no safe places in Frinton and the beds are very comfortable, besides being respectable places to die in.' When the next false alarm sounded at night, 'I slept through it.'

They returned to Ayot. He went to London. It seemed that everyone had reluctantly acquiesced to this war. Public libraries and schools were commandeered, petrol was rationed, mortgage rates raised. All were exhorted to make sacrifices – the *Daily Telegraph* gave up its book reviews. A National Service Bill came into force conscripting men between eighteen and forty-one. Up and down the daylight streets paraded army officers, their boots and belts aggressively polished; and the King opened Parliament wearing a splendid naval uniform.

Shaw studied the papers and listened to the news bulletins on the wireless which were becoming a focal point of the day in every home. Unlike the last war, everything was unnaturally dark and quiet. 'The psychology of September 1939 was terribly different from that of August 1914,' wrote Leonard Woolf. During the 1930s one political crisis had piled upon another until people now waited for the catastrophe with feelings of helplessness. 'Yet the catastrophe we braced ourself to face did not happen,' recorded Cecil Beaton in his diary. On 10 December Sir Henry Channon, a Parliamentary Private Secretary in the Foreign Office, noted that 'the war is 100 days old, and a damned bore it is . . . ' As these months of what Churchill called the 'pretended war' lengthened into 1940 with all their tension of boredom-and-anxiety, unnatural detachment and the tightening strain of inactivity, London began to fill with 'pathetic couples having last flings together', crowds of bony youths, airmen on leave, debutantes, tarts, all jostling to the jazz bands of the nightclubs, gazing at naked *artistes* in the London Casino and the *tableaux vivants* at the Windmill Theatre.

'I daresay you will get through,' Shaw signalled Trebitsch. 'You always do.' Now a fully accredited Frenchman, Trebitsch turned up in London that spring and settled as usual into the Dorchester Hotel. He brought with him an electric torch with which to pierce the blackout. 'I shall pay your bill,' Shaw told him. ' . . . Do not trouble to economize.'

'when there is a moon the risks are negligible . . . You need not bother about evening dress: the place is full of men on leave in Khaki . . . If you stand on the kerb and keep calling Taxi, one will stop for you and miraculously carry you to your destination as if it were broad daylight. The drivers have developed eyes like owls . . . '

Could the war itself have been a false alarm? Shaw took what advantage he could of this 'phoney war' to argue for an immediate peace conference. 'There is still half a chance of a negotiation before we are landed in a war in which the odds may be against us,' he wrote to Kingsley Martin, editor of the *New Statesman*. He saw this war as simply a renewal of hostilities between the same enemies, using the same maps, and proceeding from the same fear of one another with its accompanying cry for security that did not exist 'in a world dominated by mankind, which is a dangerous species'. He saw Neville Chamberlain as having been bullied by British imperialists, without the ghost of a mandate from the people, into challenging Hitler with an unconvincing ultimatum when Britain was unprepared for war. He saw the British guarantee to Poland as 'thoughtless' because it had nerved the Polish army to put up a desperate resistance to the German invasion, leading to the loss of many thousand lives on both sides, while Britain, without 'a soldier within hundreds of miles of her frontiers nor a sailor in the Baltic', could not use her bombers for fear of starting a series of retaliatory raids.

By the end of September the war was over, Shaw declared, because Poland had been completely occupied. When, early in October, Hitler extended peace feelers to Britain and France, he responded at once with an article 'Uncommon Sense about the War' in the *New Statesman*. This proposed setting up truce negotiations (accompanied by a suspension of hostilities) to which Britain would go 'with quite as big a bundle of demands as Herr Hitler' to find out whether another world war was truly unavoidable. 'If it is, we can fight as easily after a conference as before it.' That much was owed to those who had known the heartbreak of the last war.

Some readers found Shaw's uncommon sense appealing. There was little enthusiasm for war in the country. 'Everyone I speak to seems utterly bewildered and downcast,' Beatrice Webb wrote in her diary, '– far more so than in the early days of the great war.' Harold Nicolson, then a National Labour Member of Parliament, shared this apprehension. Like Leonard and Virginia Woolf, he privately supplied himself and his wife Vita Sackville-West with the means of committing suicide, but kept up a brave face in public. 'I do not really see how we can win this war, yet if we lose it, we lose everything,' he confided. '...But one thing I do know and it comforts me. I would rather go down fighting and suffering than creep out after a month or two at the cost of losing our pride...'

Nicolson hated Shaw for his lack of pride. Others too thought his determination to break their patriotic code irresponsible and possibly dangerous. 'I think old Shaw really ought to dry up,' protested the industrialist Samuel Courtauld. The proper behaviour for those who shared Shaw's views was that of Sir Nevile Henderson, the British ambassador in Berlin, who had made a similar analysis of Hitler's political skills and Chamberlain's vacillation in the manuscript of his book *Failure of a Mission*, but who loyally accepted drastic pruning of his text by the Foreign Office before publication. G.B.S. felt no such loyalty and accepted nothing. Instead, he reminded Maynard Keynes that 'I am an Irishman and you an Englishman ... bear with me. I am sometimes useful.'

On this occasion, however, Keynes was convinced that Shaw's uncommon sense might do harm 'both to the chances of success in peace and the prospects of success in war', and he recommended that his article for the *New Statesman* be forwarded to the official censor. When Kingsley Martin consulted the Foreign Office, he found to his surprise that Lord Halifax, the Foreign Secretary, was 'strongly in favour of publication'. The Cabinet, some of whom wanted to 'cease fighting Hitler and join Germany against Stalin', was evidently curious to see what this debate between 'responsible writers' would reveal about public opinion. The correspondence columns of the *New Statesman* prolonged the debate for two months, and Shaw's article was read out on the floor of the United States Senate as part of an isolationist attack on President Roosevelt. Keynes had accused G.B.S. of leaving 'the defence of freedom to Colonel Blimp and the Old School Tie'. But Shaw still hoped that the defence of freedom might be left to the German people themselves. Surely they must wake up soon from the spell of Hitler's eloquence. 'Leave Germany to itself, and there will be a reaction against Hitlerism,' he was to predict. Keynes, too, though he quarrelled with Shaw's mischievous tone and tactics, did not yet 'rule out the ideal peace. It may fall within our grasp,' he wrote in the *New Statesman*, 'in ways we cannot yet foresee. And then we could indeed cease fire . . .'

*

. . . and turn up the lights. At the beginning of the war the Home Secretary had decided to close all 'places of amusement' – art galleries, cinemas, concert halls, museums, theatres. Only churches and public houses were exempt. Shaw, who believed that the arts and learned professions must be defended against any presumption that they were 'an immoral luxury', reminded his fellow authors that 'war is only a ripple of slaughter and destruction on the surface of the world's necessary work, most of which must carry on without a moment's intermission'. He advised the Royal Academy of Dramatic Art to follow the example of the Windmill Theatre and stay open every day, backing up his advice with a cheque for £1,000. He objected to proposals for banning Wagner, as well as to the doubling of purchase tax on musical instruments, and urged the government not to turn the 'irreplaceably rare and highly skilled' dancers at the Sadler's Wells ballet into unskilled labourers for the army.

In the silent black streets of London, blocks of featureless buildings stood like fateful emanations of a civilization that might soon be vanishing. 'It was as if the awful prospect of another war had to be marked by some sort of penitential ritual,' wrote the Director of the National Gallery. Shaw vehemently protested against this total blackout. In letters to *The Times* and *Daily Telegraph* he recalled that during the First World War the theatres had been overflowing with soldiers on leave desperately needing recreation after their miseries in the trenches. 'Are there to be no theatres for them this time?' he asked. 'We have hundreds of thousands of evacuated children to be kept out of mischief and traffic dangers. Are there to be no pictures for them?'

He was confident that this 'ridiculous funk ... will soon pass'. And then turn up the lights. These war years, which began and ended with productions of *Saint Joan*, were to witness an extraordinary refuelling of Shaw's popularity in the theatre. At the end of 1939 the curtain went up on *Major Barbara* at the Westminster Theatre, and the following summer *The Devil's Disciple*, with Robert Donat appearing as Dick Dudgeon, came in after a successful tour to the Piccadilly Theatre. During 1942 *The Doctor's Dilemma*, with Vivien Leigh playing Jennifer Dubedat and John Gielgud replacing Cyril Cusack as Louis Dubedat, ran for 474 performances at the Haymarket Theatre. Outstanding among the four London revivals the next year was a luxurious production of *Heartbreak House* at the Cambridge Theatre, with costumes by Cecil Beaton and starring Edith Evans and Deborah Kerr, which ran for 236 performances. But the topmost year was 1944 when no fewer than nine of Shaw's plays were put on in London, including the Old Vic Company's production of *Arms and the Man* with Laurence Olivier, Ralph Richardson, Sybil Thorndike and Margaret Leighton – all players lured back to the stage after making their names on the screen. 'The London stage is transformed out of knowledge,' wrote the avant-garde theatrical manager Ashley Dukes. ' ... We laugh at the Balkans with a good conscience, and the shafts of wit aimed at heroism fall lightly at the feet of the returning warriors.'

'I dare not face another revival,' Shaw cried out. ' ... Another "success" would ruin me.' On incomes of over £30,000, after the deduction of income tax at ten shillings in the pound, every two pounds of gross income yielded one pound of net income, on which nineteen shillings of surtax was payable – giving the Shavian total of one pound and nineteen shillings taxation on one pound of net income. 'I am driven to the conclusion that our Chancellor is not much of a financier,' G.B.S. pointed out. ' ... a policy of knocking the linchpin out of Capitalism without substituting Socialism leads not to victory but to Queer Street.' Far from being fabulously rich, as everyone supposed, he represented himself as leading the straitened existence of a tax collector for the British government, which 'allows me to retain the merest trifle by way, I suppose, of commission'.

Equality of income would have rescued him from this sense of subsidizing his own success. Nevertheless he let his reputation boom, with occasional reminders to the press that he was paying handsomely for everyone's fun. A touring Bernard Shaw Company took seven of his plays round the country in 1942 and 1943, and half a dozen of them were also regularly performed by the Travelling Repertory Theatre which went to villages and munitions factories, mining towns and blitzed towns, and established 'Plays in the Parks' in support of the Lord Mayor's War Relief

Fund. 'Whenever business lagged or we were in need of a play for a hastily prepared fit-up tour, we turned to the plays of Shaw,' remembered Basil Langton, actor-manager of the Travelling Repertory Theatre. 'They were a delight to do because they filled the theatre with laughter, required little scenery or lighting, and provided wonderful acting parts for every member of the company...'

'Shaw wrote plays for actors ... If you learned your lines and picked up your cues, the play took care of itself, much like a well-composed piece of music. This was to be my first real clue as to how to act the plays of Shaw ... Character in a Shaw play is more in the character of the voice than it is in the actor's physical appearance.'

It was his unconventionality, Beatrice Webb believed, and his illuminating fun that had relit this interest in his work. Revivals of his comedies, romances, fables, fantasias were appearing everywhere to meet the needs of a new public educated by the wireless. But there were to be no new plays during the war. 'I have written nothing for the stage since Charles,' he told Beatrice in 1941, 'and will perhaps not write for it again.'

*

'Meanwhile all my writing energy is expended on the war controversy,' Shaw told Trebitsch. As in the First World War, he poured forth journalism – over 250 broadsides, obituaries, contributions to symposiums, answers to questionnaires, reacting to almost every aspect of the war and examining how best to secure peace afterwards. 'Shaw's views on the conduct of the war may not seem particularly useful to the Cabinet. We do not know,' declared the front page of *Cavalcade*. 'What we do know is that his views are of great interest to a vast number of people, and that in total war it is the will of the people that ought to prevail.'

In his fashion Shaw sought to fill the role Carlyle had occupied in the nineteenth century as keeper of the public conscience. But the world was larger, more uncertain, fragmented. 'One has to gather any major news nowadays by means of hints and allusions,' wrote George Orwell in 1940. Shaw used these hints and allusions as best he could, resenting his exclusion from more central sources of information. 'It was indeed a wonder to note how carefully the old man watched the news and kept up with events,' observed the Labour Member of Parliament Emrys Hughes.

One of the new war posters warned the populace that 'Careless Talk Costs Lives'. But the most careless talk of all, to Shaw's mind, came from Cabinet Ministers. 'There must be no more nonsense about our being certain to win, and God being on our side, as in that case we have nothing to do but sit down in our armchairs and let God win,' he wrote. 'God helps those who help themselves.' Hitler had helped himself so energetically that we would have to 'put the last ounce of our weight into the fight with him'. This was a sample of Shaw's alternative patriotism. Britain needed an alternative because, as Sir Henry Channon was to write from the Ministry of Information in March 1940, 'we are being defeated all along the diplomatic line'. At a conference on war aims, Shaw proposed a new ministry of propaganda – 'a Council of British Policy and a National Orator or Oratress' – whose business it would be to take the words out of Chamberlain's mouth and give precise replies to Hitler and Stalin. 'A speaker who takes it on himself to be the mouthpiece of a nation must know the meaning of his words ... We know our Neville Chamberlain and make allowances for his seldom meaning what he says, but the Germans and their leader do not.'

This job of advocating Britain's cause before Europe, and elucidating it to the people, was one Shaw offered himself. He recommended a different set of guidelines on 'how to talk intelligently about the war' and disentangle the mesh of enemy-impregnated words – appeasement, communism, fascism, Hitlerism and National Socialism. 'We must not let Adolf give Socialism a bad name,' he rallied Beatrice Webb. In the Shavian dictionary appeasement on a grand scale was to be read as Britain's war aim (rather than a defeatist term carrying 'accidental associations with unpopular bygones at Munich'); and he defined Hitlerism as a government founded on the idolatry of one person laying claim to the world on behalf of Germans as the Chosen Race. Such personal autocracy had no special connection with either fascism (which was the imposition of state-assisted privatization), or democracy (government in the interests of everybody and not a privileged class) or communism. 'If you are a Communist then the word requires a new definition,' Lord Alfred Douglas was to press him. But Shaw's definition was pre-war, catholic, non-combatant, free from party political commitment, and unaffected by the abuse of power or the fall of empires. 'Communism has a hundred doors; and they do not all open and close at the same moment,' he wrote. 'Everywhere already we have communism in roads, bridges, street lighting, water supply, police protection, military, naval and air services ... Civilization could not exist for a fortnight except on a basis of Communism.'

Early in the war G.B.S. was generally seen to be a combatant pacifist, a view sharpened in 1941 by his campaign to outlaw the reciprocal bombing of cities. In *The Times* and other newspapers he called on Britain to initiate this agreement with the German government, claiming that no military advantage could possibly be won by a new method of warfare that stiffened the resistance of the attacked and gratified, at enormous cost, passions among the attackers 'which civilised nations should not gratify'. Since both sides were depending for victory on famine by blockade, he characteristically added, any reduction in the number of civilian mouths to feed would be a tactical gain. 'The way to end the bombing match is to drop leaflets telling the Germans that as they are killing only 233 of us per day it will take them 470 years to exterminate us, and it will take us longer to exterminate them.'

More serious, from the government's view, was Shaw's persistent support of Stalin and his urging of a conciliatory policy towards the Soviet Union. He represented Stalin's invasion of Finland as inevitable once the Finnish government had refused Russia's proposal for a readjustment of their frontier. After all, Finland had allowed herself to be used by the United States and Western Allies, he pointed out, and 'no Power can tolerate a frontier from which a town such as Leningrad could be shelled'. To reinforce this argument, he asked his readers to imagine what England would do if threatened from the West. 'Ireland is the British Finland,' he wrote. 'Rather than allow Ireland to be occupied or invaded or even threatened by a foreign Power ... England would be strategically obliged to reoccupy Ireland ... That is exactly the Russo–Finnish situation.'

'If we cannot agree, we must, I suppose, fight it out, in which case my position will be simplified,' he had written in the *New Statesman*. '... [and] I must strive for a British win as if I were the rabidest of Jingoes.' By the early summer of 1940, when the war had settled into its routine and Churchill's Cabinet replaced Chamberlain's, Shaw was invited to broadcast on the Overseas Service of the British Broadcasting Corporation. Though he believed he could get the better of William Joyce – the notorious 'Lord Haw-Haw' who broadcast Nazi propaganda into Britain – 'I should scare the wits out of the official home front', he warned. 'Better let this sleeping dog lie.' But the BBC persisted. It wanted someone whose vivacity and insight would stir foreign listeners as J. B. Priestley's broadcasts had inspired audiences in Britain. At the beginning of June, Shaw sent in his script. It was an exhortation to the Allies as orthodox as he could contrive. He portrayed the British as 'champion fighters for humanity', defended Britain's unpreparedness for war ('Heaven defend us from Governments who can think of nothing but the next war and do nothing but prepare for it!'), and gave, as the Big Idea that 'we must risk our lives for', the need to defeat anti-Semitism ('We ought to have declared war on Germany the moment Mr Hitler's police stole Einstein's violin'). A year before Germany invaded Soviet Russia and eighteen months before the United States came into the war, he inserted one passage that sounded peculiarly Shavian in its unorthodoxy. 'The friendship of Russia is vitally important to us just now. Russia and America may soon have the fate of the world in their hands; that is why I am always so civil to Russia.'

The Ministry of Information immediately vetoed this broadcast. 'Shaw's main theme is that the only thing Hitler has done wrong is to persecute the Jews,' explained Harold Nicolson, then Parliamentary Secretary to the Ministry of Information and later to be appointed a Governor of the BBC. 'As the Minister [Duff Cooper] remarks, millions of Americans and some other people [believe] that this is the only thing he has done right.' The Controller of Overseas Programmes, Sir Stephen Tallents, tried to reverse this decision. 'The value, especially in America, of a broadcast talk by Shaw endorsing the war against Germany and Italy would be very high,' he explained. '... Australia, too, urged me some months ago to secure a talk by him.' But Duff Cooper 'still sees grave objection to any talk of this sort going across', Harold Nicolson answered. In an attempt to free Shaw from a total ban at the microphone, Tallents sent the Ministry of Information what he called 'the sequel to the G.B.S. story'. Shaw had 'responded with entire good temper and generosity' to the cancellation of his talk, said that he 'would have been willing to alter the text at any points which had been felt to give difficulty', and left the BBC producer Anthony Weymouth with 'the impression that his one anxiety was to serve the national cause'. But Duff Cooper was adamant: 'I won't have that man on the air.'

'I shall have to confine myself to articles in The Daily Worker,' Shaw wrote to Anthony Weymouth. But when, at the beginning of 1941, this English Communist Party newspaper was banned for twenty months, another wartime outlet closed. Not wishing to embarrass Kingsley Martin again at the *New Statesman*, he gave much of his war journalism to *Forward*, a socialist weekly edited in Glasgow by Keir Hardie's son-in-law Emrys Hughes. Here he denounced the *Daily Worker*'s suppression as a blow against the free democracy for which Britain was fighting, and carried on its work by warning the public against any government alliance with the Axis to destroy Russian socialism. Friendly relations with the USSR were 'of vital importance', he insisted, because one day Churchill would have to sit down with Stalin – and preferably Roosevelt also – to settle the ceasefire.

*

'The world wars were largely Hollywood products,' Shaw later asserted. He had continued to permeate America through the Hearst press because Hearst took his newspaper empire seriously as a source of power. But Hearst had been moving into Hollywood, pursuing a grand plan for mythologizing the United States and demonizing Germans and communists in the dreams of vast cinema congregations. Here he became Shaw's opponent. G.B.S. wanted to turn up his own lights and put these dream-makers in the shade. 'I do not concern myself with Hollywood,' he said. 'I write for America, a quite different country.'

By 1939, having joined the Screenwriters' Association, he gave Gabriel Pascal the go-ahead to film *Major Barbara*. 'We must show the Hollywood distributors that we are independent of them as far as capital is concerned,' he wrote. The invasion of Holland and Belgium had put a stop to Pascal's plans for European financing, and Shaw agreed to let his syndicate, including General Film Distributors and J. Arthur Rank, use £12,774 of his royalties from the *Pygmalion* film until it could raise in Britain the full £125,000 that Pascal reckoned was needed. 'In permitting Barbara to be filmed I have made a heroic sacrifice for the good of British films,' he wrote afterwards.

The sixteen new film sequences Shaw supplied to help modernize his play were almost his only dramatic writing during these war years. The theme of his play, which had been an attempt to move the thinking man, Cusins, up the evolutionary ladder beyond the point of wanting power, seemed a genuine contribution to the anti-war effort. It could 'hardly be considered good propaganda', remarked Kenneth Clark, Director of the Film Division and Controller of Home Publicity at the Ministry of Information, when turning down Pascal's appeal for money. But G.B.S. was quick to reassure Blanche Patch that she could not 'possibly be more usefully employed than in helping Gabriel and myself with the Barbara film and keeping the theatres going. And you will be giving people pleasure instead of helping to kill them.'

Another reason for making this film was Wendy Hiller's desire to play the title role. Shaw vetoed Pascal's choice of the romantic Leslie Howard for Cusins ('quite out of the question') and suggested 'a young actor named [Alec] Guinness' who had recently come to lunch at Whitehall Court. But eventually the part went to Rex Harrison, and Undershaft was played by Robert Morley.

These were precarious times for film-making. 'My film future depends on you,' Shaw appealed to Pascal. 'Ought I have your life insured?' But wars were little deterrent to Pascal. Towards the end of the 1930s *Time* magazine had placed him, along with Hitler and the Pope, among the ten most famous men in the world. With Shaw's help he had become a naturalized British subject, bought (out of his personal losses on *Pygmalion*) a large Tudor house in Buckinghamshire and, so G.B.S. hoped, 'shifted the artistic center of gravity of the film industry from Hollywood to Middlesex'. Between marriages and engagements to marry, he would claim that because 'the greatest sacrifice in marriage is the sacrifice of the adventurous attitude towards life' he would 'never get married'. To which Shaw would nod his head and say: 'He is wed to my plays.'

On 26 May 1940, as the British prepared to evacuate Dunkirk, the location shooting of *Major Barbara* began on the Dartington Hall Estate in South Devon, later moving to Tower Bridge for some Salvation Army scenes and round Sheffield for distant views of Undershaft's factory. 'I am quite guiltless of letting him [Pascal] loose on you,' Shaw apologized to Leonard Elmhirst, chairman of the Dartington Hall Trust, 'but now that he has found you out he is enchanted with the great hall and the other attractions of the place ... As there is no limit to his imagination and to his powers of transmogrification you must keep your eyes on him lest he should make Dartington disappear from the earth like a transformation scene in a pantomime.'

It was hard finding actors in 1940: many did not want exemption and were called up. Three weeks after the studio started shooting at Denham on 17 June, the Nazi bombing of Britain began. '*Major Barbara* was filmed under fire,' Bernard Dukore has written. Pascal was to count 125 bombs that fell in the vicinity of Denham Studios while they were making the picture. 'I was surprised when I learned that Denham gets so large a share of bombing,' Shaw wrote to him. 'The truth seems to be that the German pilots, flying blind and trusting to their instruments, are convinced that they are bombing Whitehall.' Technical equipment was destroyed, transportation often made impossible by land mines and railway disruptions, and when they did get to London to take exterior shots they would find everything in rubble the next day before their shooting was completed. Everyone agreed with Wendy Hiller that 'without Pascal's courage and almost demoniac energy the film would never have beaten all the difficulties of wartime production'.

The cast and crew bedded down 'as close to the studio as possible: dressing rooms, pubs, the homes of friends'. Whenever air-raid warnings interrupted a scene they would go to ground in a concrete shelter under the floor of the sound studio. Here Robert Morley filled the dim light with tales of Pascal's adventures culminating in a fantasy of his luxurious private shelter nearby, lined by tiger skins and crowded with '*lovvly vimmen*', where they imagined him to be taking his ease.

In fact Pascal never went to a shelter but would hold his infatuated scenario editor, Marjorie Deans, on the lawn in extended discussion of the script as the bombers raced overhead. 'Pascal bullied everyone,' Robert Morley remembered. Each morning his shouts of 'You are ruining my picture – you are crucifying me!' would greet the actors and at the end of the day the empty sets still rang to his cries. 'Has Pascal driven you mad?'

G.B.S. asked Wendy Hiller. Frequently she would be called to calm him down. 'Gaby often screamed and raged – but never at me,' she wrote. Deborah Kerr, however, whose first film this was and whom Pascal berated as 'a constipated virgin', was sometimes in tears; and all the actors felt nervous, not knowing what on earth he would do next. During the course of the film he sacked almost everyone and then, with a kiss and a grin, made it up with them again – though he didn't get this opportunity with the actor Donald Calthrop, who died.

What ruined Pascal, in the opinion of Alexander Korda, was his mania to be a director. He was determined to direct as well as produce *Major Barbara*. 'I was sadly missing the helpful direction of "Puffin" Asquith which I had on *Pygmalion*', wrote Wendy Hiller. 'Pascal was no director.' He had, however, two directorial assistants: Harold French, who rehearsed the actors with their lines; and David Lean, who was in charge of the shooting. When Pascal ordered impossible camera angles, Lean and the crew would turn over the camera with no film in it to keep him happy and these were referred to as 'Gaby's takes'.

'Leave it to me . . . to keep my faithfulness to you as an artist,' Pascal urged G.B.S. ' . . . believe me, my dearest Maestro, I have an unfailing instinct for pictures.' But Shaw was determined that his wishes should not be circumvented as in *Pygmalion*. Some of Pascal's suggestions struck him as being 'beyond the wildest dreams of Sam Goldwyn'. He feared that the interest of the film might be shifted to a lower class of audience, spoiling it for all audiences. 'Beware of the temptation to overdo every good effect . . . the fault of Hollywood,' he warned. Regularly during the shooting Pascal would 'go see Bernashaw' and they would discuss what Pascal called 'the iron law of movement, which is the basic element of the cinema (and the reason why it is also called "movies")'. Between these visits Shaw continued to revise the dialogue, making cuts, transpositions, interpolations as he accepted, modified or rejected Pascal's advice: 'for I can stand up to you and none of the rest can'. For this reason, Pascal would eventually arrive with only those changes proposed by his shooting-script team that he thought had a fair chance of getting Shaw's approval.

On his eighty-fourth birthday G.B.S. was invited to the Albert Hall to watch the shooting of the Salvation Army revival meeting. 'Everyone wanted to be in that,' wrote the theatrical historian Joe Mitchenson who was one of 500 extras assembled for the scene. Leading actors who were taking cameo parts, such as Sybil Thorndike in the role of a Salvation Army General and Emlyn Williams as the derelict Snobby Price were there, and G.B.S. was greatly fussed and fêted. Getting over-excited he plunged into the sound equipment, spreading silent but expensive chaos, and played with the camera mounted on a trolley with a boom. Raising himself into its chair he began pulling handles and pressing buttons, lifting and swivelling and tilting himself until, grabbing at some weights, he almost crashed to the floor. After that he sheepishly climbed down and tried to behave better. But when the large band began to play, remembering perhaps the Salvation Army festival in which he had joined so happily at the Albert Hall thirty-five years earlier when finishing his play, he darted down the main aisle and dived in among the chorus, voice uplifted, arms flailing. Next day he sent Pascal his 'apologies for interfering on Friday. I tried to keep quiet; but suddenly felt twenty years younger, and couldn't.'

Originally scheduled for ten weeks, the film eventually took six months to shoot, while the costs rose to almost £300,000 and the backers vainly tried to replace Pascal with Anthony Asquith. 'The more outrageously expensive you make the film the easier it will be to get the money,' Shaw had predicted. '...it will pay to outdo Korda in extravagance.' Now, faced with a real financial crisis, he gave terser instructions.

'You will finish screening my script *without a single retake*, until you have it complete ... you will go through the rushes and be satisfied with what is good enough ... Any sequences that are really unpresentable you can then retake ... You must finish, finish, finish at all sacrifices until *a* Barbara film is ready for release, no matter how far it may fall short of *the* film of which you dream.'

Flushed with modified triumph, Pascal accompanied Katharine Hepburn to the grand opening in Nassau on 20 March 1941 'under the aegis of the Duke and Duchess of Windsor'. But *Major Barbara* was not to be the film of his or Shaw's dreams. Unauthorized cuts demanded by the distributors reduced Pascal's 137-minute print to 121 minutes at the British première and, in the United States, where censorship objections were raised to the film's irreverence towards religious institutions, the première was shortened to 115 minutes. Both these versions appear 'choppy and unfocused', as Bernard Dukore writes, with 'motivations and connections between scenes missing'. Only six of Shaw's sixteen new sequences were used and his social criticism was severely weakened. 'They cut the last third of the film all to pieces,' he told Gilbert Murray, 'and left Barbara's and Undershaft's position so hopelessly confused that I am inundated with letters accusing me of making Barbara sell out, and glorifying a scoundrelly war profiteer.'

'I saw the finished film once only – I wept with disappointment,' wrote Wendy Hiller. But Gilbert Murray was 'moved and thrilled' by parts of it, Beatrice Webb found its 'expression of the brutal power of mass murder in

437

modern war' dramatically topical, and the general public relished the performance by Robert Newton as the 'rough customer' Bill Walker, the burlesque playing of Robert Morley's Undershaft and Wendy Hiller's achievement in catching Barbara's idealism yet making it so humorously attractive. Seldom had a film sought such sustained intellectual engagement with its audience. The final vision of Perivale St Andrews looked forward to the socialist-inspired plans for post-war reconstruction. 'The house was packed ... and you could not have had a more responsive audience,' H. G. Wells wrote. 'They laughed at all the right places. Mostly young people in uniform they were ... We shall rise again sooner than Marx did and for a better reason.'

Some of the best acting came from G.B.S. impersonating himself in a three-minute 'visual prologue' made for American audiences. On the morning of 12 September 1940, he had presented himself at Denham Studios as an Arrangement in Monochrome, wearing a grey Norfolk jacket, grey knee-breeches, long grey stockings and brogues and woollen tie. 'I was immensely impressed by his appearance,' remembered Rex Harrison. '...His hair was quite white, and his beard also. With him came his famous secretary, Miss Patch, an old lady who appeared to me to be growing a small white moustache to match his.'

By now reluctantly convinced that the only way of gaining peace was simply to defeat Hitler and Mussolini, and that 'a single handed victory would not be so good for us as an Anglo-American one', Shaw recorded a preface that was seen by many Americans as a rallying call for them to come and fight. The British argument was simple, he told one United States correspondent: 'there is a very dangerous madman loose in Europe who must, we think, be captured and disabled. If we are right, he is as dangerous to you as to us; so we ask you to join the hunt.'

Made a few days after the exchange of U.S. destroyers for the lease of naval bases in Newfoundland and the Caribbean, Shaw's prologue announces his own contribution to the deal: 'I am sending you my old plays, just as you are sending us your old destroyers.' The Battle of Britain had reached its peak the previous month and more than a hundred German planes were shot down over London three days after Shaw made his recording. 'I am within forty minutes' drive of the center of London, and at any moment a bomb may crash through this roof and blow me to atoms,' he told the United States.

'...I can't absolutely promise you such a delightful finish to this news item. Still ... don't give up hope – yet ... it will not matter very much to me ... I have done my work ... But if my films are still being shewn in America, my soul will go marching on ...'

438

25 Pascal filming *Caesar and Cleopatra*, 1944

26 Beatrice and Sidney Webb

27 Just before his 90th birthday, in the garden at Ayot St Lawrence

28A Gene Tunney; B Dame Laurentia McLachlan; C Siegfried Trebitsch;
D F.E. Loewenstein

G.B.S.

G.B.S.

to Clara Higgs
the trusty and well beloved, with
gratitude for all she has done for me

G. Bernard Shaw

Christmas 1940.

to Harry Batchelor Higgs
who has kept my gardens for 38 years
and been a good friend and helpful
housemate all that time

G. Bernard Shaw

Christmas 1940.

29C Fred Day, the chauffeur; D Alice Laden with Bunch

30A *The Simpleton of the Unexpected Isles*, Warsaw, 1935; B *Village Wooing*, London, 1934

31 Shaw in 1948

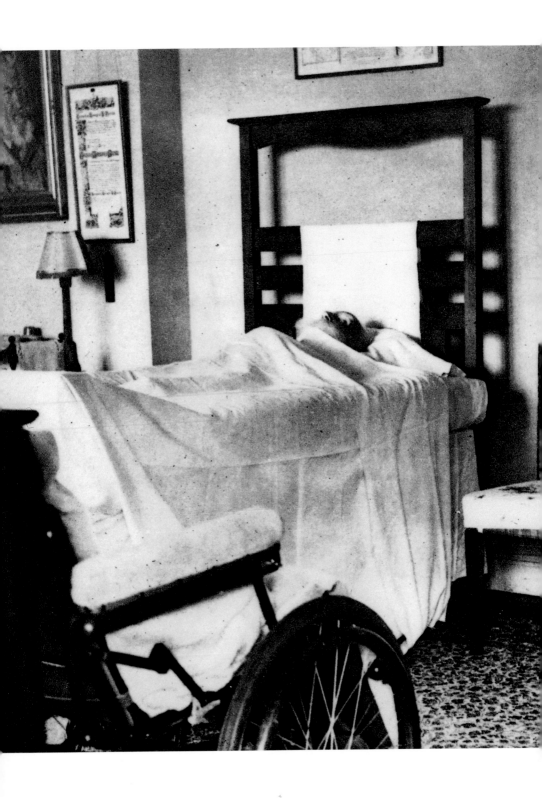

32 On his deathbed, 2 November 1950

An air-raid warning sounded while he was speaking and Pascal charged forwards – then stopped as G.B.S. imperturbably went on ('We'll keep it in the picture') against the grunting of the enemy planes. For this was a valedictory to which he had summoned his unseen audiences before the darkness rushed in. When he was a little boy, he continued, the Dublin newspapers reported how America had abolished black slavery. When he grew up 'I determined to devote my life as far as I could to the abolition of white slavery,' – the sort of slavery to economic dictatorship that had erupted in this war.

Then he lifted one hand, trembling slightly, to his forehead and held it there in a salute. 'When my mere bodily stuff is gone, I should like to imagine that you are still working with me ... at that particular job ... farewell!'

[2]

Think of us always as we were...

Shaw and Charlotte felt a strong moral obligation to be 'pigheaded' about the war and 'pretend we don't care a dump for Adolf...' After Dunkirk and the Battle of Britain '[we] are snapping our fingers at Hitler and his threat of invasion', Shaw notified Trebitsch. During this first year they carried on normally: from Wednesday noon to Saturday afternoon at Whitehall Court, then at Ayot from Saturday afternoon to Wednesday morning, sleeping through the all-night air-raids in both places. 'My wife does not give a damn for bombs,' G.B.S. wrote to Alfred Douglas, 'but dreads shelters and prefers death to getting up and dressing.'

So it was business as usual until, one Saturday afternoon early in September 1940, arriving at Ayot a day before the German Blitzkrieg opened on London, Charlotte fell heavily on the gravel. For the rest of that month she was unable to walk and could go upstairs only backwards, with G.B.S. precariously at the helm. 'I have accidents,' she wrote to Nancy Astor, '– but they seem to do me good.' This accident, G.B.S. added, had given them 'an excuse for skulking down here instead of coming up to town for half the week in our regular routine'.

By the time Charlotte recovered it seemed foolish to go back to London at all. They were 'too old to do anything, and might be a casualty and a trouble'. Ayot had a small squeaky siren that importantly echoed all the alarms from the capital thirty miles away, and they could see the flashes in the sky and hear the thunder of the guns, like far-off celebrations. Stray

439

raiders would occasionally float overhead and release a bomb near enough to shiver the house, and Charlotte, 'who hates the distant sounds, is infuriated by the big bangs, which she takes as personal insults', Shaw told Nancy Astor.

'To-morrow, or indeed to-day, we may be blown to bits; but really at our ages, it does not matter,' he had written to Maurice Colbourne that October. In London one bomb destroyed almost 90,000 unbound sets of sheets of his Collected Edition ('plus their dustwrappers', his bibliographer notes) and threw up enough insurance money for him to pay off his supertax. Another bomb whistled past Blanche Patch's bedroom ceiling, spilling her on to the floor and shattering a house nearby. Feeling rather 'out of sorts', she hurried down to join Shaw and Charlotte; and continued living with them at Ayot till the summer of 1943.

'Until the war I had not been down to Ayot,' Miss Patch wrote, 'for there was never any need for me to go.' Compared to London it felt quiet at first, only some desultory manoeuvres by the Women's Land Army or an occasional challenge from the reserve policeman (an ex-gardener in uniform) who inspected one's identity card. But the notorious Wheathampstead rubbish dump, which even in peacetime had reminded G.B.S. of Stromboli, was now converted into a zone for detonating delayed-action bombs, and the loud bangs at uneven intervals kept them all jumping. Then, in the middle of November, came a 'full dress bombardment' with eight high-explosives crashing on to the roads and fields around them, a shower of incendiary shells, and the rattle of shrapnel on the roof. The house trembled but 'we are more frightened than hurt', Shaw wrote. As for Miss Patch, '[I] wondered if my last hour had come.' G.B.S., who blamed a new searchlight in the village, seemed chiefly worried by the effect all this was beginning to have on Charlotte. He did what he could to calm her. 'All through the war his nerve remained steady,' Miss Patch conceded, 'and often in the late evening when we heard the wail of the Alert siren, and the planes were droning overhead, he would sit down at the piano and play and sing the old Italian operas. The piano was an ordinary upright ... It was always in the hall because Charlotte liked to lie in her room upstairs and listen to him.'

The mingling of these arias with the noise of the siren was peculiarly trying for Miss Patch, though she was too polite to say so. The fact was that of the three of them she alone wasn't going deaf ('a great point in her favor at the telephone', Shaw admitted). But at least the old man wasn't under her feet so much as in Whitehall Court. After breakfast he would stalk down to the curious 'toolshed' at the end of the garden which gave him his solitude. Here he arranged himself in his wicker chair at a simple flap table with all

440

the innocent technology of his work tidily deployed around him – a thermo-meter and paste pot, some paperclips and scissors, red ink, alarm clock and portable Remington typewriter ('Could that typewriter type a play?' he had asked the demonstrator when buying it. 'Of course it could,' she indignantly replied. 'It could type anything.'). But he only used two fingers and of course he couldn't touch-type like Miss Patch. 'He loved his red ink, paste pot and paper clips,' she observed. '... the alarm clock was set each day to remind him when it was time for lunch. He never took any notice of it.'

His principal work during the war was *Everybody's Political What's What?* 'I find myself in a world in which everyone knows the XYZ of politics, philosophy, religion, science and art, and nobody knows the ABC of them,' he wrote to Upton Sinclair. On his eighty-fifth birthday he told the *Daily Telegraph* that this work was to be 'an elementary text-book' on politics. Who better, then, to write a 'Child's Guide' than someone already well advanced into second childhood? 'Perhaps my second childhood may go down with the mob better than my maturity did.' He wanted to survey the natural laws governing political action and itemize those subjects every member of a responsible democracy should understand before voting or becoming eligible for public work. 'In my book I am insisting that statesmanship is entirely metaphysical fundamentally,' he wrote to Beatrice Webb, 'and consists in devising means whereby all our egotisms shall be subject to an obligation to do justice and love mercy and walk humbly with whatever we call the urge in this direction without which we are scoundrels.'

Like much of his later political writings, *Everybody's Political What's What?* was to enquire after egalitarianism in the future while turning away from contemporary heartbreak and helplessness. 'It is better to work away at my book, and at my business affairs, and leave myself no time to attend to the endless misfortunes brought by the war on people whom I know,' he appealed to Trebitsch, 'and people whom I dont know ... but who in desperation appeal to me as if my reputation made me a sort of political and financial Providence.'

He would work at this book until lunch, to which he was summoned by the clanging of a loud handbell from the house (sometimes panicking the villagers). Then he slept for an hour in the early afternoon and would afterwards 'go about the lanes and woods with a secateur and a little saw and clear up overgrown paths' until the blackout came down. In spite of the world's miseries, these spring and summer months were 'altogether wonderful', and he did not find his old age or this 'cottage life' unhappy – at least not unbearably so, as his youth had been.

'G.B.S. is like a lion,' Charlotte wrote to Nancy Astor. 'I fear the country agrees with him! He is working as hard as ever, & he has taken to lopping &

pruning trees. I wish you could see him when he comes in from the woods – dripping & smiling.' Most evenings he liked to settle down to his correspondence and over dinner would come up with schemes involving deliveries of sand or the addition of longhandled spades, tall ladders and a stirrup pump for making Ayot war-proof. 'No one took any notice of him,' said Miss Patch.

She had a difficult time wrestling with his shorthand which every month appeared to be growing smaller, though not less. 'My heart sinks when I see these masses of shorthand you are pouring out,' she reprimanded him. 'I am writing to Judy [Musters],' he replied. So Miss Patch was obliged, for the most part, to swallow her complaints and carry on.

To Shaw's eyes the 'Patient Patch' carried on very well. She was 'at home in every house in the village', he reported to Beatrice Webb. 'At the end of 35 days she knew more about it than we did at the end of 35 years.' As for Shaw himself, he didn't care 'if I never set foot in London again'; but between Charlotte and Miss Patch there arose something of a competition as to who more wholeheartedly disliked living in this remote village. 'Week after week I get more impatient of being kept here & find it harder to bear the deadly inactivity of the place,' Charlotte confessed; while to Miss Patch Ayot seemed like 'utter banishment' after the amenities of London. 'Charlotte may not have felt so strongly about it as I did,' she emphasized. But Charlotte could hardly go out of doors at all now – it seemed like 'years I have been shut up here!' It was always chilly at Ayot, the two women agreed. One of the reasons Miss Patch visited 'every house in the village' was that every house was warmer.

Charlotte now 'felt the cold intensely'. For many weeks that winter she was bedridden, in horrible pain, unable even to write letters 'as her back will not stand the writing posture'. As winter passed this pain receded. She raged against her confinement but her dread of bringing back the pain by too much movement slowed her recuperation. 'I have been ill for 2 years,' she told Hugh Walpole. 'The trouble is I don't believe I have arthritis, & everyone else does.'

G.B.S. played for her, sat with her, read to her. 'Charlotte had better be left alone just now,' he cautioned Nancy Astor on 30 January 1941. '... Her nerves are all in rags.' Nancy had offered them a home at Cliveden but 'it must remain a lovely dream for us', Charlotte thought – 'I wish it could come true, but it cant.' By August, however, she felt so much better that they decided to go for three weeks' holiday there. Both of them were nervous: 'we are like people coming out of a dark cellar', Charlotte warned Nancy. And Shaw wrote: 'We shall be a horrid imposition. Ten years ago I could still earn my keep by entertaining your guests by my celebrated performances as G.B.S. Now if I attempt to talk my teeth fall out. I am a decrepit old bore and you must hide me in a corner . . . ' What he had never accepted was that people might value him without all his self-dramatizing funniments and gallantries. 'He *is* older but he is incredible for eighty-five,' wrote Nancy Astor's thirty-year-old niece Joyce Grenfell who was also staying at Cliveden. 'Looks wonderfully pink and white and fresh and beautifully dandified . . .'

'Both the Shaws take trouble over their appearance. The more I see of them the more I like them and find their company stimulating. When he isn't putting on his act . . . then he is a charmer and what he has to say is worth hearing . . . Mrs Shaw is very deaf, which means that conversation takes time and must be executed *fortissimo* . . .'

They returned to Ayot. 'Back again in our little prison,' Charlotte wrote. Shaw had hoped to finish *Everybody's Political What's What?* by the end of 1941, but the book hung fire. Sometimes it seemed to him all 'senile ramblings and repetitions', and he despaired of ever being able to get it into an intelligent sequence. 'I am too old to know whether I can still write or not,' he confessed to Wells. He had tried to start another play but themes and stories eluded him: 'I seem to have dried up at last: I am absolutely barren.'

He had found some pleasure however in preparing a *Graduates' Keepsake & Counsellor* for Diploma Students at the Royal Academy of Dramatic Art, contributing a long unsigned introduction, editing the twelve 'messages of advice' and underwriting the costs of publication. A land mine had exploded at the RADA building in Gower Street in 1941 completely destroying the students' theatre that backed on to Malet Street. Shaw had immediately gone up to see the extent of the damage, picking his way through the splintered door, past the blown-out windows to the debris of the Principal's office and remarking: 'Well, they made a good job of it.' Workmen were boarding up the windows and through a slit between the wooden planks the actor Laurence Irving, also arriving to inspect the devastation, saw a shaft of sunlight through scintillating dust pierce the gloom and focus on G.B.S. huddled in a chair. 'The cocksure mobile features of the old champion of the RADA were pinched and aged,' he remembered; 'the challenging and mocking eyes were lustreless and evasive in undisguised dejection . . .'

But this would never do. He returned to Ayot, and after the publication of his *Graduates' Keepsake*, took up his 'Child's Guide' again, a little anxiously, as the bombardment of British and German cities intensified and he struggled in his garden for new evidence to illustrate his theme that

443

politically 'the matter with mankind is not incorrigible natural depravity but just ignorance – flat earth ignorance'.

After his eightieth birthday G.B.S. had finally given up platform speaking and resigned his 'frightful responsibility' as chairman of the British Broadcasting Corporation's Advisory Committee on Spoken English. On his eighty-fifth birthday ('the limit set by public decency as well as by my infirmity') he retired from all committee work, including the Council of the Shakespeare Memorial Theatre and the RADA Council. 'You must endure my going hence even as my coming hither,' he wrote to Kenneth Barnes, Principal of RADA. He had been offered the Presidency of RADA in the 1920s, and was now offered an honorary Presidency, but preferred to remain an Associate Member, signifying something potentially useful rather than honorific. He could now work on his political textbook with fewer diversions and, whenever this writing became troublesome, he would renew his experiments (like the experiments of a literary alchemist) to discover an alphabet capable of spelling the English language.

One day was like another at Ayot. Miss Patch knitted for the soldiers, made soft dolls for the Red Cross and when not filling chinks in the housekeeping typed up Shaw's shorthand for the printer. 'We just potter along from day to day,' Charlotte wrote. One day was like another; but each day grew shorter and 'the darkness is hard to bear'. Charlotte longed to be back in Whitehall Court, but Shaw feared the effect on her of more bombing – his newspaper campaign against reprisal raids on cities was largely prompted by Charlotte's alternating impatience and nervousness. Perhaps 'a bomb could be the easiest way to end', she had speculated in a letter to Beatrice Webb, but how could she be 'sure of its making a complete job': one bomb that broke the windows of Whitehall Court would simply have shattered a few bones and made things worse. 'I have not enough skill in Christian Science to cure Charlotte's worrying,' Shaw wrote to Nancy Astor.

This was a gruelling winter for Charlotte. The rheumatic attacks grew more severe, sometimes driving her crazy with the pain. She seemed to be shrinking into infirmity. 'Her case is graver than you think,' Shaw wrote to Nancy Astor in April 1942. 'Her spine has collapsed to such an extent that she cannot stand without hurting herself unbearably by a one-sided stoop...'

When summing up their condition – 'very old and muddled...always late or wrong or both' – G.B.S. liked to add their ages together. By the spring of 1942 they were one hundred and seventy. While she was 'bowed and crippled, furrowed and wrinkled', he still stood strikingly erect yet was so unsubstantial he appeared like Coleridge's 'a man all light, a seraph man'. In his prime his weight had been almost eleven stone; by the beginning of the war it had fallen to ten stone, and two years later it was barely nine stone. 'I am losing weight so fast that I shall presently have totally disappeared,' he wrote to Beatrice Webb. 'I look when stripped like a native in a famine picture, an imperfectly concealed skeleton.'

There were still moments when he felt 'nearly – only nearly – equal to anything'. Yet Charlotte remained incapacitated until fitted with a reinforced corset designed by her osteopath. 'I am crawling through this old spell like a half dead fly, still – I *am* getting through,' she wrote. Gradually her powers of recovery reasserted themselves. Could the two of them visit Cliveden again? They dreaded being stared at by strangers. But Nancy Astor had been their friend now for fifteen years and was 'a unique and amusing phenomenon', Shaw told Upton Sinclair, ' . . . [whose] philosophy begins and ends with her being a good sort'. With Charlotte becoming more fractious and complaining that the doctors were fools, Shaw explained the predicament to Nancy: 'A change would be good for her [Charlotte] one way, and in another possibly kill her.' Nancy urged them on and that July they decided to risk it, G.B.S. having first made arrangements for their cremation in case 'we die on your hands . . .'

One of their complaints was that Charlotte's doctors had done little but call her illness names such as arthritis, lumbago, or fibrositis. While at Cliveden they were both medically examined by the Canadian military staff billeted there. 'I was passed sound in wind and limb,' Shaw wrote to Beatrice Webb. But after four years of torment Charlotte was found to have been suffering from *osteitis deformans* or Paget's disease. 'Crawling about with difficulty and sometimes in pain, [she] was pronounced incurable at her age,' he informed Beatrice. This inexorable breaking down of the bone structure had probably been caused by an accident in her youth and 'the prognosis was terrible', he told Wells, 'ending with double pneumonia'.

They went home to Ayot, 'surprisingly small after Cliveden . . . strangely still and dull', and dug in for another winter.

The weeks flew past 'like Hurricanes and Spitfires' to the cries of the siren, the distant crackle of gunfire and bumping rhythm of the air-raids. Once they were back, Miss Patch took herself off for a short holiday to a warm hotel, but her predecessor Judy Musters suddenly turned up at Ayot 'in high spirits, her ailing mother and husband having just died and set her free. She is a darling,' Shaw enthused. Miss Patch hastened back, took out her knitting needles, arranged her pens and typewriter, and was soon rapping out letters to *The Times* on Scottish water-power, seconding G.B.S. through a resounding duel in *The Listener* with the zoologist Julian Huxley, and deciphering answers to 'Questions on the Future' from the *Sunday*

Express. Skeletal and erect, Shaw's almost transparent figure flickered between his workshed and the wireless, pulled back and forwards by the hyperactivity of this second childhood. He could not quell his beating spirit of enquiry. 'The war is interesting all the same, diabolical, senseless, useless as it now seems,' he wrote to Sidney Webb. ' . . . I am rather curious to see how it will end.'

But for Charlotte, horribly hunchbacked, unable to walk without help, unable to reach the garden, the collapsed wreck of her body held in her armoured corset, there was nothing to desire except a happy end. As the disease progressed, her bones felt as if they were cracking and splintering whenever she moved or breathed too deeply. Fiercely as she resented her invalidism, she had come to fear the pain more. 'The difficulty with which she crawls about is heartbreaking,' Shaw wrote. ' . . . But her vitality does not seem to diminish.'

By 1943 they were approaching their forty-fifth wedding anniversary. For much of this marriage Charlotte had remained unseen by the general public. Responding to this invisibility – her refusal to be photographed, and her virtual absence from the biographies of G.B.S. – many onlookers of the Shavian phenomenon imagined her a prisoner of wedlock. Accompanying her husband to his first nights, publishing *Selected Passages* from his works, nursing him through illnesses, keeping obscurely in the background, she seemed to have given up her life to his career. 'I am certain that Shaw's success owed a very great deal to Mrs Shaw – far more than is generally realised,' said Mrs Tuke, wife of the Chairman of Barclays Bank, who occasionally saw them together at Ayot.

Such a conclusion followed naturally from the initial scepticism that had been aroused by Shaw's facetiously happy announcement of their marriage ('Years of married bliss to them'). It was impossible that they would ever 'rise to the loftier heights of wedded love', predicted W. A. S. Hewins, a political economist at the London School of Economics, though he allowed them a little 'refreshment on the lower slopes'. Everyone agreed that their marriage had not been made in heaven. 'He [Shaw] is too clever to be really in love with Lottie, who is nearly clever but not quite,' Charlotte's cousin Edith Somerville had written. 'However it may be better than it seems.'

And it had been better, this childless partnership of a middle-aged couple. At Adelphi Terrace and Whitehall Court they had arranged their lives like characters from a previous century. No wonder Shaw had set the scene of their marriage as the finale to '*In Good King Charles's Golden Days*'. He would introduce Charlotte in the grand manner, then sprint to open doors for her and bow as she passed from one room to another. 'She had decided views on etiquette,' noticed one of their neighbours, Captain Ames, and she led a life 'rather like that of a Queen Consort', Lady Rhondda thought. '...she had a number of the attributes of a Queen.' Another neighbour observed that she held 'an "upper-class" outlook, which contrasted with her husband's socialistic cosmopolitanism'. Beatrice Webb had described her temperament as volcanic; and later Charlotte called Beatrice's refusal to be known as Lady Passfield 'absolutely disgraceful and utterly inexcusable conduct'.

'My wife is a woman of strong mentality,' Shaw answered one questioner, 'and expresses strong opinions to me twelve or thirteen times a day.' Many of her strongest opinions, such as her view that they should not have children, had been expressions of her anxieties. She looked forward to a time when women need not be involved in the process of childbirth. 'Sometimes I have been sorry that I was not more insistent on the point,' Shaw later conceded.

Not everyone thought her charming. Sean O'Casey, for example, was disgusted by the sight of her leaning determinedly forward, covering a huge pile of food in thick sauce and swallowing it down with sluggish energy – Johnsonian eating habits that some saw as a compensatory substitute for sex.

Others ridiculed her quest, in the wake of her guru James Porter Mills, to locate the Great Architect in the works of Ouspensky and others. When Mills died in the 1920s, his teaching had been taken up by Charlotte's friend, the former actress Lena Ashwell who had created the Polish aviator in *Misalliance* and whose father suggested Captain Shotover to Shaw. 'I am working to achieve a wireless set which will respond to the music of the spheres,' she wrote in Shotover style, pursuing Mills's merging of Eastern religions with Western technology. With a 'Cosmic Ray', she explained in 1936, 'the character could be changed and the means of escape made plain from all the slavery of our little lives'. Such mystical tunings-in, which had once provided Charlotte with a means of escape from the anxieties of being married alive to G.B.S., seemed eventually to invade Shaw's own work as he progressed from the *Pygmalion* romance between an East End flower girl and a West End gentleman to the surreal marriage of East and West in *The Simpleton of the Unexpected Isles*.

'It takes a long time for two people to get to know each other,' Shaw remarked. Sometimes the knowledge seemed to filter in unconsciously. As a Fabian with a 'full-size social conscience', Charlotte had always admired the egalitarian vision of her husband's socialism. But it was as 'a dreamer of wonderful dreams' that he had become a great man to her. Perhaps something of her own intuitions quietly permeated those dreams. In any event 'something quite indestructible' had grown up between them. 'Finally a marriage consolidates itself until the two lose all sense of separateness, and the married life becomes one life,' they wrote to a friend, echoing the words of Pra and Prola at the end of *The Simpleton*.

G.B.S. was the direct opposite of what the world believed, Charlotte informed a journalist in 1914. 'He is not the blatant, bombastic person of the popular conception. He is bashful and retiring, quiet and reserved by nature. But he does not let this part of his nature overrule him. He sweeps it aside ... when he thinks it is the only way to propagate his ideas and beliefs.'

Few people got through the zone of bombast to the ordinariness of their married life. Blanche Patch had once come across G.B.S. sitting with his arms round Charlotte singing an impromptu version of 'Oh, Mr Porter' – and quietly stole away. Barry Jackson, calling round unexpectedly, found them sitting side by side on a sofa looking through a large picture book, themselves the picture of a happy marriage. To Lawrence Langner, Charlotte appeared like 'a kindly mother whose grown son was distinguishing himself before an appreciative audience'. Her family, which had starred Granville-Barker and T. E. Lawrence as sons apparent, was mostly played by the servants at Ayot. They knew this marriage better than anyone. They saw how Shaw's daily routine during these war years had become determined by Charlotte's health. They saw his tenderness, her solicitude. Each morning he would go to her bedroom for a talk before breakfast, and she would insist on arranging the pillows for his siesta between their lunch and tea together. In the late afternoon, when he liked to stride outdoors in the pursuit of air and exercise, she would wait anxiously for him until he presented himself to her before dinner 'to show that nothing has happened to me'. In the evenings he sometimes played for her the songs his mother had sung during his boyhood in Dublin; and they would read together books she had chosen, such as Gerald Heard's *Pain, Sex and Time*. Heard's attempt to combine science and religion, nature and supernature, impressed Shaw as though it had been a work by Conrad Barnabas in *Back to Methuselah*, and it came to Charlotte as a revelation – a final ascent in the long flight of her mystical readings. The book 'lighted up the whole pile of little personal discoveries', she wrote, 'and made them glow with new lights'.

Shaw's anxieties rose to the surface as financial problems. 'I am living on my capital and will end in the workhouse if the war lasts,' he declared to Nancy Astor. 'This makes me anxious as to what is happening to your income,' he added in a letter to Beatrice Webb, ' ... so if you get into a too tight corner let me know and I may be able to tide you over. We must sink or swim together.'

Charlotte's anxieties were generally exercised over her servants at Ayot. She became distracted by the thought that one of the housemaids, a 'good girl' whom everyone liked, might be taken away for war service. It was as if she felt that human life could no longer be sustained without a housekeeper and cook, gardener and two maids. By bombarding the local authorities and persuading Nancy Astor to intercede with the Ministry of Labour and National Service, G.B.S. managed to postpone the call-up date. But when the maid finally left Ayot in the summer of 1943, it seemed to Charlotte like the end of the world. Shaw wanted to bring in a nurse to relieve the other domestics, but Charlotte feared a newcomer might be resented and not fit comfortably into their household. 'I have not engaged the nurse but I have talked to her about the loneliness of the place,' she explained to Mrs Higgs, the housekeeper. '... you will know best and advise me.'

Charlotte was beset by such fears. 'There is not much joy in life for her,' Shaw admitted to Sidney Webb. Beatrice, too, suffering from advanced kidney disease, was finding prolonged living a painful experience. 'You can't cure old age,' she had reflected when considering Charlotte's condition as well as her own. But of course there was a cure. Once Sidney was dead she could easily kill herself. 'It will suit the public interest,' she reasoned. But on 30 April 1943, after a few days in a coma, it was Beatrice who died. 'I could not bring myself to write funereally about her ... we were all young together and never thought of ourselves as great people,' Shaw wrote to Sidney. '... I used to take it as a matter of course that if Beatrice died you would come and live with us; for I never counted on our living to this ridiculous age and being incapable of taking care of ourselves or anyone else.'

In the same way as he weeded out hostile references in the press or shielded her from the news that he had been robbed in the street, Shaw kept Beatrice's death secret from Charlotte in case it released a swarm of new anxieties. Such protection was not difficult. Her handwriting had grown so illegible that she seldom wrote to anyone these days. 'It is such a bitter humiliation to me not to be able to write properly,' she complained. Bent forwards 'like an old witch', she seemed to have shrunk to half her size, yet was still not reconciled to her condition and would not stay in bed.

At the beginning of June 1943, Shaw wrote to tell Nancy Astor that 'Cliveden is quite impossible for us this summer ... Dont bother any more about us: there is nothing to be done.' But Charlotte still longed to escape her 'little prison' at Ayot and, after much hesitation, Shaw agreed to move her back for a spell to Whitehall Court. If this plan worked, he could give the staff at Ayot a holiday and engage a professional nurse in London. The doctors had warned him that the journey would be risky, and 'I am anxious about her,' he admitted. She was driven up, fortified by her powerful corset, on his eighty-seventh birthday. It was 'quite an adventure', he told Wells; 'but it came off successfully and she is happier here'.

They had planned to remain in London three weeks, but arranged to stay on another month when Mrs Higgs fell ill and entered hospital for an operation. 'This *contretemps*, instead of upsetting Charlotte, has given her something to think about, which is very good for her,' Shaw wrote to Nancy Astor. In the past Shaw's trick for distracting Charlotte from her illnesses had been to fall ill himself. 'If Charlotte were dying, I know an infallible way to restore her to health,' he had told St John Ervine. 'I should simply go to bed and say I was dying.' But now her condition was complicated by distressing hallucinations, and his sustained health became vital to whatever peace of mind she could grasp. He consulted friends for the names of new doctors and psychotherapists who might banish the animals and evil spectres which filled her imagination and added to her terrors. 'She saw crowds of strangers in the room, and kept asking me to remonstrate with the managers and housekeeper here for allowing them to come up and intrude,' he wrote to Almroth Wright. 'She also spoke to me of imaginary kittens and little dogs in my lap. She was, however, perfectly reasonable on every point except the actual existence of these phantoms. Her best hope was to die before she became worse.'

Though he made light of it ('Mrs Shaw is . . . rather scatterbrained in the mornings') the cumulative strain of these weeks in London grew almost unendurable. Then, helping her to get up from dinner on the evening of Friday 10 September, he noticed to his great surprise and relief what seemed an extraordinary change coming over Charlotte. She appeared calmer and did not complain as usual when he took her through to the drawing-room. A miracle was rising before his eyes. He saw the furrows and wrinkles on her forehead vanish, and sensed that her worries, cares, distresses were vanishing too as she smiled easily at him and he heard her speaking again with the voice of her happiest hours. In a short time she seemed to look forty years younger, and was the woman he had known at the time of their marriage when his own life seemed to be fading. Looking in wonder at her perfectly smooth face, he told her she was beautiful and that the illness was leaving her. 'She talked to me insistently and joyously, and, though it was almost all unintelligible, she heard and understood what I said to her, and was delighted by my assurances that she was getting well, that all our troubles were over.'

Thinking she was still at Ayot, Charlotte asked him to take her upstairs to her bedroom, and he settled her in for the night earlier than usual. Next morning he was woken by the nurse with the news that Charlotte had been found lying at the foot of her bed clutching her alarm clock and with her face bleeding. He helped to get her back into bed and immediately engaged a night nurse. In spite of this fall, she was still smiling and happy, and the mysterious process by which she appeared to be discarding her years went on: 'I had never known her so young.' He realized she was dying – 'at this moment it looks as if the patient were beyond all professional help' he wrote that Saturday to James Bridie. He kept with her every possible minute and she talked to him incessantly, 'babbling to me like a happy child', he wrote to Mrs Higgs. '. . . you may be sure I said everything to please her.'

Again he settled her in early for the night and slept well himself. At a quarter past eight on Sunday morning the night nurse came to his bedroom and told him he had been a widower for almost six hours. He went to her room and, looking down at the body, saw that Charlotte's face was that of a young girl – like the portrait painted of her by Sartorio in Rome before Shaw had known her. 'I was amazed. I have never seen anything so beautiful.' She appeared so very much alive that he could not stop himself from going into her room again and again that day, and the next day, continuing to speak softly to her. 'Once, I thought that her eyes opened slightly while I was talking to her' and he took out his microscope glass and held it to her lips. 'I could not believe she was dead.'

All sorts of associations – an echo from Cordelia at the end of *King Lear*, a reversal of Wilde's ending for *The Picture of Dorian Gray* – mingled in this strange experience. He felt the need to tell everyone about her marvellous rejuvenation. 'She had thirty hours of happiness and heaven,' he wrote to H. G. Wells. 'It was a blessedly happy ending,' he wrote to Granville-Barker, breaking almost twenty years of silence. '. . . You will not, I know, mind my writing this to you.' The woman whose face had been likened to a muffin by the Regius Professor of Modern History at Oxford at the time of her marriage had flowered on the day of her death into an 'incredibly beautiful' young girl. It was like a fairy story in which Shaw's search for love was finally to be fulfilled. 'I did not know I could be so moved,' he wrote to Wells. This vivid trance lasted nearly two days. Then Charlotte's body, which had shed with its physical history her relationship with himself, became a wax figure: the jaw dropped open and she was gone.

'No flowers; no black clothes; no service,' she had requested. Shaw arranged for a private cremation, as he had for his mother and his sister. There was cheerful weather for the cremation, but Shaw was disappointed that he could not go behind the scenes, as he had done after his mother's death, to see the coffin spring into Pentecostal flames and see Charlotte become that garnet-coloured fire.

Nancy Astor and Blanche Patch accompanied him to Golders Green. Not a word was spoken and the ceremony lasted only a few minutes. Handel, the composer Charlotte loved most, provided the music: 'But Thou didst not leave His soul in hell' from *Messiah* for the committal; 'Ombra ma fù' from *Serse* for the voluntary. 'Who could ask for more?' At the end 'Shaw lifted up his arms and softly sang the words as if to Charlotte whose coffin was just in front of him,' Blanche Patch noticed. 'It was a really beautiful sight.' Then, as the anthem neared its close, the coffin moved out and Shaw continued standing there, still singing, his arms outstretched.

[3]

I still regard myself as Charlotte's property. I really could not ask her to mix our ashes with those of a third party.
Shaw to Nancy Astor (11 August 1944)

Shaw kept the news of Charlotte's death out of the newspapers until after her cremation. 'I could not stand flowers . . . and a crowd at Golders Green,' he told Wells. Once the news broke he was overwhelmed with letters and had to acknowledge them collectively in a notice to *The Times* assuring everyone that 'a very happy ending to a very long life has left him awaiting his own turn in perfect serenity'.

He had been tempted, he told Sean O'Casey, to insert 'No letters: no congratulations' into his *Times* notice. For he felt more thankful than unhappy. 'What I dreaded was her lingering in distress,' he wrote to Sidney Webb. He could admit that 'when I come across something intimate of her belongings I have a welling of emotion and quite automatically say something endearing to her'. But, he added in a letter to Alfred Douglas, 'I am not in the least desolate.'

A few of these belongings he gave to Charlotte's friends ('two priceless evening dresses ... will henceforth dazzle society on the shoulders of B[lanche] P[atch]'). He invited them to call at Whitehall Court 'just as if nothing had happened'. But he could not stop speaking of Charlotte. Death was long familiar and had been an everyday possibility, he reminded people, so there was now no sorrow, only a flow of deep feeling. He took care to barricade himself against the possibility of grief. 'I do not grieve,' he insisted; 'but then neither do I forget.' He did not forget that Charlotte's end had been transparently happy. Yet the armour that had shone so brightly for so long was suddenly pierced. 'He missed her far more than he had ever imagined he could miss anybody,' wrote St John Ervine.

He fought this enemy, grief, with every Shavian contrivance. Until a man loses his wife he does not discover how completely his habits have been subjected to hers, he pointed out. As a widower he was free to return to his bachelor life, eat when he was hungry, dress as he fancied, work without consulting anyone but himself and 'go to bed when I like', which usually meant after midnight. His mother had never gone to bed before midnight 'and I won't either'. People thought he was lonely: but he was simply indulging the talent for solitude he had inherited from his parents. He had replaced emotion with money as his mother's motive for leaving him in Dublin, and he covered his emotional deprivation now with obsessional talk of death duties. Charlotte's death had been a great loss, he agreed, a great financial loss.

'So away with melancholy!' he chided William Maxwell. The method by which he strove to reverse his feelings, outwit them, transmute them into something else – at any rate keep them under control – could sound oddly callous. 'Now we can play our merriest tunes to celebrate a very happy ending to a very long life,' he exhorted Otto Kyllmann. Yet, it was 'funny', he told the composer Rutland Boughton three years later, that 'I have not touched the piano since Charlotte died'. He would nevertheless sing hilariously, have his photograph taken cheerfully ('Miss Patch also posed') and boast that his health was improving markedly since Charlotte's death 'set me free'. Even so he could not always prevent himself from crying in the street. Over the next two or three years he 'seemed extraordinarily "caved in" ', a local bookseller near Ayot noticed. ' . . . He looked very sad. I did not think he was capable of such emotional feeling, but he showed it quite obviously.'

*

There is a suspicion, widely shared, that after forty years of marriage a widower must be in want of a second attachment. On several occasions Shaw had protested that he was not naturally a marrying man. But was he not protesting a little too much? When young, it was true, he had been forced into singular isolation, but then gradually learned what he called 'the technique of marriage'. It was a triumph of experience. So there should be little surprise that people were already reflecting on the possibility of a natural sequel. Such a possibility played on the minds of both Lady Astor and Miss Patch as they drove back from Golders Green.

Indeed Lady Astor was hardly out of the crematorium before, to Miss Patch's disgust, she invited G.B.S. to Cliveden where she could see he was properly cared for. Miss Patch knew her game. She had never forgotten the time when her ladyship 'upset my plans' by coming at the last moment to one of Shaw's performances at the Kingsway Hall and taking the best seat, reserved for Miss Patch herself, so that 'I had to sit in a hateful position just behind the speaker and chairman'. With characteristic tactlessness, Lady Astor was now doing virtually the same thing again.

Standing with G.B.S. over Charlotte's body only three days before, Miss Patch had asked him whether he wished to invite anyone else to Golders Green 'and his reply was that he and I would go together and he wanted the ceremony to be absolutely quiet'. Why, then, had Lady Astor 'insisted on coming with us' if she wasn't trying to supplant Miss Patch as G.B.S.'s closest, quietest, female friend? She had to admit that Lady Astor was 'invariably kind to me'. But these acts of kindness – proposals that she must be looked after by a nurse or given a new suit of clothes – were curiously disconcerting and seldom prevailed on G.B.S. 'Don't worry about her: she is jolly well provided for,' he replied on one occasion. ' . . . I could detect no trace of the half starved, raggedly dressed, cruelly exploited, moribund victim I had been led to expect from recent conversations.' Neither did Miss Patch see herself as a patient needing charity. Her needs were more ambitious. When G.B.S. presented her with certain likenesses of himself – in short, his Max Beerbohm caricatures – or handed her Charlotte's £100 fur coat, it was surely obvious that these were not charitable provisions but tokens of a special attachment. She had been with him now for quarter of a century, sharing what he most prized: his work. And it was his work, she was pleased to note, that he cited when fending off Lady Astor's advances. 'I am full of unfinished jobs, some of them unbegun; and I must take my own advice and not attempt to combine them with visits to Cliveden . . . ' During this transitory period it was not difficult to read into such unfinished business a new beginning for herself.

Even in her tweed suit, sweater and pearls, Miss Patch was now so thin she barely cast a shadow. Her Picasso-esque features, framed by a face 'like two profiles stuck together', were formidable. 'Piercing blue eyes,' one dismayed visitor noted, 'a nose like a knife blade, lipless mouth.'

Towards the end of 1943 Shaw left Whitehall Court and settled himself at Ayot. Miss Patch stayed uneasily in London while Lady Astor gave notice of whirlwind swoops on G.B.S. 'Don't come down here yet,' he pleaded at the beginning of 1944. ' . . . for a month or two I must be let alone.' But Lady Astor was not a waiting woman. She remembered how Charlotte had trusted her to look after G.B.S. in Russia ('It will be difficult: but if anyone can keep him in hand *you* can!') and she believed that after her death Charlotte had implicitly bequeathed her this duty. So she persisted with her efforts to police Shaw's life. When he wrote explaining that 'I cannot entertain anyone, not even you, for more than an hour at teatime,' she invited herself instead for the night – in which case, he quickly amended, he would have to call in Lady Rhondda, Ellen Pollock, Blanche Patch and Judy Musters 'to chaperone us; and there would be only one bed for them'. So Nancy began to vary her tactics, dealing out offers of excursions to Cornwall and holidays at Sandwich. 'I shall never see these places again,' Shaw answered. 'The garden and plantation here are my world now.'

Occasionally she would dangle before him someone he could not resist, such as the ex-Vice-President of the United States, Henry Wallace, who was soon to run for the presidency as leader of his new Progressive Party. But though she sometimes got through his defences, she found the encircling routine at Ayot difficult to penetrate and the sort of beneficial changes Charlotte would have approved almost impossible to inflict on G.B.S. 'If I am uprooted I shall probably die immediately,' he threatened her. 'That is how I feel about it.'

Besides there had been enough changes at Ayot in the year following Charlotte's death.

Early in June 1944 sinister robot planes began flying over London and the south of England. These were the Germans' mysterious new secret weapons, pilotless rockets or flying bombs nicknamed 'doodlebugs', that roared overhead like express trains illuminated by searchlights, then suddenly cut their engines, descended silently and hit the ground with shattering explosions. One of these 'buzzer bombs', as Blanche Patch called them, fell near Charing Cross and next morning she arrived to find that the blast from Hungerford Bridge had blown in the study windows of Shaw's flat, broken the grandfather clock in the hall and covered everything with debris. As the bombardment went on, she began to feel 'decidedly shaky as the result of sleepless nights'. Over 200,000 houses, mostly in the London area, had been made uninhabitable by the end of the month. 'The pilotless bombs have driven everyone out of London, including Blanche, who has returned to Ayot,' Shaw wrote to Nancy Astor. 'The village is crowded with refugees. But the bombs in their blindness stray this way: two came down near enough to shake the house last week.'

Two months after Miss Patch arrived at Ayot, Henry and Clara Higgs, the gardener and housekeeper who had been with Shaw forty-two years, gave in their notice. 'My wife felt the work had become too much for us,' Higgs said. They had put off going as long as they could. Though terribly lame, Higgs could not bear to leave his garden until he had seen it through one more summer. It had been a matter of special pride to him that Shaw felt so attached to this garden: he liked to find out things about it, such as whether the large red poppies' seeds were poisonous. 'We must get a packet and send them off to Hitler,' he said after being told they were.

455

Higgs's place in the garden was to be taken in 1946 by his pupil Fred Drury. As a lad of nineteen, Drury had come to work as assistant gardener in 1934, then been called up six years later, and eventually returned to Ayot after the war, not wishing 'to work for anyone else'.

Mrs Higgs's place in the kitchen was immediately filled by Alice Laden, a plump, capable, grey-haired and pink-complexioned widow who had nursed Charlotte through her last weeks at Whitehall Court. 'You are just the person I'm looking for,' Shaw told her. 'I want you to come and look after me till *I* die.' It was a tall order, but Mrs Laden had felt lonely after losing her husband in the war, and besides, she reckoned that she knew how to handle G.B.S. better than anyone since Charlotte. 'I could sense his moods,' she said. '. . . I had a way with him.' Shaw sent his Rolls to fetch her and her cat Bunch and waited with Mrs Higgs who had volunteered to stay on for a fortnight to train her. But after two devastating days with this fiercely efficient Scottish newcomer, Mrs Higgs fled, driven out with her husband 'before a terrible New Woman, of a species unknown to them, from the house where they had been supreme indoors and out . . . [to] fend for themselves in a world in which they are museum pieces'.

When the day came to shake hands and say goodbye, Higgs could see that the old man was upset. 'They went away in a handsome cab, beautifully dressed, with the dog on its lead, greatly excited,' Shaw wrote to Nancy Astor.

'I kissed her goodbye, and waved after them until the car disappeared round the corner. Always acting, you will say. I thought so myself; but I must have felt the part: for when I went to the shelter to write, I found that my pen wobbled a little in my hand.'

Next day he was resolutely G.B.S. again: 'it was as if they had been gone twenty years'.

Shaw made no secret of finding Mrs Laden a good-looking woman and she was soon speaking of him as 'a vur-r-r-ee good man'. Before long whispers began to breeze through the village that he was allowing her the intimacy of trimming his beard and buying his elastic braces ('without them my dignity would disappear altogether', he apologized to Blanche Patch). Where would it end? 'I shall probably have to marry Mrs Laden,' he confided to Nancy Astor.

Both Lady Astor and Miss Patch felt qualms over this new regime. After Higgs left there was no other man on the premises – only Mrs Laden, Miss Patch and the Irish parlourmaid Margaret Cashin. It was a delicate situation. Miss Patch had urged Shaw to establish Mrs Laden's employment on a proper business basis. Accordingly he went to her and explained that, as he could not do without her and she could do without him, her strong position entitled her to a blank cheque. 'I had to cover my ignorance with this stage effect,' he explained to Nancy Astor.

At the start Mrs Laden settled for two pounds and fifteen shillings a week. Before many weeks passed she had calmed Lady Astor's and Miss Patch's suspicions. They were particularly thankful that she knew her place so well. She never allowed G.B.S. into the kitchen. 'Your job is to write plays and mine is to keep house,' she instructed him. '... You mind your business and I'll mind mine.' Some people were terrified of G.B.S. but she didn't appear frightened of him at all, indeed he seemed a little afraid of her. If he wanted anything he had to ask her for it through the kitchen hatch or leave a note for her on the hall table.

'I've got a good manager. She looks after me well,' Shaw acknowledged. Both were intractable characters and they had some commendable fights, 'I am a rank Tory and I heartily disagree with all Socialist views,' she told him. He seemed delighted. Her vigilant manner and strong Aberdonian accent were wonderfully effective when discouraging callers on the telephone and at the front door. There was no bribing her. Journalists were usually sent away with a flea in their ear. 'If I didn't have Mrs Laden I'd have an Alsatian watchdog,' Shaw told visitors. In the village she was referred to as 'the Dragon' and, accepting this as a compliment, bought herself a brooch in the form of a green dragon, telling G.B.S. he was 'St George to my Dragon'.

In these days of food rationing Mrs Laden's job was not easy. Shaw never allowed her to buy black-market goods and he insisted that the calories in each dish must be carefully calculated – though she often found him eating sweets or chocolates, or with a large chunk of iced cake in his hand, between meals. 'Sugar I stole,' he had written of his childhood. When he was past ninety, Mrs Laden would come across him in the evening spooning sugar into his mouth from a bowl. For the most part he lived off soups, eggs, milk, honey, cheese, fruit, cream, biscuits and lemon juice. Mrs Laden's husband had been a vegetarian and she had gone through a course of training in vegetarian cookery. Even Miss Patch melted somewhat at the new fare. 'Blanche and I have been gorging,' Shaw wrote to Nancy Astor. '... After Mrs Higgs's two or three dishes over and over again, Mrs Laden's meals are the masterpieces of a beribboned chef. Her soups! Her sweets! Her savouries! We have to wait on ourselves; but we eat too much and enjoy doing it.'

'Do not be nervous about the ladies,' G.B.S. had advised Nancy. Both Blanche and Nancy were agitated by his perpetual teasing. 'I'm trying to school myself to be indifferent to his pin pricks,' Miss Patch told Hesketh Pearson, though she had to agree with Gabriel Pascal when he called

G.B.S. 'ze Vorld's greatest Zadist'. In her post as secretary she sometimes opened proposals of marriage posted by complete strangers, and G.B.S. would forward one or two of them to Nancy Astor with a note: 'You see, I am still in demand.' Would he really be silly enough to marry again in old age? 'Second marriages are the quietest and happiest,' he wrote and Miss Patch agreed. Hadn't Lloyd George married his secretary Frances Stevenson in 1943? But Miss Patch wondered whether her employer might suddenly attach himself to the wrong person, while Lady Astor felt convinced that any second marriage would be disastrous. There was no telling, they agreed, where his vanity might lead him. But to Shaw's mind he was simply 'a tremendous catch for spinsters looking out for a rich widowhood'. He continued to escape 'like Joseph from Potiphar's wife', advising one acquaintance who had briefly returned to England from the United States and invited herself to tea that she must overcome these impulses. 'Mrs [Laden] has now to be mistress of the house.' According to Shavian economics he was growing increasingly attractive to these women as his life-expectancy shortened. 'I am rather a catch now,' he explained to Molly Tompkins, 'having only a few years at most to live (quite probably a few days)'.

Old flames such as Molly caused Miss Patch and Lady Astor most apprehension. Having gone to Rome at the end of the 1920s, Molly had, like Sweetie (alias Susan Simpkins and the 'Countess Valbrioni') in *Too True to be Good*, led the life of a flamboyant aristocrat until, tired and lonely, she suddenly attempted to kill herself. Shaw had been apprised of her story by Cecil Lewis who still saw her occasionally in Italy. The Wall Street crash forced Molly to give up the palazzo on their magical Isolino San Giovanni and during the 1930s Shaw paid for the education in England of her unruly son Peter. 'You may send me Peter's bills until I am broke,' he wrote to the headmaster of Ferndale, a private school in Surrey. 'This is of course retrospective ... The Principal of Stowe estimates the annual needs of the Scholar at about £135. I have let myself in for this ... '

Molly had meanwhile turned to playwrighting and sent Shaw a melodrama in which, as at the end of *Tosca*, the heroine leaps from a parapet and is drowned in the lake – only to be revived by G.B.S., who changed the plot into a farce like *Jitta's Atonement*. When Laurence mislaid this tragicomedy, Molly had took up another career, arriving in London early in the 1930s for a one-woman exhibition of her paintings at the Leicester Galleries. 'How terrifying!' Shaw greeted her. 'What on earth am I to do with you?' He took her round the art galleries and bought one of her pictures, 'The Road to Stresa', which he still called The Road to Baveno. 'I found him his old self,' Molly wrote, 'if anything more dear and charming than ever.' To Charlotte she displayed her nude studies of Adam done in the manner of D. H. Lawrence whose exhibition had been raided by police two years previously. But her show, with temporary fig leaves attached, was a success and Charlotte had written to congratulate her: 'I feel that you are "all right", and that you will go on from triumph to triumph!'

But she had not gone on; she had come back and after more wanderings, more conquests and a divorce from Laurence, rented a studio in Chelsea at the end of 1937. 'You mustn't come near us,' Shaw commanded her. 'Why are you so terrified?', she asked, and he replied that he did not want her to see him at eighty-two 'and shatter your memories'. So leaving him her love and 'many more things' she did 'not know how to say', she went to Rome again and then eventually sailed into New York as the Japanese attacked Pearl Harbor.

Now surely, like the love-goddess Maya who was conceived from her and came to life on the *Unexpected Isles*, she must vanish. And so she did until Shaw summoned her up after Charlotte's death. 'Let me have a line occasionally. We can write more freely now that Charlotte can never read our letters.' So she wrote to him freely, proposing a last adventure. She would cross the Atlantic. She would come to him. They would make up for lost time and be free as air ... 'Your letters always knock me endways,' he was to answer her. 'I am too old for such shocks.' She was an atom bomb exploding in a havoc of romantic ridicule. If she stayed even one night at Ayot, he warned her, his stern Scottish housekeeper and devout Irish Catholic housemaid – to say nothing of Miss Patch herself – would leave instantly and his dignified retirement would be shattered.

'No woman shall ever live with me again in that sense ... The scandal in the village, the degradation to Literature, the insult to Charlotte's memory would be such that I should be justified in shooting you if there were no other way of preventing you from crashing my gates.'

'I am ashamed of you for being afraid,' Molly replied. Besides, he had misconstrued her proposal monstrously. What she wanted was a short visit, she told him, not the Baveno Road again which she would always have 'deep and sweet in my heart'. 'You must cast me off like a laddered stocking,' he pleaded, 'and get a younger correspondent.' But she seemed unable to do this. 'When I can't write to you I am always a little lost.' So they continued their 'heart-to-heart correspondence', playing on each other's emotions, conjuring up their phantom island and an apparition of the endless road to Baveno. 'Have you not yet discovered that the only roads that remain beautiful are those that never led anywhere?' he had once asked her. 'For you never come to the end of them.'

'Everyone knows that its a mistake to live at your job,' Blanche Patch acknowledged. Early in 1945 she decided to brave the bombs, move back to London and into a private apartment at the Onslow Court Hotel, a highly respectable address in Queen's Gate soon to be made notorious by John Haig's acid bath murders.

There were several reasons for this retreat. The fearful cold and isolation of Ayot had begun to make her 'melancholy mad', particularly over Christmas which Shaw refused to celebrate ('I am a lifelong advocate of its abolition'). Then there was the ticklish question of who was in charge of the house now that Mrs Laden had settled in. Not wanting Mrs Laden for an enemy, Miss Patch judged it best to 'make a stand' – which was to say, take her leave and assign all household duties to 'our cook'. There was also the matter of her special relationship with G.B.S. Very few people were privileged to be intimate with him or could understand how such intimacy was enhanced by a judicious distance. She felt nervous over leaving, but 'I think the poor old dear wants to be left alone & will be thankful when I move off,' she confided to Hesketh Pearson. It was also true that she could protect his interests and uphold her own status by keeping a regular eye on Whitehall Court where Judy Musters was apparently free to stay any time she fancied. Finally Miss Patch was better placed to drop in for 'a chit-chat' with Shaw's solicitor and accountant. From every point of view it seemed sensible to leave Ayot for London. All the same, she felt 'down in the dumps'. It was strange, she reflected, 'how indifferent he is to what makes me suffer'.

Putting aside their jealousies, Miss Patch, Mrs Laden and Lady Astor were beginning to form a wary alliance against three mysterious men whom Shaw had imported into his life to cope with the extra work created by 'Charlotte's death and the near prospect of my own'.

The first of these new men was John Wardrop, a twenty-year-old Scottish journalist who had arrived on 17 December 1939 at Whitehall Court after a seventeen-hour journey from Edinburgh, crumpled, unshaven, 'like the hero in fiction . . . with something around a shilling in my pocket and a picture in my heart'. Sending up his National Union of Journalists card to Shaw's apartment ('with its record of arrears of contributions all complete'), he had it promptly sent back down to him by Miss Patch with a note that Shaw was out of town.

Wardrop had no friends in London, no job and no plans other than that of attaching himself to G.B.S. He wanted to interview him, write articles about him, become his friend. 'There are forty-odd millions of people in this country, mostly freelance journalists,' Shaw had protested. 'How long do you think it would take me to see them all?' But Wardrop felt unique. He wrote incessantly and over the next two years did get to see G.B.S., though Charlotte would never admit him to her sitting-room. He also introduced himself to Gabriel Pascal, Hesketh Pearson and J. Arthur Rank as Shaw's prospective literary agent and sought to make his attachment indefinably closer after tracking down Erica Cotterill, then living under an assumed name in a North Devon farmhouse. 'Be kind to her,' Shaw advised: 'she is a nonpareil.'

So perhaps was Wardrop. In any event Shaw tried to be kind to him. Yet he was difficult to employ, being 'too good for one level and not schooled enough for the other'. 'Have you made the best of me?' Wardrop had wanted to know. He dreamed of editing Shaw's correspondence, advising on the productions of his plays, representing him on the sets of his films. By 1942, however, he was working less exaltedly as Shaw's editorial assistant and proof-reader on *Everybody's Political What's What?*

Wardrop was keen, excitable, bright with promise. 'He lacked neither brains nor devotion,' Shaw judged, 'but age, experience, training, and polish.' While waiting for his Shavian future to expand, Wardrop had begun living with Eleanor O'Connell, a capable woman fifteen years older than himself, at a house in Park Village West next to the one occupied by Lucinda Elizabeth Shaw during her last years. G.B.S. liked Eleanor whom he treated as Wardrop's common-law wife. He had gone round to their house after Charlotte's death and invited them to visit Whitehall Court. To Miss Patch's annoyance he showed them round Charlotte's bedroom and gave Wardrop a key to the apartment so that he could work there in the evenings cataloguing Charlotte's books. This would be another of those jobs for which he was unschooled that nevertheless proved not good enough for him – in Miss Patch's view it was 'quite beyond his powers'. Desiring more, he gained Shaw's permission to carry off various papers from the study files 'for greater safety'. This was almost the last straw for Miss Patch. 'We had some really good rows over the Wardrops when Charlotte died,' she told Hesketh Pearson.

Convinced that G.B.S. would be unable to 'get me out of your hair', Wardrop sought the posthumous appointment as Shaw's official biographer. He saw the original 'shilling in my pocket' spinning into a magical fortune, while the early 'picture in my heart' now shone like a cloud-capped castle-in-the-air where he lived as Shaw's twin brother, his future self. 'You are to have my house and everything in it, including my Rolls Royce car, which you are already driving in your dreams,' Shaw was to tell him. ' . . . happy as the dream is, I must wake you up.'

Then, just as Miss Patch felt she had checked Wardrop's trespass into her territory, Shaw 'inflicts the Jew on me', she complained.

The Jew was Dr Fritz Loewenstein. He too had been circling round G.B.S. before Charlotte's death, soliciting his help as early as 1936 in the compilation of a bibliography. Unfortunately, Shaw was 'a man who had no understanding of or respect for the responsibilities of scholarship'. He shied away from the 'appalling grave digging' of such deep work, agreeing merely to look through Loewenstein's opus list 'when you have completed it, and see whether I can add anything to it'.

The war, though delaying bibliographical progress, advanced Loewenstein's moral position. He had left Germany in 1933 with little more than a doctorate from the University of Würzburg for a thesis on Japanese prints, and after the declaration of war was briefly interned as an enemy alien on the Isle of Man. 'I am a Jewish refugee,' he wrote to Shaw in 1942, '... and I am 41 years of age. I am married and have three children. I am as poor as a church mouse and make at present my living as a motor mechanic-trainee.' Listening to his fellow mechanics he had been aghast at their ignorance of Shaw's 'priceless goods'. From his home in north-west London he set out to remedy matters through the creation of a Shaw Society, making up for lost time by backdating its foundation to Shaw's eighty-fifth birthday. By means of lectures and exhibitions, bulletins and publications such as Loewenstein's own bibliography, this Shaw Society was to work 'for the creation of a new Civilisation based on Shavian principles'.

Far from flattering him, Loewenstein's invention appalled Shaw. 'I lie low and take no responsibility for the proceedings of the Society,' he made clear. 'My only hope is that nobody will join it, and therefore there will be no proceedings.' He feared Loewenstein would assemble a conventicle of evangelical ladies nosing out old documents he had supposed safely burnt, hunting up lost relations, pestering him with awful questions and unintentionally making his reputation ridiculous. 'Do not, I beg you, let me see your handwriting, much less yourself,' he advised Loewenstein early in 1943. '... Occupy yourself with your Society as much as you please, but not with G. Bernard Shaw.' However he could not altogether repudiate the wartime appeals of this German Jewish refugee to 'let me have your spiritual guidance' and 'absolve me from the sin of having formed the Shaw Society'.

Loewenstein centred his heart on the Shaw Society. It became the power base for all his throbbing plans. He would submit his ideas to G.B.S. who gave back unstinting advice: 'I deprecate any such gaffe, and will have to repudiate it publicly if you persist in it ... This shallow rubbish is exactly what it should be the business of a Shaw Society to explode ... May I beg you not to be a damned fool.' By the beginning of 1944 Shaw was calling Loewenstein 'an unholy terror: a man to be avoided beyond any other fellow creature'.

Within such reverberating descriptions there sounds a note of Shavian awe. Loewenstein was not easy to discourage. He had weathered a storm of frantic abuse and still trudged onwards. By the summer of 1944 he had advanced as far as Harpenden, three miles west of Ayot St Lawrence, where his wife was obliged to manage a house in lieu of rent. Buoyed up with the title of 'official bibliographer and remembrancer', Loewenstein put himself entirely at Shaw's disposal.

'I've now reached the stage when I can only sit back and smile at the Shaw-Wardrop-Loewenstein struggles,' Miss Patch had written that summer. But there was bitterness in her smile. The terrible rivalry between Wardrop and Loewenstein had left her with the feeling that 'I was to be pushed out or retired'. Everything was happening very differently from what she had imagined and sometimes, she admitted, 'I long to retire from G.B.S. and all his works.' But it was worth hanging on, worth bearing the humiliation of being condescended to by these newcomers as a mere typist because 'I think G.B.S. is beginning to get quite frightened as to what he has let himself in for.'

Loewenstein was an altogether different 'hero in fiction' from Wardrop – a Wellsian, almost Chaplinesque figure, middle-aged, bowler-hatted, still dapper though somewhat stout, with a homely moustache and forceful expression. While Wardrop was assuming 'not only the position of my literary agent but of my son and heir', Shaw noted, Loewenstein 'is resolved to be the oldest and dearest friend I have in the world'. His own job specifications were more ruthlessly modest. He looked for a superior 'errand boy' in Wardrop and a 'first rate office boy' in Loewenstein. Whenever Wardrop was given some menial task he looked 'amazed' and became 'infuriated'. But no task was too menial for Loewenstein who 'positively likes sorting papers and doing things that would drive you mad', Shaw told Blanche Patch. 'He gets round me and everybody else every time.'

Of these two contenders for Shaw's favour, Loewenstein appeared the more deserving, Wardrop the more attractive. By the end of 1944 Wardrop accidentally secured an advantage after Loewenstein's wife, refusing to live any longer in Harpenden, hurried her family back to London. 'I am freed from the daily visits of Loewenstein, the Jew,' Miss Patch exulted. But no sooner had she herself returned to London than Loewenstein reappeared in Hertfordshire. Released from his wife and child he was free for five days a week to walk the two and a half miles to Ayot from his room near the

Wheathampstead rubbish dump. He had overtaken Wardrop and was 'in daily attendance', Shaw reported.

Shaw hoped that Loewenstein could 'come to a co-operative under-standing with W[ardrop]'. But in the second week of February 1945, reacting to information he was given by Miss Patch, Wardrop 'burst in on me', Shaw wrote from Ayot 'with a suit case, frantic about Loewenstein, and announcing that he had come to sleep here and live with me to protect his property (ME) against the Jew'. After 'bullying him into comparative deflatedness if not into sanity', Shaw packed him back to London and drafted a note intended to resolve the crisis. Wardrop had 'proved impossible', he decided. ' ... The slightest encouragement turned his head ... A rebuff prostrated him to the verge of suicide.' Loewenstein had 'captured the tidying-up job by sheer fitness for it'.

As Shaw approached his nineties this 'scramble for the rights to be regarded as the only friend of an old celebrity who had no friends' was providing what one visitor to Ayot was to call 'a fantastic ending to the life of a very great man that is almost as sardonic as the last days of Swift'. Like coffin makers these friends jostled round, taking measurements, calculating odds, advancing terms while G.B.S. looked on quizzically at his own obsequies. From a virtuous benefactor he was transformed, like Osiris, into a god destined to be cut to pieces after death and scattered, ready for reassembly by the Shaw Society as a judge of the dead.

The three women had now largely combined their operations. Mrs Laden reported what she saw at Ayot to Miss Patch who embellished the news for Lady Astor who then blazed her way down to Ayot and confronted G.B.S. with the enormity of his crimes. 'I see,' he wrote after one of these confrontations. 'Having neither wisdom nor character I am to be placed in the care of someone gifted with both, selected by you, and willing to act as my keeper and office boy. Splendid.' Nevertheless, Lady Astor made potent use of Miss Patch's insinuations against Wardrop after he had legitimately taken away Shaw's papers from Whitehall Court ('there have been many thefts from the flats ... it might put him [in] a false position if anything couldn't be traced'). Though he would accuse her of being 'crazy about Wardrop', Shaw was amazed by the quantity of these papers when Wardrop drove them down to Ayot. 'F. E. L[oewenstein] had to pile them on the floor in the best bedroom,' he told Eleanor O'Connell.

Loewenstein was now being employed not only to complete his bibliography, but also to prepare the Shaw archive for posthumous presentation to the British Museum and the London School of Economics, as well as to take on various daily chores sorting out priceless 'old rubbish'. The vanload of papers brought by Wardrop was soon being absorbed into his empire and he hastened to prostrate himself before Lady Astor. 'My Lady ... Future Shaw-Historians (including the present writer) will be most grateful for your Ladyship's intercession. I beg to remain, your Ladyships obedient servant, F. E. Loewenstein.'

Lady Astor did not relish this falsification of her own motives. After twenty-five years in the House of Commons, she had recently been pressured into announcing her retirement from politics. 'I have said that I will not fight the next election because my husband does not want me to,' she told the newspapers. But she was finding this 'one of the hardest things I have ever done in my life'. In her torment she turned to G.B.S. What she did not know was that her family believed she had lost her grip on current politics and would be humiliated if she contested the general election in the summer of 1945. 'Winston should make you a peeress in your own right,' Shaw suggested. 'Ask him flatly to do it. Keep at him until he does.' But Churchill's response was silence, followed by an angry grunt.

At the age of sixty-six Nancy Astor was still teeming with energy. Yet her interest in public work had gone, she was without occupation and she blamed her husband for this deprivation. Seeking to regain a sense of 'positive authority', she entered aggressively into the domestic politics of Ayot. 'I don't like the company you are keeping,' she warned Shaw. '... Charlotte would rise in her grave. Mercifully I am not in my grave ... I must take active steps.'

Besides seeking cover from Lady Astor's heavy artillery, Loewenstein also had to dodge the crossfire from Mrs Laden who, being a war widow, 'has a particular antipathy to Germans', noticed Miss Patch whose own antipathy favoured the Jews. When Mrs Laden spotted Loewenstein roaming from room to room, peering into drawers, rustling wastepaper baskets, ferreting for relics in the store cupboards, when she caught him listening at the telephone or hovering behind her in the hall so as to butt in after she opened the door to visitors, her ire was kindled and she breathed out her dragon's flames. 'I dont know when I gave a man such a dressing down,' she wrote to Miss Patch. '... I will not have it when I am in charge of Mr Shaw's house.' He, who 'would have been Master of the Manor', was banished from her kitchen and, bringing a thermos flask and sandwiches each day, ate his lunch outside on the back porch. 'He seemed terrified so that's that,' Mrs Laden concluded: '... he has got his match. I am most able.'

This was a valuable letter and Miss Patch made several copies of it. But she did not share Mrs Laden's confidence. She had taken advice from Shaw's solicitor, financial adviser and accountant, and 'I dont think there is anything to be done about ousting the German as long as GBS is pleased with him,' she concluded. 'My one hope is that he will one day get such a drenching on his walk from Wheathampstead ... that he will pass out.'

But then, late in 1945, Miss Patch was provoked into uncharacteristically dramatic action after the third of Shaw's 'peculiar friends', Stephen Winsten, stepped forward.

Winsten was to fashion a career out of being Shaw's neighbour at Ayot. He was like a man 'who comes out one morning to find a meteorite in his back garden', Brian Inglis has written, 'and who turns out to be good at organising coach trips for the public to see it'. As 'lifelong conscientious objectors to everything conventional', he and his wife Clare kept an aesthetic vegetarian household and made their home 'a centre for wellknown visitors'. In their imaginations they lived through famous people, soliciting politenesses which, in the abundant retelling, swelled into exotic compliments. Shaw enjoyed occasionally calling round, meeting their guests (such as Gandhi's son Devadas), playing with their cat Fuzzia (a tortoiseshell rival to Mrs Laden's bright orange cat Bunch), sitting for Clare Winsten (who was a sculptress and painter) and chatting to her husband (who had been imprisoned as a youthful pacifist in the First World War). 'They are Bohemian Anarchists who have been in everything and know everyone in each Movement,' he wrote. Now that Apsley Cherry-Garrard had left Lamar Park, the Winstens were 'the only people in the village I can talk to or can talk to me'.

Of 'GBS's triplets – War, Win and Loew', it was really quite difficult for the three women to agree which 'parasite' (to use Mrs Laden's word) was the most absolutely dislikeable. Looking on from the sidelines, Eleanor O'Connell could see that Shaw used the Winstens 'to antagonise people, for they had trouble with all his near friends' including Wardrop and herself. Mrs Laden 'detested' the Winstens too and Loewenstein 'also hates them'. Miss Patch, however, generally remained loyal to 'the non-stop smoking German Jew', Loewenstein, as the most poisonous of them all, though when Lady Astor described him as 'a sweet, little spring lamb' in comparison to the 'Polish Jew' Winsten, she could not help laughing and spreading the amusement from her hide-out at the Onslow Court Hotel.

The Winstens' 'speciality is doing impossible things', G.B.S. reckoned. Stephen Winsten, for example, was set on being Shaw's Boswell. He had 'discussed every conceivable subject with him', so it was natural that 'many people had been pressing me to share my unique experience with them'. Inevitably Shaw had picked him out as 'the one to write about me'. Why, then, had he delayed so long? Certainly not because they had met recently. On the contrary 'for many years I desisted because I did not want to take advantage of a peculiar friendship'.

Winsten brought out what his publishers were to call three 'outstanding examples of Boswellian art', mostly chronicling the 'few hours every day' they passed together. After the first of these, *Days With Bernard Shaw*, was presented to G.B.S., 'he blushed like an adolescent; he loved it', Winsten could see. 'Whenever I called on him I would find the book beside him.' Alerted by Loewenstein to many concealed breaches of copyright, Shaw eventually picked it up and looked inside. 'In hardly any passage in the book as far as I have had time to examine it,' he wrote in *The Times Literary Supplement*, 'had Mr Winsten's art not improved on bare fact and occurrence by adding the charm of his own style to the haphazard crudity of nature.' Winsten admitted to being 'mightily amused' by his friend's letter. Shaw had been 'eager to help', he explained, and had written it to provoke sales. Indeed he even offered to draft 'a crushing answer', but Winsten 'brushed this aside' and afterwards 'went over the book most carefully with him and he was most apologetic'. The old man's memory, however, was no longer secure. Otherwise, when writing to others, he could hardly have forgotten his apology so far as to call the book 'a faggot of inaccuracies and inventions' and claim that its author 'is out of his element in Shawland'.

Winsten's element was pastiche. He was a sleight-of-hand anthologist who strolled through his acquired narrative as some editor-in-chief improving and rearranging Shaw's conversational quotations until they came to 'reveal more of himself'. Like Wardrop he grew into another version of G.B.S. Though beardless, bald-headed and half Shaw's age, he was sometimes mistaken for his neighbour in the village. This closeness enabled him instinctively 'to separate the truth from the fiction', though even in those works composed after Shaw's death 'to restore the magic of personal contact', the process was still imperfect and some specks of truth perplexingly fox his pages.

Unlike Loewenstein, who deferentially referred to Shaw as 'the Master', the Winstens traded in superiority, especially Clare who described Lady Astor as 'an American chorus girl ... grossly ignorant of how to speak to an English lady and a distinguished artist'. Though 'Inca', as Shaw called Stephen Winsten, had the pleasing style, it was Clare who was possessed of inspiration. Yet Shaw was something of a disappointment to her. It was true that he extravagantly praised her work, came to use her drawings rather than Topolski's to illustrate his books, paid for her statue of St Joan in his garden, contributed £2,000 for the education of her son at university and provided a job as theatre designer for one of her daughters. But she could not abide his lack of generosity, for it could only have been meanness that prevented Shaw from purchasing her portrait of him. 'I will not buy the portrait quite simply because I dont want it,' he had told her. '. . . I cannot cure you of valuing your work in vulgar plutocratic thousands of pounds . . .'

The history of the Winstens exacerbated Miss Patch's sense of devaluation. It was a double insult to her, since Shaw's Trust Fund of £2,000 for Christopher Winsten's education came on top of a grant-in-aid for another £2,000 to John Wardrop: while her salary had remained static over twelve years. She could not check her indignation – the injustice overwhelmed her. 'I have seen the wicked in great power,' she burst out to Shaw, quoting Psalm 34 Verse 35, 'and spreading like a great bay tree.' How had she merited such injury? Like Martha, busy about many things, she did not have the better part. When had she been brought the fatted calf? She had buried her one talent carefully for her employer and now, after half a lifetime, it was apparently to be taken away from her. One day she would tell her story – 'how I left home with less than £60 in my pocket and with that paid for my keep in Battersea as well as my tuition and examination fees at Apothecaries' Hall', she declared, 'Since passing the exams I have kept myself entirely.'

After financing the son of his old Fabian colleague Hubert Bland through Cambridge and the medical profession, Shaw had got in the habit 'of spending some of my spare money in that way', he explained to her. There had been school fees for the son of his friend Frederick Evans, the bookseller and photographer; and then for Peter Tompkins and now Christopher Winsten. 'They were all more or less Pygmalion experiments,' he told her. Admittedly the case of John Wardrop was rather different. There seemed nothing to do

'but either drop him or make a qualified professional man of him. He was willing to matriculate and qualify for the bar and fairly confident that he could get through the examinations. He estimated the cost as £5,000. I could not swallow that; but the experiment tempted me. I plunged and gave him £2,000.

'The result remains to be seen. Meanwhile he is offstage.'

But Blanche Patch was not appeased. With continual reference to Shaw's bank statements she kept her grievance hot. To each according to his greed seemed to be the Shavian rule. 'While lacking all the things required from a secretary,' she wrote, 'he [Loewenstein] possesses the racial knack of knowing how to extract money. In the past 18 months he has had about £745 from you in addition to his percentages, payments from newspapers for news of you and subscriptions from members of the Shaw Society.' What were all these peddlings compared with her issuing of licences, checking of royalties, vetting of United States plays in production, all of which had 'grown to such an extent that it might be said I am expected to manage a play-leasing bureau?'

'This is not meant as a complaint,' she ended. 'It is a feeling of resentment that you should look on me simply as a shorthand-typist.'

'My dear Blanche,' Shaw replied. 'You have given me a jolt at last.' In all their years together she had never seen anything in his socialism. Yet what more vivid illustration could there be of the curse of property, the absurd distortion of worth based on pay differentials and the disabling effects of inheritance than this unhappy scramble swirling round him since Charlotte's death? He had stopped raising Blanche Patch's salary, 'which has nothing to do with your merits' he explained, once she 'had enough for comfortably ladylike life, with a pension that would leave you rather more after my death'. Recently he had analysed her financial position with an accountant to ensure it was fair and generous. 'For emergencies and luxuries you always could depend on me for a grant-in-aid ... If you are pressed for money you have only to suggest a grant. Will that satisfy you? If not, what will?'

But how could it satisfy her? She could not say why it did not, nor what would make all the difference in the world. 'Dear, long-suffering G.B.S.,' she answered. 'I dont really want more money having quite enough for my modest needs – and, anyhow, you have always been generous in paying for things that dont come under my normal duties.' Money was a shorthand for something that could never be spelt out. She knew now that G.B.S. would pay her salary or pension whether she continued working for him or not. She also knew that he gave those jobs which had plagued her to Loewenstein so as to 'leave you free as possible'. But free for what? Now he tried to relieve her further by handing over the licensing work they shared to the Society of Authors. But there was no relief in such a loss and precious little comfort in his remedy: 'Why not prepare for my death by clearing out all my old rubbish and unwanted books?'

Hardly had Shaw recovered from Miss Patch's earthquake than Mrs Laden dropped an atom bomb on him over breakfast one summer morning by handing in her notice. For two years she had been living at Ayot like someone in solitary confinement subjected to trials by torture whenever Loewenstein or the Winstens arrived. It was too much. 'You have only to lift your little finger,' Shaw said, 'and I would double your salary.' But she told him off pretty smartly for that. 'When I want a rise I will ask for it.' She also refused his offer of a television set. But when Lady Astor gave her tickets for the Covent Garden ballet she became herself again, 'rejuvenated, smiling, and utterly repudiating the possibility of leaving me on any terms'. She needed occasional treats in London (spinning up in the Rolls), and also a Corgi motor scooter to take her to the shops and cinemas beyond Ayot. Then she found out that her salary had been doubled after all. 'She is worth the money [six pounds a week] – more, in fact,' Shaw wrote to Blanche Patch.

Money seemed to mean different things for each of them. 'Money is power. Money is security. Money is freedom,' declares the heroine of *The Millionairess*. For Shaw the love of good economy was the root of all virtue. Equality of income was equality of truth. In a bad economy, money was theft and made barren our lives. His parents had married for money; Miss Patch's fellow resident at the Onslow Court Hotel was shortly to be murdered, by John Haig, for money. Money was simply exchange value for some, and for others it was the freedom not to exchange what they valued. 'Are you fond of money?' the young doctor Harry Trench asks Blanche Satorius in *Widowers' Houses*. Around Ayot the women seemed less acutely fond of it than the men: Lady Astor pretty well took it for granted, Mrs Laden was not much exercised by it, while for Miss Patch it seemed more powerful as a symbol than an instrument for use – other people's money meant almost more to her than her own. 'The difficulty, as far as I am concerned,' she told Shaw, 'is that your other followers – Wardrops, Winstens and Pascal are all up against him [Loewenstein] and each other, lest one should get more money from you than the other.'

These followers did not see themselves as characters in a Pygmalion experiment; they behaved like investors receiving their interim dividend on a capital speculation. When Wardrop, following a term in the army, appealed in 1948 for another dividend, 'quoting my works to shew that I owe it to my character and reputation to give him £3,000 to start with in America', Shaw commented, 'I tore the letter up. He shall get no further echo out of me.'

This was refreshing news for Miss Patch. It was a relief too when in 1949 the Winstens decided to leave Ayot and go to live in Oxford. Shaw was to miss their company in the last year of his life but, as Clare Winsten made quite plain, it was really his own fault. He could have bought their bungalow for them or another place in the village. But all he did was to write on their behalf to the landlord, Lord Brocket. This was simply not enough. Indeed it was less than he had done for Loewenstein, she believed, and he was a mere employee rather than a fellow artist. 'I have not become a landlord, nor a mortgagee nor done anything for L[oewenstein] that I would not have done for Inca [Winsten] had the conditions been the same,' Shaw protested to Clare Winsten. '. . . Oxford is certainly the place for you, and so farewell, and if for ever, still for ever.'

But there was no farewell for Loewenstein. His empire expanded through a proliferation of Shaw Societies with their network of publications round Britain and in Canada, Germany, Hungary, India, Ireland and the United States. 'The Shaw Society of Argentina will shortly be established,' announced *Life Digest* in 1948. Loewenstein's bibliography expanded, too, over numberless cards of dense, sloping, semi-illegible notes which, in their swelling shopping-bag, would eventually achieve the status of a master-parody of scholarship.

It was as an assistant secretary rather than the flower of scholarship that Loewenstein strengthened his position at Ayot. 'So far, I should be poorer without him,' Shaw firmly told Blanche Patch at the end of 1945. The following year he printed a card announcing that since he had 'no time for any except the most urgent private correspondence', he must 'refer you to the Founder of the Shaw Society, Dr F. E. Loewenstein' who is 'better informed on many points than Mr Shaw himself, and will be pleased to be of assistance'.

Loewenstein never made the error of pressing hard for premature dividends. His pamphlets and papers, thickened with pedantic superfluities, added a little to the salary Shaw gave him but were principally in the nature of deeper investments in the future. He looked for pre-eminence in the posthumous phase of Shaw's copyright kingdom where he would be crowned Curator of Shaw's Corner and reign there as his representative on earth. To this end he sought a privileged place in wills that Shaw made in the late 1940s. But all G.B.S. finally guaranteed him was a favourable introduction to the Public Trustee (who as the sole executor would appoint the tenant at Ayot), the naming of him as his bibliographer and a recommendation that he be employed or consulted whenever this might prove 'desirable'.

Fearing that too much was left uncertain in this legacy, Loewenstein at last pressed Shaw to borrow money 'at $4^{1}/_{2}\%$ from my bankers and let him have it for $3^{1}/_{2}\%$ on mortgage', so that he could buy a house in St Albans. G.B.S. refused to do this, but in 1949 guaranteed a bank overdraft of £3,500 on the strength of which Loewenstein bought the house and renamed it 'Torca Cottage'. In the event of Shaw's death, he had balanced his risks between foreclosure at the bank and expulsion from Ayot. But still the risk was great and he attempted to add tenure to the prospect of tenancy by drafting a document guaranteeing him £500 a year during part of the 1950s. This document Shaw apparently tore up, but raised Loewenstein's salary to £500 for three years. 'He will have to take an overdose if he goes on pursuing you,' volunteered Lady Astor.

Lady Astor now looked on Ayot as her new constituency. 'Keep off, Keep off, Keep off, Keep off,' Shaw cautioned her. But whenever she was fuelled with fresh evidence of Loewenstein's 'disgraceful behaviour', she would take off for yet another devastating raid to remove him. All the village could hear the reverberating rumours of her tirades. 'She called him a leech and told him he was taking advantage of a poor old man.' But Loewenstein had 'as many tricks as a monkey' and never allowed Lady Astor's outbursts to disturb his ingratiating composure.

'If you will not let me manage my work and my household in my own way you must not come at all,' Shaw eventually retaliated. This letter brought Lady Astor down again at once, and almost weeping she showed Mrs Laden what G.B.S. had sent her.

'You need looking after far more than I do; and nobody knew this better than Charlotte, except perhaps your unfortunate secretaries. You must upset your own household, not mine.'

As Mrs Laden was reading, Loewenstein appeared and stood smiling in the background. Later, once Lady Astor had left, he quizzed her as to what exactly G.B.S. had written.

'I ... am rather angry with you for forcing me to put my old foot down ... As the keeper of a mental patient you are DISCHARGED.'

Though he had gently signed off 'Quite unchanged nevertheless G.B.S.' this marked the final battle in Nancy Astor's blazing campaign.

Miss Patch campaigned more discreetly. She had accepted that she could not interfere 'if GBS is satisfied with Loew's work'. But realizing that Loewenstein's long-term aim was to be appointed Custodian of the Shavian shrine, she set about sabotaging his chances with those who might advise the Public Trustee after Shaw's death.

Though Miss Patch almost lost her sanity when trying to live at Ayot, she still prized her special open invitation there. 'The place is so utterly dull for anyone but an ancient hermit like me that I cannot press visits on people,' Shaw wrote to her; 'but you are always welcome.' She had never dreamed of love in a village ('I care for nobody, no not I,' Shaw wrote; 'and nobody need care for me'). What she looked for was recognition as the First Lady in Shaw's life at the end.

Instead, she was to be granted another sort of privilege when, in his ninety-third year, G.B.S. gave her the use of his letters (and Charlotte's too if she wanted them) for a volume commemorating their thirty years together. Through the dry leaves of this ghosted memoir, in the shade of a man now 'bored with us all and eager to be gone', she would finally come to share his life.

Films, you know, are a strange business.
You can get in, but you can't get out.
Shaw to S. N. Behrman

For over two years following his film of *Major Barbara*, Pascal would
regularly 'go see Bernashaw'. Dressed in the costume of a country squire,
he liked to motor across from his rambling Tudor house at Chalfont St
Peter and extravagantly 'talk cast'. He fancied Marlene Dietrich in *The
Millionairess*, or perhaps Greer Garson 'my nearly wife' in *Candida*; he also
dreamed of fixing up Clark Gable and Cary Grant together in *The Devil's
Disciple*, and actually persuaded Ginger Rogers to appear in *Arms and the
Man* – provided a few dance numbers were added and the action moved
from Bulgaria into Canada. 'Do not argue with her,' Shaw responded; 'just
throw her out of the window and tell her not to come back.' The favourite of
all Pascal's schemes was a *Saint Joan* for which he had signed up Greta
Garbo. Unfortunately the idea took a fantastic turn after he tried to raise
money from General de Gaulle: 'instead of Garbo', Pascal reported to
Shaw, 'de Gaulle wanted to play the Saint himself'. If the heroine had been
the Blessed Virgin, commented G.B.S., 'they would probably have
suggested Miss Mae West'.

'We never met,' regretted Mae West, 'but I would have been happy to
entertain the gentleman.'

The speed with which absolutely nothing happened was often
breathtaking. But also the 'celerity with which you find a new plan of
campaign when the old one breaks down is very reassuring', G.B.S.
congratulated Pascal. By the autumn of 1943 an agreement for three Shaw
films had been signed with Arthur Rank.

Rank was looking for a lavish Technicolor challenge to Hollywood, but
he had to go along with the British government's suggestion that to make a
film showing the English burning a French patriot would be untimely. So
'we make *Caesar and Cleopatra*', Pascal announced. This sounded like the
perfect vehicle for a superspectacle to eclipse memories of *Ben Hur* and *The
Ten Commandments*. Rank assumed total responsibility for the cost,
gambling on drawing in large audiences from a war-weary public after
Hitler had finally been defeated. At the eleventh hour Pascal was in his
seventh heaven. 'But I pity poor Rank,' Shaw told him. 'The film will cost a
million.'

'John Gielgud is Caesar. Vivien Leigh is Cleopatra,' Pascal declared as he stepped off a boat at New York. 'Wonderful, no?' John Gielgud certainly thought it wasn't wonderful. Shaw wrote flatteringly to him of knowing 'no one who could follow Forbes Robertson in the part with any chance of getting away with it except yourself'. But Gielgud replied: 'I do not like filming, and should be terrified of risking giving an indifferent performance . . . So I must reluctantly say no to the film, and hope that you will let me do the *play* some time not so far distant. Then . . . perhaps the film could be undertaken with mutual confidence.' What this meant was that Gielgud disliked Pascal and had no confidence in him as a director. Six months later, in what critics were to call 'an utterly negative and phantom Caesar', Pascal cast Claude Rains who had taken the lead in *The Invisible Man* and *Phantom of the Opera*. Rains was an experienced actor who had played many leading Shavian parts at the Everyman Theatre, and was to become famous on film as the French Chief of Police in *Casablanca*.

Pascal's other choice, Vivien Leigh, was best known as Scarlett O'Hara in *Gone With the Wind*, but had recently filled the Haymarket Theatre for over a year in a revival of *The Doctor's Dilemma*. She longed to play Shaw's Cleopatra but was bound by an exclusive contract with David O. Selznick, until Pascal leased her with £50,000 of Rank's money.

The rest of the cast was largely made up from well-known Shavian performers (Ernest Thesiger as Theodotus, Esmé Percy as a Major-Domo) and Pascal's talent spotting. The fifteen-year-old Jean Simmons was led across the screen as a Harp Girl on a camel; Kay Kendall hurried around as a serving-maid; the future special agent Roger Moore stood in a red toga carrying a long spear; and Stanley Holloway marched back and forwards in the pre-Doolittle role of an Egyptian captain.

But there was some strange casting too. In his winking jewellery and shimmering purples, Stewart Granger played the aesthetic carpet dealer Apollodorus with 'many a flashing smile of perfectly formed grand piano teeth'. It seemed curious that Cleopatra never responded. Shaw had made it clear to Pascal that the sexual attraction must centre on Cleopatra's chief nurse Ftatateeta, not with the child Cleopatra herself. But Ftatateeta was played by a strong unromantic character actress, Flora Robson, who was soon to act Caesar's counterpart, Lady Cicely Waynflete, in a successful stage revival of *Captain Brassbound's Conversion*. Ftatateeta tells Cleopatra: 'Your life is changed. You are still my child; but to all others you are now a grown woman.' In this new film sequence the nurse also congratulates Cleopatra on having charmed Caesar. Then, promising to guide her 'until you learn how to guide yourself', she adds that in future Cleopatra is to have a bath every day ('You will soon get used to it, and love it'). The bathroom scene, a variation of Mrs Pearce's bathing of Eliza in *Pygmalion*, is a 'very ladylike piece of provocation', Lucy Hughes-Hallett remarks in *Cleopatra. Histories, Dreams and Distortions*, 'but it is sufficient to make an important change to the meaning of the play. Caesar has awoken Cleopatra's sexuality: she is "a grown woman" and she is being groomed to seduce him.' Seeking to steer between Rank's need for a love interest and Shaw's insistence that his work remain a play for puritans, Pascal converted Cleopatra's petulance and pouting into a flirtatiousness so infantile and ambiguous that even the Penal Code Administration of the United States could see no objection to it.

The shooting began on 12 June 1944, six days after D-Day. On 29 June Shaw visited the set at Denham Studios. Never had there been such a colossal or so splendiferous a sight as Pascal's Egypt. The interior of the Memphis Palace with its pseudo-granite columns each weighing two tons, its carvings of men with wings, hawks' heads, black marble cats, was to cover 28,000 square feet; while the palace steps and quayside were immense exterior sets constructed for the thousands of extras he had hired. All their costumes, the hieroglyphs and statues were copied from originals – even the formation of the stars behind the mighty Sphinx was designed by an astronomer. 'The film promises to be a wonder,' Shaw told Pascal. It was impossible not to be impressed. 'When I look back on my work as a young man with my colleagues in the theatre, it seems to me we were like children playing with wretched makeshift toys. Here you have the whole world to play with!'

Pascal had indeed created a wonderful toyshop for G.B.S. to play in. 'When it is all finished it will lick creation,' Shaw exclaimed. Placing a Roman helmet on his head, he posed for photographs. Then, as he left the studios accompanied by Miss Patch, a voice called out from the ranks 'Hail Caesar!' And all the soldiers stood to attention as the old man and his secretary passed by.

From the start, exotic jealousies blossomed on the imported sand and choked the production. Stewart Granger had begun an affair with Deborah Kerr and was dismayed to find that everyone knew of it when Vivien Leigh shouted out that he must concentrate on his lines rather than on Deborah. Her waspishness was probably connected to her unexpected pregnancy. 'Everyone is *very, very* cross & keeps asking me how I suppose they are going to make me look like the 16 year old Cleopatra,' Vivien wrote in mid-August. '... I think it is a very good thing really because they'll just have to hurry up with the film.'

Yet everything conspired towards delay. No sooner had Pascal rearranged the schedules to shoot Vivien Leigh's scenes first, than she suffered a miscarriage after running up and down the palace beating a slave, and he had to rearrange them all again. Blaming him for not employing a double, she tried to get Pascal replaced. Claude Rains, too, was refusing to speak to him. Amid the jungle of intrigues, his temper grew shorter, his accent more heavily impenetrable. 'I was surrounded by saboteurs,' he later grumbled.

There was also the war. Four days after filming began, the Germans launched their V2 rocket attacks. 'I am having the same gay start on the picture as I had with Major Barbara during the blitz,' Pascal wrote to Shaw. One flying bomb, exploding in a field nearby, damaged the Pharos set, another destroyed the dressmaking workrooms and a third almost killed some members of the production unit. Senior centurions changed from their armour into civilian suits and went off for Home Guard drill. Teenage girls, their costumes specially fitted, were suddenly collected by their mothers from the palace pool and taken to work in factories in the north of England. Supply depots closed; telephone lines came down; and then there was the weather. For weeks, and then months, the cast waited on the gigantic location-sets of ancient Alexandria for the sun to shine. Eventually they tried to film the summer scenes in winter. 'We had to clear away great slushes of snow,' Stanley Holloway remembered, 'and even then our breath was coming out in clouds . . . '

Exploiting Rank's belief that British films had been handicapped by 'a faintly claustrophobic indoor quality', Pascal persuaded him to move the location to Egypt itself. The enormous papier-mâché Sphinx was divided into sections, crated and sent down to the docks with all the other properties and costumes, and reassembled in the desert. As the British army reached the Rhine, Pascal came to Cairo. At Beni Ussef he waited, rather like Dunois in *Saint Joan*, for a tremendous sandstorm to subside so that he could produce a more filmic flurry of sand with the miraculous use of two aero-engines operated by the Royal Air Force. Two hundred and fifty horses had been placed at his disposal by the Egyptian government, which also supplied him with over 1,000 troops. Ephemerally dressed in the costumes brought out from England, they were charmed by the papier-mâché shields which, coated with a delicious sauce of fish glue, were quickly consumed, leaving the army defenceless.

Shaw continued to advise on all things: Caesar's smile, Cleopatra's accent, Britannus's eyebrows. 'In Heaven's name, no Egyptian music,' he appealed. Listening to the BBC's Third Programme he had kept his knowledge of twentieth-century music more up-to-date than his knowledge of contemporary literature, admiring Prokofiev and Sibelius, and praising Debussy, Schönberg, Scriabin and Stravinsky for usefully enlarging our musical material. 'Radio music has changed the world in England,' he was to write. Among British composers he was 'very much struck' by the originality of Benjamin Britten who 'had the forgotten quality of elegance'. The score for *Pygmalion* had been written by Arthur Honegger, that for *Major Barbara* by William Walton whom Shaw advised to add 'the effect of a single trombone sounding G flat quite quietly after the others have stopped. Undershaft pretending to play it. It ought to have the effect of a question mark.' But neither Walton nor Britten, nor even Prokofiev, was available for *Caesar and Cleopatra*. 'Write your Blissfullest,' Shaw urged. But Arthur Bliss took one look at Pascal and withdrew. Eventually Pascal contracted Georges Auric, a member of Les Six, who had written scores for René Clair's *A nous la liberté*, Jean Cocteau's *L'Eternel retour* and most recently Michael Balcon's *Dead of Night*. Shaw came to a recording session by the National Symphony Orchestra. When the Roman soldiers raised their swords and Caesar's galley sailed from Egypt at the end, Auric's music, he said, 'is almost Handelian'.

The end of the film coincided with Japan's formal capitulation and the end of the Second World War. During these fifteen months Pascal continued to change into his country-squire habiliments and, still looking very much himself, to go regularly to Ayot. He would bring stills and they discussed details of the next day's shooting.

'Have you killed Ftatateeta yet?' G.B.S. asked one day.

'Killed her yesterday,' said Pascal, with satisfaction.

'How did you manage her death-scream?'

'Like this,' said Pascal and began to scream at the top of his voice.

'Too high,' said Shaw. 'Lower. Like this.'

Then he too started to scream in a deeper register, and the two of them stood in the garden counter-screaming.

On 13 December 1945, exactly ten years after the signing of the *Pygmalion* agreement, *Caesar and Cleopatra* had its première at the Odeon, Marble Arch. Queen Mary attended, and there was the most chaotic traffic jam since VJ Day, so impenetrable that Pascal arrived too late to be presented. It was 'a good picture, in my opinion', said Blanche Patch. But many critics disagreed and, although the American notices were more favourable when it was shown in the United States the following year, *Caesar and Cleopatra* was to gain legendary fame as 'the biggest financial failure in the history of British cinema'. The Rank Organisation had estimated a budget of £550,000, but the shooting went on for nine months longer than expected and costs rose to £1,500,000. The loss was so disastrous that Rank cancelled his agreement with Pascal for two more Shaw films and the Association of Ciné-Technicians in Britain, passing a resolution of censure on Pascal for the 'inordinate length' of time taken to produce *Caesar and Cleopatra*, ruled that he be 'only allowed to make pictures in this country subject to special control'.

All this time and money had gone to make what Pascal himself later called 'a gorgeous bore'. Without Anthony Asquith, David Lean or Harold French to guide him, he had used his camera so inexpertly that the spectacular sets were reduced to stagey backgrounds for some ponderous acting. 'It is a triumph of technicolour and statuary, and makes quite an enjoyable illustrated chapter of Roman history,' Shaw concluded; 'but as drama it is nothing.' Unlike *Antony and Cleopatra*, it was never intended to be a love story (his job as screenwriter, Shaw later commented, was not to make love to people who could go home afterwards and do that for themselves); and unlike *Henry V*, also being made at Denham and starring Vivien Leigh's husband Laurence Olivier, it was not a patriotic adventure story. It was the 'educational history film' Shaw had once hoped to make with *Good King Charles*. But Caesar's education of Cleopatra and the development of his character vanish innocuously in a 'poor imitation of Cecil B. de Mille'. Shaw hated Hollywood with a sincere hatred, and Pascal had offered up the sincerest form of flattery. But it was Rank Shaw accused of having gone 'completely Hollywood'. In future they would have to 'rule him out of our operations'.

Whenever Pascal began speaking of these operations – *The Doctor's Dilemma* for Alexander Korda, *The Shewing-up of Blanco Posnet* for Mary Pickford – his face would glow translucently, his smile crack open and all past tribulations fall away. Yet he was soon forced to recognize that 'we have come to a crucial point . . . I have no studio space any longer at my disposal in England'.

He raced around Europe trying to raise money, find studios, sell his dreams. But the film world had lost confidence in him: what could be more ludicrous, for example, than his idea of a *Pygmalion* musical by Alan Jay Lerner and Frederick Loewe? Arriving in Italy he announced untruthfully that Shaw was to write an original screenplay on the life of Saint Francis of Assisi; stopping off in Malta and then Mexico he negotiated unsuccessfully for a film version of *Androcles and the Lion* featuring his new wife, the Hungarian actress Valerie Hidveghy. 'We must try,' Shaw advised, 'to secure an up-to-date Studio reserved (perhaps built) for our use exclusively.'

The ideal country for this Studio in the Clouds was Ireland. 'The climate, the scenery, the dramatic aptitudes of the people, all point that way,' Shaw declared. In his imagination he was returning to Keegan's holy ground, raising the tents, castles and embattlements for a final campaign against the goddams of Hollywood. They would have such revenges. For Pascal's optimism, too, rose over these imaginary Irish pastures. 'The Irish race suits my Hungarian temperament,' he wrote. It would be his 'predestination as an artist' to make *Saint Joan* there. 'I am ready,' Shaw wrote in support, 'to give Ireland the first call on my valuable film rights.' For their 'Irish principles' they soon received a wealth of praise from the Taoiseach, Éamon de Valera. But the millionaire founder of the Irish Hospital sweepstake was less bedazzled, and without him the enterprise sank.

Their adventures had been fun, but Shaw was too old for any more. He urged Pascal to find 'new friendships and new interests and activities', and to 'live in your generation, not in mine'. Yet this was now curiously difficult. 'Somehow, whenever I try to be unfaithful to you and do any other picture than yours,' Pascal explained, 'I have no luck.'

But Pascal's luck had gone. His marriage was failing; he was suffering from cancer; and it seemed to him there was 'an invisible conspiracy against me'. Each week he returned to Ayot. But he was clinging to a dying man, Shaw insisted, and must release himself. 'If you will not take care of your interests and think of your prospects when I am dead, I must do it for you,' he wrote on 3 July 1950. 'Don't force me to break with you for your own sake.'

Had Charlotte still been living it might have ended differently. 'She liked me and sold all my ideas to him,' Pascal claimed. Without Charlotte, G.B.S. had withdrawn into deeper isolation. 'I have in me the makings of a first rate hermit,' he acknowledged. 'Even a bit of an oracle.'

'Don't leave me in a vacuum,' Pascal had pleaded. But though Shaw refused to give the English language rights of his films to anyone else, 'I do not want to see you,' he wrote. 'I do not want to see ANYBODY ... Keep away, Gabriel. Keep away EVERYBODY.'

[5]

Only in dreams my prime returns.
Epigraph to *Buoyant Billions*

Shaw had originally given *Everybody's Political What's What?* the subtitle 'Machiavelli Modernised'. Besides linking him to the Italian playwright and political philosopher who got a bad name for separating private morals from political science, this was also a reference to H. G. Wells's novel *The New Machiavelli*. For the starting-point of this political testament had been Wells's 'Declaration of Rights', drafted at the beginning of the war with a committee of scientists and politicians, which he later amended and

479

repossessed in his Penguin book, *The Rights of Man, or What Are We Fighting For?*. Wells wanted to see the war converted into a social revolution. In *Everybody's Political What's What?* Shaw tried to provide a complementary basis for post-war social reconstruction. He had received his political education in the last two decades of the nineteenth century when government intervention, though setting limits to individual liberties, had brought great improvement to most people's lives. He took his lessons on reconstruction from the early years of the century. The problems of poverty and unemployment, homelessness, education and health would not be met, he believed, by a trickling down of money from the riches of privatization and profit-taking, but by collective action, investment in public services and leadership that encouraged pursuit of the common good. 'Parliament kills everyone except careerists,' he wrote. Politics for Shaw was simply the complicated business of 'organizing human society so as to secure the utmost possible welfare for everybody through a just sharing of the burden of service and the benefit of leisure'. He saw the ideological war of the mid-twentieth century being fought out between plutocracy and democracy, fascism and communism. Himself, he was a democratic communist. When asked shortly before beginning this book what was his chief aim in life, he had replied:

'My general effort has been to lay down a line of political conditions for the future. I am a Communist, but not in the sense in which it is generally misunderstood. I want to make man comfortable. He should have a reasonable remuneration for the shortest possible working hours. He should have more leisure for spiritual development and be educated for liberty.'

Everybody's Political What's What? is a ragged patchwork of autobiography, sociology, history and political economy, a rambling narrative of almost 200,000 words that repeats ideas he had given better elsewhere and then repeats itself. The book had kept Shaw company over the war years, helping to guard his solitude. He moves across its pages like a solitary wanderer through the abstract scenery of economic politics, from the false prosperity of *laissez-faire* to the imaginary riches of Social Credit. 'My method of examining any proposition is to take its two extremes, both of them impracticable,' he wrote; 'make a scale between them; and try to determine at what point on the scale it can best be put into practice.' The result was a geometry of realism with map and compass rather than sight and touch. His book advocated new thought, though 'there's nothing really new in it', he admitted. 'At my age one has nothing fresh to say.'

Yet this summary of a life's teaching was a prodigious achievement for a man who at the time of its publication was in his eighty-ninth year. When he warns us that in a commercialized world everything is bought and sold; reminds us that no state may be accounted civilized that has poor people among its citizens; instructs us that democracy must find a use for every person and not put him off with a dole: when he attacks fundamentalists as the enemies of religion and advises us to canonize our modern literature, then we can feel again a prophet of change conjuring his powers of transcendental reasonableness and compelling us to remake society in the image he has divined. His political schoolbook is most eloquent as simple rhetoric:

'Socialism is not charity nor loving-kindness, nor sympathy with the poor, nor popular philanthropy ... but the economist's hatred of waste and disorder, the aesthete's hatred of ugliness and dirt, the lawyer's hatred of injustice, the doctor's hatred of disease, the saint's hatred of the seven deadly sins.'

It was not as the adherent to a party line nor from his ideological commitment that Shaw had permeated the mind of more than one generation, but as a dreamer whose dream 'burned like a poem', Edmund Wilson remembered, '... stirring new intellectual appetites, exciting our sense of moral issues, sharpening the focus of our sight on the social relations of our world'. *Everybody's Political What's What?* is not a sacred text. But in occasional passages of his Child's Guide, when memories from earlier days invade this writing from 'my second childhood', passions stir and the embers glow.

'For some inscrutable reason there is a Shaw boom on just now,' G.B.S. reported in September 1944, the month of publication; 'all the booksellers have lost their heads in it.' Within a year the book had sold 85,000 hardback copies in Britain. 'When it is finished I shall be finished too,' he had predicted in a letter to Lillah McCarthy. Finished, all finished, nearly finished. On the last page he gestures towards the future, though the narrative would have '*to be continued by them that can*'. Yet in the prefaces he would add to *Geneva* and *Good King Charles* during 1945, and then in the articles, letters and self-drafted interviews he issued to the newspapers from his garden shed at a production rate of almost seventy a year over the next five years, he precipitated G.B.S. into the atomic age.

'Do not tell me that war profits nobody: I know better,' he wrote in *Everybody's Political What's What?* '... I have never written a line to start a war ... I feel the losses on both sides ... I have not the consolations and exultations of English patriotism; for I am an Irishman ... I loathe war.'

When asked by the US Office of War Information for a short statement on the liberation of Paris, he replied: 'Cheering, mafficking, bell ringing and the Marseillaise are appropriate; but they are not in my line.' He welcomed the defeat of Hitler and Mussolini, 'but I don't intend to celebrate at all', he told the *New York Journal-American* the following April. 'The war won't be over on VE-Day. It will go on for a long time against Japan.' On 6 August 1945 the United States exploded an atom bomb on Hiroshima. 'The war came to an end when the first atomic bomb was dropped,' Shaw stated in the *News Chronicle*. 'It is very doubtful if we have the right ever to drop another.' Another was dropped on Nagasaki three days later for experimental purposes, and even before Japan formally surrendered, G.B.S. had started on the track of Shavianizing the bomb.

It had had 'its momentary success' he wrote in the *Sunday Express* on 12 August, and now that the war with Japan was over we could see that the institution of world war was reduced to absurdity. 'The wars that threaten us in the future are not those of London or Berlin or Washington or Tokyo,' he believed. 'They are civil wars ... to say nothing of wars of religion ... fundamentalists and atheists, Moslems and Hindus, Shintos and Buddhists.' Since it was 'very unlikely that atomic bombs will be used again', he tried to move the debate from atomic warfare to atomic welfare. 'Atomic disintegration will some day make heat cheaper than can coal-burning,' he predicted in a letter to *The Times*. Yet our dreams of waking from that old power-grubbing in the mines into a dawn of nuclear power were 'frightfully dangerous'. For like the sorcerer's apprentice, 'we may still practise our magic without knowing how to stop it, thus fulfilling the prophecy of Prospero'. We would be better employed, he thought, discovering how to capture economically the power of the sun, the winds and the seas.

> I have bedimm'd
> The noontide sun, call'd forth the mutinous winds,
> And 'twixt the green sea and the azur'd vault
> Set roaring war.

Occasionally G.B.S. warmed his frail spirit in this awful glare. An atomic conflagration, flaming into temperatures 'impossible at Golders Green' and leaving 'nothing but a cloud of star dust', would 'end all our difficulties'. Like the prophetic *Book of Revelation*, this unveiling of things that might shortly come to pass was an apocalyptic vision of a time when there shall be no more sea and 'no more death, neither sorrow, nor crying, neither shall there be any more pain'. In the strange phase 'that follows second childhood', such thoughts comforted his faith in pure energy and reflected his unease in an unstable world where advances in scientific technology were not balanced by advances in human understanding.

By 1946 civilized understanding meant for Shaw an amnesty for all political prisoners and prisoners of war, without which 'we shall go on plundering and slaughtering and proclaiming peace where there is no peace'. Ever since a war crimes commission had been set up late in 1943, he had declared his opposition to putting the civil and military leaders of Nazi Germany on trial for crimes against peace and humanity. After the raining down of 200,000 tons of bombs on German cities and the gratuitous dropping of a second atom bomb on Japan, where could we find the spotless men and women to act as judges? Only by conspicuous humanity to the victims and the vanquished, he believed, could we stop hatred replacing the terror of war. When the verdicts and sentences of the first Nuremberg tribunals were announced in the autumn of 1946, Shaw gave his reaction to the press.

'We are all self righteous enough to enjoy reading denunciations of the condemned men as ... hideous freaks of German nature who deserve all they suffered and are about to suffer, and a bit more ... Instead of a row of countenances stamped from birth as murderous villains for exhibition in wax effigy in a chamber of horrors, what confront me are nothing but perfectly commonplace middle-class gentlemen who differ in no respects from any common jury or row of pewholders in the nearest church ... it is as clear as daylight that if they had been left in their natural places they would have been no worse than an equal number of Bayswater ratepayers ... Disfranchise them by all means. Disqualify them for the posts and powers they proved so tragically unfit for. I should let them loose as nobodies ... I believe they will be quite harmless and negligible. Why make martyrs of them?'

In the opinion of Mrs Laden, Shaw 'could not bring himself to believe in the German concentration camps like Dachau and Belsen. He was so very clever, yet he was a very simple man in some directions.' The darker the subject, the more light-hearted grew his tone. When he branded Hitler a 'rascal' or described the camps as if there were bad cases of overcrowding, his vocabulary became disablingly inadequate. 'It is sometimes better not to think at all than to think intensely and think wrong,' he wrote in the Preface to *Geneva*. Some thinkers were convinced that the hanging of war criminals was a final solution to war crimes. 'Ought we not rather to hang ourselves?' Shaw enquired. We were all potential criminals, he believed, and the solution lay in renewing ourselves through another morality. 'To be just and human to those we detest and dread: that is the counsel of perfection.'

In any event the job of restoring a half-ruined Europe could not be given to people with their hands full of war punishments for old defeated generals.

Shaw had supported William Beveridge's report on social insurance, which led to the Welfare State, as a modest instalment of socialism; he had prophesied Churchill's defeat at the general election of 1945, dispatched campaign testimonials to Labour candidates, and appealed for an understanding of the daunting reorganization that confronted Attlee's new government.

'Heaps of rubble to rebuild as cities ... wrecked transport systems to remake ... gangs of assassins, saboteurs and bandits, who were yesterday being encouraged as heroic patriot armies, to be policed; enormous debts to be paid as interest on barren capital that was spent on destruction and death ... Not an enviable job this for any party.'

The red-hot socialist who once delighted William Morris with his cascading oratory, who, thin as a whipping post, had marched with Annie Besant to Trafalgar Square on Bloody Sunday, made speeches at street corners with Keir Hardie, met Engels and known Eleanor Marx was a legend to many younger socialists in the late 1940s. But he was also a terrible and ubiquitous nuisance. Ordinary socialists felt embarrassed when they read him recommending Stalin for the Nobel Peace Prize. The Labour Party, too, was angered by his condemnation of its Front Bench in the House of Commons. He, who accused Churchill of being 'a century out of date', was himself 'an obsolete Old Pioneer', in the words of a future Labour Party leader Michael Foot. 'One of the foremost educators of the past,' Foot wrote, he had 'stopped thinking' in the early 1930s and become a 'blind seer' confusing his disciples just when many of his 'early dreams have started to be translated into fact'. He had bound himself into a dictionary whose terms of reference went back beyond living memory. 'I myself find it impossible to make myself understood,' Shaw agreed in a letter to *The Times* appealing for a Government Select Committee to settle Britain's political nomenclature. He wanted to see a thaw in the cold war and to see socialism, which was serious and dear to him, protected from the degenerating slapstick of parliamentary abuse. The difficulty of wording such messages without misunderstanding was sometimes 'an agony' to him. But though aggravated by age, this agony was not simply a matter of differing political dictionaries. It was caused by the defect of his qualities: what Eric Bentley was to call the 'bad fairy' that cast its spell over his gifts and brought forth the self-dramatizing G.B.S. who lived above human feelings.

'Anything I do is a Shaw event and not a political development,' he wrote in 1946. The last political initiative of his life was the Coupled Vote. Nearly twenty years after women had been granted the vote, the British people were 'misrepresented at Westminster' by twenty-four women and six hundred and sixteen men. No government, Shaw reasoned, could be democratic in the absence of women. His remedy was to make the electoral candidate not an individual but a pair, 'not a man *or* a woman but a man *and* a woman'. He called it the Coupled Vote. It was a psychological as much as a politically logical concept, uniting male and female, father mother. 'This, and this alone,' he urged, 'will secure the representation of men and women in equal numbers.' Having placed this democratic reform in the *Manchester Guardian* and his extended Preface to *Good King Charles*, Shaw handed over his plan to Lady Rhondda's Six Point Group. 'It is the right organ for it,' he wrote. '...for I want it to come from the Women's organizations and not from a man.'

'What I desire is that the Six Point Group should communicate their action to all the feminist organizations they know of in the world ... Only by making the couple the political unit by a Constitutional Amendment can 50–50 be achieved.'

At the end of 1948 the campaign was launched under the headline 'Revolutionary Political Idea' on the front page of *Wife and Citizen*. Shaw had hoped that feminists would adopt it as an expression of their own conviction. But the Six Point Group quickly ran out of money and the Coupled Vote receded into the history of Shavian fantasies.

*

The 'inscrutable Shaw boom' was also reverberating through the post-war theatres, led by a run of 312 performances of *You Never Can Tell* in the West End. 'It is the most exhilarating piece now playing in London,' wrote the *Punch* drama critic. The centre for Shaw's revivals was the Arts Theatre in Great Newport Street which, under the direction of Alec Clunes, was being spoken of as Britain's 'pocket-sized national theatre'. But in all sorts of other places, as well, Shavian fables and fantasies were springing up. *The Inca of Perusalem* received its first public presentation in London during Donald Wolfit's season of seven Shaw plays at the Bedford Theatre in Camden Town; Toynbee Hall was plunged back into the second or third century AD for a production of *Androcles and the Lion*; and George VI and Queen Elizabeth came to a showing of '*In Good King Charles's Golden Days*' at the People's Palace in the Mile End Road.

Then, a week after his eighty-ninth birthday, Shaw began writing new plays again. Playwrighting was an elixir, he sometimes felt, similar in its exotic effects to his mother's spirit communications on the planchette and ouija board. In any event, it gave him 'moments of inexplicable happiness' and when he tried to explain it to himself he was taken 'out of the realm of logic into that of magic and miracle'.

485

Buoyant Billions was a play he had started while sailing to Honolulu in February 1936. He briefly picked it up again in August 1937, then retrieved it and would continue to revise it until the middle of July 1947. In a short Preface he asked readers to forgive a 'trivial comedy which is the best I can do in my dotage ... At least it will not rub into you the miseries and sins of the recent wars, nor even of the next one.' On the contrary, it is a romance spun around the theme of avoiding warfare, a work 'not leading up to a murder, but to a thought', he told an interviewer. Shaw's thought suggests that the future lies not with the world-betterer (as Tolstoy's children described their father) but with those who can learn the universal secrets. After his educational history play celebrating the use of good manners he had characteristically come up with 'A Comedy of No Manners'. But the manners with which he was dispensing were verbal conventions that confused meaning and confined people to their social compartments. The characters in *Buoyant Billions* are neither rude nor malevolent. 'They are simply frank, which is the extremity of no manners,' Shaw explained.

In the first act a father and son, specimens of pre- and post-atomic cultures, confront each other. 'We resist changes until the changes break us,' says the son. But Mr Smith does not resist his son. He pays his fare to go round the world investigating the beneficial use of atomic fusion. By the second act Junius Smith has reached the Panama Canal, on the tropical shore of which he comes across a young woman, 'Babzy' Buoyant, who has escaped 'civilization' and charms the Punch-and-Judy-like snakes and alligators with her saxophone. They argue, but are so irresistibly attracted to each other that Babzy runs off into the third act and the safety of her father's Belgrave Square house in London. Junius pursues her and they both turn up in its curious drawing-room decorated like a Chinese temple in time to contribute to a symphonic discourse on death and its duties which is being conducted by the family solicitor. Shaw manipulates everyone's views to illustrate his harmonious belief that 'differences of creed must be tolerated, analysed, discussed, and as far as possible reconciled'. In the short fourth act, the billionaire, Old Bill Buoyant, gives his blessing to the marriage of Babzy and Junius, and this human fusion culminates in the surprise and wonder of a happy ending.

Though G.B.S. had let conversation thrive, *Buoyant Billions* was a dramatically weak comedy. 'My fans must not expect from me more than a few crumbs dropped from the literary loaves I distributed in my prime,' he wrote in the Preface to his next play, *Farfetched Fables*, 'plus a few speculations, as to what may happen in the next million light years...'

This 'batch of childish fables', written between July and August 1948, is a post-atomic fantasy in five conversation pieces and one monologue. Here the young man does not pursue the attractive young woman who is refusing to bring children into the modern world, but goes off to invent a peculiarly lethal gas. Having sold his terrible invention he retires to the safest civilized place in the world, the Isle of Wight, where unfortunately the first gas bomb is exploded. It is so devastatingly successful that human civilization is destroyed. From the Isle of Wight, which becomes another Noah's Ark, we see the Dark Ages return and values change. Scientists classify the fool as a genius, and human beings change into a breed of super-gorillas. Time moves on bringing with it the discovery that humans need not after all eat grass but can live on air and water. They evolve into a race of supermen, superwomen and superhermaphrodites, and eventually thought struggles free from the body. In the sixth and final fable a schoolroom of sixth-form children, throwbacks to the twentieth century, are visited by a disembodied mind. Impelled by intellectual curiosity it has used the power of evolution, 'which can go backwards as well as forwards', to appear before them as a feathered youth named Raphael and experience what is called the word made flesh. The lesson for audiences as well as for sixth-formers is that regardless of consequences the pursuit of knowledge and power will go on into the infinity of time.

Farfetched Fables is a toy version of Shaw's 'fascinating monster' *Back to Methuselah* and 'suitable only for little groups of amateurs', he wrote. For its first presentation he handed the play to the Shaw Society which, led by Ellen Pollock, directed by Esmé Percy and with futuristic designs by Topolski, gave it thirty performances at the Watergate Theatre in the autumn of 1950.

Farfetched Fables was to be posthumously published in Shaw's Standard Edition together with *Buoyant Billions*, which had been his last serious attempt to draw the bow of Ulysses, and *Shakes versus Shav*, a ten-minute play for puppets which he wrote during four January days in 1949.

Puppets had some natural Shavian advantages over human material. They could preserve an unvarying intensity of facial expression and sustain treatment impossible for mere living actors. 'When I first saw them in my boyhood,' Shaw wrote, 'nothing delighted me more than when all the puppets went up in a balloon and presently dropped from the skies with an appalling crash on the floor.' He gave his own puppets some glorious acrobatics – Shakes and Shav sparring and knocking each other down, while their champions Rob Roy and Macbeth dance and spin until Rob Roy cuts off Macbeth's head with a claymore and Macbeth marches off, head under arm, to the tune of 'The British Grenadiers'.

'Nothing can extinguish my interest in Shakespeare,' Shaw wrote in his miniature Preface. *Shakes versus Shav* marks the culmination of what the critic Sally Peters was to call 'Shaw's unending duel with the ghost of

Shakespeare'. In this playlet the 'real Shakespeare' is someone whose circumstances were also Shaw's, whose birthplace at Stratford he regarded as 'a supplementary birthplace' to his own in Dublin, and who 'might have been myself'.

Shakes is the darker face of Shav, a vengeful protagonist who introduces himself with excerpts from the soliloquies of his villainous Richard III and Macbeth, and whose aggressive impulses are usually hidden by the court-jesting mask of G.B.S. Their intertextual battle has Macbeth quoting Macduff from whose third son, Shaw had told his biographers Hesketh Pearson and Archibald Henderson, 'I am supposed to be descended ... hence my talent for playwrighting'. It is a duel between the contradictory impulses he had struggled all his life to reconcile. But Shaw is also one of Shakespeare's heirs and so after their jousting and rivalry comes a final plea for peace. *A light appears between them*, the stage directions tell us. Then the candle is puffed out and darkness embraces them both.

Shakes versus Shav was commissioned by England's 'chief puppet master' Waldo Lanchaster who sent G.B.S. 'figures of two puppets, Shakespeare & myself, with a request that I should supply one of my famous dramas for them'. It was performed at Lanchaster's Malvern Marionette Theatre during the 1949 Malvern Festival and in the same week as the first English presentation of *Buoyant Billions*.

The world première of *Buoyant Billions* had already been given the previous autumn in Trebitsch's translation at the Schauspielhaus in Zurich. 'The applause which after the first two acts was moderate only,' wrote the *Zürcher Zeitung*, 'grew considerably in the rest of the play and was very loud at the end.' The audience was applauding a lifetime's achievement, adding its own recognition to the rising volume of acclaim around the world. 'My vogue has never been greater,' Shaw remarked with some surprise. Throughout the Portuguese- and Spanish-speaking countries of South America and within the French- and English-speaking theatres of Canada and the Netherlands, around Scandinavia, in the Far East and Eastern Europe, as well as in the United States where his popularity had been rekindled by a spectacular *Man and Superman*, audiences were standing up and joining in this final wave of tribute.

Nowhere were his plays more enthusiastically welcomed than in German-speaking countries where most theatres had been closed down by Goebbels in 1944 as part of the 'total war' effort. Nazi attacks on Shaw's nihilism vanished and though he was praised for differing ideological virtues in East and West Germany he quickly regained his popularity throughout the divided country. Between 1945 and 1970 in the Soviet and Allied sectors of Berlin there were to be forty-nine productions of twenty-four of his plays – more than Chekhov or Ibsen, Gorki or Strindberg, Pirandello or Eugene O'Neill.

All this should have benefited Trebitsch who continued living in Zurich and was to crown his career as Shaw's translator with a revised twelve-volume edition of his plays and their prefaces for the Swiss publishing company Artemis. During the war he had appealed desperately for money to guarantee his debts at the luxurious Dolder Hotel in whose forest grounds during meditative walks over several years 'I was able to come to some sort of terms with myself'. But Shaw's replies were often delayed or misdirected since Trebitsch could not bring himself to reveal where he and his wife were living. 'I have no hope of this reaching you; but ... my silence is only apparent,' Shaw had written to Lausanne. '... Dont torment yourself with imagining that I am less friendly than when you were prosperous.' He had tried crediting money to the Trebitsches in Paris and asking the British Foreign Office to release German royalties through a neutral Swiss agent, but all these 'efforts to obtain permission to send them any [money] have failed', he admitted.

In his seventies Trebitsch did not know how to live otherwise than as a rich man and he did not really understand why G.B.S. could not help him. 'I cannot bring myself to write these heartbreaking letters – even to you – to say that I can do nothing,' Shaw had explained. '... You see, when I write to you I have nothing to say except what will depress you more than my silence, adding my troubles to your own. Be thankful when I do not write: it is the kindest thing I can do for you ... However, the war cannot last for ever.'

And when the war was over surely all their difficulties would be over too. 'I have not forgotten you and Tina in the least; you are very much in my mind at times,' Shaw wrote in 1945. But he was anxious to avoid seeing them. It was too late. He was too old. 'We must make up our minds not to meet again,' he urged.

But Trebitsch had already made up his mind to fly over, stay in a *hôtel de luxe* in London, and pay his condolences over Charlotte's death. He remembered Charlotte vividly: her devotion to 'long walks', her exploits as a 'brilliant cyclist', how she 'loved sport and enjoyed riding' like her sister who was 'one of the best-known women riders to hounds in the British Isles'. Trebitsch gloried in these memories and was eager to bring G.B.S. the comfort of them.

Shaw looked forward to his visit with dread. 'I beg you not to come,' he appealed. 'Food is rationed here ... Life is much less pleasant and healthy than in Switzerland. To come merely to see me is sentimental nonsense ...' But whatever the cost to Shaw or danger to his own health following a prostate operation, Trebitsch knew his duty. He came in the spring of 1946 and was in excellent spirits. It was six years since they had last met. 'You dont know what it is to be 90,' Shaw had warned him and it was true that Trebitsch, who was not quite eighty, did not know. He was surprised to see his old friend failing in strange ways. 'He was impatient, was afraid of falling asleep when he leaned back in his chair, and ... of showing this understandable weakness even in front of a familiar visitor as I was.' Other failings such as his inability to 'walk more than a mile, very unsteadily and leaning on a stick' were not without their advantages for the visitor. But Shaw's capacity for work had not diminished, Trebitsch noticed, nor had 'his passion to master the growing problems of a new world'.

For Trebitsch most of these growing problems were financial. His house in Vienna was returned to him later that year and he sold it to the Czech embassy. But foreign-owned funds throughout Germany continued to be blocked and it was impossible for either of them to draw on German royalties. Therefore, Shaw concluded, on no account could Trebitsch afford another sentimental journey to England. Trebitsch, however, had some important business to discuss, in particular a scheme for aiding G.B.S. with his income tax by taking over the burden of his income. 'As to guaranteeing your income I cannot even guarantee my own,' Shaw had protested. '... However, I shall not see you starve if I can help it.'

With this small encouragement Trebitsch was back again in the Dorchester Hotel in the spring of 1947 and, despite heavy Shavian defences, hurrying down all smiles to Ayot St Lawrence. It was a lesson to Shaw of how unwise he had been to offer any encouragement at all. He would never do so again. 'I am no longer the Shaw you knew,' he cautioned. He had changed from 'the vigor of my prime to the callousness & impotence of old age'. Over the next three years he went on scolding Trebitsch dreadfully. But like the ageing Falstaff, Trebitsch was ever-confident of some special favours from his old companion. He simply could not believe Shaw's 'hartless' words and responded to them like a rejected lover with spells of recovery in expensive spas. Exasperation rose in G.B.S. What was he to do except run out a string of terrible blowings-up and dressings-down?

'I am in my 90th year; and you write as if I were in my 19th ... Damn it, man, do you imagine that I am a pretty girl of 17 and you a blithering idiot of 18 ... There is nothing wrong with you except nerves ... Can you not bear the thought of my having any friend in the world except yourself? Pull yourself together ... I dont want to shake hands with you nor to contemplate your wrinkles ... I have no patience with it; and if we cannot remain good friends without it we had better not pretend to be friends at all.'

This bombardment abruptly halted Trebitsch at the Dorchester Hotel during his annual pilgrimage to England in the spring of 1948. The earnestness of his affection was being horribly tested. Despite an assurance from G.B.S. that 'I can keep my regard for you without seeing you for a hundred years,' he still sweated to see his friend for one last farewell, or perhaps two, or better still three. 'What do you suppose I care about last meetings at my age?' Shaw had demanded. 'I never see anyone now without being conscious that it is probably our last meeting . . . When the cat leaves the room it may never see me alive again.'

For Trebitsch, however, Shaw was 'the last, greatest and strangest hero of my life'. He would not be put off. He could not wait another year. In the early autumn of 1948 he slipped back into England and down to Ayot for what was to be their final meeting, leaving 'after a farewell that was kept light and airy'.

But their old business relationship had been broken up by the war and when Shaw advised Trebitsch not to 'speak or write to anyone over 40' he was trying to break his translator's dependence on royalties that must further diminish 'after my death, which is imminent'. Trebitsch could appreciate this. He had been happy to 'shuffle off the good fortune' of translating *Everybody's Political What's What?* For although these translations were 'close to my heart', yet 'at the same time I wanted to free my heart'. But like Gabriel Pascal and Molly Tompkins, he was lost without G.B.S. Shaw had been like a father to them all and they could not detach themselves. Many of Trebitsch's friends had died in the war and he felt 'alone upon this earth, except for the one man whom I still had: Bernard Shaw'.

What Shaw had called 'dismal money matters' rained down upon their last years. Trebitsch's inability to understand anything was exacerbated by Shaw's inability to remember anything and then additionally confused by their publisher's blurring of their business with that of the young American novelist Irwin Shaw. 'If imaginary riches make you happy, by all means imagine them; but they will never materialize,' Shaw wrote after the production of *Buoyant Billions* which he had made Trebitsch translate as *Zu Viel Geld* ('Too Much Money'). ' . . . You are too sentimental. And I have no money for you.'

Their misunderstandings wounded Trebitsch and maddened Shaw. 'For heaven's sake let us stop this correspondence,' G.B.S. implored, ' . . . and appoint an agent to transact our literary business.' This was the sad and irritable ending to almost fifty years of a relationship which Trebitsch still counted as 'the greatest event of my life'.

Well, goodbye, goodbye, goodbye, goodbye – all of you.
BBC television broadcast by Shaw on his ninetieth birthday

'Mr Bernard Shaw becomes a nonagenarian to-day,' announced *The Times* on 26 July 1946. He had hoped to 'spend the day as usual in solitary work and meditation', but was threatened by a bristling programme of celebrations. 'I am doing what I can to escape,' he pleaded. '... If I can survive it I can survive anything.'

He received so much food – cakes from admirers in Canada and Australia, grain cereals and molasses from vegetarians in the United States – that he felt like a pet animal. From India a Talisman and Talismi Powder arrived guaranteeing him 'the age of 125 years happily' if he followed the complex operational instructions with care. Congratulations converged on him in verse and prose by telegrams, letters, cards. The local postman at Ayot carried two large mail bags, heavy with good wishes, by the first post 'and much more followed by other deliveries', he remembered. 'Later in the day I delivered over 100 telegrams myself, and a boy was put on specially all day to deliver the several hundred others...'

There were tributes from Churchill and de Valera, salutations from the Labour Party and Trades Union Congress, sweets from local schoolchildren, greetings from anyone who had seen a play or read a paragraph. For a fortnight huge numbers of these messages and gifts went on avalanching into Ayot where Shaw desperately marshalled Loewenstein and Winsten to destroy the happy returns as if they were high explosives. Later he drafted a postcard imploring his readers 'not to celebrate his birthdays nor even to mention them to him. It is easy to write one letter or send one birthday cake; but the arrival of hundreds of them together is a calamity that is not the less dreaded because it occurs only once a year'.

A policeman had been stationed outside his house earlier that month to repulse enthusiasts. 'I am fighting off all photographers and newsreelers,' Shaw insisted. But a few wriggled through his defences. 'I hope I shall interview you again on your 100th birthday,' said a young journalist. 'I don't see why not,' Shaw answered; 'you look healthy enough to me.'

In the fourth week of July he uprooted himself from Ayot and came somewhat nervously to Whitehall Court – not for the celebrations, he explained, but to let the staff at Ayot enjoy a short rest. 'My world contracts to my garden as I grow older,' he told one of his neighbours. 'London offers me nothing but taxis and buses to run over me.'

It was impossible to overlook the birthday festivities. Newspapers and magazines were crammed with photographs, profiles, poems, interviews and editorials 'aglow not only with the warmth of a universal admiration but with the heat of latent controversial fires'. A *Times* leader praised his 'brilliantly divagating thought' which by some miracle of creative stamina was still disturbing complacent attitudes. He was 'the greatest living pamphleteer writing in English' and a playwright who 'in the teeth of critical discouragement' had used the long prose speech to create 'a serious audience' in the theatre. 'Mr Shaw is so vast a subject,' concluded *The Times*, 'that none will envy the ultimate biographer.'

He had been asked by Oxford University Press to choose the five hundredth title in its World's Classics series from among his own work and he chose his masterpiece of wishful thinking, *Back to Methuselah*, using the chance to revise the play and its Preface and to attach a postscript. Besides this new volume and the million Penguin paperbacks, there was also a symposium, *G.B.S. 90*, in the bookshops, compiled by Stephen Winsten and containing memories from old friends such as H. G. Wells and Sidney Webb, Gilbert Murray and Max Beerbohm, together with surveys of his plays and music criticism, examinations of his ideas on phonetics, economics and education by C. E. M. Joad, J. D. Bernal and others, and statements of literary goodwill from J. B. Priestley, Maynard Keynes, Aldous Huxley.

There was more. On stage the Arts Theatre was playing *Don Juan in Hell*; on radio the BBC produced *The Man of Destiny* and later broadcast a Shaw Festival for its new Third Programme; in the evening Shaw appeared on television complaining that his popularity 'shews that I am getting old and feeble and nobody is afraid of me any longer'.

And again there was more, still more. At the National Book League his ninety years were being reviewed in an exhibition of inscribed first editions, actors' rehearsal copies, first-night programmes as well as woodcuts, stage designs, caricatures, busts, posters, portraits. 'I may drop in when it is all over,' Shaw notified the Poet Laureate, John Masefield, whose poem 'On the Ninetieth Birthday of Bernard Shaw' was to be printed in *The Times* the following day; 'but I am doubtful as to how much I shall be able to get about in London.' He did drop in during the late afternoon and was cheered and flash-photographed for three-quarters of an hour. 'Now you have seen the animal,' he remarked on leaving.

Such an adulatory revival of his past focused awkwardly on a writer forever dissenting from the unanimous verdicts of the present and still resolved to establish his unsentimental vision of the future. As his dramatic vitality waned, his absorption into contemporary English politics intensified

493

and he gave warning that he would continue to offer the native Irishman's 'objective view' of England: 'that "distressful country" in whose service I am a missionary'.

At the prompting of the Irish trade unionist James Larkin, he had been offered the Honorary Freedom of Dublin and replied in his letter of acceptance: 'Dublin alone has the right to affirm that in spite of my incessantly controversial past and present I have not disgraced her.' He signed the Scroll of Freedom presented by the Irish ambassador on his birthday, but put off an official delegation which planned a special ceremony with the plea that it would find only a poor dotard who 'after a pitiable effort to rise to the occasion' would 'fall asleep in their faces'.

'If I yield an inch,' he had written to William Maxwell, 'I shall simply be killed with kindness, well meant but lethal.' A little later in the year, however, he did accept the Honorary Freedom of the Borough of St Pancras on whose vestry and borough council he had worked, and used the occasion to argue for the virtues of a local government system independent of central party political control.

'I need no publicity: I have already much more than my fair share of it,' Shaw wrote to the Liberal peer Lord Samuel a few days later. Public attention had once been his compensation for meagre family affection. Now it had expanded, he sometimes felt, into a substitute for political achievement. A few of the gifts touched him: the golden shamrock sent over by a Dublin dustman ('It is on my watch chain, and shall remain there until I myself drop off it') and the little anthology of praise later edited by his 'Honorary Proof-Reader' Allan M. Laing ('I did not know there was so much kindness in the world'). But he felt sickened by the general fanfare. The successful man 'is the one who has people doing what he wants them to do', he had told a journalist ten years earlier. ' ... But they're always doing what I don't want them to do.' He would have traded all this publicity for an Act of Parliament legalizing the Coupled Vote, and he took more pleasure from legislation in the Dáil to municipalize his Carlow estate than anything else that happened this year.

'I wish you were not too far off to be within my reach,' he had written earlier in the year to Sidney Webb. Their old colleague Sydney Olivier had died within a few months of Beatrice and Charlotte, leaving Webb and Shaw the last two Fabian musketeers. 'So let us hold on as long as we can,' G.B.S. exhorted his friend. The atom bomb appeared to have heightened the Shavian view of our political immaturity. But at a time of life when, in the world of *Back to Methuselah*, their careers would have been dawning, Webb's stroke had put an end to his work while G.B.S. was so 'groggy on my legs' that he staggered 'like a drunk' whenever he stepped outside without a stick.

494

'Everywhere I gained something,' Webb had written of their peripatetic work together. On 13 October 1947, in only his eighty-ninth year, he died at Passfield Corner. 'I hope we have been a pair of decent useful chaps as men go,' G.B.S. wrote to him in his last letter; 'but we have had too short a lifetime to qualify for real high politics.'

For the last surviving member of the Fabian Old Gang there was much day-to-day campaigning still to get through. He wanted a national basic income as part of a programme of communism with 'a top dressing of private enterprise', he wanted divorce law reform ('Why should a marriage licence be held more sacred than a driving licence?') and he wanted full rights and responsibilities for aliens residing permanently within the Commonwealth. Despite being faced with national bankruptcy after the war, Britain possessed a more promising future, it seemed to him, than when he had arrived in the country seven decades earlier. But if the discrepancy between promise and performance widened too far there would be a popular reaction against socialism. In particular Shaw feared that the bellicose personality of Ernest Bevin, so much more powerful in the public imagination than the mouselike Attlee, would turn democratic socialism into rabid trade unionism. As Secretary of State for Foreign Affairs, Bevin appeared to have little liking for diplomacy, but enjoyed knocking out his overseas opponents. 'His ability is so commanding and his record so creditable that nobody in the Cabinet can stand up against him,' Shaw warned left-wing readers of the *Daily Worker*.

'...For him Parliament is not the House of Commons but the Trades Union Congress, a monstrously undemocratic body in which trade union secretaries are the most absolute despots on earth, and old men sleep until they are wakened up to produce their union cards and cast millions of votes single-handed.

'This is neither Democracy nor Socialism: it is Capitalism in its last ditch in Transport House. To emphasise it Mr Bevin renews his declaration of irreconcilable hostility to Communism, thus playing it up for a Capitalist war on the U.S.S.R.'

In 1949 Shaw brought out a revised and expanded version of the autobiographical miscellany *Shaw Gives Himself Away* which the Gregynog Press had published in a limited edition ten years earlier. 'I have changed the title to SIXTEEN SELF SKETCHES,' he wrote to his American publisher, 'partly because there must be no suggestion of a full dress Autobiography, and also because a title must be easy to speak, easy to spell, and unmistakeable to pronounce.' The new title gives helpful evidence of Shaw's innumeracy since, as Brigid Brophy first noticed, the book contains seventeen self sketches. Then in his ninety-fifth year he completed the last of his ephemeral works for publication: a series of doggerel verses accompanying some blurred photographs of Ayot. *Bernard Shaw's Rhyming Picture Guide to Ayot* is addressed to an imaginary guest whom once

'disposed of, home I wend to
My proper business to attend to.'

Actors and authors liked coming down occasionally to see him in the belief that G.B.S. occasionally liked seeing them. 'Especially actresses,' the actress Lilli Palmer added. But when she asked him after an hour if he wanted her to 'stay a little longer, Mr Shaw', he answered truthfully: 'No. I'm always glad when people go.' Although he conducted a miniature rehearsal of *Buoyant Billions* in his garden, he put off the American showgirl Frances Day, who took the lead, from coming back to Ayot alone. 'When one is still an elderly youth of 70 romance is still possible with Old Men's Darlings,' he wrote to her. '...But for old skeletons of 90 they are unnatural, abhorrent, unbearable ... keep the old skeleton out of sight and touch as much as you can. His skinny presence is best left to itself. Only in dreams is he young. Do not disturb them.'

Burlesques were less disturbing to him than gallantries. In his young nineties he performed a garden pantomime with Danny Kaye and, his eyes sparkling, sang a duet from *Aladdin* with Gertrude Lawrence.

'Come, little girl, for a sail with me
Round and round the moon.
No one to see us behind the Clouds
Oh, what a place to spoon.'

'My voice is no penny whistle now!' he remarked to Kingsley Martin after bursting out with an aria from Verdi in the middle of the lane outside his house. His speaking voice, too, surprised some visitors: 'I had not expected the strong Irish brogue,' wrote James Lees-Milne. 'This peasant origin makes him all the more impressive ... When he smiles his face softens and becomes engaging.' To the novelist William Saroyan he appeared a 'sweet old gentleman ... a butterfly with a white beard'. To a journalist from *Palestine Post* he looked like 'a very old and rather dangerous bird ...'

'Shaw is shockingly thin now. The famous beard has shortened ... His skin is like parchment. The whole figure seems more like an echo of itself and a reflection of a famous picture.

'But ... you see the eyes of a youth. Blue, radiating, quick and alert, they are the real Bernard Shaw ... the great firebrand ... who has gradually become an object of admiration and love, first in the world and then in his country.'

Once 'erect as an exclamation point' he now stooped slightly, 'hanging his head when he talks as though it were too heavy for him', another visitor observed. 'Wobbling from subject to subject' much as he 'swayed in his walking', he was Britain's legendary patriarch who 'has somehow kept his wit and his brilliance, above all his gaiety', Alan Moorehead noticed. 'It is his *extreme* niceness that affects the most.'

Despite this aura of benevolence many of his visitors felt like invaders in the separate world he inhabited. He 'looked more alone than any man I have ever seen', wrote the American drama critic John Mason Brown. Even Nancy Astor conceded that he was happier by himself. 'It was sometimes a trouble to him to be with other people,' St John Ervine noticed. '... he did not need people.' 'I can always tell myself stories,' he explained, 'and so am never lonely.'

Sometimes he would listen to other people's stories. Not long after Charlotte's death he had received the first instalment of a remarkable story-in-letters by Margaret Wheeler, a thirty-five-year-old housewife from Workington in Cumberland. 'I wanted an intelligent man to discuss things with,' she later said, 'so I deliberately picked him up.' Her only chance, she reckoned, was to choose something close to his heart. So she wrote to him about phonetic alphabets. It was a sprat to catch a whale. 'I should like to give you my thanks now, anyway,' she ended her letter, 'for the enjoyment of reading and the stimulus of thought you have given to me many and many a time.'

'Not at all a bad beginning this of yours ... Keep at it: it's a good indoor hobby,' Shaw answered. He was referring to her alphabet, but his words would fit their correspondence. For with her next letter she began unburdening herself of an obsession that had been haunting her for seven years. 'My problem is concerned with my little daughter, whom I believe to have been swopped by accident in the Nottingham nursing home where she was born, for another child born at the same time ... I have been endeavouring to persuade the other parents to join with me in scientific tests ... and they have refused ... on the grounds that they are fond of the child they have and don't wish to give her up.'

Margaret Wheeler was a strong-willed, independent-minded, working-class woman, full of energy and argument, and 'in the grip of a passion to know about things'. In short, she was a species of genuine Shavian. She placed G.B.S. on the throne of a latter-day Solomon. 'Altogether a very difficult case,' he summed up, 'for which there is no harmless solution

497

possible.' But she was determined to find a solution. He warned her 'not to prove your case legally and publicly', reminded her that 'unsuitable arrangements sometimes last longest', suggested the possibility of a 'reciprocal adoption' only if both sets of parents agreed it was best for the children, and counselled her to be 'content with the establishment of a private understanding between the two families'.

It was all sensible advice, though 'my letters will not help you', he promised. Yet they were soon doing her 'no end of good' and she felt justified in having appealed to him. 'I am serene in my confidence that you will not do anything against the interests of the two children whose future you have helped me to consider,' she assured him.

She did not want his money. She did not want to marry him – with five children and a husband she was sufficiently married already. 'I am perfectly happy just writing to you,' she told him. 'I cannot go on writing for ever,' he protested, 'and really should not indulge in this correspondence at all'. Yet he was interested by her curious situation. Orphans, foundlings, outcasts, changelings had always fascinated him. 'The serial keeps up its interest,' he admitted. 'I am still interested,' he added two years later.

This was partly because Margaret Wheeler was a natural writer. Shaw recommended her to take it up professionally. 'I don't care a damn about seeing myself in print,' she replied. ' . . . I like having you around to practise on.' Writing to G.B.S. was like talking to someone over a garden wall. 'I should never have written to you in the first instance had I not felt completely safe with you.'

They exchanged photographs. He let her know she was 'an attractively intelligent woman . . . able to get round bank managers, solicitors, literary celebrities, and susceptible males generally with great ease; and you know it. You are what experienced men call a dangerous woman. This does not matter with me: I have been a dangerous man myself.' But looking at his photograph she could not see that he was dangerous at all. 'I'm not in the least frightened,' she boasted.

She was young enough to be his grand-daughter. 'But pray don't be alarmed; I am not going to propose to be a grand-daughter to you . . . I have heard of people who have been rash enough to make odd proposals to you, and of what happened to them.' She was wonderfully undemanding, 'a joyous creature, a charmer', and she laughed so much at what he wrote and was so immensely bucked up that she 'felt like charging everybody else sixpence to look at me'.

So they kept up their indoor hobbies, teasing and scolding each other and covering every subject from marriage and food rationing to hospital procedures and the control of floods. Over six years this correspondence unfolded into the story of a woman's life isolated and over-burdened with housework in post-war northern England. Writing to Shaw she could put that problem of the jactitated children to the back of her mind, post off her medical and marital problems, and relieve for a time 'the very strong feeling I carry around with me of being utterly completely and absolutely alone'.

Shaw's own letters were often echoes from the past where ghosts of friends long dead played out their comedies again for a new companion. 'As long as I live I must write,' he had said. His letters to 'Dear Mrs Wheeler, not to say Margaret or Maggie or Meg' became part of this process of living, lightening a little the solitude of these last years.

*

These last years were framed by two controversial wills. The net value of Charlotte's estate amounted to £150,976 13s. 9d. out of which £49,702 9s. 5d. was to be paid in death duties. Apart from a number of small annuities for the servants, there was also a legacy of £1,000 to Sidney Webb and £20,000 to Charlotte's niece. By selling some of his own investments Shaw had paid these legacies almost immediately. He was appointed joint-executor with the National Provincial Bank and given a life interest in Charlotte's estate. But since this would simply have raised his own supertax, he relinquished his role as beneficiary and strengthened Charlotte's residuary estate.

After Shaw's death, Charlotte's money was to be left in trust to an Irish bank for the development of Irish culture. The National City Bank was directed to use the residual £94,000 to make grants to institutions having as their objective 'the bringing of the masterpieces of fine art within the reach of the Irish people', the teaching of 'self control, elocution, oratory, and deportment, the arts of personal contact, of social intercourse', and the establishment of a 'Chair or Readership' at an Irish university to give instruction in those subjects. It was Charlotte's version of the *Pygmalion* experiment.

What incensed potential beneficiaries were the reasons Charlotte advanced for these charitable endeavours. In the course of a long life she had been given many opportunities for observing how 'the most highly instructed and capable persons' had their efficiency defeated and their authority derided by 'their awkward manners ... by vulgarities of speech and other defects as easily corrigible by teaching and training as simple illiteracy', and how the lack of this teaching and training 'produces not only much social friction but grave pathological results'.

The will had been partly worded by Sidney Webb (seldom singled out for his tact), but the blame was loaded on to G.B.S. His international fame and popularity became spurs to Irish derision. People lamented that the bright hopes of a well-intentioned, sweetly-nurtured, not-to-say-gently-connected Irish lady should have been tarnished by a 'counterfeit Irishman' with a 'bad temper'. G.B.S. was pictured as a wicked wizard changing her gift into an insult. In *The Irish Times* Myles na Gopaleen was to elucidate how Mrs Shaw 'found herself married and living in the same house with a conceited boor of an Irishman ... the very strange will is her posthumous gesture of revenge'. The American-Irish Historical Society stated in the *New York Times* however that Mrs Shaw had been 'undoubtedly influenced by the timidity and awkwardness of her husband ... She did a wonderful job on him'. And the *New Yorker* concluded: 'anybody who thinks the Irish can be taught self-control is a crazy optimist, and anybody who thinks they need to be taught elocution is just plain crazy'. But Shaw maintained that the will had been 'misunderstood only by simpletons who thought they were being accused of eating peas with a knife'. Those who made fun of it, he suggested, were proving their need for deportment and self-control so convincingly that he was seriously thinking of doing the same thing for the English.

In the event, he did something many English people felt was almost equally provoking.

Shaw's last will, which he completed shortly before his ninety-fourth birthday, has connections with Charlotte's over its disposal of papers, its complementary annuities to servants (with a clause allowing for inflation) and a charitable trust challenging England to mind its language. It is an extraordinarily public-spirited document giving works of art by Augustus John, Rodin, Strobl, Sargent, Troubetzkoy to public galleries and theatres in Britain, Ireland and the United States, his furniture to the National Trust, papers of sociological interest to the British Library of Political Science at the London School of Economics, and an enormous collection of literary papers to the British Museum 'where all the would-be biographers can find it and do their worst or their best'.

'Drafting the will has been more trouble than ten plays,' Shaw wrote happily to Sydney Cockerell. The most original feature was its disposal of his royalties over the posthumous fifty-year copyright period. He directed that these earnings should be used during the first twenty-one years following his death for the creation and promotion of a new phonetic alphabet containing at least forty letters, 'one symbol for each sound'. Over the following twenty-nine years his copyright income was to be shared equally by three residuary legatees: the National Gallery of Ireland 'to which I owe much of the only real education I ever got as a boy in Eire'; the Royal Academy of Dramatic Art (on whose Council he had served for thirty years) representing the theatre where he had derived his livelihood; and the

British Museum 'in acknowledgement of the incalculable value to me of my daily resort to the Reading Room of that Institution at the beginning of my career'.

Shaw was convinced that unless phonetic spelling was introduced with sufficient boldness the reform would die of ridicule. By appointing the Public Trustee as his executor and making him responsible for challenging English orthography, he hoped to give his proposal additional authority. He knew that people, 'being incorrigibly brain lazy, just laugh at spelling reformers as silly cranks'. So he attempted to reverse this prejudice and exhibit a phonetic alphabet as native good sense while making traditional spelling sound foreign and absurd. 'Let people spell as they speak without any nonsense about bad or good or right or wrong spelling and speech,' he recommended. He would writhe and wrinkle his face into the most terrible shapes while pronouncing the word 'though' with six letters instead of two, and confess the impossibility of discussing it 'as it is outside the range of common sanity'. He also liked to explain that what was wrong with the atomic bomb was its entirely senseless last sign which 'suggests an absurd mis-pronunciation of the word, exactly as if the word "gun" were to be spelt "gung" '. But when an enthusiastic convert suggested that 'ghoti' would be a reasonable way to spell 'fish' under the old system (*gh* as in 'tough', *o* as in 'women' and *ti* as in 'nation'), the subject seemed about to be engulfed in the ridicule from which Shaw was determined to save it.

He had become interested in English spelling reform as early as page 102 of the first volume of this biography, where he had met the phonetic enthusiast James Lecky ('jeemz leki'). For a time he tried respelling the old alphabet in his plays to convey the pompous intonation of the vulgarian Burgess in *Candida*, the flavour of Kerry brogue underlying Hector Malone's international American in *Man and Superman*, the rough working-class accent of Bill Walker in *Major Barbara* and, most unsuccessful of all, the fluent nasal delivery of Drinkwater's sea-and-city slum talk in *Captain Brassbound's Conversion*. 'The fact that English is spelt conventionally and not phonetically makes the art of recording speech almost impossible,' he complained in his notes to that play. When he came to *Pygmalion*, which romanticized the science of phonetics, he quickly abandoned his 'desperate attempt' to represent Eliza Doolittle's broad cockney speech with transliterated 'nu speling' because it looked illiterate, sometimes even indecent, and was 'unintelligible outside London'. All these experiments confused readers and baffled actors. 'I have given up trying to write these dialects phonetically,' he stated in 1936: 'it cannot be done with our alphabet.'

This failure grew into one of the 'everyday workshop grievances' which ventilated his alphabetical campaign. His attempt to overcome the clumsy,

501

pseudo-etymological misspelling stabilized by Dr Johnson's latinate dictionary – scaling 'the Johnsonian mountain', as he called it – had begun as early as 1901 with letters to the *Morning Leader*. Five years later he arrived at the essential conclusions for a better word notation that were to be expressed in his last will. We must 'enlarge the alphabet until our consonants and vowels are for all practical purposes separately represented, and defined by rhyming with words in daily use', he wrote to *The Times* in 1906. '... The new letters must be designed by an artist with a fully developed sense of beauty in writing and printing.'

From his years policing pronunciation for the British Broadcasting Corporation he knew that his battles with the 'mob of spelling cranks' would be hard and long. 'The only danger I can foresee in the establishment of an English alphabet is the danger of civil war,' he wrote. '... Still, we must take that risk.' Like any good commander he represented victory as assured. 'We cannot get away from phonetic spelling, because spelling is as necessarily and inevitably phonetic as moisture is damp.' Though his tactics were to change significantly, he remained consistent. 'The English have no respect for their language, and will not teach their children to speak it,' he objected in the 1912 Preface to *Pygmalion*. In 1927 he advised the Simplified Spelling Society that 'we must have an English alphabet and a new script to match. And the script must not be shorthand' which was merely a code of ticks and dashes for jotting down some of the sounds uttered by public speakers. By 1938 he was writing to the journalist Hannen Swaffer: 'I should like to do something for the English language.' But after forty years he had concluded that 'no British Government will ever be stirred to action in the matter until the economies of a phonetically spelt scientific and scholarly Pidgin are calculated and stated in terms of time, labour and money'.

Providing this economic argument was Shaw's unique contribution to the spelling reform debate. Earlier appeals had failed to make the subject alluring. But if he could demonstrate a financial saving, large enough perhaps to pay for a third world war, what government could resist?

Between Charlotte's death and his own he returned to this alphabetical windmill and tilted at it with heroic persistence. 'I am at present making my will ... I am a citizen desirous of bequeathing my property to the public for public good,' he announced in a public letter which was printed in 1944 and sent to twenty-two government departments as well as to colleges, trusts, societies and 'all other stones I could think of to turn'. He tempted readers by estimating his property as running into six figures. But 'I am up against the difficulty of ascertaining which public department or committee, or what learned Society, I should nominate as an executant of my scheme'.

This circular elicited 'letters mostly polite and even sympathetic, but all to the same effect: "An interesting project, but not our job" ', he described it to James Pitman. '. . . It is clear that if I wait for a solution before making my will I shall die intestate as far as the alphabet is concerned.'

There was gathering interest after the war in adult literacy, initial teaching alphabets for children and the reform of language. This interest was to reach its conclusion in 1975 with the Bullock Report, *A Language for Life*. But already by the late 1940s it seemed that a change in English lettering was more likely than changes in coinage, the measurements of weights or distances, fluid volumes or temperatures. Shaw planned his will so as to give 'the alphabet question a good standing advertisement for 20 years'. Otherwise 'I wash my hands of the business'.

Yet he could not wash his hands of it. Unharnessed languages rushed in at him from everywhere and he beat them off with volleys of withering advice on blue printed postcards, statements for debates in Parliament, letters to *Tit-Bits* and *The Times*, and an ultimate brochure launched at all members of the House of Commons, every active section of the House of Lords, at the entire Dáil and sixty Irish senators. But still they came at him, the champions of Basic English and Simplified Spelling, knights of Interglossa and Esperanto, Novial and Volapük, ancient lords of Visible Speech, irascible young linguists, strange panoptic conjugators, calligraphers, mathematical symbolists, firers of pistics, shorthanders, Pidgin fanciers. He spread his dramatic skills and left them all for dead.

Was there any sense in all this warring of signs and sounds? That a man of letters might want to improve his implements is not obviously unreasonable. It could be an advantage for writers to lessen the disparity in speed between written and spoken language, between thought and its communication on to paper. Shaw took many sensible precautions in his will. He did not call for an infinite vista of reform that might waste his money on planning committees, but defined a limited experiment to place a new alphabet into competition with the old (as Arabic numerals had competed successfully with Roman numerals), 'until one of the two proves the fitter to survive'. Neither was he deaf to the many regional accents in Britain, nor did he claim that one was better, or any ideal: he simply relied on what was generally intelligible. He never contemplated designing the new alphabet himself or appropriating the reform personally.

Yet in spite of all this surrounding sense, the scheme remains incredible.

This was partly because he omitted from his will any mention of the familiar virtues of alphabetical improvement, such as its educational benefits for infants and the environmental saving of trees. He believed that a good phonetic script would make English easier for foreigners and improve its chances of emerging by natural selection from international Babel to become the lingua franca of the world: 'the language with the best spelling and the least grammar will win', he predicted. But this too is omitted from the will.

The reason Shaw gave for his omissions was that these benefits had failed to win public opinion. What hampered reform, he thought, was the apparently enormous cost. He therefore argued that any operation for rescuing the handicapped language should be led by economists. In the past he had tried to get a Chair of Languages established at the London School of Economics for Henry Sweet. Now he put his trust in a Member of Parliament, James Pitman, grandson of the inventor of the phonographic system of shorthand. 'You are, I should say, by far the best equipped adventurer in the field,' he wrote to Pitman. '... You have no enemies and a great phonetic name. My name is well known; but it raises clouds of savage prejudices; and I am too old, too old.'

Some admirers of Shaw believed this alphabetical craze to be a product of his old age. 'What is happening to you?' demanded Hesketh Pearson. 'Is reason tottering on her throne, or has the heart ceased to function?' Under the 'incoherence' and 'inanity' of Shaw's proposals, the American writer Jacques Barzun was to detect a more fundamental motive. 'His expressed purpose was not his real purpose,' Barzun wrote; 'he did not want to save ink and paper, help the child and favor the foreigner. What did he want to do? Simply to get rid of the past, to give a part of mankind a fresh start by isolating it from its own history and from the ancestral bad habits of the other nations ...'

Shaw had his reasons and he had his needs. He wanted to renew the future as well as get rid of the past. Alphabetical reform became not the letter but the very spirit of change which was itself the beat of life. In old age a peculiar passion enters his crusade and ties it to his family name. 'All round me I hear the corruption of our language,' he writes, 'produced by the absurd device of spelling the first sound in my name with the two letters sh.' This impurity weighs on him like a defect in the blood. 'My surname has two sounds: but I have to spell it with four letters: another 100 per cent. loss of time, labour, ink and paper.' But as Barzun says 'he did not want to save ink and paper', so in the will his desire is expressed purely as an equation involving labour, cost and time: the orgasm of mental labour to which he had been so ecstatically if regretfully addicted; the cost into which he had protectively transferred much emotional profit and loss; and the time that was running out. 'Saving time is of no significance,' protested Hesketh Pearson. But at ninety it may be. Shaw calculated that phonetic spelling would 'add years' to a writer's life. Its significance was that of a magic symbol arising from the long-life Utopia of *Back to Methuselah* and, like an algebraic spell, conjuring his name out of recognition, altering his identity.

He had shed a good deal that belonged to his past before he came to sign his will. He gave, for example, the surviving holographs of his novels to the National Library of Ireland. 'Your invitation as national librarian is in the nature of a command,' he wrote to its director.

Then there was his property. 'I own the freehold of a ten roomed house in the village of Ayot St Lawrence in Herts,' he had written to the secretary of the National Trust shortly after Charlotte's death ' . . . Has such a trifle any use or interest for the National Trust?' A member of the Trust, James Lees-Milne, came down one dismal day early 1944, glanced at the exterior of this 'ugly, dark red-brick villa', glanced through its 'far from beautiful' rooms with their pinched fireplaces, flaking walls, and decided that the National Trust was positively interested. 'I am not neglecting the matter,' Shaw wrote six weeks later, 'as I am in mortal dread of dying before it is settled.'

Not wishing the house to decline into a hollow museum, he transferred many of his possessions from Whitehall Court to add zest to what he called 'the birthplace'. The hydra-headed hatstand in the hall wore a noble collection of town and country headgear, from the soft Homburg to the beekeeper's black veil, above its glove box and his sticks. The rooms brimmed with memorabilia and mementoes conveying a cluttered recapitulation of his life. Here is the Bechstein piano on which he played to Charlotte; the scales that registered his decreasing weight; his fountain pen, gold propelling pencil, mittens, cameras, steel-rimmed spectacles and the typewriter that could type plays. Here are the colour-coded postcards on Capital Punishment, Vegetarian Diet, Temperance and the Forty-Letter British Alfabet. Here too is a Staffordshire figure of Shakespeare picked up cheap at the seaside, an ancient exercise bicycle bought in France, a filing cabinet with its drawers marked 'Ayot', 'Russia', 'Keys and Contraptions', together with his admission card to the Reading Room of the British Museum for 1880 and his membership of the Cyclist Touring Club renewed in 1950. There are his books, the framed parchment scrolls of his honorary freedoms of Dublin and St Pancras; his Hollywood Oscar and Nobel Prize for Literature as well as a medal from the Irish Academy of Letters and the master key to the Malvern Festival. In the meagre writing-hut stand a wicker chair, narrow bed, flap table, telephone, thermometer, toothbrush. Everywhere, from the brass door-knocker inwards, there are images of G.B.S., and pictures of those he knew: the Sartorio portrait of Charlotte; photographs of the two heralds of his career, William Morris and Sidney Webb; his special friends and loves, Archer and Barker, Ellen and

Stella; his sparring partners Chesterton and Wells; fellow playwrights and compatriots, Ibsen and Barrie, Sean O'Casey, W. B. Yeats, Lady Gregory; and others he admired such as Lenin, Gene Tunney, Gandhi, Lawrence of Arabia, Einstein and Uncle Joe Stalin.

Whatever was superfluous could be auctioned to pay for repairs. Shaw wanted the house to be held alienably so that if only few visitors came it could be sold. In the summer of 1944 he signed the vesting deed, retaining a life interest for himself. Then, early in 1949, he notified the managing director of Whitehall Court that he wanted to be transferred to a smaller flat in the building. He had last come up to Whitehall Court at the end of 1946 'and it is unlikely that I shall ever see London again', he wrote. '... all I need is a study for Miss Patch to work in, a lavatory, and perhaps a bedroom in case I should be burnt out here and need a place to sleep in an emergency'.

He finally gave up number 130 Whitehall Court in May 1949 and became the absentee tenant of number 116, a rather dark, two-roomed furnished flat downstairs which at ten guineas a month was half the cost. 'I shall put nothing in except Miss Patch's equipment,' he informed the management, 'and some special bedding that I use.'

He was impatient to sell 'every stick and stone' not needed at Ayot so that the new flat could be handed back with ease for re-letting 'after my transfer to Golders Green'. Loewenstein stood wringing his hands in despair over the swirling litter of precious papers strewn across the floor; Miss Patch wandered distracted around the moving furniture; and Lady Astor, whose bust by Strobl was listed as a terra cotta likeness of Beatrice Webb, felt deeply confused. 'I did not bother to study the catalogues,' Shaw wrote to her, 'as I would have paid anybody handsomely to rid me of my superfluous belongings.' At the furniture auction 'the best bed: Charlotte's: a beauty' made only £18 and 'my splendid Hepplewhites (first class fakes), fit for Windsor or Chatsworth ... fetched shillings'.

There were 1,100 books at Whitehall Court and Shaw was determined to make them 'more saleable by every trick in my power'. Into eight of the more valuable volumes he inserted reminiscences. The Cranwell Edition of T. E. Lawrence's *Seven Pillars of Wisdom* went for £460, a facsimile set of four folios of Shakespeare's plays for £163. Apsley Cherry-Garrard bought the Ashendene Press edition of Dante's *Tutte le Opere* for £115, and Gertrude Lawrence snapped up Malory's *Le Morte Darthur* (illustrated by Beardsley) for only £58. After forty years of inflation and vaulting literary reputations, some of the prices now look small. Except for Wilde's *The Importance of Being Earnest* (which fetched £125), the first edition authors' presentation copies went modestly: £7 10s. 0d. for Yeats's *The Trembling of the Veil*, £6 10s. 0d. for Virginia Woolf's *A Room of One's Own*; £6 for O'Casey's

506

Juno and the Paycock. 'I am out for money: HARD,' Shaw told Sydney Cockerell; 'for the rest of the year my name is Harpagon.' His books raised £2,649 15s. od.: which he used to offset the Capital Levy (a tax of between two and ten shillings in the pound on all incomes over £2,000 of which investment income exceeded £250) which the Labour government introduced in 1948 to avoid national bankruptcy.

The Labour government was also appealing to the population for increased productivity, and in the last year of his life Shaw responded patriotically, boosting his exports with contributions to the *Negro Digest*, *Amrita Bazar Patrika*, *Neue Schweizer Rundschau* and *Atlantic* among overseas papers. He began 1950 by including among his choices as men of the half-century 'one whom I cannot modestly name', gave campaign testimonials for the less orthodox socialist candidates in the February general election (which Labour won with a reduced majority), reviewed G. D. H. Cole's *The Essential Samuel Butler* for the *Observer*, turned his attention to the Korean War and in May won a half-guinea consolation prize in a *New Statesman* competition for a short essay on 'The Happiest Day of My Holidays' in the style of Bernard Shaw.

Also in the *New Statesman* that month he published an evocative defence of the 'Play of Ideas', responding to Terence Rattigan and making a final analysis of his own dramaturgy. 'Theatre technique begins with the circus clown and ringmaster and the Greek tribune, which is a glorified development of the pitch from which the poet of the market place declaims his verses,' he wrote.

' ... Wherever there is a queue waiting for the doors of a theatre to open you may see some vagabond artist trying to entertain it in one way or another ... I myself have done the same on Clapham Common, and collected sixteen shillings in my hat at the end for the Socialist cause. I have stopped on the Thames Embankment; set my back to the river wall; and had a crowd listening to me in no time ...

'Now I, the roofless pavement orator, ended in the largest halls in the country with overcrowds that filled two streets ... Why do I tell this tale? Because it illustrates the development of the theatre from the pavement to the tribune and the cathedral, and the promotion of its outcasts to palaces ...

' ... The truth was I was going back atavistically to Aristotle, to the tribune stage, to the circus, to the didactic Mysteries, to the word music of Shakespear, to the forms of my idol Mozart, and to the stage business of the great players whom I had actually seen acting, from Barry Sullivan, Salvini, and Ristori to Coquelin and Chaliapin ... I know my business both historically and by practice.'

Perhaps affected by this testimony, Shaw wrote the five small scenes of a 'little comedy' in one July week, calling it *Why She Would Not*. The reason why the good-looking Serafina White will not marry the rich and improving young man is that 'I am afraid of you,' she tells him. He is incredulous: 'I coerce nobody,' he protests: 'I only point out the way.' The play is a Christian allegory. In the first scene the man appears as a chivalrous 'newcomer', in the second he is revealed as 'a carpenter of sorts', in the third he acts an apparently 'unemployable walking gentleman', in the fourth he becomes 'a very smart city man' dealing in real estate, and in the fifth he is finally 'a wonder', admired but alone. Shaw's hero is like a miniature of Los in Blake's Symbolic poems: the voice of eternal prophecy, the spectre of reasoning, the creator of alphabets, divorced from the Female Principle and hammering out the future in his creator's shade. His Shavian name is Henry Bossborn, a good surname to adopt for a writer once unsure of his legitimacy who had won natural authority through the power of language. His fearful solitude is the solitude G.B.S. had regained seven years after Charlotte's death.

Shaw's nature was rooted in solitude. 'His mind was always busy with his thoughts,' Mrs Laden noticed. He was never lonely. 'No such luck!' But he wanted deeper seclusion, for his privacy was ringed with crowds of people, as if he lived in the eye of a perpetual storm. On 26 July 1950, three days after he completed *Why She Would Not*, *The Times*, which now recorded his birthdays in its Court Circular, described his ninety-fourth birthday as restful.

'Restful!!! Restful, with the telephone and the door bell ringing all day! With the postmen staggering under bushels of letters and telegrams! With immense birthday cakes ... falling on me like millstones! With the lane blocked by cameramen, televisors, photographers, newsreelers, interviewers, all refusing to take No for an answer. And I with a hard day's work to finish in time for the village post. Heaven forgive *The Times*. I cannot.'

He lived, Mrs Laden thought, like 'a prisoner in his own house. He could not even poke his head out of the window without someone spotting it.' Mrs Laden would have refused 'the King of England' had he driven up without an appointment. But she could not stop people climbing the trees and peering down, or prevent photographers breaking through hedges and setting up their cameras on the lawn, or silence the persistent telephone calls. 'I don't want to speak to anybody,' Shaw cried out, 'alive or dead.'

He had always been fastidious and could not bear people detecting signs of his infirmities – the egg stain on his tie, the weak bladder. Neither Pascal nor Trebitsch, Nancy Astor nor Molly Tompkins had been able to accept that he was 'no longer a desirable acquaintance'. But nothing was hidden from Mrs Laden. She had noticed pools in the lavatory and observed how the old man would empty the chamber pot from under his bed each morning. Suspecting he was suffering from renal trouble or perhaps a failure of the prostate gland, she collected a specimen of his urine, saw that it contained blood, and sent it to the doctor. He advised immediate treatment. But she knew it was hopeless. G.B.S. did not want to speak about such things.

Apart from these secrets, he was not unhappy. 'Life is worth my while: if it were not I should end it.' Death did not frighten him. Quite the contrary. 'For you as for me "la morte e nulla",' he wrote to Dean Inge. '. . . I sleep well, always in the hope that I may not wake again.'

India's first Prime Minister, Jawaharlal Nehru, had visited Ayot, but Shaw had to refuse Thakin Nu, the Prime Minister of Burma, that summer because 'I am being treated in hospital for an attack of lumbago which is disabling at my great age.' By the beginning of September he had recovered and was busy making bonfires in the garden. One of the neighbours rang up to complain about the smoke and Mrs Laden roared 'with the ferocity of a lioness' down the telephone. 'Your phone to Mrs Laden reached her in a moment when a terrible misfortune had just overtaken her,' Shaw wrote to pacify him. 'Our pet cat had died in the night; and she was overwhelmed with grief. Forgive her if she vented any of it on you.'

The death of Bunch, her orange cat, at last persuaded Mrs Laden to go on holiday up to Scotland. 'It was the first holiday I'd taken for years,' she remembered. 'I was entitled to at least two weeks a year, but I usually felt that something would happen to him if I wasn't there.' Margaret Cashin Smith, the recently married Irish parlourmaid, bicycled back to look after him while Mrs Laden was away. 'Mr Shaw was very pleased to see me,' she said, 'and I to see him.' Everything was prepared. All seemed well. Mrs Laden coached G.B.S. on the things he must not do in her absence, and left at the end of the week.

'I can hardly walk through my garden without a tumble or two,' Shaw had written in his preface to *Buoyant Billions*. In the late afternoon of Sunday 10 September, once it had stopped raining, he walked in the garden with his secateurs. 'Pruning with the secateurs was his chief interest,' the gardener Fred Drury had reckoned. But this time, while cutting a projecting branch, he slipped, fell on the path, and began blowing the whistle he carried for emergencies. 'I ran out into the garden and found him on the ground,' the

Irish parlourmaid remembered. 'I had him sitting on my knees for fifteen minutes. "Put me down and go and fetch someone," he said, but I wouldn't put him on the wet grass and blew and blew at the whistle till my husband, who happened to be near, came and helped Mr Shaw into the house.'

His doctor arrived and sent for a radiologist who was driven to the house by Shaw's chauffeur Fred Day. A portable X-ray machine revealed that Shaw's left thigh was fractured, and his leg was put in a splint. The doctor sedated him for the night and later arranged for an ambulance to take him next morning to the Luton and Dunstable Hospital. He also telephoned Mrs Laden who flew back the following day.

'He was in great pain, but most stoical,' said one of the doctors at the hospital. Feeling that he would oppose any attempt to treat him by surgery, Shaw's doctor had a long consultation with the resident orthopaedic surgeon, but rather to their surprise G.B.S. agreed to everything they suggested and at 5.15 on the Monday afternoon he was operated on, the surgeon joining the broken surfaces of the neck of his thigh bone. Next day, the *Manchester Guardian* reported him to be 'fairly comfortable' and the *Lancashire Evening Post* as 'very comfortable', but the *Daily Express* predicted that 'Shaw may never walk again'.

As soon as the newspapers heard of the accident 'all hell broke loose'. So many telephone calls came in from all parts of the world that the hospital had to employ an extra switchboard operator. The corridors and waiting-room seethed with reporters. Photographers offered the management £1,000 for a picture of Shaw in bed surrounded by the flowers sent by Winston Churchill and others, and when this did not succeed they put ladders against the outside wall in an attempt to climb into his room. Mrs Laden, arriving with fruit and pyjamas, wool blankets and an electrically-heated bed warmer, felt quite scared as they all pressed round her.

To deal with the chaos, the hospital management set aside its boardroom for regular bulletins. Journalists soon filled the local accommodation and 'a few of the reporters were found room in a jail cell at the police station'. Their stories were remorselessly cheerful. They quoted the hospital staff as being 'amazed' at Shaw's 'grand colour', his 'lively and talkative' behaviour and other signs of his rapid recovery: 'G.B.S. Gets Out of Bed – and Stands', miraculously announced one newspaper. When two nurses did lift him for a few seconds he cautioned them to tell no one or else 'they will say I've walked a mile'.

It quickly became apparent to surgeons and doctors at the hospital that Shaw was suffering from longstanding kidney and bladder trouble. They took temporary measures to relieve the condition and then, on 21 September, operated on him again. Though his fractured thigh was mending well, he was described as being only 'fairly satisfactory in the circumstances' and his doctor remembered that shortly after this second operation he became 'quite unmanageable'. The Sister tried 'her best to make him drink as she had been instructed to do, but her attempts were being met with violent opposition'. He now had a silver catheter attached to his bladder which had to be cleaned each week and which he was told he must use for the rest of his life. He pestered Mrs Laden to let him come home. Eleanor O'Connell, who visited the hospital on 2 October, observed that he looked 'so fragile and strangely enough not a bit peaceful', and also that 'his voice was very low, not exactly feeble, but lowly hoarse and tremulous'. The only way to catch his words, she found, was to lean her elbows on the bed and put her head on the pillow next to his head. She asked him how he was.

'Everyone asks me that, and it's so silly when all I want is to die, but this damned vitality of mine won't let me.'

She asked him whether he was looking forward to dying.

'Oh so much, so much (tremulously like a child) if *only* I could die, this is all such a waste of time, a waste of food, a waste of attention – but they won't leave me alone – I'm in HELL (loudly) here, they wash me all the time ... when I'm asleep they wake me, and when I'm awake they ask why I'm not asleep. Each time they pounce on me they tell me it will be just the same as last time and then I find they have added a new torture ... (beating feebly against his thigh). Ah if only I could walk I would get up at once and go, but this leg is only held together with a pin ... I tell you I am in hell. I want to die and I can't (Here there was almost a sob in his voice and such a pleading that I felt it was a prayer).'

She reminded him that he was to leave the hospital in a couple of days, told him that his room at Ayot was ready and that he would be happier there.

'Happier? No, but at least I will be able to die in peace.'

According to the orthopaedic surgeon, Shaw 'might have lived till a hundred' had he stayed in hospital, allowed them to feed him up with butcher's meat, and enjoyed another visit or two to the operating theatre. 'G.B.S.: Tells doctors, "Read my prefaces"', reported the *Daily Express*. In his Preface to *The Doctor's Dilemma* he had written: 'in surgery all operations are recorded as successful if the patient can be got out of the hospital or nursing home alive...' The last hospital bulletin proclaimed his 'satisfactory progress'. And it was true that he was still alive, though such a shadow of G.B.S. he seemed a ghost. 'He died in effect the day he fell in his garden,' said the village postmistress Jisbella Lyth. '...He died in his garden, like my husband, just as he had always told me he wanted to do. It wasn't physical death yet ... but it was death to Bernard Shaw.'

After twenty-four days in hospital, the ambulance drove him back to Ayot where, hidden from the crowd behind a white canvas screen held by his gardener and chauffeur, he was carried into the dining-room which Mrs Laden had fitted up as a bedroom.

Two nurses looked after him day and night, and Margaret Cashin Smith again came back to help. 'He is very well, thank you,' Mrs Laden brusquely informed a journalist from the *Manchester Guardian*. But in fact she could see that he was not at all himself. His face had fallen in, he was pale and quiet, a vacant thing, ghastly. Everyone saw it. 'It was pitiful to see him the last time I cut his hair,' said the man who had been his regular barber for almost twenty years. '... He was very thin – he couldn't have had less flesh on him. Formerly he enjoyed having his hair cut, but that last time he was completely miserable. I don't know how I got through it. He was a changed man – just like a child. I hope I never have an experience like that again.'

'Shaw's last days were agony for me,' said Mrs Laden. Life was no longer worth his while, but he could not end it. Passing his room one morning Mrs Laden heard him ask the nurse not to prolong his life as he was a very old man. So she went in at once to upbraid him.

'You're much more than an old man, you are a national institution.'

'What's the good of trying to repair an ancient monument?' he asked.

Then she burst out: 'I wish it was I that was dying and not you.'

In the kitchen she set to preparing some 'vur-r-r-ee special' soups with something secretly added to buck him up, but he would only take a little so as to whisper a compliment to her. He did not want to eat or drink but to make what haste he could and be gone. 'How much longer do you want me to lie here paralyzed and be watched like a monkey by those outside?' he suddenly demanded. He hated the degradations that made him so dependent on others, 'like a baby in swaddling clothes', as he called it. 'His mental worry about his kidney trouble killed him as much as the illness itself,' Mrs Laden could tell. Yet she had to keep trying to make him eat and drink: there was nothing else for her to do.

Blanche Patch went on with her secretarial work as best she might, coming down and reading some of his mail to him, deciphering a few instructions and holding his wrist as she got a signature out of him. One of the first signatures he wrote after getting back to Ayot was on a large cheque to be divided among the hospital telephonists, porters and nurses whose duties had been so stretched by their newsworthy patient. One of his last signatures was on a tax document. 'I don't think I shall ever write anything more,' he said.

They had placed his narrow bed facing a long window so that he could see the lawn. Wearing a light saffron nightgown with wide sleeves he looked 'a

Blake-like figure', thought Esmé Percy visiting him there. 'He took my hand and pressed it against his heart. How thin his body was. He just said, "Good luck, good-bye", and then a brief but heart-rending pause, and "Now get along with you".'

Visitors had begun arriving at the hospital and would continue coming to Ayot, though they did not always get to see him. First they came to cheer him on, then to make their farewells. Loewenstein hovered near the bedroom and eventually took up his vigil in the next room. Nancy Astor came and went bringing many flowers, but got into a fight with the actress Frances Day over who should be regarded as the chief mourner. 'I don't want visitors. They tire me too much,' Shaw had said to Eleanor O'Connell. But a few people, mostly women, were briefly welcome. 'Think of the enjoyment you've given and the stimulus,' said Judy Musters. 'You might say the same,' he replied, 'of any Mrs Warren.' Sean O'Casey's beautiful wife Eileen also came to see him and stroked his aching head. It was wonderful, he told her. She felt he was 'back again as a small child wanting a mother's comfort'. He asked her to kiss him. 'Goodbye and God bless you,' she said as she wiped away the lipstick from his face. 'He has blessed you already,' he answered.

It was Nancy Astor who alerted the newspapers. ' "Shaw is Dying", Says Lady Astor', announced the *Daily Express*. 'I want to sleep,' he had said to her, and for much of the last week he did sleep. Then his temperature rose rapidly, and in the early hours of 1 November, shortly before going into a coma, he spoke his last words: 'I am going to die.'

Mrs Laden asked the rector of Ayot to read the twenty-third Psalm over him as he lay on his bed snorting and snoring and looking dreadful, and the rector agreed for 'the man was surely no atheist'. Shaw had summed up his religious beliefs the week before when speaking to Judy Musters: 'I believe in life everlasting; but not for the individual.' For twenty-six hours he remained unconscious. Then, early on 2 November, Mrs Laden walked out through the morning mist and told the reporters waiting with their blinding flash bulbs at the gate that, shortly before five o'clock, G.B.S. had died.

*

'Life goes on as usual at Shaw's Corner' the *Daily Herald* reported that morning. Outside Fred Drury was brushing up the dead leaves. The windows of the house stood open but there were no hushed voices. Inside, the nurses began packing and Lady Astor soon arrived. So, rather later, did Pascal, flying in from New York with a suitcase full of vitamins, then bursting into tears, and stating that he would film the life of G.B.S. 'I shall write it myself,' he declared before driving off.

Death suited G.B.S. He hadn't appeared so well for a long time. 'When he was dead he looked wonderful – quite different,' said Mrs Laden; 'clear of complexion and with a sort of whimsical smile on his face . . . ' Lady Astor, giving an excellent performance 'as if she was the widow', went out later that morning and invited almost twenty reporters into the house. 'I think you ought to see him, he looks so lovely.' At noon the rector conducted a short service at the bedside and seven women from the village came to pay their last respects. In the afternoon Shaw's body was driven to the Chapel of Rest at Welwyn. It was dressed in his mauve pyjamas and on Lady Astor's instructions a death mask was made.

Next day the extraordinary outpouring of memories and obituaries began on the wireless, the new-fangled television sets, and in the newspapers. The Indian cabinet adjourned; theatre audiences in Australia rose for two minutes' silence; the Swedish National Theatre delivered a statement to the British ambassador in praise of Shaw's creative life; and on Broadway and in Times Square the lights were briefly blacked out. 'There was a singular sense of loss,' recorded St John Ervine. Shaw himself would have preferred to be remembered 'as Sonny than as the ghastly old skeleton of a celebrity I now am'. But there was no one alive who knew him as Sonny – certainly not the presidents and prime ministers, the famous actors and impresarios whose fine opinions were being blazed round the world. On the other hand, it was strange that such a dry, unsentimental phenomenon as G.B.S. could have touched ordinary people unless something of Sonny had lived on. 'I sobbed my socks off,' said the housewife from Workington. 'It was a great loss to me,' said the village postmistress at Ayot.

Shaw had wanted the funeral service at Golders Green to be private, but almost forty distant relatives, official representatives, and old colleagues claimed cards of admission. Outside in the Garden of Remembrance some 500 people haphazardly gathered. 'We'll never see his like again,' platitudinized a Cockney woman. 'Madam, we must never underrate posterity,' an Irishman corrected her. A representative of the women's movement who unfurled a green, purple and white striped flag proclaiming G.B.S. 'one of our best friends during our fight for the vote' was hustled off by police.

The music was relayed to those outside: the hymn at the beginning of Humperdinck's *Hansel and Gretel* overture, the *Libera me* from Verdi's *Requiem*, extracts from Elgar's *The Music Makers* and the 'Nimrod' section from his *Enigma Variations*. There was no religious ceremony, but Sydney Cockerell read the final passage of Mr Valiant for Truth from *The Pilgrim's Progress*. So he passed over.

'My ghost would be bored by big buildings like the [Westminster] Abbey or St Patrick's Cathedral,' Shaw had written to Sydney Cockerell. '... I need seasons: trees and birds.' Charlotte had directed in her will that her ashes 'shall be taken to Ireland and scattered on Irish ground', but after the war started Shaw proposed that their ashes be mixed inseparably and distributed round the garden at Ayot. 'It pleased her, and she agreed.'

Charlotte's ashes had been waiting in a bronze casket at the Golders Green columbarium, and his were placed in a smaller casket which fitted exactly on top of hers in the niche. Early in the morning of 23 November, the two caskets were taken down to Ayot. The Public Trustee emptied his ashes into hers at the dining-room sideboard, and stirred them together. Then, with his two deputies, Charlotte's executor from the bank, the local doctor, a news agency reporter representing the public, and Mrs Laden, he went into the garden. The doctor shook the aluminium sprinkler and a grey cloud drifted into the air and was carried to the ground by the falling rain. He led them past the flower beds, emptying the ashes along the path and round the revolving hut at the end where G.B.S. had recently paraded with a famous actress and, waving her goodbye, asked:

'Well, did I give a good performance?'

BIBLIOGRAPHICAL NOTE
AND ACKNOWLEDGEMENTS

I would like to renew my special thanks to the team that has assisted me throughout the three volumes of this biography. Sarah Johnson continued typing the narrative and became perhaps the only person capable of reading my raw handwriting. Richard Bates expertly conveyed the corrected typescript on to disc and later married my style with the publisher's house style. Vivian Elliot has helped greatly in the checking of quotations and the supplying of photographs. Margery Morgan read each chapter, pulling me up and setting me straight where I was blown off course. I am sincerely grateful to them all.

The Lure of Fantasy has been carefully and sympathetically edited at Chatto & Windus by Alison Samuel assisted by Robert Lacey who also worked with my previous editor Hilary Laurie on *The Search for Love* and *The Pursuit of Power*. At Random House U.S.A. Joe Fox has persisted heroically with his editorial 'nitpickings' to the end.

The standard biographies of Bernard Shaw by Hesketh Pearson and St John Ervine have no references. This biography will have some ten thousand reference notes. To those readers who would have preferred to see them incorporated into the three volumes, or placed at the end of this third volume, I offer my apologies. I know how irritating the failure to locate at once the source of a quotation can be. To offset this I have tried to indicate sources within the text where it has been possible to do so without overloading my narrative.

My decision to publish the notes separately arises from what I believe is the hybrid nature of biography. As a genre, it appears to have two categories of reader. My intention was to offer the general reader who does not greatly use references a less expensive non-fiction story in line with Shavian principles of publishing, while allowing myself the space and time to provide more specialist and academic readers with a greater number of references in a form that will in due course be easier for them to use. Some aesthetic considerations were also involved in this decision. I wanted to present a 'pure' narrative that was neither interrupted by sequences of numbers nor undermined by a series of footnotes.

Since the Bibliographical Note and Acknowledgements to *The Search for Love* were drafted, a number of useful works on Shaw have become available. These include *G. B. Shaw: An Annotated Bibliography of Writings about Him* Volume I: 1871–1930 compiled and edited by J. P. Wearing; Volume II: 1931–1956 compiled and edited by Elsie B. Adams with Donald C. Haberman; Volume III: 1957–1979 compiled and edited by Donald C. Haberman (Northern Illinois University Press, 1986, 1987, 1986); *Bernard Shaw Collected Letters 1926–1950* edited by Dan H. Laurence (Max Reinhardt, 1988); *Shaw's Sense of History* by J. L. Wisenthal (Clarendon Press, 1988); *File on Shaw* compiled by Margery Morgan (Methuen Drama, 1989); *Shaw on Photography* edited, with an introduction, by Bill Jay and Margaret Moore (Gibbs Smith, 1989); *Bernard Shaw on the London Art Scene 1885–1950* edited, with an introduction, by Stanley Weintraub (Pennsylvania State University Press, 1989); *GBS & Company* by Aubrey Hampton (Organica Press, 1989); *Shaw: Interviews and Recollections* edited by

A. M. Gibbs (Macmillan Press, 1990). I am also much indebted to the invaluable *Annual of Bernard Shaw Studies* (Pennsylvania State University Press) the last three issues of which have been edited by Stanley Weintraub and Fred D. Crawford separately and together. I have found *The Shavian* (journal of the Shaw Society, edited by T. F. Evans) and *The Independent Shavian* (journal of the Bernard Shaw Society, Inc., edited by Richard Nickson) of great interest and use.

To the people listed in my original acknowledgements to whom I am indebted for help I would like to add the following: E. I. Allen, Micki Amick, Stephen Barrett, Ian Britain, Jane Brownrigg, Peter Catrell, A. Cherepansky; L. W. Conolly, Patricia Cooke, Sister Felicitas Corrigan, Barbro Edwards, Anne-Marie Ehrlich, Christopher Fry, Jonathan Fryer, B. J. M. Fulliot, Jane S. Home, Yuli Kagarlitsky, Joe Keenan, Carol Kroch-Rhodes, Basil Langton, Joan Larkin, Violet E. M. Liddle, James McNeish, Claire Madden, Susanna Marcus, Catherine Moody, Victor Moody, A. Obraztsova, Brendan O'Byrne, Theodore M. Pasca, Mary Pless, Liz Rich, Peter Rowland, Max Rutherston, Margaret Scott, Frank Singleton, Mrs Roy M. Stewart, Anna Surmach, Peter Symms, Neil Titley, Diane Uttley, Herbert Whittaker.

To the institutions holding Shaw material that were listed in my acknowledgements the following must be added: Bath Reference Library; Bedford Dramatic Club; Birmingham Reference Library; University of Bristol Library; British Theatre Association, London (Regent's College); Brotherton Library, Leeds (Brotherton Collection); BSSR Central State Archives Museum, Minsk; Clifton College Library, Bristol; University College Dublin; Dublin Public Libraries; Edinburgh City Libraries; Edinburgh University Library; University of Essex; University of Glasgow Library; The *Guardian* Archives, Manchester; University of Guelph Library, Ontario; Walter Hampden – Edwin Booth Theatre Collection Library (The Players Club); Hull Central Library (Winifred Holtby Collection); The Hyde Collection, Somerville, New Jersey; India Office Library and Records, London; International Institute of Social History, Amsterdam; Keats' House; Frederick R. Koch Foundation; Lambeth Palace Library, London; Liddell Hart Centre For Military Archives (Kings College London); City of London Polytechnic (Fawcett Library); University College London; University of London Library; Longleat House, Warminster; Malvern Public Library; Manchester College Library, Oxford; Raymond Mander and Joe Mitchenson Theatre Collection; Mitchell Library (Glasgow District Libraries); National Archive of Ireland; National Sound Archive, London; Nehru Memorial Museum and Library, New Delhi; Newport Central Library, Gwent; Norfolk Record Office; University of Nottingham Library; Nottinghamshire Record Office; Oxford University Press Archives; Paul Robeson Archive, New York; Royal Literary Fund; Royal Society of Literature; Ruskin Galleries, Bembridge School, Isle of Wight; University of St Andrews Library; Science Fiction Foundation, North East London Polytechnic; Sheffield City Libraries; Shepherd's Bush Public Library; Street Public Library, Somerset; Surrey Record Office, Kingston Upon Thames; West Sussex Record Office, Chichester; Swedish Embassy, London; Swiss Cottage Public Library (Local History Library); Taylor Institution Library, University of Oxford; Ellen Terry Memorial Museum; Trinity College Library, Cambridge; Trinity College Library, Dublin; University of Warwick, Modern Records Centre; Victoria and Albert Museum (National Art Library); Westfield College Library, London; Winchester College Library.

MICHAEL HOLROYD. Porlock Weir. October 1990.

517

24 Courtesy of the Nancy Astor Archives, Reading University Library, Reading. 6B, 11B, 15A, 16, 23, 26, 31 Courtesy of the British Library. 32 Courtesy of the British Library, Colindale. 6A, 29A, 29B Courtesy of Allan Chappelow *Shaw the Villager and Human Being*, Charles Skilton, London, 1961. 17 Courtesy of Constable & Co., London, 1932. 22 Courtesy of Valerie Delacorte (Valerie Pascal *The Disciple and his Devil*, Michael Joseph, London, 1971). 4 Courtesy of Vivian Elliot. 9 Courtesy of Professor A. M. Gibbs *Shaw: Interviews and Recollections*, Macmillan, London, 1990, and F. E. Loewenstein *Bernard Shaw Through the Camera*, B & H White Publications Ltd, London, 1948. 21 Courtesy of Archibald Henderson *Playboy and Prophet*, Appleton, New York, 1932. 12, 27, 28A, 30B Courtesy of the Hulton Picture Company, London. 11A Courtesy of the Sir Barry Jackson Trust, Birmingham. 2 Courtesy of the Dan H. Laurence Collection, University of Guelph Library, Guelph, Ontario. 28D Courtesy of *Life* magazine, November 1950. 3, 13, 14A, 14B, 19A, 25, 29C, 30A Courtesy of the London School of Economics and Political Science, British Library of Political and Economic Science, and the Society of Authors, London. 10 Courtesy of the Malvern Festival Programme, 1980. Front endpaper, Back endpaper, 1 Courtesy of Mander & Mitchenson Theatre Collection, Beckenham. 5 (head of St Maurice, once thought to be St Joan) Courtesy of Musée d'Orléans, Orléans, and Photographie Lauros-Giraudon, Paris. 29D Courtesy of the National Anti-Vivisection Society Ltd, London (*Shaw on Vivisection: Abolish It*, Allen & Unwin, London, 1949). 19B Courtesy of the National Portrait Gallery, London. 15B Courtesy of Pictorial Parade Inc., New York. 8 Courtesy of *Punch*, London. 7 Courtesy of *Smithsonian* magazine, Washington DC. 20 Courtesy of Southern Historical Collection, Wilson Library, University of North Carolina at Chapel Hill. 28B Courtesy of Stanbrook Abbey, Worcester. 28C Courtesy of Siegfried Trebitsch *Chronicle of a Life*, William Heinemann, London, 1953. 18 Courtesy of the Victoria & Albert Museum Theatre Collection, London.

INDEX

Abbey Theatre Company, Dublin, 195, 196, 197, 199

Achurch, Janet (Mrs Charles Charrington) 77, 79, 128

Actresses Franchise League, 183

Adam, Ronald, 395

Adelphi Terrace, London, Shaw's flat in, 27, 79, 138, 446

Adler, Alfred, 265

Adler, Friedrich, 145; Shaw to, 144

Adventures of the Black Girl in Her Search for God, The, see Shaw: *Works*

Agate, James, 24, 58, 98, 415

Alexander, King of Yugoslavia, 181

Altringham, Lord, 160

American-Irish Historical Society, 500

American Vegetarian, The, 364

Ames, Captain (neighbour), 447

Amrita Bazar Patrika, 507

Amundsen, Captain Roald, 104, 105

Androcles and the Lion, see Shaw: *Works*

Anglo-Irish Treaty, 61

Anglo-Swedish Literary Foundation, 93

Annajanska, see Shaw: *Works*

Apple Cart, The, see Shaw: *Works*

Araki, General, 300, 301

Arandora Star, S.S., 313–14

Archer, William, 54, 80, 94–6; death of, 97, 99; *The Old Drama and the New,* 95; 'The Psychology of G.B.S.', 95–8

Arms and the Man, see Shaw: *Works*

Armstrong, William, Shaw to, 352

Ashwell, Lena, 9, 447

Asquith, Anthony, 391, 392, 436, 437

Asquith, 'Beb', 391

Asquith, Elizabeth, 391

Asquith, Herbert Henry, 4, 47, 58, 221

Assembly of Ireland, *see* Dáil Éireann

Association of Cine-Technicians, 477

Astor, David, 233, 240

Astor, Lady (Nancy), 102, 140, 470; as first woman MP, 140; relationship with Shaw, 139, 233, 236–7, 140–1,

142; invites Shaws to Cliveden, 140, 141–2, 442–3; attitude to Charlotte, 140; influences Shaw's characters, 155, 334; on trip to Russia with Shaw, 233–7, 239, 241–2, 248, 369; meets Stalin, 244–5, 284; Blanche Patch on, 385, 453–4; Shaw on, 445; at Charlotte's funeral, 452; attempts to police Shaw's life, 454–5; worried that Shaw will marry again, 456, 457, 458; allies herself with Miss Patch and Mrs Laden against Shaw's new friends, 460, 464, 465; attitude to Loewenstein, 466, 471–2; Clare Winsten on, 467; gives Mrs Laden ballet tickets, 469; concedes Shaw is happier by himself, 497; confused at Shaw's selling of belongings, 506; alerts press that Shaw is dying, 513; after Shaw's death, 513, 514. *See also* Charlotte's letters to, *under* Shaw, Charlotte; Shaw's letters to, *under* Shaw

Astor, Waldorf, 140, 233–42, 247; Shaw to, 234

Athenaeum, 22

Athens, Shaw's visit, 286

Atkinson, Brooks, 406, 415

Atlantic (Monthly), 507

Attlee, Clement, 373, 484, 495

Auckland, Shaw's visit, 315, 317

Auric, Georges, 477

Australia, productions of Shaw's plays in, 351, 358

Austria, productions of Shaw's plays in, *see* Vienna

Ayliff, H. K., 57, 400; Shaw to, 406, 409

Ayot St Lawrence, 70, 79, 82, 86, 87, 98, 99–100, 103, 140–1, 328–32, 419; in wartime, 439–42, 444, 445–6, 448, 449, 454, 455, 460; *Bernard Shaw's Rhyming Picture Guide to Ayot,* 496; Shaw makes museum of, 505–6

Butler, Samuel, 38–40, 41, 289; *Life and Habit*, 38; *Luck or Cunning?*, 38; *Notebooks*, 39; *Erewhon*, 39, 40; *The Way of All Flesh*, 39, 208

Caesar and Cleopatra, see Shaw: *Works*
Cai Yuan-pei, 294
Cairnes, John Eliot, 131
Calthrop, Donald, 436
Calvin, John: *Institution*, 403
Campbell, Alan, 152
Campbell, Mrs Patrick (Stella), 182; as model for Hesione in *Heartbreak House*, 17; on *Heartbreak House*, 20–1; and the publication of Shaw's letters in *My Life and Some Letters*, 115–17, 121, 150; as model for Orinthia in *The Apple Cart*, 150, 151, 153–4; lack of money, 150–1; meets Shaw again after 15 years, 151–2; Shaw reads *The Apple Cart* to, 152, 187; appeals to Shaw again for his letters, 187; death, 187; will, 187–8; her daughter publishes *Bernard Shaw and Mrs Patrick Campbell: Their Correspondence*, 188
Campbell, R. M., Shaw to, 315
Candida, see Shaw: *Works*
Cape, Jonathan, 372
Cape Argus, 272, 274, 277, 282
Cape Times, 271, 272, 273, 283
Cape Town, Shaw in, 272–7, 282–3
Čapek, Karel: *Insect Play*, 57; *Makropoulos Secret*, 42
Captain Brassbound's Conversion, see Shaw: *Works*
Carlyle, Thomas, 430; *Sartor Resartus*, 413
Carnarvon Castle, 272
Casement, Roger, 20, 194
Cashel Byron's Profession, see Shaw: *Works*
Cashin, Margaret, see Smith, Margaret
Casson, Christopher, 342
Casson, Lewis, 79, 82, 341–2, 375
Catholic Action, 381, 382
Caute, David, 223, 252
Cavalcade, 430
Chamberlain, Sir Austen, 402
Chamberlain, Neville, 143, 395, 396, 408, 424, 426, 431
Channon, Sir Henry, 426, 431
Chaplin, Charlie, 143, 314, 385
Chardin, Pierre Teilhard de, 289
Charles II, King of England, 157–8, 410, 413

Chatto & Windus, 372
Chaudhuri, Nirad, 288
Chekhov, Anton, 24; *The Cherry Orchard*, 8–9, 14
Cherry-Garrard, Apsley, 103–6, 385, 466, 506; Charlotte Shaw to, 122, 363; *The Worst Journey in the World*, 103–5, 373
Chesterton, G. K., 99, 139, 203, 219, 327, 367; Shaw to, 117, 324; *Shaw*, 173, 178, 179, 366
Cheston, Dorothy, see Bennett, Dorothy
Chevalier, Maurice, 385
Chiang Kai-shek, 293
China, Shaw's visit, 293, 294–7
Chocolate Soldier, The, 377, 418–19
Cholmondeley, Mary, 129, 210
Churchill, Winston, 211, 260; relationship with Shaw, 226–8, 384, 492, 510; anti-Soviet obsession, 253; opposed to constitutional reform in India, 286; in Second World War, 426, 432; refuses to make Lady Astor a peeress, 465; Shaw prophesies his defeat in 1945 Election, 484
Cibber, Colly, 393
Clair, René: *A nous la liberté*, 477
Clarence, O. B., 391
Clark, Kenneth, 428, 434
Clark, Norman: Shaw to, 2
Clark, R. & R., 373
Clemenceau, Georges, 5, 33
Cliveden and the Cliveden Set, 102, 140, 141–3, 146, 445
Clunes, Alec, 485
Coates, Albert, 122, 126
Coates, Madelon, 122
Cockburn, Claud, 142
Cockerell, Douglas, 130
Cockerell, Sydney, introduces Shaw to Quicherat's *Procès*, 80, 81; introduces T. E. Lawrence to Shaw, 84–5; at Hardy's funeral, 202, 203; introduces Shaw to Dame Laurentia McLachlan, 212–14; and interest in their subsequent relationship, 215–16; on '*In Good King Charles's Golden Days*', 415; reads at Shaw's funeral, 514. *For Shaw's letters to, see under Shaw*
Cocteau, Jean: *L'Éternel retour*, 477
Coffey, Denise, 352
Cohen, Harriet, 98, 166; Shaw to, 122

Einstein, Albert, 107, 133, 217, 218,
219–20, 399, 411, 432
Eisenstein, Sergei, 307; *Battleship
Potemkin*, 240
Elder, Ann, 25, 26, 27
Elder, Una, 25
Election, General (1918), 3–4
Elgar, Edward, 99, 102, 159, 163–8;
death, 168; Shaw to, 14, 23
Eliot, T. S., 21, 54, 84, 160; *The Waste
Land*, 20
Ellis, Havelock, 130
Elmhirst, Leonard, Shaw to, 435
Ely, Gertrude, 234
Empress of Britain, Shaws' cruise on the,
285–6, 291, 294, 296, 297, 303,
306, 308–9, 312–13, 325
Encyclopaedia Britannica, 232
Engels, Friedrich, 224, 484
English Players' Company, Zürich, 199
Ervine, Leonora, Shaw to, 341, 354
Ervine, St John, 30, 80, 98; criticizes
Heartbreak House, 24, and *Back to
Methuselah*, 44; on Mary
Hankinson, 83; finds flat for Shaws,
138; member of Irish Academy of
Letters, 197; on Wells's obituary of
Shaw, 207; reviews *Too True to be
Good*, 270; Shaw tries to abort
biography, 366–7, 368; on Shaw
after Charlotte's death, 452, 497;
on Shaw's death, 514. *See also*
Shaw's letters to, *under* Shaw
Evans, Caradoc, 177
Evans, Edith, 23, 57–8, 149, 151, 342,
358, 429; Shaw to, 94, 356, 358
Evans, Frederick, 468
Evans, Geoffrey, 363
Evening Standard, 94
Everybody's Political What's What?, *see*
Shaw: *Works*

Fabian Essays in Socialism, *see* Shaw:
Works
Fabian Tracts, *see* Shaw: *Works*
Fabian Women's Group, 84, 119
Fabians, 18–19, 39, 60, 82, 83, 111,
143, 224, 229, 232, 365; Shaw to,
230; Summer Schools, 33, 82:
Penlee (1919), 82; Godalming
(1922), 119, 122; Scarborough
(1922), 120
Fagan, J. B., 23, 24–5
Fairbanks, Douglas, 235

Fanny's First Play, *see* Shaw: *Works*
Farfetched Fables, *see* Shaw: *Works*
Farleigh, John, 323
Farr, Florence (Mrs Edward Emery), 77,
128, 194, 265
Fascinating Foundling, The, *see* Shaw:
Works
Fenton, James, 339
Feuchtwanger, Leon, 417
Ffrangcon-Davies, Gwen, 57
Flecker, James Elroy, Shaw to, 367
Foch, Marshal, 86
Foot, Michael, 484
Forbes, G. W., 315
Forbes-Robertson, Johnston, 121, 474
Forster, E. M., 98, 399
Forsyth, Matthew, Shaw to, 355
Forward, 433
Fox, George, 83, 288, 410, 413
France, Anatole, 134, 252; *Vie de Jeanne
d'Arc*, 73, 84
Franco, General, 403, 422
Fraser, Peter, 316
French, Harold, 436
French, Lord, 60
Freud, Sigmund, 170, 265;
Psychopathology of Everyday Life, 373
Frinton-on-Sea, England, Shaws at, 30,
425
Froissart, Jean: *Chronicles*, 353
Fry, Christopher, 341
Fry, Roger, 164

Gabor, Zsa Zsa, 385
Gallacher, William, 231
Galsworthy, John, 99, 119, 147, 202
Gamble, Sidney D., 234
Gandhi, Devadas, 466
Gandhi, Mahatma, 233, 286, 287
Garbo, Greta, 473
Garden City Movement, the, 16
Garson, Greer, 473
Gaulle, General Charles de, 473
G.B.S. 90, 493
General Strike (1926), 29, 135
Geneva, *see* Shaw: *Works*
Geneva, Shaw in, 170, 396–7, 398
Genn, Leo, 390
George V, King, 157, 283, 383
Gerhardie, William, Shaw to, 242–3
German Society for Education in State
Citizenship, 64
Germania, 420

Hitchcock, Alfred: *Rope*, 377
Hitler, Adolf, 113, 396, 417, 418, 420,
    427; Shaw on, 113, 143, 144, 421,
    422, 423, 424, 426, 427, 431, 433,
    482, 483; Shaw's portrayal in
    Geneva, 400, 403–5
Ho Tung, Sir Robert, 292
Hogarth, D. G., 86
Holloway, Stanley, 474, 476
Hollywood: Shaw in, 307; Shaw on, 307,
    310, 376–7, 381
Hone, Joseph, 197
Honegger, Arthur, 477
Hong Kong, Shaws visit, 291–3, 294
Hong Kong Telegraph, 293
Honolulu, Shaw in, 306, 314
Hoover, President Herbert, 305
Housman, A. E., 202
How He Lied to Her Husband, *see* Shaw:
    Works
Howard, Ebenezer, 16, 98; *To-morrow,*
    A Peaceful Path to Rural Reform, 16
Howard, Leslie, 390, 392, 434
Hughes, Emrys, 430, 433
Hughes-Hallett, Lucy: *Cleopatra.*
    Histories, Dreams and Distortions,
    475
Hugo, Leon, 273, 277
Huizinga, Johan, 78
Hulbert, Jack, 166
Huntley, Raymond, 57
Huxley, Aldous, 160, 493
Huxley, Julian, 373, 445
Hyndman, Henry Mayers, 231

Ibsen, Henrik, 53, 131; *The Master*
    Builder, 21; *When We Dead Awaken*,
    257; *Rosmersholm*, 338
Illesh, Bela, 234
Immaturity, see Shaw: *Works*
'In Good King Charles's Golden Days', *see*
    Shaw: *Works*
Inca of Perusalem, The, see Shaw: *Works*
Independent Labour Party, 131;
    Summer School at Digswell Park,
    248, 251
India, Shaw's visit, 286–91
Inge, Dean W. R., 50, 256, 263, 264,
    385; Shaw to, 509
Inglis, Brian, 466
Intelligent Woman's Guide, The, see Shaw:
    Works

International Labour Organization, 397,
    398
IRA, *see* Irish Republican Army
Ireland: the Shaws at Parknasilla, 32–3,
    59, 63, 79, 80; Dáil Éireann
    (Assembly of Ireland), 59, 61;
    Dominion League, 59, 61; Shaw
    on, 59, 60, 61, 62, 64, 494;
    partitioning of, 60–1; Abbey
    Theatre Company, Dublin, 195,
    196, 197, 199. *See also* Irish
    Academy of Letters
Irish Academy of Letters, 102, 196–8,
    324
Irish Free State Army, 62
Irish Peace Conference (1920), Dublin,
    60
Irish Republican Army (IRA), 61, 62
Irish Statesman, 59, 60, 62
Irish Times, 61, 500
Irrational Knot, The, see Shaw: *Works*
Irvine, William, 8
Irving, Henry, 182, 183, 185, 186, 393,
    394
Irving, Laurence, 391, 443
Isaacs, Harold, 294, 295
Isolino San Giovanni, Italy, 123, 126
Izvestia, 231, 236, 237

Jackson, (Sir) Barry, 56–7, 91, 99, 162,
    163, 147–9, 256, 268, 351, 385,
    448
Jainism, Shaw's interest in, 288–91
James, Henry: *The Saloon*, 355
Japan, 291, 292; Shaws visit, 297–301
Jazz Singer, The, 375
Jeans, Sir James, 413; *The Mysterious*
    Universe, 373
Jewish Chronicle, 422
Jitta's Atonement, see Shaw: *Works*
Joad, C. E. M., 252, 493
John, Augustus, 100, 500; portrait of
    Shaw, 80, 85
John, Dorelia, 100
John Bull's Other Island, see Shaw: *Works*
Johnson, Amy, 385
Johnson, Samuel, 134, 224, 502
Jones, Barry, 377, 406
Jones, Daniel, 118
Jones, Festing, Shaw to, 40
Jordan, Shaws in, 216–17
Jordans, Buckinghamshire, 83

Lyttelton, Edith, 151, 152; Shaw to, 130
Lytton, Edward Bulwer: *The Coming Race*, 50

Macaulay, Lord: *History of England*, 413
MacCarthy, Desmond, 98; *reviews*: *Heartbreak House*, 12; *Back to Methuselah*, 54, 58–9; *Saint Joan*, 78, 84; *The Apple Cart*, 160; *Too True to be Good*, 269, 270; *Geneva*, 407–8
McCarthy, Lillah, 91, 103; Shaw to, 10, 332, 481
Macdermot, Norman, 147
Macdona, Charles, 341, 343
Macdona Players, 147, 341, 342, 391
MacDonald, Ramsay: Shaw campaigns for, 3–4; loses 1918 Election, 4; political career in the 1920s, 108; attitude to Russia, 108, 222, 231; Shaw's attitude to, 108–9, 110, 111, 112, 225, 250, 315; on *The Intelligent Woman's Guide*, 133; Shaw caricatures in *The Apple Cart*, 156–7; at Hardy's funeral, 202; portrayal in *On the Rocks*, 334
McDowell, Frederick P. W., 333, 349
MacGowan, Kenneth, Shaw to, 379
Mackaye, Percy: *Jeanne d'Arc*, 73
McKenna, Siobhan, 333
McLachlan, Dame Laurentia, 211–16; effect of Shaw's *Black Girl* on, 324–7; upset by *The Simpleton of the Unexpected Isles*, 351–2. *See also* Shaw's letters to, *under* Shaw
McMahon Players, 358
McRory, Desmond, 218
'Madame Sun', *see* Soong Ching Ling
Madeira, 94; Reid's Palace Hotel, 97
Madge, Charles, 252
Major Barbara, *see* Shaw: *Works*
Mallin, J. W., 234
Malory, Sir Thomas: *Morte d'Arthur*, 335
Malvern, England, 79, 125; Festival, 147–9, 161–4, 166, 256, 268–9, 326, 351, 358, 378, 405, 488; Bernard Shaw Exhibition, 148, 164
Man and Superman, *see* Shaw: *Works*
Man of Destiny, The, *see* Shaw: *Works*
Manchester Guardian, 111, 159, 485, 510, 512
Mann, Thomas, 107, 160

Mansfield, Katherine, 98, 252
Maoris, the, 318
Martin, Kingsley, 337–8, 427, 433; Shaw to, 426, 496
Marx, Eleanor, 484
Marx, Karl, 231, 289, 370; *Das Kapital*, 229, 367
Mary, Queen, 477
Masefield, John, 147; 'On the 90th Birthday of Bernard Shaw', 493
Massingham, Hugh W., 97
Matteoti, Giacomo, 144
Maurras, Charles: *Jeanne d'Arc...*, 84
Maxwell, William, 322, 323; Shaw to, 108, 146, 373, 453, 494
Mayer, Louis B., 388
Mazzini, Giuseppe, 20
Meher Baba, 388
Meisel, Martin, 414
Millionairess, The, *see* Shaw: *Works*
Mills, James Porter, 447
Misalliance, *see* Shaw: *Works*
Mitchenson, Joe, 436
Monck, Nugent, Shaw to, 14
Montagu, Ivor, 252
Moody, Vincent, Shaw to, 361
Mooney, Thomas, 306
Moor, Ethel, 82, 83
Moore, George, 387; Shaw to, 9
Moore, Roger, 474
Moorehead, Alan, 497
Morgan, Charles, 269
Morgan, Margery, 160, 337, 349
Morley, Robert, 434, 435, 438
Morning Leader, 502
Morning Post, 164, 337, 360
Morris, William, 133, 134, 158, 195, 212, 214, 229, 231, 251, 289, 322, 484
Moscicki, Ignacy, 149
Moscow, Shaw's visit to (1931), 233–9, 241–8, 369
Mosley, Cynthia, 142, 170
Mosley, Sir Oswald, 109–13, 142, 170, 337; *Wagner and Shaw*, 109
Mrs Warren's Profession, *see* Shaw: *Works*
Muggeridge, Malcolm, 253
Munthe, Dr Axel, 363
Murphy, James: trs. *Mein Kampf*, 403
Murray, Gilbert, 99; and League of Nations, 291, 399; on treatment of anaemia, 363; and *Geneva*, 400, 401, 408; on film of *Major Barbara*, 437; participates in *G.B.S. 90*, 493

528

Hugh Walpole, on her illness, 442
Beatrice Webb, on Shaw, 122, 123;
on being bombed, 444
H. G. Wells, on Jane, 204; on Shaw's
behaviour, 205, 207
Shaw, George Bernard: gets inspiration
for *Saint Joan* (*see Works*) in Orléans
(1913), 73–4; at Wyndham Croft
with Webbs and Woolfs (1916),
18–19; works on *Heartbreak House*
(*see Works*), 20; campaigns in 1918
Election on behalf of MacDonald,
3–4; at Parknasilla with Charlotte
(*q.v.*), 59; visits Horace Plunkett
(*q.v.*) in Ireland, 59.

1919:
brings out *Peace Conference Hints*, 4
(*see Works*); response to the War
revealed in *Heartbreak House*, 8;
sympathetic to Germany, 64; tries
to help Trebitsch (*q.v.*), 64–5;
translates *Jitta's Atonement* (*see
Works*), 65–8; welcomes Trebitsch
to England, 70; reads *Saint Joan* to
him, 70–1; reluctance to have
Heartbreak House performed, 22.

1920:
public and private life in the 1920s,
97–9; signs contract with Theatre
Guild, 22–3; employs Blanche
Patch (*q.v.*) as his secretary, 25, 26;
treatment of her, 26–7, 29, 30

1921:
directs rehearsals of Court Theatre
production, 23–4; hobbies, 28;
obsession with writing, 28;
continues to employ Judy Musters
(*q.v.*), 29; postwar tours with
Charlotte, 30; as a motorcyclist, 30,
99, and a car driver, 30–2;
completes *Back to Methuselah*, 32–3,
34 (*see Works*); sends copy to Lenin,
54; interests Langner (*q.v.*) in
staging *Back to Methuselah*, 55;
agrees to censorship, 58; meets
Molly Tompkins (*q.v.*), 114; Stella
Campbell (*q.v.*) presses to be
allowed to publish their
correspondence, 115.

1922:
meets Michael Collins, 62–3; at
Fabian Summer Schools, 119, 120;
collaborates with Cherry-Garrard
(*q.v.*) on *Worst Journey in the World*,

103–5; finds his Saint Joan, 79, 82;
introduced to Lawrence (*q.v.*), 84,
and reads *Seven Pillars of Wisdom*,
85.
1923:
depressed at reception of *Heartbreak
House*, 9–10; meets Jackson (*q.v.*),
56, 57; happy with Birmingham
production of *Back to Methuselah*,
58; has a fall in Ireland, 63; meets
Dame Laurentia McLachlan (*q.v.*),
213.
1924:
chairs Archer's (*q.v.*) lecture, 94;
sails to Madeira with Charlotte, 94,
96–7; reads *O'Flaherty V.C.* on the
radio, 106 (*see also* British
Broadcasting Corp.); begins *The
Intelligent Woman's Guide to
Socialism* (*see Works*), 128–9.
1925:
Charlotte takes him to Scotland,
122; Charlotte blames his illness on
the *Guide*, 122.
1926:
70th birthday celebrations, 93,
107–8; in Italy, 122–4; sits for
statuette by Troubetzkoy (*q.v.*), 123;
awarded the Nobel Prize, 92–5.
1927:
stays with the Webbs (*q.v.*), 125–6;
finishes *Guide*, 129; 'behaves badly'
over Jane Wells's death and funeral,
204–7; back in Italy, 126–8; moves
from Adelphi Terrace to Whitehall
Court, 138–9; at Cliveden with the
Astors (*q.v.*), 140, 141–3.
1928:
at Hardy's funeral, 201–3;
negotiations over Terry–Shaw
correspondence (1928–31), 183–6;
on the Riviera with Charlotte,
169–70; meets Frank Harris (*q.v.*),
170, 172; completes *The Apple Cart*,
146 (*see Works*); and founding of
Malvern Festival (*q.v.*), 147, 148;
goes to League of Nations Palace in
Geneva, 396–7; meets Tunney
(*q.v.*), 209.
1929:
meeting with Stella Campbell,
151–2; lays foundation stone of
Shakespeare Memorial Theatre,
149; supports Malvern Festival,

533

149, 161, 162, 163; friendship with Elgar (*q.v.*), 163; with Charlotte on Island of Brioni, 180, 209, 210; makes embarrassing speech in Yugoslavia, 180–1; spends a week in Venice, 181; finishes preface to Ellen Terry (*q.v.*) correspondence, 181.

1930:
brings out Limited Collected Edition, 189; rehearses film *How He Lied* (*see Works*), 376; toasts Einstein (*q.v.*) at Savoy Hotel dinner, 219–20.

1931:
begins *Too True to be Good*, 255 (*see Works*); visits the Holy Land, 216–17; campaigns against rubbish dump at Ayot, 329–30; visits Russia with Lady Astor, 233–40; meets Stanislavsky, Gorki and Lenin's widow, 240; 'exploited to the last inch', 240–1; unresponsive to Krynins' plight, 241–2; meets Stalin, 244–5; gives speeches on Lenin and in tribute to Russia, 246–7; returns to England, 248; gives speech at ILP Summer School, 248, 250, 251; converts the Webbs to Soviet Communism, 248–51; gives 'A Little Talk on America', 305; brings out *The Rationalization of Russia*, 255 (*see Works*); tries *Too True* out on friends, 256; meets Gandhi, 286; sails for South Africa, 271–2.

1932:
gives 'stupendous lecture on Russia', 273; popularity in Cape Town, 273, 274; is taken flying, 274–5; gives disastrous broadcast, 275–7; crashes the car, 277–8; stays at Knysna, 278–9, 282; writes *The Adventures of the Black Girl* (*see Works*), 279; works on film of *Arms and the Man* (*see Works*), 377–8; at Malvern for the première of *Too True to be Good*, 256, 268, 269; elected President of the Irish Academy of Letters, 197; gives speech 'in praise of Guy Fawkes', 111–12; publishes *Black Girl* in cheap edition, 322–4; cruises on

Empress of Britain, 285–6; in Italy and Athens, 286.

1933:
begins *Village Wooing* (*see Works*), 332, and *On the Rocks* (*see Works*), 333; in India, 286–8: interest in Jainism, 288–90; in Hong Kong, 291–3; in China, 293–4: meets 'Madame Sun', 294–5; gives talk to Shanghai PEN club, 293, 295; attends theatre in Peking, 296; enjoys the Tientsin band, 296; is flown over the Great Wall, 296–7; arrives exhausted in Japan, 297; 'conquers press by kindness', 297; is embarrassingly critical of Japanese policies, 297–9; meets Federation of Labour delegation, 299, Admiral Saito, 299–300, and General Araki, 300–1; visits Buddhist temples, Shinto shrines and Noh theatre, 301; arrives in North America, 302, 303, 306; stays with Hearst, 306; visits Hollywood, 307–8; mobbed by press in New York, 308–9, 312–13; gives lecture for the Academy of Political Science at Metropolitan Opera House, 308, 309–12.

1934:
works on filmscript of *The Devil's Disciple* (*see Works*), 379; on *RMS Rangitane* to New Zealand, 314; lectures Wellington Fabian Society, 315–16; recommends free milk for schoolchildren, 316; criticizes and pays tribute to New Zealand, 316–17, 319–20; goes on motor tour, 317–18; visits Truby King Karitane Hospital, 318–19; at rehearsals of première of *On the Rocks*, 341, 343; works on filmscripts of *Pygmalion* and *Saint Joan*, 380–2; 'drops dead on 24th Nov', 359.

1935:
tries to reduce volume of work, 360; has portrait painted by Moody, 361; gives Sidney Webb £1,000, 361–2; returns to South Africa, 283–4; life at Ayot, *see* Ayot St Lawrence, and at Whitehall Court, 382–6; renews acquaintance with Pascal (*q.v.*), 386; gives him *Pygmalion* 'to experiment with', 388–9.

and fascism, 143; on his speech in
Cape Town, 273; on Charlotte's
accident, 278; on their world cruise,
285–6; on *The Millionairess*, 356; on
his sudden collapse, 364; on
Pearson, 368; on Charlotte, 440,
444, 450; on his financial problems,
448
Waldorf Astor, on their arrival in
Moscow, 234
H. K. Ayliff, on *Geneva*, 406, 409
Julius Bab, on appeals from abroad,
33
Stanley Baldwin, on Ramsay
MacDonald, 109
Henri Barbusse, on the League of
Nations, 231, 399
John Barrymore, on acting his plays,
357; on British films, 379
S. N. Behrman, on films, 473
Rutland Boughton, on Elgar, 163; on
Russia, 233, 254; on Charlotte's
death, 453
James Bridie, on Czinner and *Saint
Joan*, 382; on Charlotte, 451
Fenner Brockway, on using *The
Intelligent Woman's Guide* for
election pamphlets, 130–1
Mrs Patrick (Stella) Campbell, on
Heartbreak House, 17; on Blanche
Patch, 26; on *Saint Joan*, 74; on his
visit to Yugoslavia, 180
R. M. Campbell, on lecturing, 315
G. K. Chesterton, on Stella's
publication of his letters, 117; on
the Bible, 324
Norman Clark, on himself, 2
Sydney Cockerell, on Dame Laurentia
McLachlan, 216, 327, 352; on
Charlotte, 359–60, 361; on his will,
500; on making money, 507; on his
ghost, 515
Harriet Cohen, on being ill, 122
Maurice Colbourne, on being
bombed, 440
Constance Collier, on the New York
press, 309, 312–13
Noël Coward, on getting 'clean away
from me', 98
Lord Alfred Douglas, on *Heartbreak
House*, 9; on religion, 217; on
Charlotte, 439; on himself, 452
Edward Elgar, on *Heartbreak House*,
14, 23

Leonard Elmhirst, on Gabriel Pascal,
435
Leonora Ervine, on playwriting, 341;
on *The Millionairess*, 354
St John Ervine, on cutting *Heartbreak
House*, 24; on *Back to Methuselah*,
52; on Ramsay MacDonald, 110;
on *Too True to be Good*, 260; on
Americans, 305; on 'impossibility',
344; on Charlotte, 450
Edith Evans, on *Saint Joan*, 94; on *The
Millionairess*, 356, 358
James Elroy Flecker, on geniuses, 367
Matthew Forsyth, on *The Millionairess*,
355
William Gerhardie, on his inability to
help political prisoners, 242
Maxim Gorki, on the Revolution, 222
Harley Granville-Barker, on the
theatre, 73; on Charlotte, 451
Lady Gregory, on being a failure, 63;
on Lawrence's *Seven Pillars of
Wisdom*, 85; on Charlotte, 317
Stephen Gwynn, on Yeats, 195
Augustin Hamon, on *Heartbreak
House*, 23; on Nobel Prize, 93; on
Stalin, 245; on Socialism, 250; on
'talkies', 380; on Gabriel Pascal,
390
Florence Hardy, on Hardy's funeral,
202–3
Frank Harris, on himself, 169; on his
letters, 186; on the Russian
Revolution, 221
Nellie Harris, on his doctoring of
Shaw, 178
Theresa Helburn, on *On the Rocks*,
338; on Hollywood, 379; on the
Saint Joan script, 381
Archibald Henderson, on writing *The
Intelligent Woman's Guide*, 129; on
publishing his correspondence, 186;
on his career and Voltaire's, 280; on
Dickens, 302; on being descended
from Macduff, 488
Clara Higgs, on Charlotte, 451
W. R. Inge, on death, 509
Festing Jones, on Samuel Butler, 40
Lord Kennet, on Cherry-Garrard's
view of Scott, 104
Kathleen Kennet, *see* Scott, Kathleen
John Maynard Keynes, on himself,
327
Gertrude Kingston, on *On the Rocks*,
343

Otto Kyllmann, on *The Intelligent Woman's Guide*, 130; on the Collected Edition, 189; on *Too True to be Good*, 256; on his reception in New York, 309; on lowering book prices, 323; on Charlotte's death, 453

Lawrence Langner, on *Jitta's Atonement*, 68; on *The Millionairess*, 358

T. E. Lawrence, on retiring, 169; on *Too True to be Good*, 260

Cecil Lewis, on writing *The Apple Cart*, 146; on film-script writing, 378

Roy Limbert, on *Geneva*, 406

Lady Londonderry, on being morally dead, 364

Lady Ebba Low, on Nobel Prize, 93

Edith Lyttelton, on *The Intelligent Woman's Guide*, 130

Lillah McCarthy, on *Heartbreak House*, 10; on *Village Wooing*, 332; on *Everybody's Political What's What?*, 481

Ramsay MacDonald, on Mussolini, 144, 145; on boycotting Communism, 231–2

Kenneth MacGowan, on British films, 379

Dame Laurentia McLachlan, on the Holy Land, 216–17; on Russia, 221; on Jainism, 290; on *The Black Girl* 324, 325, 326

Kingsley Martin, on peace negotiations, 426; on his voice, 496

William Maxwell, on his 70th birthday, 108; on beginning *The Apple Cart*, 146; on Penguin wanting *The Intelligent Woman's Guide*, 373; on Charlotte's death, 453; on accepting official invitations, 494

Nugent Monck, on *Heartbreak House*, 14

Vincent Moody, on himself, 361

George Moore, on *The Cherry Orchard*, 9

Gilbert Murray, on *Major Barbara* (film), 437

Karel Musek, on sales of *Back to Methuselah*, 53

Bertha Newcombe, on life around him, 35

Carl Otto, on the war, 64

Blanche Patch, on the French Riviera, 169; on Brioni, 180; on Charlotte, 258; on *On the Rocks*, 333; on Frinton, 425; on useful wartime employment, 434

Hesketh Pearson, on Charlotte, 102; on *The Apple Cart*, 158; on Inge, 263; on *The Simpleton of the Unexpected Isles*, 290

Esmé Percy, on *Heartbreak House*, 22

Sir Arthur Wing Pinero, on 'talkies', 375

James Pitman, on simplified spelling, 503, 504

Horace Plunkett, on his Russian trip, 233

Ezra Pound, on Joyce, 199

Herbert Prentice, on *The Millionairess*, 356

John Reith, on Elgar, 168; on his heart attack, 359

William Rothenstein, on Madeira, 97; on Malvern, 163; on getting peace during a cruise, 314

Michael Sadleir, on lowering prices, 323

'Christopher St John', on *Too True to be Good*, 269

Catherine Salt, on Henry Salt's death, 366

Henry Salt, on *Peace Conference Hints*, 4; on Hardy's funeral, 202; on the human race, 253; on his heart attack, 359; on taking liver extract, 363, 364; on his anorexia, 365

Lord Samuel, on publicity, 494

Kathleen Scott, on Lenin, 8; on Scott, 105; on himself, 106; on curing his anaemia, 364

Upton Sinclair, on historical facts, 413; on politics, 441; on Nancy Astor, 445

Floryan Sobieniowski, on his avoidance of his own plays, 161; on *The Simpleton of the Unexpected Isles*, 349

J. C. Squire, on *Heartbreak House*, 14; on his playwriting, 357

Alfred Sutro, on *The Apple Cart*, 150

Hannen Swaffer, on his death, 359; on simplified spelling, 502

Rabindranath Tagore, on India, 287

Ellen Terry, on giving her a part, 181–2

Sybil Thorndike, on *The Millionairess*, 358

Molly Tompkins, on *The Intelligent Woman's Guide*, 129; on his first visit to Cliveden, 141; on Mussolini, 144; on her refusal to behave tactfully, 179

Siegfried Trebitsch, on Keynes, 7; on *Heartbreak House*, 13; on *Back to Methuselah*, 43; on *Saint Joan*, 76; on *The Apple Cart*, 158; on the French Riviera, 169; on his insensitivity in old age, 254; on *Too True to be Good*, 256; on illustrations for *The Black Girl*, 322–3; on *On the Rocks* and *Village Wooing*, 344; on *The Simpleton of the Unexpected Isles*, 346; on films, 372; on a film of *Arms and the Man*, 378; on Gabriel Pascal, 386, 389; on *Geneva*, 405; on Reinhardt's production of *The Apple Cart*, 418; on 'keeping out of the mêlée', 420–1; on the effects of the war, 430, 439, 441

Sir Emery Walker, on Blacks in South Africa, 276

Revd Ensor Walters, on Russian equality, 255; on Hinduism, 289

Beatrice Webb, on Blanche Patch, 26, 442; on growing old, 63; on *The Intelligent Woman's Guide*, 130; on Jane Wells, 205; on Pearson's biography, 368, 369; on sixpenny journals, 372; on the League of Nations, 398; on *'In Good King Charles's Golden Days'*, 413; on 'eugenic experiments', 422; on Socialism, 431; on *Everybody's Political What's What?*, 441; on himself, 445; on giving her money, 448

Sidney Webb, on *The Millionairess*, 356; on the war, 446; on Beatrice's death, 449; on Charlotte, 452

H. G. Wells, on Nobel Prize, 93

Arthur Wontner, on working together, 341

Virginia Woolf, on *Heartbreak House*, 19; on himself, 327

Sir Almroth Wright, on Charlotte, 450

W. B. Yeats, on censorship of *Black Girl*, 324

Sir Francis Younghusband, on finding religion in the east, 257

Shaw's views and attitudes on:
Americans, 302–3, 304–6, 310–12
appeals for help and/or money, 33, 242
Lady Astor, 445
the atom bomb, 482
biographers and biographies, 172, 366–9
Blacks in South Africa, 276–7, 279, 281–2, 283, 284
Samuel Butler, 38–40
capitalism, 8, 133–4, 232
Winston Churchill, 226–8
Anton Chekhov, 8–9, 14
civilization, 271–2, 321
communism, 113, 229, 231, 232, 243–4, 249, 250, 251, 254–5, 272, 273, 306, 322, 369–70, 431, 480
creative evolution, 35, 36, 38, 40
Darwinism, 38, 40–2
democracy, 8, 47, 136, 143, 158, 315–16
Charles Dickens, 302
dictatorships, 75, 113–14, 143–4, 321, 416; *see also* Hitler; Mussolini; Stalin (*below*)
economics, 132, 136, 137; *see also* money (*below*)
Fascism, 113, 143, 431; *see also* Hitler (*below*)
feminism, 84, 132–3
films and the film industry, 374–5, 376, 379, 473; *see also* Hollywood (*below*)
James Keir Hardie, 315
Frank Harris, 170, 172, 177
history and historical accuracy, 353, 412–13
Adolf Hitler, 113, 143, 144, 400, 403–5, 421–7 *passim*, 431, 433, 482
Hollywood, 307, 310, 376–7, 381
Ireland, 59, 60, 61, 62, 64
his Irishness, 481, 493–4
Japan, 297–9, 300–1
Jesus, 280–1
Jews and anti-Semitism, 113, 406, 407, 418, 420, 421, 422
James Joyce, 170, 198, 199
the League of Nations, 5, 6, 12, 179, 230–1, 291, 292, 396–8, 400, 406, 421, 422–3
V. I. Lenin, 8, 225, 226, 228, 229–30, 246, 249, 289
David Lloyd George, 47–8, 58, 226

Michael Holroyd was born in 1935 and is half-Swedish and partly Irish. In 1968 his *Lytton Strachey* was acclaimed as a landmark in contemporary biography and, six years later, his *Augustus John* confirmed his place as one of the most influential modern biographers. He has worked for fifteen years on the research and writing of *Bernard Shaw*. The first volume, published in 1988, was hailed by George Painter as 'one of the finest literary biographies of our half-century ... It may well turn out to be the greatest of them all.'

Michael Holroyd lives in London and is married to Margaret Drabble.

The title on page iii is set in
Caslon Old Face,
the design favoured by Bernard Shaw
when he was directing the manufacture
of his books at R. & R. Clark, Edinburgh.
The text is set in Linotron Ehrhardt,
a typeface derived from similar seventeenth-century
Dutch sources as Caslon Old Face.